CONCEPTS
IN PSYCHOLOGY

CONCEPTS IN PSYCHOLOGY

Introductory Readings Edited by

Paul Mussen & Mark R. Rosenzweig
University of California, Berkeley

Elliot Aronson
University of Texas

David Elkind
University of Rochester

Seymour Feshbach
University of California, Los Angeles

Stephen E. Glickman
University of California, Berkeley

Bennet B. Murdock, Jr.
University of Toronto

Michael Wertheimer
University of Colorado

D.C. HEATH AND COMPANY
Lexington, Massachusetts   Toronto   London

PREFACE

This volume of readings is intended to provide students who are beginning their study of psychology with a fairly well-rounded, representative sample of articles, both theoretical and empirical, drawn from eight fields of psychology—social, personality, developmental, cognitive and educational, learning and memory, perception, biological, and comparative. The purpose of the collection is to supplement and enrich the student's understanding of psychology by exposing him directly to a broad range of articles that demonstrate how psychological investigators and theorists think, conceptualize their problems, and formulate and test hypotheses, as well as how they do research, analyze their data, interpret their findings, and communicate their results.

The articles in each of the substantive sections of the book (Sections Two–Nine) were carefully selected by an expert in that particular area. We used four main criteria for selection: (1) Each article is a contemporary one that makes some significant contribution to our comprehension of an interesting, and, wherever possible, socially relevant issue in that area. (2) We wanted articles that are not too technical or too difficult for students to understand. (3) Each article is self-contained so that the reader can understand it without reading other, related articles. (4) Within each area, we sought some diversity of subject matter so that many varieties of research and thinking are represented.

The papers are arranged in an order that parallels the sections of our text *Psychology: An Introduction* (D.C. Heath), beginning with social psychology and personality, the areas that are closest to the student's own experience and interests and thus intrinsically meaningful to him. These sections contain articles that deal with some of the major problems of psychology, but they require very little technical or specialized background. Even though the table of contents of this volume is directly related to our own introductory text, the book can be used independently of that text, because the readings in it, fulfilling the criteria listed above, will prove interesting and enlightening to all students of psychology.

Credit is given to the authors and publishers of each of the papers in appropriate footnotes. We gratefully acknowledge their generosity in granting permission to reprint the material and thus make this book possible. We are also indebted to Vivien March for her patient work in preparing the manuscript for publication.

CONTENTS

CONCEPTS IN PSYCHOLOGY

Section One
PSYCHOLOGY: THE STUDY OF BEHAVIOR

The most satisfactory, comprehensive, and accurate definition of psychology is probably found in the many activities of psychologists—in what they actually do as they study behavior, and as they apply the findings of scientific research to problems such as mental illness, racial prejudice, and the education of the disadvantaged. Psychology as we know it today consists of a number of fields or subdisciplines. The basic ones are *social,* the study of relationships among people; *personality,* the investigation of factors *within* the individual that affect behavior and personal characteristics; *developmental,* focusing on growth and change in cognitive functions, personality, and social behavior; *cognitive and educational,* the first is concerned with the processes of thinking, reasoning, and problem solving, the second with learning and teaching in educational settings; *learning,* research on how we profit from experience; *perception,* the study of how we organize and interpret stimuli received from the environment; *biological,* probing the physiological, neural, and endocrinal roots of behavior; *comparative,* discovering the form, sources, and functions of different kinds of behaviors in various species of animals.

Most textbooks used in introductory psychology courses present some of the fundamental concepts and well-established facts from all these major fields. Accounts of research are usually given in condensed form and findings are summarized. But these accounts generally provide very little information about critically important aspects of research such as the investigator's thinking, the ideas and hypotheses underlying his work, or the

1

details of the methods and techniques used in the study. The complexity of research work and the care that goes into each study are seldom stated explicitly.

This book of readings attempts to make up for some of these inevitable shortcomings in introductory textbooks by giving you examples of original theoretical and research articles in different fields of psychology. Each of the eight major sections following this introduction includes three to five articles from one particular field. The articles, selected by experts in each particular area, were included because they are of general interest and, at the same time, are considered to be important contributions. Each article brings you some of the flavor of a particular subdiscipline and shows how psychologists in that field work—the research questions they ask, their ways of analyzing data and interpreting their findings, and their style of communication. By reading these articles, you can "listen in" on psychologists as they discuss their research with each other.

In making selections for this book of readings, we attempted to avoid articles that are too difficult for the introductory student either because they are too technical or because they do not communicate sufficiently clearly. Nevertheless, some of the passages in some of the articles may appear difficult, obscure, or highly technical when you read them for the first time. In these cases, you should begin by skimming the article to get the most significant ideas and pay less attention to specific details of the methods used. These will become clearer on the second reading.

This introductory section includes only two articles, based on presidential addresses given at meetings of the American Psychological Association. The first, by George A. Miller, is concerned with the social relevance of psychology, its enormous potential for aiding in the solution of major social problems and in promoting human welfare. The second, by Donald Marquis, clearly shows how broad principles of scientific method are applied to the study of behavior. Marquis describes six steps in a complete research program from the initial formulation of a behavioral problem to the application of research findings. Most of the articles in this book do not include all six steps; some start with a research problem that is already past the initial stage, and some stop short of application. You will find it illuminating to measure each research report against Marquis's six-step scheme.

Paul Mussen
Mark R. Rosenzweig

*How can the methods and findings of psychology best be used to pro-
mote human welfare? In this first article, George A. Miller argues that the best
method will be to "give psychology away." By that phrase he means that it is less
important for psychologists to act as experts trying to supervise the applications of
psychology than to help nonpsychologists become able to practice psychology in a
valid way. If we can accomplish that, we can really bring about a psychological and
a social revolution. In discussing these questions in his presidential address to the
American Psychological Association in 1969, Miller broke with tradition by not
discussing his own research. A pioneer in the field of psycholinguistics and in the
application of mathematical concepts to the study of behavior, he has received
much recognition for his imaginative research. But in this influential paper he
pushes out beyond the confines of the laboratory to the social world—the world
that, according to Miller, cries for solutions to the problems we have ourselves
created. Most of the later selections in this book restrict themselves to a much
narrower scope, but Miller's article reveals the revolutionary intellectual potential
of psychology that each of its subfields is helping to create.*

Psychology as a Means of Promoting Human Welfare

George A. Miller

The most urgent problems of our world today are the problems we
have made for ourselves. They have not been caused by some heedless or
malicious inanimate Nature, nor have they been imposed on us as punishment
by the will of God. They are human problems whose solutions will require us
to change our behavior and our social institutions.

As a science directly concerned with behavioral and social processes, psychology might be expected to provide intellectual leadership in the
search for new and better personal and social arrangements. In fact, however,
we psychologists have contributed relatively little of real importance—even
less than our rather modest understanding of behavior might justify. We should
have contributed more; although our scientific base for valid contributions is
far from comprehensive, certainly more is known than has been used intel-
ligently.

Source: Reprinted by permission from *American Psychologist*, 1969, *24* (12) 1063–1075.
Copyright © 1969 by the American Psychological Association.

Note: Presidential Address to the American Psychological Association in Washington,
D.C., September 1969. It is customary on this occasion to summarize one's own research.
Although that would be a more comfortable role, I have decided instead to take this
opportunity to express some personal opinions about the current state of our discipline
and its potential role in meeting the human problems of our society. This departure from
tradition is intended to honor the theme of the 1969 Convention, "Psychology and the
Problems of Society." I am indebted to several friends, and especially to J. A. Varela,
for critical comments on earlier drafts.

This is the social challenge that psychologists face. In the years immediately ahead we must not only extend and deepen our understanding of mental and behavioral phenomena, but we must somehow incorporate our hard-won knowledge more effectively into the vast social changes that we all know are coming. It is both important and appropriate for us, on occasions such as this, to consider how best to meet this social challenge.

In opening such a discussion, however, we should keep clearly in mind that society has not commissioned us to cure its ills; a challenge is not a mandate. Moreover, there is nothing in the definition of psychology that dedicates our science to the solution of social problems. Our inability to solve the pressing problems of the day cannot be interpreted as an indictment of the scientific validity of our psychological theories. As scientists we are obliged to communicate what we know, but we have no special obligation to solve social problems.

Our obligations as citizens, however, are considerably broader than our obligations as scientists. When psychological issues are raised in this broader context, we cannot evade them by complaining that they are unscientific. If we have something of practical value to contribute, we should make every effort to insure that it is implemented.

I believe that the majority of American psychologists have accepted this broader interpretation of our responsibilities and have been eager—perhaps, sometimes, overly eager—to apply our science to social problems. We have not been aloof or insensitive; the bulk of our profession works full time on exactly such problems. And I do not wish to discount the many and often successful efforts toward application that we have made already. Yet I cannot escape the impression that we have been less effective than we might have been. "Why" and "what more might be done" are questions that have troubled me increasingly in recent years.

First, however, I would like to raise a somewhat parochial question.

Role of the American Psychological Association

If we accept this challenge to use psychology to solve social problems, what role should we expect the American Psychological Association to play? I raise this question because my experience as an officer of APA has taught me that many of our members look to their national organization for leadership in insuring that our scientific and professional activities have greater social relevance.

Psychologists have been well represented among those who sign petitions of political protest (Ladd, 1969), and they have not failed to make their opinions heard in their own national headquarters. Scarcely a meeting of the Board of Directors in recent years has not featured one or more petitions from concerned members, committees, boards, divisions, or state associations requesting some action related to public affairs. These matters range all the way from the proper use of psychological tests, where APA usually has something to say, to the endorsement of particular political candidates, where APA usually does not.

These demands have imposed considerable strain on the Association, which was not created to be an instrument for social action and which responds hesitantly to any suggestion that it should become something more than a scientific and professional organization. But it does respond. I was surprised to discover how seriously APA regards any legitimate request from its membership, and how sensitive it is to the social implications of its actions, policies, and communications. Some members wish APA would do more, some less. On balance, I think APA has reflected reasonably accurately the general consensus of its members with respect to its role in public affairs.

It is not my intention to raise here any of the specific issues of public policy that have concerned the Board of Directors and the Council of Representatives, or even to offer a general formula for deciding what the public role of the APA should be. Procedurally, I am willing to stand on the thoughtful recommendations of the ad hoc Committee on Public Affairs (Tyler, 1969).

A point of general interest, however, and one that relates more directly to the theme I wish to discuss, is the frequently heard argument that APA should take some action or other because the first article of our Bylaws states that the Association shall have as its object to promote human welfare, a goal that is echoed in our statement of the *Ethical Standards of Psychologists.*

This argument is usually made by those who recommend that APA should publicly advocate some particular social reform. When these recommendations are appropriate, the action is adopted—the necessary letters are written, public statements are released to the press, etc. But not every recommendation is acceptable. It has been my impression that the less related the issue is to the scientific and professional interests of our membership, the greater is the likelihood that the promotion of human welfare will be invoked in the course of the discussion.

In most cases this argument has not persuaded me; I have traced my skepticism to two sources.

First, even the most cursory study of welfare economics will show that human welfare has never been operationally defined as a social concept. If there is such a thing as human welfare in the general sense, it must be some kind of weighted average. In difficult cases, where disagreement is most probable, something that advances the welfare of one group may disadvantage another group. The problem is to decide whose welfare we wish to promote. The APA is committed to advancing the welfare of psychologists, of course, but we dare not assume blindly that whatever is good for psychology must always be good for humanity.

Vague appeals to human welfare seldom answer specific questions because we seldom have sufficient information to decide which actions will have the desired result. And even when we do have sufficient wisdom to know in advance which actions will promote human welfare most effectively, we still face the ethical question of whether such actions are morally permissible.

My first reason for distrusting appeals to human welfare, therefore, is that they do little to clarify the logical, informational, or ethical bases for making difficult decisions. Something more is required than a sincere declaration that our heart is in the right place.

My second reason has to do with the fact that the phrase is usually quoted out of context. At the risk of losing your attention, therefore, I would like to state Article I of our Bylaws in full:

> The objects of the American Psychological Association shall be to advance psychology as a science and as a means of promoting human welfare by the encouragement of psychology in all its branches in the broadest and most liberal manner; by the promotion of research in psychology and the improvement of research methods and conditions; by the improvement of the qualifications and usefulness of psychologists through high standards of professional ethics, conduct, education, and achievement; by the increase and diffusion of psychological knowledge through meetings, professional contacts, reports, papers, discussions, and publications; thereby to advance scientific interests and inquiry, and the application of research findings to the promotion of the public welfare [APA, 1968, xii].

As I understand Article I, our corporate aim is to promote psychology. We justify that aim by our belief that psychology can be used for the public good. I do not understand Article I as a general license to endorse social actions or positions, however meritorious on other grounds, that do not advance psychology as a science and as a means of promoting human welfare. The APA is our own creature, of course; we can change our Bylaws any way we like. As presently conceived, however, APA does not have a charter to intervene on behalf of every good cause that comes along.

There are many things of social value that APA can do, and many that it has already done. If your officers have not always seemed hungry for innovation, eager to reshape APA to meet every new social issue, they have certainly been open to constructive change within the scope of our charter. I believe they have reflected the wishes of the bulk of the membership, and I feel no need to apologize for what has been accomplished. The APA has been doing what its membership wanted to do, and doing it rather well.

Of course, the membership has been far from unanimous in these matters. For example, there has been a running debate in recent years concerning the proper role for individual psychologists to play in the initiation of social reforms. We have been divided as to whether psychologists should remain expert advisers or should take a more active, participatory responsibility for determining public policy. An adviser is expected to summarize the arguments pro and con, but to leave the policy decisions to others; a participant wants to make the policy decisions himself.

Those who favor more active participation by individual psychologists tend to argue that APA should also become directly involved in advocating particular social policies. This whole debate seems to presuppose, however, that social reforms can occur only as a result of policy decisions by government or industry. This presupposition should not go unchallenged. Perhaps our options for promoting human welfare are broader than this debate would suggest.

It was E. G. Boring who first impressed on me the importance of a clear distinction between Psychology with a capital P and psychology with a small p. Capital-P Psychology refers to our associations, departments, laboratories, and the like. Small-p psychology refers to the discipline itself. Capital-P Psychology can do little to promote human welfare, outside of its faithful promotion of small-p psychology. We should not, through impatience or bad judgment, try to use capital-P Psychology where only small-p psychology could succeed. Let us by all means do everything we can to promote human welfare, but let us not forget that our real strength in that cause will come from our scientific knowledge, not from our national Association.

In my opinion, our Association can never play more than a supporting role in the promotion of social change. I do not conclude from this that APA has become irrelevant or useless, or, even worse, that it has tacitly endorsed a political bureaucracy that presides over the inequitable distribution of health, wealth, and wisdom in our society. The fact that APA has not reformed society does not mean that it approves the status quo; it means simply that there is relatively little such an association can do. When one considers the magnitude and urgency of the problems mankind faces, the question of what positions APA takes is, after all, a minor matter.

The important question, to my mind, is not what APA is doing, but what psychologists are doing. What Psychology can do as an association depends directly on the base provided by psychology as a science. It is our science that provides our real means for promoting human welfare.

So let me turn now to broader aspects of my topic.

Revolutionary Potential of Psychology

I will begin by stating publicly something that I think psychologists all feel, but seldom talk about. In my opinion, scientific psychology is potentially one of the most revolutionary intellectual enterprises ever conceived by the mind of man. If we were ever to achieve substantial progress toward our stated aim—toward the understanding, prediction, and control of mental and behavioral phenomena—the implications for every aspect of society would make brave men tremble.

Responsible spokesmen for psychology seldom emphasize this revolutionary possibility. One reason is that the general public is all too ready to believe it, and public resistance to psychology would be all too easy to mobilize. Faced with the possibility that revolutionary pronouncements might easily do more harm than good, a prudent spokesman finds other drums to march to.

Regardless of whether we agree that prudence is always the best policy, I believe there is another reason for our public modesty. Anyone who claims that psychology is a revolutionary enterprise will face a demand from his scientific colleagues to put up or shut up. Nothing that psychology has done so far, they will say, is very revolutionary. They will admit that psychometric tests, psychoanalysis, conditioned reflexes, sensory thresholds, implanted electrodes, and factor analysis are all quite admirable, but they can scarcely be compared to gunpowder, the steam engine, organic chemistry, radio-telephony, computers, atom bombs, or genetic surgery in their revolutionary consequences for society. Our enthusiastic spokesman would have to retire in confused embarrassment.

Since I know that rash statements about the revolutionary potential of psychology may lead to public rejection and scientific ridicule, why do I take such risks on this occasion? My reason is that I do not believe the psychological revolution is still pie in the sky. It has already begun.

One reason the psychological revolution is not more obvious may be that we have been looking for it in the wrong place. We have assumed that psychology should provide new technological options, and that a psychological revolution will not occur until someone in authority exercises those options to attain socially desirable goals. One reason for this assumption, perhaps, is that it follows the model we have inherited from previous applications of science to practical problems. An applied scientist is supposed to provide instrumentalities for modifying the environment—instrumentalities that can then, under public regulation, be used by wealthy and powerful interests to achieve certain goals. The psychological revolution, when it comes, may follow a very different course, at least in its initial stages.

Davis (1966) has explained the difference between applied social science and applied natural science in the following way:

> Applied science, by definition, is instrumental. When the human goal is given, it seeks a solution by finding what effective means can be manipulated in the required way. Its function is to satisfy human desires and wants; otherwise nobody would bother. But when the science is concerned with human beings—not just as organisms but as goal-seeking individuals and members of groups—then it cannot be instrumental in this way, because the object of observation has a say in what is going on and, above all, is not willing to be treated as a pure instrumentality. Most so-called social problems are problems because people want certain things or because there is a conflict of desires or interests [p. 26].

Davis goes on to argue that once conflicts of interest have developed, applied social science is helpless; that it is only when people are agreed on their goals that our information can be usefully applied.

Although I agree with Davis that behavioral and social sciences cannot be applied to people and institutions in the same way physical and biological sciences are applied to objects and organisms, I do not agree with his view that we must remain impotent in the face of conflict. We know a great deal about the prevention and resolution of conflicts, and that information could certainly be put to better use than it has been. Indeed, sometimes what is needed is not to resolve conflict but to foster it, as when entrenched interests threaten segments of the public that have no organizational identity. And there, in turn, we know a great deal about the creation of appropriate constituencies to defend their common interests. Behavioral and social scientists are far from helpless in such situations.

More important, however, I believe that the real impact of psychology will be felt, not through the technological products it places in the hands of powerful men, but through its effects on the public at large, through a new and different public conception of what is humanly possible and what is humanly desirable.

I believe that any broad and successful application of psychological knowledge to human problems will necessarily entail a change in our conception of ourselves and of how we live and love and work together. Instead of inventing some new technique for modifying the environment, or some new product for society to adapt itself to however it can, we are proposing to tamper with the adaptive process itself. Such an innovation is quite different from a "technological fix." I see little reason to believe that the traditional model for scientific revolutions should be appropriate.

Consider, for example, the effect that Freudian psychology has already had on Western society. It is obvious that its effects, though limited to certain segments of society, have been profound, yet I do not believe that one can argue that those effects were achieved by providing new instrumentalities for achieving goals socially agreed upon. As a method of therapy, psychoanalysis has had limited success even for those who can afford it. It has been more successful as a method of investigation, perhaps, but even there it has been only one of several available methods. The impact of Freud's thought has been due far less to the instrumentalities he provided than to the changed conception of ourselves that he inspired. The wider range of psychological problems that Freud opened up for professional psychologists is only part of his contribution. More important in the scale of history has been his effect on the broader intellectual community and, through it, on the public at large. Today ✱ we are much more aware of the irrational components of human nature and much better able to accept the reality of our unconscious impulses. The importance of Freudian psychology derives far less from its scientific validity than from the effects it has had on our shared image of man himself.

I realize that one might argue that changes in man's conception of himself under the impact of advances in scientific knowledge are neither novel nor revolutionary. For example, Darwin's theory changed our conception of ourselves, but not until the past decade has it been possible to mount a truly scientific revolution based on biological science. One might argue that we are now only at the Darwinian stage in psychology, and that the real psychological revolution is still a century or more in the future. I do not find this analogy appropriate, however.

To discover that we are not at the center of the universe, or that our remote ancestors lived in a tree, does indeed change our conception of man and society, but such new conceptions can have little effect on the way we behave in our daily affairs and in our institutional contexts. A new conception of man based on psychology, however, would have immediate implications for the most intimate details of our social and personal lives. This fact is unprecedented in any earlier stage of the Industrial Revolution.

The heart of the psychological revolution will be a new and scientifically based conception of man as an individual and as a social creature. When I say that the psychological revolution is already upon us, what I mean is that we have already begun to change man's self-conception. If we want to further that revolution, not only must we strengthen its scientific base, but we must also try to communicate it to our students and to the public. It is not the industrialist or the politician who should exploit it, but Everyman, every day.

The enrichment of public psychology by scientific psychology constitutes the most direct and important application of our science to the promotion of human welfare. Instead of trying to foresee new psychological products that might disrupt our existing social arrangements, therefore, we should be self-consciously analyzing the general effect that our scientific psychology may have on popular psychology. As I try to perform this analysis for myself, I must confess that I am not altogether pleased with the results.

I would like now to consider briefly some of the effects we are having and where, in my view, our influence is leading at the present time. Let me begin with a thumbnail sketch of one major message that many scientific psychologists are trying to communicate to the public.

Control of Behavior

One of the most admired truisms of modern psychology is that some stimuli can serve to reinforce the behavior that produces them. The practical significance of this familiar principle arises from the implication that if you can control the occurrence of these reinforcing stimuli, then you can control the occurrence of adaptive behavior intended to achieve or avoid them. This contingency between behavior and its consequences has been demonstrated in many studies of animal behavior, where environmental conditions can be controlled, or at least specified, and where the results can be measured with some precision.

Something similar holds for the human animal, of course, although it is complicated by man's symbolic proclivities and by the fact that the disparity between experimenter and subject changes when the subject is also a man. Between men, reinforcement is usually a mutual relation and each person controls the other to some extent. This relation of mutual reinforcement, which man's genius for symbols has generalized in terms of money or the promise of money, provides the psychological basis for our economic system of exchange. Psychologists did not create this economic system for controlling behavior, of course. What we have tried to do is to describe its psychological basis and its limits in terms sufficiently general to hold across different species, and to suggest how the technique might be extended to educational, rehabilitative, therapeutic, or even political situations in which economic rewards and punishments would not normally be appropriate. Once a problem of behavior control has been phrased in these terms, we may then try to discover the most effective schedule of reinforcements.

My present concern has nothing to do with the validity of these ideas. I am concerned with their effect on the public at large, for it is there, if I am right, that we are most likely to achieve a psychological revolution.

In the public view, I suspect, all this talk about controlling behavior comes across as unpleasant, if not actually threatening. Freud has already established in the public mind a general belief that all behavior is motivated. The current message says that psychologists now know how to use this motivation to control what people will do. When they hear this, of course, our scientific colleagues are likely to accuse us of pseudoscientific claims; less scientific segments of the public are likely to resent what they perceive as a threat to their personal freedom. Neither reaction is completely just, but neither is completely unjustifiable.

I believe these critics see an important truth, one that a myopic concentration on techniques of behavior control may cause us to overlook. At best, control is but one component in any program for personal improvement or social reform. Changing behavior is pointless in the absence of any coherent plan for how it should be changed. It is our plan for using control that the public wants to know about. Too often, I fear, psychologists have implied that acceptable uses for behavior control are either self-evident or can be safely left to the wisdom and benevolence of powerful men. Psychologists must not surrender the planning function so easily. Humane applications of behavior control must be based on intelligent diagnosis of the personal and social problems we are trying to solve. Psychology has at least as much, probably more, to contribute to the diagnosis of personal and social problems as it has to the control of behavior.

Regardless of whether we have actually achieved new scientific techniques of behavior control that are effective with human beings, and regardless of whether control is of any value in the absence of diagnosis and planning for its use, the simple fact that so many psychologists keep talking about control is having an effect on public psychology. The average citizen is predisposed to believe it. Control has been the practical payoff from the other sciences. Control must be what psychologists are after, too. Moreover, since science is notoriously successful, behavior control must be inevitable. Thus the layman forms an impression that control is the name of the road we are traveling, and that the experts are simply quibbling about how far down that road we have managed to go.

Closely related to this emphasis on control is the frequently repeated claim that living organisms are nothing but machines. A scientist recognizes, of course, that this claim says far more about our rapidly evolving conception of machines than it says about living organisms, but this interpretation is usually lost when the message reaches public ears. The public idea of a machine is something like an automobile, a mechanical device controlled by its operator. If people are machines, they can be driven like automobiles. The analogy is absurd, of course, but it illustrates the kind of distortion that can occur.

If the assumption that behavior control is feasible in some precise scientific sense becomes firmly rooted in public psychology, it could have unfortunate consequences, particularly if it is coupled with an assumption that control should be exercised by an industrial or bureaucratic elite. Psychologists must always respect and advocate the principle of *habeas mentem*—the right of a man to his own mind (Sanford, 1955). If we really did have a new scientific way to control human behavior, it would be highly immoral to let it fall into the hands of some small group of men, even if they were psychologists.

Perhaps a historical analogy would be appropriate. When the evolution of species was a new and exciting idea in biology, various social theorists took it up and interpreted it to mean that capitalistic competition, like the competition between species, was the source of all progress, so the great wealth of the new industrialists was a scientifically necessary consequence of the law of the survival of the fittest. This argument, called "social Darwinism," had unfortunate consequences, both for social science and for society generally (Hofstadter, 1944).

If the notion should now be accepted that it is a scientifically necessary consequence of the law of reinforcement that industrialists or bureaucrats must be allowed the same control over people that an experimenter has over his laboratory animals, I fear that a similar period of intolerable exploitation might ensue—if, indeed, it has not already begun.

The dangers that accompany a science of behavior control have been pointed out many times. Psychologists who study motivation scientifically are usually puzzled by this widespread apprehension that they might be successful. Control is not something invented by psychologists. Everyone is "controlled" all the time by something or other. All we want is to discover how the controls work. Once we understand that, society can use the knowledge in whatever manner seems socially advantageous. Our critics, on the other hand, want to know who will diagnose our problems, who will set our social goals, and who will administer the rewards and punishments.

All that I have tried to add to this familiar dialogue is the observation that the social dangers involved need not await the success of the scientific enterprise. Behavior control could easily become a self-fulfilling prophecy. If people generally should come to believe in the scientific control of behavior, proponents of coercive social programs would surely exploit that belief by dressing their proposals in scientific costumes. If our new public conception of human nature is that man's behavior can be scientifically controlled by those in positions of power, governments will quickly conform to that conception. Thus, when I try to discern what direction our psychological revolution has been taking, some aspects of it disturb me deeply and lead me to question whether in the long run these developments will really promote human welfare.

This is a serious charge. If there is any truth to it, we should ask whether any other approaches are open to us.

Personally, I believe there is a better way to advertise psychology and to relate it to social problems. Reinforcement is only one of many important ideas that we have to offer. Instead of repeating constantly that reinforcement leads to control, I would prefer to emphasize that reinforcement can lead to satisfaction and competence. And I would prefer to speak of understanding and prediction as our major scientific goals.

In the space remaining, therefore, I want to try to make the case that understanding and prediction are better goals for psychology than is control—better both for psychology and for the promotion of human welfare—because they lead us to think, not in terms of coercion by a powerful elite, but in terms of the diagnosis of problems and the development of programs that can enrich the lives of every citizen.

Public Psychology: Two Paradigms

It should be obvious by now that I have somewhere in the back of my mind two alternative images of what the popular conception of human nature might become under the impact of scientific advances in psychology. One of these images is unfortunate, even threatening; the other is vaguer, but full of promise. Let me try to make these ideas more concrete.

The first image is the one I have been describing. It has great appeal to an authoritarian mind, and fits well with our traditional competitive ideology based on coercion, punishment, and retribution. The fact that it represents a serious distortion of scientific psychology is exactly my point. In my opinion, we have made a mistake by trying to apply our ideas to social problems and to gain acceptance for our science within the framework of this ideology.

The second image rests on the same psychological foundation, but reflects it more accurately; it allows no compromise with our traditional social ideology. It is assumed, vaguely but optimistically, that this ideology can be modified so as to be more receptive to a truer conception of human nature. How this modification can be achieved is one of the problems we face; I believe it will not be achieved if we continue to advertise the control of behavior through reinforcement as our major contribution to the solution of social problems. I would not wish to give anyone the impression that I have formulated a well-defined social alternative, but I would at least like to open a discussion and make some suggestions.

My two images are not very different from what McGregor (1960) once called Theory X and Theory Y. Theory X is the traditional theory which holds that because people dislike work, they must be coerced, controlled, directed, and threatened with punishment before they will do it. People tolerate being directed, and many even prefer it, because they have little ambition and want to avoid responsibility. McGregor's alternative Theory Y, based on social science, holds that work is as natural as play or rest. External control and threats are not the only means for inspiring people to work. People will exercise self-direction and self-control in the service of objectives to which they are committed; their commitment is a function of the rewards associated with the achievement of their objectives. People can learn not only to accept but to seek responsibility. Imagination, ingenuity, and creativity are widely distributed in the population, although these intellectual potentialities are poorly utilized under the conditions of modern industrial life.

McGregor's Theory X and Theory Y evolved in the context of his studies of industrial management. They are rival theories held by industrial managers about how best to achieve their institutional goals. A somewhat broader view is needed if we are to talk about public psychology generally, and not merely the managerial manifestations of public psychology. So let me amplify McGregor's distinction by referring to the ideas of Varela, a very remarkable engineer in Montevideo, Uruguay, who uses scientific psychology in the solution of a wide range of personal and social problems.

Varela (1970) contrasts two conceptions of the social nature of man. Following Kuhn's (1962) discussion of scientific revolutions, he refers to these two conceptions as "paradigms." The first paradigm is a set of assumptions on which our social institutions are presently based. The second is a contrasting paradigm based on psychological research. Let me outline them for you very briefly.

Our current social paradigm is characterized as follows: All men are created equal. Most behavior is motivated by economic competition, and conflict is inevitable. One truth underlies all controversy, and unreasonableness is best countered by facts and logic. When something goes wrong, someone is to blame, and every effort must be made to establish his guilt so that he can be punished. The guilty person is responsible for his own misbehavior and for his own rehabilitation. His teachers and supervisors are too busy to become experts in social science; their role is to devise solutions and see to it that their students or subordinates do what they are told.

For comparison, Varela offers a paradigm based on psychological research: There are large individual differences among people, both in ability and personality. Human motivation is complex and no one ever acts as he does for any single reason, but, in general, positive incentives are more effective than threats or punishments. Conflict is no more inevitable than disease and can be resolved or, still better, prevented. Time and resources for resolving social problems are strictly limited. When something goes wrong, how a person perceives the situation is more important to him than the "true facts," and he cannot reason about the situation until his irrational feelings have been toned down. Social problems are solved by correcting causes, not symptoms, and this can be done more effectively in groups than individually. Teachers and supervisors must be experts in social science because they are responsible for the cooperation and individual improvement of their students or subordinates.

No doubt other psychologists would draw the picture somewhat differently. Without reviewing the psychological evidence on which such generalizations are based, of course, I cannot argue their validity. But I think most of you will recognize the lines of research on which McGregor's Theory Y and Varela's second paradigm are based. Moreover, these psychologically based paradigms are incompatible in several respects with the prevailing ideology of our society.

Here, then, is the real challenge: How can we foster a social climate in which some such new public conception of man based on psychology can take root and flourish? In my opinion, this is the proper translation of our more familiar question about how psychology might contribute to the promotion of human welfare.

I cannot pretend to have an answer to this question, even in its translated form, but I believe that part of the answer is that psychology must be practiced by nonpsychologists. We are not physicians; the secrets of our trade need not be reserved for highly trained specialists. Psychological facts should be passed out freely to all who need and can use them. And from successful applications of psychological principles the public may gain a better appreciation for the power of the new conception of man that is emerging from our science.

If we take seriously the idea of a peaceful revolution based on a new conception of human nature, our scientific results will have to be instilled in the public consciousness in a practical and usable form so that what we know can be applied by ordinary people. There simply are not enough psychologists, even including nonprofessionals, to meet every need for psychological services. The people at large will have to be their own psychologists, and make their own applications of the principles that we establish.

Of course, everyone practices psychology, just as everyone who cooks is a chemist, everyone who reads a clock is an astronomer, everyone who drives a car is an engineer. I am not suggesting any radical departure when I say that nonpsychologists must practice psychology. I am simply proposing that we should teach them to practice it better, to make use self-consciously of what we believe to be scientifically valid principles.

Our responsibility is less to assume the role of experts and try to apply psychology ourselves than to give it away to the people who really need it—and that includes everyone. The practice of valid psychology by nonpsychologists will inevitably change people's conception of themselves and what they can do. When we have accomplished that, we will really have caused a psychological revolution.

How to Give Psychology Away

I am keenly aware that giving psychology away will be no simple task. In our society there are depths of resistance to psychological innovations that have to be experienced to be believed (Graziano, 1969).

Solving social problems is generally considered to be more difficult than solving scientific problems. A social problem usually involves many more independent variables, and it cannot be finally solved until society has been persuaded to adopt the solution. Many who have tried to introduce sound psychological practices into schools, clinics, hospitals, prisons, or industries have been forced to retreat in dismay. They complain, and with good reason, that they were unable to buck the "System," and often their reactions are more violent than sensible. The System, they say, refuses to change even when it does not work.

This experience has been so common that in my pessimistic moments I have been led to wonder whether anything less than complete reform is possible.

Deutsch (1969) has made an interesting case that competitive and cooperative social relationships tend to be mutually exclusive. He summarizes the result of considerable research in the following terms:

> The strategy of power and the tactics of coercion, threat, and deception result from and also result in a competitive relationship. Similarly, the strategy of mutual problem solving and the tactics of persuasion, openness, and mutual enhancement elicit and also are elicited by a cooperative orientation [p. 4].

Each orientation has its own internal consistency; elements of one are not easily injected into the other.

Perhaps a similar pressure toward internal coherence lies at the root of public resistance to many of our innovative suggestions. It often seems that any one of our ideas taken alone is inadequate. Injected into the existing social paradigm it is either a foreign body, incompatible with the other presuppositions that shape our social institutions, or it is distorted and trivialized to fit the preexisting paradigm.

One of the most basic ideas in all the social sciences is the concept of culture. Social anthropologists have developed a conception of culture as an organic whole, in which each particular value, practice, or assumption must be understood in the context of the total system. They tell terrible tales about the consequences of introducing Western reforms into aboriginal cultures without understanding the social equilibria that would be upset.

Perhaps cultural integrity is not limited to primitive cultures, but applies also to our own society here and now. If so, then our attempts at piecemeal innovation may be doomed either to fail or to be rejected outright.

I label these thoughts pessimistic because they imply a need for drastic changes throughout the whole system, changes that could only be imposed by someone with dangerous power over the lives of others. And that, I have argued, is not the way our psychological revolution should proceed.

In my more optimistic moments, however, I recognize that you do not need complete authority over a social organization in order to reform it. The important thing is not to control the system, but to understand it. Someone who has a valid conception of the system as a whole can often introduce relatively minor changes that have extensive consequences throughout the entire organization. Lacking such a conception, worthwhile innovations may be total failures.

For example, if you institute a schedule of rewards and punishments in the psychiatric ward of a Veterans Hospital, you should not be indignant when the American Legion objects on the grounds that you cannot withhold food and clothing from veterans. If you had had a more adequate understanding of the hospital as a social system, you would have included the interests and influence of the American Legion in your diagnosis of the problem, and you would have formulated a plan to gain their endorsement as part of your task as a social engineer. You should not demand inordinate power just because you made an inadequate diagnosis of the problem. Understanding must come first.

In my optimistic moments I am able to convince myself that understanding is attainable and that social science is already at a stage where successful applications are possible. Careful diagnosis and astute planning based on what we already know can often resolve problems that at first glance seemed insurmountable. Many social, clinical, and industrial psychologists have already demonstrated the power of diagnosis and planning based on sound psychological principles.

Varela has illustrated such applications by his work in Uruguay. Diagnosis involves not only a detailed analysis of the social organization and of the perceptions and goals of all the people caught up in the problem, but also the description of their abilities and personalities. Planning involves the explicit formulation of a series of steps that will lead these people to consider the problem together and will help them to discover a solution that respects everyone's hopes and aspirations. If, in the course of this plan, it becomes necessary to persuade someone, this is not to be accomplished by coercion or by marshaling facts, but by a gradual, step-by-step process that enables him to reduce his reactance little by little as he convinces himself of the virtues of the alternative view and broadens his conception of the range of acceptable solutions (Zimbardo & Ebbeson, 1969, pp. 114–121). This is not the place and I am not the person to describe the ingenuity with which Varela has constructed such plans and carried them out, but such applications give me some reason for optimism.

Diagnosing practical problems and developing detailed plans to deal with them may or may not be more difficult than solving scientific problems, but it is certainly different. Many psychologists, trained in an empiricist, experimental tradition, have tried to serve two masters at once. That is to say, they have tried to solve practical problems and simultaneously to collect data of scientific value on the effects of their interventions. Other fields, however, maintain a more equitable division of labor between scientist and engineer. Scientists are responsible for the validity of the principles; engineers accept them and try to use them to solve practical problems.

Although I recognize the importance of evaluating an engineer's product, in this domain it is no easy thing to do. Assessing social innovations is a whole art in itself, one that we are only beginning to develop. Economic considerations are relevant, of course, but we must also learn to evaluate the subtler psychological and social implications of our new solutions (Bauer, 1966). Technological assessment in this sense will not be achieved by insisting that every reform should resemble a well-designed experiment. In particular, the need for assessment should not be allowed to discourage those who enjoy and have a talent for social engineering.

We are in serious need of many more psychological technologists who can apply our science to the personal and social problems of the general public, for it is through them that the public will eventually discover the new paradigm that psychologists are developing. That is to say, it is through the success of such practical applications that we have our best hope for revolutionizing public psychology.

Obviously, we must avoid the evils of superficiality; we must continue as scientists to refine, clarify, and integrate our new paradigm. Most importantly, we must self-consciously recognize that it *is* a new and revolutionary conception that we are working toward, so that isolated discoveries can be related to and evaluated in terms of that larger context. But all that would be futile, of course, if the general public did not accept it, or if public psychology were not altered by it.

There is no possibility of legislating the changes I have in mind. Passing laws that people must change their conceptions of themselves and others is precisely the opposite of what we need. Education would seem to be our only possibility. I do not mean only education in the schoolroom, although that is probably the best communication channel presently at our disposal. I have in mind a more ambitious program of educating the general public.

It is critically important to shape this education to fit the perceived needs of the people who receive it. Lectures suitable for graduate seminars are seldom suitable for laymen, and for a layman facing a concrete problem they are usually worse than useless. In order to get a factory supervisor or a ghetto mother involved, we must give them something they can use. Abstract theories, however elegant, or sensitivity training, however insightful, are too remote from the specific troubles they face. In order to get started, we must begin with people where they are, not assume we know where they should be. If a supervisor is having trouble with his men, perhaps we should teach him how to write a job description and how to evaluate the abilities and personalities of those who fill the job; perhaps we should teach him the art of persuasion, or the time and place for positive reinforcement. If a ghetto mother is not giving her children sufficient intellectual challenge, perhaps we should teach her how to encourage their motor, perceptual, and linguistic skills. The techniques involved are not some esoteric branch of witchcraft that must be reserved for those with Ph.D. degrees in psychology. When the ideas are made sufficiently concrete and explicit, the scientific foundations of psychology can be grasped by sixth-grade children.

There are many obvious and useful suggestions that we could make and that nonpsychologists could exploit. Not every psychological problem in human engineering has to be solved by a professional psychologist; engineers can rapidly assimilate psychological facts and theories that are relevant to their own work. Not every teaching program has to be written by a learning theorist; principles governing the design and evaluation of programmed materials can be learned by content specialists. Not every personnel decision has to be made by a psychometrician; not every interview has to be conducted by a clinical psychologist; not every problem has to be solved by a cognitive psychologist; not every reinforcement has to be supervised by a student of conditioning. Psychological principles and techniques can be usefully applied by everyone. If our suggestions actually work, people should be eager to learn more. If they do not work, we should improve them. But we should not try to give people something whose value they cannot recognize, then complain when they do not return for a second meeting.

Consider the teaching of reading, for example. Here is an obviously appropriate area for the application of psychological principles. So what do we do? We assemble experts who decide what words children know, and in what order they should learn to read them; then we write stories with those words and teachers make the children read them, or we use them in programmed instruction that exploits the principles of reinforcement. But all too often the children fail to recognize the value of learning these carefully constructed lessons.

Personally, I have been much impressed with the approach of Ashton-Warner (1963), who begins by asking a child what words he wants. Mummy, daddy, kiss, frightened, ghost, their own names—these are the words children ask for, words that are bound up with their own loves and fears. She writes each child's word on a large, tough card and gives it to him. If a child wants words like police, butcher, knife, kill, jail, and bomb, he gets them. And he learns to read them almost immediately. It is *his* word, and each morning he retrieves his own words from the pile collected each night by the teacher. These are not dead words of an expert's choosing, but words that live in a child's own experience. Given this start, children begin to write, using their own words, and from there the teaching of reading follows naturally. Under this regimen, a word is not an imposed task to be learned with reinforcements borrowed from some external source of motivation. Learning the word is itself reinforcing; it gives the child something he wants, a new way to cope with a desire or fear. Each child decides where he wants to start, and each child receives something whose value he can recognize.

Could we generalize this technique discovered by an inspired teacher in a small New Zealand school? In my own thinking I have linked it with something that White (1959) has called competence motivation. In order to tap this motivational system we must use psychology to give people skills that will satisfy their urge to feel more effective. Feeling effective is a very personal thing, for it must be a feeling of effectiveness in coping with personal problems in one's own life. From that beginning some might want to learn more about the science that helped them increase their competence, and then perhaps we could afford to be more abstract. But in the beginning we must try to diagnose and solve the problems people think they have, not the problems we experts think they ought to have, and we must learn to understand those problems in the social and institutional contexts that define them. With this approach we might do something practical for nurses, policemen, prison guards, salesmen—for people in many different walks of life. That, I believe, is what we should mean when we talk about applying psychology to the promotion of human welfare.

If you tell me that such a program is too ambitious or too foreign to our conception of ourselves as scientists and practitioners, I must agree that I do not know where to place our fulcrum to move the world. My goal is to persuade you that this is the problem we face, and that we dare not leave it for bureaucrats or businessmen to solve. We will have to cope with it however we can, and I hope that someone has better ideas than I about how to do it.

I can see some promise for innovations in particular subcultures. If we apply our new paradigm in particular institutions—in schools, hospitals, prisons, industries—we can perhaps test its validity and demonstrate its superiority. Many such social experiments are already in progress, of course. And much of the recent surge of interest in community psychology (Bennett, 1966) has been stimulated by the realization that we really do have something to contribute to community life. Perhaps all this work will eventually have a cumulative effect.

One trouble, of course, is that we are trying to reverse the natural direction of influence. Ordinarily, an institution or a community models its own subculture more or less automatically after the larger culture in which it is embedded, and new members require little indoctrination in order to understand the tacit assumptions on which the institution is based. Whether the new paradigm will be powerful enough to reverse this direction is, I suppose, a matter for pure speculation at the present time. It seems unlikely that we will succeed, however, if each application of the new paradigm is viewed as unrelated to every other, and no attempt is made to integrate these experiments into a paradigm for society as a whole.

It is possible, however, that our society may not by quite as resistant as we anticipate. The demand for social relevance that we have been voicing as psychologists is only one aspect of a general dissatisfaction with the current state of our society. On every hand we hear complaints about the old paradigm. People are growing increasingly alienated from a society in which a few wise men behind closed doors decide what is good for everyone. Our system of justice based on punishment and retribution is not working. Even those most blessed by economic rewards are asking for something more satisfying to fill their lives. We desperately need techniques for resolving conflicts, and for preventing them from becoming public confrontations from which reasonable retreat is impossible. Anyone who reads the newspapers must realize that vast social changes are in the making, that they must occur if civilized society is to survive.

Vested interests will oppose these changes, of course, but as someone once said, vested interests, however powerful, cannot withstand the gradual encroachment of new ideas. If we psychologists are ready for it, we may be able to contribute a coherent and workable philosophy, based on the science of psychology, that will make this general agitation less negative, that will make it a positive search for something new.

I recognize that many of you will note these ambitions as little more than empty rhetoric. Psychologists will never be up to it, you will say. We should stay in our laboratories and do our own thing. The public will work out its own paradigms without us. Perhaps such skepticism is justified.

On the other hand, difficulty is no excuse for surrender. There is a sense in which the unattainable is the best goal to pursue. So let us continue our struggle to advance psychology as a means of promoting human welfare, each in our own way. For myself, however, I can imagine nothing we could do that would be more relevant to human welfare, and nothing that could pose a greater challenge to the next generation of psychologists, than to discover how best to give psychology away.

References

AMERICAN PSYCHOLOGICAL ASSOCIATION. Bylaws of the American Psychological Association. *1968 Directory*. Washington, D.C.: Author, 1968.

ASHTON-WARNER, S. *Teacher*. New York: Simon & Schuster, 1963.

BAUER, R. A. (Ed.) *Social indicators*. Cambridge: M.I.T. Press, 1966.

BENNETT, C. C. *Community psychology*. Report of Boston Conference on the Education of Psychologists for Community Mental Health. Boston: Boston University, 1966.

DAVIS, K. The perilous promise of behavioral science. In *Research in the service of man: Biomedical knowledge, development, and use*. A conference sponsored by the Subcommittee on Government Research and the Frontiers of Science Foundation of Oklahoma for the Committee on Government, Operations of the U.S. Senate, October 1966. Washington, D.C.: U.S. Government Printing Office, 1967.

DEUTSCH, M. Reflections on some experimental studies of interpersonal conflict. Presidential Address to the Eastern Psychological Association, New York, April 11, 1969.

GRAZIANO, A. M. Clinical innovation and the mental health power structure: A social case history. *American Psychologist*, 1969, *24*, 10–18.

HOFSTADTER, R. *Social Darwinism in American thought*. Philadelphia: University of Pennsylvania Press, 1944.

KUHN, T. *The structure of scientific revolutions*. Chicago: University of Chicago Press, 1962.

LADD, E. C., JR. Professors and political petitions. *Science*, 1969, *163*, 1425–1430.

McGREGOR, D. *The human side of enterprise*. New York: McGraw-Hill, 1960.

SANFORD, F. H. Creative health and the principle of *habeas mentem*. *American Psychologist*, 1955, *10*, 829–835.

TYLER, L. An approach to public affairs: Report of the ad hoc Committee on Public Affairs. *American Psychologist*, 1969, *24*, 1–4.

VARELA, J. A. *Introduction to social science technology.* New York: Academic Press, 1970.

WHITE, R. W. Motivation reconsidered: The concept of competence. *Psychological Review,* 1959, *66,* 297–333.

ZIMBARDO, P., & EBBESON, E. *Influencing attitudes and changing behavior.* Reading, Mass.: Addison-Wesley, 1969.

As the articles in this book demonstrate, many different research methods are used in the various fields of psychology. Scientific research is not limited to the use of certain specific techniques such as laboratory equipment or methods of measurement. Rather science refers to a way of doing things that involves certain basic general principles and procedures.

What then are the essential components of scientific research? What are the actual processes involved in accumulating scientific knowledge and arriving at scientific generalizations? In the following selection, the late Donald G. Marquis, an eminent psychologist who served for many years as chairman of the Psychology Department at the University of Michigan and professor of psychology at MIT, as well as president of the APA, described a sequence of six steps that can be identified in any complete research program. Together, these steps serve as a kind of idealized model or paradigm of the scientific process.

As the author points out, most published research does not fulfill all the criteria of a complete scientific program. Most research is distinguished by competent achievement of one or two of the six steps but is incomplete with respect to one or more of the other steps.

Research Planning at the Frontiers of Science

Donald G. Marquis

Psychology today faces a task of a different order from any before. During its brief period of development it has been relatively free to grow at its own pace and in self-chosen directions. Nutured by steadily expanding college enrollments and with occasional odd-jobs in industry and the clinic, psychology developed its methods, facts, principles and technical skills to a point that enabled it during the crisis of the last war to join with the older sciences in making a significant and effective contribution to the common goal. Psychology has demonstrated its maturity; it can now expect to be called upon to assume the responsibilities of an adult science.

The nature of these responsibilities is now being made clear. Many of the crucial problems facing our society are problems of human relations and social organization. The great advances which have been made in industrial production, in transportation and in communication do not by themselves guarantee the general welfare—indeed, they create such rapid changes in our way of life that the traditional trial and error methods of social adaptation are totally inadequate. Critical gaps in our knowledge are found in mental

Source: Reprinted by permission from *American Psychologist,* 1948, *3* (10), 430–438. Copyright © 1948 by the American Psychological Association.

Note: Address of the president of the American Psychological Association at Boston, September 9, 1948.

hygiene, in designing machines with respect to their operators, in industrial relations, in minority tensions, in educational methods, in social and political organization, and in military defense. Leaders in various activities, impressed by the achievements of science in physical and biological fields, are asking what science can contribute in the psychological and social fields.

The call for new knowledge of human relations is not just a rhetorical call—it is backed up by money and other support. The great philanthropic foundations such as Carnegie and Rockefeller have deliberately allocated a larger share of their resources to research in the social sciences. And the national government has called for tremendous expansion in this field. Every one of the federal departments with the exception of the Post Office is now supporting research on human behavior. The Veterans Administration and the U.S. Public Health Service are spending between two and three million dollars annually in developing the field of clinical psychology through fellowships, hospital and clinic positions, research funds, and training grants to universities. The Department of Army, Navy and Air Forces, now the biggest customers for research of all kinds, have budgeted between 6 and 7 millions this year for studies in psychology and social science which are being carried out partly by military research agencies and partly by contract with university departments and research institutes. There is good reason to believe that the total level of support will have to be doubled or trebled before the clearly recognized needs of the nation will be even approximately met.

This general picture might be considered a source of gratification except for one reservation: there is no guarantee that we can deliver what is expected. Our resources of research know-how are concentrated in the older and better established areas of science while the call now is for knowledge in the less explored fields of human relations and social behavior.

In the title of this paper I used the phrase "frontiers of science." Although all research is by definition at the frontier of knowledge, it seems to me that science itself has a frontier. The scientific method first became clearly established in astronomy, physics and mathematics, and later was extended into biology, agriculture, medicine and psychology—encroaching on areas formerly considered the province of philosophy, religion or practical common sense. In the span of our own lives we have seen this frontier move through the field of psychology. Many of us learned the method of science in studying biology, physics or physiology and brought it to bear on problems of psychology. As late as the decade of the 1920's the most methodologically defensible research was done in the related areas of comparative, sensory or physiological psychology. The frontier has now passed through the areas of learning and of mental abilities and may be recognized somewhere in the fields of interpersonal relations and social psychology, with extensions into anthropology, sociology, economics and political science.

Let us recognize clearly that frontier research is not easy. A useful contribution in the field of human relations will loom large in relation to the present meager level of verified knowledge, but it is not a simple thing to achieve. The eager researcher finds no adequate structure of theory to guide his inquiry; not even a terminology with commonly accepted meanings. He is thwarted by the lack of standard measurement techniques for the relevant variables, and dismayed at the absence of even the simplest kinds of taxonomic data on the materials of his study. The scientist who would forsake the security of a well established research field with the prospect of one sound publication a year must have a certain amount of courage or else a full professorship.

It is not surprising to find that the quality and the product of research in frontier fields appears relatively inferior. Although hundreds of competent individuals are publishing thousands of books and articles each year, one cannot escape the impression that it does not always add up to any very clear and usable result. The intriguing problems are so numerous and diverse that research effort becomes scattered rather than focused. And the individual researches are difficult to put into a cumulative integrated structure because the concepts used are not the same, the observational data are not commensurate, and the samples studied are not chosen or described in such a way as to permit combination.

I can find no reason to doubt that steady progress will continue to be made in the research fields which are now being initially explored. Eventually certain concepts will come into common use, definitions and measures will become more standardized, and a coherent body of knowledge will be built. For those who are content to wait patiently for the inevitable blossoming of the science of human relations I have nothing more to say. For those who share my feeling that the urgencies of our contemporary society demand an accelerated rate of scientific advance I propose to discuss some possible steps toward its achievement.

Scientific progress can not of course be speeded up by command nor by exhortation, nor even by money alone. If the number of scientists and the amount of financial support were doubled there would be twice as much of what we have now, but that may not be enough to keep pace with the needs of our swiftly changing society. And since there are very definite limits on the rate of training additional research experts, it becomes imperative to examine any other possible means of increasing the effectiveness of scientific work. It is my thesis that more attention to planning can greatly accelerate the rate of development of frontier research.

Research planning can be carried out at different levels. I would like to distinguish three levels which I will call experimental design, program design and policy design. Experimental design is the planning of a single specific project. Program design is the planning of an integrated set of projects focused on a central problem. Policy design is a new word for overall planning of the distribution of effort among programs, areas or fields. Planning at the first or project level is a universally accepted requirement of scientific method —it is what distinguishes an experiment from objective openminded common sense observation. In the past decade, following R. A. Fisher's monograph (3), we have all become very much aware of the design of experiments, and statistical method is now taught with as much concern for the planning of research as for the analysis of collected data. Psychologists have shown an unusual interest in and capacity for experimental design. Among the younger members of the profession at least we find widespread sophistication on tests of significance, methods of drawing a sample, null hypothesis and factorial design. You can seldom catch a psychologist without an estimate of the error variance.

At the other end of the scale is the level of policy planning of the broad directions of scientific effort. Psychology and the other sciences have had little experience with this type of planning. General trends in the growth of a science have been the complex resultant of a multitude of individual decisions by scientists about their own work, influenced unsystematically by social needs and pressures such as university policy and available financial support.

There is clear evidence now, that with the growing recognition of the relevance of scientific research to national welfare, the major agencies of research support are assuming responsibility for policy planning. Foundations have always distributed their funds in a pattern designed to stimulate work in certain fields. We have seen the valuable results in psychology of the support of child welfare research institutes during the 1920's. Industrial associations, pharmaceutical firms and organizations such as the cancer or infantile paralysis funds also operate to expand research in selected areas, but so far have had only incidental influence in psychology. The most important planning agency now is the federal government. As it assumes a larger and larger share of the support of scientific research, it establishes planning boards to make sure that funds are allocated wisely. The Office of Scientific Research and Development, created during the last war, undertook responsibility for allocation of money and personnel to the several objectives of the national effort. The OSRD is now succeeded by the Research and Development Board, under the chairmanship of Vannevar Bush, with the task of planning an overall research program for the Army, Navy and Air Force. One of the 15 committees of the Board is the Committee on Human Resources, covering the field of psychology and the social sciences. During the past year the Committee, through its central staff and its numerous advisory panels, has surveyed the current national research activities and has recommended an expansion and redistribution of research effort designed to contribute maximally to both the immediate and the long-range needs of the country. Other evidences of national planning are found in the Bush report (2), and in the report last year by the President's Scientific Research Board (7), and in the recent appointment by the President of an Interdepartmental Committee for Scientific Research. If and when Congress eventually approves the creation of a National Science Foundation there will be an agency with authority and responsibility for planning on an even broader scale.

I do not propose to discuss the procedures or the desirability of policy planning. With the growing tendency toward centralization of research support in federal funds, it is inevitable that allocation of such funds must be made on some basis. At the present time there are no adequate objective procedures for evaluating programs or fields of research, and the most we can expect is that scientists will participate in policy decisions on the distribution of funds. I hope that a few years hence someone will address you on the subject of the criteria and methods of research policy design—but it cannot be done today.

Between the level of experimental design and policy design there is a large gap which neither of them can fill. Policy planning, by virtue of its breadth, can not be a specific guide to actual research. Experimental design, on the other hand, is concerned with the investigation of a restricted question and cannot be a guide in choosing the most significant problems for research attack. I believe that the greatest present need for planning exists as this intermediate level which I call *program design,* and I believe that by exploiting this type of planning we can accelerate the development of frontier research in areas critical for human welfare.

By program design I mean the planning of an integrated series of research activities, focused on a central problem, and involving a number of scientists for several years. This is not, of course, an original idea. There have been outstanding examples of good program design in frontier research, but they are few. Usually they are found in the work of an investigator who keeps his eyes steadily on a central problem throughout his lifetime. One thinks immediately of Ebbinghaus's studies of memorizing, of Pavlov's work on conditioning, of Terman's research on intelligence, on Thurstone's analysis of human abilities, of Hull's and Tolman's programs in rote learning, of Maier's work on reasoning, of Kurt Lewin's studies in group organization. The fruitfulness of such integrated programs of research is what convinces me that it would be worth while to study the characteristics of program design so that the procedure could be more widely used.

I do not believe that it takes a genius to design a research program, nor is it necessary to wait for that rare flash of scientific insight. An example from another field of science may indicate more clearly what I mean. In meteorology there is no theory comparable to that in physics or chemistry. It is conceivable that hundreds of students of weather could carry out in their individual laboratories and field stations a multitude of little unrelated studies. One of them would clock the sunrise in Central standard time; another would report the movement of the moon in Eastern daylight saving time; one of them would record wind velocity on a 7-point descriptive scale; another would devise a windmill gadget and report velocities in reliable but arbitrary units of revolutions per minute. One would study temperature in Albuquerque, another rainfall in Cheyenne. In spite of all the diligence and individual ingenuity of this earnest band of researchers it would be a slow and wasteful process to accumulate useful meteorological knowledge. But because the problem is sufficiently important, the meteorologists have gotten together and agreed to collect commensurate data by standardized methods in all parts of the world. With these data available there has been steady growth in theory and in the accuracy of prediction. This is an extreme example. In most frontier fields it may not be possible to undertake so comprehensive a program but rather to have many programs proceeding simultaneously, each large enough to provide an adequate test of the conceptual theory involved but permitting several alternative approaches to the same general problem.

What, then, is the essential feature of program design? It is the attempt to plan a comprehensive, integrated series of studies in relation to a particular set of concepts focused on a central problem. It is the attempt to broaden and lengthen the scope of a research sufficiently so that we can tell whether it is really getting anywhere. It is scientific method in its full and complete form. I shall list six steps in program design. The temporal sequence of the steps is not fixed although there is a natural order.

1. The first step may be called *problem formulation*. In the selection of a problem there appears to be no restriction on the kind of topic which can be attacked scientifically. "The religious attitudes of middle-west farmers" is as acceptable a problem as the limits of their visual sensitivity. There are, however, two important limitations governing the formulation of a problem for scientific study. The first is that a value proposition cannot be verified by any present scientific methods. It is necessary therefore to separate the value assumptions from the factual propositions which can be investigated. Most of the problems arising from the practical situations of living come to us with a mixture of value and factual questions. We cannot, for example, test the proposition that spaced practice is better than massed practice. Analyzing this problem into its components, we formulate the proposition that spaced practice results in more rapid learning than massed practice, and we do not examine the question of whether rapid learning is desirable or not. Such analysis of a problem poses few difficulties in physical and biological science but is a frequent source of confusion in dealing with topics like labor relations, race prejudice, and therapy.

A second limitation on the scientific method of inquiry is that the phenomenon under study must exist in replication. There is no known method by which a single unique event can be the subject of research. If we are interested in what appears to be a unique situation, such as the explanation of the suicide of a particular individual or the form of organization of the world state, it is necessary to reformulate the problem in terms of those aspects of the situation which can be identified in several instances. This is a serious limitation on the scope of scientific investigation and one which is not completely accepted by all persons who become interested in the significant and real problems of practical life.

2. The second step is *review of knowledge*—of what has been learned or said by others about the topic. The library is the usual source of this material but personal informants are often utilized, for example, in anthropological field work. Although this step is clearly recognized by everyone, the difficulties of achieving it are becoming serious as a result of the tremendous growth in the literature of every field. Abstract journals, bibliographies, sum-

maries and reviews are important aids in this respect and should be extended into frontier fields more adequately than at present. If research is organized into programs it becomes feasible for each to undertake a comprehensive review of current knowledge, and the Office of Naval Research has recognized this need in arranging contracts which include specific provision for literature summaries.

3. The third step is *preliminary observation* of the events under study. This may be quite unstructured observation which enriches the second-hand library knowledge and suggests new leads for investigation. It may also be more controlled observation in the nature of trying out methods of measurement, formulating codes for classification of data, identifying sub-samples of the population and pretesting promising hypotheses. In its most developed form it may be methodological research—a comparison of two or more ways of describing, measuring or scoring the phenomena. A variety and diversity of observational methods is desirable at this point in order to explore most fruitfully the best possible ways of formulating and categorizing the data.

4. The fourth step is *theory construction*—the formulation of specific and rigorous hypotheses for subsequent test. Now the investigator draws upon everything that he has learned from his review of previous work and from preliminary observation. While theory construction can sometimes be achieved in the comfort of the armchair, I do not want to imply that it is easy or routine. It is indeed the crucial test of the creative scientist.

I think we are beginning to realize more clearly that a theory, to be useful, must be built around concepts which have specific and unequivocal relation to empirical observation and measurement. Only in this way can theory be verified. Most of what we have called theory in the new fields of psychology has not been of this type. Our theories have a long life span of controversy because of the difficulties of testing them. Their concepts are not such as can be identified or measured. They were invented on the basis of a priori considerations rather than being abstracted from empirical study and as a result, they do not lend themselves to unequivocal test. It is certainly typical, and perhaps inevitable, that the first theories in a new field, since they aim at broad understanding, are speculative and untestable. Man's desire for explanation does not permit a vacuum in his comprehension of the world. Hence the crystal spheres theory in astronomy; the earth, air, fire and water theory in physical science; the demonological theory of mental disease; the social contract theory of the state; and the instinct theory of human behavior. In the history of science it has usually been necessary to abandon such theories completely rather than to try to modify them to a form which permits testing. We can perhaps accelerate the long-range development of scientific knowledge in frontier fields by emphasis upon the construction of theory out of empirical or operationally-defined concepts. Such theories will necessarily be limited in scope. It is inevitable that the most useful theories will, for some time to come, be small conceptual systems dealing with a restricted range of phenomena.

5. The fifth step is *verification*—the testing of the hypotheses or of deductions from them. If our concepts have been properly chosen and if methods of measurement have been devised, we find adequate guides for verification in our present knowledge of statistical methods. This step in program design is the one which has received the most extensive attention and while it is crucial for science, it is not the primary topic of my discussion. Perhaps the most frequent present limitation in the verification stage is found in the selection of a population for study. Too often in the formulation of a problem we fail to think through the definition of the universe to which our theory is applicable and we are apt to overlook the necessity to select a representative sample of that universe for verification purposes. Considerations of convenience, habit and inadequate funds usually determine that the research will be carried out on any available group of college sophomores, nursery school children, or military personnel. Such studies may be very fruitful and have a definite place in the preliminary observation step. Usually, however, they cannot be made a coordinate part of a total integrated body of knowledge.

The processes of verification may take quite different forms, of which the controlled experiment is only one example. Correlation studies, comparative studies, genetic studies, surveys, intensive case studies, and field studies each have a definite place if they are relevant tests of the theory which has been formulated.

The results of the verification process do not all turn out as the theory predicted. This is not entirely unfortunate, since it provides the clue for reformulation of the theory and hence advance in knowledge. The scientist then proceeds with further tests of his revised theory and in this manner theory construction goes along with experiment and observation in a continuous reciprocal alternation.

6. The sixth and last step in program design is *application* of the verified theory. In pure research, of course, application is not involved since the results are used only to modify the theory. But pure research is rare in frontier fields and application must usually be made directly from the research results rather than indirectly through the theory. Application involves three processes itself: first is a value decision on the desired objective, second is the diagnosis of the specific situation, and third is the selection of the relevant verified knowledge and its application. Consider, for example, the clinical psychologist dealing with a client requesting vocational counseling. A decision must first be made whether a job is to be chosen on the basis of salary, status, interests or some combination of factors. Scientific theory does not determine what job the individual should take; it can only point out the probability of certain consequences of a vocational choice. The decision must be made by the counselor or, better, by the client, in reference to his value system. The diagnosis requires pertinent information about the individual and about the possible jobs. It is then possible to apply knowledge such as "the greater the congruence of a person's abilities with the requirements of an occupation, the greater are the chances of that individual's success and satisfaction in that occupation."

This analysis makes apparent that those persons who are charged with the application of science must have two qualifications over and above their knowledge of research findings: moral responsibility and diagnostic skill. For this reason a class of professionals is created whose long careful training helps to insure effective application of science. The steps in application are usually not very explicit or clear and merge together in what we often call the art of psychological practice. But it seems clear to me that advance in professional psychology will come only with the development of verified theory and of techniques for diagnosing specific situations to determine when the theory is relevant. A complete program design must therefore take account of these needs and make provision for effective application of its results. It is not enough to establish the fact that training first-line supervisors in human relations will result in improved employee morale. If application is to be successful the research program should include studies of the acceptability to management and to unions of supervisor training, and manuals for the training itself. If the nature of the optimal training is different in different situations, there must be diagnostic measures for identification of those situations.

Here, then, is the pattern of program design—the strategy which supplements the tactics of research planning. Its objective is to promote in the undeveloped frontier fields of research what comes naturally in well-established fields. The distinction I am making between effective research and less effective research is not based on the field or topic or practical significance, but only on the basis of its potential incorporation into the body of scientific knowledge. Some studies become a part of the developing science; others are not only forgotten but they leave no trace of any influence. Science can well afford to support work on wild guesses and bizarre hunches, but it cannot afford the wasted effort of indeterminate research—the kind which is not carried far enough to find out whether it is any good or not. If a particular project cannot be clearly related to an existing body of rigorous concepts and theory—and this is the defining condition of frontier research—it is then necessary to design and carry out a program of research. Anything less is apt to join the company of incomplete and forgotten research.

The responsibility for program design falls clearly on the original researcher. Often a suggestive study ends with the statement that "present results are inconclusive and it is hoped that future investigation will throw more light on the problem." I have not made a tally, but I suspect that in nine cases out of ten no other researcher will take up the challenge.

It may be worth while to look briefly at some of the characteristics of research which does not fulfill the criteria of complete program design. Such research is often distinguished by exceptionally competent achievement of one of the six steps in program design but is incomplete with respect to one or more of the other steps. There are certain types which occur frequently enough so they are easily recognizable.

One of these, which I might call *wisdom research,* concentrates on steps 2 and 3, with thorough library study combined with first-hand experience and unsystematic observation. This paper is an example of what I mean and many of the essays and books in anthropology, sociology and political science are of this kind. I do not mean to imply that they are not worth while, but only that as science they are incomplete. Such studies are valuable guides to immediate understanding and fruitful sources of hypotheses, but the absence of systematic data precludes any verification in the scientific sense. It would be unfortunate if good work of the wisdom type were permitted to block the best work of the scientific type.

Another frequent kind of incomplete program is one which fails to formulate a central problem. Although there is collection of numerous data, there is no adequate criterion to which the data can be related. We might call this *unfocused research*. For example, one might lay out an elaborate research to compare lecture with discussion methods of teaching, arranging equated groups of students, random assignment of instructors and elaborate records of teaching procedures. But what will be the criterion of better teaching? It will probably turn out that the students will do equally well on the final examination, at which point we protest that that is no measure of what we mean by good teaching. But unless such a measure is included in the research, the extensive data serve no function. Sometimes the failure to identify and measure the ultimate criterion is an oversight from lack of planning; more often it is just too difficult to measure as in the case of the air crew selection research program (4). But whatever the reason, we will not have adequate program design in problems such as counseling, supervisor training and leader selection until adequate criterion measures are included.

Practical research is a special case—it may be complete with respect to the specific local problem which it undertakes to investigate and at the same time be incomplete from the standpoint of its contribution to the development of science. When existing knowledge does not provide a solution to some immediate and local question it becomes necessary to try out new hypotheses. Although the new knowledge may be adequate for the solution of the specific problem, it is not usually in such form as to permit its general application. For example, the research division of company A may find out that music during the morning rest period in the shipping department results in increased output. This finding is all that is necessary to answer the particular problem, but its application beyond that department is limited. There is no basis for diagnosing other situations to determine which ones would be similar and which different.

The distinction between practical research and theoretical or pure research is a matter of degree—the degree of generality of the results. Theoretical research often finds useful practical application, and there is no necessary reason why practical research should not have theoretical significance. But theory is always general, and practical research can contribute to theory only if deliberate design provides adequate statement of the variables in general terms and verification with samples that can be related to known general universes.

Descriptive research is another example of incomplete program design. A full, accurate, unbiased record of observations is of course desirable, but it does not constitute the ultimate objective of research. Examples of descriptive research are often found in clinical case studies, community studies and public opinion polls. Such data are invaluable when they are collected in order to test theoretical propositions, but by themselves they represent an incomplete scientific program. It may be worth while to note the several places in program design where description is appropriate, using clinical case studies for an example. They may be useful in step 3 as a rich source of theoretical concepts and hypotheses; they may be useful in step 5 for verification, provided that commensurate data are secured from a number of individuals; they may be valuable in step 6 as a guide to the diagnosis which is necessary for application of scientific knowledge. The further possibility that case study can be used to construct and verify a theory for a single individual has been explored by Allport (1). The necessary replication of instances is secured by observing repeated behaviors of the same individual, and this becomes an example of practical or local research.

A special case of descriptive research is that in which the investigators seem rigidly tied to a particular technique or method which is applied over and over again to new populations without sufficient regard to its adequacy for the problem being studied. There was a period which most of us can remember when this seemed to be true of animal maze research and conditioning research. And there may be some who wonder if there is similar danger in the present utilization of the Rorschach test, attitude tests, or sociometric ratings. Another evidence of rigidity in research planning comes from the habitual identification of a method with a particular kind of problem. Because a question falls in the field of clinical psychology does not necessarily mean that methods for its investigation are limited to diagnostic tests and interviews. It is encouraging to see more and more examples of the use of laboratory methods in clinical problems, of clinical methods in social problems, and of social methods in industrial problems.

Theoretical studies of a certain kind represent another type of incomplete research. Theory is an indispensable part of science but the elaborate analysis of concepts which have no clear referents in observation or measurement has limited utility in the development of a scientific body of knowledge. Such an analysis provides a systematization of a field which leads to a feeling of understanding but which carries no very clear guides for the next steps in the scientific process. An outstanding example of the highest type of theoretical analysis is found in Charles Morris' recent book on *Signs, Languages and Behavior*. If I am right, his book will stand for many years as the best treatment of the subject, but the developments and changes in our theory of language behavior will find their origins elsewhere.

My last example of incomplete research may be called *critical ratio research*. There are many studies impeccable in their experimental design, unassailable in their careful controls, ending up with a significant difference at a probability level less than .01—and not much else. I sometimes wonder if the critical ratio has been more harmful than helpful in its seductive implication that it signifies a completed research. If we find that there is a significant difference between carpenters and machinists in their attitude toward unionization, we have established a scientific fact, but what do we know? We know very little about the differences between carpenters and machinists if that is what we are interested in, and we know only a tiny fraction of what determines attitudes toward unionization, if that is what we are interested in. Perhaps it may help us to see our problems in their totality if we make more widespread use of the technique of expressing the effect of a variable in terms of the proportion of the total variance which it determines.

It should be apparent now that the burden of my thesis is that each phase or step of scientific research is essential and valuable, but that only in planned combination do they yield the kind of knowledge which becomes a part of the body of science. The pattern of total research is not easy to achieve and it involves definite compromises and limitations. In order to secure commensurate data on many instances for verification it is necessary to give up the ideal of complete description. To get a theory which is testable it is necessary to sacrifice breadth and scope. To do research which is relevant to the critical problems of practical living it is necessary to give up some degree of rigor and the security of working in the better established fields. To achieve the complete pattern of program design it is necessary to give up the desire to get a scientific answer tomorrow to problems like labor unrest, divorce, or world organization.

I would like to be able to suggest some mechanisms and procedures which would be helpful in program design. Although I have participated in planning several researches, I do not have any systematic data on the best ways of doing it. Certain procedural necessities, however, seem to follow naturally from the conception of program design.

The first requisite of program design is that projects must be planned on a bigger scale than that to which we are accustomed. They must extend over a period of years and must involve a number of investigators if they are to meet the requirements. And if they are going to deal scientifically with critical current problems they must have facilities for the extensive collection of data on adequate samples of the population studied. Under present conditions of scarcity of research talent it is desirable to make maximal utilization of every competent researcher by the provision of sufficient assistants, clerks and technicians. In comparing several projects, I have found that it is possible to plan an effective rate of expenditure of $15,000–$20,000 per year for each experienced professional scientist.

A program of such size does not offer any serious problems of administration but it requires the services of a director who will coordinate the planning and the component projects in such a way that the focus of the research is always clear. The professional personnel may number three, four or five to secure a well coordinated yet diversified group. The diversity of backgrounds is a particular advantage of program research.

I am convinced that planning by a group of scientists is superior to individual planning. It seems desirable to take advantage of a variety of skills and experiences in order not to overlook any possible hypotheses and techniques. In talking with persons who have had experiences in planning, I have not found one who did not believe that the outcome of group discussion was superior to the ideas with which he went into the conference. In the planning phase the research team may be supplemented by consultants who are appointed specifically for this function. Such a procedure enables the research to take advantage of the abilities of university staff members whose teaching duties do not permit more than part time or occasional association with the project. The advantage of a diverse team of scientists will be equally clear in the preliminary observation and verification steps. The available research methods are many and no one person is master of all those which may turn out to be relevant for the research. Frontier research is frequently interdisciplinary. The traditional academic fields of knowledge are a reflection and crystallization of the work of the past fifty years, but frontier research is breaking into new problem areas.

The program design should contain a schedule of the several phases of the work. The time allotted to preliminary library work, observation, planning, methodological work, and pretesting should undoubtedly be greater than is usually allowed. In many instances this phase will be longer than that devoted to collection of verification data, and it seems reasonable to expect a research project of the size we are talking about to spend at least a year in preliminary work. When the verification stage is once begun the concepts, measures and hypotheses are no longer changeable. A continuous project might very well plan for a recurring cycle of operations in which planning, data collecting, and application are repeated more than once. This enables each phase of the program to profit from what is learned in the other phases. It helps to guard against the occasional tragedy in which, at the end, you discover that you have failed to take account of the most important variable.

Research planning today should also make provision for the systematic training of young scientists, in view of their current shortage. Advanced graduate students on half-time assistantships and post-doctoral psychologists on well-paid internships are the most available possibilities for training. Training in program or large scale group research is not the traditional pattern for the doctoral dissertation, but I hope that graduate schools will recognize the value of such training and permit reasonable flexibility in their requirements. I shall count it a mark of distinct advance when some university awards the doctoral degree to three students who worked together to achieve a significant program of research and submitted only one thesis.

Program design, with the objectives and procedures which I have tried to outline, is not intended of course to replace individual and small scale studies. This would be impossible as well as undesirable. It is intended rather that an increased number of large and well planned research programs will carry the scientific development of a frontier topic to the point where theory and data can provide guides for the individual researcher and make possible the incorporation of his work in the growing integrated body of scientific knowledge. The urgent requirement for new verified knowledge of interpersonal relations and social organization calls for acceleration in the development of the frontier fields of psychology, and if we are to meet our responsibilities we must exploit every possible means of speeding this advance.

References

1. ALLPORT, G. W. *The use of personal documents in psychological science.* New York: Social Science Research Council, 1942.
2. BUSH, V. *Science, the endless frontier.* U.S. Govt. Printing Office, 1945.
3. FISHER, R. A. *The design of experiments.* Edinburgh: Oliver and Boyd, 1935.
4. JENKINS, J. G. Validity for what? *J. Consult. Psychol.,* 1946, *10,* 93–98.
5. NATIONAL RESOURCES PLANNING BOARD. *Research—A national resource.* 3 vols. U.S. Govt. Printing Office, 1938 and 1941.
6. PRESIDENT'S COMMISSION ON HIGHER EDUCATION, George F. Zook, chairman. *Higher education for American democracy.* 6 vols. U.S. Govt. Printing Office, 1947.
7. PRESIDENT'S SCIENTIFIC RESEARCH BOARD, John R. Steelman, chairman. *Science and public policy.* 6 vols. U.S. Govt. Printing Office, 1947.

Section Two
SOCIAL PSYCHOLOGY

In a real sense, virtually all people are social psychologists. That is, people tend to be interested in the topics of social psychology: why people like or dislike one another, how other people's opinions are best influenced, how prejudices are formed or eliminated, how children acquire and practice an enduring set of values, and so forth.

This is, of course, another way of saying that social psychology is a highly relevant science—it deals with topics and issues of paramount importance in our everyday life. But when I say "virtually all people are social psychologists," I mean to underscore far more than the relevance of social psychology as a science. I mean, in addition, that almost everyone actively forms theories and tests hypotheses about the effects of various social behaviors. The adolescent girl who spends hours in front of a mirror practicing her smile is testing an implicit theory of interpersonal attraction; the political candidate (or her speechwriter) is testing her ideas of persuasion every time she appears before her constituents, and every mother has some notion of what she can do to help her child grow into a decent, ethical person rather than a liar or a cheat.

Moreover, this is not a recent phenomenon. It is a safe guess that people have always been social psychologists. We do know that our earliest literature—from Eve's successful influence attempt on Adam to Moses' use of magic tricks to build up his credibility in the eyes of the Pharaoh—is replete with evidence of concern with these topics. In a more systematic sense, Aristotle laid out some of the basic principles of persuasion some 2300 years ago, while in the much more recent past, Benedictus Spinoza came out with a systematic theory of why people like each other.

And this is the exciting part. While systematic theories relevant to social psychological phenomena have existed at least since Aristotle, it has

only been in the past forty years or so that social psychologists have developed
the tools and the techniques to test these theories in a vigorous scientific
manner! Thus, while Aristotle's ideas have excited students for 2300 years,
we were not certain of their exact truth until they were tested scientifically by
Carl Hovland and Walter Weiss, as recently as 1951; and while Spinoza had
some remarkable insights about attraction in the seventeenth century, these
were first examined rigorously by Elliot Aronson and Darwyn Linder in 1965.

The articles in this section were carefully selected to capture the
sweep of social psychology as a science and to broaden and deepen the reader's
knowledge of social psychology. Intending to choose original writings of
central importance, I selected four articles that can best be described as
contemporary classics. Each article in this section has not only withstood the
test of time, but, in addition, each is as important today as it was on the day
it was published—important both for the advancement of social psychology as
a science as well as for its application to the problems of the world. The topics
represented in these articles cover a wide range of areas, including how to
understand the effects of desegregation on racial prejudice, how to implant
values in children, how to influence people, and how to win friends.

A word of caution to the reader: scholarly articles are often written
in a scholarly manner—complete with detailed descriptions of the research
methods employed in building the experiment as well as an analysis of statistics
employed to help understand the data. As a reader, you may be interested
in every detail of all aspects of each article, and then again you may not.
Accordingly, you may have to train yourself to read selectively. If you are
interested in the details of the methodology, then you will want to read the
sections on methods carefully; if you are interested in the techniques of social
psychologists only in the most general sense, then you may want to skim
through the methods section. In short, the articles will be difficult to read
only if you allow yourself to become bogged down in the aspects of the
readings which are of peripheral concern to you.

Elliot Aronson

In the following article, Thomas Pettigrew surveys desegregation as a social psychological phenomenon. He shows how prejudiced racial attitudes are beginning to soften, and he discusses the role that desegregation has played in the reduction of prejudice. Pettigrew attributes a good deal of prejudice to the tendency people have to conform to the social norms of the community. Thus, as norms begin to shift (through desegregation, for example), prejudice gradually diminishes. According to Pettigrew, many individuals are "latent liberals"—that is, they do not have a deep-seated need to be prejudiced but will become more liberal as soon as they perceive the norm shifting toward the acceptance, rather than the rejection, of ethnic minorities.

Social Psychology and Desegregation Research

Thomas F. Pettigrew

What one hears and what one sees of southern race relations today are sharply divergent. Consider some of the things that occur in interviews with white Southerners.

"As much as my family likes TV," confided a friendly North Carolina farmer, "we always turn the set off when they put them colored people on." But as the two of us were completing the interview, a series of famous Negro entertainers performed on the bright, 21-inch screen in the adjoining room. No one interrupted them.

A rotund banker in Charleston, South Carolina, was equally candid in his remarks: "Son, under no conditions will the white man and the black man ever get together in this state." He apparently preferred to ignore the government sponsored integration at his city's naval installation, just a short distance from his office.

Another respondent, this time a highly educated Chattanooga businessman, patiently explained to me for over an hour how race relations had not changed at all in his city during the past generation. As I left his office building, I saw a Negro policeman directing downtown traffic. It was the first Negro traffic cop I had ever seen in the South.

The South today is rife with such contradictions; social change has simply been too rapid for many Southerners to recognize it. Such a situation commands the attention of psychologists—particularly those in the South.

Source: Reprinted by permission from *American Psychologist*, 1961, *16*, 105–112. Copyright © 1961 by the American Psychological Association.

Note: This paper was given as an invited address at the Annual Meeting of the Southeastern Psychological Association, Atlanta, Georgia, March 31, 1960. The author wishes to express his appreciation to Gordon W. Allport of Harvard University, E. Earl Baughman of the University of North Carolina, and Cooper C. Clements of Emory University for their suggestions.

There are many other aspects of this sweeping process that should command our professional attention. To name just two, both the pending violence and the stultifying conformity attendant with desegregation are uniquely psychological problems. We might ask, for instance, what leads to violence in some desegregating communities, like Little Rock and Clinton, and not in others, like Norfolk and Winston-Salem? A multiplicity of factors must be relevant and further research is desperately needed to delineate them; but tentative early work seems to indicate that desegregation violence so far has been surprisingly "rational." That is, violence has generally resulted in localities where at least some of the authorities give prior hints that they would gladly return to segregation if disturbances occurred; peaceful integration has generally followed firm and forceful leadership.[1]

Research concerning conformity in the present situation is even more important. Many psychologists know from personal experience how intense the pressures to conform in racial attitudes have become in the present-day South; indeed, it appears that the first amendment guaranteeing free speech is in as much peril as the fourteenth amendment. Those who dare to break consistently this conformity taboo must do so in many parts of the South under the intimidation of slanderous letters and phone calls, burned crosses, and even bomb threats. Moreover, this paper will contend that conformity is the social psychological key to analyzing desegregation.

It is imperative that psychologists study these phenomena for two reasons: first, our psychological insights and methods are needed in understanding and solving this, our nation's primary internal problem; second, this process happening before our eyes offers us a rare opportunity to test in the field the psychological concomitants of cultural stress and social change. Thus I would like in this paper to assess some of the prospects and directions of these potential psychological contributions.

Role of Social Science in the Desegregation Process to Date

The role of social science, particularly sociology and psychology, in the desegregation process has been much publicized and critized by southern segregationists.[2] Many of these critics apparently think that sociology is synonymous with socialism and psychology with brainwashing. In any event, their argument that we have been crucially important in the Supreme Court desegregation cases of the fifties is based largely on the reference to seven social science documents in Footnote 11 of the famous 1954 *Brown* v. *Board of Education* decision. It would be flattering for us to think that our research has

---

[1] Clark (1953) predicted this from early border-state integration, and a variety of field reports have since documented the point in specific instances.

[2] For instance, once-liberal Virginius Dabney (1957, p. 14), editor of the *Richmond Times-Dispatch,* charged that "the violence at Little Rock . . . never would have happened if nine justices had not consulted sociologists and psychologists, instead of lawyers, in 1954, and attempted to legislate through judicial decrees."

had such a dramatic effect on the course of history as segregationists claim, but in all truth we do not deserve such high praise.

In making their claim that the 1954 decision was psychological and not legal, the segregationists choose to overlook several things. The 1954 ruling did not come suddenly "out of the blue"; it was a logical continuation of a 44-year Supreme Court trend that began in 1910 when a former private in the Confederate Army, the liberal Edward White, became Chief Justice (Logan, 1956). When compared to this backdrop, our influence on the 1954 ruling was actually of only footnote importance. Furthermore, the language and spirit of the 1896 *Plessy* v. *Ferguson,* separate-but-equal decision, so dear to the hearts of segregationists, were as immersed in the jargon and thinking of the social science of that era as the 1954 decision was of our era. Its 1896, Sumnerian argument that laws cannot change "social prejudices" (Allport, 1954, pp. 469–473) and its use of such social Darwinism terms as "racial instincts" and "natural affinities" lacked only a footnote to make it as obviously influenced by the then current social science as the 1954 ruling.

A final reason why we do not deserve the flattering praise of the segregationists is our failure to make substantial contributions to the process since 1954. The lack of penetrating psychological research in this area can be traced directly to three things: the lack of extensive foundation support, conformity pressures applied in many places in the South that deter desegregation research, and the inadequacy of traditional psychological thinking to cope with the present process. Let us discuss each of these matters in turn.

A few years ago Stuart Cook (1957) drew attention to the failure of foundations to support desegregation research; the situation today is only slightly improved. It appears that a combination of foundation fears has produced this situation. One set of fears, as Cook noted, may stem from concern over attacks by southern Congressmen on their tax free status; the other set may stem from boycotts carried out by some segregationists against products identified with the foundations. In any case, this curtailment of funds is undoubtedly one reason why social scientists have so far left this crucial process relatively unstudied. Recently, however, a few moderate sized grants have been made for work in this area; hopefully, this is the beginning of a reappraisal by foundations of their previous policies. And it is up to us to submit competent research proposals to them to test continually for any change of these policies.

It is difficult to assess just how much damage has been done to desegregation research in the South by segregationist pressures. Probably the number of direct refusals to allow such research by southern institutions outside of the Black Belt has actually been small. More likely, the greatest harm has been rendered indirectly by the stifling atmosphere which prevents us from actually testing the limits of research opportunities. Interested as we may be in the racial realm, we decide to work in a less controversial area. Perhaps it is less a matter of courage than it is of resignation in the face of what are thought to be impossible barriers. If these suspicions are correct, there is real hope for overcoming in part this second obstacle to desegregation research.

In some situations, there should be little resistance. In racially integrated veterans' hospitals, for instance, much needed personality studies comparing Negro and white patients should be possible. In other situations, the amount of resistance to race research may be less than we anticipate. Since Little Rock, many so-called "moderates" in the South, particularly businessmen, have become more interested in the dynamics of desegregation. This is not to say that they are more in favor of racial equality than they were; it is only to suggest that the bad publicity, the closing of schools, and the economic losses suffered by Little Rock have made these influential Southerners more receptive to objective and constructive research on the process. It is for this reason that it is imperative the limits for the southern study of desegregation be tested at this time.

Finally, psychological contributions to desegregation research have been restricted by the inadequacy of traditional thinking in our discipline. More specifically, the relative neglect of situational variables in interracial behavior and a restricted interpretation and use of the attitude concept hinder psychological work in this area.

The importance of the situation for racial interaction has been demonstrated in a wide variety of settings. All-pervasive racial attitudes are often not involved; many individuals seem fully capable of immediate behavioral change as situations change. Thus in Panama there is a divided street, the Canal Zone side of which is racially segregated and the Panamanian side of which is racially integrated. Biesanz and Smith (1951) report that most Panamanians and Americans appear to accommodate without difficulty as they go first on one side of the street and then on the other. Likewise in the coal mining county of McDowell, West Virginia, Minard (1952) relates that the majority of Negro and white miners follow easily a traditional pattern of integration below the ground and almost complete segregation above the ground. The literature abounds with further examples: southern white migrants readily adjusting to integrated situations in the North (Killian, 1949), northern whites approving of employment and public facility integration but resisting residential integration (Reitzes, 1953), etc. Indeed, at the present time in the South there are many white Southerners who are simultaneously adjusting to bus and public golf course integration and opposing public school integration. Or, as in Nashville, they may have accepted school integration but are opposing lunch counter integration.

This is not to imply that generalized attitudes on race are never invoked. There are some Panamanians and some Americans who act about the same on both sides of the Panamanian street. Minard (1952) estimated about two-fifths of the West Virginian miners he observed behave consistently in either a tolerant or an intolerant fashion both below and above ground. And some whites either approve or disapprove of all desegregation. But these people are easily explained by traditional theory. They probably consist of the extremes in authoritarianism; their attitudes on race are so generalized and so salient that their consistent behavior in racial situations is sometimes in defiance of the prevailing social norms.

On the other hand, the "other directed" individuals who shift their behavior to keep in line with shifting expectations present the real problem for psychologists. Their racial attitudes appear less salient, more specific, and more tied to particular situations. Conformity needs are predominantly important for these people, and we shall return shortly to a further discussion of these conformists.

One complication introduced by a situational analysis is that interracial contact itself frequently leads to the modification of attitudes. A number of studies of racially integrated situations have noted dramatic attitude changes, but in most cases the changes involved specific, situation linked attitudes. For example, white department store employees become more accepting of Negroes in the work situation after equal status, integrated contact but not necessarily more accepting in other situations (Harding & Hogrefe, 1952). And *The American Soldier* studies (Stouffer, Suchman, DeVinney, Star, & Williams, 1949) found that the attitudes of white army personnel toward the Negro as a fighting man improve after equal status, integrated contact in combat, but their attitudes toward the Negro as a social companion do not necessarily change. In other words, experience in a novel situation of equal status leads to acceptance of that specific situation for many persons. Situations, then, not only structure specific racial behavior, but they may change specific attitudes in the process.

One final feature of a situational analysis deserves mention. Typically in psychology we have tested racial attitudes in isolation, apart from conflicting attitudes and values. Yet this is not realistic. As the desegregation process slowly unfolds in such resistant states as Virginia and Georgia, we see clearly that many segregationist Southerners value law and order, public education, and a prosperous economy above their racial views. Once such a situation pits race against other entrenched values, we need to know the public's hierarchy of these values. Thus a rounded situational analysis requires the measures of racial attitudes in the full context of countervalues.[3]

A second and related weakness in our psychological approach is the failure to exploit fully the broad and dynamic implications of the attitude concept. Most social psychological research has dealt with attitudes as if they were serving only an expressive function; but racial attitudes in the South require a more complex treatment.

In their volume, *Opinion and Personality,* Smith, Bruner, and White (1956) urge a more expansive interpretation of attitudes. They note three attitude functions. First, there is the *object appraisal* function; attitudes aid in understanding "reality" as it is defined by the culture. Second, attitudes can

[3] A popular treatment of this point has been made by Zinn (1959).

play a *social adjustment* role by contributing to the individual's identification with, or differentiation from, various reference groups. Finally, attitudes may reduce anxiety by serving an expressive or *externalization* function.

> Externalization occurs when an individual . . . senses an analogy between a perceived environmental event and some unresolved inner problem . . . [and] adopts an attitude . . . which is a transformed version of his way of dealing with his inner difficulty (pp. 41–44).

At present the most fashionable psychological theories of prejudice —frustration-aggression, psychoanalytic, and authoritarianism—all deal chiefly with the externalization process. Valuable as these theories have been, this exclusive attention to the expressive component of attitudes has been at the expense of the object appraisal and social adjustment components. Moreover, it is the contention of this paper that these neglected and more socially relevant functions, particularly social adjustment, offer the key to further psychological advances in desegregation research.[4]

The extent to which this psychological concentration on externalization has influenced the general public was illustrated recently in the popular reaction to the swastika desecrations of Jewish temples. The perpetrators, all agreed, must be juvenile hoodlums, or "sick," or both. In other words, externalization explanations were predominantly offered.[5] Valid though these explanations may be in many cases, is it not also evident that the perpetrators were accurately reflecting the anti-Semitic norms of their subcultures? Thus their acts and the attitudes behind their acts are socially adjusting for these persons, given the circles in which they move.

Much less the public, some sociologists, too, have been understandably misled by our overemphasis on externalization into underestimating the psychological analysis of prejudice. One sociologist (Rose, 1956) categorically concludes:

> There is no evidence that . . . any known source of "prejudice" in the psychological sense is any more prevalent in the South than in the North (p. 174).

Two others (Rabb & Lipset, 1959) maintain firmly:

> the psychological approach, as valuable as it is, does not explain the preponderance of people who engage in prejudiced behavior, but do *not* have special emotional problems (p. 26).

---

[4] Though this paper emphasizes the social adjustment aspect of southern attitudes toward Negroes, the equally neglected object appraisal function is also of major importance. Most southern whites know only lower class Negroes; consequently their unfavorable stereotype of Negroes serves a definite reality function.

[5] Such explanations also serve for many anti-Semitic observers as an ego-alien defense against guilt.

Both of these statements assume, as some psychologists have assumed, that externalization is the only possible psychological explanation of prejudice. These writers employ cultural and situational norms as explanatory concepts for racial prejudice and discrimination, but fail to see that conformity needs are the personality reflections of these norms and offer an equally valid concept on the psychological level. To answer the first assertion, recent evidence indicates that conformity to racial norms, one "known source of prejudice," is "more prevalent in the South than in the North." To answer the second assertion, strong needs to conform to racial norms in a sternly sanctioning South, for instance, are *not* "special emotional problems." Psychology is not just a science of mental illness nor must psychological theories of prejudice be limited to the mentally ill.

Conformity and Social Adjustment in Southern Racial Attitudes

Evidence of the importance of conformity in southern attitudes on race has been steadily accumulating in recent years. The relevant data come from several different research approaches; one of these is the study of anti-Semitism. Roper's (1946, 1947) opinion polls have twice shown the South, together with the Far West, to be one of the least anti-Semitic regions in the United States. Knapp's (1944) study of over 1,000 war rumors from all parts of the country in 1942 lends additional weight to this finding. He noted that anti-Semitic stories constituted 9% of the nation's rumors but only 3% of the South's rumors. By contrast, 8.5% of the southern rumors concerned the Negro as opposed to only 3% for the nation as a whole. Consistent with these data, too, is Prothro's (1952) discovery that two-fifths of his white adult sample in Louisiana was quite favorable in its attitudes toward Jews but at the same time quite unfavorable in its attitudes toward Negroes. But if the externalization function were predominant in southern anti-Negro attitudes, the South should also be highly anti-Semitic. Externalizing bigots do not select out just the Negro; they typically reject all out-groups, even, as Hartley (1946) has demonstrated, out-groups that do not exist.

Further evidence comes from research employing the famous F Scale measure of authoritarianism (Adorno, Frenkel-Brunswik, Levinson, & Sanford, 1950). Several studies, employing both student and adult samples, have reported southern F Scale means that fall well within the range of means of comparable nonsouthern groups (Milton, 1952; Pettigrew, 1959; Smith & Prothro, 1957). Moreover, there is no evidence that the family pattern associated with authoritarianism is any more prevalent in the South than in other parts of the country (Davis, Gardner, & Gardner, 1941; Dollard, 1937). It seems clear, then, that the South's heightened prejudice against the Negro cannot be explained in terms of any regional difference in authoritarianism. This is not to deny, however, the importance of the F Scale in predicting individual differences; it appears to correlate with prejudice in southern samples at approximately the same level as in northern samples (Pettigrew, 1959).

The third line of evidence relates conformity measures directly to racial attitudes. For lack of a standardized, nonlaboratory measure, one study defined conformity and deviance in terms of the respondents' social characteristics (Pettigrew, 1959). For a southern white sample with age and education held constant, potentially conforming respondents (i.e., females or church attenders) were *more* anti-Negro than their counterparts (i.e., males or nonattenders of church), and potentially deviant respondents (i.e., armed service veterans or political independents) were *less* anti-Negro than their counterparts (i.e., nonveterans or political party identifiers). None of these differences were noted in a comparable northern sample. Furthermore, Southerners living in communities with relatively small percentages of Negroes were less anti-Negro than Southerners living in communities with relatively large percentages of Negroes, though they were *not* less authoritarian. In short, respondents most likely to be conforming to cultural pressures are more prejudiced against Negroes in the South but not in the North. And the percentage of Negroes in the community appears to be a fairly accurate index of the strength of these southern cultural pressures concerning race.

Thus all three types of research agree that conformity to the stern racial norms of southern culture is unusually crucial in the South's heightened hostility toward the Negro.[6] Or, in plain language, it is the path of least resistance in most southern circles to favor white supremacy. When an individual's parents and peers are racially prejudiced, when his limited world accepts racial discrimination as a given of life, when his deviance means certain ostracism, then his anti-Negro attitudes are not so much expressive as they are socially adjusting.

This being the case, it is fortunate that a number of significant laboratory and theoretical advances in the conformity realm have been made recently in our discipline. Solomon Asch's (1951) pioneer research on conformity, followed up by Crutchfield (1955) and others, has provided us with a wealth of laboratory findings, many of them suggestive for desegregation research. And theoretical analyses of conformity have been introduced by Kelman (1958, 1961), Festinger (1953, 1957), and Thibaut and Kelley (1959); these, too, are directly applicable for desegregation research. Indeed, research in southern race relations offers a rare opportunity to test these empirical and theoretical formulations in the field on an issue of maximum salience.

Consider the relevance of one of Asch's (1951) intriguing findings. Asch's standard situation, you will recall, employed seven pre-instructed assistants and a genuine subject in a line judgment task. On two-thirds of the judgments, the seven assistants purposely reported aloud an obviously incorrect estimate; thus the subject, seated eighth, faced unanimous pressure to conform by making a similarly incorrect response. On approximately one-third of such judgments, he yielded to the group; like the others, he would estimate a 5-inch

---

[6] Similar analyses of South African student data indicate that the social adjustment function may also be of unusual importance in the anti-African attitudes of the English in the Union (Pettigrew, 1958, 1960).

line as 4 inches. But when Asch disturbed the unanimity by having one of his seven assistants give the correct response, the subjects yielded only a tenth, rather than a third, of the time. Once unanimity no longer existed, even when there was only one supporting colleague, the subject could better withstand the pressure of the majority to conform. To carry through the analogy to today's crisis in the South, obvious 5-inch lines are being widely described as 4 inches. Many Southerners, faced with what appears to be solid unanimity, submit to the distortion. But when even one respected source—a minister, a newspaper editor, even a college professor—conspicuously breaks the unanimity, *perhaps* a dramatic modification is achieved in the private opinions of many conforming Southerners. Only an empirical test can learn if such a direct analogy is warranted.

Consider, too, the relevance of recent theoretical distinctions. Kelman (1958, 1961), for example, has clarified the concept of conformity by pointing out that three separate processes are involved: *compliance, identification,* and *internalization*. Compliance exists when an individual accepts influence not because he believes in it, but because he hopes to achieve a favorable reaction from an agent who maintains surveillance over him. Identification exists when an individual accepts influence because he wants to establish or maintain a satisfying relationship with another person or group. The third process, internalization, exists when an individual accepts influence because the content of the behavior itself is satisfying; unlike the other types of conformity, internalized behavior will be performed without the surveillance of the agent or a salient relationship with the agent. It is with this third process that Kelman's ideas overlap with authoritarian theory.

We have all witnessed illustrations of each of these processes in the acceptance by Southerners of the region's racial norms. The "Uncle Tom" Negro is an example of a compliant Southerner; another example is furnished by the white man who treats Negroes as equals only when not under the surveillance of other whites. Identification is best seen in white Southerners whose resistance to racial integration enables them to be a part of what they erroneously imagine to be Confederate tradition. Such identifiers are frequently upwardly mobile people who are still assimilating to urban society; they strive for social status by identifying with the hallowed symbols and shibboleths of the South's past. Southerners who have internalized the white supremacy dictates of the culture are the real racists who use the issue to gain political office, to attract resistance group membership fees, or to meet personality needs. Southerners with such contrasting bases for their racial attitudes should react very differently toward desegregation. For instance, compliant whites can be expected to accept desegregation more readily than those who have internalized segregationist norms.

On the basis of this discussion of conformity, I would like to propose a new concept: *the latent liberal*. This is not to be confused with the cherished southern notion of the "moderate"; the ambiguous term "moderate" is presently used to describe everything from an integrationist who wants to be socially accepted to a racist who wants to be polite. Rather, the latent liberal refers to the Southerner who is neither anti-Semitic nor authoritarian but whose conformity habits and needs cause him to be strongly anti-Negro. Through the processes of compliance and identification, the latent liberal continues to behave in a discriminatory fashion toward Negroes even though such behavior conflicts with his basically tolerant personality. He is at the present time *il*liberal on race, but he has the personality potentiality of becoming liberal once the norms of the culture change. Indeed, as the already unleashed economic, legal, political, and social forces restructure the South's racial norms, the latent liberal's attitudes about Negroes will continue to change. Previously cited research suggests that there are today an abundance of white Southerners who meet this latent liberal description; collectively, they will reflect on the individual level the vast societal changes now taking place in the South.

Some Suggested Directions for Future Psychological Research on Desegregation [7]

We are in serious need of research on the Negro, both in the North and in the South. Most psychological research in this area was conducted during the 1930s and directed at testing racists' claims of Negro inferiority. But the most sweeping advances in American Negro history have been made in the past generation, requiring a fresh new look—particularly at the Negro personality.

Two aspects of this research make it complex and difficult. In the first place, the race of the interviewer is a complicating and not as yet fully understood factor. Further methodological study is needed on this point. Moreover, special problems of control are inherent in this research. Not only are there some relatively unique variables that must be considered (e.g., migration history, differential experience with the white community, etc.), but such simple factors as education are not easy to control. For instance, has the average graduate of a southern rural high school for Negroes received an education equal to the average graduate of such a school for whites? No, in spite of the South's belated efforts to live up to separate-but-equal education, available school data indicate that the graduates have probably not received equivalent educations. Yet some recent research on Negro personality has been based on the assumption that Negro and white education in the South are equivalent (e.g., Smith & Prothro, 1957).

Fortunately, the Institute for Research in the Social Sciences at the University of North Carolina has embarked on a large study of many of these content and methodological problems. It is to be hoped that their work will stimulate other efforts.

Some of the most valuable psychological data now available on desegregation have been collected by public opinion polls. But typically these

[7] For other suggestions, see the important analysis of desegregation by Cook (1957).

data have been gathered without any conceptual framework to guide their coverage and direction.

For example, one of the more interesting poll findings is that a majority of white Southerners realize that racial desegregation of public facilities is inevitable even though about six out of seven strongly oppose the process (Hyman & Sheatsley, 1956). The psychological implications of this result are so extensive that we would like to know more. Do the respondents who oppose desegregation but accept its inevitability have other characteristics of latent liberals? Are these respondents more often found outside of the Black Belt? Typically, we cannot answer such questions from present poll data; we need to build into the desegregation polls broader coverage and more theoretical direction.

The third direction that psychological research in desegregation could usefully take concerns measurement. Save for the partly standardized F Scale, we still lack widely used, standardized field measures of the chief variables in this realm. Such instruments are necessary both for comparability of results and for stimulation of research; witness the invigorating effects on research of the F Scale, the Minnesota Multiphasic Inventory, and the need achievement scoring scheme. Mention of McClelland's need achievement scoring scheme should remind us, too, that projective and other indirect techniques might answer many of these measurement requirements—especially for such sensitive and subtle variables as conformity needs.

Finally, the definitive interdisciplinary case study of desegregation has yet to be started. Properly buttressed by the necessary foundation aid, such a study should involve comparisons before, during, and after desegregation of a wide variety of communities. The interdisciplinary nature of such an undertaking is stressed because desegregation is a peculiarly complex process demanding a broad range of complementary approaches.

Any extensive case project must sample three separate time periods: before a legal ruling or similar happening has alerted the community to imminent desegregation, during the height of the desegregating process, and after several years of accommodation. Without this longitudinal view, desegregation as a dynamic, ongoing process cannot be understood. This time perspective, for instance, would enable us to interpret the fact that on overwhelming majority of Oklahoma whites in a 1954 poll sternly objected to mixed schools, but within a few years has accepted without serious incident integrated education throughout most of the state (Jones, 1957).

A carefully selected range of communities is required to test for differences in the process according to the characteristics of the area. Recent demographic analyses and predictions of the South's school desegregation pattern (Ogburn & Grigg, 1956; Pettigrew, 1957; Pettigrew & Campbell, 1960) could help in making this selection of communities. Comparable data gathered in such a selected variety of locations would allow us to pinpoint precisely the aspects of desegregation unique to, say, a Piedmont city, as opposed to a Black Belt town.

Compare the potential value of such a broad research effort with the limited case studies that have been possible so far. Low budget reports of only one community are the rule; many of them are theses or seminar projects, some remain on the descriptive level, all but a few sample only one time period, and there is almost no comparability of instruments and approach. A comprehensive case project is obviously long overdue.

This has been an appeal for a vigorous empirical look at southern race relations. Despite segregationists' claims to the contrary, social psychological contributions to desegregation research have been relatively meager. There are, however, grounds for hoping that this situation will be partly corrected in the near future—particularly if psychologists get busy.

Foundations appear to be re-evaluating their previous reluctance to support such research. And we can re-evaluate our own resignation in the face of barriers to conduct investigations in this area; the tragedy of Little Rock has had a salutary effect on many influential Southerners in this respect.

Recognition of the importance of the situation in interracial behavior and the full exploitation of the attitude concept can remove inadequacies in the traditional psychological approach to the study of race. In this connection, an extended case for considering conformity as crucial in the Negro attitudes of white Southerners was presented and a new concept—the latent liberal —introduced. One final implication of this latent liberal concept should be mentioned. Some cynics have argued that successful racial desegregation in the South will require an importation of tens of thousands of psychotherapists and therapy for millions of bigoted Southerners. Fortunately for desegregation, psychotherapists, and Southerners, this will not be necessary; a thorough re-patterning of southern interracial behavior will be sufficient therapy in itself.

References

ADORNO, T. W., FRENKEL-BRUNSWIK, E., LEVINSON, D. J., & SANFORD, N. *The authoritarian personality.* New York: Harper, 1950.

ALLPORT, G. W. *The nature of prejudice.* Cambridge, Mass.: Addison-Wesley, 1954.

ASCH, S. E. Effects of group pressure upon the modification and distortion of judgments. In H. Guetzkow (Ed.), *Groups, leadership and men.* Pittsburgh: Carnegie, 1951.

BIESANZ, J., & SMITH, L. M. Race relations of Panama and the Canal Zone. *Amer. J. Sociol.,* 1951, *57,* 7–14.

CLARK, K. B. Desegregation: An appraisal of the evidence. *J. Soc. Issues,* 1953, *9,* 1–76.

COOK, S. W. Desegregation: A psychological analysis. *Amer. Psychologist,* 1957, *12,* 1–13.

CRUTCHFIELD, R. S. Conformity and character. *Amer. Psychologist,* 1955, *10,* 191–198.

DABNEY, V. The violence at Little Rock. *Richmond Times-Dispatch,* 1957, *105,* September 24, 14.

DAVIS, A., GARDNER, B., & GARDNER, MARY. *Deep South.* Chicago: Univer. Chicago Press, 1941.

DOLLARD, J. *Caste and class in a southern town.* New Haven: Yale Univer. Press, 1937.

FESTINGER, L. An analysis of compliant behavior. In M. Sherif & M. O. Wilson (Eds.), *Group relations at the crossroads.* New York: Harper, 1953.

————. *A theory of cognitive dissonance.* Evanston, Ill.: Row, Peterson, 1957.

HARDING, J., & HOGREFE, R. Attitudes of white department store employees toward Negro co-workers. *J. Soc. Issues,* 1952, *8,* 18–28.

HARTLEY, E. L. *Problems in prejudice.* New York: King's Crown, 1946.

HYMAN, H. H., & SHEATSLEY, P. B. Attitudes toward desegregation. *Scient. Amer.* 1956, *195,* 35–39.

JONES, E. City limits. In D. Shoemaker (Ed.), *With all deliberate speed.* New York: Harper, 1957.

KELMAN, H. C. Compliance, identification, and internalization: Three processes of attitude change. *J. Conflict Resolut.,* 1958, *2,* 51–60.

————. *Social influence and personal belief.* New York: Wiley, 1961.

KILLIAN, L. W. Southern white laborers in Chicago's West Side. Unpublished doctoral dissertation, University of Chicago, 1949.

KNAPP, R. H. A psychology of rumor. *Publ. Opin. Quart.,* 1944, *8,* 22–37.

LOGAN, R. W. The United States Supreme Court and the segregation issue. *Ann. Amer. Acad. Pol. Sci.,* 1956, *304,* 10–16.

MILTON, O. Presidential choice and performance on a scale of authoritarianism. *Amer. Psychologist,* 1952, *7,* 597–598.

MINARD, R. D. Race relations in the Pocahontas coal field. *J. Soc. Issues,* 1952, *8,* 29–44.

OGBURN, W. F., & GRIGG, C. M. Factors related to the Virginia vote on segregation. *Soc. Forces,* 1956, *34,* 301–308.

PETTIGREW, T. F. Demographic correlates of border-state desegregation. *Amer. Sociol. Rev.,* 1957, *22,* 683–689.

————. Personality and sociocultural factors in intergroup attitudes: A cross-national comparison. *J. Conflict Resolut.,* 1958, *2,* 29–42.

————. Regional differences in anti-Negro prejudice. *J. Abnorm. Soc. Psychol.,* 1959, *59,* 28–36.

————. Social distance attitudes of South African students. *Soc. Forces,* 1960, *38,* 246–253.

PETTIGREW, T. F., & CAMPBELL, E. Q. Faubus and segregation: An analysis of Arkansas voting. *Publ. Opin. Quart.,* 1960, *24,* 436–447.

PROTHRO, E. T. Ethnocentrism and anti-Negro attitudes in the deep South. *J. Abnorm. Soc. Psychol.,* 1952, *47,* 105–108.

RABB, E., & LIPSET, S. M. *Prejudice and society.* New York: Anti-Defamation League of B'nai B'rith, 1959.

REITZES, D. C. The role of organizational structures: Union versus neighborhood in a tension situation. *J. Soc. Issues,* 1953, *9,* 37–44.

ROPER, E. United States anti-Semites. *Fortune,* 1946, *33,* 257–260.

————. United States anti-Semites. *Fortune,* 1947, *36,* 5–10.

ROSE, A. M. Intergroup relations vs. prejudice: Pertinent theory for the study of social change. *Soc. Probl.,* 1956, *4,* 173–176.

SMITH, C. U., & PROTHRO, J. W. Ethnic differences in authoritarian personality. *Soc. Forces,* 1957, *35,* 334–338.

SMITH, M. B., BRUNER, J. S., & WHITE, R. W. *Opinion and personality.* New York: Wiley, 1956.

STOUFFER, S. A., SUCHMAN, E. A., DEVINNEY, L. C., STAR, SHIRLEY A., WILLIAMS, R. M., JR. *Studies in social psychology in World War II*. Vol. 1. *The American soldier: Adjustment during army life*. Princeton: Princeton Univer. Press, 1949.

THIBAUT, J. W., & KELLEY, H. H. *The social psychology of groups*. New York: Wiley, 1959.

ZINN, H. A fate worse than integration. *Harper's*, 1959, *219*, August, 53–56.

The late Carl Hovland and his associates were the first investigators to subject the area of propaganda to rigorous experimental analysis. One of the most important determinants of opinion change is the prestige of the communicator. In this classic study, Hovland and Weiss clearly demonstrate that if a communication is attributed to individuals having high credibility—that is, individuals who are expert as well as trustworthy—far more people will be influenced than if the identical communication is attributed to sources which have lower credibility. At the same time, their findings show the effects of prestige may be only temporary; people seem to forget the source while they remember the content of the communication. Hovland and Weiss dub this phenomenon "the sleeper effect"—specifically, a communication is not believed immediately after it's heard if it is attributed to a source having low prestige, but over time, as one forgets the source and continues to remember the communication, one's opinions begin to change.

The Influence of Source Credibility on Communication Effectiveness

Carl I. Hovland and Walter Weiss

In a new test of the process of forgetting, the authors found that subjects, at the time of exposure, discounted material from "untrustworthy" sources. In time, however, the subjects tended to disassociate the content and the source with the result that the original scepticism faded and the "untrustworthy" material was accepted. Lies, in fact, seemed to be remembered better than truths.

An important but little-studied factor in the effectiveness of communication is the attitude of the audience toward the communicator. Indirect data on this problem come from studies of "prestige" in which subjects are asked to indicate their agreement or disagreement with statements which are attributed to different individuals.[1] The extent of agreement is usually higher when the statements are attributed to "high prestige" sources. There are few studies in which an identical communication is presented by different commu-

Source: Reprinted by permission from *Public Opinion Quarterly*, Winter 1951/52, *15*, 635–650.

Note: This study was done as part of a coordinated research project on factors influencing changes in attitude and opinion being conducted at Yale University under a grant from the Rockefeller Foundation. (See Hovland, C. I., "Changes in Attitude Through Communication," *Journal of Abnormal and Social Psychology*, Vol. 46 (1951), pp. 424–437.) The writers wish to thank Prof. Ralph E. Turner for making his class available for the study.
[1] See e.g. Sherif, M., "An Experimental Study of Stereotypes," *Journal of Abnormal and Social Psychology*, Vol. 29 (1935), pp. 371–375; Lewis, H. B., "Studies in the Principles of Judgments and Attitudes": IV. The Operation of "Prestige Suggestion." *Journal of Social Psychology*, Vol. 14 (1941), pp. 229–256; Asch, S. E., "The Doctrine of Suggestion, Prestige, and Imitation in Social Psychology," *Psychological Review*, Vol. 55 (1948), pp. 250–276.

nicators and the relative effects on opinion subsequently measured without explicit reference to the position taken by the communicator. Yet the latter research setting may be a closer approximation of the real-life situation to which the results of research are to be applied.

In one of the studies reported by Hovland, Lumsdaine and Sheffield, the effects of a communication were studied without reference to the source of the items comprising the opinion questionnaire. They found that opinion changes following the showing of an Army orientation film were smaller among the members of the audience who believed the purpose of the film was "propagandistic" than among those who believed its purpose "informational."[2] But such a study does not rule out the possibility that the results could be explained by general predispositional factors; that is, individuals who are "suspicious" of mass-media sources may be generally less responsive to such communications. The present study was designed to minimize the aforementioned methodological difficulties by experimentally controlling the source and by checking the effects of the source in a situation in which the subject's own opinion was obtained without reference to the source.

A second objective of the present study was to investigate the extent to which opinions derived from high and low credibility sources are maintained over a period of time. Hovland, Lumsdaine and Sheffield showed that some opinion changes in the direction of the communicator's position are larger after a lapse of time than immediately after the communication. This they refer to as the "sleeper effect." One hypothesis which they advanced for their results is that individuals may be suspicious of the motives of the communicator and initially discount his position, and thus may evidence little or no immediate change in opinion. With the passage of time, however, they may remember and accept *what* was communicated but not remember *who* communicated it. As a result, they may then be more inclined to agree with the position which had been presented by the communicator. In the study referred to, only a single source was used, so no test was available of the differential effects when the source was suspected of having a propagandistic motive and when it was not. The present experiment was designed to test differences in the retention, as well as the acquisition, of identical communications when presented by "trustworthy" and by "untrustworthy" sources.

Procedure

The overall design of the study was to present an identical communication to two groups, one in which a communicator of a generally "trustworthy" character was used, and the other in which the communicator was generally regarded as "untrustworthy." Opinion questionnaires were administered before the communication, immediately after the communication, and a month after the communication.

---

[2] Hovland, C. I., A. A. Lumsdaine and F. D. Sheffield, *Experiments on Mass Communication*. Princeton: Princeton University Press, 1949, pp. 101f.

Because of the possibility of specific factors affecting the relationship between communicator and content on a single topic, four different topics (with eight different communicators) were used. On each topic two alternative versions were prepared, one presenting the "affirmative" and one the "negative" position on the issue. For each version one "trustworthy" and one "untrustworthy" source was used. The topics chosen were of current interest and of a controversial type so that a fairly even division of opinion among members of the audience was obtained.

The four topics and the communicators chosen to represent "high credibility" and "low credibility" sources were as follows:

	"High Credibility" Source	"Low Credibility" Source
A. *Anti-Histamine Drugs*: Should the anti-histamine drugs continue to be sold without a doctor's prescription?	*New England Journal of Biology and Medicine*	Magazine A* [A mass circulation monthly pictorial magazine]
B. *Atomic Submarines:* Can a practicable atomic-powered submarine be built at the present time?	Robert J. Oppenheimer	*Pravda*
C. *The Steel Shortage*: Is the steel industry to blame for the current shortage of steel?	*Bulletin of National Resources Planning Board*	Writer A* [A widely syndicated anti-labor, anti-New Deal, "rightist" newspaper columnist]
D. *The Future of Movie Theaters*: As a result of TV, will there be a decrease in the number of movie theaters in operation by 1955?	*Fortune* magazine	Writer B* [An extensively syndicated woman movie-gossip columnist]

* The names of one of the magazines and two of the writers used in the study have to be withheld to avoid any possible embarrassment to them. These sources will be referred to hereafter only by the letter designations given.

In some cases the sources were individual writers and in others periodical publications, and some were fictitious (but plausible) and others actual authors or publications.

The "affirmative" and "negative" versions of each article presented an equal number of facts on the topic and made use of essentially the same material. They differed in the emphasis given the material and in the conclusion drawn from the facts. Since there were two versions for each topic and these were prepared in such a way that either of the sources might have written either version, four possible combinations of content and source were available on each topic.

The communication consisted of a booklet containing one article on each of the four different topics, with the name of the author or periodical given at the end of each article. The order of the topics within the booklets was kept constant. Two trustworthy and two untrustworthy sources were included in each booklet. Twenty-four different booklets covered the various combinations used. An example of one such booklet-combination would be:

Topic	Version	Source
The Future of Movie Theaters	Affirmative	*Fortune*
Atomic Submarines	Negative	*Pravda*
The Steel Shortage	Affirmative	*Writer A*
Anti-Histamine Drugs	Negative	*New England Journal of Biology and Medicine*

The questionnaires were designed to obtain data on the amount of factual information acquired from the communication and the extent to which opinion was changed in the direction of the position advocated by the communicator. Information was also obtained on the subject's evaluation of the general trustworthiness of each source, and, in the after-questionnaires, on the recall of the author of each article.

The subjects were college students in an advanced undergraduate course in History at Yale University. The first questionnaire, given five days before the communication, was represented to the students as a general opinion survey being conducted by a "National Opinion Survey Council." The key opinion questions bearing on the topics selected for the communication were scattered through many other unrelated ones. There were also questions asking for the subjects' evaluations of the general trustworthiness of a long list of sources, which included the critical ones used in the communications. This evaluation was based on a 5-point scale ranging from "very trustworthy" to "very untrustworthy."

Since it was desired that the subjects not associate the experiment with the "before" questionnaire, the following arrangement was devised: The senior experimenter was invited to give a guest lecture to the class during the absence of the regular instructor, five days after the initial questionnaire. His remarks constituted the instructions for the experiment:

> Several weeks ago Professor [the regular instructor] asked me to meet with you this morning to discuss some phase of Contemporary Problems. He suggested that one interesting topic would be The Psychology of Communications. This is certainly an important problem, since so many of our attitudes and opinions are based not on direct experience but on what we hear over the radio or read in the newspaper. I finally agreed to take this topic but on the condition that I have some interesting live data on which to base my comments. We therefore agreed to use this period to make a survey of the role of newspaper and magazine reading as a vehicle of communication and then to report on the results and discuss their implications at a later session.

Today, therefore, I am asking you to read a number of excerpts from recent magazine and newspaper articles on controversial topics. The authors have attempted to summarize the best information available, duly taking into account the various sides of the issues. I have chosen up-to-date issues which are currently being widely discussed and ones which are being studied by Gallup, Roper and others interested in public opinion.

Will you please read each article carefully the way you would if you were reading it in your favorite newspaper and magazine. When you finish each article write your name in the lower right hand corner to indicate that you have read it through and then go on to the next. When you finish there will be a short quiz on your reaction to the readings.

Any questions before we begin?

The second questionnaire, handed out immediately after the booklets were collected, differed completely in format from the earlier one. It contained a series of general questions on the subjects' reactions to the articles, gradually moving toward opinion questions bearing on the content discussed in the articles. At the end of the questionnaire there was a series of fact-quiz items. Sixteen multiple choice questions, four on each content area, were used together with a question calling for the recall of the author of each of the articles.

An identical questionnaire was administered four weeks after the communication. At no prior time had the subjects been forewarned that they would be given this second post-test questionnaire.

A total of 223 subjects provided information which was used in some phase of the analysis. Attendance in the history course was not mandatory and there was considerable shrinkage in the number of students present at all three time periods. For the portions of the analysis requiring before-and-after information, the data derived from 61 students who were present on all three occasions were used. Thus for the main analysis a sample of 244 communications (four for each student) was available. Since different analyses permitted the use of differing numbers of cases, the exact number of instances used in each phase of the analysis is given in each table.

Results

Before proceeding to the main analyses it is important to state the extent to which the sources selected on *a priori* grounds by the experimenters as being of differing credibility were actually reacted to in this manner by the subjects. One item on the questionnaire given before the communication asked the subjects to rate the trustworthiness of each of a series of authors and publications. Figure 1 gives the percentages of subjects who rated each of the sources "trustworthy."

The first source named under each topic had been picked by the experimenters as being of high credibility and the second of low. It will be observed that there is a clear differentiation of the credibility in the direction

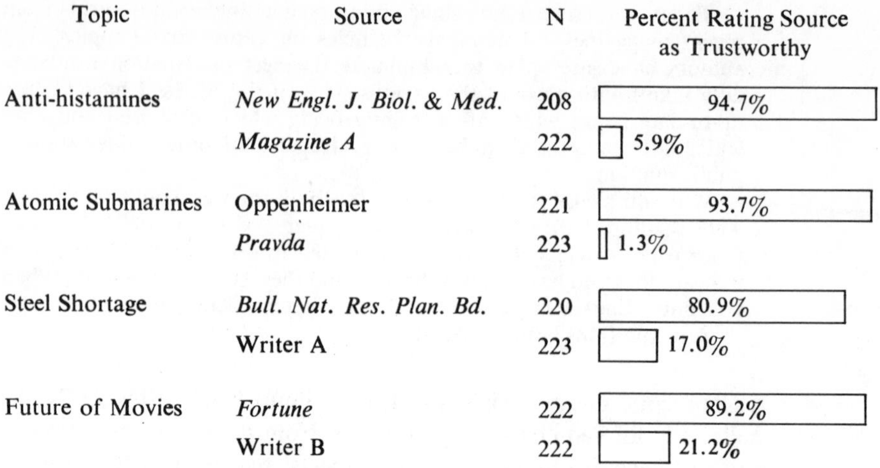

Topic	Source	N	Percent Rating Source as Trustworthy
Anti-histamines	*New Engl. J. Biol. & Med.*	208	94.7%
	Magazine A	222	5.9%
Atomic Submarines	Oppenheimer	221	93.7%
	Pravda	223	1.3%
Steel Shortage	*Bull. Nat. Res. Plan. Bd.*	220	80.9%
	Writer A	223	17.0%
Future of Movies	*Fortune*	222	89.2%
	Writer B	222	21.2%

FIGURE 1.   Credibility of sources

of the initial selection by the experimenters. The differences between members of each pair are all highly significant (t's range from 13 to 20). The results in Figure 1 are based on all of the subjects present when the preliminary questionnaire was administered. The percentages for the smaller sample of subjects present at all three sessions do not differ significantly from those for the group as a whole.

Differences in Perception of Communication of Various Audience Sub-groups

Following the communication, subjects were asked their opinion about the fairness of the presentation of each topic and the extent to which each communicator was justified in his conclusion. Although the communications being judged were *identical*, there was a marked difference in the way the subjects responded to the "high credibility" and "low credibility" sources. Their evaluations were also affected by their personal opinions on the topic before the communication was ever presented. Audience evaluations of the four communications are presented in Table 1. In 14 of the 16 possible comparisons the "low-credibility" sources are considered less fair or less justified than the corresponding high credibility sources. The differences for the low credibility sources for the individuals initially holding an opinion different from that advocated by the communicator and those for the high credibility sources for individuals who initially held the same position as that advocated by the communicator are significant at less than the .004 level.[3]

[3] The probability values given in the table, while adequately significant, are calculated conservatively. The two-tailed test of significance is used throughout, even though in the case of some of the tables it could be contended that the direction of the differences is in line with theoretical predictions, and hence might justify the use of the one-tail test. When analysis is made of *changes*, the significance test takes into account the internal corre-

TABLE 1. Evaluation of "fairness" and "justifiability" of identical communications when presented by "high credibility" and "low credibility" sources among individuals who initially agreed and individuals who initially disagreed with position advocated by communicator

A. Per Cent Considering Author "Fair" in His Presentation*

Topic	High Credibility Source		Low Credibility Source	
	initially agree	initially disagree (or don't know)	initially agree	initially disagree (or don't know)
Anti-Histamines	76.5%	50.0%	64.3%	62.5%
Atomic Submarines	100.0	93.7	75.0	66.7
Steel Shortage	44.4	15.4	12.5	22.2
Future of Movies	90.9	90.0	77.8	52.4
Mean	78.3%	57.9%	60.5%	51.9%
N =	46	76	43	79

B. Per Cent Considering Author's Conclusion "Justified" by the Facts**

Topic	High Credibility Source		Low Credibility Source	
	initially agree	initially disagree (or don't know)	initially agree	initially disagree (or don't know)
Anti-Histamines	82.4%	57.1%	57.1%	50.0%
Atomic Submarines	77.8	81.2	50.0	41.2
Steel Shortage	55.6	23.1	37.5	22.2
Future of Movies	63.6	55.0	55.6	33.3
Mean	71.7%	50.0%	51.2%	36.7%
N =	46	76	43	79

* Question: Do you think that the author of each article was fair in his presentation of the facts on both sides of the question or did he write a one-sided report?
** Question: Do you think that the opinion expressed by the author in his conclusion was justified by the facts he presented or do you think his opinion *was not* justified by the facts?

Effect of Credibility of Source on Acquisition of Information and on Change in Opinion

Information

There is no significant difference in the amount of factual information acquired by the subjects when the material is attributed to a high credibility source as compared to the amount learned when the same material is attributed to a low credibility source. Table 2 shows the mean number of items correct on the information quiz when material is presented by "high credibility" and "low credibility" sources.

lation (Hovland, Sheffield and Lumsdaine, *op. cit.,* pp. 318ff.), but the analyses of cases of post-communication agreement and disagreement are calculated on the conservative assumption of independence of the separate communications.

TABLE 2.   Mean number of items correct on four-item information quizzes on each of four topics when presented by "high credibility" and "low credibility" sources (test immediately after communication)

| | Mean Number of Items Correct | | | |
Topic	High Credibility Source		Low Credibility Source	
Anti-Histamines	(N = 31)	3.42	(N = 30)	3.17
Atomic Submarines	(N = 25)	3.48	(N = 36)	3.72
Steel Shortage	(N = 35)	3.34	(N = 26)	2.73
Future of Movies	(N = 31)	3.23	(N = 30)	3.27
Average	(N = 122)	3.36	(N = 122)	3.26
Per cent of items correct		84.0		81.5
$p$diff. M.		.35		

Opinion

Significant differences were obtained in the extent to which opinion on an issue was changed by the attribution of the material to different sources. These results are presented in Table 3. Subjects changed their opinion in the direction advocated by the communicator in a significantly greater number of cases when the material was attributed to a "high credibility" source than when attributed to a "low credibility" source. The difference is significant at less than the .01 level.

From Figure 1 it will be recalled that less than 100 per cent of the subjects were in agreement with the group consensus concerning the trustworthiness of each source. The results presented in Table 3 were reanalyzed using the individual subject's own evaluation of the source as the independent variable. The effects on opinion were studied for those instances where the source was rated as "very trustworthy" or "moderately trustworthy" and for those where it was rated as "untrustworthy" or "inconsistently trustworthy."

TABLE 3.   Net changes of opinion in direction of communication for sources classified by experimenters as "high credibility" or "low credibility" sources*

| | Net Percentage of Cases in Which Subjects Changed Opinion in Direction of Communication | | | |
Topic	High Credibility Sources		Low Credibility Sources	
Anti-Histamines	(N = 31)	22.6%	(N = 30)	13.3%
Atomic Submarines	(N = 25)	36.0	(N = 36)	0.0
Steel Shortage	(N = 35)	22.9	(N = 26)	−3.8
Future of Movies	(N = 31)	12.9	(N = 30)	16.7
Average	(N = 122)	23.0%	(N = 122)	6.6%
Diff.		16.4%		
$p$diff.		<.01		

* Net changes = positive changes *minus* negative changes.

TABLE 4. Net changes of opinion in direction of communication for sources judged "trustworthy" or "untrustworthy" by individual subjects

Topic	Net Percentage of Cases in Which Subjects Changed Opinion in Direction of Communication			
	"Trustworthy" Sources		"Untrustworthy" Sources	
Anti-Histamines	(N = 31)	25.5%	(N = 27)	11.1%
Atomic Submarines	(N = 25)	36.0	(N = 36)	0.0
Steel Shortage	(N = 33)	18.2	(N = 27)	7.4
Future of Movies	(N = 31)	12.9	(N = 29)	17.2
Average	(N = 120)	22.5%	(N = 119)	8.4%
Diff.			14.1%	
$p$diff.			<.03	

Results from this analysis are given in Table 4. The results, using the subject's own evaluation of the trustworthiness of the source, are substantially the same as those obtained when analyzed in terms of the experimenters' *a priori* classification (presented in Table 3). Only minor shifts were obtained. It appears that while the variable is made somewhat "purer" with this analysis this advantage is offset by possible increased variability attributable to unreliability in making individual judgments of the trustworthiness of the source.

Retention of Information and Opinion in Relation to Source

Information

As was the case with the immediate post-communication results (Table 2), there is no difference between the retention of factual information after four weeks when presented by high credibility sources and low credibility sources. Results in Table 5 show the mean retention scores for each of the four topics four weeks after the communication.

TABLE 5. Mean number of items correct on four-item information quizzes on each of four topics when presented by "high credibility" and "low credibility" sources (recall four weeks after communication)

Topic	Mean Number of Items Correct			
	High Credibility Source		Low Credibility Source	
Anti-Histamines	(N = 31)	2.32	(N = 30)	2.90
Atomic Submarines	(N = 25)	3.08	(N = 36)	3.06
Steel Shortage	(N = 35)	2.51	(N = 26)	2.27
Future of Movies	(N = 31)	2.52	(N = 30)	2.33
Average	(N = 122)	2.58	(N = 122)	2.67
Per cent of items correct		64.5		66.7
$p$diff.			.46	

Opinion

Extremely interesting results were obtained for the retention of opinion changes. Table 6 shows the changes in opinion from immediately after the communication to those obtained after the four-week interval. It will be seen that compared with the changes immediately after the communication, there is a *decrease* in the extent of agreement with the high credibility source, but an *increase* in the case of the low credibility source. This result, then, is similar to the "sleeper effect" found by Hovland, Lumsdaine and Sheffield.[4] The results derived from Tables 3 and 6 are compared in Figure 2, which shows the changes in opinion from before the communication to immediately afterwards and from before to four weeks afterwards.

TABLE 6.   Net changes of opinion from immediately after communication to four weeks later in direction of "high credibility" and "low credibility" sources

Topic	High Credibility Source (A)	Low Credibility Source (B)	Difference (B-A)
Anti-Histamines	(N = 31) − 6.5%	(N = 30) + 6.7%	+13.2%
Atomic Submarines	(N = 25) −16.0	(N = 36) +13.9	+29.9
Steel Shortage	(N = 35) −11.4	(N = 26) +15.4	+26.8
Future of Movies	(N = 31) − 9.7	(N = 30) − 6.7	+ 3.0
Average	(N = 122) −10.7%	(N = 122) + 7.4%	+18.1%
^{p}diff.			.001

The loss with the "trustworthy" source and the gain with the "untrustworthy" source are clearly indicated. A parallel analysis using the individual's own evaluation of the source credibility (similar to the method of Table 4) showed substantially the same results.

Retention of Name of Source

One hypothesis advanced for the "sleeper effect" involved the assumption that forgetting of the source would be more rapid than that of the content. This is a most difficult point to test experimentally because it is almost impossible to equate retention tests for source and for content. It is, however, possible to make a comparison of the retention of the name of the source where the subjects initially agreed with the source's position and considered the communicator a "trustworthy" source, and those where they disagreed and considered the source "untrustworthy." Data on this point are presented in Table 7.

No clear differences are obtained immediately after the communication, indicating comparable initial learning of the names of the different sources. At the time of the delayed test, however, there appears to be a clear difference in the retention of the names of "untrustworthy" sources for the

---

[4] *Op. cit.*

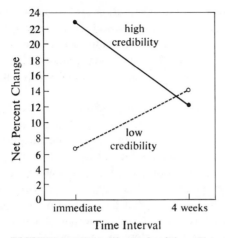

FIGURE 2. "Retention" of opinion. Changes in extent of agreement with position advocated by "high credibility" and "low credibility" sources

TABLE 7. Recall of source immediately after communication and after four weeks

Recall	Trustworthy Source		Untrustworthy Source	
	Individuals initially holding position advocated by communicator	Individuals not initially holding position advocated by communicator	Individuals initially holding position advocated by communicator	Individuals not initially holding position advocated by communicator
Immediately after communication	93.0% (N = 43)	85.7% (N = 77)	93.0% (N = 43)	93.4% (N = 76)
Four weeks after communication	60.5 (N = 43)	63.6 (N = 77)	76.7 (N = 43)	55.3 (N = 76)

group initially agreeing with the communicator's position as compared with that for the group disagreeing with the communicator's position ($p = .02$). Since the "sleeper effect" occurs among the group which initially disagrees with an unreliable source (but subsequently comes to agree with it), it is interesting to note that among this group the retention of the source name is poorest of all. Too few subjects were available to check whether retention was poorer among the very subjects who showed the "sleeper effect," but no clearcut difference could be seen from the analysis of the small sample.

Discussion

Under the conditions of this experiment, neither the acquisition nor the retention of factual information appears to be affected by the trustworthiness of the source. But changes in opinion are significantly related to the trustworthiness of the source used in the communication. This difference is in line with the results of Hovland, Lumsdaine and Sheffield, who found a clear distinction between the effects of films on information and opinion.[5] In the case of factual information they found that differences in acquisition and retention were primarily related to differences in learning ability. But in the case of opinion, the most important factor was the degree of "acceptance" of the material. In the present experiment, this variable was probably involved as a consequent of the variation in source credibility.

The present results add considerable detail to the Hovland-Lumsdaine-Sheffield findings concerning the nature of the "sleeper effect." While they were forced to make inferences concerning possible suspicion of the source, this factor was under experimental control in the present experiment and was shown to be a significant determinant of subsequent changes in opinion. In terms of their distinction between "learning" and "acceptance," one could explain the present results by saying that the content of the communication (premises, arguments, etc.) is learned and forgotten to the same extent regardless of the communicator. But the extent of opinion change is influenced by both learning and acceptance, and the effect of an untrustworthy communicator is to interfere with the acceptance of the material ("I know what he is saying, but I don't believe it"). The aforementioned authors suggest that this interference is decreased with the passage of time, and at a more rapid rate than the forgetting of the content which provides the basis for the opinion. This could result in substantially the same extent of agreement with the position advocated by trustworthy and by untrustworthy sources at the time of the second post-test questionnaire. In the case of the trustworthy source, the forgetting of the content would be the main factor in the decrease in the extent of opinion change. But with the untrustworthy source the reduction due to forgetting would be more than offset by the removal of the interference associated with "nonacceptance." The net effect would be an increase in the extent of agreement with the position advocated by the source at the time of the second post-communication questionnaire. The present results are in complete agreement with this hypothesis; there is a large difference in extent of agreement with trustworthy and untrustworthy sources immediately after the communication, but the extent of agreement with the two types of source is almost identical four weeks later.

The Hovland-Lumsdaine-Sheffield formulation makes forgetting of the source a critical condition for the "sleeper" phenomenon. In the present analysis the critical requirement is a decreased tendency over time to reject the material presented by an untrustworthy source.[6] This may or may not require

---

[5] *Ibid.*

[6] In the present analysis the difference in effects of trustworthy and untrustworthy source is attributed primarily to the *negative* effects of rejection of the untrustworthy source. On the other hand, in prestige studies the effects are usually attributed to the *positive* enhancement of effects by a high prestige source. In both types of study only a difference in effect of the two kinds of influence is obtained. Future research must establish an effective "neutral" baseline to answer the question as to the absolute direction of the effects.

that the source be forgotten. But the individual must be less likely with the passage of time to associate spontaneously the content with the source. Thus the passage of time serves to remove recall of the source as a mediating cue that leads to rejection.[7]

It is in this connection that the methodological distinction mentioned earlier between the procedure used in this experiment and that customarily employed in "prestige" studies becomes of significance. In the present analysis, the untrustworthy source is regarded as a cue which is reacted to by rejection. When an individual is asked for his opinion at the later time he may not spontaneously remember the position held by the source. Hence the source does not then constitute a cue producing rejection of his position. In the usual "prestige" technique, the attachment of the name of the source to the statement would serve to reinstate the source as a cue; consequently the differential effects obtained with the present design would not be expected to obtain. An experiment is now under way to determine whether the "sleeper effect" disappears when the source cue is reinstated by the experimenter at the time of the delayed test of opinion change.

Finally, the question of the generalizability of the results should be discussed briefly. In the present study the subjects were all college students. Other groups of subjects varying in age and in education will be needed in future research. Four topics and eight different sources were used to increase the generality of the "source" variable. No attempt, however, was made to analyze the differences in effects for different topics. Throughout, the effects of the "Atomic Submarine" and "Steel Shortage" communications were larger and more closely related to the trustworthiness of source variable than those of the "Future of Movies" topic. An analysis of the factors responsible for the differential effects constitutes an interesting problem for future research. A repetition of the study with a single after-test for each time interval rather than double testing after the communication would be desirable, although this variation is probably much less significant with opinion than with information questions. The generality of the present results is limited to the situation where individuals are experimentally exposed to the communication; i.e., a "captive audience" situation. An interesting further research problem would be a repetition of the experiment under naturalistic conditions where the individual himself controls his exposure to communications. Finally for the present study it was important to use sources which could plausibly advocate either side of an issue. There are other combinations of position and source where the communicator and his stand are so intimately associated that one spontaneously recalls the source when he thinks about the issue. Under these conditions, the

[7] In rare instances there may also occur a change with time in the attitude toward the source, such that one remembers the source but no longer has such a strong tendency to discount and reject the material. No evidence for the operation of this factor in the present experiment was obtained; our data indicate no significant changes in the evaluation of the trustworthiness of the sources from before to after the communication.

forgetting of the source may not occur and consequently no "sleeper effect" would be obtained.

Summary

1. The effects of credibility of source on acquisition and retention of communication material were studied by presenting identical content but attributing the material to sources considered by the audience to be of "high trustworthiness" or of "low trustworthiness." The effects of source on factual information and on opinion were measured by the use of questionnaires administered before, immediately after, and four weeks after the communication.

2. The immediate reaction to the "fairness" of the presentation and the "justifiability" of the conclusions drawn by the communication is significantly affected by both the subject's initial position on the issue and by his evaluation of the trustworthiness of the source. Identical communications were regarded as being "justified" in their conclusions in 71.7 per cent of the cases when presented by a high credibility source to subjects who initially held the same opinion as advocated by the communicator, but were considered "justified" in only 36.7 percent of the cases when presented by a low credibility source to subjects who initially held an opinion at variance with that advocated by the communicator.

3. No difference was found in the amount of factual information learned from the "high credibility" and "low credibility" sources, and none in the amount retained over a four week period.

4. Opinions were changed immediately after the communication in the direction advocated by the communicator to a significantly greater degree when the material was presented by a trustworthy source than when presented by an untrustworthy source.

5. There was a *decrease* after a time interval in the extent to which subjects agreed with the position advocated by the communication when the material was presented by trustworthy sources, but an *increase* when it was presented by untrustworthy sources.

6. Forgetting the name of the source is less rapid among individuals who initially agreed with the untrustworthy source than among those who disagreed with it.

7. Theoretical implications of the results are discussed. The data on post-communication changes in opinion (the "sleeper effect") can be explained by assuming equal *learning* of the content whether presented by a trustworthy or an untrustworthy source but an initial resistance to the *acceptance* of the material presented by an untrustworthy source. If this resistance to acceptance diminishes with time while the content which itself provides the basis for the opinion is forgotten more slowly, there will be an increase after the communication in the extent of agreement with an untrustworthy source.

How do you bring up children so that they will develop the "right" values? While direct experimentation on value formation is virtually nonexistent, some research has been done on how children come to value or devalue anything—toys, for example. The experiment by Jonathan Freedman is an extension and elaboration of the rather striking finding that mild threats, when used to prevent children from playing with toys, will induce those children to dislike the toys to a much greater extent than severe threats (Aronson & Carlsmith, 1963). In Freedman's study, he goes one step farther: he shows that those children who receive mild threats actually refrain from playing with the crucial toy long after the threat is administered—and long after the threatening adult has left the scene. Severe threats are not nearly as effective as a way of preventing transgressions over the long run.

Long-Term Behavioral Effects of Cognitive Dissonance

Jonathan L. Freedman

Since the publication of *A Theory of Cognitive Dissonance* (Festinger, 1957), a large number of studies have been conducted to test a variety of deductions from the theory. Although not all of the results have been positive, in general the published research has supported the basic theory (see Brehm and Cohen, 1962, for a review).

There is, however, one quite serious limitation in this research. Virtually all of the results supporting dissonance theory have involved attitudes of one sort or another as measured by paper and pencil questionnaires, and all of the significant effects were found a very short time after the experimental manipulation. The authors of these studies have made the explicit or implicit assumption that the same results would also hold for appropriate behavioral measures and that with sufficiently powerful manipulations the effects would endure for some time. Unfortunately, there is little or no evidence supporting such an assumption.

Only two published studies have aroused dissonance in an attempt to produce behavioral changes. Although both of these (Cohen, Greenbaum, and Mansson, 1963; and Wieck, 1964) report positive results, the experimental situations were quite unusual; and the effects were obtained very soon after the

Source: Reprinted by permission of Academic Press from *Journal of Experimental Social Psychology*, 1965, *1*, 145–155.

Note: This study was begun in collaboration with the late Dr. Arthur R. Cohen. The author is grateful for the stimulation and advice he received from Bob Cohen, and considers himself privileged to have known and worked with him. Thanks are also due to Dr. Helen Bee and Mr. Thomas Schweitzer for serving as experimenters, and to the Los Altos School system for generously providing space and time for the running of the experimental sessions. The study was supported in part by grant GS-196 from the National Science Foundation.

manipulation. The data on long-term effects are less consistent. Aronson and Carlsmith (1963) report that 45 days after an initial manipulation there was still some tendency for a dissonance effect to remain. Opposed to this is the result of a study by Walster (1964). Post-decisional changes in attitudes were taken at various intervals after a choice, and it was found that after ninety minutes attitudes were the same as before the decision was made.

The issue of whether or not dissonance theory applies to important, enduring, behavior is particularly important because of the nature of the theory. It is clearly a cognitive theory, and is stated in terms of thoughts, opinions, beliefs, etc. A person's awareness of his own behavior is a cognitive element and fits into the theoretical framework, but the theory does not deal directly with the behavior itself. It is assumed, of course, that changes in cognitions will tend to produce corresponding changes in relevant behavior and vice versa; but as Festinger has recently pointed out (1964), this remains to be shown. The present study, therefore, was designed primarily to demonstrate that the arousal and subsequent reduction of cognitive dissonance can affect relatively important behavior and that this effect can endure over a reasonably long period of time.

One of the most ubiquitous and important problems in behavior modification is the attempt to shape a child's behavior so that it is in accordance with the moral, legal, and social values of society. It is relatively easy to make the child behave correctly when he is offered a reward or threatened with punishment, but this is far from enough. For the socialization process to be successful, the child must also behave correctly in the absence of any such direct pressure, and this is considerably more difficult to accomplish. It has been suggested (Aronson and Carlsmith, 1963; Festinger and Freedman, 1964; Mills, 1958) that the theory of cognitive dissonance provides one possible framework within which to consider this problem.

Attempts to shape a child's behavior often occur in a type of forced compliance situation. The child is told not to do something[1] and is under varying amounts of pressure to obey. The parent or authority giving this restriction may strengthen it with a promise of a reward if the child obeys, a threat of punishment if he does not obey, or some other justification for obeying such as that the toy is fragile and may break if not used correctly. Any of these justifications may vary in magnitude. The rewards may be large or small, the threats mild or severe, the reasons good or bad, etc. If the child obeys the restriction, he is in a potentially dissonant situation because he wanted to perform the forbidden act but did not. As in other forced compliance situations, the greater the justification for obeying, the less dissonance should be aroused (cf. Festinger and Carlsmith, 1959; Freedman, 1963; Rabbie, Brehm, and Cohen, 1959; etc.).

Consider a situation in which a child is told not to play with a very

---

[1] The same arguments would hold for situations in which the child is told to do something, but for purposes of this paper the discussion will refer only to the case in which the authority attempts to prevent certain behavior.

attractive, desirable toy, and is threatened with either mild or severe punishment for disobeying. If he obeys, all those factors which made him want to play with the toy are dissonant with the knowledge that he did not play with it. However, these factors are to some extent balanced by those factors which justified not playing with it. With a severe threat, the child has a very good justification for not playing since if he played, he would have been punished severely. Since there is little or nothing dissonant about refraining from playing even with a desirable toy in order to avoid severe punishment, little or no dissonance should be aroused under a severe threat condition. With a mild threat, on the other hand, the child does not have as good a reason for refraining. If the threat is mild enough relative to the desirability of the toy, a considerable amount of dissonance should be aroused. Regardless of the absolute level of threat, more dissonance should be aroused by obeying under mild than under severe threat.

Any dissonance that is aroused may be reduced either by decreasing the desire to play with the toy or by increasing the justification for not playing with it. The most direct and obvious way of accomplishing the former is to devalue the forbidden toy or increase the value of other, nonforbidden toys or activities. Aronson and Carlsmith (1963) and Turner and Wright (1964) have recently demonstrated in a situation similar to the one described above that a forbidden toy is devalued more under mild than under severe threat. The justification for not transgressing may be increased by magnifying the perceived dangerousness of the act, by enhancing the value of the prohibiting agent, by accepting the adult's evaluation of the act as wrong, or by a variety of similar changes in the perception of the situation.

The important point for our purpose is that any of these modes of dissonance reduction would tend to make the child less likely to play with the toy in the future. A lessening in the value of the toy, an increase in the value of the authority, an acceptance of the moral value that playing with that toy was wrong will all decrease the child's tendency to play with the toy. All these modes of dissonance reduction should be reflected in one specific type of behavior—to the extent that these modes of reduction occur the child should have less inclination to play with the toy, and he should be less likely to play with it even if the original threat were no longer salient or had been removed entirely.

It should be recalled that less dissonance should be aroused by obeying under severe than under mild threat, and correspondingly, less dissonance reduction should occur in the severe threat condition. Thus, if children refrain from playing with the toy under either severe or mild threat and are then given another opportunity to play with the toy with the threats removed, more of the children in the mild threat than in the severe condition should refrain from playing in this second session.

One final point should be made. The arousal of dissonance in this situation depends upon the lack of justification for obeying the restriction. If the child never considers transgressing because he perceives the pressure against this to be too great, no dissonance should be aroused. In other words, the child must face and resist temptation in order for dissonance to be produced. If, for example, the parent made the threat, even a mild threat, but never gave the child a chance to trangress, little or no dissonance would be aroused.

The analysis in terms of cognitive dissonance may now be summarized. A child is told not to play with a toy and is threatened with severe or mild punishment if he transgresses. If he is put into a situation in which he is tempted to play with it and he does not, greater dissonance will be aroused under mild than under severe threat. If there is then another opportunity to play with the toy and the threats are removed, those children who resisted temptation under mild threat will be less likely to play with the toy than those who resisted under severe threat. This difference between mild and severe threat will not occur if the child was not exposed to temptation in the first place. The present experiment was done to test this prediction with the additional specification that the effect could be demonstrated 3 or more weeks after the initial dissonance manipulation.

Method

Design

Children were told not to play with a very desirable toy under either high or low threat for disobeying, and were given a five minute free period during which the toy was present and available. During this period half of Ss in each threat condition were left alone with the toy (experimental groups); half were not left alone (control groups). Ratings of the attractiveness of the forbidden toy and four other toys were taken before the threat instructions were given and after the free period. Several weeks later the threats were nullified by a second E and Ss were again given the opportunity to play with the forbidden toy. There were thus four groups: experimental mild and severe threat (EM and ES), and control mild and severe threat (CM and CS). The mild and severe threats served as high or low justification for obeying in the first session, and the major prediction was that fewer Ss in the EM than in the ES condition would play with the toy during the second session. The control groups were included to assess the direct effect of the threat instructions. There was presumably little or no temptation during the first session of the control condition because E was present. Since only those Ss who resisted temptation should feel any dissonance, the predicted superiority of the mild threat instructions should appear in the experimental conditions but not in the control conditions.

Procedure

The Ss were 89 boys in the second to fourth grades in the Carmel and Springer schools in Los Altos, California. They were run individually and randomly assigned to conditions. Four Ss (two in each of the experimental conditions) violated the prohibition by playing with the toy in the first session and were not included in the analysis, and two more were absent and could not be seen in the second session. The remaining 83 Ss were divided equally among the four conditions except that the CS had 20 Ss and the other groups had 21 Ss.

The procedure in the first session was quite similar to that employed by Aronson and Carlsmith (1963). The S was told that the study concerned children's preferences among various toys. He was asked to indicate his liking of each of five toys on a scale ranging from 0 ("very, very bad toy") to 100 ("very, very good toy") by pointing to a place on the scale. The five toys were a cheap plastic submarine, an extremely expensive, battery controlled robot, a child's baseball glove, an unloaded Dick Tracy toy rifle, and a Tonka tractor. The robot was the toy which was forbidden in order to maximize the temptation to transgress. It was placed on the floor with its control handle on a table, and the other toys were laid out neatly on the table. The toys were demonstrated briefly by E in the order listed above, and were then rated by S in the same order. The E recorded the ratings on a separate sheet.

At this point the procedure diverged for the various conditions. For the experimental Ss, E pretended to remember that he had an errand to do and said that he had to leave for about 10 minutes. For the control Ss, E said that he had something to do and would be busy for about 10 minutes working in the room.

In the low threat conditions E continued, "While I'm gone (or busy) you can play with the toys if you want. You can play with any of them except the robot (pointing to it). Do not play with the robot. It is wrong to play with the robot." The high threat conditions had these same instructions with the addition of the following: "If you play with the robot I'll be very angry and will have to do something about it." Note that Ss are told that it is "wrong" to play with the robot, and also that the severe threat condition depends primarily on an ambiguous, vague threat to "do something about it." It was felt that this would probably be more threatening and would be less susceptible to disbelief than any specific threat.

The E then left the room in the experimental conditions, or worked at some papers in the room in the control conditions. A concealed electric timer was attached to the control switch on the robot so that it would indicate whether or not the robot was turned on, and if so, for how long. At the end of only five minutes, E returned to the room (or finished his work) told S that we wanted a second rating of the toys, and said that sometimes ratings change and sometimes they did not change, and that S should rate them as he felt about them now. After the second rating, S was thanked, told not to talk about the study with anyone else, and sent back to his class. This first session was run by a male E.

The second session was arranged to make it appear unrelated to the first. The interval between the two sessions ranged from 23 to 64 days (Christmas vacation interrupted the course of the study) with a mean interval of 39.8 days. There were no appreciable differences among the groups in either the range of time intervals or the mean interval. This second session was run by a female E who was not described as coming from Stanford, whereas the male E who ran the first session was explicitly from Stanford. The same experimental room was used to make the presence of the toys plausible, but the furniture was rearranged somewhat. The toys were in the far corner of the room placed in a disorderly manner. The control switch for the robot was draped carelessly over a music stand, and the other toys were scattered around.

The E, who did not know what group S was in, asked him to sit at the table and told him that she wanted him to copy some drawings. She then administered five cards of the Bender Gestalt (Bender, 1938) which S copied while E timed his responses. After the Bender was finished, E said that she had to score it and might want to ask S some questions about it. She said that while she was doing that, if S wanted he could play with any of the toys that someone had left in the room (pointing to the toys). This was delivered rather casually, and she then pretended to begin scoring the test. If, as happened occasionally, S continued to sit at the table, E repeated that S could play with the toys, and finally she said that she would prefer it if S did not watch her. Most Ss played with some of the toys, but as will be discussed later, a few did not play with any. If S asked specifically if he could play with the robot, E responded that as far as she was concerned he could play with any of the toys. As before, the timing apparatus timed if and how long S played with the robot, and E also recorded from the stopwatch how many seconds the toy was running. Unfortunately, part-way through the experiment, the robot broke down and would no longer operate. This, of course, made time scores meaningless since S would immediately discontinue playing with the robot as soon as it was obvious that it was not working. Therefore, the major data are simply whether or not S pressed the control switch.

At the end of four minutes, E said she was finished scoring the drawings and that S had done quite well. She thanked him and urged him not to talk about the study. This concluded the experiment.

Results

Our original basic assumption was that less dissonance would be aroused by resisting temptation under high justification than under low justification, and that this difference would be reflected in subsequent behavior. In particular, it was predicted that the mild threat experimental condition (EM) would produce more dissonance than the severe threat experimental (ES) and that fewer Ss in the EM than in the ES would play with the forbidden toy in the second session. The relevant data are presented in Table 1, which shows the number of Ss in each group who played with the robot in

TABLE 1. Number in each condition who played with robot in second session

Group	Low Threat		High Threat	
	Played	*Did Not Play*	*Played*	*Did Not Play*
Experimental	6	15	14	7
Control	14	7	13	7

the second session. It may be seen that more than twice as many Ss in the ES condition as in the EM condition played with the previously forbidden toy. This difference is in the predicted direction and is significant ($X^2 = 6.11$, $p < .02$). In other words, the use of a mild threat in the first session more effectively prevented subsequent transgression than the use of a severe threat.

Since the presence of E during the first session should have been sufficient justification by itself to prevent the arousal of dissonance, no difference was expected between the mild and severe threat control conditions. Regardless of the severity of the threat, Ss should have felt little dissonance; and the two groups should therefore not have differed in amount of transgression during the second session. The results are consistent with this analysis —the amount of transgression in the two control conditions was virtually identical.

No prediction was made regarding differences between the experimental severe threat condition and the control groups, because the exact strength of the threat was undetermined. If the severe threat had by itself been sufficient to preclude the arousal of any dissonance, the additional justification provided by E's presence would not have made any difference. If, however, the severe threat were not this effective, additional justification could have further reduced the amount of dissonance; and the control groups would show greater transgression than the experimental severe threat group. Since the actual results show no differences between the control groups and the experimental severe threat group, it appears that the severe threat provided enough justification for not playing with the toy so that little or no dissonance was aroused.

Included in the data presented in Table 1 are some Ss who did not play with any toys in the second session. It might be argued that these Ss are not resisting the temptation to play with the robot, but rather are not interested in playing with the toys. In a sense these Ss should not be included among those who do not play with the forbidden toy since they do not play with any toy. As may be seen in Table 2, removing these Ss from the analysis does not change the main effect appreciably. The difference between EM and ES conditions is still in the predicted direction and significant ($X^2 = 5.51$, $p < .02$). There is a slight tendency for the CM Ss to transgress more than the CS Ss. Although this difference is not significant, it suggests that the effect

TABLE 2. Number in each condition who played with robot in second session, with Ss who played with no toys omitted from data

Group	Mild Threat		Severe Threat	
	Played	*Did Not Play*	*Played*	*Did Not Play*
Experimental	6	12	14	4
Control	14	1	13	7

in the experimental conditions may have occurred despite some direct effect of the threat which operated in the direction opposite to the effect of the dissonance manipulation.

The other major data are presented in Table 3 which shows the changes in evaluations of the toys from the beginning to the end of the first experimental session. The toys were rated on a scale ranging from 0 ("very, very bad toy") to 100 ("very, very good toy"). If dissonance were aroused by not playing with the forbidden toy, one possible way of reducing it would have been to devalue the forbidden toy or increase the value of the other toys. This would make the forbidden toy relatively less attractive and would decrease the temptation to play with it. As may be seen, all of the groups change their ratings significantly in the direction of dissonance reduction. This change need not, however, have been due to dissonance reduction. In the first place, the initial ratings of the robot were so high (all above 90) that an increase in its rating was highly unlikely. In addition, almost all Ss played with some of the toys but not the robot. The relative increase in the other toys might therefore have been due to greater familiarity with them, or some other factor associated with having used them.

A more meaningful way of considering these data is to compare the various groups in amount of change. Presumably the greater the dissonance that was aroused, the more change in the direction of dissonance reduction that should have occurred. Therefore, the mild threat experimental group should show more dissonance reduction than the other groups. On both

TABLE 3. Mean changes in ratings of toys

Group		Robot	Others	Total Change in Direction of Dissonance Reduction[a]
Experimental	Mild threat	−5.48[b]	+7.72	13.20
	Severe threat	−4.28	+5.90	10.18
Control	Mild threat	−4.00	+5.31	9.31
	Severe threat	−4.84	+5.93	10.77

[a] The sum of the decrease in rating of the robot and the mean increase in rating of the other toys.
[b] All changes are significantly different from no change at $p < .05$. None of the differences between experimental groups approaches significance.

individual measures and the overall change measure, the EM group does show the most change in the direction of dissonance reduction; but none of these differences are significant. Thus, although the results are consistent with the dissonance analysis, they do not provide significant support for it.

This lack of significance is in contrast with the results of the study by Aronson and Carlsmith (1963) in which a forbidden toy was devalued significantly more under mild threat than under severe threat conditions. The experimental situations are not, however, exactly comparable. In the present study the forbidden toy, the robot, was intentionally made much more attractive than any of the other toys in order to maximize the temptation to play with it. It was so much more desirable than the other toys (it was rated an average of more than ten points higher than the closest toy) that devaluing it below the other toys must have been extremely difficult and unrealistic. It seems likely that re-evaluating the toys was not an efficient or practical mode of dissonance reduction in the present experiment and was not employed to any great extent.

Discussion

Although the difference in amount of transgression between the high and low threat experimental groups is clearly consistent with the prediction from dissonance theory, other explanations of this difference are possible. A more severe threat might have called more attention to the forbidden toy or made it seem more attractive, and this would tend to make the severe threat Ss play with the toy more than did the mild threat Ss. Or, E may have been liked more or believed more when he made a mild threat than when he made a severe threat, and his original commands would have been obeyed more in the former condition. Any of these explanations sounds plausible, and there are probably a number of other reasonable possibilities that could explain the difference between the high and low threat experimental conditions.

It should be noted, however, that the control Ss received exactly the same threat instructions as the corresponding experimental Ss, and that all Ss went through exactly the same procedure with one crucial difference. In the experimental conditions, E left the room and gave S a chance to play with the forbidden toy without being observed; in the control conditions, E did not leave the room. Any explanation of the results must therefore account for the fact that only when E leaves the room during the first session do the threats have differential effects on subsequent behavior. The explanations offered above clearly would require differences in both experimental and control conditions and may thus be ruled out; and most other explanations based on surmises about the differential meaning, plausibility or direct effect of the threat instructions would probably also be eliminated.

The results do fit the analysis in terms of cognitive dissonance. When Ss are given a mild threat and they resist temptation, more dissonance is produced than when they resist temptation because of a severe threat.

This dissonance may be reduced in a number of ways, all of which would tend to make S refrain from playing with the toy in the future even in the absence of any threat. Since more dissonance is aroused in the low threat condition, more dissonance reduction occurs in that condition; and the low threat Ss should refrain from playing to a greater extent than should the high threat Ss.

When E remains in the room, there is no temptation to play with the forbidden toy since S would surely get caught. Therefore, no dissonance is aroused in either high or low threat control conditions; and the two should not differ. The lack of difference between control groups is clearly consistent with the dissonance analysis and would seem to make alternative explanations somewhat difficult.

The results thus strongly support the predictions based on the theory of cognitive dissonance. They provide a clear demonstration that the theory does apply to behavioral as well as attitudinal changes and that the arousal and reduction of differential amounts of dissonance can have a significant effect even after an interval of just under 6 weeks.

Since the data on changes in ratings of the toy indicated that this was not a major mode of dissonance reduction in the present situation, it might be interesting to speculate on what the primary mode of reduction was. One provocative possibility is that at least in part dissonance was reduced by an acceptance of the idea that it was wrong to play with the forbidden toy. In other words, the subject may have provided himself with moral justification for obeying the restriction. This would tend to make him less likely to play with the toy in the second session, even though another E said it was all right to play with it.

As Festinger and Freedman have pointed out (1964), one implication of this is that inculcating moral values will be most successful if a minimal amount of justification of any kind is offered for the relevant behavior. If the goal is to make a child accept the values of society, he should not be given a great many logical reasons supporting the valued behavior, nor threatened with severe punishment or eternal damnation if he transgresses, nor promised great rewards, eternal or otherwise, for obeying. Rather, he should be given just enough justification to cause him to obey in the presence of the justification; and then his acceptance of the value itself will be maximal. This analysis of the development of moral values is, of course, highly speculative, and the present study offers no evidence directly supporting it. The present result and that reported by Mills (1958) are, however, consistent with the analysis, and it is hoped that it will be tested more directly by additional research.

Summary

The study was conducted to investigate whether or not the arousal of cognitive dissonance can produce long-term behavioral effects. Children were told not to play with a very desirable toy under high or low threat, and were left alone with the toy. Those who did not play with it were given a second opportunity to play with the toy several weeks later, with the original threat removed. The prediction was that those subjects who had resisted temptation under mild threat would be less likely to play with the toy in this second session than would those who had resisted under severe threat. The results supported this prediction.

References

ARONSON, E., & CARLSMITH, J. M. The effect of the severity of threat on the devaluation of forbidden behavior. *J. Abnorm. Soc. Psychol.*, 1963, *66*, 584–588.

BENDER, LAURETTA. A visual motor gestalt test and its clinical use. Research Monogr. No. 3, *Amer. Orthopsychiat. Assoc.*, 1938.

BREHM, J. W., & COHEN, A. R. *Exploration in cognitive dissonance.* New York: Wiley, 1962.

COHEN, A. R., GREENBAUM, C. W., & MANSSON, H. H. Commitment to social deprivation and verbal conditioning. *J. Abnorm. Soc. Psychol.*, 1963, *67*, 410–421.

FESTINGER, L. *A theory of cognitive dissonance.* Stanford, Calif.: Univer. Press, 1957.

———. Behavioral support for opinion change. *Pub. Opin. Quart.*, 1964, *28*, 404–417.

FESTINGER, L., & CARLSMITH, J. Cognitive consequences of forced compliance. *J. Abnorm. Soc. Psychol.*, 1959, *58*, 203–210.

FESTINGER, L., & FREEDMAN, J. L. Dissonance reduction and moral values. In Worchel and Byrne (Ed.), *Personality change.* New York: Wiley, 1964.

FREEDMAN, J. L. Attitudinal effects of inadequate justification. *J. Pers.*, 1963, *31*, 371–385.

MILLS, J. Changes in moral attitudes following temptation. *J. Pers.*, 1958, *26*, 517–531.

RABBIE, J. M., BREHM, J. W., & COHEN, A. R. Verbalization and reactions to cognitive dissonance. *J. Pers.*, 1959, *27*, 407–417.

TURNER, ELIZABETH A., & WRIGHT, J. C. The effects of severity of threat and perceived availability on the attractiveness of objects. Unpublished manuscript, 1964.

WALSTER, ELAINE. The temporal sequence of post-decision processes. In L. Festinger (Ed.) *Conflict, decision and dissonance.* Stanford, Calif.: Univer. Press, 1964. pp. 112–128.

WIECK, K. E. Reduction of cognitive dissonance through task enhancement and effort expenditure. *J. Abnorm. Soc. Psychol.*, 1964, *68*, 533–539.

Interpersonal attraction (liking) is one of the most basic aspects of human interaction. The experiment by Aronson and Linder represents an attempt to investigate the relationship between liking and being liked. Anyone could tell you that one thing that determines whether Sam will like Harry is whether or not Harry like Sam. But, alas, the problem is not that simple. As Aronson and Linder point out, the sequence of the development of Harry's liking for Sam is of crucial importance in determining whether or not Sam will like Harry. Indeed, as it turns out, a totally positive expression of sentiment on Harry's part is far less effective than an expression of negative feelings followed by some positive ones.

Gain and Loss of Esteem as Determinants of Interpersonal Attractiveness

Elliot Aronson and Darwyn Linder

One of the major determinants of whether or not one person (*P*) will like another (*O*) is the nature of the other's behavior in relation to the person. Several investigators have predicted and found that if *P* finds *O*'s behavior "rewarding," he will tend to like *O* (Newcomb, 1956, 1961; Thibaut and Kelley, 1959; Homans, 1961; Byrne, 1961; Byrne and Wong, 1962). One obvious source of reward for *P* is *O*'s attitude regarding him. Thus, if *O* expresses invariably positive feelings and opinions about *P*, this constitutes a reward and will tend to increase *P*'s liking for *O*.

Although this has been demonstrated to be true (Newcomb, 1956, 1961), it may be that a more complex relationship exists between being liked and liking others. It is conceivable that the sequence of *O*'s behavior toward *P* might have more impact on *P*'s liking for *O* than the total number of rewarding acts emitted by *O* toward *P*. Stated briefly, it is our contention that the feeling of gain or loss is extremely important—specifically, that a gain in esteem is a more potent reward than invariant esteem, and similarly, the loss of esteem is a more potent "punishment" than invariant negative esteem. Thus if *O*'s behavior toward *P* was initially negative but gradually became more positive, *P* would like *O* more than he would had *O*'s behavior been uniformly positive. This would follow even if, in the second case, the sum total of rewarding acts emitted by *O* was less than in the first case.

This "gain-loss" effect may have two entirely different causes. One

Source: Reprinted by permission of Academic Press from *Journal of Experimental Social Psychology,* 1965, *1,* 156–171.

Note: This research was supported by a grant from the National Science Foundation (NSF GS 202) to Elliot Aronson. The authors wish to thank Mrs. Ellen Berscheid, who served as the experimenter during a pilot study, and Miss Darcy Oman, who served as the confederate during the experiment.

is largely affective, the other cognitive. First, when O expresses negative feelings toward P, P probably experiences some negative affect, e.g., anxiety, hurt, self-doubt, anger, etc. If O's behavior gradually becomes more positive, his behavior is not only rewarding for P in and of itself, but it also serves to reduce the existing negative drive state previously aroused by O. The total reward value of O's positive behavior is, therefore, greater. Thus, paradoxically, P will subsequently like O better *because* of O's early negative, punitive behavior.

This reasoning is similar to that of Gerard and Greenbaum (1962). Their experiment involved an Asch-type situation in which they varied the behavior of the stooge whose judgments followed those of the subject. In one condition the investigators varied the trial on which the stooge switched from disagreeing with the judgment of the subject (and agreeing with that of the majority) to agreeing with the judgment of the subject. The results showed a curvilinear relationship between the point at which the stooge switched and his attractiveness for the subjects—the subjects liked him best if he switched either very early or very late in the sequence of judgments. The investigators predicted and explained the high degree of liking for the "late-switcher" as being due to the fact that he was reducing a greater degree of uncertainty. Our reasoning is also consistent with that of Walters and Ray (1960) who, in elaborating on an experiment by Gewirtz and Baer (1958), demonstrated that prior anxiety arousal increases the effectiveness of social reinforcement on children's performance. In their experiment social approval had a greater effect on performance in the anxiety conditions because it was reducing a greater drive.

We are carrying this one step further. What we are suggesting is that the existence of a prior negative drive state will increase the attractiveness of an individual who has both created and reduced this drive state. The kind of relationship we have in mind was perhaps best expressed by Spinoza (1955) in proposition 44 of *The Ethics:* "Hatred which is completely vanquished by love passes into love: and love is thereupon greater than if hatred had not preceded it. For he who begins to love a thing, which he has wont to hate or regard with pain, from the very fact of loving feels pleasure. To this pleasure involved in love is added the pleasure arising from aid given to the endeavour to remove the pain involved in hatred, accompanied by the idea of the former object of hatred as cause."

The same kind of reasoning (in reverse) underlies the "loss" part of our notion. Here P will like O better if O's behavior toward P is invariably negative than if O's initial behavior had been positive and gradually became more negative. Although in the former case O's behavior may consist of a greater number of negative acts, the latter case constitutes a distinct loss of esteem and, therefore, would have a greater effect upon reducing P's liking for O. When negative behavior follows positive behavior, it is not only punishing in its own right, but also eradicates the positive affect associated with the rewarding nature of O's earlier behavior. Therefore, P dislikes the positive-negative O more than the entirely negative O precisely because of the fact that, in the first case, O had previously rewarded him.

The predicted gain-loss effect may also have a more cognitive cause. By changing his opinion about P, O forces P to take his evaluation more seriously. If O expresses uniformly positive or uniformly negative feelings about P, P can dismiss this behavior as being a function of O's style of response, i.e., that O likes everybody or dislikes everybody, and that is *his* problem. But if O begins by evaluating P negatively and then becomes more positive, P must consider the possibility that O's evaluations are a function of O's perception of him and not merely a style of responding. Because of this he is more apt to be impressed by O than if O's evaluation had been invariably positive. It is probably not very meaningful to be liked by a person with no discernment or discrimination. O's early negative evaluation proves that he has discernment and that he's paying attention to P—that he's neither blind nor bland. This renders his subsequent positive evaluation all the more meaningful and valuable.

By the same token, if O's evaluation of P is entirely negative, P may be able to write O off as a misanthrope or a fool. But if O's initial evaluation is positive and then becomes negative, P is forced to conclude that O can discriminate among people. This adds meaning (and sting) to O's negative evaluation of P and, consequently, will decrease P's liking for O.

The present experiment was designed to test the major prediction of our gain-loss notion, that is, the primary intent of this experiment was to determine whether or not *changes* in the feelings of O toward P have a greater effect on P's liking for O than the total number of rewarding acts emitted by O. A secondary purpose was to shed some light on the possible reasons for this relationship. The specific hypotheses are (1) P will like O better if O's initial attitude toward P is negative but gradually becomes more positive, than if his attitude is uniformly positive; (2) P will like O better if his attitude is uniformly negative than if his initial attitude toward P is positive and becomes increasingly negative.

Method

Subjects and Design

In order to provide a test of the hypotheses, it was necessary to design an experiment in which a subject interacts with a confederate over a series of discrete meetings. During these meetings the confederate should express either a uniformly positive attitude toward the subject, a uniformly negative attitude toward the subject, a negative attitude which gradually becomes positive, or a positive attitude which gradually becomes negative. It was essential that the interactions between subject and confederate be constant throughout experimental conditions except for the expression of attitude. At the close of the experiment, the subject's liking for the confederate could be assessed.

The subjects were 80 female students[1] at the University of Minnesota. Virtually all of them were sophomores; they were volunteers from introductory classes in psychology, sociology, and child development. All subjects were randomly assigned to one of the four experimental conditions.

Procedure

The experimenter greeted the subject and led her to an observation room which was connected to the main experimental room by a one-way window and an audio-amplification system. The experimenter told the subject that two students were scheduled for this hour, one would be the subject and the other would help the experimenter perform the experiment. He said that since she arrived first, she would be the helper. He asked her to wait while he left the room to see if the other girl had arrived yet. A few minutes later, through the one-way window, the subject was able to see the experimenter enter the experimental room with another female student (the paid confederate). The experimenter told the confederate to be seated for a moment and that he would return shortly to explain the experiment to her. The experimenter then returned to the observation room and began the instructions to the subject. The experimenter told the subject that she was going to assist him in performing a verbal conditioning experiment on the other student. The experimenter explained verbal conditioning briefly and told the subject that his particular interest was in the possible generalization of conditioned verbal responses from the person giving the reward to a person who did not reward the operant response. The experimenter explained that he would condition the other girl to say plural nouns to him by rewarding her with an "mmm hmmm" every time she said a plural noun. The experimenter told the subject that his procedure should increase the rate of plural nouns employed by the other girl. The subject was then told that her tasks were: (1) to listen in and record the number of plural nouns used by the other girl, and (2) to engage her in a series of conversations (not rewarding plural nouns) so that the experimenter could listen and determine whether generalization occurred. The experimenter told the subject that they would alternate in talking to the girl (first the subject, then the experimenter, then the subject) until each had spent seven sessions with her.

The experimenter made it clear to the subject that the other girl must not know the purpose of the experiment lest the results be contaminated. He explained that, in order to accomplish this, some deception must be used. The experimenter said that he was going to tell the girl that the purpose of the experiment was to determine how people form impressions of other people. He said that the other girl would be told that she was to carry on a series of seven short conversations with the subject, and that between each of these conversations both she and the subject would be interviewed, the other girl

---

[1] Actually, 84 subjects were run in these four conditions. Four of the subjects were unusable because they were able to guess the real purpose of the experiment.

by the experimenter and the subject by an assistant in another room, to find out what impressions they had formed. The experimenter told the subject that this "cover story" would enable the experimenter and the subject to perform their experiment on verbal behavior since it provided the other girl with a credible explanation for the procedure they would follow. In actuality, this entire explanation was, in itself, a cover story which enabled the experimenter and his confederate to perform their experiment on the formations of impressions.

The independent variable was manipulated during the seven meetings that the experimenter had with the confederate. During their meetings the subject was in the observation room, listening to the conversation and dutifully counting the number of plural nouns used by the confederate. Since the subject had been led to believe that the confederate thought that the experiment involved impressions of people, it was quite natural for the experimenter to ask the confederate to express her feelings about the subject. Thus, without intending to, the subject heard herself evaluated by a fellow student on seven successive occasions.

There were four experimental conditions: (1) Negative-Positive, (2) Positive-Negative, (3) Negative-Negative, and (4) Positive-Positive. In the Negative-Positive condition the confederate expressed a negative impression of the subject during the first three interviews with the experimenter. Specifically, she described her as being a dull conversationalist, a rather ordinary person, not very intelligent, as probably not having many friends, etc. During the fourth session she began to change her opinion about her. The confederate's attitude became more favorable with each successive meeting until, in the seventh interview, it was entirely positive. In the Positive-Positive condition the confederate's stated opinions were invariably positive. During the seventh interview her statements were precisely the same as those in the seventh meeting of the Negative-Positive condition. In the Negative-Negative condition the confederate expressed invariably negative feelings about the subject throughout the seven interviews. The Positive-Negative condition was the mirror image of the Negative-Positive condition. The confederate began by stating that the subject seemed interesting, intelligent, and likeable, but by the seventh session she described the subject as being dull, ordinary, etc.

In the Positive-Positive condition the confederate made 28 favorable statements about the subject and zero unfavorable statements. In the Negative-Negative condition the confederate made 24 unfavorable statements about the subject and zero favorable ones. In both the Negative-Positive and Positive-Negative conditions the confederate made 14 favorable and 8 unfavorable statements about the subject.

At the opening of the first interview, the experimenter informed the confederate that she should be perfectly frank and honest and that the subject would never be told anything about her evaluation. This was done so that the subject, upon hearing favorable statements, could not readily believe that the confederate might be trying to flatter her.

Interactions between Subjects and Confederate

Prior to each interview with the experimenter, the confederate and the subject engaged in a 3-minute conversation. This provided a credible basis upon which the confederate might form and change her impression of the subject. During these sessions it was essential that the confederate's conversations with the subject be as uniform as possible throughout the four experimental conditions. This was accomplished by informing the subject, prior to the first session, of the kind of topics she should lead the confederate into. These included movies, teachers, courses, life goals, personal background information, etc. Once the subject brought up one of these topics, the confederate spewed forth a prepared set of facts, opinions, and anecdotes which were identical for all experimental subjects. Of course, since a social interaction was involved, it was impossible for the confederate's conversations to be entirely uniform for all of the subjects. Occasionally the confederate was forced to respond to a direct question which was idiosyncratic to a particular subject. However, any variations in the statements made by the confederate were minor and nonsystematic.

The subject and confederate met in the same room but they were separated at all times by a cardboard screen which prevented visual communication. This was done for two reasons. First, it made it easier for the confederate to play the role of the naive subject. We feared that the confederate, after saying negative things about the subject, might be reluctant to look her squarely in the eye and engage in casual conversation. In addition, the use of the screen allowed for a more precise control of the conversation of the confederate by enabling her to read her lines from a prepared script which was tacked to the screen. The use of the screen was easily explained to the subject (in terms of the verbal reinforcement cover story) as a necessary device for eliminating inadvertent nonverbal reinforcement, like nods and smiles.

The confederate carried on her end of the conversation in a rather bland, neutral tone of voice, expressing neither great enthusiasm nor monumental boredom. The same girl (an attractive 20-year-old senior) was used as the confederate throughout the experiment. In order to further convince the subject of the validity of the cover story, the confederate used increasingly more plural nouns throughout the course of the experiment.

The Dependent Variable

At the close of the experiment the experimenter told the subject that there was some additional information he needed from her, but that it was also necessary for him to see the other girl to explain the true nature of the experiment to her. He said that, since he was pressed for time, the subject would be interviewed by his research supervisor while he, the experimenter, explained the experiment to the other girl. The experimenter then led the subject into the interviewer's office, introduced them, and left.

A separate interviewer[2] was used in order to avoid bias, the interviewer being ignorant of the subject's experimental condition. The purpose of the interview was to measure the subject's liking for the confederate; but this could not be done in any simple manner because the bare outlines of this experiment were extremely transparent: the confederate evaluated the subject, then the subject evaluated the confederate. Unless the interviewer could provide the subject with a credible rationale (consistent with the cover story) for asking her to evaluate the other girl, even the most naive of our subjects might have guessed the real purpose of the experiment. Therefore, the interviewer took a great deal of time and trouble to convince the subject that these data were essential for an understanding of the other girl's verbal behavior. The essence of his story was that the attitudes and feelings that the "helpers" in the experiment had for the "subjects" in the experiment often found expression in such subtle ways as tone of voice, enthusiasm, etc. "For example, if you thought a lot of the other girl you might unwittingly talk with warmth and enthusiasm. If you didn't like her you might unwittingly sound aloof and distant." The interviewer went on to explain that, much to his chagrin, he noticed that these subtle differences in inflection had a marked effect upon the gross verbal output of the other girls, that is, they talked more when they were conversing with people who seemed to like them than when they were conversing with people who seemed not to like them. The interviewer said that this source of variance was impossible to control but must be accounted for in the statistical analysis of the data. He explained that if he could get a precise indication of the "helpers' " feelings toward the "subjects," he could then "plug this into a mathematical formula as a correction term and thereby get a more or less unbiased estimate of what her gross verbal output would have been if your attitude toward her had been neutral."

The interviewer told the subject that, in order to accomplish this, he was going to ask her a number of questions aimed at getting at her feelings about the other girl. He emphasized that he wanted her *feeling*, her "gut response"; i.e., that it was essential that she give her frank impression of the other girl regardless of whether or not she had solid, rational reasons for it.

After the subject indicated that she understood, the interviewer asked her whether she liked the other girl or not. After she answered, the interviewer showed her a card on which was printed a 21-point scale, from −10 to +10. The interviewer asked her to indicate the magnitude of her feeling as precisely as possible. He verbally labeled the scale: "+10 would

[2] It should be reported that in an earlier attempt to test this hypothesis, a questionnaire was administered instead of an interview. This was a more economical procedure, but it proved to be less effective. Although the results in the four experimental conditions were in the predicted order, the variance was extremely large. Postexperimental discussions with the subjects led us to suspect that one reason for the large variance might be due to the fact that the subjects were treating the questionnaires in a rather casual manner, believing that this aspect of the experiment was of little importance. It was primarily for this reason that we decided to use a high-status interviewer, whose earnest presence forced the subjects to treat the interview seriously and to respond in an honest and thoughtful manner.

mean you like her extremely, -10 that you dislike her extremely. Zero means that you are completely indifferent. If you liked her a little, you'd answer $+1$, $+2$, or $+3$; if you liked her moderately well, you'd answer $+4$, $+5$, or $+6$; if you liked her quite a bit, you'd answer with a higher number. What point on the scale do you feel reflects your feeling toward the girl most accurately?"

This was the dependent measure. In addition, the interviewer asked the subjects to rate the confederate on 14 evaluative scales including intelligence, friendliness, warmth, frankness, etc. Most of these were asked in order to ascertain whether or not general liking would manifest itself in terms of higher ratings on specific attributes; a few were asked as possible checks on the manipulations.

Finally, the interviewer asked the subject if it bothered, embarrassed, annoyed, or upset her to hear the other girl evaluate her to the experimenter. After recording her answer, the interviewer probed to find out whether or not the subject suspected the real purpose of the experiment. He then explained, in full, the true nature of the experiment and the necessity for the deception. The subjects, especially those who had been negatively evaluated, were relieved to learn that it was not "for real." Although several of the girls admitted to having been quite shaken during the experiment, they felt that it was a worthwhile experience, inasmuch as they learned the extent to which a negative evaluation (even by a stranger) can affect them. They left the interview room in good spirits.

In most cases the interviewer remained ignorant of which of the four experimental conditions the subject was in until the conclusion of the interview. On a few occasions, however, a subject said something casually, in the midst of the interview, from which the interviewer could infer her experimental condition. It should be emphasized, however, that the dependent variable was the first question asked; in no case was the interviewer aware of a subject's experimental condition before she responded to that question.

Results and Discussion

Our hypotheses were that the confederate would be liked better in the Negative-Positive condition than in the Positive-Positive condition and that she would be liked better in the Negative-Negative condition than in the Positive-Negative condition. To test these hypotheses we compared the subjects' ratings of their liking for the confederate across experimental conditions. The significance of the differences were determined by t-test.[3] Table 1 shows

---

[3] A t-test was used because it is the most direct statistical technique and it also allowed us to perform an internal analysis to be described later. However, it is not the most powerful method of analyzing the data. An analysis of variance was also performed, and the results were slightly more significant than those of the t-test. The difference between Negative-Positive and Positive-Positive conditions reached the .02 level of significance; the difference between the Negative-Negative and the Positive-Negative conditions reached the .07 level of significance. The overall treatment effect was highly significant ($p < .0005$).

TABLE 1. Means and standard deviations for liking of the confederate

Experimental condition	Mean	SD	t-values	
1. Negative-Positive	+7.67	1.51	1 vs. 2	2.71**
2. Positive-Positive	+6.42	1.42	2 vs. 3	7.12***
3. Negative-Negative	+2.52	3.16	3 vs. 4	1.42*
4. Positive-Negative	+0.87	3.32		

* $p < .15$.
** $p < .02$.
*** $p < .001$ (all p levels are two-tailed).

the means, SDs, t-values, and significance levels. An examination of the table reveals that the means are ordered in the predicted direction. Moreover, it is clear that the confederate was liked significantly more in the Negative-Positive condition than in the Positive-Positive condition ($p < .02$, two-tailed). The difference between the Negative-Negative condition and the Positive-Negative condition showed a strong trend in the predicted direction, although it did not reach an acceptable level of significance ($p < .15$, two-tailed). There is a great deal of variability in these two conditions. This large variability may be partly a function of the well-known reluctance of college students to express negative feelings about their fellow students, even when the behavior of the latter is objectively negative (e.g., Aronson and Mills, 1959). Typically, in social psychological experiments, regardless of how obnoxiously a stooge behaves toward a subject, many subjects find it difficult to verbalize negative evaluations of the stooge. In these two conditions the behavior of the stimulus person would seem to have brought forth a negative evaluation; although most of the subjects were able to do this, several came out with highly positive evaluations. Thus, the range for the Negative-Negative and Positive-Negative conditions was 15 scale units (from +7 to −7). In the other two conditions negative evaluations were *not* in order; thus, this difficulty was not encountered. The range for these two conditions was only seven scale units (from +9 to +3). Therefore, although the mean difference between the Positive-Negative and Negative-Negative conditions was actually larger than the mean difference between the Positive-Positive and Negative-Positive conditions, it fell short of statistical significance.

Table 1 also indicates that there is a very large difference between those conditions in which the confederate ended by expressing a positive feeling for the subject and those in which she ended with a negative feeling for the subject. For example, a comparison of the Positive-Positive condition with the Negative-Negative condition yields a *t* of 7.12, significant at far less than the .001 level. As predicted, the widest mean difference occurs between the Negative-Positive condition (M = +7.67) and the Positive-Negative condition (M = +0.87). This is interesting in view of the fact that the confederate made the same number of positive and negative statements in these two conditions; only the sequence was different.

It will be recalled that the subjects were asked to rate the confederate on 14 evaluative scales in order to ascertain whether or not greater liking would manifest itself in terms of higher ratings on specific attributes. No evidence for this was found; e.g., although the subjects liked the confederate better in the Negative-Positive condition than in the Positive-Positive condition, they did not find her significantly more intelligent or less conceited. In fact, the only ratings that reached an acceptable level of significance showed a reverse effect: In the Positive-Positive condition the confederate was rated more friendly ($p < .01$), nicer ($p < .01$), and warmer ($p < .01$) than in the Negative-Positive condition. Our failure to predict this effect may be attributable to a naive belief in generalization which served to blind us to more obvious factors. Thus, although we did not predict this result, it is not startling if one considers the simple fact that in the Positive-Positive condition the confederate's evaluations of the subject, because they were entirely positive, *did* reflect greater friendliness, niceness, and warmth. That is, when forced to consider such things as friendliness, niceness, and warmth, the subjects in the Negative-Positive condition could not give the confederate a very high rating. The confederate, here, is not the kind of person who exudes niceness; by definition she is capable of saying negative things. Nevertheless, when asked for their "gut-response" regarding how much they liked the confederate, the subjects in the Negative-Positive condition tended to give her a high rating. To speculate, we might suggest the following: When one is asked to rate a person on a particular attribute, one tends to sum the person's relevant behavior in a rather cognitive, rational manner. On the other hand, when one is asked how much one likes a person, one tends to state a current feeling rather than to add and subtract various components of the person's past behavior.

Degree of Liking as a Function of "Upset"

The major results are consistent with the hypotheses derived from the gain-loss notion. Although, in this experiment, it was not our intention to test the underlying assumptions of this notion, there are some data which may be of relevance. Recall that one of the suggested causes of the gain-loss effect is that, in the negative conditions, the subjects experienced negative feelings such as anxiety, anger, self-doubt, etc. That is, it was predicted that the subjects in the Negative-Positive condition would like the confederate better than would the subjects in the Positive-Positive condition because in the Negative-Positive condition the confederate's behavior was reducing a negative drive state. If this assumption is correct, the effect should not occur if, for some reason, the confederate's negative behavior did not produce a negative drive state in the subjects. For example, in the Negative-Positive condition, if the subjects did not take the negative evaluation personally there would be no negative drive state to be reduced. Similarly, in the Positive-Negative condition, loss would not be experienced if the confederate's negative behavior, for some reason, were not taken personally by the subject. As mentioned earlier, near the end of the experiment the interviewer asked the subject if it bothered, embarrassed, or upset her to listen to herself being evaluated by the other girl. As one might expect, in the Positive-Positive condition none of the subjects were at all bothered, upset, or embarrassed by the situation. In the Negative-Positive condition, however, 11 subjects admitted to having been somewhat upset when the other girl was evaluating them negatively; similarly, nine girls in the Negative-Negative condition and nine in the Positive-Negative condition admitted that they were upset by the negative evaluation. In these latter conditions the subjects who claimed that they were not upset by the negative evaluation tended to explain this by saying that the situation was so restricted that they lacked the freedom and relaxation to "be themselves" and "make a good impression" on the other girl. Typically, they felt that it was reasonable for the other girl to think of them as dull and stupid—the situation *forced* them to appear dull. Thus, many of the girls refused to take a negative evaluation personally; instead, they felt that the confederate would have liked them better if the situation had been freer, allowing them to express their usual, loveable personalities.

For what it is worth, let us compare those who were upset by a negative evaluation with those who were not in terms of how much they liked the confederate. Within the Negative-Positive condition those subjects who were upset by the negative evaluation liked the confederate *more* than those who were not upset ($t = 3.36$, $p < .01$, two-tailed). Similarly, within the Positive-Negative condition those who were upset by the negative evaluation liked the confederate *less* than those who were not upset ($t = 4.44$, $p < .01$). In the Negative-Negative condition, as might be expected, there was a tendency for those who were not upset to like the confederate better than those who were upset ($t = 1.26$, N.S.). We can also compare degree of liking across experimental conditions, eliminating those subjects who were not upset by a negative evaluation. The difference between the Negative-Positive and Positive-Positive conditions is highly significant ($t = 4.57$, $p < .005$, two-tailed). When the "upset" subjects only are compared, the difference between the Negative-Negative and Positive-Negative conditions approaches significance ($t = 1.91$, $p < .08$, two-tailed).

These data are consistent with the affective assumption of the gain-loss notion inasmuch as they suggest that a feeling of upset is a necessary precondition for the great liking in the Negative-Positive condition and the great dislike in the Positive-Negative condition. However, since these data are based on an internal analysis, they are not unequivocal; those subjects who were upset (strictly speaking, those who admitted to being upset) by a negative evaluation may be different kinds of animals from those who did not admit to being upset. The differences in their liking for the stimulus person may be a reflection of some unknown individual differences rather than of the manipulated differences in the independent variable. For example, considering the explanations given by those subjects who were not upset, it is conceivable that these individuals may be extreme on "ego-defensiveness"; or, conversely, those subjects who *were* upset may be extremely "hypersensitive." From our data it is impossible to judge whether or not such individual differences could be correlated with the dependent variable. In sum, although the results from the internal analysis are suggestive, they are equivocal because they do not represent a systematic experimental manipulation.

A Neutral-Positive Condition

If, for the moment, one ignores the internal analysis, the possibility exists that *any* increase in the confederate's positive evaluation of the subject would have produced an increase in the subject's liking for the confederate, even if pain had not been involved. For example, suppose the confederate's initial evaluation of the subject had been neutral rather than negative, and then had become increasingly positive; would the subject like the confederate as much in this condition as in the Negative-Positive condition? If so, then, clearly, pain and suffering are not necessary factors. To test this possibility, 15 additional subjects were run in a Neutral-Positive condition.[4] This condition is identical to the Negative-Positive condition except that during the first three meetings, instead of expressing negative evaluations of the subject, the confederate was noncommital, saying such things as "She seems to be pretty intelligent, but perhaps just a little on the dull side. . . ." "I'm not sure; she kind of strikes me both ways. . . ." "I just can't make up my mind about her. My feelings are rather neutral." The subjects were randomly assigned to this condition, although assignment did not commence until after two or three subjects had been run in each of the other four conditions. In this condition the mean liking score was 6.66. This is almost identical with the mean in the Positive-Positive condition. The difference between the Neutral-Positive and Negative-Positive conditions approaches statistical significance ($t = 1.96$, $p < .07$, two-tailed).

These data, coupled with the data from the internal analysis, suggest that some upset on the subjects part increased her liking for the stimulus person. However, other factors may contribute to the effect. One such contributing factor has already been discussed as the cognitive assumption underlying the gain-loss notion. Specifically, when O changes in evaluation of P, it is indicative of the fact that he (O) has some discernment and that his evaluation is a considered judgment. Consequently, his evaluation of P should have greater impact on P than an invariably positive or invariably negative evaluation. This would lead to greater liking in the Negative-Positive condition and less liking in the Positive-Negative condition. We made no great attempt to investigate the validity of this assumption in the present experiment. We did ask the subjects to rate the degree of discernment of the stimulus person. Here, we found a faint glimmer of support. There was some

---

[4] We wish to thank Ellen Berscheid, who first suggested this condition.

tendency for the subjects in the Negative-Positive condition to rate the stimulus person higher (M = 6.75) than did the subjects in the Positive-Positive condition (M = 5.35), but this difference was not statistically significant ($t = 1.40$, $p < .15$). There was no difference in the ratings made by the subjects in the other two conditions.

Alternative Explanations

FLATTERY.   Recent work by Jones (1964) on flattery and ingratiation suggests the possibility that a person who makes exclusively positive statements might be suspected of using flattery in order to manipulate the subject, and therefore might be liked less than someone whose evaluation include negative statements. However, this is not a compelling explanation of the results of the present experiment because the subject was led to believe that the confederate was unaware that she (the subject) was eavesdropping during the evaluation. One cannot easily attribute these ulterior motives to a person who says nice things about us in our absence.

CONTRAST.   Another possible alternative explanation involves the phenomenon of contrast (Helson, 1964). After several negative and neutral statements, a positive evaluation may seem more positive than the same statement preceded by other positive statements. Similarly, a negative evaluation following several positive and neutral statements may appear to be more negative than one that formed part of a series of uniformly negative statements. Thus, a contrast effect, if operative, could have contributed to our results. At the same time, it should be noted that in the Neutral-Positive condition, where some degree of contrast should also occur, there is little evidence of the existence of this phenomenon. Specifically, the mean liking score in the Neutral-Positive condition was almost identical to that in the Positive-Positive condition and quite different from that in the Negative-Positive condition ($p < .07$). These data suggest that, although a contrast effect could conceivably have contributed to the results, it is doubtful that such an effect was strong enough, in this experimental situation, to have generated the results in and of itself.

COMPETENCE.   In the Negative-Positive condition the subject has succeeded in showing the confederate that he (the subject) is not a dull clod but is, in fact, a bright and interesting person. This is no mean accomplishment and therefore might lead the subject to experience a feeling of competence or efficacy (White, 1959). Thus, in this condition, part of the reason for O's great attractiveness may be due to the fact that he has provided the subject with a success experience. Indeed, during the interview many subjects in this condition spontaneously mentioned that, after hearing O describe them as dull and stupid, they tried hard to make interesting and intelligent statements in subsequent encounters with O. It is reasonable to suspect that they were gratified to find that these efforts paid off by inducing a change in O's evaluations. This raises an interesting theoretical question; it may be that the feeling of competence is not only a contributing factor to the "gain" effect but may actually be a necessary condition. This possibility could be tested in future experimentation by manipulating the extent to which the subject feels that O's change in evaluation is contingent upon the subject's actual behavior.

Possible Implications

One of the implications of the gain-loss notion is that "you always hurt the one you love," i.e., once we have grown certain of the good will (rewarding behavior) of a person (e.g., a mother, a spouse, a close friend), that person may become less potent as a source of reward than a stranger. If we are correct in our assumption that a gain in esteem is a more potent reward than the absolute level of the esteem itself, then it follows that a close friend (by definition) is operating near ceiling level and therefore cannot provide us with a gain. To put it another way, since we have learned to expect love, favors, praise, etc. from a friend, such behavior cannot possibly represent a gain in his esteem for us. On the other hand, the constant friend and rewarder has great potential as a punisher. The closer the friend, the greater the past history of invariant esteem and reward, the more devastating is its withdrawal. Such withdrawal, by definition, constitutes a loss of esteem.

An example may help clarify this point. After 10 years of marriage, if a doting husband compliments his wife on her appearance, it may mean very little to her. She already knows that her husband thinks she's attractive. A sincere compliment from a relative stranger may be much more effective, however, since it constitutes a gain in esteem. On the other hand, if the doting husband (who used to think that his wife was attractive) were to tell his wife that he had decided that she was actually quite ugly, this would cause a great deal of pain since it represents a distinct loss of esteem.

This reasoning is consistent with previous experimental findings. Harvey (1962) found a tendency for subjects to react more positively to a stranger than a friend when they were listed as sources of a relatively positive evaluation of the subject. Moreover, subjects tended to react more negatively to a friend than a stranger when they were listed as sources of negative evaluations of the subject. Similarly, experiments with children indicate that strangers are more effective as agents of social reinforcement than parents, and that strangers are also more effective than more familiar people (Shallenberger and Zigler, 1961; Stevenson and Knights, 1962; Stevenson, Keen and Knights, 1963). It is reasonable to assume that children are accustomed to receiving approval from parents and familiar people. Therefore, additional approval from them does not represent much of a gain. However, approval from a stranger *is* a gain and, according to the gain-loss notion, should result in a greater improvement in performance. These latter results add credence to our speculations regarding one of the underlying causes of the gain-loss effect. Specifically, children probably experience greater social anxiety in the presence of a stranger than a familiar person. Therefore, social approval from a stranger may be reducing a greater drive than social approval from a friend. As previously noted, this reasoning is identical to that of Walters and his colleagues regarding the effect of prior anxiety on subsequent performance (Walters and Ray, 1960; Walters and Foote, 1962).

Summary

In a laboratory experiment, coeds interacted in two-person groups over a series of brief meetings. After each meeting the subjects were allowed to eavesdrop on a conversation between the experimenter and her partner in which the latter (actually a confederate) evaluated the subject. There were four major experimental conditions: (1) the evaluations were all highly positive; (2) the evaluations were all quite negative; (3) the first few evaluations were negative but gradually became positive; (4) the first few evaluations were positive but gradually became negative.

The major results showed that the subjects liked the confederate best when her evaluations moved from negative to positive and least when her evaluations moved from positive to negative. The results were predicted and discussed in terms of a "gain-loss" notion of interpersonal attractiveness.

References

ARONSON, E., & MILLS, J. The effect of severity of initiation on liking for a group. *J. Abnorm. Soc. Psychol.*, 1959, *59*, 177–181.

BYRNE, D. Interpersonal attraction and attitude similarity. *J. Abnorm. Soc. Psychol.*, 1961, *62*, 713–715.

BYRNE, D., & WONG, T. J. Racial prejudice, interpersonal attraction, and assumed dissimilarity of attitudes. *J. Abnorm. Soc. Psychol.*, 1962, *65*, 246–253.

GERARD, H. B., & GREENBAUM, C. W. Attitudes toward an agent of uncertainty reduction. *J. Pers.*, 1962, *30*, 485–495.

GEWIRTZ, J. L., & BAER, D. M. The effect of brief social deprivation on behaviors for a social reinforcer. *J. Abnorm. Soc. Psychol.*, 1958, *56*, 49–56.

HARVEY, O. J. Personality factors in resolution of conceptual incongruities. *Sociometry*, 1962, *25*, 336–352.

HELSON, H. Current trends and issues in adaptation-level theory. *Amer. Psychologist*, 1964, *19*, 26–38.

HOMANS, G. *Social behavior: Its elementary forms.* New York: Harcourt, Brace, and World, 1961.

JONES, E. E. *Ingratiation: A social psychological analysis.* New York: Appleton-Century-Crofts, 1964.

NEWCOMB, T. M. *The acquaintance process.* New York: Holt, Rinehart and Winston, 1961.

———. The prediction of interpersonal attraction. *Amer. Psychologist*, 1956, *11*, 575–586.

SHALLENBERGER, PATRICIA, & ZIGLER, E. Rigidity, negative reaction tendencies and cosatiation effects in normal and feebleminded children. *J. Abnorm. Soc. Psychol.*, 1961, *63*, 20–26.

SPINOZA, B. *The ethics*. New York: Dover Press, 1955. Prop. 44, p. 159.

STEVENSON, H. W., KEEN, RACHEL, & KNIGHTS, R. M. Parents and strangers as reinforcing agents for children's performance. *J. Abnorm. Soc. Psychol.*, 1963, *67*, 183–185.

STEVENSON, H. W., & KNIGHTS, R. M. Social reinforcement with normal and retarded children as a function of pretraining, sex of *E,* and sex of *S. Amer. J. Ment. Defic.*, 1962, *66*, 866–871.

THIBAUT, J., & KELLEY, H. H. *The social psychology of groups*. New York: Wiley, 1959.

WALTERS, R. H., & FOOTE, ANN. A study of reinforcer effectiveness with children. *Merrill-Palmer Quart. Behav. Develpm.*, 1962, *8*, 149–157.

WALTERS, R. H., & RAY, E. Anxiety, social isolation, and reinforcer effectiveness. *J. Pers.*, 1960, *28*, 258–267.

WHITE, R. W. Motivation reconsidered: the concept of competence. *Psychol. Rev.*, 1959, *66*, 297–334.

Section Three
PERSONALITY

Personality study is the area of psychology that is most closely related to the layman's impressions of psychology. It concerns what each of us is like—the feelings and goals that we share with other people as well as the motivations and traits that make us unique. The psychology of personality attempts to take account of individual differences in behavior as well as universal human tendencies. Personality psychologists ask whether there are general tendencies in individual behavior. Is an individual's behavior consistent only within a specific situation or are there more general traits that characterize a person's behavior in many different situations?

They are also interested in the organization and structure of personality. They want to know what kinds of behavior are related to each other and tend to appear in conjunction with one another. For example, if an individual is hostile, is he also likely to be anxious? Or if someone is highly conforming, is he also likely to be highly repressed? In determining the interrelationships among behavior traits, psychologists at the same time ask which traits are central and basic to the individual's personality and which are minor and peripheral.

To study these questions, the psychologist must be able to describe and measure personality. A variety of procedures have been developed to help describe human personality. These procedures range from judgments or ratings, to questionnaires, inkblots, and elegant laboratory instruments. A great deal of research effort is devoted to the development of personality measures and to testing their usefulness.

The study of the *organization* of personality is frequently coupled with the study of the *dynamics* of personality. Organization refers to the "anatomy" of personality—how the different elements of personality are linked together; while dynamics is concerned with the *function* of behavior—the purpose of an act, the *why* of the individual's behavior. Questions of dynamics are typically addressed to the immediate situation in which action is taking place, while questions of organization generally deal with relatively enduring and stable aspects of behavior. Dynamics and structure are closely related. Thus you might be interested in determining the effects of anxiety-evoking stimuli on perception, judgment, and memory (dynamics). In addition, you might be able to show that people with certain kinds of personalities are predictably different in the way in which they respond to anxiety (structure). In either instance, you have to have tools for measuring anxiety and the response to it.

Questions about personality cannot be answered simply. Consequently, there are many theories that attempt to explain personality structure and dynamics. Perhaps the best known and most influential of these is *psychoanalysis,* originally formulated and elaborated by Sigmund Freud. A number of important and well-known theorists, such as Carl Jung and Erich Fromm, are psychoanalytically oriented but have developed their own unique views. Major alternatives to the psychoanalytic approach are offered by Carl Rogers and related personality theorists who emphasize the importance of self-actualizing tendencies in behavior and the importance of present experiences, as contrasted to the role of early childhood, in determining behavior. Another major approach is offered by learning theory as represented in the works of B. F. Skinner and Neal Miller, who emphasize simpler, empirically established principles of behavior in their explanations of human personality. A difficult but challenging task for a student is to select the personality theory (or theories) that seems most valid and to understand why.

Personality theories must explain abnormal as well as normal behavior. They help in deciding when behavior should be considered abnormal, how one diagnoses abnormality, and especially, how one treats abnormal behavior. The study of abnormal behavior and its treatment or therapy is a major interest of the psychology of personality.

The readings in this section have been chosen to illustrate the variety of issues with which personality psychologists are concerned, some of the methods they use in studying these issues, and some of the theoretical approaches that influence personality research.

Seymour Feshbach

The article by Ernest Hilgard has become a classic statement of the need for a concept of the self in order to explain many personality phenomena. Historically important, it was an outstanding experimental psychologist's presidential address to the American Psychological Association.

A cogent argument is presented for a theory of human motivation based on human experience rather than upon models of animal behavior. Professor Hilgard shows how the self-concept is critical to an understanding of defense mechanisms and describes the devious routes people sometimes take to maintain their self-image. He then goes on to discuss how self-awareness explains such behavior as self-criticism and guilt reactions and how the concept of self provides a basis for understanding the organization of personality and the continuity in behavior patterns. In this selection a link is made between psychoanalytic approaches to personality and the approaches of actualization theorists such as Carl Rogers.

Human Motives and the Concept of the Self

Ernest R. Hilgard

No problems are more fascinating than those of human motivation, and none are more in need of wise solution. To understand the struggles which go on within economic enterprise, to interpret the quarrels of international diplomacy, or to deal with the tensions in the daily interplay between individuals, we must know what it is that people want, how these wants arise and change, and how people will act in the effort to satisfy them.

American psychologists typically believe that adult motivational patterns develop through the socialization of organic drives. Our preference for such an interpretation is understandable because our science is rooted in biology. Man is assuredly a mammal as well as a member of society, and we begin to understand him by studying what he has in common with other animals. When we accept as the biological basis for motivation the drives present at birth or developing by maturation, it is natural to think of the learned social motives as grafted upon these or in some way derived from them. Despite the variations in the detailed lists of primary drives which different ones of us offer, and some alternative conceptions as to the ways in which socialization takes place, we find it easy to agree that adult motives are to be understood through an interaction between biology and culture.

Without reviewing any further the genetic development of motives, I wish to turn to some of the problems arising as we attempt to understand

Source: Reprinted by permission from *American Psychologist,* 1949, *4,* 374–382. Copyright © 1949 by the American Psychological Association.

Note: Address of the president of the American Psychological Association at Denver, September 6, 1949.

how these motives affect conduct. In our textbooks there is usually some important material left over after we have finished the chapters on physiological drives and social motives. I refer to the problems raised by the so-called defense mechanism or mechanisms of adjustment.

The Mechanisms of Adjustment in Motivational Theory

The mechanisms of adjustment were the features of Freudian theory that we earliest domesticated within American academic psychology. They now have a respectable place in our textbooks, regardless of the theoretical biases of our textbook writers.

The mechanisms did not burst all at once upon the psychological scene. Freud had begun to write about them in the '90's, and by the time of his *Interpretation of dreams* (1900) he had named repression, projection, displacement, identification, and condensation. In his *Three contributions to the theory of sex* (1905) he added fixation, regression, and reaction formation. It remained for Ernest Jones to give the name rationalization to that best-known of the mechanisms. He assigned this name in an article in the *Journal of Abnormal Psychology* in 1908. Among the books which brought the mechanisms together and called them to the attention of psychologists none was more popular than Bernard Hart's *Psychology of insanity,* which appeared in 1912 and went through several editions and many reprintings. Hart treated especially the manifestations of identification, projection, and rationalization, and introduced that by now familiar friend, logic-tight compartments.

It remained for Gates to collect the mechanisms into a list in a textbook intended for the general student. The evolution of his chapter on mechanisms is itself instructive by showing how styles change in psychology. In his *Psychology for students of education* (1923), Gates called the chapter "The dynamic role of instincts in habit formation." In the first edition of his *Elementary psychology* (1925) he changed the title to "The dynamic role of the dominant human urges in habit formation." Then in the next edition (1928) he used the contemporary sounding title: "Motivation and adjustment." The content of the chapter underwent only minor revisions with these changes in title. These widely used books did much to place the mechanisms on the tips of the tongues of psychology students and professors twenty years ago, for by that time the mechanisms were already part of the general equipment of psychology, and not reserved for abnormal psychology or the clinic.

Some of the tendencies found in Gates' early treatment have persisted in more recent discussions of the mechanisms. For one thing, we took over the mechanisms when as a profession we were hostile to other aspects of psychoanalytic teaching. As a consequence, we often gave only halting recognition to their psychoanalytic origins. Nearly all the mechanisms do in fact derive from Freud, Jung, Adler, and their followers. Among the mechanisms in Gates' 1928 list, psychoanalytic writers originated introversion, identification, rationalization, projection, defense mechanisms, and compensation. Yet

Gates' only mention of psychoanalysis was in some disparaging remarks about the "alleged adjustment by repression to the unconscious," an explanation of adjustment which he rejected as neither true nor useful.

In subsequent discussions of the mechanisms, textbook writers have seldom felt called upon to take responsibility for serious systematic treatment. In order to avoid a mere listing of mechanisms, many writers have attempted some sort of classificatory simplification, but there has been little agreement on which mechanisms belong together. Gates, for example, had included four mechanisms under rationalization: projection, sour grapes, sweet lemon, and logic-tight compartments. He gave defense and escape mechanisms separate places, although psychoanalytic practice has been to consider all the mechanisms as forms of defense. Shaffer (19) separated adjustments by defense from adjustments by withdrawing, but he took back much of the distinction by treating withdrawing as a defense. In his recent books concerned with the mechanisms, Symonds (23, 24) provides a rich collection of descriptive material, frankly psychoanalytic in orientation, but he succeeds little better than those who preceded him in giving a unified treatment of the mechanisms in relation to motivation.

The lack of systematic treatment of the mechanisms has had consequences for their development as part of psychological science. When there is no effort to be systematic, problems are not sharply defined. When problems are not sharply defined, anecdotal evidence is used loosely, and sometimes irresponsibly. A consequence is that very little evidence of experimental sort is introduced into the chapters on the mechanisms. This does not mean that evidence does not exist. It means only that problems have to be more carefully formulated before the relevance of existing evidence is seen, and before gaps in knowledge are discovered which evidence can fill.

The Mechanisms and the Self

It would take us too far afield to review the individual mechanisms at this time, and to consider evidence in relation to them. Instead, we may examine some of their most general characteristics, as they relate to motivational theory. These characteristics lend support to a thesis which I propose to defend: the thesis that all the mechanisms imply a self-reference, and that the mechanisms are not understandable unless we adopt a concept of the self.

The thesis that the mechanisms imply a self-reference need come as no surprise. Psychoanalysts have thought of the mechanisms as protecting the ego. Anna Freud's book on the subject bears the title: *The ego and the mechanisms of defense* (6). Non-psychoanalysts have occasionally endorsed a similar thesis. In their recent text, for example, Guthrie and Edwards have given a very straightforward account of the defense mechanisms. Although their text remains within the broad framework of behaviorism, they do not hesitate to relate the mechanisms to the ego. In fact they define defense mechanisms as "the reaction patterns which reestablish the ego" (7, p. 137).

Let us examine two of the characteristics of the mechanisms to see how the thesis of self-reference is implied. We may choose to view the mechanisms as defenses against anxiety, or we may see them as self-deceptive.

1. *The mechanisms as defenses against anxiety.* The natural history of anxiety in relation to learning has been much illuminated by the series of experiments with animal subjects performed by Mowrer, *e.g.* (13), Miller, *e.g.* (12), and their collaborators.

A white rat is confined in a rectangular box of one or more compartments. The animal can escape electric shock either by some action within the shock compartment (such as depressing a lever to shut off the current), or by escaping from the dangerous place (as by leaping a barrier). Both Mowrer and Miller find that in situations like this a new drive is acquired, sometimes called anxiety, sometimes called fear. This new drive can motivate learning very much like any other drive. They accept the general position that drive-reduction is reinforcing. Anything which reduces the fear or anxiety will reinforce the behavior leading to this reduction. Thus any sort of activity or ritual which would reduce fear or anxiety might be strengthened. Such activities or rituals might have the characteristics of defense mechanisms.

The natural history of anxiety, according to this view, is somewhat as follows. First, the organism has experiences of pain and punishment—experiences to be avoided. These are followed in turn by *threats* of pain and punishment, which lead to *fear* of the situations in which such threats arise. Other situations are assimilated to these fear-provoking ones, so the added circumstances may lead to apprehension. Fears with these somewhat vaguer object-relations become known as anxiety states. Sometimes as the apprehensive state becomes more and more detached from particular frightening situations, clinicians refer to it as a state of free-floating anxiety. All of these acquired states of fear, apprehension or anxiety are tension-states. Any one of them may serve as an acquired drive and motivate learning. Activities which lessen fear and anxiety are reinforced because tension is reduced. Thus behavior mechanisms become reinforced and learned as ways of reducing anxiety.

The Mowrer-Miller theory of the origin of fear, and of its role as an acquired drive, is acceptable as far as it goes. But it needs to be carried one step further if it is to deal with the kinds of anxiety which are found in the clinic. This step is needed because in man anxiety becomes intermingled with *guilt-feelings*. The Mowrer and Miller experiments with animals carry the natural history of anxiety through the stages of fear and apprehension, but not to the stage of guilt-feelings.

In many cases which come to the clinic, the apprehension includes the fear lest some past offense will be brought to light, or lest some act will be committed which deserves pain and punishment. It is such apprehensions which go by the name of guilt-feelings, because they imply the responsibility of the individual for his past or future misbehavior. To feel guilty is to conceive of the self as an agent capable of good or bad choices. It thus appears that at the point that anxiety becomes infused with guilt-feelings, self-reference enters. If we are to understand a person's defenses against guilt-feelings, we must know something about his image of himself. This is the kind of argument which supports the thesis that if we are to understand the mechanisms we shall have to come to grips with a concept of the self.

2. *The mechanisms as self-deceptive.* Another way of looking at the mechanisms is to see them as bolstering self-esteem through self-deception. There is a deceptive element in each of the mechanisms. Rationalization is using false or distorted reasons to oneself as well as to the world outside; using reasons known to be false in order to deceive someone else is not rationalization but lying. It is entirely appropriate to consider self-deception as one of the defining characteristics of a mechanism. As another example of what I mean, let us consider when aggression should be thought of as a mechanism. Aggressive behavior which is a form of fighting directly for what you want or as a protest against injustice is not a mechanism at all, even if it is violent and destructive. It is then simply a direct attempt at problem-solving. But displaced aggression has the characteristics of a mechanism, because false accusations are made, and the object of aggression may be related only remotely to the source of the need to express aggression. Displaced aggression thus contains the elements of self-deception, and fits the pattern of the mechanisms.

There are two chief ways in which we deceive ourselves. One is by *denial* of impulses, or of traits, or of memories. The second is through *disguise,* whereby the impulses, traits, or memories are distorted, displaced, or converted, so that we do not recognize them for what they are. Let us see what evidence there is for denial and for disguise.

The clearest evidence for denial comes through amnesia, in which memories are temporarily lost. If such memories can later be recovered without relearning, support is given to an interpretation of forgetting as a consequence of repression. Often in amnesia the memories lost are the personal ones, while impersonal memories remain intact.

The man studied by Beck (2), for example, had no trouble in carrying on a conversation, in buying railroad tickets, or in many other ways conducting himself like a mature adult with the habits appropriate to one raised in our culture. It is a mistake to say that he lost his memory, for without memory he would have been unable to talk and make change and do the other things which are based upon past experience with arbitrary symbols and meanings. But he did lose *some* of his memories. He could not recall his name, and he could not recall the incidents of his personal biography. The highly selective nature of the memory loss is an important feature of many amnesias. Under treatment, the man referred to recovered most of his memories, except for one important gap. This gap was for a period in his career in which he conducted himself in a manner of which he was thoroughly ashamed.

Disguise, as the second form of self-deception, shows in many ways. The most pertinent evidence from the laboratory comes in the studies of projection defined as the attribution of traits. Undesirable traits of his own of which the person prefers to remain unaware are assigned in exaggerated measure to other people (Sears, 18). In some cases, the deception goes so far as to become what Frenkel-Brunswik calls "conversion to the opposite." In one of her studies (4) it was found that a person who said, "Above all else I am kind," was one likely to be rated unkind by his acquaintances. In the studies of anti-Semitism which she later carried on collaboratively with the California group she presents evidence that anti-Semitism is sometimes a disguise for deepseated attitudes of hostility and insecurity having to do with home and childhood, and nothing to do directly with experience with Jews (5).

If self-deception either by denial or by disguise is accepted as characteristic of a mechanism, the problem still remains as to the source of or reasons for the self-deception. The obvious interpretation is that the need for self-deception arises because of a more fundamental need to maintain or to restore self-esteem. Anything belittling to the self is to be avoided. That is why the memories lost in amnesia are usually those with a self-reference, concealing episodes which are anxiety or guilt-producing. What is feared is loss of status, loss of security of the self. That is why aspects of the self which are disapproved are disguised.

In this discussion of the mechanisms I have tried to point out that they may be integrated with other aspects of motivation and learning provided their self-reference is accepted. Then it can be understood how they provide defenses against anxiety, and why they are self-deceptive through denial and disguise.

The Self Present in Awareness

The mechanisms are comprehensible only if we accept a conception of the self. This poses us the problem of the nature of the self-concept that we may find acceptable. Two main approaches lie before us. One approach is to look for the self in awareness, to see if we can find by direct observation the self that is anxious, that feels guilty, that tries various dodges in order to maintain self-respect. The second approach is to infer a self from the data open to an external observer, to construct a self which will give a coherent account of motivated behavior. Let us examine these two possibilities in turn.

We enter upon the task of discovering the self in awareness with the warnings from past failures. Any naive person who started out to develop a psychology of the self would expect to find the task relatively easy because self-awareness seems to be commonplace. Everybody knows that people are proud or vain or bashful because they are self-conscious. But the psychologist knows that this self-evident character of self-awareness is in fact most illusive. You presently find yourself as between the two mirrors of a barber-shop, with each image viewing each other one, so that as the self takes a look at itself taking a look at itself, it soon gets all confused as to the self that is doing the looking and the self which is being looked at. As we review the efforts of Miss Calkins (3) and her students to demonstrate that there was a self discoverable in every act of introspection, and find how little convinced Titchener and his students were, we are well advised not to enter that quarrel with the same old weapons. Introspection was taken seriously in those days and psychologists worked hard at it. There is little likelihood that we can succeed where they failed.

Their difficulty was not due to the insistence upon trained observers. Self-observation of a much freer type by naive subjects is little more satisfactory. Horowitz' study of the localization of the self as reported by children was not very encouraging in this respect (9). Children located their selves in the head or the stomach or the lower jaw or elsewhere, each individual child being reasonably consistent, but the whole picture not being very persuasive as to the fruitfulness of an approach through naive self-observation.

But the reason for rejecting a purely introspective approach to the search for the self is not limited to the historical one that earlier attempts have proved fruitless. It is based also on the recognition that defense mechanisms and self-deception so contaminate self-observation that unaided introspection is bound to yield a distorted view of the self.

Having said all this by way of warning, we may still allow some place for self-awareness in arriving at our concept of the self. Two aspects of the self as seen by the experiencing person appear to be necessary features in understanding self-organization.

The first of these is the continuity of memories as binding the self, as maintaining self-identity. To the external observer, the continuity of the bodily organism is enough to maintain identity, but the person himself needs to have continuous memories, dated in his personal past, if he is to have a sense of personal identity. One of the most terrifying experiences in the clinical literature is the state known as depersonalization, in which experiences are no longer recognized as belonging to the self. Break the continuity of memories and we have dissociation, split personalities, fugue states, and other distortions of the self.

The second feature of self-awareness which cannot be ignored in forming our concept of the self is that of self-evaluation and self-criticism. I earlier pointed out that we need to understand the feelings of guilt which go beyond mere anxiety. Guilt-feelings imply that the self is an active agent, responsible for what it does, and therefore subject to self-reproof. The other side of self-evaluation is that the self must be supported and must be protected from criticism. One component of the self is provided by those vigilant attitudes which are assumed in order to reduce anxiety and guilt. It is this vigilant self-criticism in its harshest form which is implied in Freud's concept of the super-ego. Evaluative attitudes toward the self, including both positive and negative self-feelings, come prominently to the fore in the interviews recorded by Rogers and his students (16, 17).

Another way of putting this is to state that the self of awareness is an object of value. McDougall referred to the sentiment of self-regard, as in some sense the master sentiment. Murphy, Murphy, and Newcomb put it tersely: "The self is something we like and from which we expect much." (15,

p. 210.) Perhaps I might amend the statement to read: "To some people the self is something they dislike and from which they expect little." In any case it is an object about which attitudes of appreciation and depreciation are organized. Snygg and Combs state as the basic human need the preservation and enhancement of the phenomenal self (21, p. 58). It would be easy to multiply testimony that one of the fundamental characteristics of self-awareness is an evaluative or judging attitude toward the self, in which the self is regarded as an object of importance and preferably of worth (1, 14, 20).

Despite the difficulties in introspective approaches to the self, we find that our self-concept needs to include some information based on private experience. The continuity of memories maintains personal identity, and the awareness of the self as an object of value organizes many of our attitudes. More is needed, however, to enrich the concept of the self and to make it square with all that we know about human motivation.

The Inferred Self

This points up the need for a more inclusive self-concept, one which will make use of all the data. Such a self-concept I shall call the inferred self. Like any other scientific construct, it will prove to be valid to the extent that it is systematically related to data, and it will be useful to the extent that it simplifies the understanding of events.

I wish to suggest three hypotheses needed in arriving at an inferred self. Each of these, although plausible, is not self-evident, and therefore requires demonstration. In order to be scientifically useful, it is important that the inferred self should go beyond the obvious. The inferred self will prove acceptable only if these hypotheses, or closely related ones are supported.

The first hypothesis is that of *the continuity of motivational patterns.* This means that the organization of motives and attitudes that are central to the self is one which persists and remains recognizable as the person grows older. Reactions to present situations will be coherent with reactions to past situations. For those who prefer the habit concept, the inferred self may be thought of as a pattern of persisting habits and attitudes. The organization or structure which is implied is a learned one, and like any habit structure it carries the marks of the past in the present. When new goals are substituted for old ones, there is continuity with the past in the ways in which the goals are selected and in the ways in which gratification is obtained. This is all plausible, but it is by no means self-evident, and it is greatly in need of empirical study. It is a matter for study and demonstration whether or not a continuity can be traced between nursing arrangements, thumb-sucking, nail-biting, cigarette-smoking, and overt sexual behavior. The first hypothesis implies that there is such a continuity, whatever motivational strands are being followed, so that one form of gratification shades imperceptibly into the next. If we but knew enough, we could trace the continuity throughout the life span.

The second hypothesis supporting the inferred self is that of *the genotypical patterning of motives.* This hypothesis suggests that motives unlike in their overt or phenotypical expression may represent an underlying similarity. It will do no good to try to appraise personality by a study confined to its superficial expression. What we know about the mechanisms of denial and disguise tells us that the genotypical pattern will have to be inferred. Unless we move at the level of inference and interpretation, much behavior will be baffling or paradoxical.

The inferred self goes beyond the self of awareness by including for purposes of inference much that is excluded from self-awareness. Awareness includes the not-self as well as the self. In dreams and hallucinations we have products of the self, present in awareness, but products for which the self takes neither credit nor responsibility. It is hard to see the self as giving the stage-directions for the dream, or as selecting the epithets hurled by the hallucinated voices. Yet in making a reconstruction of genotypical motives, these products of the self enter as evidence. Some items, then, remain in awareness, but are not part of self-awareness. Other items are excluded from awareness by inattention or amnesia. Facts such as these necessitate indirection in the inference to motivational organization. A description of overt conduct is not enough to permit an accurate appraisal of motivational patterning.

These assertions may be made with some confidence, but again confidence of assertion does not constitute proof. We need to show by rigorous proof that predictions based on the concept of genotypical patterning of motives will account for behavior either more economically or more accurately than predictions based on phenotypical manifestations of motivated action.

3. The third hypothesis is that *the important human motives are inter-personal both in origin and in expression.* Despite the fertility of Freud's mind and the penetration of his observations, this is one hypothesis about the self which he never fully grasped. By good fortune he laid his emphasis upon the one organic need—sex—which is inevitably interpersonal in its fullest expression. Even so, he remained within the instinct tradition. Once we reject the self as the unfolding of an inevitable pattern, but see it instead as an individual acquisition, we are impressed by the part which other people play in the shaping of an individual self. Because the parents and others who transmit the culture are themselves a part of the culture, there are some uniformities in socialization, producing pressure in the direction of a modal personality (10). In addition, there are diverse roles which are ready-made for the individual, to which he conforms with greater or less success. There are the roles of man and of woman, of eldest and youngest child, or mother and father and in-law, of employer and employee, of craftsman and white-collar worker. Finally there are the individualizing influences of heredity, of birth accidents, of childhood experiences. There are many details to be filled in, but there is little doubt about the general course of socialization, leading in the end to internalizing much of the culture in the form of personal ideals and standards of conduct.

The self is thus a product of interpersonal influences, but the question remains whether the end-product is also interpersonal in its expression.

Does the self have meaning only as it is reflected in behavior involving other people, either actually or symbolically? Is it true that you can describe a self only according to the ways in which other selves react to it? I am inclined to believe that the self, as a social product, has full meaning only when expressed in social interaction. But I do not believe that this is obvious, because I can conceive that it might not be true, or might be true in a limited sense only.

These uncertainties about the truth of the hypotheses regarding the inferred self need not be regarded as signs of weakness in the concept. On the contrary, the concept has greater potential richness of meaning precisely because it goes beyond the self-evident and requires empirical study and justification. If it turns out that in some meaningful sense motivational patterns are continuous, that we can unravel their genotypical organization, and that we can know in what precise way they are interpersonal, then we will have a concept of an inferred self that will be genuinely useful.

What does the inferred self imply as to the unity of personality? It does not necessarily imply unity. Conflict as well as harmony may be perpetuated through genotypical organization. The healthy self, however, will achieve an integrative organization. Note that I say integrative and not integrated. It is the integrative personality which can handle the complexity of relationships with other persons in a culture like ours, a culture which makes plural demands. An integrated personality soon leads to its own isolation or destruction if it is not also integrative. Lest this seem to be an idle play on words, let me point out that the paranoid psychotic with highly systematized delusions is among the best integrated of personalities. He is integrated but not integrative. The genotypical patterns of motivation which comprise the inferred self may or may not be integrative.

A Laboratory for the Study of Psychodynamics

I have argued that we need a self-concept if we are to understand the richness of human motivation, and I have proposed that we adopt an inferred self as the unifying concept. Now what shall we do about it?

Perhaps this all sounds very much like clinical psychology, so that the answer might come: "Leave it to the clinicians." I believe this to be the wrong answer, not because I have any lack of confidence in clinicians, but because I believe it represents a faulty conception of the appropriate division of labor within psychology. The problems of human motivation and personality belong to all psychologists. The problems of the self-concept are general problems of psychological science.

Instead of assigning these problems to any one group of psychologists, I propose that we proceed to establish laboratories for the study of psychodynamics fully commensurate with laboratories for the study of perception or learning or other problems of general psychology (11).

A laboratory for the study of psychodynamics differs from the clinic in its intent, though there will be overlap in staff, in procedures, and in prob-

lems. I am assuming that people are referred to a clinic or come there volun-
tarily in order to be helped with their personal problems. By contrast, subjects
are invited to come to a laboratory because they fit into an experimental design. The laboratory permits delimitation of problems and control of variables
in a manner usually less possible in a situation geared to service.

In order to make the picture of the psychodynamics laboratory
concrete, we may sketch a few specimen problems likely to be worked upon.
Many of these problems will have had their origin in clinical experience, and
many fruitful hypotheses will have come from the clinic. But the task of achieving precision in the testing of scientific generalizations belongs to the laboratory.

Of first moment are the problems involved in the natural history of
the self. This will mean concentrated study of young children, under arrangements which permit the testing of hypotheses. For many years we have given
assent to the importance of language as an instrument of socialization, but we
have a paucity of data. Piaget asked many of the right questions, but his con-
jectures have to be refined and put to the test in a manner more convincing to
American psychologists. I should assign the study of the child's language as a
task of high priority in the psychodynamics laboratory. This is but one aspect
of discovering in what ways the self is a social product.

Other problems include the details of influence by important people
in the child's environment. Some studies now under way at Stanford (8) suggest that patterns of sibling rivalry among young children are often traceable
to unresolved rivalries going back to the parents' childhoods. A parent may
act as a director of the drama, assigning the roles to the children, and calling
the turns on a new performance that largely reenacts one of a previous generation. While there is satisfactory evidence from case histories that this sort of
parental influence goes on, just how it comes about, and just how the parent is
protected from becoming aware of what is being done, need to be studied
under laboratory-type controls.

Another developmental problem worthy of careful exploration has
to do with the magical ideas of childhood, sometimes referred to as the feeling
of omnipotence. While the stubborn realities of the environment soon trim
down the sense of power to more finite proportions, magical conceptions continue even into adult life, influencing the interpretations of causal sequences.
I do not refer simply to superficial manifestations, as in the prevalence of
superstition. When the investigator begins to look, he finds that there are many
ways in which individuals believe themselves to have magical powers, to be
among the specially gifted, to be so precious as to be specially vulnerable, to
be able to shape events through willing them to be. In a scientific age like ours,
these magical ideas are taboo, and consequently may influence behavior while
being largely out of awareness. If we understand this desire to gain satisfaction
through the expression of magical power, we would better understand some of
the most puzzling aspects not only of an individual's behavior, but of the dynamics of economic and political life.

I have chosen these few illustrations (language, sibling rivalry, and the magic of power) to illustrate the sorts of problems which can be studied in arriving at a natural history of the self.

Let me turn now to a set of problems in the answer to which experiments with animal subjects are particularly promising. These are defining experiments on the concepts of anxiety, shame, and guilt. I have already referred to the excellent start made by experiments on fear and anxiety in rats. It may take a more sociable animal, such as the dog, to exhibit the behavior we call shame. There is no doubt that the dog can act as if ashamed. I do not know whether or not a dog can act as if guilty. Shame may be thought of as a response to being caught by someone else in socially disapproved behavior; guilt may be thought of as a response to catching yourself in behavior discordant with your own conscience. Can both shame and guilt go on outside of awareness, or is guilt alone subject to unconscious expression? Is the concept of guilt applicable only to man? We need better definitions, but we also need to know what is the case. I should like to see the psychodynamics laboratory work on the problem of clarifying what is meant by anxiety, shame, and guilt, and instructing us about the principles according to which these processes occur.

The psychodynamics laboratory is the place in which to make a direct study of the self-organization which permits conflicts within the self as dramatized in the Freudian notions of id, ego, and superego. This particular partitioning of the self is probably too rigid to be acceptable, but they are genuine problems which the partitioning is designed to explain, and these problems are still in need of explanation. Anna Freud suggests that under hypnosis the hypnotist sets aside the subject's ego. Others have suggested that the superego is soluble in alcohol. If appropriate hypotheses are clearly stated, it ought to be possible to design experiments to test them by biasing the outcome of the wars within the self. That is, through appropriate techniques, perhaps using hypnosis or alcohol, one or the other of the fighters in the battle could be strengthened or weakened. Thus it should be possible to determine with greater precision the nature of the participants in self-conflict.

Another problem is that of rapport which arises because we need to know the circumstances under which a person can freely report private experience with a minimum of distortion. Consider the following three situations. First is the administration of projective tests, say the Rorschach or the TAT. It is assumed, rightly or wrongly, that rapport with the test-administrator can be established fairly promptly. It is also assumed, rightly or wrongly, that once rapport is established, responses are primarily to the stimulus cards rather than to the test administrator. All this needs study, but we may accept this situation as involving a relatively low order of rapport. Next in our scale is the ordinary interviewing situation, in which the subject, alone with the psychologist, reports private experiences. Here it is plausible to assume that rapport is more important than in the test situation, so that what the person reveals becomes more closely related to the inter-personal situation the interviewer is able to create. The third situation, with rapport at a maximum, is that of hypnosis, in which rapport is exaggerated beyond that ordinarily found in the interviewing situation. These graded situations provide an excellent series in which to study what rapport does to the possibility of reporting personal experiences with varying degrees of distortion.

Another problem is that of insight as a factor in personality reorganization. Here we have a problem directly pertinent to clinical practices, and to psychotherapy, but there is pertinence to general psychology also. How is the insight of which the psychotherapist speaks related to that of which the animal psychologist speaks? There is a similarity in that both have to do with sensible problem-solving, based on the ways in which situations are perceived.

In studying the achievement of insight we have an opportunity to compare the self present in awareness with the inferred self. What we mean by insight in this context is essentially that the self of which the person is aware comes to correspond to the inferred self,—in other words, that the person comes to see himself as an informed other person sees him. This is what is meant by an objective attitude toward the self. The self may be granted the privilege of privacy, but even the view of the self held in private is such as could be communicated to a trusted outsider. This explains the enigmatic statement of the late Harry Stack Sullivan that one achieves mental health to the extent that one becomes aware of one's inter-personal relations (22, p. 102). When the relations to other people become communicable to oneself and potentially to another, then these relations are no longer confused by the distortions of neurotic mechanisms.

It is sometimes said that the mechanisms are blind and inflexible, little subject to the ordinary principles of learning (25). But they can be unlearned; this is, in fact, one of the chief tasks of psychotherapy. There are perhaps two main ways in which, through insight, the mechanisms can be defeated.

The first of these methods is to become aware of the mechanisms, so that the person can catch himself using them. He may learn to interpret his own headaches and his own outbursts of temper. Because he knows what he is doing, he is able to control his conduct. Insight here is into symptoms and the chain of events of which these symptoms are a part. Following insight the chain of events may be broken, so that the sequences do not flow to their usual conclusions. Guthrie has made use of a notion very like this (despite his discomfort with insight as a concept) in urging that the way to gain control over a habit sequence is to identify the cues. By alienating these cues, the objectional habit sequence is interrupted.

The second method overlooks the detailed action of the mechanisms entirely, while seeking insight into whatever has made the mechanisms necessary. There is a reevaluation of the self and its motives, a willingness to accept features of the self which were previously unacceptable. If more security can be achieved by abandoning the mechanisms than was achieved by them, they do not have to be fought. The mechanisms simply dissolve because they are no longer needed.

It is important to know whether or not this is a two-stage process, or an interaction between two methods of solving the same problem. This is not something to be debated, but something to be studied and understood.

We are ready today, as we might not have been a few years ago, to establish psychodynamic laboratories to attack and answer many of the questions which I have raised. Such laboratories will provide opportunities for cooperation between experimental and clinical psychologists on problems of mutual concern. The staff to be invited to work in these laboratories will include psychologists with a variety of backgrounds, united in their acknowledgment that the search for the self is a significant scientific endeavor.

References

1. ALLPORT, G. W. The ego in contemporary psychology. *Psychol. Rev.*, 1943, *50*, 451–478.
2. BECK, L. F. Hypnotic identification of an amnesia victim. *Brit. J. Med. Psychol.*, 1936, *16*, 36–42.
3. CALKINS, M. W. The self in scientific psychology. *Amer. J. Psychol.*, 1915, *26*, 495–524.
4. FRENKEL-BRUNSWIK, ELSE. Mechanisms of self-deception. *J. Soc. Psychol.*, 1939, *10*, 409–420.
5. ———. A study of prejudice in children. *Human Relations*, 1948, *1*, 295–306.
6. FREUD, ANNA. *The ego and the mechanisms of defence*. London: Hogarth Press, 1937.
7. GUTHRIE, E. R., & EDWARDS, A. L. *Psychology*. New York: Harper, 1949.
8. HILGARD, JOSEPHINE R. Sibling rivalry and pseudoheredity. *Psychiatry* (To appear).
9. HOROWITZ, E. L. Spatial localization of the self. *J. Sec. Psychol.*, 1935, *6*, 379–387.
10. KARDINER, A. *The psychological frontiers of society*. New York: Columbia Univ. Press, 1945.
11. MACKINNON, D. W., & HENLE, MARY. *Experimental studies in psychodynamics; a laboratory manual*. Cambridge: Harvard Univ. Press, 1948.
12. MILLER, N. E. Studies of fear as an acquirable drive: I. Fear as motivation and fear reduction as reinforcement in the learning of new responses. *J. Exp. Psychol.*, 1948, *38*, 89–101.
13. MOWRER, O. H. Anxiety-reduction and learning. *J. Exp. Psychol.*, 1940, *27*, 497–516.
14. MURPHY, G. *Personality: A biosocial approach to origin and structure*. New York: Harper, 1947.
15. MURPHY, G., MURPHY, LOIS B., & NEWCOMB, T. *Experimental social psychology*. New York: Harper, 1937.
16. ROGERS, C. R. Some observations on the organization of personality. *Amer. Psychologist*, 1947, *2*, 358–368.
17. ROGERS, C. R., et al. A coordinated research in psychotherapy. *J. Consulting Psychol.*, 1949, *13*, 149–220.
18. SEARS, R. R. Experimental studies of projection: I. Attribution of traits. *J. Soc. Psychol.*, 1936, *7*, 151–163.
19. SHAFFER, L. F. *The psychology of adjustment*. Boston: Houghton Mifflin, 1936.
20. SHERIF, M., & CANTRIL, H. *The psychology of ego-involvements*. New York: Wiley, 1947.
21. SNYGG, D., & COMBS, A. W. *Individual behavior*. New York: Harper, 1949.

22. SULLIVAN, H. S. Conceptions of modern psychiatry. *Psychiatry,* 1940, *3,* 1–117.
23. SYMONDS, P. M. *The dynamics of human adjustment.* New York: Appleton-Century, 1946.
24. ———. *Dynamic psychology.* New York: Appleton-Century-Crofts, 1949.
25. TOLMAN, E. C. *Drives toward war.* New York: Appleton-Century, 1942.

This article describes two experiments designed to clarify the effects of children's experiences of fear on their perception of other people. The authors are interested in studying how fear distorts one's perceptions of other people. Their specific objective is to determine the conditions under which people attribute their own feelings to others (supplementary projection) and the conditions under which the distortion in social perception complements their feeling (complementary projection). Their findings indicate that frightened boys show supplementary projection (that is, attribute fear to others) when judging boys, but show complementary projection (attribute malice to others) when judging adult males.

A methodological point to note is their incidental observation of the tightening of the circle when the children told ghost stories. An observation of this kind is called an "unobtrusive measure." The note on the use of naturally occurring fear situations instead of inducing fear experimentally is also of interest. Most psychologists now prefer, on ethical and other grounds, using naturally occurring unpleasant or noxious events in research rather than experimentally inducing them.

Influence of the Stimulus Object upon the Complementary and Supplementary Projection of Fear

Seymour Feshbach and Norma Feshbach

Two studies were conducted bearing on the hypothesis that frightened boys attribute malice to male adults but attribute fear to other boys. In the 1st experiment, a Halloween setting was used to elicit fear. The experimental group, in comparison to a matched control group, manifested a reliable increment in attribution of maliciousness to pictures of men and boys but no significant change in attribution of fear. Because of possible complications due to hostility arousal, a 2nd experiment was carried out in which judgments were elicited from boys who thought they were going to participate in a study involving frightening equipment. Under these conditions, the experimental Ss attributed reliably more maliciousness to men and reliably more fear to boys.

Clinical observation as well as experimental studies (Feshbach & Singer, 1957; Murray, 1933; Singer & Feshbach, 1962) indicate that a frightened individual tends to distort his judgments of other people. The factors that determine the degree and type of distortion that will take place have yet to be specified. The present study proposes to investigate the influence of the stimulus person upon the projective process under conditions in which fear has been

Source: Reprinted by permission from *Journal of Abnormal and Social Psychology,* 1963, *66,* 498–502. Copyright © 1963 by the American Psychological Association.

Note: This study was supported by Research Grant M3213 from the National Institute of Mental Health, United States Public Health Service. The authors wish to thank Samuel Cameron and Louise Irwin for their assistance in carrying out these experiments.

112

aroused and in which social interaction between the perceiver and the stimulus is minimized.

At least two different kinds of changes in social judgment have been observed in response to fear arousal. Murray (1933), in his pioneer study, found that frightened girls perceived pictures of adults, primarily male, as malicious and threatening. Murray described this effect as "complementary projection" to distinguish it from the more classic form of "supplementary projection" in which characteristics of the perceiver are directly attributed to the stimulus. In a study by Feshbach and Singer (1957), using college males who were subjected to electric shocks as the subjects and a film of an adult male taking some psychological tests as the stimulus, evidence of supplementary as well as complementary projection was obtained; that is, under conditions of fear arousal, the subjects tended to attribute both fear and hostility to the stimulus person.

Although the above cited studies are concerned with the problem of projection, the processes involved are probably quite distinct from that mediating psychoanalytic projection (Murstein, 1959). In the case of the latter, the attributed trait is unacceptable and the function of the projection is the reduction of anxiety. In the case of the fear arousal studies, one appears to be dealing with a process which is more akin to stimulus generalization in that the perceiver generalizes from his own state to that of the person being judged. In terms of this process which has been previously labeled "infusion" (Feshbach & Singer, 1957), the degree of "projection" will be a function of the degree of similarity between the perceiver and the stimulus person. From this point of view, egocentricity of the perceiver or the extent to which he is preoccupied with his own feelings should exaggerate the influence of his feelings upon his judgment.

While these assumptions can account for the phenomenon of supplementary projection, they do not explain the attribution of maliciousness found by Murray (1933) under conditions of fear arousal. A comparison of the differences between the Murray and the Feshbach and Singer studies provides some suggestions as to the conditions which elicit a particular type of "projection." There are a number of differences in procedure and subject population between these two experiments which may have been responsible for the differences in results including the very obvious fact that Murray had not obtained ratings of the degree to which the stimuli appeared anxious or fearful. However, we suggest that even if Murray had obtained judgments of fearfulness, changes in the ratings of this dimension would have been less marked than the observed changes in the ratings of maliciousness, because the children judged only adults. It is the principal contention of this paper that a critical variable determining the kind of distortion in judgment that is likely to take place under conditions of fear arousal is the relationship between the perceiver and the stimulus person.

More specifically, a frightened child who is observing an adult, in the absence of information about the adult, is likely to attribute to him those feelings and attitudes which adults displayed in previous situations in which he had been frightened. If the past experience of fear has been associated with a punitive adult, then, under subsequent conditions of fear arousal, the child will tend to attribute maliciousness to similar adults; that is, he will manifest complementary projection. However, when a child judges another child, the psychological situation is markedly different. The similarity of the stimulus person to the perceiver is likely to foster the direct attribution of the affect of the perceiver to the stimulus. Also, the variable of past experience, although less clear in its consequences than in the case of interaction with adults, would probably facilitate the direct attribution of the child's feelings to the stimulus child; that is, when children judge others who are similar to them in age and sex, supplementary projection should be manifested.

On the basis of these considerations, it is hypothesized that frightened boys tend to perceive other boys as fearful and tend to perceive adults, particularly males, as malicious. The prediction regarding adult males is based upon Murray's previous findings and upon the assumption that, in general, boys in our culture are likely to be more frightened of male figures, particularly their fathers, than female figures. This assumption receives some support from Kagan's (1956) finding that 6–10 year old children view their mothers as friendlier and less punitive than their fathers.

Experiment I

Method

The first experiment to be described which bears upon these hypotheses is essentially a replication of various features of Murray's (1933) original study with some important modifications. Ten neighborhood boys, ranging in age from 9 to 12, were invited to a Halloween party at the home of the experimenters. The parents of the children had previously been informed of the purpose of this "party" and had consented to their children participating, being reassured by the fact that the experimenters' son was also to be a subject in the study.

When the boys arrived, they found themselves in a completely darkened house except for one room which was illuminated by a jack-o'-lantern. The eeriness of the atmosphere was further enhanced by having the children form a circle and relate ghost stories to each other. The second author sat in the center of the circle and initiated the stories. (Although the diameter of the circle was about 11 feet at the beginning of the story telling, by the time the last ghost story was completed, it had been spontaneously reduced to approximately 3 feet.) After the ghost stories, she introduced the boys to a game called "murder" in which they were required to hide alone and conceal themselves from the individual who, without their knowledge, was designated as the murderer. Immediately after he was caught, the child was taken to the "testing" room where he was presented a series of 16 pictorial stimuli consisting of an equal number of men, women, boys, and girls, arranged in a random sequence with the restriction that no two pictures within the same age-sex category should follow each other. Three such random sequences were employed. The pictures were first rated for fearfulness and then for maliciousness. Each rating scale consisted of seven alternatives which in the case of fearfulness ranged from "fearless" to "extremely scared" and in the case of maliciousness ranged from "extremely good and kind" to "extremely bad and cruel."

A control group of 10 boys was obtained from the same school which the experimental subjects attended. The controls and experimental subjects were matched on the basis of age, intelligence, school performance, religion, and race. Each control subject was seen individually and after rapport was established, the subject rated the standard set of stimuli. Both control and experimental subjects were subsequently retested under relaxed conditions with the same stimuli after an interval of 4 weeks.

Results

Scores ranging from one to seven were assigned to each judgment of a photograph, a higher score reflecting a higher rating of maliciousness or fearfulness, according to the scale being used. Ratings of a particular characteristic for each set of four photographs within an age-sex grouping were separately summed for each child. For every subject, then, judgments of men, women, boys, and girls were determined for each of the two testing sessions. Change scores were obtained by subtracting the second set of ratings from the corresponding initial set so that for the experimental group, for example, a positive score reflects a greater degree of attribution of the trait or affect in question under conditions of fear arousal than under relaxed conditions. Mean changes in attribution of maliciousness and fear by the experimental and control groups are reported in Table 1. With respect to attribution of fear, although the experimental group displays larger positive increments than does the control group, the differences are not significant. However, there are marked, statistically significant differences in the attribution of maliciousness. The increments in perception of maliciousness are significantly greater for the

TABLE 1. Mean change scores in attribution of maliciousness and fearfulness as a function of experimental treatment and sex and age of the stimulus (Experiment I)

Group	Attribution of Maliciousness				Attribution of Fear			
	Boys	Men	Girls	Women	Boys	Men	Girls	Women
Experimental	+ .9	+2.6	+ .4	−1.0	+2.3	+2.6	+ .9	+1.3
Control	−2.7	−2.3	−2.3	−3.5	+ .9	+ .5	+1.7	− .4
p^a	<.01	<.02	<.10	<.10	—	—	—	—

[a] All p values presented in the tables are based on a two-tailed Mann-Whitney U test. Dash entry indicates p value greater than .10.

experimental than for the control group in response to male stimuli, but are not significant for the judgments of girls and women.

The data then provide evidence of complementary projection only and fail to support the prediction of supplementary projection when judging similar age boys. In addition, the results are not consistent with a simple model of complementary projection since distortions of this type were evidenced in judgments of boys as well as adult males. The data can be accounted for within the proposed theoretical framework if one assumes that the experimental situation aroused hostile impulses as well as fear. The telling of ghost stories and the murder game may well have aroused aggressive fantasies. As an incidental but pertinent note, the boys were rather aggressive and unrestrained when dessert was served following completion of the experiment. (The experimenters, at least, interpreted as aggressive the use of the white dining room walls as targets for chocolate ice cream balls fired from improvised sling shots). The attribution of malice to the male stimuli may then have been a function of generalization of hostile impulses as well as, in the case of the adult males, the redintegration of negative percepts associated with previous fear arousal situations.

Experiment II

Method

Because of the ambiguous nature of the findings in this initial study, it was felt desirable to obtain similar data but under conditions in which fear arousal would be maximized and hostility arousal minimized. This second study was conducted in a YMCA setting. Twenty-seven volunteers from several boys' clubs were assigned at random to an experimental or control condition. These boys ranged in age from 8 to 12. The subjects in the experimental or fear arousal condition entered a room in which in one corner was situated a black stool to which were attached a number of metallic extensions. Several wires led from the stool to an adjacent black box which had elaborate dials and a series of flickering colored lights. A long hypodermic needle placed on a white napkin near the box was also visible to the subjects. Midway in the experiment, a male assistant dressed in a white coat entered the room and conspicuously filled the hypodermic with a milky white fluid. The experimental subjects were initially told by the senior author that there were two phases to the experiment, the first consisting of judgments of a series of pictures and the second having "something to do with the equipment in the corner." As in the first study, the subjects were given a series of stimuli to rate on scales of fearfulness and then maliciousness, except that in this second experiment, the photographs were projected onto a screen. The photographs used in this second study were the same as those initially employed except that a new, male adult photograph was substituted for one used in the Halloween study. There was an additional variation in procedure: before either of the ratings was made, the subjects were asked to select an adjective from the following list—relaxed, mean, pleased, scared, kind, unhappy—which best fitted the person in the picture. Thus, the photographs were presented three times—once for the adjective description, and once for the ratings of fearfulness, and finally once more for the ratings of maliciousness. It is important to note that the judgments of the experimental group were elicited while the fear arousing stimuli were in clear view. The "second part" of the experiment involving these stimuli was, of course, never carried out and a party was substituted instead. The control group followed the same procedure as the experimental group except for the absence of the fear inducing objects that were present in the experimental room.

Results

The ratings obtained in the YMCA study were summed and analyzed according to the age and sex of the stimulus person. The pertinent data are presented in Table 2. These results are much more consistent with the experimental hypotheses than was the case for the Halloween data. As Table 2 indicates, the experimental subjects attributed significantly more maliciousness to the adult male photographs than did the control subjects. The attribution of maliciousness to adult males is quite specific since in no other instance did the differences in ratings of maliciousness approach statistical significance. One notes that under control conditions, a markedly greater degree of malice was attributed to boys than to any of the other stimuli. While it is possible that the absence of an experimental effect in the judgment of boys is due to these high ratings, the fact that the Halloween subjects who also attributed greater maliciousness to boys under control conditions manifested a reliable increment under experimental conditions argues against this possibility.

TABLE 2.   A comparison of experimental and control mean ratings of fearfulness and maliciousness as a function of sex and age of the stimulus (Experiment II)

Group	Attribution of Maliciousness				Attribution of Fear			
	Boys	*Men*	*Girls*	*Women*	*Boys*	*Men*	*Girls*	*Women*
Experimental	19.0	17.6	13.2	14.1	14.8	12.1	10.8	15.1
Control	18.0	13.4	12.4	13.5	11.6	10.1	9.1	12.0
p	—	$<.01$	—	—	.053	—	—	$<.10$

When the fearfulness ratings are examined, a quite different pattern emerges. The experimental group perceives boys as more frightened, the *p* value of the difference being .053. In addition, the experimental subjects tend to attribute more fear to women than do the controls, the difference being significant at the .10 level.

Inspection of the adjective choice data revealed that the only substantial differences occurred in the attribution of the adjectives "scared" and

"unhappy" to boys. The experimental subjects used these adjectives significantly more frequently than did the controls, a finding which supports the
difference obtained in the direct ratings of fearfulness of boys. The mean
frequency with which "scared" and "unhappy" were employed for the various
age and sex groups is presented in Table 3. Although the difference is unreliable, one notes that the experimental subjects tend to attribute more of these
same adjectives to women than do the controls, a trend consistent with the
rating results.

TABLE 3. A comparison of mean frequencies of attribution of "scared" and "unhappy" descriptions to stimuli of varying age and sex by the experimental and control groups (Experiment II)

Group	Boys	Men	Girls	Women
Experimental	2.4	1.2	1.2	2.1
Control	1.4	1.1	1.5	1.6
p	<.05	—	—	—

Discussion

The data of the YMCA study conform rather well to the experimental predictions. Fear arousal is seen to result in qualitatively different
distortions depending upon characteristics of the stimulus being judged. Complementary projection is observed in the judgments of adult males; that is,
the frightened boys tended to perceive men as malicious. Supplementary projection is observed in the judgments of the young males similar in age to the
perceiver; that is, the frightened boys tended to perceive other boys as similarly frightened and unhappy. The greater attribution of fear to boys was
reflected by both the adjective choice measure and the ratings of fearfulness.
Significant differences in the attribution of malice to men were obtained for
ratings of maliciousness but not for adjective choice. The lack of sensitivity
of the adjective choice measure in the latter instance may have been due to
the fact that only one adjective—"mean"—out of the six provided could be
used as an index of complementary projection while two adjectives—"scared"
and "unhappy"—were available as indices of supplementary projection, thus
providing a more reliable datum.

Although an attempt was made in the second experiment to maximize fear arousal and reduce hostility arousal, the conditions for arousing fear
are so similar to the conditions under which hostility is elicited that one cannot
be certain that the boys, in addition to being frightened, were not also aggressive. However, the possibility that the complementary projection observed was
actually a case of supplementary projection—namely, the boys directly attributing their aggressive impulses to the adult male figures—seems unlikely
for the following reason. If supplementary projection of aggressive impulses

was the essential process, then one might have expected the attribution of maliciousness to boys as well as to men. In contrast to the results from the Halloween study, this effect did not take place. The results of the YMCA study are more readily accounted for by the predicted interaction of fear arousal with the type of stimulus person being judged.

The interpretation of this interaction which is offered here stresses past rather than current sources of threat. The latter may also be a relevant variable and, under some circumstances, could override the influence of past experience. A child recently frightened by a very hostile female may tend to generalize and attribute malice to other females rather than to males. One could argue that the perception of male adults as malicious by the experimental subjects in the YMCA experiment was due to the fact that while a female associate was present during part of the experimental session, a male acted as the primary experimenter. The force of this argument is weakened when one considers that the primary experimenter in the Halloween experiment was female and yet there was an increase in attribution of maliciousness to males and not to females.[1]

Still another interpretation of the data could be offered in terms of Heider's (1958) balance theory. From this point of view, the primary mechanism would be the need to maintain cognitive consistency. The child's perception of other children and adults balances as it were his perception of his own emotional state. Since what constitutes an appropriate match for the child's affective state may well depend upon past experience, the implications drawn from balance theory could be quite similar to those based upon the redintegration hypothesis.

The tendency of the frightened boys to attribute a greater degree of fear to women, while never reaching the .05 level, seems sufficiently consistent to warrant some comment. It may be that women, particularly mothers, are more likely than men to have occasion in which they share dysphoric feelings of their children; that is, in the past, when a child has been frightened and upset he has perceived similar affects in his mother. If the present analysis is correct, it should be possible by obtaining prior information as to the perception by the child of his parents—whether he perceives his mother as more sympathetic than his father, whether he views his father as a more severe punitive agent than his mother—to predict more precisely the specific kind of distortion that a particular child will manifest when he is frightened.

In conclusion, perhaps the most significant implication that one can draw from this study is that the influence of fear upon the cognitive functions involved in judging the motives and feelings of other people is specific and

---

[1] The issue could be readily resolved by repeating the YMCA study, using a female as the primary experimenter. However, it is the opinion of the present authors that the procedure used in the YMCA study may be too disturbing for some children. The authors feel rather fortunate in that they were readily able to reduce the anxiety of two boys who were quite upset by the experimental situation. In investigating future problems in this area, one could take advantage of natural fear producing situations such as children awaiting a polio shot or some form of surgery.

ordered, rather than pervasive and erratic. Under conditions of fear arousal the perception of only certain classes of people reflect the influence of complementary and supplementary projection. The subjects' perception of girls, for instance, in both the Halloween and YMCA studies was unaffected by the experimental conditions. These results point up the importance of the role of the stimulus in determining the influence of subjective factors upon social judgments. The subject's judgment represents the outcome of the interaction of so-called subjective and objective variables and both must be considered in order to adequately predict his behavior.

References

FESHBACH, S., & SINGER, R. The effects of fear arousal and suppression of fear upon social perception. *J. Abnorm. Soc. Psychol.*, 1957, *55*, 283–288.

HEIDER, F. *The psychology of interpersonal relations.* New York: Wiley, 1958.

KAGAN, J. The child's perception of the parent. *J. Abnorm. Soc. Psychol.*, 1956, *53*, 257–258.

MURRAY, H. A. The effect of fear on the estimates of the maliciousness of other personalities. *J. Soc. Psychol.*, 1933, *4*, 310–329.

MURSTEIN, B. I. The concept of projection: A review. *Psychol. Bull.*, 1959, *56*, 353–371.

SINGER, R., & FESHBACH, S. The effects of anxiety arousal in psychotics and normals upon the perception of anxiety in others. Paper read at Western Psychological Association, San Francisco, April 1962.

The following two articles, one by Pearl Mayo Gore and Julian B. Rotter and one by Bonnie Ruth Strickland, form a logical pair demonstrating how one validates a personality measure. The articles also show how personality scales can be used to explain and predict socially relevant behaviors. Both selections bear upon the I-E Scale, which is a measure of a generalized attitude of internal versus external control of the locus of reinforcement. It is instructive to look at some of the items in the scale, at the definition of the I-E construct, and at the propositions used by the authors in making predictions from the scale to various indices of social action. In the selection by Gore and Rotter, the criterion of social action was the verbalized commitment of students to social action-taking behavior. These data show that individuals who obtain higher "internal" scores on the I-E Scale are more likely to commit themselves to social action than those who tend to believe their fate is controlled by external forces. In the second article, Strickland extends these findings and shows that persons actually involved *in social action obtain higher internal scores on the I-E Scale than a control group of persons not engaged in social action.*

A Personality Correlate of Social Action

Pearl Mayo Gore and Julian B. Rotter

Social scientists have long been interested in the conditions under which the initiation of social change will take place. It has fallen to the social psychologist in particular to attempt predictions of individual differences in behavior directed toward a changing of the social structure. Usually, the problem has been approached through the measurement of the intensity or strength of attitudes. However, it is now widely recognized that the apparent desirability of some social outcome is a poor predictor of the degree to which an individual will commit himself toward action to obtain the desired goal. This is particularly true when the social action runs counter to majority opinion and entails risk of rejection, failure, or other punishment.

The concept of internal vs. external control of reinforcement may be of value in predicting social action behavior. This dimension distributes individuals according to the degree to which they attribute what happens to themselves to their own behaviors or characteristics vs. the degree to which they attribute what happens to themselves to forces outside their own control. Such forces would be represented by ideas of fate, chance, powerful others,

Source: Reprinted by permission of Duke University Press from *The Journal of Personality*, 1963, *31*, 58–64. Copyright © 1963 by Duke University Press.

Note: This research was supported in part by the United States Air Force under Contract No. AF 49 (638)-741 monitored by the Air Force Office of Scientific Research, Office of Aerospace Research. This paper was read at the Midwestern Psychological Association Meeting, 1962.

or a general inability to understand the world. In social learning theory (Rotter, 1954), this variable is viewed as a generalized expectancy relating behavior to reinforcement in a large number of learning situations, cutting across specific need areas. In other words, it involves a higher-level learning skill affecting behavior in a wide variety of problem-solving situations.

Previous research by Phares (1957, 1962), James and Rotter (1958), James (1957), Rotter, Liverant, and Crowne (1961) and others have shown unequivocally that the growth and extinction of expectancies for reward vary considerably in different laboratory tasks if the tasks are perceived by S as chance, luck, or controlled by E vs. those which are seen as skill tasks with reinforcement dependent upon the individual's ability.

In addition to the findings from studies of expectancy changes, it has been hypothesized that individuals differ in a stable personality characteristic of whether they expect reward in a large variety of situations to be the function of external forces or their own behavior or attributes. The first attempt to measure such a generalized characteristic was made by Phares (1957). His test was revised by James (1957) into a longer Likert type scale, and Liverant, Rotter, Crowne, and Seeman have developed successive forms of a forced choice scale starting from the James-Phares test (Rotter, Seeman, & Liverant, 1962). The test now being used at Ohio State for research with adults consists of twenty-three items with six filler items (I-E Scale). Illustrative items are as follows:

I more strongly believe that:
    6. a. Without the right breaks one cannot be an effective leader.
      b. Capable people who fail to become leaders have not taken advantage of their opportunities.
    9. a. I have often found that what is going to happen will happen.
      b. Trusting to fate has never turned out as well for me as making a decision to take a definite course of action.
    17. a. As far as world affairs are concerned, most of us are the victims of forces we can neither understand, nor control.
      b. By taking an active part in political and social affairs the people can control world events.
    23. a. Sometimes I can't understand how teachers arrive at the grades they give.
      b. There is a direct connection between how hard I study and the grades I get.

Approaches to the assessment of individual differences along these lines with children have been developed by Bialer (1961), Crandall, Katkovsky, and Preston (1962), and Battle and Rotter (1963). Previous studies with adult and child scales have shown predictiveness in some learning situations (Phares, 1957; James, 1957; Bialer, 1961), an achievement situation (Crandall & Katkovsky, in press), a conformity situation (Crowne & Liverant, 1963), risk taking tasks (Liverant & Scodel, 1960), logical relationships to other tests

(Holden, 1958; Simmons, 1959), and mean differences among known groups, (Battle and Rotter, 1963); Cromwell, Rosenthal, Shakow, & Zahn, 1961).

The most closely related research to the present study, however, was conducted by Seeman and Evans (1962) who related the concept and measure of internal vs. external control to the sociological concept of alienation, in the sense of powerlessness. Using one revision of the current test, Seeman and Evans studied patients in a tuberculosis hospital. They found statistical support for their general hypothesis that those patients who scored toward the internal control end of the dimension would know more about their own condition, would be better informed about the disease of tuberculosis in general, and would be regarded by the ward personnel as being better patients and better informed about their own condition. These predictions held in spite of the fact that none of the items in the questionnaire dealt with tuberculosis specifically or any disease or attitude toward disease. If patients' efforts to find out about their own serious physical condition can be affected by such a generalized attitude, it seems likely that where people are highly involved in desire for certain social change, as Negroes are in desegregation, social action-taking behavior could be likewise predicted from a generalized attitude of internal vs. external control of the locus of reinforcement. This is the major hypothesis of the present study. It should be emphasized that no test items in the I-E Scale deal directly with political liberalness,[1] prejudice, attitudes toward Negro rights, or the Ss' own present or past social action behavior.

In addition, it was hypothesized that predictiveness of this behavior would be improved by a knowledge of the social desirability motives of the Ss. Hence, a secondary hypothesis was that Ss high in measured social desirability motive (high SD) would be less likely to participate in actions toward social change than Ss low in this trait.

Since it appeared likely that the assumed high reinforcement value of the social change might be differently affected by the individual's social class membership, a measure of social class was included in the investigation. The direction of the relationship between social class membership and social action taking behavior was not hypothesized.

Method

Ss of the present study were students at a Southern Negro college that has featured prominently in recent social protest movements. Three psychology classes, including 62 males and 54 females, were given the Internal-External Control of Reinforcements Scale (I-E), and the Marlowe-Crowne

---

[1] Data recently collected by Rotter show no significant difference in the I-E Scale scores of Ohio State University students who identify themselves as Republicans from those who identify themselves as Democrats.

Social Desirability Scale (S-D) (Crowne & Marlowe, 1960). Socioeconomic status and religious preference data were also obtained.

Four weeks (including two weeks of vacation) after the questionnaires were given, a student confederate went into all three classes on the same day, five minutes prior to dismissal and made the following statement, "Thank you, Dr. ———, for allowing me this time. I would like to ask the cooperation of each of you in a Students for Freedom Movement. To that end, I will pass out slips for you to fill out and hand back to me as you leave." The questions on the slip are shown in Table 1. Class attendance was used to identify S who turned in slips without signing them.

TABLE 1.   Questionnaire to determine degree of social action-taking behavior

Students for Freedom Rally

Please check any or all aspects of our program in which you would be willing to participate.

I would be interested in: Check here:

   (A)   Attending a rally for civil rights.
   (B)   Signing a petition to go to local government and/or news media calling for full and immediate integration of all facilities throughout Florida.   _____
   (C)   Joining a silent march to the capitol to demonstrate our plea for full and immediate integration of all facilities throughout Florida.   _____
   (D)   Joining a Freedom Riders Group for a trip during the break.   _____
   (E)   I would not be interested in participating in any of the foregoing.   _____

                Signature: _____
                Address: _____
                Tel. No.:   _____

Ss were divided into groups according to their category of social action-taking behavior. Is a S checked more than one item, he was placed in the category of highest commitment, in the order A, B, C, D. The mean I-E, S-D, and Social Class (Warner) of each group was then determined. F and t tests were computed.

Results

The means and sigmas for each category of social action-taking are given in Table 2. Using the "mean square ratio" for unequal N's (Lindquist, 1953), a significant F relationship between scores on the I-E scale and social action-taking behavior was found. ($F = 2.89$, $df = 4$ and 111, $p = < .05$).

The following t tests were significant (all two-tailed): categories of high commitment B, C, and D vs. little commitment A ($p = < .05$); category of no commitment E vs. high commitment B, C, and D ($p = < .05$); category A vs. category C alone ($p = < .01$), and category C vs. category E ($p = < .01$).

TABLE 2.   Mean scores by categories of commitment

Category	I-E		S-D		Social Class		N
	Mean	Sigma	Mean	Sigma	Mean	Sigma	
A	10.3	3.1	18.10	6.4	4.76	1.6	20
B	9.2	3.4	17.05	5.5	5.00	1.5	20
C	7.4	2.9	16.95	6.4	5.95	1.3	24
D	8.1	3.8	16.82	4.4	5.29	1.5	20
E[a]	10.0	3.9	18.74	4.9	5.50	1.4	32

[a] E category includes those who did not sign a slip but were present.

In general, it can be seen that the means on the I-E test follow closely the order of degree of social action-taking involved in the various alternatives shown in Table 1.[2] The order is C and D most; B in the middle; and A and E least. Those individuals who were more inclined to see themselves as the determiners of their own fate tended to commit themselves to more personal and decisive social action. There was a trend, not reaching statistical significance, for persons high in measured social desirability motive to commit themselves to less social action.

An analysis of these data by sex indicates that the same trend was present for males and females. The males provided slightly more differentiation of groups than females.

Little class difference in this essentially homogeneous population was present. Class V was the modal class position (Warner scale). A nonsignificant curvilinear trend was noted. Ss at both extremes of the social action-taking continuum obtained the lowest social class ratings.

Summary

Students in a Southern Negro college very much involved in the current social protest movement against segregation were used as Ss of a study of prediction of social action-taking behavior. A forced choice test of a generalized attitude toward internal or external control of reinforcements, not specifically dealing with the issue studied, predicted the type and degree of commitment behavior manifested to effect social change. The social desirability motive and social class showed a weak trend in the predicted direction in the case of the former and a logically consistent one on an ad hoc basis in the case of the latter. These findings may serve as an impetus for much needed research in the important area of ongoing social action and social change.

[2] Shortly before the time of testing, a large number of Negroes were arrested and placed in jail for a similar march on the state house of a nearby state.

The Prediction of Social Action from a Dimension of Internal-External Control

Bonnie Ruth Strickland

A. Introduction

Of importance in a time of increased political and social upheaval is an adequate description of the persons initiating action in an attempt to change existing conditions. While it is interesting to speculate on the motivation of the people in the forefront of activity, little empirical evidence is available to support explanations. From a social-learning expectancy theory, one rather clear personality variable can be expected to delineate social action takers from nonaction takers. Rotter, Seeman, and Liverant (1962) have described a dimension of internal versus external control of reinforcement in which a person may be characterized according to the degree to which he attributes the events that happen to him as a function of his own control, skills, or behaviors as opposed to these events being the result of luck, chance, fate, or powers beyond his control.

Gore and Rotter (1963) have demonstrated that those individuals who are inclined to see themselves as determiners of their own fate tend to commit themselves to personal and decisive action. The foregoing experimenters had a student confederate go into classes at a Southern Negro college that had figured prominently in social-protest movements. The students were asked by the confederate to sign a questionnaire designed to elicit commitment to civil-rights movements. Students designated their willingness to participate in mass rallies, to sign petitions, to embark on freedom rides, and so on. Prior to and independent of the civil rights questionnaire the students had completed a scale designed to assess degree of internal versus external control of reinforcement as well as a social-desirability questionnaire assessing a dimension for approval. In general, the group means on the internal-external scale followed closely the order of degree of verbalized commitment to social action on the questionnaire, with the more-internal subjects being those stating the most commitment. The need-for-approval motive showed weak trends across the degrees of social action, with the higher-need-for-approval subjects being less likely to verbalize willingness to become involved in civil-rights action.

Source: Reprinted by permission from *The Journal of Social Psychology*, 1965, *66*, 353–358. Copyright © 1965 by the Journal Press.

Note: The author gratefully acknowledges the valuable assistance and advice of William A. Coppedge, James H. Harris, and Wendy Richardson who served as examiners. The author is also indebted to Mrs. Charles Perkins, Jr., Dr. Dorothy Rowley, Dr. Ralph McC. Chinn, and the members of the Student Nonviolent Coordinating Committee.

The purpose of the present study is to elaborate on Gore and Rotter's findings, with one essential refinement of their research. The persons described as action takers in the present experiment are those individuals actively engaged in civil-rights movements. Gore and Rotter have shown that verbalized commitment may be predicted by the internal-external dimension. It seems appropriate to extend Gore and Rotter's research to a prediction of behavioral commitment. It is hypothesized that persons engaged in social action are characterized as more internal than a comparable group of persons who are not involved.

B. Method

1. *Subjects and Procedure*

All of the subjects of the present study were Negroes, predominantly college students, who were in one of two groupings. One was an active or experimental group composed of individuals who were engaged in civil-rights movements throughout the Southern part of the United States in February and March of 1963. Approximately 33 subjects were active members of the Student Nonviolent Coordinating Committee (SNCC) predominantly engaged in voter registration. Civil-rights leaders suggested 20 other subjects known to be active in protest movements. Two independent samples were collected. The first sample consisted of the students designated by the leaders plus six SNCC members. These subjects were asked individually by three white college students (one female and two males), who served as examiners in the experiment, to complete two personality inventories and a questionnaire designed to assess the degree of activity in which they were engaged. The second sample of 27 subjects consisted of SNCC members who were attending a civil-rights rally in a large southern city during April of 1963. These persons came from many areas in the United States, with the majority being from the Northeast and South. Again the personality inventories and the activity questionnaire were administered by the white college students mentioned earlier. It should be noted that both samples consisted of subjects who in a sense volunteered to participate in the study. The subjects were told that they were being asked to complete the scales and questionnaire in conjunction with a large-scale research project. Cooperation ranged from fair to good. All subjects who indicated that they were willing to participate completed the inventories. Nineteen female subjects and 34 male subjects comprised the total active sample. Every active subject slated on the civil-rights questionnaire that he had participated in some phase of civil-rights protest, such as voter registration, sit-ins, and demonstrations. The mean number of arrests per person in conjunction with civil-rights activities was about five, with a range from zero to 62. Nineteen of the subjects answered that because of their involvement they had received threats of violence directed either at themselves or their families.

The control group of 105 subjects consisted of students at three

Negro colleges in a large Southern city. These subjects were tested while enrolled in three different required classes within their colleges. The three white
examiners who tested the active group distributed the inventories. Professors
within the institutions active in civil-rights movements assured examiners that
the classes tested would include few, if any, students active in protest movements. Thirty-three females and 72 males in the control group completed the
personality inventories.

2. *Measures*

The Internal-External Scale[1] is a 29-item forced-choice scale assessing the degree to which a person attributes the events that happen to him as
being within or beyond his personal control and understanding. An illustrative
item is "I more strongly believe that: (a) I have often found that what is going
to happen will happen. (b) Trusting to fate has never turned out well for me
as making a decision to take a definite course of action."

The inventory used as a measure of the approval motive is the
Marlowe-Crowne Social Desirability Scale. This scale is a 33-item true-false
questionnaire containing descriptions of highly socially sanctioned behaviors
that are improbable of occurrence. An illustrative item is "I am always cour-
teous even to people who are disagreeable."

The activity questionnaire that was completed by the experimental
group was a short-answer inventory asking subjects to indicate the kinds of
civil-rights movements in which they had been active, the amount of activity
in which they had engaged, the number of arrests in connection with civil
rights, and any threats of violence that had been directed toward them or their
families.

Each subject was asked to state his age and the number of school
grades completed. These data served as control variables.

C. Results

The data were first analyzed for sex differences across the personality inventories. No significant differences were found; so the data were subsequently analyzed without regard to sex. The two different samples of active
subjects were examined for significant differences on the two personality inventories. No differences were found, and the two separate samples were combined into one active group for the overall analysis of the data.

Means and standard deviations of the experimental and control
groups for the personality inventories, age, and education are presented in
Table 1. In the control group, four subjects failed to state their age, and 12
subjects did not give the number of grades in school that they had completed.
To simplify computations, these subjects were given the mean age or educa-

---

[1] A scale developed but not published by S. Liverant, J. B. Rotter, M. Seeman, and
D. P. Crowne, Spring, 1961.

TABLE 1. Means and standard deviations for active and nonactive groups

	Group			
	Active (N = 53)		Nonactive (N = 105)	
Variable	Mean	SD	Mean	SD
Internal-external scale	7.49	3.49	9.64	3.70
Marlowe-Crowne Scale	18.41	5.75	17.00	4.98
Age	21.47	4.19	19.17	1.56
Education	14.26	1.64	12.69	.70

tion of the group in which they were members. As expected, the great majority of the control subjects were of freshman or sophomore standing.

Comparison of the active and the nonactive groups on internal-external control scores produces a t of 3.58, significant beyond the .01 level. A biserial correlation between internal-external control scores and activity status is .35 ($p < .01$). Active group members are significantly more likely to be assessed as internal than are the nonactive group members.

TABLE 2. Correlations of the internal-external scores with activity and the control variables
(N = 158)

Variable	r
Activity status	.35*
Age	−.04
Education	−.14

* $p < .01$.

Active-group members appear to be higher in need for approval than do nonactive-group members; however, the difference is not significant. Active-group members are significantly older and have completed more grades in school than the nonactive-group members ($t = 3.83$, $p < .01$; $t = 6.54$; $p < .01$). Pearsonian correlations were computed between internal-external scores and age and amount of education. No significant relationships were found. See Table 2.

D. Discussion

It was hypothesized that persons involved in social action would be assessed as more internal in their feelings of personal control and understanding of the events that happen to them than would a control group of persons not engaged in social action. Results confirm the hypothesis, with Negro students who were known to be active in civil-rights demonstrations being significantly more internal than Negro students who had had no experience in protest movements. The study validates a personality inventory assessing internal control versus external control of reinforcement, as well as adding to a description of the persons involved in social action.

Comparisons between active groups and nonactive groups were complicated by the fact that the active group was found to be older and to have completed more grades of school. While this finding may be due to the sampling procedures or to the fact that commitment to social action attracts an older or more educated person, it still poses a problem with respect to prediction from the personality variable alone. However, no significant relationships were found between the internal-external score and age and amount of education.

The dimension of need for approval, as measured by the Marlowe-Crowne Social Desirability Scale offers little to a prediction of social action. The trend within the present study for the more-active students to be assessed higher in the approval motive than were members of the control group is a reversal of the trend reported by Gore and Rotter (1963). However, in neither study does the relationship attain significance.

As an essential refinement of Gore and Rotter's study, it was necessary to test persons behaviorally active in social movements. The experimental group in the present study consisted of persons clearly and dramatically committed to direct action. Many of the students, some of whom were working only for subsistent pay for SNCC, were everyday in situations of danger and harassment to themselves and their families. A few were field secretaries for SNCC, spending long months in pressure areas engaged in voter registration. Many had participated in demonstrations in Albany, Georgia, and sit-ins throughout the South. It should be noted, also, that the data were collected in the spring of 1963 before a large general onset of protest demonstrations that gained strong support within Negro communities. The persons tested were pioneers in the movements and were members of an organization that came into being not only as a positive force toward integration but as a protest against early civil-rights organizations that were not moving in a sufficiently aggressive manner for the original SNCC members. Further research might be pointed toward testing other groups of varying commitment to social action, including the White Citizen's Councils.

Clearly, the internal-external scale appears to be a useful instrument for the prediction of social action. Of primary importance, however, are the implications of the research in regard to identifying variables, such as internality-externality, that underlie behavioral commitment.

E. Summary

Two personality inventories, the Internal-External Scale and the Marlowe-Crowne Social Desirability Scale were given to a group of 53 Negroes actively engaged in civil-rights movements in the South and a control group of 105 Negroes who were not active. The Marlowe-Crowne Scale did not differentiate the active and the nonactive groups, but a significant relationship was found between internal-external scores and social action. The more internal the subject, the more likely was he to be a member of the active group. The study validates a dimension of internal-external control, as well as adding to a description of the persons involved in social action.

This article should be read from two perspectives. The data bear on the criteria for mental health, providing information on the kinds of traits that professional clinicians, as well as lay people, believe to be indicative of mental health. The article also speaks to the issue of "sexism" in modern society, showing how the stereotype of the psychologically healthy person is much more closely matched to the image of the psychologically healthy male than to the image of the psychologically healthy female. The authors' approach to this issue is an interesting and innovative one. First they show that male and female clinicians have similar definitions of a psychologically normal and healthy male, female, and adult (sex unspecified). They then show that the lay student's judgment of the social desirability of various traits correspond to the professional concepts of mental health. Finally, they show how male-valued items are more likely to be perceived as socially desirable than female-valued items. Finally, there is an impressive demonstration of a significant difference between the concepts of mental health held for females and that held for a sex-unspecified adult, while no such difference was found between the adult and masculine concepts of mental health. The content of the particular traits that are deemed healthy for females but not for males is also of considerable interest.

Sex-Role Stereotypes and Clinical Judgments of Mental Health

Inge K. Broverman, Donald M. Broverman, Frank E. Clarkson, Paul S. Rosenkrantz, and Susan R. Vogel

A sex-role Stereotype Questionnaire consisting of 122 bipolar items was given to actively functioning clinicians with one of three sets of instructions: To describe a healthy, mature, socially competent (*a*) adult, sex unspecified, (*b*) a man, or (*c*) a woman. It was hypothesized that clinical judgments about the characteristics of healthy individuals would differ as a function of sex of person judged, and furthermore, that these differences in clinical judgments would parallel stereotypic sex-role differences. A second hypothesis predicted that behaviors and characteristics judged healthy for an adult, sex unspecified, which are presumed to reflect an ideal standard of health, will resemble behaviors judged healthy for men, but differ from behaviors judged healthy for women. Both hypotheses were confirmed. Possible reasons for and the effects of this double standard of health are discussed.

Evidence of the existence of sex-role stereotypes, that is, highly consensual norms and beliefs about the differing characteristics of men and women, is abundantly present in the literature (Anastasi & Foley, 1949; Fernberger, 1948; Komarovsky, 1950; McKee & Sheriffs, 1957; Seward, 1946; Seward & Larson, 1968; Wylie, 1961; Rosenkrantz, Vogel, Bee, Broverman,

Source: Reprinted by permission from *Journal of Consulting and Clinical Psychology,* 1970, *34* (1), 1–7. Copyright © 1970 by the American Psychological Association.

& Broverman, 1968). Similarly, the differential valuations of behaviors and characteristics stereotypically ascribed to men and women are well established (Kitay, 1940; Lynn, 1959; McKee & Sherriffs, 1959; Rosenkrantz et al., 1968; White, 1959), that is, stereotypically masculine traits are more often perceived as socially desirable than are attributes which are stereotypically feminine. The literature also indicates that the social desirabilities of behaviors are positively related to the clinical ratings of these same behaviors in terms of "normality-abnormality" (Cowen, 1961), "adjustment" (Wiener, Blumberg, Segman, & Cooper, 1959), and "health-sickness" (Kogan, Quinn, Ax, & Ripley, 1957).

Given the relationships existing between masculine versus feminine characteristics and social desirability, on the one hand, and between mental health and social desirability on the other, it seems reasonable to expect that clinicians will maintain parallel distinctions in their concepts of what, behaviorally, is healthy or pathological when considering men versus women. More specifically, particular behaviors and characteristics may be thought indicative of pathology in members of one sex, but not pathological in members of the opposite sex.

The present paper, then, tests the hypothesis that clinical judgments about the traits characterizing healthy, mature individuals will differ as a function of the sex of the person judged. Furthermore, these differences in clinical judgments are expected to parallel the stereotypic sex-role differences previously reported (Rosenkrantz et al., 1968).

Finally, the present paper hypothesizes that behavioral attributes which are regarded as healthy for an adult, sex unspecified, and thus presumably viewed from an ideal, absolute standpoint, will more often be considered by clinicians as healthy or appropriate for men than for women. This hypothesis derives from the assumption that abstract notions of health will tend to be more influenced by the greater social value of masculine stereotypic characteristics than by the lesser valued feminine stereotypic characteristics.

The authors are suggesting, then, that a double standard of health exists wherein ideal concepts of health for a mature adult, sex unspecified, are meant primarily for men, less so for women.

Method

Subjects

Seventy-nine clinically-trained psychologists, psychiatrists, or social workers (46 men, 33 women) served as Ss. Of these, 31 men and 18 women had PhD or MD degrees. The Ss were all actively functioning in clinical settings. The ages varied between 23 and 55 years and experience ranged from internship to extensive professional experience.

Instrument

The authors have developed a Stereotype Questionnaire which is described in detail elsewhere (Rosenkrantz et al., 1968). Briefly, the questionnaire consists of 212 bipolar items each of which describes, with an adjective or a short phrase, a particular behavior trait or characteristic such as:

Very aggressive	Not at all aggressive
Doesn't hide emotions at all	Always hides emotions

One pole of each item can be characterized as typically masculine, the other as typically feminine (Rosenkrantz et al., 1968). On 41 items, 70% or better agreement occurred as to which pole characterizes men or women, respectively, in both a sample of college men and in a sample of college women (Rosenkrantz et al., 1968). These items have been classified as "stereotypic."

The questionnaire used in the present study differs slightly from the original questionnaire. Seven original items seemed to reflect adolescent concerns with sex, for example, "very proud of sexual ability . . . not at all concerned with sexual ability." These items were replaced by seven more general items. Since three of the discarded items were stereotypic, the present questionnaire contains only 38 stereotypic items. These items are shown in Table 1.

Finally, in a prior study, judgments have been obtained from samples of Ss as to which pole of each item represents the more socially desirable behavior or trait for an adult individual in general, regardless of sex. On 27 of the 38 stereotypic items, the masculine pole is more socially desirable, (male-valued items), and on the remaining 11 stereotypic items, the feminine pole is the more socially desirable one (female-valued items).

Instructions

The clinicians were given the 122-item questionnaire with one of three sets of instructions, "male," "female," or "adult." Seventeen men and 10 women were given the "male" instructions which stated "think of normal, adult men and then indicate on each item the pole to which a mature, healthy, socially competent adult man would be closer." The Ss were asked to look at the opposing poles of each item in terms of directions rather than extremes of behavior. Another 14 men and 12 women were given "female" instructions, that is, they were asked to describe a "mature, healthy, socially competent adult woman." Finally, 15 men and 11 women were given "adult" instructions. These Ss were asked to describe a "healthy, mature, socially competent adult person" (sex unspecified). Responses to these "adult" instructions may be considered indicative of "ideal" health patterns, without respect to sex.

TABLE 1.   Male-valued and female-valued stereotypic items

Male-valued Items	
Feminine Pole	*Masculine Pole*
Not at all aggressive	Very aggressive
Not at all independent	Very independent
Very emotional	Not at all emotional
Does not hide emotions at all	Almost always hides emotions
Very subjective	Very objective
Very easily influenced	Not at all easily influenced
Very submissive	Very dominant
Dislikes math and science very much	Likes math and science very much
Very excitable in a minor crisis	Not at all excitable in a minor crisis
Very passive	Very active
Not at all competitive	Very competitive
Very illogical	Very logical
Very home oriented	Very worldly
Not at all skilled in business	Very skilled in business
Very sneaky	Very direct
Does not know the way of the world	Knows the way of the world
Feelings easily hurt	Feelings not easily hurt
Not at all adventurous	Very adventurous
Has difficulty making decisions	Can make decisions easily
Cries very easily	Never cries
Almost never acts as a leader	Almost always acts as a leader
Not at all self-confident	Very self-confident
Very uncomfortable about being aggressive	Not at all uncomfortable about being aggressive
Not at all ambitious	Very ambitious
Unable to separate feelings from ideas	Easily able to separate feelings from ideas
Very dependent	Not at all dependent
Very conceited about appearance	Never conceited about appearance

Female-valued Items	
Feminine Pole	*Masculine Pole*
Very talkative	Not at all talkative
Very tactful	Very blunt
Very gentle	Very rough
Very aware of feelings of others	Not at all aware of feelings of others
Very religious	Not at all religious
Very interested in own appearance	Not at all interested in own appearance
Very neat in habits	Very sloppy in habits
Very quiet	Very loud
Very strong need for security	Very little need for security
Enjoys art and literature very much	Does not enjoy art and literature at all
Easily expresses tender feelings	Does not express tender feelings at all

Scores

Although Ss responded to all 122 items, only the stereotypic items which reflect highly consensual, clear distinctions between men and women, as perceived by lay people were analyzed. The questionnaires were scored by counting the number of Ss that marked each pole of each stereotypic item, within each set of instructions. Since some Ss occasionally left an item blank, the proportion of Ss marking each pole was computed for each item. Two types of scores developed: "agreement" scores and "health" scores.

The agreement scores consisted of the proportion of Ss on that pole of each item which was marked by the majority of the Ss. Three agreement scores for each item were computed; namely, a "masculinity agreement score" based on Ss receiving the "male" instructions, a "femininity agreement score," and an "adult agreement score" derived from the Ss receiving the "female" and "adult" instructions, respectively.

The health scores are based on the assumption that the pole which the majority of the clinicians consider to be healthy for an adult, independent of sex, reflects an ideal standard of health. Hence, the proportion of Ss with either male or female instructions who marked that pole of an item which was most often designated as healthy for an adult was taken as a "health" score. Thus, two health scores were computed for each of the stereotypic items: a "masculinity health score" from Ss with "male" instructions, and a "femininity health score" from Ss with "female" instructions.

Results

Sex Differences in Subject Responses

The masculinity, femininity, and adult health and agreement scores of the male clinicians were first compared to the comparable scores of the female clinicians via t tests. None of these t tests were significant (the probability levels ranged from .25 to .90). Since the male and female Ss did not differ significantly in any way, all further analyses were performed with the samples of men and women combined.

Agreement Scores

The means and sigmas of the adult, masculinity, and femininity agreement scores across the 38 stereotypic items are shown in Table 2. For each of these three scores, the average proportion of Ss agreeing as to which pole reflects the more healthy behavior or trait is significantly greater than the .50 agreement one would expect by chance. Thus, the average masculinity agreement score is .831 ($z = 3.15$, $p = .001$), the average femininity agreement score is .763 ($z = 2.68$, $p < .005$), and the average adult agreement score is .866 ($z = 3.73$, $p < .001$). These means indicate that on the stereotypic

TABLE 2. Means and standard deviations for adult, masculinity, and femininity agreement scores on 38 stereotypic items

Agreement Score	M	SD	Deviation from Chance	
			Z	p
Adult	.866	.116	3.73	< .001
Masculinity	.831	.122	3.15	< .001
Femininity	.763	.164	2.68	< .005

items clinicians strongly agree on the behaviors and attributes which characterize a healthy man, a healthy woman, or a healthy adult independent of sex, respectively.

Relationship between Clinical Judgments of Health and Student Judgments of Social Desirability

Other studies indicate that social desirability is related to clinical judgments of mental health (Cowen, 1961; Kogan et al., 1957; Wiener et al., 1959). The relation between social desirability and clinical judgment was tested in the present data by comparing the previously established socially desirable poles of the stereotypic items (Rosenkrantz et al., 1968) to the poles of those items which the clinicians judged to be the healthier and more mature for an *adult*. Table 3 shows that the relationship is, as predicted, highly significant ($\chi^2 = 23.64$, $p < .001$). The present data, then, confirm the previously reported relationships that social desirability, as perceived by nonprofessional Ss, is strongly related to professional concepts of mental health.

TABLE 3. Chi-square analysis on social desirability versus adult health scores on 38 stereotypic items

Item	Pole Elected by Majority of Clinicians for Healthy Adults
Socially desirable pole	34
Socially undesirable pole	4

Note.—$\chi^2 = 23.64$, $p < .001$.

The four items on which there is disagreement between health and social desirability ratings are: to be emotional; not to hide emotions; to be religious; to have a very strong need for security. The first two items are considered to be healthy for adults by clinicians but not by students; the second two items have the reverse pattern of ratings.

Sex-Role Stereotype and Masculinity versus
Femininity Health Scores

On 27 of the 38 stereotypic items, the male pole is perceived as more socially desirable by a sample of college students (male-valued items); while on 11 items, the feminine pole is seen as more socially desirable (female-valued items). A hypothesis of this paper is that the masculinity health scores will tend to be greater than the femininity health scores on the male-valued items, while the femininity health scores will tend to be greater than the masculinity health scores on the female-valued items. In other words, the relationship of the clinicians' judgments of health for men and women are expected to parallel the relationship between stereotypic sex-role behaviors and social desirability. The data support the hypothesis. Thus, on 25 of the 27 male-valued items, the masculinity health score exceeds the femininity health score; while 7 of the 11 female-valued items have higher femininity health scores than masculinity health scores. On four of the female-valued items, the masculinity health score exceeds the femininity health score. The chi-square derived from these data is 10.73 ($df = 1$, $p < .001$). This result indicates that clinicians tend to consider socially desirable masculine characteristics more often as healthy for men than for women. On the other hand, only about half of the socially desirable feminine characteristics are considered more often as healthy for women rather than for men.

On the face of it, the finding that clinicians tend to ascribe male-valued stereotypic traits more often to healthy men than to healthy women may seem trite. However, an examination of the content of these items suggests that this trite-seeming phenomenon conceals a powerful, negative assessment of women. For instance, among these items, clinicians are more likely to suggest that healthy women differ from healthy men by being more submissive, less independent, less adventurous, more easily influenced, less aggressive, less competitive, more excitable in minor crises, having their feelings more easily hurt, being more emotional, more conceited about their appearance, less objective, and disliking math and science. This constellation seems a most unusual way of describing any mature, healthy individual.

Mean Differences between Masculinity Health
Scores and Femininity Health Scores

The above chi-square analysis reports a significant pattern of differences between masculine and feminine health scores in relationship to the stereotypic items. It is possible, however, that the differences, while in a consistent, predictable direction, actually are trivial in magnitude. A *t* test, performed between the means of the masculinity and femininity health scores, yielded a *t* of 2.16 ($p < .05$) indicating that the mean masculinity health score (.827) differed significantly from the mean femininity health score (.747). Thus, despite massive agreement about the health dimension per se, men and women appear to be located at significantly different points along this well-defined dimension of health.

Concepts of the Healthy Adult versus Concepts of Healthy Men and Healthy Women

Another hypothesis of this paper is that the concepts of health for a sex-unspecified adult, and for a man, will not differ, but that the concepts of health for women will differ significantly from those of the adult.

This hypothesis was tested by performing t tests between the adult agreement scores versus the masculinity and femininity health scores. Table 4 indicates, as predicted, that the adult and masculine concepts of health do not differ significantly ($t = 1.38$, $p > .10$) whereas, a significant difference does exist between the concepts of health for adults versus females ($t = 3.33$, $p < .01$).

TABLE 4.   Relation of adult health scores to masculinity health scores and to femininity health scores on 38 stereotypic items

Health Score	M	SD
Masculinity	.827	.130
		$t = 1.38*$
Adult	.866	.115
		$t = 3.33**$
Femininity	.747	.187

* $df = 74, p > .05$.
** $df = 74, p < .01$.

These results, then, confirm the hypothesis that a double standard of health exists for men and women, that is, the general standard of health is actually applied only to men, while healthy women are perceived as significantly less healthy by adult standards.

Discussion

The results of the present study indicate that high agreement exists among clinicians as to the attributes characterizing healthy adult men, healthy adult women, and healthy adults, sex unspecified. This agreement, furthermore, holds for both men and women clinicians. The results of this study also support the hypotheses that (a) clinicians have different concepts of health for men and women and (b) these differences parallel the sex-role stereotypes prevalent in our society.

Although no control for the theoretical orientation of the clinicians was attempted, it is unlikely that a particular theoretical orientation was disproportionately represented in the sample. A counterindication is that the clinicians' concepts of health for a mature adult are strongly related to the concepts of social desirability held by college students. This positive relationship between social desirability and concepts of health replicates findings by a number of other investigators (Cowen, 1961; Kogan et al., 1957; Wiener et al., 1959).

The clinicians' concepts of a healthy, mature man do not differ significantly from their concepts of a healthy adult. However, the clinicians' concepts of a mature healthy woman do differ significantly from their adult health concepts. Clinicians are significantly less likely to attribute traits which characterize healthy adults to a woman than they are likely to attribute these traits to a healthy man.

Speculation about the reasons for and the effects of this double standard of health and its ramifications seems appropriate. In the first place, men and women do differ biologically, and these biological differences appear to be reflected behaviorally, with each sex being more effective in certain behaviors (Broverman, Klaiber, Kobayashi, & Vogel, 1968). However, we know of no evidence indicating that these biologically-based behaviors are the basis of the attributes stereotypically attributed to men and to women. Even if biological factors did contribute to the formation of the sex-role stereotypes, enormous overlap undoubtedly exists between the sexes with respect to such traits as logical ability, objectivity, independence, etc., that is, a great many women undoubtedly possess these characteristics to a greater degree than do many men. In addition, variation in these traits within each sex is certainly great. In view of the within-sex variability, and the overlap between sexes, it seems inappropriate to apply different standards of health to men compared to women on purely biological grounds.

More likely, the double standard of health for men and women stems from the clinicians' acceptance of an "adjustment" notion of health, for example, health consists of a good adjustment to one's environment. In our society, men and women are systematically trained, practically from birth on, to fulfill different social roles. An adjustment notion of health, plus the existence of differential norms of male and female behavior in our society, automatically lead to a double standard of health. Thus, for a women to be healthy, from an adjustment viewpoint, she must adjust to and accept the behavioral norms for her sex, even though these behaviors are generally less socially desirable and considered to be less healthy for the generalized competent, mature adult.

By way of analogy, one could argue that a black person who conformed to the "pre-civil rights" southern Negro stereotype, that is, a docile, unambitious, childlike, etc., person, was well adjusted to his environment and, therefore, a healthy and mature adult. Our recent history testifies to the bankruptcy of this concept. Alternative definitions of mental health and maturity are implied by concepts of innate drives toward self-actualization, toward mastery of the environment, and toward fulfillment of one's potential (Allport, 1955; Bühler, 1959; Erikson, 1950; Maslow, 1954; Rogers, 1951). Such innate drives, in both blacks and women, are certainly in conflict with becoming adjusted to a social environment with associated restrictive stereotypes. Acceptance of an adjustment notion of health, then, places women in the conflictual position of having to decide whether to exhibit those positive characteristics considered desirable for men and adults, and thus have their "femininity" questioned, that is, be deviant in terms of being a woman; or to behave in the prescribed feminine manner, accept second-class adult status, and possibly live a lie to boot. .

Another problem with the adjustment notion of health lies in the conflict between the overt laws and ethics existing in our society versus the covert but real customs and mores which significantly shape an individual's behavior. Thus, while American society continually emphasizes equality of opportunity and freedom of choice, social pressures toward conformity to the sex-role stereotypes tend to restrict the actual career choices open to women, and, to a lesser extent, men. A girl who wants to become an engineer or business executive, or a boy who aspires to a career as a ballet dancer or a nurse, will at least encounter raised eyebrows. More likely, considerable obstacles will be put in the path of each by parents, teachers, and counselors.

We are not suggesting that it is the clinicians who pose this dilemma for women. Rather, we see the judgments of our sample of clinicians as merely reflecting the sex-role stereotypes, and the differing valuations of these stereotypes, prevalent in our society. It is the attitudes of our society that create the difficulty. However, the present study does provide evidence that clinicians do accept these sex-role stereotypes, at least implicitly, and, by so doing, help to perpetuate the stereotypes. Therapists should be concerned about whether the influence of the sex-role stereotypes on their professional activities acts to reinforce social and intrapsychic conflict. Clinicians undoubtedly exert an influence on social standards and attitudes beyond that of other groups. This influence arises not only from their effect on many individuals through conventional clinical functioning, but also out of their role as "expert" which leads to consultation to governmental and private agencies of all kinds, as well as guidance of the general public.

It may be worthwhile for clinicians to critically examine their attitudes concerning sex-role stereotypes, as well as their position with respect to an adjustment notion of health. The cause of mental health may be better served if both men and women are encouraged toward maximum realization of individual potential, rather than to an adjustment to existing restrictive sex roles.

References

ALLPORT, G. W. *Becoming*. New Haven, Conn.: Yale University Press, 1955.

ANASTASI, A., & FOLEY, J. P., JR. *Differential psychology*. New York: Macmillan, 1949.

BROVERMAN, D. M., KLAIBER, E. L., KOBAYASHI, Y., & VOGEL, W. Roles of activation and inhibition in sex differences in cognitive abilities. *Psychological Review*, 1968, *75*, 23–50.

BÜHLER, C. Theoretical observations about life's basic tendencies. *American Journal of Psychotherapy*, 1959, *13*, 561–581.

COWEN, E. L. The social desirability of trait descriptive terms: Preliminary norms and sex differences. *Journal of Social Psychology*, 1961, *53*, 225–233.

ERIKSON, E. H. *Childhood and society*. New York: Norton, 1950.

FERNBERGER, S. W. Persistence of stereotypes concerning sex differences. *Journal of Abnormal and Social Psychology*, 1948, *43*, 97–101.

KITAY, P. M. A comparison of the sexes in their attitudes and beliefs about women. *Sociometry*, 1940, *34*, 399–407.

KOGAN, W. S., QUINN, R., AX, A. F., & RIPLEY, H. S. Some methodological problems in the quantification of clinical assessment by Q array. *Journal of Consulting Psychology*, 1957, *21*, 57–62.

KOMAROVSKY, M. Functional analysis of sex roles. *American Sociological Review*, 1950, *15*, 508–516.

LYNN, D. B. A note on sex differences in the development of masculine and feminine identification. *Psychological Review*, 1959, *66*, 126–135.

MASLOW, A. H. *Motivation and personality*. New York: Harper, 1954.

MCKEE, J. P., & SHERRIFFS, A. C. The differential evaluation of males and females. *Journal of Personality*, 1957, *25*, 356–371.

————. Men's and women's beliefs, ideals, and self-concepts. *American Journal of Sociology*, 1959, *64*, 356–363.

ROGERS, C. R. *Client-centered therapy; Its current practice, implications, and theory*. Boston: Houghton, 1951.

ROSENKRANTZ, P., VOGEL, S., BEE, H., BROVERMAN, I., & BROVERMAN, D. Sex-role stereotypes and self-concepts in college students. *Journal of Consulting and Clinical Psychology*, 1968, *32*, 287–295.

SEWARD, G. H. *Sex and the social order*. New York: McGraw-Hill, 1946.

SEWARD, G. H., & LARSON, W. R. Adolescent concepts of social sex roles in the United States and the two Germanies. *Human Development*, 1968, *11*, 217–248.

WHITE, L., JR. *Educating our daughters*. New York: Harper, 1950.

WIENER, M., BLUMBERG, A., SEGMAN, S., & COOPER, A. A judgment of adjustment by psychologists, psychiatric social workers, and college students, and its relationship to social desirability. *Journal of Abnormal Social Psychology*, 1959, *59*, 315–321.

WYLIE, R. *The self concept*. Lincoln: University of Nebraska Press, 1961.

Section Four
DEVELOPMENTAL PSYCHOLOGY

The field of developmental psychology is devoted to the study of the origins of behavior, development, and change. The central concerns of this area are the changes in behavior with age, the processes underlying these changes, and the sources of individual differences among people. Questions such as these are fundamental: What biological factors and what social experiences produce the striking and rapid changes in the child's abilities, personalities, motives, goals, and social behaviors? What forces mold the individual's unique patterns of interests, motives, goals, desires, personality characteristics, and social attitudes? To what extent are the differences between people products of the forces of "nature" (genetic or constitutional factors), and to what extent are they due to "nurture" (environmental factors, early experiences, training, and learning)?

These are age-old questions. Many classical philosophers, among them Plato, speculated and wrote on the origin of personality characteristics and abilities, and they had theories about the determinants of psychological development. While these are still vital issues even today, the developmental psychologists do not merely think and speculate on these problems; they attempt to solve problems scientifically. Of course, they formulate hypotheses and theories, but then they *test* their ideas by means of systematic research.

The aims or goals of modern scientific development psychology can be stated rather simply. The first is to describe, as completely and precisely as possible, children's psychological functions (for example, sensory, motor, and intellectual abilities; personality characteristics; and social behavior) and to discover how these functions change with age. Does progress toward intellectual maturity involve continuous, gradual increments in ability or is it marked by a series of rather abrupt changes (stages)? The second goal is to *explain* these age changes, that is, to determine the mechanisms or processes (the *determinants*) underlying such changes. Why, for example, does the child become more fluent in speech and more efficient and logical in solving problems as he grows older? A third objective of developmental psychology is to understand individual differences and the factors producing them. For example, why is it that some preschool children are explorative, daring, and creative in their activities while others are inhibited, fearful, and conforming?

The readings in this section were carefully selected to illustrate some of these objectives and to show you how the developmental psychologist theorizes, formulates and tests hypotheses, and interprets and integrates findings. One of the articles is based on Erikson's influential thinking about developmental changes in personality and interpersonal attitudes, not just in childhood but throughout the human being's life-cycle. It should also be noted that some of the readings in other sections of the book are highly relevant to the field of developmental psychology. See, for example, Scarr-Salapatek's article on "Race, Social Class, and IQ" in Section Five and the Feshbachs' report of a study of children's fear reactions in Section Three.

Paul Mussen

*Erik Erikson is a psychoanalyst who has worked extensively with chil-
dren in several cultures and has published notable books in the field of psycho-
history, attempting to apply psychoanalytic principles to an understanding of the
achievements and the influence of Gandhi and Martin Luther. Students of developmental psychology have been most influenced by Erikson's theory of the development of personal and social adjustment. According to Erikson, there are eight
major stages in this development during the course of the individual's life, beginning
in early infancy. Each stage is characterized by a specifiable central problem or
conflict. If the problem is solved reasonably well, at least temporarily, the individual
gains strength and proceeds with "vigor and confidence" to the next stage. Erikson's
theory is the basis for the following report which was prepared for a White House
Conference on Children and Youth in 1950.*

A Healthy Personality for Every Child

The following was adapted from the writings of Erik H. Erikson, and
was originally prepared for a White House conference.

Many attempts have been made to describe the attributes of healthy
personality. They have been put succinctly as the ability to love and the ability
to work. A recent review of the literature suggests that the individual with a
healthy personality is one who actively masters his environment, shows a
unity of personality, and is able to perceive the world and himself correctly.
Clearly, none of these criteria applies to a child. It seemed to us best, then, to
present for the Conference's consideration an outline that has the merit of indicating at one and the same time the main course of personality development
and the attributes of a healthy personality.

This developmental outline was worked out by Erik H. Erikson, a
psychologist and practicing psychoanalyst who has made anthropological field
studies and has had much experience with children. It is an analysis that derives from psychological theory, to which is added knowledge from the fields
of child development and cultural anthropology. The whole is infused with the
author's insight and personal philosophy.

In each stage of child development, the author says, there is a central problem that has to be solved, temporarily at least, if the child is to proceed with vigor and confidence to the next stage. These problems, these conflicts of feeling and desire, are never solved in entirety. Each shift in experience
and environment presents them in a new form. It is held, however, that each
type of conflict appears in its purest, most unequivocal form at a particular

Source: Reprinted by permission of Health Publications Institute from *A Healthy Personality for Every Child: A Fact Finding Report to the Midcentury White House Conference on Children and Youth*, 1951, 6–25.

stage of child development, and that if the problem is well solved at that time the basis for progress to the next stage is well laid.

In a sense personality development follows biological principles. Biologists have found that everything that grows has a groundplan that is laid out at its start. Out of this groundplan the parts arise, each part having its time of special ascendancy. Together these parts form a functioning whole. If a part does not arise at its appointed time, it will never be able to form fully, since the moment for the rapid outgrowth of some other part will have arrived. Moreover, a part that misses its time of ascendancy or is severely damaged during its formative period is apt to doom, in turn, the whole hierarchy of organs. Proper rate and normal sequence is necessary if functional harmony is to be secured.

Personality represents the most complicated functioning of the human organism and does not consist of parts in the organic sense. Instead of the development of organs, there is the development of locomotor, sensory, and social capacities and the development of individual modes of dealing with experience. Nevertheless, proper rate and proper sequence are as important here as in physical growth, and functional harmony is achieved only if development proceeds according to the groundplan.

In all this it is encouraging for parents and others who have children in charge to realize that in the sequence of his most personal experiences, just as in the sequence of organ formation, the child can be trusted to follow inner laws of development, and needs from adults chiefly love, encouragement, and guidance.

The operation of biological laws is seen, also, in the fact that there is constant interplay between organism and environment and that problems of personality functioning are never solved once and for all. Each of the components of the healthy personality to be described below is present in some form from the beginning, and the struggle to maintain it continues throughout life.

For example, a baby may show something like "autonomy" or a will of his own in the way he angrily tries to free his head when he is tightly held. Nevertheless, it is not until the second year of life that he begins to experience the whole conflict between being an autonomous creature and a dependent one. It is not until then that he is ready for a decisive encounter with the people around him, and it is not until then that they feel called upon to train him or otherwise curb his free-questing spirit. The struggle goes on for months and finally, under favorable circumstances, some compromise between dependence and independence is reached that gives the child a sense of well-being.

The sense of autonomy thus achieved is not a permanent possession, however. There will be other challenges to that sense and other solutions more in keeping with later stages of development. Nevertheless, once established at two or three years of age, this early sense of autonomy will be a bulwark against later frustrations and will permit the emergence of the next developmental problem at a time that is most favorable for its solution.

So it is with all the personality components to be described. They appear in miniature early in life. The struggle to secure them against tendencies to act otherwise comes to a climax at a time determined by emergence of the necessary physical and mental abilities. There are, throughout life, other challenges and other responses but they are seldom so serious and seldom so decisive as those of the critical years.

In all this, it must be noted in addition, there is not the strict dichotomy that the analysis given below suggests. With each of the personality components to be described, it is not all or nothing: trust *or* mistrust, autonomy *or* doubt, and so on. Instead, each individual has some of each. His health of personality is determined by the preponderance of the favorable over the unfavorable, as well as by what manner of compensations he develops to cope with his disabilities.

The Sense of Trust

The component of the healthy personality that is the first to develop is the sense of trust. The crucial time for [its] emergence is the first year of life. As with the other personality components to be described, the sense of trust is not something that develops independent of other manifestations of growth. It is not that the infant learns how to use his body for purposeful movement, learns to recognize people and objects around him, and also develops a sense of trust. Rather, the concept "sense of trust" is a short-cut expression intended to convey the characteristic flavor of all the child's satisfying experiences at this early age. Or, to say it another way, this psychological formulation serves to condense, summarize, and synthesize the most important underlying changes that give meaning to the infant's concrete and diversified experience.

Trust can exist only in relation to something. Consequently a sense of trust cannot develop until the infant is old enough to be aware of objects and persons and to have some feeling that he is a separate individual. At about three months of age a baby is likely to smile if somebody comes close and talks to him. This shows that he is aware of the approach of the other person, that pleasurable sensations are aroused. If, however, the person moves too quickly or speaks too sharply the baby may look apprehensive or cry. He will not "trust" the unusual situation but will have a feeling of uneasiness, of mistrust, instead.

Experiences connected with feeding are a prime source for the development of trust. At around four months of age a hungry baby will grow quiet and show signs of pleasure at the sound of an approaching footstep, anticipating (trusting) that he will be held and fed. This repeated experience of being hungry, seeing food, receiving food, and feeling relieved and comforted assures the baby that the world is a dependable place.

Later experiences, starting at around five months of age, add another dimension to the sense of trust. Through endless repetitions of attempts to grasp for and hold objects, the baby is finally successful in controlling and adapting his movements in such a way as to reach his goal. Through these and other feats of muscular coordination the baby is gradually able to trust his own body to do his bidding.

The baby's trust-mistrust problem is symbolized in the game of peek-a-boo. In this game, which babies begin to like at about four months of age, an object disappears and then reappears. There is a slightly tense expression on the baby's face when the object goes away; its reappearance is greeted by wriggles and smiles. Only gradually does a baby learn that things continue to exist even though he does not see them, that there is order and stability in his universe. Peek-a-boo proves the point by playful repetition.

Studies of mentally ill individuals and observations of infants who have been grossly deprived of affection suggest that trust is an early-formed and important element in the healthy personality. Psychiatrists find again and again that the most serious illnesses occur in patients who have been sorely neglected or abused or otherwise deprived of love in infancy. Simliarly, it is a common finding of psychological and social investigators that individuals diagnosed as a "psychopathic personality" were so unloved in infancy that they have no reason to trust the human race and, therefore, no sense of responsibility toward their fellow men.

Observations of infants brought up in emotionally unfavorable institutions or removed to hospitals with inadequate facilities for psychological care support these findings. A recent report says: "Infants under six months of age who have been in an institution for some time present a well-defined picture. The outstanding features are listlessness, emaciation and pallor, relative immobility, quietness, unresponsiveness to stimuli like a smile or a coo, indifferent appetite, failure to gain weight properly despite ingestion of diets which are entirely adequate, frequent stools, poor sleep, an appearance of unhappiness, proneness to febrile episodes, absence of sucking habits."[1]

Another investigation of children separated from their mothers at six to twelve months and not provided with an adequate substitute comes to much the same conclusion: "The emotional tone is one of apprehension and sadness, there is withdrawal from the environment amounting to rejection of it, there is no attempt to contact a stranger and no brightening if a stranger contacts him. Activities are retarded and the child often sits or lies inert in a dazed stupor. Insomnia is common and lack of appetite universal. Weight is lost, and the child becomes prone to current infections."[2]

Most significant for our present point, these reactions are most likely to occur in children who up to the time of separation at six to nine months of age had a happy relation with their mothers, while those whose relations were unhappy are relatively unaffected. It is at about this age that the struggle between trusting and mistrusting the world comes to a climax, for it is

[1] Harry Bakwin, "Emotional Deprivation in Infants," *Journal of Pediatrics,* October, 1949, *35,* 512–529.
[2] John Bowlby, M.D., Summary of Dr. René Spitz's observations, unpublished manuscript.

then that the child first perceives clearly that he and his environment are things apart. That at this time formerly happy infants should react so badly to separation suggests, indeed, that they had a faith which now was shattered. Happily, there is usually spectacular change for the better when the maternal presence and love are restored.

It is probably unnecessary to describe the numerous ways in which stimuli from without and from within may cause an infant distress. Birth is believed by some experts to be a painful experience for the baby. Until fairly recently doctors were likely to advise that babies be fed on schedule and that little attention be paid to their cries of hunger at other times. Many infants spent many of the waking hours of the first four months doubled up with colic. All of them had to be bathed and dressed at stated times, whether they liked it or not. Add to these usual discomforts the fact that some infants are handled rather roughly by their parents, that others hear angry words and loud voices, and that a few are really mistreated, and it will not be difficult to understand why some infants may feel the world is a place that cannot be trusted.

In most primitive societies and in some sections of our own society the attention accorded infants is more in line with natural processes. In such societies separation from the mother is less abrupt, in that for some time after birth the baby is kept close to the warmth and comfort of its mother's body and at its least cry the breast is produced. Throughout infancy the baby is surrounded by people who are ready to feed it, fondle it, otherwise comfort it at a moment's notice. Moreover, these ministrations are given spontaneously, wholeheartedly, and without that element of nervous concern that may characterize the efforts of young mothers made self-conscious and insecure by our scientific age.

We must not exaggerate, however. Most infants in our society, too, find smiles and the comfort of mother's soft, warm body accompanying their intake of food, whether from breast or bottle. Coldness, wetness, pain, and boredom—for each misfortune there is prompt and comforting relief. As their own bodies come to be more dependable, there is added to the pleasures of increasing sensory response and motor control the pleasure of the mother's encouragement.

Moreover, babies are rather hardy creatures and are not to be discouraged by inexperienced mothers' mistakes. Even a mother cat has to learn, and the kittens endure gracefully her first clumsy efforts to carry them away from danger. Then, too, psychologists tell us that mothers create a sense of trust in their children not by the particular techniques they employ but by the sensitiveness with which they respond to the children's needs and by their overall attitude.

For most infants, then, a sense of trust is not difficult to come by. It is the most important element in the personality. It emerges at the most vulnerable period of a child's life. Yet it is the least likely to suffer harm, perhaps because both nature and culture work toward making mothers most maternal at that time.

The Sense of Autonomy

The sense of trust once firmly established, the struggle for the next component of the healthy personality begins. The child is now twelve to fifteen months old. Much of his energy for the next two years will center around asserting that he is a human being with a mind and will of his own. A list of some of the items discussed by Spock under the heading, "The One Year Old," will serve to remind us of the characteristics of that age and the problems they create for parents. "Feeling his oats." "The passion to explore." "He gets more dependent and more independent at the same time." "Arranging the house for the wandering baby." "Avoiding accidents." "How do you make him leave certain things alone?" "Dropping and throwing things." "Biting humans." "The small child who won't stay in bed at night."

What is at stake throughout the struggle of these years is the child's sense of autonomy, the sense that he is an independent human being and yet one who is able to use the help and guidance of others in important matters. This stage of development becomes decisive for the ratio between love and hate, between cooperation and wilfulness, for freedom of self-expression and its renunciation in the makeup of the individual. The favorable outcome is self-control without loss of self-esteem. The unfavorable outcome is doubt and shame.

Before the sense of autonomy can develop, the sense of trust must be reasonably well-established and must continue to pervade the child's feeling about himself and his world. Only so dare he respond with confidence to his new-felt desire to assert himself boldly, to appropriate demandingly, and to hurl away without let or hindrance.

As with the previous stage, there is a physiological basis for this characteristic behavior. This is the period of muscle-system maturation and the consequent ability (and doubly felt inability) to coordinate a number of highly conflicting action patterns, such as those of holding on and letting go, walking, talking, and manipulating objects in ever more complicated ways. With these abilities come pressing needs to use them: to handle, to explore, to seize and to drop, to withhold and to expel. And, with all, there is the dominant will, the insistent "Me do" that defies help and yet is so easily frustrated by the inabilities of the hands and feet.

For a child to develop this sense of self-reliance and adequacy that Erikson calls autonomy, it is necessary that he experience over and over again that he is a person who is permitted to make choices. He has to have the right to choose, for example, whether to sit or whether to stand, whether to approach a visitor or to lean against his mother's knee, whether to accept offered food or whether to reject it, whether to use the toilet or to wet his pants. At the same time he must learn some of the boundaries of self-determination. He inevitably finds that there are walls he cannot climb, that there are objects out of reach, that, above all, there are innumerable commands enforced by powerful adults. His experience is much too small to enable him to know what he can and cannot do with respect to the physical environment, and it will take him years to discover the boundaries that mark off what is approved, what is tolerated, and what is forbidden by his elders whom he finds so hard to understand.

As problems of this period, some psychologists have concentrated particularly on bladder and bowel control. Emphasis is put upon the need for care in both timing and mode of training children in the performance of these functions. If parental control is too rigid or if training is started too early, the child is robbed of his opportunity to develop, by his own free choice, gradual control of the contradictory impulses of retention and elimination.

To others who study child development, this matter of toilet training is but a prototype of all the problems of this age-range. The sphincters are only part of the whole muscle system, with its general ambiguity of rigidity and relaxation, of flexion and extension. To hold and to relinquish refer to much more than the bowels. As the child acquires the ability to stand on his two feet and move around, he delineates his world as me and you. He can be astonishingly pliable once he has decided that he wants to do what he is supposed to do, but there is no reliable formula for assuring that he will relinquish when he wants to hold on.

The matter of mutual regulation between parent and child (for fathers have now entered the picture to an extent that was rare in the earlier stage) now faces its severest task. The task is indeed one to challenge the most resourceful and the most calm adult. Firmness is necessary, for the child must be protected against the potential anarchy of his as yet untrained sense of discrimination. Yet the adult must back him up in his wish to "stand on his own feet," lest he be overcome by shame that he has exposed himself foolishly and by doubt in his self-worth. Perhaps the most constructive rule a parent can follow is to forbid only what "really matters" and, in such forbidding, to be clear and consistent.

Shame and doubt are emotions that many primitive peoples and some of the less sophisticated individuals in our own society utilize in training children. Shaming exploits the child's sense of being small. Used to excess it misses its objective and may result in open shamelessness, or, at least, in the child's secret determination to do as he pleases when not observed. Such defiance is a normal, even healthy response to demands that a child consider himself, his body, his needs, or his wishes evil and dirty and that he regard those who pass judgment as infallible. Young delinquents may be produced by this means, and others who are oblivious to the opinion of society.

Those who would guide the growing child wisely, then, will avoid shaming him and avoid causing him to doubt that he is a person of worth. They will be firm and tolerant with him so that he can rejoice in being a person of independence and can grant independence to others. As to detailed procedures, it is impossible to prescribe, not only because we do not know and because every situation is different but also because the kind and degree of autonomy that parents are able to grant their small children depends on feelings about themselves that they derive from society. Just as the child's sense of trust is a reflection of the mother's sturdy and realistic faith, so the child's sense of autonomy is a reflection of the parents' personal dignity. Such appears to be the teaching of the comparative study of cultures.

Personal autonomy, independence of the individual, is an especially outstanding feature of the American way of life. American parents, accordingly, are in a particularly favorable position to transmit the sense of autonomy to their children. They themselves resent being bossed, being pushed around; they maintain that everybody has the right to express his opinion and to be in control of his affairs. More easily than people who live according to an authoritarian pattern, they can appreciate a little child's vigorous desire to assert his independence and they can give him the leeway he needs in order to grow up into the upstanding, look-you-in-the-eye kind of individual that Americans admire.

It is not only in early childhood, however, that this attitude toward growing children must be maintained. As was said at the outset, these components of the healthy personality cannot be established once and for all. The period of life in which they first come into being is the most crucial, it is true. But threats to their maintenance occur throughout life. Not only parents, then, but everybody who has significant contact with children and young people must respect their desire for self-assertion, help them hold it within bounds, and avoid treating them in ways that arouse shame or doubt.

This attitude toward children, toward all people, must be maintained in institutional arrangements as well. Great differences in educational and economic opportunity and in access to the law, discrimination of all kinds are threats to this ingredient of mental health. So, too, may be the overmechanization of our society, the depersonalization of human relations that is likely to accompany large-scale endeavor of all kinds.

Parents, as well as children, are affected by these matters. In fact, parents' ability to grant children the kind of autonomy Americans think desirable depends in part on the way they are treated as employees and citizens. Throughout, the relation must be such as affirms personal dignity. Much of the shame and doubt aroused in children result from the indignity and uncertainty that are an expression of parents' frustrations in love and work. Special attention must be paid to all these matters, then, if we are to avoid destroying the autonomy that Americans have always set store by.

The Sense of Initiative

Having become sure, for the time being, that he is a person in his own right and having enjoyed that feeling for a year or so, the child of four or five wants to find out what kind of person he can be. To be any particular kind of person, he sees clearly, involves being able to do particular kinds of things. So he observes with keen attention what all manner of interesting adults do (his parents, the milkman, the truck driver, and so on), tries to imitate their behavior, and yearns for a share in their activities.

This is the period of enterprise and imagination, an ebullient, creative period when phantasy substitutes for literal execution of desires and the meagerest equipment provides material for high imaginings. It is a period of intrusive, vigorous learning, learning that leads away from the child's own limitations into future possibilities. There is intrusion into other people's bodies by physical attack, into other people's ears and minds by loud and aggressive talking. There is intrusion into space by vigorous locomotion and intrusion into the unknown by consuming curiosity.

By this age, too, conscience has developed. The child is no longer guided only by outsiders; there is installed within him a voice that comments on his deeds, and warns and threatens. Close attention to the remarks of any child of this age will confirm this statement. Less obvious, however, are experts' observations that children now begin to feel guilty for mere thoughts, for deeds that have been imagined but never executed. This, they say, is the explanation for the characteristic nightmares of this age period and for the over-reaction to slight punishment.

The problem to be worked out in this stage of development, accordingly, is how to will without too great a sense of guilt. The fortunate outcome of the struggle is a sense of initiative. Failure to win through to that outcome leaves the personality overburdened, and possibly over-restricted by guilt.

It is easy to see how the child's developing sense of initiative may be discouraged. So many of the projects dreamed up at this age are of a kind which cannot be permitted that the child may come to feel he is faced by a universal "No." In addition he finds that many of the projects are impossible of execution and others, even if not forbidden, fail to win the approval of the adults whom he has come to love. Moreover, since he does not always distinguish clearly between actuality and phantasy, his over-zealous conscience may disapprove of even imaginary deeds.

It is very important, therefore, for healthy personality development that much leeway and encouragement be given to the child's show of enterprise and imagination and that punishment be kept at a minimum. Boys and girls at this stage are extraordinarily appreciative of any convincing promise that someday they will be able to do things as well, or maybe better, than father and mother. They enjoy competition (especially if they can win) and insistence on goal; they get great pleasure from conquest. They need numerous examples of the kinds of roles adults assume, and they need a chance to try them out in play.

The ability that is in the making is that of selecting social goals and persevering in the attempt to reach them.

If enterprise and imagination are too greatly curbed, if severe rebukes accompany the frequently necessary denial of permission to carry out desires, a personality may result that is over-constricted. Such a personality cannot live up to its inner capacities for imagination, feeling, or performance, though it may over-compensate by immense activity and find relaxation impossible.

Constriction of personality is a self-imposed constriction, an act of the child's over-zealous conscience. "If I may not do this, I will not even think it," says conscience, "for even thinking it is dangerous." Resentment and bitterness and a vindictive attitude toward the world that forces the restriction may accompany this decision, however, and become unconscious but functioning parts of the personality. Such, at least, is the warning of psychiatrists who have learned to know the inmost feelings of emotionally handicapped children and adults.

This developmental stage has great assets as well as great dangers. At no time in life is the individual more ready to learn avidly and quickly, to become big in the sense of sharing obligation and performance. If during this preschool period the child can get some sense of the various roles and functions that he can perform as an adult, he will be ready to progress joyfully to the next stage, in which he will find pleasurable accomplishment in activities less fraught with phantasy and fear.

There is a lesson in this for later periods of personality development as well. As has been said before, these conflicts that come to a head at particular periods of a child's life are not settled once and for all. The sense of initiative, then, is one that must be continually fostered, and great care must be taken that youngsters and young people do not have to feel guilty for having dared to dream.

Just as we Americans prize autonomy, so too do we prize initiative; in fact, we regard it as the cornerstone of our economic system. There is much in the present industrial and political mode of life that may discourage initiative, that may make a young person think he had best pull in his horns. What these tendencies are and what they may do to youngsters and to their parents, who too must feel free if they are to cultivate the sense of initiative in their children, is a subject that warrants much serious discussion.

The Sense of Accomplishment

The three stages so far described probably are the most important for personality development. With a sense of trust, a sense of autonomy, and a sense of initiative achieved, progress through the later stages is pretty well assured. Whether this is because children who have a good environment in their early years are likely to continue to be so favored, or whether it is because they have attained such strength of personality that they can successfully handle later difficulties, research has not yet made clear. We do know that nearly all children who get a good start continue to develop very well, and we know that some of those who start off poorly continue to be handicapped. Observations of this sort seem to support psychological theory in the conclusion that personality is pretty well set by about six years of age. Since, however, some children develop into psychologically healthy adults in spite of a bad start, and since some who start well run into difficulties later, it is clear that much research is needed before this conclusion can be accepted as wholly correct.

To return to the developmental analysis, the fourth stage, which begins somewhere around six years of age and extends over five or six years, has as its achievement what Erikson calls the sense of industry. Perhaps "sense of accomplishment" would make the meaning clearer. At any rate, this is the period in which preoccupation with phantasy subsides, and the child wants to be engaged in real tasks that he can carry through to completion. As with the other developmental stages, there are foreshadowings of this kind of interest long before six years of age. Moreover, in some societies and in some parts of our own society children are trained very early to perform socially useful tasks. The exact age is not the point at issue. What is to be pointed out is that children, after a period characterized by exuberant imagination, want to settle down to learning exactly how to do things and how to do them well.

In contrast to the preceding stages and to the succeeding ones, this stage does not consist of a swing from a violent inner upheaval to a new mastery. Under reasonably favorable circumstances this is a period of calm, steady growth, especially if the problems of the previous stages have been well worked through. Despite its unspectacular character, this is a very important period, for in it is laid a firm basis for responsible citizenship. It is during this period that children acquire not only knowledge and skills that make for good workmanship but also the ability to cooperate and play fair and otherwise follow the rules of the larger social game.

The chief danger of this period is the presence of conditions that may lead to the development of a sense of inadequacy and inferiority. This may be the outcome if the child has not yet achieved a sense of initiative, or if his experiences at home have not prepared him for entering school happily, or if he finds school a place where his previous accomplishments are disregarded or his latent abilities are not challenged. Even with a good start the child may later lapse into discouragement and lack of interest if at home or school his individual needs are overlooked—if too much is expected of him, or if he is made to feel that achievement is beyond his ability.

It is most important for health of personality, therefore, that schools be conducted well, that methods and courses of instruction be such as will give every child the feeling of successful accomplishment. Autobiographies of juvenile delinquents show time and again a boy who hated school—hated the fact that he was marked out as stupid or awkward, as one who was not as good as the rest. Some such boys find in jobs the sense of accomplishment they miss at school and consequently give up their delinquent ways. Others, however, are handicapped in job finding and keeping by the very fact that in school they did not develop the sense of industry; hence they have work failure added to their other insecurities. Nor is delinquency the only or the most likely outcome of lack of success in school. Many children respond in a quieter way, by passive acceptance of their inferiority. Psychologically they are perhaps even more harmed.

Our Puritan tradition maintains that children will not work except under the spur of competition, so we tend to fear the suggestion that all should succeed. To help children develop a sense of accomplishment does not mean, however, merely giving all of them good marks and passing them on to the next grade. Children need and want real achievement. How to help them secure it, despite differences in native capacity and differences in emotional development, is one of the school's most serious challenges.

School, of course, is not the only place in which children at this stage of development can secure the sense of industry. In work at home there are many opportunities for a child to get a feeling of mastery and worthwhile endeavor. Rural youth groups and their urban counterparts cater to this need, and many recreation programs put as much emphasis on work as on play. School, however, is the legally constituted arrangement for giving instruction to the young, so it is upon teachers that the professional responsibility for helping all children achieve a sense of industry and accomplishment rests.

In addition to aiding personality development in this way, teachers have many opportunities for reconfirming their pupils' sense of trust, autonomy, and initiative or for encouraging its growth in children who have been somewhat hampered by previous life experiences. Teachers cannot work alone, of course, either in aiding a child in the development of new capacities or in strengthening old ones. Jointly with parents and others they can do much, not only for children of already healthy personality but also for many whose development has been handicapped.

The Sense of Identity

With the onset of adolescence another period of personality development begins. As is well known, adolescence is a period of storm and stress for many young people, a period in which previous certainties are questioned and previous continuities no longer relied upon. Physiological changes and rapid physical growth provide the somatic base for the turmoil and indecision. It may be that cultural factors also play a part, for it has been observed that adolescence is less upsetting in some societies than in others.

The central problem of the period is the establishment of a sense of identity. The identity the adolescent seeks to clarify is who he is, what his role in society is to be. Is he a child or is he an adult? Does he have it in him to be someday a husband and father? What is he to be as a worker and an earner of money? Can he feel self-confident in spite of the fact that his race or religion or national background makes him a person some people look down upon? Over all, will he be a success or a failure? By reason of these questions adolescents are sometimes morbidly preoccupied with how they appear in the eyes of others as compared with their own conception of themselves, and with how they can make the roles and skills learned earlier jibe with what is currently in style.

In primitive societies adolescents are perhaps spared these doubts and indecisions. Through initiation rites, often seemingly cruel in character, young people are tested out (and test themselves out) and are then welcomed into a socially recognized age category in which rights and duties and mode of living are clearly defined. In our society there are few rituals or ceremonies that mark the change in status from childhood to youth. For those who have religious affiliations, confirmation, joining the church, may serve this purpose in part, since the young people are thereby admitted, in this one segment of their lives at least, to the company of adults. Such ceremonies serve, in addition, to reaffirm to youth that the universe is trustworthy and stable and that a way of life is clearly laid out.

Graduation ceremonies might play a part in marking a new status were it not that, in present-day America, status is so ill defined. What rules of law and custom exist are too diverse to be of much help. For example, legal regulations governing age of "consent," age at which marriage is permitted, age for leaving school, for driving a car, for joining (or being required to join) the Army or Navy mark no logical progressions in rights and duties. As to custom, there is so much variation in what even families who live next door to each other expect or permit that adolescents, eager to be on their way, are practically forced into standardizing themselves in their search for status. In this they are ably abetted by advertisers and entertainers who seek their patronage, as well as by well-meaning magazine writers who describe in great detail the means by which uniformity can be achieved.

In this urge to find comfort through similarity, adolescents are likely to become stereotyped in behavior and ideals. They tend to form cliques for self-protection and fasten on petty similarities of dress and gesture to assure themselves that they are really somebody. In these cliques they may be intolerant and even cruel toward those they label as different. Unfortunate as such behavior is and not to be condoned, intolerance serves the important purpose of giving the group members at least the negative assurance that there is something they are not.

The danger of this developmental period is self-diffusion. As Biff puts it in *The Death of a Salesman,* "I just can't take hold, Mom. I can't take hold of some kind of a life." A boy or girl can scarcely help feeling somewhat diffuse when the body changes in size and shape so rapidly, when genital maturity floods body and imagination with forbidden desires, when adult life lies ahead with a diversity of conflicting possibilities and choices.

Whether this feeling of self-diffusion is fairly easily mastered or whether, in extreme, it leads to delinquency, neurosis or outright psychosis, depends to a considerable extent on what has gone before. If the course of personality development has been a healthy one, a feeling of self-esteem has accrued from the numerous experiences of succeeding in a task and sensing its cultural meaning. Along with this, the child has come to the conviction that he is moving toward an understandable future in which he will have a definite role to play. Adolescence may upset this assurance for a time or to a degree but fairly soon a new integration is achieved, and the boy or girl sees again (and with clearer vision) that he belongs and that he is on his way.

The course is not so easy for adolescents who have not had so fortunate a past or for those whose earlier security is broken by a sudden awareness that as members of minority groups their way of life sets them apart. The former, already unsure of themselves, find their earlier doubt and mistrust reactivated by the physiological and social changes that adolescence brings. The latter, once secure, may feel that they must disavow their past and try to develop an "American" personality.

Much has been learned and written about the adolescent problems of the boys and girls whose early personality development has been impaired. How they can be helped, if their disorders are not too severe, is also fairly well known. The full implications of these findings for parents, teachers, and others who would guide youth are still to be worked out but, even so, there is considerable information.

Less well understood are the difficulties and the ways of helping adolescents who grew up in cultures that are not of the usual run. These boys and girls may have been privileged in having had a childhood in which there was little inhibition of sensual pleasures, and in which development proceeded by easy, unself-conscious stages. For them, difficulties arise if their parents lose trust in themselves or if their teachers apply sudden correctives, or if they themselves reject their past and try to act like the others. The new role of middle-class adolescent is often too hard to play. Delinquency or bizarre behavior marks the failure.

How to reach these boys and girls, how to help them attain their desire, is a matter not well understood. It is clear, however, that they should not be typed by pat diagnoses and social judgments, for they are ever ready to become the "bums" that they are called. Those who would guide them must understand both the psychology of adolescence and the cultural realities of the day. There is trust to be restored and doubt and guilt and feelings of inferiority to be overcome. The science of how to do this is still pretty much lacking, though here and there teachers, clergymen, probation officers and the like are highly successful in the task.

Hard though it be to achieve, the sense of identity is the individual's only safeguard against the lawlessness of his biological drives and the authority of an over-weening conscience. Loss of identity, loss of the sense that there is some continuity, sameness, and meaning to life, exposes the individual to his childhood conflicts and leads to emotional upsets. This outcome was observed time and again among men hard pressed by the dangers of war. It is clear, then, that if health of personality is to be preserved much attention must be given to assuring that America makes good on its promises to youth.

The Sense of Intimacy

After the sense of identity, to a greater or less extent, is achieved it becomes possible for the next component of the healthy personality to develop. This is the sense of intimacy, intimacy with persons of the same sex or of the opposite sex or with one's self. The youth who is not fairly sure of his identity shies away from interpersonal relations and is afraid of close communion with himself. The surer he becomes of himself, the more he seeks intimacy, in the form of friendship, love and inspiration.

In view of the early age at which boy and girl attachments are encouraged today, it may seem strange to put the critical period for the development of the sense of intimacy late in adolescence. The explanation is that, on the one hand, sexual intimacy is only one part of what is involved, and, on the other, boy-girl attachments of earlier age periods are likely to be of a somewhat different order. Regarding the latter point, it has been observed by those who know young people well that high-school age boys and girls often use each other's company for an endless verbal examination of what the other thinks, feels, and wants to do. In other words, these attachments are one means of defining one's identity.

In contrast to this use of friendship and companionship, boys and girls late in adolescence usually have need for a kind of fusion with the essence of other people and for a communion with their own inner resources. If, by reason of inadequacies in previous personality development, this sense of intimacy cannot be achieved, the youth may retire into psychological isolation and keep his relations with people on a formal, stereotyped level that is lacking in spontaneity and warmth or he may keep trying again and again to get close to others, only to meet with repeated failure. Under this compulsion he may even marry, but the role of mate is one he can rarely sustain, for the condition of true two-ness is that each individual must first become himself.

In this area of personality development as in the others, cultural factors play a part in sustaining or in discouraging the individual in his development. American culture is unusually successful in encouraging the development of the feelings of independence, initiative, industry, and identity. It is somewhat less successful in the area of intimacy, for the culture's ideal is the subordination of sexuality and sensuality to a life of work, duty, and worship.

Consequently, American adolescents are likely to be unsupported by their parents and find little confirmation in story or song for their desire to sense intimately the full flavor of the personality of others. In many of them, then, the sense of intimacy does not develop highly and they have difficulty in finding in close personal relations the outlet for tension that they need.

There is some evidence that a change in conventions and customs in this respect is in the making, however. Too abrupt change in any such cultural matter is not to be urged, but it is to be hoped that gradual, frank discussion can bring about gradual alteration in attitude and overcome the dangers inherent in the traditional rigidity.

The Parental Sense

"Parental sense" designates somewhat the same capacity as that implied in the words, creativity or productivity. The individual has normally come to adulthood before this sense can develop fully.

The parental sense is indicated most clearly by interest in producing and caring for children of one's own. It may also be exhibited in relation to other people's children or by a parental kind of responsibility toward the products of creative activity of other sorts. The mere desire for or possession of children does not indicate that this component of the healthy personality has developed. In fact, many parents who bring their children to child guidance clinics are found not to have reached this stage of personality development.

The essential element is the desire to nourish and nurture what has been produced. It is the ability to regard one's children as a trust of the community, rather than as extensions of one's own personality or merely as beings that one happens to live with.

Failure to develop this component of the healthy personality often results in a condition which has not been adequately categorized clinically. Although a true sense of intimacy has not developed, the individual may obsessively seek companionship. There is something of egotism in this as in his other activities, a kind of self-absorption. The individual is inclined to treat himself as a child and to be rivalrous with his children, if he has any. He indulges himself, expects to be indulged, and in general behaves in an infantile or immature manner.

There are both individual and social explanations of the failure to develop an adequate parental sense. Individually, the explanation may be found in the inadequate development of the personality components previously described. In some people this failure goes far back. Because of unfortunate experiences in childhood they did not arrive at a firm sense of trust, autonomy, and the rest. In others it is only inadequacies in later stages especially in the development of the sense of intimacy, that are at fault.

Socially, as has been suggested throughout this analysis, healthy personality development depends upon the culture's ideals and upon the economic arrangements of the society. In order that most people may develop fully the sense of being a parent, the role of parent, both mother and father, must be a respected one in the society. Giving must rank higher than getting, and loving than being loved. The economy must be such that the future can be depended upon and each person can feel assured that he has a meaningful and respected part to play. Only so can most individuals afford to renounce selfish aims and derive much of their satisfaction from rearing children.

The Sense of Integrity

The final component of the healthy personality is the sense of integrity. In every culture the dominant ideals, honor, courage, faith, purity, grace, fairness, self-discipline, become at this stage the core of the healthy personality's integration. The individual, in Erikson's words, "becomes able to accept his individual life cycle and the people who have become significant to it as meaningful within the segment of history in which he lives."

To continue Erikson's description, "Integrity thus means a new and different love of one's parents, free of the wish that they should have been different, and an acceptance of the fact that one's life is one's own responsibility. It is a sense of comradeship with men and women of distant times and of different pursuits, who have created orders and objects and sayings conveying human dignity and love. Although aware of the relativity of all the various life styles that have given meaning to human striving, the possessor of integrity is ready to defend the dignity of his own life style against all physical and economic threats. For he knows that, for him, all human dignity stands or falls with the one style of integrity of which he partakes."

The adult who lacks integrity in this sense may wish that he could live life again. He feels that if at one time he had made a different decision he could have been a different person and his ventures would have been successful. He fears death and cannot accept his one and only life cycle as the ultimate of life. In the extreme, he experiences disgust and despair. Despair expresses the feeling that time is too short to try out new roads to integrity. Disgust is a means of hiding the despair, a chronic, contemptuous displeasure with the way life is run. As with the dangers and the solutions of previous periods, doubt and despair are not difficulties that are overcome once and for all, nor is integrity so achieved. Most people fluctuate between the two extremes. Most, also, at no point, either attain to the heights of unalloyed integrity or fall to the depths of complete disgust and despair.

Even in adulthood a reasonably healthy personality is sometimes secured in spite of previous misfortunes in the developmental sequence. New sources of trust may be found. Fortunate events and circumstances may aid the individual in his struggle to feel autonomous. Imagination and initiative may be spurred by new responsibilities, and feelings of inferiority be overcome by successful achievement. Even late in life an individual may arrive at a true sense of who he is and what he has to do and may be able to win through to a feeling of intimacy with others and to joy in producing and giving.

Evidence of such changes is found in the case records of psychiatrists and social wrokers. Common sense observation attests that similar changes in health of personality are sometimes accomplished without benefit of any form of psychotherapy. Much remains to be learned about this, however, especially about how life itself may serve as therapeusis.

For the healthy personality development of children and youth it is necessary that a large proportion of adults attain a sense of integrity to a considerable degree. Not only parents but all who deal with children have need of this quality if they are to help children maintain the feeling that the universe is dependable and trustworthy. Integrity is relatively easily atttained and sustained when the culture itself gives support, when a meaning to life is clearly spelled out in tradition and ceremony, and roles are clearly defined. Our culture, with its rapidly changing technology and its diversity of value standards, leaves much for the individual to work out for himself. In the American dream, however, and the Judaeo-Christian tradition on which it is based there are values and ideals aplenty. In the interest of the welfare of children and youth, in order that a generation of happy individuals and responsible citizens be reared, it is highly important that these values and ideals be brought into prominence and that the promise of American life be kept.

How and why do infants become attached to their mothers or to their mother surrogates (substitutes)? What factors promote strong attachment and what factors inhibit its development? Obviously, for ethical reasons, we cannot experiment with human infants to answer these questions, but Professor Harry Harlow of the University of Wisconsin, an ingenius investigator, has conducted many studies of the effects of different kinds of social contacts and mothering in infancy on the later behavior of monkeys. The research has many important implications for the study of attachment behavior in human beings.

In the studies reported here, Harlow and his coinvestigators carefully observed the behavior of infant monkeys responding to different features of surrogate mothers. Data clearly show that the infant monkey responds visually to the first form of mother he encounters; he grows accustomed to this mother and he relies on "her." He also prefers surrogate mothers made of cloth rather than other materials and those who rock rather than remain stationary.

Nature of Love—Simplified

Harry F. Harlow and Stephen J. Suomi

The cloth surrogate and its wire surrogate sibling (see Figure 1) entered into scientific history as of 1958 (Harlow, 1958). The cloth surrogate was originally designed to test the relative importance of body contact in contrast to activities associated with the breast, and the results were clear beyond all expectation. Body contact was of overpowering importance by any measure taken, even contact time, as shown in Figure 2.

However, the cloth surrogate, beyond its power to measure the relative importance of a host of variables determining infant affection for the mother, exhibited another surprising trait, one of great independent usefulness. Even though the cloth mother was inanimate, it was able to impart to its infant such emotional security that the infant would, in the surrogate's presence, explore a strange situation and manipulate available physical objects (see Figure 3), or animate objects (see Figure 4). Manipulation of animate objects leads to play if these animate objects are age-mates, and play is the variable of primary importance in the development of normal social, sexual, and material functions, as described by Harlow and Harlow (1965). It is obvious that surrogate mothers, which are more docile and manipulative than real monkey mothers, have a wide range of experimental uses.

Source: Reprinted by permission from *American Psychologist*, 1970, 25, 161–168. Copyright © 1970 by the American Psychological Association.

Note: This research was supported by United States Public Health Service Grants MH–11894 and FR–0167 from the National Institutes of Health to the University of Wisconsin Primate Laboratory and Regional Primate Research Center, respectively.

FIGURE 1. Cloth and wire surrogate mothers. (Photo by Wisconsin Primate Center and Laboratory)

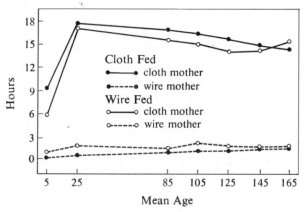

FIGURE 2. Contact time to cloth and wire surrogate

FIGURE 3. Infant monkey security in presence of cloth surrogate.
(Photo by Wisconsin Primate Center and Laboratory)

Simplified Surrogate

Although the original surrogates turned out to be incredibly efficient dummy mothers, they presented certain practical problems. The worst
of the problems was that of cleanliness. Infant monkeys seldom soil their real
mothers' bodies, though we do not know how this is achieved. However, infant
monkeys soiled the bodies of the original cloth surrogates with such efficiency
and enthusiasm as to present a health problem and, even worse, a financial
problem resulting from laundering. Furthermore, we believed that the original
cloth surrogate was too steeply angled and thereby relatively inaccessible for
cuddly clinging by the neonatal monkey.

In the hope of alleviating practical problems inherent in the original
cloth surrogate, we constructed a family of simplified surrogates. The simplified surrogate is mounted on a rod attached to a lead base 4 inches in diameter,
angled upward at 25°, and projected through the surrogate's body for 4 inches,
so that heads may be attached if desired. The body of the simplified surrogate
is only 6 inches long, 2½ inches in diameter, and stands approximately 3
inches off the ground. Figure 5 shows an original cloth surrogate and simplified surrogate placed side by side.

. . . infants readily cling to these simplified surrogates of smaller

FIGURE 4.   Infant play in presence of surrogate. (Photo by Wisconsin
Primate Center and Laboratory)

body and decreased angle of inclination. Infant monkeys do soil the simplified
surrogate, but the art and act of soiling is very greatly reduced. Terry cloth
slipcovers can be made easily and relatively cheaply, alleviating, if not eliminating, laundry problems. Thus, the simplified surrogate is a far more practical dummy mother than the original cloth surrogate.

Surrogate Variables

Lactation

Although the original surrogate papers (Harlow, 1958; Harlow &
Zimmermann, 1959) were written as if activities associated with the breast,
particularly nursing, were of no importance, this is doubtlessly incorrect.
There were no statistically significant differences in time spent by the babies
on the lactating versus nonlactating cloth surrogates and on the lactating
versus nonlactating wire surrogates, but the fact is that there were consistent
preferences for both the cloth and the wire lactating surrogates and that these
tendencies held for both the situations of time on surrogate and frequency

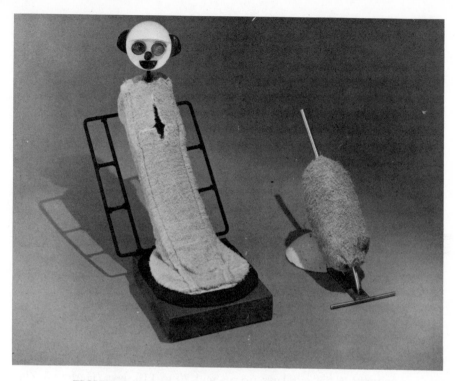

FIGURE 5. Original surrogate and simplified surrogate. (Photo by Wisconsin Primate Center and Laboratory)

of surrogate preference when the infant was exposed to a fear stimulus. Thus, if one can accept a statistically insignificant level of confidence, consistently obtained from four situations, one will properly conclude that nursing is a minor variable but one of more than measurable importance operating to bind the infant to the mother.

To demonstrate experimentally that activities associated with the breasts were variables of significant importance, we built two sets of differentially colored surrogates, tan and light blue; and using a 2 × 2 Latin square design, we arranged a situation such that the surrogate of one color lactated and the other did not. As can be seen in Figure 6, the infants showed a consistent preference for the lactating surrogate when contact comfort was held constant. The importance of the lactational variable probably decreases with time. But at least we had established the hard fact that hope springs eternal in the human breast and even longer in the breast, undressed.

Facial Variables

In the original surrogates we created an ornamental face for the cloth surrogate and a simple dog face for the wire surrogate. I was working with few available infants and against time to prepare a presidential address

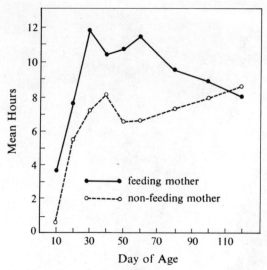

FIGURE 6. Infant preference for lactating cloth surrogate

for the 1958 American Psychological Association Convention. On the basis of sheer intuition, I was convinced that the ornamental cloth-surrogate face would become a stronger fear stimulus than the dog face when fear of the unfamiliar matured in the monkeys from about 70 to 110 days (Harlow & Zimmermann, 1959; Sackett, 1966). But since we wanted each surrogate to have an identifiable face and had few infants, we made no effort to balance faces by resorting to a feebleminded 2 × 2 Latin square design.

Subsequently, we have run two brief unpublished experiments. We tested four rhesus infants unfamiliar with surrogate faces at approximately 100 days of age and found that the ornamental face was a much stronger fear stimulus than the dog face. Clearly, the early enormous preference for the cloth surrogate over the wire surrogate was not a function of the differential faces. Later, we raised two infants on cloth and two on wire surrogates, counterbalancing the ornamental and dog faces. Here, the kind of face was a nonexistent variable. To a baby all maternal faces are beautiful. A mother's face that will stop a clock will not stop an infant.

The first surrogate mother we constructed came a little late, or phrasing it another way, her baby came a little early. Possibly her baby was illegitimate. Certainly it was her first baby. In desperation we gave the mother a face that was nothing but a round wooden ball, which displayed no trace of shame. To the baby monkey this featureless face became beautiful, and she frequently caressed it with hands and legs, beginning around 30–40 days of age. By the time the baby had reached 90 days of age we had constructed an appropriate ornamental cloth-mother face, and we proudly mounted it on the surrogate's body. The baby took one look and screamed. She fled to the back of the cage and cringed in autistic-type posturing. After some days of terror the infant solved the medusa-mother problem in a most ingenious manner. She revolved the face 180° so that she always faced a bare round ball! Furthermore, we could rotate the maternal face dozens of times and within an hour or so the infant would turn it around 180°. Within a week the baby resolved her unfaceable problem once and for all. She lifted the maternal head from the body, rolled it into the corner, and abandoned it. No one can blame the baby. She had lived with and loved a faceless mother, but she could not love a two-faced mother.

These data imply that an infant visually responds to the earliest version of mother he encounters, that the mother he grows accustomed to is the mother he relies upon. Subsequent changes, especially changes introduced after maturation of the fear response, elicit this response with no holds barred. Comparisons of effects of babysitters on human infants might be made. [Many parents have a new sitter visit the home in advance of the sitting engagement to get acquainted with the infant or young child in the reassuring presence of of the mother or father. The parents thus seek to prevent a fearful response in the child at the time they leave.—EDITOR]

Body-surface Variables

We have received many questions and complaints concerning the surrogate surfaces, wire and terry cloth, used in the original studies. This mountain of mail breaks down into two general categories: that wire is aversive, and that other substances would be equally effective if not better than terry cloth in eliciting a clinging response.

The answer to the first matter in question is provided by observation: Wire is not an aversive stimulus to neonatal monkeys, for they spend much time climbing on the sides of their hardware-cloth cages and exploring this substance orally and tactually. A few infants have required medical treatment from protractedly pressing their faces too hard and too long against the cage sides. Obviously, however, wire does not provide contact comfort.

In an attempt to quantify preference of various materials, an exploratory study[1] was performed in which each of four infants was presented with a choice between surrogates covered with terry cloth versus rayon, vinyl, or rough-grade sandpaper. As shown in Figure 7, the infants demonstrated a clear preference for the cloth surrogates, and no significant preference difference between the other body surfaces. An extension of this study is in progress in which an attempt is being made to further quantify and rank order the preference for these materials by giving infants equal exposure time to all four materials.

[1] We wish to thank Carol Furchner, who conducted this experiment and the described experiment in progress.

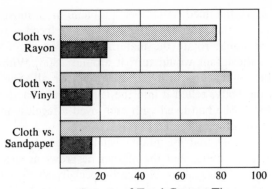

Percent of Total Contact Time

FIGURE 7.   Effect of surface on surrogate contact

Motion Variables

In the original two papers, we pointed out that rocking motion, that is, proprioceptive stimulation, was a variable of more than statistical significance, particularly early in the infant's life, in binding the infant to the mother figure. We measured this by comparing the time the infants spent on two identical planes, one rocking and one stationary (see Figure 8) and two identical cloth surrogates, one rocking and one stationary (see Figure 9).

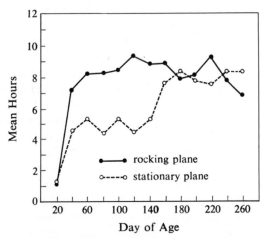

Day of Age

FIGURE 8.   Infant contact to stationary and rocking planes

Temperature Variables

To study another variable, temperature, we created some "hot mamma" surrogates. We did this by inserting heating coils in the maternal bodies that raised the external surrogate body surface about 10° F. In one experiment, we heated the surface of a wire surrogate and let four infant

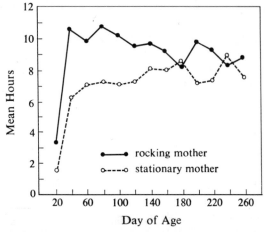

FIGURE 9.   Infant contact to stationary and rocking surrogates

macaques choose between this heated mother and a room-temperature cloth mother. The data are presented in Figure 10. The neonatal monkeys clearly preferred the former. With increasing age this difference decreased, and at approximately 15 days the preference reversed. In a second experiment, we used two differentially colored cloth surrogates and heated one and not the other. The infants preferred the hot surrogate, but frequently contacted the room-temperature surrogate for considerable periods of time.

More recently, a series of ingenious studies on the temperature variable has been conducted by Suomi, who created hot- and cold-running surrogates by adaptation of the simplified surrogate. These results are important not only for the information obtained concerning the temperature variable but also as an illustration of the successful experimental use of the simplified surrogate itself.

The surrogates used in these exploratory studies were modifications of the basic simplified surrogate, designed to get maximum personality out of

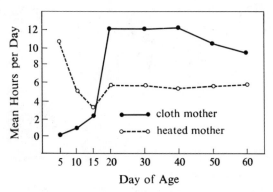

FIGURE 10.   Infant contact to heated-wire and room-temperature cloth surrogates

the minimal mother. One of these surrogates was a "hot mamma," exuding warmth from a conventional heating pad wrapped around the surrogate frame and completely covered by a terry cloth sheath. The other surrogate was a cold female; beneath the terry cloth sheath was a hollow shell within which her life fluid—cold water—was continuously circulated. The two surrogates are illustrated in Figures 11 and 12, and to the untrained observer they look remarkably similar. But looks can be deceiving, especially with females, and we felt that in these similar-looking surrogates we had really simulated the two extremes of womanhood—one with a hot body and no head, and one with a cold shoulder and no heart. Actually, this is an exaggeration, for the surface temperature of the hot surrogate was only 7° F. above room temperature, while the surface temperature of the cold surrogate was only 5° F. below room temperature.

In a preliminary study, we raised one female infant from Day 15 on the warm surrogate for a period of four weeks. Like all good babies she quickly and completely became attached to her source of warmth, and during this time she exhibited not only a steadily increasing amount of surrogate contact but also began to use the surrogate as a base for exploration (see Figure 11). At the end of this four-week period, we decided that our subject had become spoiled enough and so we replaced the warm surrogate with the cold version for one week. The infant noticed the switch within two minutes, responding by huddling in a corner and vocalizing piteously. Throughout the

FIGURE 11.   Infant clinging to and exploring from warm simplified surrogate. (Photos by Wisconsin Primate Center and Laboratory)

FIGURE 12.   Typical infant reactions to cold simplified surrogate. (Photo by Wisconsin Primate Center and Laboratory)

week of bitter maternal cold, the amount of surrogate contact fell drastically; in general, the infant avoided the surrogate in her feeding, exploratory, and sleeping behaviors. Feeling somewhat guilty, we switched surrogates once more for a week and were rewarded for our efforts by an almost immediate return to previously high levels of surrogate contact. Apparently, with heart-warming heat, our infant was capable of forgiveness, even at this tender age. At this point, we switched the two surrogates daily for a total two weeks, but by this time the infant had accepted the inherent fickle nature of her mothers. On the days that her surrogate was warm, she clung tightly to its body, but on the days when the body was cold, she generally ignored it, thus providing an excellent example of naive behaviorism.

   With a second infant we maintained this procedure but switched the surrogates, so that he spent four weeks with the cold surrogate, followed by one week with the warm, an additional week with the cold, and finally a two-week period in which the surrogates were switched daily. This infant became anything but attached to the cold surrogate during the initial four-week period, spending most of his time huddling in the corner of his cage and generally avoiding the surrogate in his exploratory behavior (see Figure 12). In succeeding weeks, even with the warm surrogate, he failed to approach the levels of contact exhibited by the other infant to the cold surrogate. Apparently, being raised with a cold mother had chilled him to mothers in general, even those beaming warmth and comfort.

Two months later both infants were exposed to a severe fear stimulus in the presence of a room-temperature simplified surrogate. The warm-mother infant responded to this stimulus by running to the surrogate and clinging for dear life. The cold-mother infant responded by running the other way and seeking security in a corner of the cage. We seriously doubt that this behavioral difference can be attributed to the sex difference of our subjects. Rather, this demonstration warmed our hopes and chilled our doubts that temperature may be a variable of importance. More specifically, it suggested that a simple linear model may not be adequate to describe the effects of temperature differences of surrogates on infant attachment. It is clear that warmth is a variable of major importance, particularly in the neonate, and we hazard the guess that elevated temperature is a variable of importance in the operation of all the affectional systems: maternal, mother-infant, possibly age-mate, heterosexual, and even paternal.

Prospectives

Recently we have simplified the surrogate mother further for studies in which its only function is that of providing early social support and security to infants. This supersimplified surrogate is merely a board 1½ inches in diameter and 10 inches long with a scooped-out, concave trough having a maximal depth of ¾ inch. . . . the supersimplified surrogate has an angular deviation from the base of less than 15°, though this angle can be increased by the experimenter at will. The standard cover for this supremely simple surrogate is a size 11, cotton athletic sock, though covers of various qualities, rayon, vinyl (which we call the "linoleum lover"), and sandpaper, have been used for experimental purposes.

> Linoleum lover, with you I am through
> The course of smooth love never runs true.

This supersimplified mother is designed to attract and elicit clinging responses from the infant during the first 15 days of the infant's life.

We have designed, but not yet tested, a swinging mother that will dangle from a frame about 2 inches off the floor and have a convex, terry cloth or cotton body surface. Observations of real macaque neonates and mothers indicate that the infant, not the mother, is the primary attachment object even when the mother locomotes, and that this swinging mother may also elicit infantile clasp and impart infant security very early in life. There is nothing original in this day and age about a swinger becoming a mother, and the only new angle, if any, is a mother becoming a swinger.

Additional findings, such as the discovery that six-month social isolates will learn to cling to a heated simplified surrogate, and that the presence of a surrogate reduces clinging among infant-infant pairs, have substantiated use of the surrogate beyond experiments of its own sake. At present, the heated simplified surrogate is being utilized as a standard apparatus in studies as varied as reaction to fear, rehabilitation of social isolates, and development of play. To date, additional research utilizing the cold version of the simplified surrogate has been far more limited, possibly because unused water faucets are harder to obtain than empty electrical outlets. But this represents a methodological, not a theoretical problem, and doubtlessly solutions will soon be forthcoming.

It is obvious that the surrogate mother at this point is not merely a historical showpiece. Unlike the proverbial old soldier, it is far from fading away. Instead, as in the past, it continues to foster not only new infants but new ideas.

References

HARLOW, H. F. The nature of love. *American Psychologist,* 1958, *13,* 673–685.

HARLOW, H. F., & HARLOW, M. K. The affectional systems. In A. M. Schrier, H. F. Harlow, & F. Stollnitz (Eds.), *Behavior of nonhuman primates.* Vol. 2. New York: Academic Press, 1965.

HARLOW, H. F., & ZIMMERMANN, R. R. Affectional responses in the infant monkey. *Science,* 1959, *130,* 421–432.

SACKETT, G. P. Monkeys reared in visual isolation with pictures as visual input: Evidence for an innate releasing mechanism. *Science,* 1966, *154,* 1468–1472.

Parents, as well as professional developmental psychologists, have long been interested in what they could do in their child-rearing practices to help their children achieve optimal adjustment, and at the same time, become competent, independent, self-reliant, responsible, and contented people. This problem has been the focus of an intensive ten-year research program conducted by Dr. Diana Baumrind of the University of California's Institute of Human Development. She has described three major patterns of parental authority—the authoritarian, the authoritative, and the permissive—and has studied the outcomes of these three types of child rearing. The following article summarizes many of her findings and applies them particularly to the development of competence (or incompetence) in young girls.

Socialization and Instrumental Competence in Young Children

Diana Baumrind

For the past 10 years I have been studying parent-child relations, focusing upon the effects of parental authority on the behavior of preschool children. In three separate but related studies, data on children were obtained from three months of observation in the nursery school and in a special testing situation; data on parents were obtained during two home observations, followed by an interview with each parent.

In the first study, three groups of nursery school children were identified in order that the child-rearing practices of their parents could be contrasted. The findings of that study (Baumrind, 1967) can be summarized as follows:

1. Parents of the children who were the most self-reliant, self-controlled, explorative, and content were themselves controlling and demanding; but they were also warm, rational, and receptive to the child's communication. This unique combination of high control and positive encouragement of the child's autonomous and independent strivings can be called *authoritative* parental behavior.

2. Parents of children who, relative to the others, were discontent, withdrawn, and distrustful, were themselves detached and controlling, and somewhat less warm than other parents. These may be called *authoritarian* parents.

Source: Reprinted by permission of the National Association for the Education of Young Children from W. W. Hartup (Ed.), *The Young Child: Reviews of Research*, Vol. 2, pp. 202–224.

Note: The research by the author reported in this paper was supported in part by research grant HD 02228 from the National Institute of Child Health and Development, U.S. Public Health Service.

3. Parents of the least self-reliant, explorative, and self-controlled children were themselves noncontrolling, nondemanding, and relatively warm. These can be called *permissive* parents.

A second study, of an additional 95 nursery school children and their parents, also supported the position that "authoritative control can achieve responsible conformity with group standards without loss of individual autonomy or self-assertiveness" (Baumrind, 1966, p. 905). In a third investigation (Baumrind, 1971), patterns of parental authority were defined so that they would differ from each other as did the authoritarian, authoritative, and permissive combinations which emerged from the first study.

Patterns of Parental Authority

Each of these three authority patterns is described in detail below, followed by the subpatterns that have emerged empirically from the most recent study. The capitalized items refer to specific clusters obtained in the analysis of the parent behavior ratings.

The *authoritarian* parent[1] attempts:

> to shape, control and evaluate the behavior and attitudes of the child in accordance with a set standard of conduct, usually an absolute standard, theologically motivated and formulated by a higher authority. She values obedience as a virtue and favors punitive, forceful measures to curb self-will at points where the child's actions or beliefs conflict with what she thinks is right conduct. She believes in inculcating such instrumental values as respect for authority, respect for work, and respect for the preservation of order and traditional structure. She does not encourage verbal give and take, believing that the child should accept her word for what is right (Baumrind, 1968, p. 261).

Two subpatterns in our newest study correspond to this description; they differ only in the degree of acceptance shown the child. One subpattern identifies families who were Authoritarian but Not Rejecting. They were high in Firm Enforcement, low in Encourages Independence and Individuality, low in Passive-Acceptance, and low in Promotes Nonconformity. The second subpattern contained families who met all the criteria for the first subpattern except that they scored high on the cluster called Rejecting.

The *authoritative* parent, by contrast with the above, attempts:

> to direct the child's activities but in a rational, issue-oriented manner. She encourages verbal give and take, and shares with the child the reasoning behind her policy. She values both expressive and instrumental attributes, both autonomous self-will and disciplined conformity. Therefore, she exerts firm control at points of parent-child divergence,

[1] In order to avoid confusion, when I speak of the parent I will use the pronoun "she," and when I speak of the child, I will use the pronoun "he," although, unless otherwise specified, the statement applies to both sexes equally.

but does not hem the child in with restrictions. She recognizes her own special rights as an adult, but also the child's individual interests and special ways. The authoritative parent affirms the child's present qualities, but also sets standards for future conduct. She uses reason as well as power to achieve her objectives. She does not base her decisions on group consensus or the individual child's desires; but also, does not regard herself as infallible, or divinely inspired (Baumrind, 1968, p. 261).

Two subpatterns correspond to this description, differing only in the parents' attitudes towards normative values. One subpattern contained families who were Authoritative and Conforming. Like the Authoritarian parents described above, these parents had high scores in Passive-Acceptance. However, they also had high scores in Encourages Independence and Individuality. The second subpattern contained parents who met the criteria for the first subpattern, but who also scored high in Promotes Nonconformity.

The *permissive* parent attempts:

to behave in a nonpunitive, acceptant and affirmative manner towards the child's impulses, desires, and actions. She consults with him about policy decisions and gives explanations for family rules. She makes few demands for household responsibility and orderly behavior. She presents herself to the child as a resource for him to use as he wishes, not as an active agent responsible for shaping or altering his ongoing or future behavior. She allows the child to regulate his own activities as much as possible, avoids the exercise of control, and does not encourage him to obey externally-defined standards. She attempts to use reason but not overt power to accomplish her ends (Baumrind, 1968, p. 256).

We were able to locate three subpatterns reflecting different facets of this prototypic permissiveness. One subpattern, called Nonconforming, typified families who were nonconforming but who were not extremely lax in discipline and who did demand high performance in some areas. The second subpattern, called Permissive, contained families who were characterized by lax discipline and few demands, but who did not stress nonconformity. The third subpattern contained families who were both nonconforming and lax in their discipline and demands; hence, they are referred to as Permissive-Nonconforming.

Instrumental Competence

Instrumental Competence refers to behavior which is socially responsible and independent. Behavior which is friendly rather than hostile to peers, cooperative rather than resistive with adults, achievement rather than nonachievement-oriented, dominant rather than submissive, and purposive rather than aimless, is here defined as instrumentally competent. Middle-class parents clearly value instrumentally competent behavior. When such parents were asked to rank those attributes that they valued and devalued in children, the most valued ones were assertiveness, friendliness, independence, and obedience, and those least valued were aggression, avoidance, and dependency (Emmerich & Smoller, 1964). Note that the positively valued attributes promote successful achievement in United States society and, in fact, probably have survival value for the individual in any subculture or society.

There are people who feel that, even in the United States, those qualities which define instrumental competence are losing their survival value in favor of qualities which may be called *Expressive Competence*. The author does not agree. Proponents of competence defined in terms of expressive, rather than instrumental, attributes, value feelings more than reason, good thoughts more than effective actions, "being" more than "doing" or "becoming," spontaneity more than planfulness, and relating intimately to others more than working effectively with others. At present, however, there is no evidence that emphasis on expressive competence, at the expense of instrumental competence, fits people to function effectively over the long run as members of any community. This is not to say that expressive competence is not essential for effective functioning in work as well as in love, and for both men and women. Man, like other animals, experiences and gains valid information about reality by means of both noncognitive and cognitive processes. Affectivity deepens man's knowledge of his environment; tenderness and receptivity enhance the character and effectiveness of any human being. But instrumental competence is and will continue to be an essential component of self-esteem and self-fulfillment.

One subdimension of instrumental competence, here designated *Responsible vs. Irresponsible,* pertains to the following three facets of behavior, each of which is related to the others:

(a) *Achievement-oriented vs. Nonachievement-oriented.* This attribute refers to the willingness to persevere when frustration is encountered, to set one's own goals high, and to meet the demands of others in a cognitive situation as opposed to withdrawal when faced with frustration and unwillingness to comply with the teaching or testing instructions of an examiner or teacher. Among older children, achievement-orientation becomes subject to autogenic motivation and is more closely related to measures of independence than to measures of social responsibility. But in the young child, measures of cognitive motivation are highly correlated with willingness to cooperate with adults, especially for boys. Thus, in my study, resistiveness towards adults was highly negatively correlated with achievement-oriented behavior for boys, but not for girls. Other investigators (Crandall, Orleans, Preston & Rabson, 1958; Haggard, 1969) have also found that compliance with adult values and demands characterizes young children who display high achievement efforts.

(b) *Friendly vs. Hostile Behavior Towards Peers.* This refers to nurturant, kind, altruistic behavior displayed toward agemates as opposed to bullying, insulting, selfish behavior.

(c) *Cooperative vs. Resistive Behavior Towards Adults.* This refers to trustworthy, responsible, facilitative behavior as opposed to devious, impetuous, obstructive actions.

A second dimension of child social behavior can be designated *Independent vs. Suggestible*. It pertains to the following three related facets of behavior:

(a) *Domineering vs. Tractable Behavior*. This attribute consists of bold, aggressive, demanding behavior as opposed to timid, nonintrusive, undemanding behavior.

(b) *Dominant vs. Submissive Behavior*. This category refers to individual initiative and leadership in contrast to suggestible, following behavior.

(c) *Purposive vs. Aimless Behavior*. This refers to confident, charismatic, self-propelled activity vs. disoriented, normative, goalless behavior.

The present review is limited to a discussion of instrumental competence and associated antecedent parental practices and is most applicable to the behavior of young children rather than adolescents. Several ancillary topics will be mentioned, but not discussed in depth, including:

THE RELATION OF IQ TO INSTRUMENTAL COMPETENCE. My own work and that of others indicate that, in our present society, children with high IQs are most likely to be achievement-oriented and self-motivated. The correlations between IQ and measures of purposiveness, dominance, achievement-orientation, and independence are very high even by ages three and four. In my study Stanford-Binet IQ tests were administered to 122 preschool boys and girls as part of an investigation of current patterns of parental authority and their effects on the behavior of preschool children. White children with IQs of at least 96 were grouped within sex on the basis of IQ to form five continuous groups for both boys and girls. Groups were compared on child behavior and parent socialization practices. Higher and lower IQ groups differed significantly from each other on measures of social responsibility and independence, notably with regard to clusters designated Achievement Oriented and Independence.[2]

THE RELATION OF MORAL DEVELOPMENT AND CONSCIENCE TO INSTRUMENTAL COMPETENCE. This area of research, exemplified by some of the work of

[2] A paper entitled "The relationship of cognitive ability as measured by IQ tests to interpersonal competence: educational implications" (1971, in preparation) discusses this area in full. In that paper social implications of IQ as a predictor of adult achievement, interpersonal competence, and level of moral development, are discussed. The possible effects of different types of educational environment on achievement, in particular "discovery" vs. direct training methods, and ability groups vs. integrated classrooms, are explored. The importance of evaluating current programs in which the classroom is integrated (e.g., Berkeley) is emphasized.

Aronfreed, Kohlberg, Mussen, and Piaget, is of special importance with older age groups and will be covered tangentially when the antecedents of social responsibility are explored.

THE RELATION OF WILL TO INSTRUMENTAL COMPETENCE. This topic, which overlaps with the previous one, has received very little direct attention during the past 30 years. In the present review, this area is discussed to some extent along with antecedents of independence.

THE ANTECEDENTS OF CREATIVE OR SCIENTIFIC GENIUS. Socialization practices which lead to competence are not the same as those associated with the development of high creativity or scientific genius. Most studies, such as those by Roe (1952) and Eiduson (1962), suggest that men of genius are frequently reared differently from other superior individuals. It has been found, for example, that as children men of genius often had little contact with their fathers, or their fathers died when they were young; they often led lonely, although cognitively enriched, existences. Such rearing cannot be recommended, however, since it is unlikely that the effects on most children, even those with superior ability, will be to produce genius or highly effective functioning.

THE DEVELOPMENT OF INSTRUMENTAL COMPETENCE IN DISADVANTAGED FAMILIES. The assumption cannot be made that the same factors relate to competence in disadvantaged families as in advantaged families. The effect of a single parental characteristic is altered substantially by the pattern of variables of which it is a part. Similarly, the effect of a given pattern of parental variables may be altered by the larger social context in which the family operates. The relations discussed here are most relevant for white middle-class families and may not always hold for disadvantaged families. In my study of current patterns of parental authority and their effects on the behavior of preschool children, the data for the 16 black children and their families were analyzed separately, since it was assumed that the effect of a given pattern of parental variables would be altered by the larger social context in which the family operates. The major conclusion from this exploratory analysis was that if black families are viewed by white norms they appear deviant, and yet, judged by the same norms, their so-called authoritarian methods seem to produce self-assertive, independent girls (1972b).

Development of Instrumental Incompetence in Girls

Rapid social changes are taking place in the United States which are providing equal opportunity for socially disadvantaged groups. If a socially disadvantaged group is one whose members are discouraged from fully developing their potentialities for achieving status and leadership in economic, academic, and political affairs, women qualify as such a group.

There is little evidence that women are biologically inferior to men in intellectual endowment, academic potential, social responsibility, or capacity for independence. Constitutional differences in certain areas may exist, but they do not directly generate sex differences in areas such as those mentioned. The only cognitive functions in which females have been shown consistently to perform less well than males are spatial relations and visualizations. We really do not know to what extent the clearly inferior position women occupy in United States society today should be attributed to constitutional factors. The evidence, however, is overwhelming that socialization experiences contribute greatly to a condition of instrumental *incompetence* among women. It follows that if these conditions were altered, women could more nearly fulfill their occupational and intellectual potential. The interested reader should refer to Maccoby's excellent "Classified Summary of Research in Sex Differences" (1966, pp. 323–351).

FEW WOMEN ENTER SCIENTIFIC FIELDS AND VERY FEW OF THESE ACHIEVE EMINENCE. According to the President's Commission on the Status of Women in 1963, the proportion of women to men obtaining advanced degrees is actually dropping. Yet there is little convincing evidence that females are constitutionally incapable of contributing significantly to science. Girls obtain better grades in elementary school than boys, and perform equally to boys on standard achievement tests, including tests of mathematical reasoning. By the high school years, however, boys score considerably higher than girls on the mathematical portion of the *Scholastic Aptitude Test* (Rossi, 1969). It is interesting to note that a high positive relation between IQ and later occupational levels holds for males, but does not hold for females (Terman & Oden, 1947). According to one study of high school physics students, girls scored higher on understanding scientific processes, while boys scored higher on a test of physics achievement (Walberg, 1969). As Rossi has argued:

> If we want more women to enter science, not only as teachers of science but as scientists, some quite basic changes must take place in the way girls are reared. If girls are to develop the analytic and mathematical abilities science requires, parents and teachers must encourage them in independence and self-reliance instead of pleasing feminine submission; stimulate and reward girls' efforts to satisfy their curiosity about the world as they do those of boys; encourage in girls not unthinking conformity but alert intelligence that asks why and rejects the easy answers (Rossi, 1969, p. 483).

FEMININITY AND BEING FEMALE IS SOCIALLY DEVALUED. Both sexes rate men as more worthwhile than women (e.g., McKee & Sherriffs, 1957). While boys of all ages show a strong preference for masculine roles, girls do not show a similar preference for feminine roles, and indeed, at certain ages, many girls as well as boys show a strong preference for masculine roles (Brown, 1958). In general, both men and women express a preference for having male children (Dinitz, Dynes & Clarke, 1954). Masculine status is so to be preferred to feminine status that girls may adopt tomboy attributes and be admired for doing so, but boys who adopt feminine attributes are despised as sissies. Feminine identification in males (excluding feminine qualities such as tenderness, expressiveness, and playfulness) is clearly related to maladjustment. But even in females, intense feminine identification may more strongly characterize maladjusted than adjusted women (Heilbrun, 1965). Concern about population control will only further accelerate the devaluation of household activities performed by women and decrease the self-esteem of women solely engaged in such activities.

INTELLECTUAL ACHIEVEMENT AND SELF-ASSERTIVE INDEPENDENT STRIVINGS IN WOMEN ARE EQUATED WITH LOSS OF FEMININITY BY MEN AND WOMEN ALIKE. Women, as well as men, oppose the idea of placing women in high-status jobs (Keniston & Keniston, 1964). One researcher (Horner, 1968) thinks that women's higher test anxiety reflects the conflict between women's motivation to achieve and their motivation to fail. She feels that women and girls who are motivated to fail feel ambivalent about success because intellectual achievement is equated with loss of femininity by socializing agents and eventually by the female herself.

GENERALLY, PARENTS HAVE HIGHER ACHIEVEMENT EXPECTATIONS FOR BOYS THAN THEY DO FOR GIRLS. Boys are more frequently expected to go to college and to have careers (Aberle & Naegele, 1952). The pressure towards responsibility, obedience, and nurturance for girls, and towards achievement and independence for boys which characterizes United States society also characterizes other societies, thus further reinforcing the effect of differential expectations for boys and girls (Barry, Bacon & Child, 1957). In the United States, girls of nursery school age are not less achievement-oriented or independent than boys. By adolescence, however, most girls are highly aware of, and concerned about, social disapproval for so-called masculine pursuits. They move toward conformity with societal expectations that, relative to males, they should be nonachievement-oriented and dependent.

GIRLS AND WOMEN CONSISTENTLY SHOW A GREATER NEED FOR AFFILIATION THAN DO BOYS AND MEN. The greater nurturance toward peers and cooperation with adults shown by girls is demonstrable as early as the preschool years. In general, females are more suggestible, conforming, and likely to rely on others for guidance and support. Thus, females are particularly susceptible to social influences, and these influences generally define femininity to include such attributes as social responsibility, supportiveness, submissiveness, and low achievement striving.

There are complex and subtle differences in the behavior of boys and girls from birth onward, and in the treatment of boys and girls by their caretaking adults. These differential treatments are sometimes difficult to identify because, when the observer knows the sex of the parent or child, an automatic adjustment is made which tends to standardize judgments about the two sexes. By the time boys enter nursery school, they are more resistant to adult authority and aggressive with peers. Thus, a major socialization task for preschool boys consists of developing social responsibility. While preschool girls (in my investigations) are neither lacking in achievement-orientation nor in independence, the focal socialization task for them seems to consist of maintaining purposive, dominant, and independent behavior. Without active intervention by socializing agents, the cultural stereotype is likely to augment girls' already well-developed sense of cooperation with authority and eventually discourage their independent strivings towards achievement and eminence. As will be noted later, there is reason to believe that the socialization practices which facilitate the development of instrumental competence in *both* girls and boys have the following attributes: (a) they place a premium on self-assertiveness but not on anticonformity; (b) they emphasize high achievement and self-control but not social conformity; (c) they occur within a context of firm discipline and rationality with neither excessive restrictiveness nor over-acceptance. For a more complete discussion of changes in socialization practices which might produce greater competence in girls, see the author's paper entitled "From each woman in accord with her ability" (Baumrind, 1972a).

Socialization Practices Related to Responsible vs. Irresponsible Behavior

The reader will recall that I have defined Responsible vs. Irresponsible Behavior in terms of Friendliness vs. Hostility Towards Peers, Cooperation vs. Resistence Towards Adults, and High vs. Low Achievement Orientation. Socialization seems to have a clearer impact upon the development of social responsibility in boys than in girls, probably because girls vary less in this particular attribute. In my own work, parents who were authoritative and relatively conforming, as compared with parents who were permissive or authoritarian, tended to have children who were more friendly, cooperative, and achievement-oriented. This was especially true for boys. Nonconformity in parents was not necessarily associated with resistant and hostile behavior in children. Neither did firm control and high maturity demands produce rebelliousness. In fact, it has generally been found that close supervision, high demands for obedience and personal neatness, and pressure upon the child to share household responsibilities are associated with responsible behavior rather than with chronic rebelliousness. The condition most conducive to antisocial aggression, because it most effectively rewards such behavior, is probably one in which the parent is punitive and arbitrary in his demands, but inconsistent in responding to the child's disobedience.

Findings from several studies suggest that parental demands provoke rebelliousness only when the parent both restricts autonomy of action and does not use rational methods of control. For example, Pikas (1961), in a survey of 656 Swedish adolescents, showed that differences in the child's acceptance of parental authority depended upon the reason for the parental directive. Authority based on rational concern for the child's welfare was accepted well by the child, but arbitrary, domineering, or exploitative authority was rejected. Pikas' results are supported by Middleton and Snell (1963) who found that discipline regarded by the child as either very strict or very permissive was associated with rebellion against the parents' political views. Finally, Elder (1963), working with adolescents' reports concerning their parents, found that conformity to parental rules typified subjects who saw their parents as having ultimate control (but who gave the child leeway in making decisions) and who also provided explanations for rules.

Several generalizations and hypotheses can be drawn from this literature and from the results of my own work concerning the relations of specific parental practices to the development of social responsibility in young children. The following list is based on the assumption that it is more meaningful to talk about the effects of *patterns* of parental authority than to talk about the effects of single parental variables.

1. *The modeling of socially responsible behavior facilitates the development of social responsibility in young children, and more so if the model is seen by the child as having control over desired resources and as being concerned with the child's welfare.*

The adult who subordinates his impulses enough to conform with social regulations and is himself charitable and generous will have his example followed by the child. The adult who is self-indulgent and lacking in charity will have his example followed even if he should preach generous, cooperative behavior. Studies by Mischel and Liebert (1966) and by Rosenhan, Frederick and Burrowes (1968) suggest that models who behave self-indulgently produce similar behavior in children and these effects are even more extensive than direct reward for self-indulgent behavior. Further, when the adult preaches what he does not practice, the child is more likely to do what the adult practices. This is true even when the model preaches unfriendly or uncooperative behavior but behaves toward the child in an opposite manner. To the extent that the model for socially responsible behavior is perceived as having high social status (Bandura, Ross & Ross, 1963), the model will be most effective in inducing responsible behavior.

In our studies, both authoritative and authoritarian parents demanded socially responsible behavior and also differentially rewarded it. As compared to authoritative parents, however, authoritarian parents permitted their own needs to take precedence over those of the child, became inaccessible when displeased, assumed a stance of personal infallibility, and in other ways showed themselves often to be more concerned with their own ideas than with the child's welfare. Thus, they did not exemplify prosocial behavior, although they did preach it. Authoritative parents, on the other hand, both preached and practiced prosocial behavior and their children were significantly more responsible than the children of authoritarian parents. In this regard, it is interesting that nonconforming parents who were highly individualistic and professed anticonforming ideas had children who were more socially responsible than otherwise. The boys were achievement-oriented and the girls were notably cooperative. These parents were themselves rather pacific, gentle people who were highly responsive to the child's needs even at the cost of their own; thus, they modeled but did not preach prosocial behavior.

> 2. *Firm enforcement policies, in which desired behavior is positively reinforced and deviant behavior is negatively reinforced, facilitate the development of socially responsible behavior, provided that the parent desires that the child behave in a responsible manner.*

The use of reinforcement techniques serves to establish the potency of the reinforcing agent and, in the mind of the young child, to legitimate his authority. The use of negative sanctions can be a clear statement to the child that rules are there to be followed and that to disobey is to break a known rule. Among other things, punishment provides the child with information. As Spence (1966) found, nonreaction by adults is sometimes interpreted by children as signifying a correct response. Siegel and Kohn (1959) found that nonreaction by an adult when the child was behaving aggressively resulted in an increased incidence of such acts. By virtue of his or her role as an authority, the sheer presence of parents when the child misbehaves cannot help but affect the future occurrence of such behavior. Disapproval should reduce such actions, while approval or nonreaction to such behavior should increase them.

In our studies, permissive parents avoided the use of negative sanctions, did not demand mannerly behavior or reward self-help, did not enforce their directives by exerting force or influence, avoided confrontation when the child disobeyed, and did not choose or did not know how to use reinforcement techniques. Their sons, by comparison with the sons of authoritative parents, were clearly lacking in prosocial and achievement-oriented behavior.

> 3. *Nonrejecting parents are more potent models and reinforcing agents than rejecting parents; thus, nonrejection should be associated with socially responsible behavior in children provided that the parents value and reinforce such behavior.*

It should be noted that this hypothesis refers to nonrejecting parents and is not stated in terms of passive-acceptance. Thus, it is expected that nonrejecting parental behavior, but not unconditionally acceptant behavior, is associated with socially responsible behavior in children. As Bronfenbrenner pointed out about adolescents, "It is the presence of rejection rather than the lack of a high degree of warmth which is inimical to the development of responsibility in both sexes" (1961, p. 254). As already indicated, in our study authoritarian parents were more rejecting and punitive, and less devoted to the child's welfare than were authoritative parents; their sons were also less socially responsible.

4. *Parents who are fair, and who use reason to legitimate their directives, are more potent models and reinforcing agents than parents who do not encourage independence or verbal exchange.*

Let us consider the interacting effects of punishment and the use of reasoning on the behavior of children. From research it appears that an accompanying verbal rationale nullifies the special effectiveness of immediate punishment, and also of relatively intense punishment (Parke, 1969). Thus, by symbolically reinstating the deviant act, explaining the reason for punishment, and telling the child exactly what he should do, the parent obviates the need for intense or instantaneous punishment. Immediate, intense punishment may have undesirable side effects, in that the child is conditioned through fear to avoid deviant behavior, and is not helped to control himself consciously and willfully. Also, instantaneous, intense punishment produces high anxiety which may interfere with performance, and in addition may increase the likelihood that the child will avoid the noxious agent. This reduces that agent's future effectiveness as a model or reinforcing agent. Finally, achieving behavioral conformity by conditioning fails to provide the child with information about cause and effect relations which he can then transfer to similar situations. This is not to say that use of reasoning alone, without negative sanctions, is as effective as the use of both. Negative sanctions give operational meaning to the consequences signified by reasons and to rules themselves.

Authoritarian parents, as compared to authoritative parents, are relatively unsuccessful in producing socially responsible behavior. According to this hypothesis, the reason is that authoritarian parents fail to encourage verbal exchange and infrequently accompany punishment with reasons rather than that they use negative sanctions and are firm disciplinarians.

Socialization Practices Related to Independent vs. Suggestible Behavior

The reader will recall that Independent vs. Suggestible Behavior was defined with reference to: (a) Domineering vs. Tractable Behavior, (b) Dominance vs. Submission, (c) Purposive vs. Aimless Activity, and (d) Independence vs. Suggestibility. Parent behavior seems to have a clearer effect upon the development of independence in girls than in boys, probably because preschool boys vary less in independence.

In my own work, independence in girls was clearly associated with authoritative upbringing (whether conforming or nonconforming). For boys, nonconforming parent behavior and, to a lesser extent, authoritative upbringing were associated with independence. By independence we do not mean anticonformity. "Pure anticonformity, like pure conformity, is pure dependence behavior" (Willis, 1968, p. 263). Anticonforming behavior, like negativistic behavior, consists of doing anything but what is prescribed by social norms. Independence is the ability to disregard known standards of conduct or normative expectations in making decisions. Nonconformity in parents may not be associated in my study with independence in girls (although it was in boys) because females are especially susceptible to normative expectations. One can hypothesize that girls must be trained to act independently of these expectations, rather than to conform or to anticonform to them.

It was once assumed that firm control and high maturity demands lead to passivity and dependence in young children. The preponderance of evidence contradicts this. Rather, it would appear that many children react to parental power by resisting, rather than by being cowed. The same parent variables which increase the probability that the child will use the parent as a model should increase the likelihood that firm control will result in assertive behavior. For example, the controlling parent who is warm, understanding, and supportive of autonomy should generate less passivity (as well as less rebelliousness) than the controlling parent who is cold and restrictive. This should be the case because of the kinds of behavior reinforced, the traits modeled, and the relative effectiveness of the parent as a model.

Several generalizations and hypotheses can be offered concerning the relations between parental practices and the development of independence in young children:

1. *Early environmental stimulation facilitates the development of independence in young children.*

It took the knowledge gained from compensatory programs for culturally disadvantaged children to counteract the erroneous counsel from some experts to avoid too much cognitive stimulation of the young child. Those Head Start programs which succeed best (Hunt, 1968) are those characterized by stress on the development of cognitive skills, linguistic ability, motivational concern for achievement, and rudimentary numerical skills. There is reason to believe that middle-class children also profit from such early stimulation and enrichment of the environment. Fowler (1962) pointed out, even prior to the development of compensatory programs, that concern about the dangers of premature cognitive training and an over-emphasis on personality development had delayed inordinately the recognition that the ability to talk, read, and compute increase the child's self-respect and independent functioning.

Avoidance of anxiety and self-assertion are reciprocally inhibiting responses to threat or frustration. Girls, in particular, are shielded from stress and overstimulation, which probably serves to increase preferences for avoidant rather than offensive responses to aggression or threat. By exposing a child to stress or to physical, social, and intellectual demands, he or she becomes more resistant to stress and learns that offensive reactions to aggression and frustration are frequently rewarding. In our studies, as the hypothesis would predict, parents who provided the most enriched environment, namely the noncon-forming and the authoritative parents, had the most dominant and purposive children. These parents, by comparison with the others studied, set high standards of excellence, invoked cognitive insight, provided an intellectually stimulating atmosphere, were themselves rated as being differentiated and individualistic, and made high educational demands upon the child.

2. *Parental passive-acceptance and overprotection inhibits the development of independence.*

Passive-acceptant and overprotective parents shield children from stress and, for the reasons discussed above, inhibit the development of assertiveness and frustration tolerance. Also, parental anxiety about stress to which the child is exposed may serve to increase the child's anxiety. Further, willingness to rescue the child offers him an easy alternative to self-mastery. Demanding and nonprotective parents, by contrast, permit the child to extricate himself from stressful situations and place a high value on tolerance of frustration and courage.

According to many investigators (e.g., McClelland, Atkinson, Clark & Lowell, 1953), healthy infants are by inclination explorative, curious, and stress-seeking. Infantile feelings of pleasure, originally experienced after mild changes in sensory stimulation, become associated with these early efforts at independent mastery. The child anticipates pleasure upon achieving a higher level of skill, and the pleasure derived from successfully performing a somewhat risky task encourages him to seek out such tasks.

Rosen and D'Andrade (1959) found that high achievement motivation, a motivation akin to stress-seeking, was facilitated both by high maternal warmth when the child pleased the parent and high maternal hostility and rejection when the child was displeasing. Hoffman et al. (1960), found that mothers of achieving boys were more coercive than those who performed poorly, and it has also been found (Crandall, Dewey, Katkovsky & Preston, 1964) that mothers of achieving girls were relatively nonnurturant. Kagan and Moss (1962) reported that achieving adult women had mothers who in early childhood were unaffectionate, "pushy," and not protective. Also, Baumrind and Black (1967) found paternal punitiveness to be associated positively with independence in girls. Finally, in a recent study (Baumrind, 1971), there were indications for girls that parental nonacceptance was positively related to independence. That is, the most independent girls had parents who were either not passive-acceptant or were rejecting.

Authoritarian control and permissive noncontrol both may shield the child from the opportunity to engage in vigorous interaction with people. Demands which cannot be met, refusals to help, and unrealistically high standards may curb commerce with the environment. Placing few demands on the child, suppression of conflict, and low standards may understimulate him. In either case, he fails to achieve the knowledge and experience required to desensitize him to the anxiety associated with nonconformity.

3. *Self-assertiveness and self-confidence in the parent, expressed by an individual style and by the moderate use of power-oriented techniques of discipline, will be associated with independence in the young child.*

The self-assertive, self-confident parent provides a model of similar behavior for the child. Also, the parent who uses power-oriented rather than love-oriented techniques of discipline achieves compliance through means other than guilt. Power-oriented techniques can achieve behavioral conformity without premature internalization by the child of parental standards. It may be that the child is, in fact, more free to formulate his own standards of conduct if techniques of discipline are used which stimulate resistiveness or anger rather than fear or guilt. The use of techniques which do not stimulate conformity through guilt may be especially important for girls. The belief in one's own power and the assumption of responsibility for one's own intellectual successes and failures are important predictors of independent effort and intellectual achievement (Crandall, Katkovsky & Crandall, 1965). This sense of self-responsibility in children seems to be associated with power-oriented techniques of discipline and with critical attitudes on the part of the adult towards the child, provided that the parent is also concerned with developing the child's autonomy and encourages independent and individual behavior.

In my study, both the authoritative and the nonconforming parents were self-confident, clear as well as flexible in their child-rearing attitudes, and willing to express angry feelings openly. Together with relatively firm enforcement and nonrejection, these indices signified patterns of parental authority in which guilt-producing techniques of discipline were avoided. The sons of nonconforming parents and the daughters of authoritative parents were both extremely independent.

4. *Firm control can be associated with independence in the child, provided that the control is not restrictive of the child's opportunities to experiment and to make decisions within the limits defined.*

There is no logical reason why parents' enforcing directives and demands cannot be accompanied by regard for the child's opinions, willingness to gratify his wishes, and instruction in the effective use of power. A policy of firm enforcement may be used as a means by which the child can achieve a high level of instrumental competence and eventual independence. The controlling, demanding parent can train the child to tolerate increasingly intense and prolonged frustration; to broaden his base of adult support to include neighbors, teachers, and others; to assess critically his own successes and failures and to take responsibility for both; to develop standards of moral conduct; and to relinquish the special privileges of childhood in return for the rights of adolescence.

It is important to distinguish between the effects on the child of restrictive control and of firm control. *Restrictive control* refers to the use of extensive proscriptions and prescriptions, covering many areas of the child's life; they limit his autonomy to try out his skills in these areas. By *firm control* is meant firm enforcement of rules, effective resistance against the child's demands, and guidance of the child by regime and intervention. Firm control does not imply large numbers of rules or intrusive direction of the child's activities.

Becker (1964) has summarized the effects on child behavior of restrictiveness vs. permissiveness and warmth vs. hostility. He reported that warm-*restrictive* parents tended to have passive, well-socialized children. This author (Baumrind, 1967) found, however, that warm-*controlling* (by contrast with warm-*restrictive*) parents were not paired with passive children, but rather with responsible, assertive, self-reliant children. Parents of these children enforced directives and resisted the child's demands, but were not restrictive. Early control, unlike restrictiveness, apparently does not lead to "fearful, dependent and submissive behaviors, a dulling of intellectual striving, and inhibited hostility," as Becker indicated was true of restrictive parents (1964, p. 197).

5. *Substantial reliance upon reinforcement techniques to obtain behavioral conformity, unaccompanied by use of reason, should lead to dependent behavior.*

To the extent that the parent uses verbal cues judiciously, she increases the child's ability to discriminate, differentiate, and generalize. According to Luria (1960) and Vygotsky (1962), the child's ability to "order" his own behavior is based upon verbal instruction from the adult which, when heeded and obeyed, permits eventual *cognitive* control by the child of his own behavior. Thus, when the adult legitimizes power, labels actions clearly as praiseworthy, explains rules and encourages vigorous verbal give and take, obedience is not likely to be achieved at the cost of passive dependence. Otherwise, it may well be.

It is self-defeating to attempt to shape, by extrinsic reinforcement, behavior which by its nature is autogenic. As already mentioned, the healthy infant is explorative and curious, and seems to enjoy mild stress. Although independent mastery can be accelerated if the parent broadens the child's experiences and makes certain reasonable demands upon him, the parent must take care not to substitute extrinsic reward and social approval for the intrinsic pleasure associated with mastery of the environment. Perhaps the unwillingness of the authoritative parents in my study to rely solely upon reinforcement techniques contributed substantially to the relatively purposive, dominant behavior shown by their children, especially by their daughters.

6. *Parental values which stress individuality, self-expression, initiative, divergent thinking, and aggressiveness will facilitate the development of independence in the child, provided that these qualities in the parent are not accompanied by lax and inconsistent discipline and unwillingness to make demands upon the child.*

It is important that adults use their power in a functional rather than an interpersonal context. The emphasis should be on the task to be done and the rule to be followed rather than upon the special status of the powerful adult. By focusing upon the task to be accomplished, the adult's actions can serve as an example for the child rather than as a suppressor of his independence. Firm discipline for both boys and girls must be in the service of training for achievement and independence, if such discipline is not to facilitate the development of an overconforming, passive life style.

In our study, independence was clearly a function of nonconforming but nonindulgent parental attitudes and behaviors, for boys. For girls, however, nonconforming parental patterns were associated with independence only when the parents were also authoritative. The parents in these groups tended to encourage their children to ask for, even to demand, what they desired. They themselves acquiesced in the face of such demands provided that the demands were not at variance with parental policy. Thus, the children of these parents were positively reinforced for autonomous self-expression. In contrast to these results, the authoritarian parents did not value willfulness in the child, and the permissive parents were clearly ambivalent about rewarding such behavior. Further, the permissive parents did not differentiate between mature or praiseworthy demands by the child and regressive or deviant demands. These permissive parents instead would accede to the child's demands until patience was exhausted; punishment, sometimes very harsh, would then ensue.

Conclusions

Girls in Western society are in many ways systematically socialized for instrumental incompetence. The affiliative and cooperative orientation of girls increases their receptivity to the influence of socializing agents. This influence, in turn, is often used by socializing agents to inculcate passivity, dependence, conformity, and sociability in young females at the expense of independent pursuit of success and scholarship. In my studies, parents designated as authoritative had the most achievement-oriented and independent daughters. However, permissive parents whose control was lax, who did not inhibit tomboy behavior, and who did not seek to produce sex-role conformity in girls had daughters who were nearly as achievement-oriented and independent.

The following adult practices and attitudes seem to facilitate the development of socially responsible and independent behavior in both boys and girls:

1. Modeling by the adult of behavior which is both socially responsible and self-assertive, especially if the adult is seen as powerful by the child and as eager to use the material and interpersonal resources over which he has control on the child's behalf.

2. Firm enforcement policies in which the adult makes effective use of reinforcement principles in order to reward socially responsible behavior and to punish deviant behavior, but in which demands are accompanied by explanations, and sanctions are accompanied by reasons consistent with a set of principles followed in practice as well as preached by the parent.

3. Nonrejecting but not overprotective or passive-acceptance parental attitudes in which the parent's interest in the child is abiding and, in the preschool years, intense; and where approval is conditional upon the child's behavior.

4. High demands for achievement and for conformity with parental

policy, accompanied by receptivity to the child's rational demands and willingness to offer the child wide latitude for independent judgment.

5. Providing the child with a complex and stimulating environment offering challenge and excitement as well as security and rest, where divergent as well as convergent thinking is encouraged.

These practices and attitudes do not reflect a happy compromise between authoritarian and permissive practices. Rather, they reflect a synthesis and balancing of strongly opposing forces of tradition and innovation, divergence and convergence, accommodation and assimilation, cooperation and autonomous expression, tolerance and principled intractability.

References

ABERLE, D. F., & NAEGELE, K. D. Middle-class fathers' occupational role and attitudes toward children. *Am. J. Orthopsychiat.*, 1952, *22*, 366–378.

BANDURA, A., ROSS, D., & ROSS, S. A. A comparative test of the status envy, social power, and the secondary-reinforcement theories of identificatory learning. *J. Abnorm. Soc. Psychol.*, 1963, *67*, 527–534.

BARRY, H., BACON, M. K., & CHILD, I. L. A cross-cultural survey of some sex differences in socialization. *J. Abnorm. Soc. Psychol.*, 1957, *55*, 327–332.

BAUMRIND, D. Effects of authoritative parental control on child behavior. *Child Develpm.*, 1966, *37*, 887–907.

———. Child care practices anteceding three patterns of preschool behavior. *Genet. Psychol. Monogr.*, 1967, *75*, 43–88.

———. Authoritarian vs. authoritative parental control. *Adolescence*, 1968, *3*, 255–272.

———. Current patterns of parental authority. *Develpm. Psychol. Monogr.*, 1971, *4*(1), 1–102.

———. From each woman in accord with her ability. *School Rev.*, Feb. 1972(a).

———. An exploratory study of socialization effects on black children: Some black-white comparisons. *Child Develpm.*, 1972(b).

BAUMRIND, D., & BLACK, A. E. Socialization practices associated with dimensions of competence in preschool boys and girls. *Child Develpm.*, 1967, *38*, 291–327.

BECKER, W. C. Consequences of different kinds of parental discipline. In M. L. Hoffman & L. W. Hoffman (Eds.), *Review of child development research*, Vol. 1. New York: Russell Sage Foundation, 1964. Pp. 169–208.

BRONFENBRENNER, U. Some familial antecedents of responsibility and leadership in adolescents. In L. Petrullo & B. M. Bass (Eds.), *Leadership and interpersonal behavior*. New York: Holt, Rinehart & Winston, 1961. Pp. 239–271.

BROWN, D. Sex role development in a changing culture. *Psychol. Bull.*, 1958, *55*, 232–242.

CRANDALL, V., DEWEY, R., KATKOVSKY, W., & PRESTON, A. Parents' attitudes and behaviors and grade school children's academic achievements. *J. Genet. Psychol.*, 1964, *104*, 53–66.

CRANDALL, V., KATKOVSKY, W., & CRANDALL, V. J. Children's beliefs in their own control of reinforcements in intellectual-academic achievement situations. *Child Develpm.*, 1965, *36*, 91–109.

CRANDALL, V., ORLEANS, S., PRESTON, A., & RABSON, A. The development of social compliance in young children. *Child Develpm.*, 1958, *29*, 429–443.

DINITZ, S., DYNES, R. R., & CLARKE, A. C. Preference for male or female children: Traditional or affectional. *Marriage & family living*, 1954, *16*, 128–130.

EIDUSON, B. T. *Scientists, their psychological world.* New York: Basic Books, 1962.

ELDER, G. H. Parental power legitimation and its effect on the adolescent. *Sociometry*, 1963, *26*, 50–65.

EMMERICH, W., & SMOLLER, F. The role patterning of parental norms. *Sociometry*, 1964, *27*, 382–390.

FOWLER, W. Cognitive learning in infancy and early childhood. *Psychol. Bull.*, 1962, *59*, 116–152.

HAGGARD, E. A. Socialization, personality, and academic achievement in gifted children. In B. C. Rosen, H. J. Crockett, & C. Z. Nunn (Eds.), *Achievement in American society.* Cambridge, Mass.: Schenkman Publishing, 1969. Pp. 85–94.

HEILBRUN, A. B. Sex differences in identification learning. *J. Genet. Psychol.*, 1965, *106*, 185–193.

HOFFMAN, L., ROSEN, S., & LIPPITT, R. Parental coerciveness, child autonomy, and child's role at school. *Sociometry*, 1960, *23*, 15–22.

HORNER, M. S. Sex differences in achievement motivation and performance in competitive situations. Unpubl. doctoral dissertation, Univ. of Michigan, 1968.

HUNT, J. McV. Toward the prevention of incompetence. In J. W. Carter, Jr. (Ed.), *Research contributions from psychology to community mental health.* New York: Behavioral Publications, 1968.

KAGAN, J., & MOSS, H. A. *Birth to maturity: A study in psychological development.* New York: John Wiley, 1962.

KENISTON, E., & KENISTON, K. An American anachronism: the image of women and work. *Am. Scholar*, 1964, *33*, 355–375.

LURIA, A. R. Experimental analysis of the development of voluntary action in children. In *The central nervous system and behavior.* Bethesda, Md.: U.S. Dept. of Health, Education, & Welfare, National Institutes of Health, 1960. Pp. 529–535.

Maccoby, E. E. (Ed.), *The development of sex differences.* Stanford, Calif.: Stanford Univ. Press, 1966.

MCCLELLAND, D., ATKINSON, J., CLARK, R., & LOWELL, E. *The achievement motive.* New York: Appleton-Century-Crofts, 1953.

MCKEE, J. P., & SHERRIFFS, A. C. The differential evaluation of males and females. *J. Pers.*, 1957, *25*, 356–371.

MIDDLETON, R., & SNELL, P. Political expression of adolescent rebellion. *Am. J. Sociol.*, 1963, *68*, 527–535.

MISCHEL, W., & LIEBERT, R. M. Effects of discrepancies between observed and imposed reward criteria on their acquisition and transmission. *J. Pers. Soc. Psychol.* 1966, *3*, 45–53.

PARKE, R. D. Some effects of punishment on children's behavior. *Young Children*, 1969, *24*, 225–240.

PIKAS, A. Children's attitudes toward rational versus inhibiting parental authority. *J. Abnorm. Soc. Psychol.*, 1961, *62*, 315–321.

ROE, A. *The Making of a Scientist.* New York: Dodd, Mead, 1952.

ROSEN, B. C., & D'ANDRADE, R. The psychological origins of achievement motivation. *Sociometry*, 1959, *22*, 185–218.

ROSENHAN, D. L., FREDERICK, F., & BURROWES, A. Preaching and practicing: Effects of channel discrepancy on norm internalization. *Child Develpm.*, 1968, *39*, 291–302.

Rossi, A. Women in science: why so few? In B. C. Rosen, H. J. Crockett, & C. Z. Nunn (Eds.), *Achievement in American society*. Cambridge, Mass.: Schenkman Publishing, 1969. Pp. 470–486.

Siegel, A. E., & Kohn, L. G. Permissiveness, permission, and aggression: The effects of adult presence or absence on aggression in children's play. *Child Develpm.*, 1959, *36*, 131–141.

Spence, J. T. Verbal-discrimination performance as a function of instruction and verbal reinforcement combination in normal and retarded children. *Child Develpm.*, 1966, *37*, 269–281.

Terman, L. M., & Oden, H. H. *The gifted child grows up*. Stanford, Calif.: Stanford Univ. Press, 1947.

Vygotsky, L. S. *Thought and language*. Cambridge, Mass.: M.I.T. Press, 1962.

Walberg, H. J. Physics, femininity, and creativity. *Develpm. Psychol.*, 1969, *1*, 47–54.

Willis, R. H. Conformity, independence, and anticonformity. In L. S. Wrightsman, Jr. (Ed.), *Contemporary issues in social psychology*. Belmont, Calif.: Brooks/Cole Publishing, 1968. Pp. 258–272.

For the last decade Professor Lawrence Kohlberg of Harvard University's School of Education has been the leading American theorist and researcher in the field of moral development. In his first major paper, which is reprinted here, he suggests that moral development progresses through a sequence of six stages that evolve in a regular and predictable order. Kohlberg does not believe that moral development depends on a process of learning and internalization of the culture's basic sanctions and prohibitions. Rather, he interprets his findings in accordance with a "cognitive-developmental" point of view in which each new step involves "a restructuring of preceding types of thought." Attainment of the lower types of thought is prerequisite to attainment of the higher types. The author postulates that there is "a series of internally patterned or organized transformations of social concepts and attitudes, transformations that constitute a developmental process."

The Development of Children's Orientations Toward a Moral Order: I. Sequence in the Development of Moral Thought

Lawrence Kohlberg

Since the concept of a moral attitude forms the basic building block of the social psychological theories of *Freud* (1922), *Durkheim* (1906), *Parsons* (1960) and others, there is reason to agree with *McDougall* (1908) that "the fundamental problem of social psychology is the moralization of the individual by the society."

Following the leads of *Freud* and *Durkheim,* most social scientists have viewed moralization as a process of *internalizing* culturally given external rules through rewards, punishments, or identification. Without questioning the view that the end point of the moralization process is one in which conduct is oriented to internal standards, one may well reject the assumption that such internal standards are formed simply through a process of "stamping in" the external prohibitions of the culture upon the child's mind. From the perspective of a developmental psychology such as that of *Piaget* (1932) or *J. M. Baldwin* (1906), internal moral standards are rather the outcome of a set of transformations of primitive attitudes and conceptions. These transformations accompany cognitive growth in the child's perceptions and orderings of a social world with which he is continuously interacting.

Source: Reprinted by permission from *Vita Humana*, 1963, 6, 11–33.

Note. Part II. Social Experience, Social Conduct and the Development of Moral Thought appears in a subsequent issue of *"Vita Humana."*

Directed by this developmental conception of the moralization process, our research has been oriented to the following tasks:

1. The empirial isolation of sequential stages in the development of moral thought.
2. The study of the relation of the development of moral thought to moral conduct and emotion.
3. The application of a stage analysis of moral judgment to subcultural differences as well as pathological deviance in moral orientations.
4. The isolation of the social forces and experiences required for the sequential development of moral orientations.

In the present paper, we shall summarize our findings as they relate to moralization as an age-developmental process, and we shall compare this characterization with that of *Piaget*.

The Isolation of Six Stages of Development in Moral Thought

Our developmental analysis of moral judgment is based upon data obtained from a core group of 72 boys living in Chicago suburban areas. The boys were of three age groups: 10, 13, 16. Half of each group was upper-middle class; half, lower to lower-middle class. For reasons to be discussed in the sequel to this paper, half of each group consisted of popular boys (according to classroom sociometric tests), while half consisted of socially isolated boys. All the groups were comparable in I.Q.

We have also used our procedures with a group of 24 delinquents aged 16, a group of 24 six-year-olds, and a group of 50 boys and girls aged 13 residing outside of Boston.

The basic data were two-hour tape-recorded interviews focussed upon hypothetical moral dilemmas. Both the content and method of the interviews were inspired by the work of *Piaget* (1932). The ten situations used were ones in which acts of obedience to legal-social rules or to the commands of authority conflicted with the human needs or welfare of other individuals. The child was asked to choose whether one should perform the obedience-serving act or the need-serving act and was then asked a series of questions probing the thinking underlying his choice.

Our analysis of results commenced with a consideration of the action alternatives selected by the children. These analyses turned out to shed little light on moral developments. Age trends toward choice in favor of human needs, such as might be expected from *Piaget's* (1932) theory, did not appear. The child's reason for his choice and his way of defining the conflict situations did turn out to be developmentally meaningful, however.

As an example, one choice dilemma was the following:

Joe's father promised he could go to camp if he earned the $50 for it, and then changed his mind and asked Joe to give him the money he had earned. Joe lied and said he had only earned $10 and went to camp using the other $40 he had made. Before he went, he told his younger brother Alex about the money and about lying to their father. Should Alex tell their father?

Danny, a working class 10-year-old of I.Q. 98 replied: "In one way it would be right to tell on his brother or his father might get mad at him and spank him. In another way it would be right to keep quiet or his brother might beat him up."

Obviously whether Danny chooses to fulfill his "obligation" to adult authority or to peer loyalty will depend on which action he perceives as leading to the greater punishment. What interests us most, however, is the fact that Danny does not appear to have a conception of moral obligation. His judgments are predictions; they are not expressions of moral praise, indignation, or obligation. From one to the next of the situations presented him, Danny was not consistently "authoritarian" or "humanistic" in his choices, but he was consistent in choosing in terms of the physical consequences involved.

A careful consideration of individual cases eventually led us to define six developmental types of value-orientation. A Weberian ideal-typological procedure was used to achieve a combination of empirical consistency and logical consistency in defining the types. The six developmental types were grouped into three moral levels and labelled as follows:

Level I. Pre-Moral Level

Type 1. Punishment and obedience orientation.
Type 2. Naive instrumental hedonism.

Level II. Morality of Conventional Role-Conformity

Type 3. Good-boy morality of maintaining good relations, approval of others.
Type 4. Authority maintaining morality.

Level III. Morality of Self-Accepted Moral Principles

Type 5. Morality of contract and of democratically accepted law.
Type 6. Morality of individual principles of conscience.

These types will be described in more detail in subsequent sections of this paper. The typology rests upon 30 different general aspects of morality which the children brought into their thinking. One such aspect was the child's use of the concept of rights, another his orientation toward punitive justice, a third his consideration of intentions as opposed to consequences of action, etc. Each aspect was conceived as a dimension defined by a six-level scale, with each level of the scale corresponding to one of the six types of morality just listed.

A "motivational" aspect of morality was defined by the motive mentioned by the subject in justifying moral action. Six levels of motive were isolated, each congruent with one of the developmental types. They were as follows:

1.   Punishment by another.
2.   Manipulation of goods, rewards by another.
3.   Disapproval by others.
4.   Censure by legitimate authorities followed by guilt feelings.
5.   Community respect and disrespect.
6.   Self-condemnation.

These motives fall into three major levels. The first two represent on the verbal level what *McDougall* (1905) termed "the stage in which the operation of the instinctive impulses is modified by the influence of rewards and punishments." The second two correspond to *McDougall's* second stage "in which conduct is controlled in the main by anticipation of social praise and blame." The fifth, and especially the sixth, correspond to *McDougall's* third and "highest stage in which conduct is regulated by an ideal that enables a man to act in the way that seems to him right regardless of the praise or blame of his immediate social environment."

A more cognitive aspect of morality, conceptions of rights, was defined in terms of the following levels:

1.   No real conception of a right. "Having a right" to do something equated with "being right," obeying authority.
2.   Rights are factual ownership rights. Everyone has a right to do what they want with themselves and their possessions, even though this conflicts with rights of others.
3.   Same as the second level concept but qualified by the belief that one has no right to do evil.
4.   Recognition that a right is a claim, a legitimate exception, as to the actions of others. In general, it is an earned claim, e.g., for payment for work.
5.   A conception of unearned, universal individual or human rights in addition to rights linked to a role or status.
6.   In addition to level 5 conceptions, a notion of respecting the individual life and personality of the other.

Each of the 50 to 150 moral ideas or statements expressed by a child in the course of an interview could be assigned to one of 180 cells (30 dimensions × 6 levels per dimension) in the classification system. This classification yielded scores for each boy on each of the six types of thought based on the percentage of all his statements which were of the given type. Judges were able to assign responses to the moral levels with an adequate degree of agreement, expressed by product moment correlations between judges ranging from .68 to .84.

In spite of the variety of aspects of morality tapped by the 30 dimensions, there appeared to be considerable individual consistency in level of thought. Thus 15 boys in our original group of 72 were classified (in terms of their modal response) as falling in the first of our six types. On the average, 45% of the thinking of these 15 boys could be characterized as Type 1.

The differences between our age groups offer evidence concerning the developmental nature of the typology. The age trends for usage of the six type of thought are presented in Figure 1.

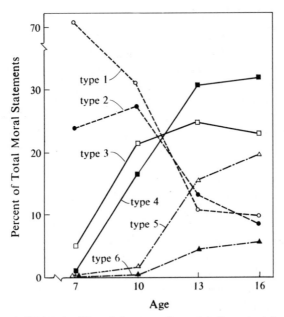

FIGURE 1.   Use of six types of moral judgments at four ages

It is evident that our first two types of thought decreased with age, our next two types increase until age 13 and then stabilize, and our last two types increase until age 16. Analyses of variance of the percentage usage of each type of thought by the 10-, 13-, and 16-year-old groups were carried out.[1] The differences between the three age groups in usage of all types of thought but one (Type 3) were found to be significant beyond the .01 level.

If our stages of moral thinking are to be taken as supporting the developmental view of moralization, evidence not only of age trends, but of sequentiality is required. While the age trends indicate that some modes of thought are generally more difficult or advanced than other modes of thought, they do not demonstrate that attainment of each mode of thought is prerequisite to the attainment of the next higher in a hypothetical sequence.

---

[1] The means in Figure 1 for age 7 are based on only 12 boys and a limited number of responses per child, compared to the older group.

Because the higher types of moral thought replace, rather than add to, the lower modes of thought, the *Guttman* (1950) scaling technique used by other investigators to establish certain cognitive developmental sequences (*Schuessler and Strauss, 1950; Wohlwill,* 1960) is not appropriate for our material. A more appropriate statistical model is derived from *Guttman's* (1954) quasi-simplex correlation matrix. The "simplex" pattern of intercorrelations derives from the expectation that the more two types of thought are separated from one another in a developmental sequence, the lower should be the correlations between them. This expectation can be compared with the actual intercorrelations obtained among the six types of thought.

Each child had a profile showing the percent of his responses that fell within each of the six types of thought. These profiles permitted us to correlate each of the six types of thought with each of the others across the sample of 72 boys, aged 10 to 16. The resulting product-moment correlation matrix is presented in Table 1. Each correlation reflects the extent to which the individuals who use the type of thought identified by the numbers at the left margin of the matrix also use a second type of thought identified by the numbers above the matrix.

TABLE 1.   Matrix of intercorrelations between six types of moral judgment

Type	1	2	3	4	5	6
1	x					
2	55	x				
3	−41	−19	x			
4	−52	−41	18	x		
5	−52	−58	09	00	x	
6	−37	−43	−29	−07	23	x

The expectation applied to the matrix is that the correlations between two types of thought should decrease as these two types are increasingly separated in the developmental hierarchy. The matrix presented in Table 1 indicates general agreement with the expectation. The correlations diminish as we move away from the main diagonal entries, whether we go across the columns or down the rows. (The correlations are markedly negative, partially because of the necessity for one percentage score to decrease as another increases.) Furthermore, correlations of types within the three main levels are higher than between levels, supporting our distinction of levels.[2]

[2] These cross-sectional findings need to be supplemented by a longitudinal analysis if we are to accept the stages as a genuine developmental sequence. We are presently engaged in a semilongitudinal analysis, in which we have reinterviewed 54 of our original subjects after a three-year interval. The findings will be reported in a subsequent publication.

The First Two Stages Compared with Piaget's Stages

Our proposed sequence of stages must have logical as well as empirical support. In characterizing our stages, we shall attempt a logical justification of their location in the hierarchy and at the same time, a comparison of our stages and concepts with *Piaget's* (1932) theory of developmental stages of moral judgment.[3]

Piaget (1932) starts from a conception of morality as respect for rules, a respect derived from personal respect for the authorities who promulgate and teach the rules. The young child's respect for authority and rules is originally unilateral and absolutistic, but in the 8- to 12-year-olds, this respect becomes mutual, reciprocal and relativistic. Unilateral respect for adults is said to inspire a *heteronomous* attitude toward adult rules as sacred and unchangeable. This attitude is believed to be supported by two cognitive defects in the young child's thought. One defect, egocentrism, the confusion of one's own perspective with that of others, leads to an inability to see moral value as relative to various persons or ends. The other defect, realism, the confusion of subjective phenomena with objective things, leads to a view of moral rules as fixed, eternal entities rather than as psychosocial expectations. The moral ideology resulting from the interaction of heteronomous respect and cognitive realism is described as "moral realism."

Piaget believes that the development of mutual respect toward other individuals in the 8- to 12-year-olds leads to an "autonomous" regard for the rules as products of group agreement and as instruments of cooperative purposes. "Mutual respect" is believed to be associated with the cognitive capacity to differentiate one's own value perspective from that of others (decline of egocentrism) and both of these trends are believed to arise largely through peer-group interaction.

Several of the thirty dimensions characterizing our six types are based on *Piaget's* conceptions. Our Moral Type 1 shares such characteristics of *Piaget's* heteronomous as concern for consequences rather than intentions, lack of awareness of relativity of value, definition of right as obedience to authority. These and other Type 1 characteristics are illustrated by an excerpt from an interview with Tommy (age 10, working class, I.Q. 128). The excerpt also illustrates how the interview method traces back the child's immediate judgments to the unstated but basic assumptions or "principles" behind them.

This portion of the interview is in response to the third of the 10 moral dilemmas:

In Europe, a woman was near death from a special kind of cancer. There was one drug that the doctors thought might save her. It was a form of radium that a druggist in the same town had recently discovered. The drug was expensive to make, but the druggist was charging ten times what

---

[3] There are a number of other recent typologies of moral judgment relevant to our own, briefly discussed elsewhere (*Kohlberg*, 1963).

the drug cost him to make. He paid $200 for the radium and charged $2000 for a small dose of the drug. The sick woman's husband, Heinz, went to everyone he knew to borrow the money, but he could only get together about $1000 which is half of what it cost. He told the druggist that his wife was dying and asked him to sell it cheaper or let him pay later. But the druggist said: "No, I discovered the drug and I'm going to make money from it." So Heinz got desperate and broke into the man's store to steal the drug for his wife. Should the husband have done that?

The interview proceeded as follows:

> His wife was sick and if she didn't get the drug quickly, she might die. Maybe his wife is an important person and runs a store and the man buys stuff from her and can't get it any other place. The police would probably blame the owner that he didn't save the wife. That would be like killing with a gun or knife.
>
> (Interviewer: Would it be all right to put the druggist in the electric chair for murder?)
>
> If she could be cured by the drug and they didn't give it to her, I think so, because she could be an important lady like Betsy Ross, she made the flag. And if it was President Eisenhower, he's important, and they'd probably put the man in the electric chair because that isn't fair.
>
> (Should the punishment be more if she's an important person?)
>
> If someone important is in a plane and is allergic to heights and the stewardess won't give him medicine because she's only got enough for one and she's got a sick one, a friend, in back, they'd probably put the stewardess in a lady's jail because she didn't help the important one.
>
> (Is it better to save the life of one important person or a lot of unimportant people?)
>
> All the people that aren't important because one man just has one house, maybe a lot of furniture, but a whole bunch of people have an awful lot of furniture and some of these poor people might have a lot of money and it doesn't look it.

On the one hand we notice Tommy's reasoning ability, his utilitarian calculation of the economics of the greater good. On the other hand we notice that the calculation of value is based on a "primitive" assumption as to the basis of moral values. A prosaic and commendable concern about the wife's life is eventually based on the notion that the value of a life is determined by its "importance" and that such importance is essentially a function of the amount of furniture owned.

Why are we justified in using the term "primitive" in describing the derivation of the value of life from the value of furniture? Awarding moral value to furniture involves a failure to differentiate the self's point of view from that of others, or to differentiate what the community holds as a shared or moral value (the value of life) and what the individual holds as a private value (the desire for furniture). Such a lack of a sense of subjectivity of value is also suggested by Tommy's definition of culpability in terms of consequences rather than intentions (the wickedness of the druggist depends on his causing the loss of an important life).

It seems warranted then to view our Type 1 responses as reflecting cognitively primitive value assumptions.

Type 1 value assumptions, furthermore, are externalized from the motivational point of view, as indicated by definitions of right and wrong in terms of punishment and conformity to power-figures. As an example, Tommy defines the druggist's wrong in terms of a prediction with regard to punishment, and in terms of conformity to the wishes of important persons.

Such an interpretation of Tommy's responses as involving external motives is open to question, however. *Piaget* would see these responses as re-reflecting the young's child's deep respect for authority and rules. *Piaget* sees the young child's morality as externally oriented only in a cognitive sense, not in a motivational sense. According to *Piaget,* the strong emotional respect the young child feels for authority and rules make him feel unable to judge for himself, and forces him to rely on external adult sanctions and commands to define what is right and wrong. In the *Piaget* view, the child is oriented to punishment only because punishment is a cue to what is disapproved by adults or by the "sacred World-Order."

In contrast to *Piaget's* interpretation, it has seemed to us simpler to start with the assumption that the Type 1 definition of wrong in terms of punishment reflects a realistic-hedonistic desire to avoid punishment, rather than a deep reverence for the adult "World-Order." The children of 10 and older who represent Type 1 morality did not in fact seem to show strong respect for adult authority. A case in point is Danny who, in a situation of conflict between brother and father, defined the right choice in terms of a prediction as to which one would retaliate more heavily. Danny went on to say:

> My brother would say, "If you tell on me, I'll whip you with my belt real hard."
> (What would you do then?)
> Well, if I was to tell my Dad if my brother Butchie was still hurting me, my brother Butchie would go find another house to live in.

Danny scores high on various attributes of *Piaget's* "moral realism," but it is hard to see Danny as expressing what *Piaget* terms "the sacredness of rules," "unilateral respect for adults," or a "belief in a World-Order."

We have concluded that it is possible to interpret all our observations with regard to "moral realism" without invoking *Piaget's* notion of the child's sense of the sacredness of authority and rules. This conclusion is consistent with the findings of other studies of *Piaget's* moral judgment dimensions, as is documented elsewhere (*Kohlberg,* 1963).

Regardless of the validity of *Piaget's* interpretation of "moral realism," *Piaget's* assumption that the young child feels a strong idealized moral respect for adult authority requires direct investigation. *Piaget* shares this assumption with psychoanalysts, and some form of the assumption seems critical for widely accepted notions as to the early childhood origins of adult neurotic guilt. In collaboration with *B. Brener,* we attempted a direct study of the validity of the *Piaget* assumption of "heteronomous respect" to explain the moral judgments of children aged four to eight. Earlier work with children of six and seven indicated that these children defined right and wrong mainly by reference to punishment when faced with simplified versions of our moral dilemmas. Did this indicate a basically "hedonistic" view of right or wrong or did it rather reflect a lack of cognitive resources in answering "why" questions in the context of a concern for conformity to sacred authority (*Piaget's* view)?

To investigate this issue, 96 children, aged 4, 5, and 7 were confronted with doll-enactments of stories in which disobedience to a rule (or adult) was followed by reward, and other stories in which obedience to a rule was followed by punishment. One such story was of a boy who was ordered to watch a baby on a couch while his mother left the house. The boy in the story proceeded to run out of the house and play outside. The *S* was asked to complete the story. The *S* was told that the mother returned and gave the disobedient boy some candy. *S* was then asked whether the child-doll had done good or bad, and a series of related questions.

In general, the 4-year-olds defined the story act as good or bad according to the reward or punishment rather than according to the rule or adult command. The older children showed considerable conflict, some of the 7-year-olds defining right and wrong in terms of the rule and showing concern about the "injustice" of punishing good and rewarding evil. These older children, however, still explained the rightness and wrongness of the act in relation to sanctions, but took a long-range or probabilistic view of this relation. Disobedience might have been rewarded in that situation, the children said, but in general it would still lead to punishment.

These results, while not consistent with *Piaget's* assumptions, should not be used to conclude that the moral decisions of 4–5-year-olds are based on crafty hedonism. Only as children reach a level of cognitive development at which the meaning of moral concepts can be differentiated from punishment can they attain either a definite hedonism or a degree of disinterested respect for authority.

The emergence of individualistic hedonism out of such growing cognitive differentiation is suggested by the responses which fall in our Type 2. Just as our first stage of morality coincides descriptively with *Piaget's* "heteronomous stage" but differs from it in interpretation, so our second stage coincides descriptively with *Piaget's* autonomous stage but differs from it in interpretation. Like *Piaget* and others, we found an increase in the use of reciprocity (exchange and retaliation) as a basis for choice and judgment in the years six to ten, though not thereafter. We also found age increases in notions of relativism of value, and in egalitarian denial of the moral superiority of authorities.

These reactions were common enough and well enough associated in our 10-year-olds to help define our Type 2. The tendency to define value relative to private needs is reflected in the response of Jimmy (a 10-year-old working-class boy, I.Q. 105) to our test situation about mercy-killing. The story continues the plight of the wife dying of cancer as follows:

The doctor finally got some of the radium drug for Heinz's wife. But it didn't work, and there was no other treatment known to medicine which could save her. So the doctor knew that she had only about six months to live. She was in terrible pain, but she was so weak that a good dose of a pain-killer like ether or morphine would make her die sooner. She was delirious and almost crazy with pain, and in her calm periods, she would ask the doctor to give her enough ether to kill her. She said she couldn't stand the pain and she was going to die in a few months anyway.

Should the doctor do what she asks and make her die to put her out of her terrible pain?

Jimmy replied:

> It's according to how you look at it. From the doctor's point of view, it could be a murder charge. From her point of view, it isn't paying her to live anymore if she's just going to be in pain.
> (How about if there were a law against it?)
> It should be up to her; it's her life. It's the person's life, not the law's life.

In this situation Jimmy defines right action instrumentally, as means to individual values; he defines it relativistically, in relation to the conflicting values of various individuals; and he defines it hedonistically, in terms of "paying" in pleasure and pain. The woman has ownership rights over herself, she is her own property. In more mature types of thought rights are defined relative to duties, the law is seen as defending and defining rights, and the law's respect for the woman's rights represents a respect for her personality and life.

Jimmy also relied heavily on reciprocity in defining role relations as indicated by such remarks as the following:

> (Why should someone be a good son?)
> Be good to your father and he'll be good to you.

The advance in cognitive differentiation of this type of response over that of Type 1 seems evident. It seems clear that such definition of value in terms of ego-need and reciprocity of needs is in a sense internal; i.e., it is not simply a reflection of direct teaching by others. It reflects rather Type 2's increasing awareness of its own ego-interests and of the exchange of ego-interests underlying much of social organization.

It also seems evident, however, that the Type 2 modes of thought are far from constituting an adequate or mature basis for morality. We find in a number of our older delinquent boys that further intellectual development seems to carry this Type 2 morality to the cynicism which is its logical endpoint. For example, John, a bright 17-year-old working-class delinquent (I.Q. 131), said in response to the story about stealing a drug for one's wife:

> Should the husband steal the drug for his wife? I would eliminate that into whether he wanted to or not. If he wants to marry someone else, someone young and good-looking, he may not want to keep her alive.

John's hedonistic relativism was also associated with a view of rights and law which was the systematic endpoint of Jimmy's views:

> (Should the law make a worse punishment for stealing $500 or for cheating that amount by making a personal loan with no intention to repay it?)
> I don't see that they have a right to decide anything. Who are they? They didn't get robbed and they don't do the stealing. It's vanity, they like the feeling of saying what's right. Laws are made by cowards to protect themselves.

Insofar as John was willing to make judgments not based completely on hedonistic relativism, they involved some notion of equality or reciprocity, e.g.:

> If a buddy of mine loans me something I'd do anything for him. If he double-crosses me, I'll do anything against him.[4]

From a developmental view, then, the Type 2 morality of need and reciprocity reflects both cognitive advance and a firmer internal basis of judgments than does the Type 1 morality. It does not, however, give rise to any of the characteristics usually attributed to moral judgment, or to a sense of obligation. While possessing the basic attributes stressed by *Piaget* as characterizing the stage of moral autonomy, this type of thought is not based on mutual (or any other type) moral respect (as *Piaget* had hypothesized).

The Intermediate Stages of Moral Development

It is clear that Type 1 and Type 2 children do not express attitudes toward "the good" and "the right" like those we take for granted in adults and which we often regard as moral clichés or stereotypes. These stereotypes first appear in our Type 3 and Type 4 preadolescents, whose verbal judgments and decisions are defined in terms of a concept of a morally good person (the implication of labelling Type 3 as a "good boy" morality).

A fairly typical Type 3 "good boy" response to the story about stealing the drug is the following response by Don (age 13, I.Q. 109, lower-middle class):

---

[4] Such use of reciprocity by delinquents should not be considered evidence of a genuine morality of peer loyalty or "mutual respect" however. John says elsewhere, "I'm a natural leader. I understand how kids are made and I just pull the right strings and make monkeys out of them."

> It was really the druggist's fault, he was unfair, trying to overcharge and letting someone die. Heinz loved his wife and wanted to save her. I think anyone would. I don't think they would put him in jail. The judge would look at all sides, and see that the druggist was charging too much.

Don's response defines the issues in terms of attitudes toward the kinds of people involved; "the loving husband," "the unfair druggist," "the understanding judge," "what anyone would do," etc. He assumes that the attitudes he expresses are shared or community attitudes.

Don carries his moral-stereotypical definition of the social world into material not explicitly moral, e.g. into a series of questions we asked concerning the status of various occupational roles. Don tells us:

> President Eisenhower has done a good job and worked so hard he got a heart attack and put himself in the grave, just about, to help the people.

Don sees expected role-performances as expressions of a virtuous self, and bases respect for authority on a belief in the good intentions and wisdom of the authority figure, rather than in his power. It is also clear that his definition of the good and right has moved from a simple classification of outward acts (Type 1) and their need-related consequences (Type 2) to a definition in terms of "intentions," of inner attitudes of liking and "helping other people" (Type 3), or attitudes of "showing your respect for authority" (Type 4). These concerns imply a definition of good and right which involves an active concern for the social goals behind the rules.

In terms of motivation, this second level is one in which conduct is controlled in the main by anticipation of praise and blame. Praise and blame are, of course, effective reinforcers even in the child's earliest years. In these early years, however, disapproval is but one of the many unpleasant external consequences of action that are to be avoided. In contrast, our Type 3 and Type 4 preadolescents attempt to make decisions and define what is good for themselves by *anticipating* possible disapproval in thought and imagination and by holding up approval as a final internal goal. Furthermore, the preadolescent is bothered only by disapproval if the disapproval is expressed by legitimate authorities. This attitude is naively expressed by Andy (age 16, working class, I.Q. 102) in his reply to the second story about telling one's father about one's brother's lie:

> If my father finds out later, he won't trust me. My brother wouldn't either, but I wouldn't have *a conscience* that he (my brother) didn't.

Andy equates his "conscience" with avoidance of disapproval by authorities, but not by peers. The growth of self-guidance in terms of consciously anticipated moral praise or blame seems to be part of a larger process of development expressed in the active use of moral praise and blame to-ward others expressed at this stage. There is also a close relationship between approval-sensitivity and what is often termed "identification with authority." This is evident with regard to Andy who tells us:

> I try to do things for my parents, they've always done things for you. I try to do everything my mother says, I try to please her. Like she wants me to be a doctor and I want to, too, and she's helping me to get up there.

Unlike the statements of compliance to the wishes of superiors (as in Level I). Andy's statements imply an identification of his own goals with his parent's wishes and a desire to anticipate them, somewhat independent of sanctions.

To summarize, we have mentioned the following "cognitive" characteristics of moral definitions at our second level:

(a) Moral stereotyping. Definition of the good in terms of kinds of persons and a definition of persons and roles in terms of moral virtues.
(b) Intentionalism. Judgments of moral worth based on intentions.
(c) Positive, active and empathic moral definition. Duty and moral goodness defined in terms going beyond mere obedience to an actual service to other persons or institutions, or to a concern about the feelings of others.

On the motivational side we have mentioned:

(d) Sensitivity to and self-guidance by anticipated approval or disapproval.
(e) Identification with authority and its goals.

All of these characteristics imply that moral judgments at this level are based on *role-taking,* on taking the perspective of the other person with legitimate *expectations* in the situation, as these expectations form part of a *moral order*.

For children dominantly Type 3, this order and its associated role-taking is mainly based on "natural" or familistic types of affection and sym-pathy, as our examples have suggested. For children Type 4, the moral order is seen as a matter of rules; and role-taking is based on "justice," on regard for the rights and expectations of both rule-enforcers and other rule-obeyers. The distinction between Type 3 and Type 4 styles of role-taking in moral judgment may be illustrated by two explanations as to the wrong of stealing from a store. Carol (13, I.Q. 108, lower-middle class, Type 3) says:

> The person who owns that store would think you didn't come from a good family, people would think you came from a family that didn't care about what you did.

James (13, I.Q. 111, lower-middle class, Type 4) says:

You'd be mad, too, if you worked for something and someone just came along and stole it.

Both Carol and James define the wrong of stealing by putting themselves in the role of the victim. James, however, expresses the "moral indignation" of the victim, his sense that the rights of a community member have been violated, rather than expressing merely the owner's disapproval of the thief as a bad and unloved person. In both, Type 3 and Type 4, regard for rules is based upon regard for an organized social order. For Type 3, this order is defined primarily by the relations of good or "natural" selves; for Type 4 it is rather defined by rights, assigned duties, and rules.

Moral Orientation at the Third Developmental Level

It is often assumed by psychologists that moral conflicts are conflicts between community standards and egoistic impulses. If this were true, it seems likely that the Type 3 and 4 moral orientations would persist throughout life. The story situations we used, however, placed in conflict two standards or values simultaneously accepted by large portions of the community. Many of the children at stages 3 and 4 went to great lengths to redefine our situations in such a way as to deny the existence of such conflicts between accepted norms, no matter how glaringly this conflict was presented. Both types of children took the role of the authority figure in defining right and wrong, tending to insist that the authority figure would adjust the rule in the interests of the various individuals involved.

In contrast, children of Types 5 and 6 accept the possibility of conflict between norms, and they attempt something like a "rational" decision between conflicting norms. This is most clear in our Type 6 children who attempt to choose in terms of moral principles rather than moral rules. Conventional examples of moral principles are the Golden Rule, the utilitarian principle (the greatest good for the greatest number) and Kant's categorical imperative. A moral principle is an obligatory or ideal rule of choice between legitimate alternatives, rather than a concrete prescription of action (*Dewey and Tufts,* 1936; *Kohlberg,* 1958). Philosophically such principles are designed to abstract the basic element that exists in various concrete rules, and to form an axiomatic basis for justifying or formulating concrete rules.[5] Moral principles, of course, are not legally or socially prescribed or sanctioned, they are social ideals rather than social realities.

An example of the use of the utilitarian maxim as a moral principle is provided by Tony (age 16, I.Q. 115, upper-middle class). He is replying to a situation involving a choice of leaving or staying at a civilian air-defense post after a heavy bombing raid may have endangered one's family:

[5] It is historically true that all philosophic formulations of moral principles, such as those just mentioned, are variations of a basic prescription to take the role of all others involved in the moral situations.

> If he leaves, he is putting the safety of the few over the safety of many. I don't think it matters that it's his loved ones, because people in the burning buildings are someone's loved ones too. Even though maybe he'd be miserable the rest of his life, he shouldn't put the few over the many.

Tony says that leaving the post is wrong, not because of the actual consequences, but because he evaluated the situation wrongly, and "put the few over the many." This is not merely a matter of utilitarian economics but of the requirement of justice that all lives be treated as of equal value.

Moral principles are principles of "conscience," and Type 6 children tend to define moral decisions in these terms. When Type 6 children are asked "What is conscience?", they tend to answer that conscience is a choosing and self-judging function, rather than a feeling of guilt or dread.

A more easily attained "rationality" in moral choice than that of Type 6 is embodied in the Type 5 orientation of social contract legalism. Type 5 defines right and wrong in terms of legal or institutional rules which are seen as having a rational basis, rather than as being morally sacred. Laws are seen as maximizing social utility or welfare, or as being necessary for institutional functioning. It is recognized that laws are in a sense arbitrary, that there are many possible laws and that the laws are sometimes unjust. Nevertheless, the law is in general the criterion of right because of the need for agreement.

While Type 5 relies heavily on the law for definitions of right and wrong, it recognizes the possibility of conflict between what is rationally "right" for the individual actor, and what is legally or rationally right for the society. George (16, upper-middle class, I.Q. 118) gives a fairly typical response to the questions as to whether the husband was wrong to steal the drug for his dying wife:

> I don't think so, since it says the druggist had a right to set the price since he discovered it. I can't say he'd actually be right; I suppose anyone would do it for his wife though. He'd prefer to go to jail than have his wife die. In my eyes he'd have just cause to do it, but in the law's eyes he'd be wrong. I can't say more than that as to whether it was right or not.
> (Should the judge punish the husband if he stole the drug?)
> It's the judge's duty to the law to send him to jail, no matter what the circumstances. The laws are made by the people and the judge is elected on the basis that he's agreed to carry out the law.

George's belief is that the judge must punish even though the judge may not think the act is wrong. This is quite consistent with his belief that the act was individually "just," but legally wrong. It reflects a typical distinction made at this level between individual person and social role, a distinction which contrasts with the earlier fusion of person and role into moral stereotypes. The judge's role is seen as a defined position with a set of agreed-upon rules which the role-occupant contractually accepts on entering office. At the level of definition of role-obligation, then, contract replaces earlier notions of helping the role-partner, just as legality replaces respect for social authority in defining more general norms.

All these aspects of a Type 5 orientation seem to be, in part, reactions to a cognitive advance in social concepts to what *Inhelder* and *Piaget* (1958) describe as the level of formal operations. Such a cognitive advance permits a view of normative judgment as deriving from a formal system derived from a set of agreed-upon assumptions. Any given set of norms or roles is then seen as one of many possibilities, so that the major requirement of normative definition becomes that of clarity and consistency.

Implications of the Stages for Conceptions of the Moralization Process

We may now briefly consider some of the implications of our stages for conceptions of the process and direction of moral development. Our age trends indicate that large groups of moral concepts and ways of thought only attain meaning at successively advanced ages and require the extensive background of social experience and cognitive growth represented by the age factor. How is this finding to be interpreted?

From the internalization view of the moralization process, these age changes in modes of moral thought would be interpreted as successive acquisitions or internalizations of cultural moral concepts. Our six types of thought would represent six patterns of verbal morality in the adult culture which are successively absorbed as the child grows more verbally sophisticated.

In contrast, we have advocated the developmental interpretation that these types of thought represent structures emerging from the interaction of the child with his social environment, rather than directly reflecting external structures given by the child's culture. Awareness of the basic prohibitions and commands of the culture, as well as some behavioral "internalization" of them, exists from the first of our stages and does not define their succession. Movement from stage to stage represents rather the way in which these prohibitions, as well as much wider aspects of the social structure, are taken up into the child's organization of a moral order. This order may be based upon power and external compulsion (Type 1), upon a system of exchanges and need satisfactions (Type 2), upon the maintenance of legitimate expectations (Types 3 and 4), or upon the maintenance of legitimate expectations (Type 3 and 4), or upon ideals or general logical principles of social organization (Types 5 and 6). While these successive bases of a moral order do spring from the child's awareness of the external social world, they also represent active processes of organizing or ordering this world.

We have cited two major results from our quantitative analyses which support this developmental interpretation. The first result was the approximation of the matrix of type intercorrelations to a quasi-simplex form.

This suggested that individual development through the types of moral thought proceeded stepwise through an invariant sequence. If our moral types form an invariant sequence, acquisition of a higher type is not likely to be a direct learning of content taught by cultural agents, but is rather a restructuring of preceding types of thought. This interpretation is strengthened by the trend toward negative correlations between the higher and lower types of thought. Such negative relations suggest that higher modes of thought replace or inhibit lower modes of thought rather than being added to them. This in turn suggests that higher types of thought are reorganizations of preceding types of thought.

More strongly than the quantitative data, we believe that the qualitative data and interpretations contained in our stage descriptions makes the notion of developmental transformations in moral thought plausible and meaningful. We have described characteristics of the types which suggest that each type is qualitatively different than previous types. Such qualitative differences would not be expected were development simply a reflection of greater knowledge of, and conformity to, the culture. We have also attempted a logical analysis of the characteristics of the types which allows us to see each type as a conceptual bridge between earlier and later types.

The developmental conception of the moralization process suggested by our analysis of age changes has some definite further implications. Implications as to relations of the development of moral thought to social environmental factors on the one hand, and to the development of moral conduct on the other, will be considered in the sequel to this paper.

Summary

The paper presents an overview of the author's findings with regard to a sequence of moral development. It is based on empirical data obtained mainly from boys aged 10, 13, and 16 in lengthy free interviews around hypothetical moral dilemmas. Ideal-typological procedures led to the construction of six types of moral thought, designed to form a developmental hierarchy. The first two types parallel *Piaget's* heteronomous and autonomous moral stages, but various findings fail to support *Piaget's* view that these stages are derived from heteronomous or mutual respect.

More mature modes of thought (Types 4–6) increased from age 10 through 16, less mature modes (Types 1–2) decreased with age. Data were analyzed with regard to the question of sequence, e.g., to the hypothesis that attainment of each type of thought is the prerequisite to attainment of the next higher type. A quasi-simplex pattern of intercorrelations supported this hypothesis.

Such evidence of developmental sequence in moral attitudes and concepts is believed to be of great importance for conceptions of the process of moralization. It indicates the inadequacy of conceptions of moralization as a process of simple internalization of external cultural rules, through verbal teaching, punishment, or identification. In contrast, the evidence suggests the existence of a series of internally patterned or organized transformations of social concepts and attitudes, transformations which constitute a developmental process.

References

BALDWIN, J. M. *Social and ethical interpretations in mental development*. New York: Macmillan, 1906.

DEWEY, J., & TUFTS, J. *Ethics*. New York: Holt, 1932.

DURKHEIM, E. *Sociology and philosophy*. Glencoe, Illinois: Free Press, 1953. Originally published 1906.

FREUD, S. *Group psychology and the analysis of the ego*. New York: Liveright, 1949. Originally published 1922.

GUTTMAN, L. The basis for scalogram analysis. In Stoufer, S. A., et al., *Measurement and prediction*. Princeton: Princeton University Press, 1950. Pp. 60–90; in Lazarsfeld, P. (Ed.), *Mathematical thinking in the social sciences*. Glencoe: Free Press, 1954.

INHELDER, B., & PIAGET, J. *The growth of logical thinking*. New York: Basic Books, 1958.

KOHLBERG, L. The development of modes of moral thinking and choice in the years 10 to 16; unpublished doctoral dissertation, Chicago (1958).

————. Moral development and identification; in Stevenson, H. (Ed.), *Child psychology, 1963*. Yearbook of Nat. Soc. for the Study of Education. Chicago: University of Chicago Press, 1963.

McDOUGALL, W. *An introduction to social psychology*. London: Methuen, 1905.

PARSONS, T. The superego and the theory of social systems. In Bell, N., & Vogel, E. (Eds.), *A modern introduction to the family*. Glencoe: Free Press, 1960.

PIAGET, J. *The moral judgment of the child*. Glencoe: Free Press, 1948. Originally published 1932.

SCHUESSLER, K., & STRAUSS, A. L. A study of concept learning by scale analysis. *Amer. Soc. Rev.*, 1950, *15*, 752–762.

WOHLWILL, J. A study of the development of the number concept by scalogram analysis. *J. Genet. Psychol.*, 1960, *97*, 345–377.

Section Five
COGNITIVE AND EDUCATIONAL PSYCHOLOGY

It is really very difficult to convey, with four readings, anything of the full scope of theoretical and research issues that are prominent today in cognitive and educational psychology. Even a larger number of articles would not really do justice to these dynamic, rapidly changing and growing fields. All that one can do here is suggest a few of the major trends in these fields and hint at where things may be going in the future. Crystal-ball gazing, however, particularly in science, is always hazardous and the ideas offered here are, at most, tentative.

In many ways cognitive psychology seems to be replacing the "learning" psychology that for so long dominated the scene in American psychology. Interest in animal learning, qua learning, is diminishing as human learning, memory, and cognitive functioning generally become major foci of research. As a result of the amout of work currently being carried out in the field of cognitive psychology, we can expect new conceptualizations of relevant issues and breakthroughs in research and methodology.

Nowhere is the evidence of rapid growth and change in the field more evident than in the domain of psycholinguistics. Our ways of thinking about language acquisition, about the relations between language and thought, and about the symbolic dimension of language have changed markedly in less than a decade. Our recognition that even young children's speech follows some grammatical rules has raised, in new forms, the old questions about nature and nurture or about maturation and experience. Some of the challenging, exciting, and important problems in psychology today are to be found in interface between the development of language and cognition. The Shenker and Houston articles reprinted in this section deal with quite different issues in the field of psycholinguistics.

Another area that has become equally important, with respect to both research and practical application, concerns the role of genetics in human behavior. The extreme environmentalism of psychology that once dominated the field, is no longer so prevalent, and most psychologists recognize that genetic endowment does make a difference. Given that psychologists today are more accepting of the dynamic role genetics plays in behavior, the demonstration and explanation of these effects are still fairly rough and ready. The article by Scarr-Salapatek, however, suggests a new level of sophistication both in theory and in research methodology in this very difficult field. interpersonal dimensions of the classroom are beginning to receive the research

Finally, in the field of educational psychology, the social and interpersonal dimensions of the classroom are beginning to receive the research and theoretical attention they have so badly needed. The child in the classroom, after all, is involved in a dynamic group process that undoubtedly affects his success as a learner. Teachers, as group leaders, have an impact over and above any influence as skilled educational practitioners. The "atmosphere" of the classroom in particular, as well as that of the school in general, plays an important part in the learning process and in how children feel about themselves and about their work. In the article by Harvey *et al.*, the atmosphere effects created by the teacher's personality are shown to be significantly related to the academic achievement and interpersonal behavior of children.

Cognitive psychology (particularly psycholinguistics), the genetic component of behavior and personality, and the social components in classroom behavior appear to this psychologist at least, to be themes and problems that will continue to be major preoccupations of many psychologists in the 1970's.

David Elkind

*The following material serves as an introduction to Noam Chomsky—
the man and his ideas—much of it in his own words. Chomsky has created something of a revolution in linguistics and has been a major impetus to the establishment of the new discipline of psycholinguistics. Central to his theory is that there
exists a "universal grammar" governing all languages which supports his contention that the language capacity is innate.*

Noam Chomsky's View of Linguistics as a Branch of Psychology

Israel Shenker

As a boy of nine, in 1938, Noam Chomsky used to sit in the front
row of the Hebrew class at Mikveh Israel, in Philadelphia, paying little attention to the teacher.

He was not disrespectful, but he had covered the ground long
before, at home, with his parents. His mother was the teacher in this class,
and his father was the school's principal. I was a backward classmate, aged
thirteen.

As a young boy, Chomsky used to proofread his father's work
on medieval Hebrew grammar. It was only natural—one might say almost
genetically fated—that he became interested in linguistics. Since he was no
less interested in man's place in the world, he almost quit the University of
Pennsylvania as a sophomore to go to Palestine and live on a kibbutz (he
knew Hebrew and was studying Arabic).

If he happens to be the most famous professor of linguistics in
the world, that is in part because his work in the field has been original, even
revolutionary. It is also because of his second passion—an overpowering interest in politics and recent history. He is a ranking theorist and polemicist
of the New Left, a determined opponent of the Vietnam war. This less scholarly eminence followed closely upon publication of an article, in *The New
York Review of Books* in 1967, that dealt with the political responsibility of
American intellectuals. In 1969 his political essays were published in *American
Power and the New Mandarins*. He is constantly importuned for articles,
statements, speeches—and his work is an extraordinary amalgam of the
polemical (Chomsky on Songmy) and the esoteric (Chomsky on the Algebraic
Theory of Context-Free Languages).

At the Massachusetts Institute of Technology, where he is the
Ferrari P. Ward Professor of Modern Languages and Linguistics, Noam

Source: "Chomsky is difficult to please," "Chomsky is easy to please," "Chomsky is
certain to please" by Israel Shanker is reprinted by permission from *Horizon* (Spring
1971), Vol. XIII, No. 2. © 1971 by American Heritage Publishing Co., Inc.

217

Chomsky could pass as an aging student. His office is unkempt and weary—torn green shades, dusty volumes, a chair in the final stages of disintegration—but he presides with blithe unconcern over such externals, and with intense devotion to what he considers essentials.

One must listen carefully when he speaks, not only because of the complexity of his thought, but because—having mentally reviewed his own reasoning so often—he tends in conversation to omit some intermediate steps. What is more, he speaks very softly.

"Linguistics," he says, "is concerned with the description of a particular language, so its fundamental concept is the knowledge of a language. And a person who knows a language has somehow mastered a system of principles that determine the sound and meaning of infinitely many sentences."

"New sentences often pass between us—but we understand, and this is perfectly normal. What's exotic is repetition of old sentences." There are few examples of simple repetition in ordinary speech. Though there are stereotyped expressions, such as greetings, these are incidentals and do not overwhelm the characteristic inventiveness of speech.

"It's often said that language and other aspects of human behavior involve habit structures. But you can't innovate by habit. The first task of a linguistic is therefore to grasp and characterize what makes innovation—that is, normal usage—possible; what allows us—free of detectable stimuli, external or internal—to speak our minds in an original, appropriate, and coherent way."

The linguist tries to make explicit what the child grasps intuitively, and therefore tries to construct a "generative grammar"—a system of rules and principles that determine the connection of sound and meaning for the indefinitely large number of sentences that constitute a single language.

But the linguist also tries to establish the principles of "universal grammar," which governs all human languages. As Chomsky explains: "Universal grammar tries to specify the constraints and principles which determine what makes a possible system of grammar into a humanly accessible system. It tries to distinguish the essence of human language from arbitrary systems that might be imagined."

But what leads Chomsky to believe there is an essence? He replies: "The best evidence is the very fact that a child acquires knowledge of a language—an astonishing feat which is beyond the capacity of an otherwise intelligent ape." Chomsky holds that language has not evolved from simpler systems in nonhuman organisms. The child acquires and constructs for himself a very specific generative grammar and does so, on the basis of degenerate and limited data, in an extremely short time.

"The data are degenerate in the sense that a good deal of the material that the child hears is not even properly constructed: normal language consists very largely of false starts and fragments and hesitations. But the grammar the child constructs tells him what is a well-formed sentence and how such sentences can be used and understood.

"The child is in a much worse situation than a scientist who experiments and has good data—he is rather like a physicist who can do no experiments but nonetheless tries to construct theories about the world. The child develops a very complex and articulated theory of enormous predictive scope and explanatory power—he takes an incredible inductive leap."

Chomsky suggests that the child brings to this enormously difficult problem "a very rich system of expectations—a very rich innate system that tells him how to interpret data as a possible language." He argues that if a child were initially uninformed as to the nature of the system he has to construct, if his mind were totally plastic—as the behavioral psychologists believe—the acquisition of language would be a miracle. Since he rigorously refuses to believe in miracles, Chomsky has another explanation. He says that the mind of a child is not plastic, but has intrinsic properties that are the subject of universal grammar.

Chomsky's work in linguistics is a highly complex attempt to fill in the details for the particular grammar of English and for a universal grammar for all possible languages. His work with the grammar of English is much less controversial than are his theories about universal grammar and its significance for a theory of mind and psychology.

What he has attempted to show—in opposition to earlier "structural linguistics" and behavioral psychology and indeed the whole tradition of empiricism in psychology—is that the principles of a grammar are deep and abstract, and that only an organism initially (i.e., at birth) informed of the nature of these principles (in fact, "preset") could have discovered them in a particular case. Such principles tell us something about the intrinsic nature of the human mind and define one capacity of that mind: the language capacity.

All of this puts Chomsky at odds with an older linguistic tradition that holds there is nothing universal about the form of language, and that the collection of sounds that transmit meaning is arbitrary rather than mind-determined, the result of environment and teaching rather than of natural structure. Though the earlier tradition has accumulated lots of material from particular languages, Chomsky maintains that it fails to ask or answer the really hard questions.

Had such iconoclasm been discussed within the confines of a linguistic discipline, it would have created much less fuss. Chomsky's views have aroused academicians because of his repeated intimations of generality—the suggestion that his approach is the right one for other aspects of human behavior, such as ethics, psychology, aesthetics, sociology, and logic.

Thus he says: "Universal grammar is a hypothesis about the essential nature of man—what it means to be a human being, what psychology is about. It tells you it's hopeless, or at best marginal, to try to explain anything about humans in terms of habit formation, or stimulus and response, or associations, or the shaping of behavior by environment. It tells us that we don't acquire knowledge the way empiricists think we do—through experience by association of stimuli, stimulus-response connections, and training. Language is not a matter of know-how established by habit.

"If you want to find out what it means to be a human being, you have to examine free creation within a system of rules, acquisition of knowledge within the framework of restrictive conditions imposed by the mind. The human mind is thus a kind of schematism, or framework, within which learning and behavior take place. Linguistic competence—knowledge of a language —is an abstract system, a generative grammar, consisting of rules or constraints that determine the form and meaning of an infinite number of sentences."

To show what he means by constraints—or innate principles—Chomsky proposes two simple sentences:

(1) Mary believed (that John had read *the book*).
(2) Mary believed (the claim that John had read *the book*).

The general rule for forming questions is to take the italicized phrase, replace *the book* by *what book,* put it in front of the whole sentence (while making some adjustments of the main verb, i.e., replacing "believed" with "did . . . believe"). This works for (1) and gives us: what book did Mary believe that John had read? But it does not work for (2), since it gives us: what book did Mary believe the claim that John had read?

"I wouldn't say," explains Chomsky, "that the 'corresponding question' in the second case is 'What book did Mary claim that John had read?' Rather, that is the question corresponding, by the rule just mentioned, to 'Mary claimed that John had read the book.' "

"In fact, there is no question corresponding to (2). The problem is, how do we know this: how do we know that the simple rule just stated, which works for (1), doesn't generalize to (2)?

"The answer is that the italicized phrase, which is a noun phrase, appears within the parenthesized noun phrase in (2), but not within a larger noun phrase in (1)—rather, there the parenthesized phrase is a sentence. But the parenthesized element in (2) is just an extension of the noun phrase 'the claim.'

"There is a general principle that a noun phrase cannot be extracted from another, larger noun phrase containing it. Therefore the italicized phrase cannot be extracted from the parenthesized phrase in (2), but it can be in (1)."

Having said all this, Chomsky concludes: "The example demonstrates two important facts. First, in producing and understanding sentences we make use of abstract mental representations, such as the one indicated by the parenthesization in (1) and (2)—with the further information that the parentheses in (1) bound a sentencelike element and in (2) a noun phrase. Second, we operate with general principles; for example, you can't extract a noun phrase from within a larger noun phrase."

Retracing his argument, Chomsky is intent on showing that there is no question corresponding to (2). Thus, the sentence "What book did Mary believe the claim that John had read?" is one that we don't accept; indeed, it does not even occur to our mind to say it. In Chomsky's view this is evidence that there are general principles that guide us—though we may be unaware of their guidance.

(Indeed, when Chomsky said the sentence aloud, I *heard* it as "What book did Mary believe that John had read?" He found this further corroboration for his argument, pointing out that my mind had kept me from repeating the sentence as it was uttered. My sixteen-year-old son, who was with us, told me afterward that Chomsky himself had said the sentence as I reproduced it; I therefore suspected that Chomsky's mind had not allowed *him* to say it as he wished. Since there was no neutral observer present, we will all have to remain in the dark. But the mistake *was* made, and it is characteristic of the principle.)

The language learned has no *evidence* for any such general principle. It is unimaginable that every speaker of English has been explicitly taught that he can't form a question from (2), or explicitly taught the general principle that determines this fact, or explicitly given sufficient information to demonstrate this general principle. Rather, he just hears such sentences as (1) and (2) and lots of others and develops a knowledge of language that is governed by these general principles, which are an innate part of the structure we impose on experience.

The acquisition of knowledge is therefore a creative act by which we impose on data a structure of principles. That structure determines what we come to know on the basis of those principles. We come to know that one collection of consecutive words is a sentence and another is not.

The principles are a skeleton, and the degenerate data of language is flesh concealing the skeleton. English and all other languages have the same skeleton, Chomsky and his followers argue, and the different varieties of flesh hang where the skeleton allows them to hang, not at random.

In universal grammar the skeletal principles are unconscious, and often there seems no way to pry them into consciousness. Chomsky maintains, indeed, that the greatest defect of classical philosophy is its assumption that the mind's properties and content are accessible to introspection. This may sound obscurantist; Chomsky argues that it is realistic.

He returns to the blackboard. "When you hear a sentence you hear a noise," Chomsky notes, picking up a piece of chalk, "and when you look at the sentence you see words. But you know more."

To clarify this point, he writes down three additional collections of words that we call sentences:

"John is difficult to please."
"John is easy to please."
"John is certain to please."

In the first two sentences John is the person being pleased; in the third, John does the pleasing. The surface structure thus does not always reflect the deep structure—which relates not to the sound but to the meaning. Our knowledge of the difference is unconscious and a part of the structure of the mind, Chomsky says.

"One is not merely interested in the data of English, but in what it tells us about the structure of the mind. The mind is arranged in terms of principles of this kind—basic rules which determine systems of grammatical relations and the way to organize these deep structures into surface structures. How to determine the nature of these grammatical relations is a problem of science—difficult but not impossible."

Chomsky writes another sentence on the blackboard:

"The man will win."

The corresponding question is: "Will the man win?"

Then he writes: "The man who will arrive at six will win."

The corresponding question is: "Will the man who will arrive at six win?"

"How do I know that I take the second 'will' to form the question?" asks Chomsky, turning to his audience of two. "How do I know the question should not be formed by taking out the first 'will' and using it as the first word of the question: 'Will the man who arrive at six will win?' "

To answer his own questions, he proposed two possible formulations of the rule: first, take the left-most occurrence of "will," and put it at the head of the sentence; and second, take the occurrence of "will" that functions as "main verb" following the initial noun phrase of the sentence and invert it.

"Both rules give the same result in the case of the simpler sentences," he notes. "They give different results in the case of the longer sentence. The first, of course, gives the wrong result. But the first is by far the simpler rule. Suppose, say, you had a computer that was to perform these operations. To perform operation one, the computer would simply have to scan the sentence from left to right until it came across an occurrence of 'will,' which it would then prepose. To perform operation two, the computer would have to analyze the syntactic structure of the sentence, determining that 'the man who will arrive at six' is the noun phrase subject and 'will' is the main verbal element."

"Operation one is 'structure-independent'—it cares only about the actual content of the sentence to which it applies and doesn't care at all about its abstract structure. Operation two is 'structure-dependent'—it cares about the abstract structure of the sentence, as well as about its actual content. Though structure-dependent operations are more complex and abstract, languages appear to have only operations of this sort."

Nobody who has spoken English has ever made the mistake of opting for the first rule instead of the second, he says. "And why not? Why does our mind use a difficult rule instead of a simple one, and why does the rule apply in every language?"

His answer is that the structure of the mind tells us which operations are permissible and which are not.

In any language there are things we learn. In English, for example, we learn that a rational featherless biped is "man," and in French we learn to call this animal "*homme.*" But there are things we know without learning—such as the rule illustrated in the questions about the man who will (or will not) arrive at six.

The underlying pattern of the mind even provides us with a guide to pronunciation. If we kept only to the phonetic surface form, we could not understand why, for example, we should expect a full vowel in "rel*a*xation," and a reduced vowel in "dem*o*nstration," in the italicized position. In other related forms both these vowels are full rather than reduced: compare "rel*á*x," and "dem*ó*nstrative." In fact, as the examples "rel*á*x" and "dem*ó*nstrative" indicate, the vowels are full when they receive the main stress in the word. But in "rel*a*xátion" and "dem*o*nstrátion," the italicized vowel is unstressed in both cases, yet it is full in the first case and reduced in the second.

The reason is that "rel*a*xátion" is derived from the underlying form "rel*á*x" and "dem*o*nstrátion" is derived from the underlying form "dém*o*nstrate," and in these underlying forms the italicized vowel of "rel*á*x" is stressed, hence full, while the italicized vowel of "dém*o*nstrate" is unstressed, hence weak. In "rel*a*xátion" and "dem*o*nstrátion" the italicized vowel is unstressed in both cases, but in speaking and hearing these words, we make use of the abstract mental representation of the underlying form, with its stress pattern and consequent choice of full or reduced vowel, and in this way we determine the stress and vowel quality of the words "relaxation" and "demonstration" themselves. It turns out, then, that we hear and speak many words as if we had in mind their underlying forms.

There are probably similar things to be said about meaning, Chomsky suggests, adding, however: "We have ways for describing sounds, but we still don't have good ways for describing meaning."

"Everybody thinks his own field is the most important," Chomsky says smilingly. "Linguistics, however, does tell us interesting things about the nature of human nature, about the human mind and some of the conditions of human creativity and free thought and expression. It tells us how humans speak and understand and think, though it has not yet managed to relate its discoveries to physiological mechanisms or interpret thought in terms of 'physical causes.'"

"One might consider linguistics as a branch of psychology," Chomsky adds. "Take psychology generally. As a human being you have friends and acquaintances and have made some assessment about them, you have a theory about them, even if unconscious, about how they will act. An important part of psychology ought to be to state the theories and discover how you arrived at them. To do so, psychology should try to discover those intrinsic properties of the mind that lead us to interpret the insignificant data of experience to form rich conclusions about what people are like. I think we'd then perhaps discover something like a universal grammar not of language but of human nature."

"Psychology should thus ask: what is it we learn? Then it should ask: what is the universal system of constraints that made possible this learning? Psychology has suffered from the fact that it lacked the concept of 'what is known,' 'what is learned.' Behaviorists talk only about relations between stimulus and response. They offer no way to account for the fact that we speak intelligibly. Because of that conceptual gap, they haven't made progress."

Chomsky indeed finds it significant that we speak nowadays of "behavioral science," not of "science of the mind." It is as though, he suggests, we called natural science "the science of meter readings."

"Consider the acquisition of scientific knowledge," he says. "I'd assume there are some rather general conditions. I think that science arises when the structure of the world and the structure of the mind somehow fit together. Where the real nature of the world is such that it doesn't mesh with the structure of our mind, we don't have science."

"In science we sense intuitively that sometimes we have scientific knowledge and sometimes only intellectual technology. The difference can't be explained in terms of prediction. It has to do with comprehension, and psychology might attempt to specify the difference between scientific understanding and technology. The explanation would have to grow out of the concept of mind, and would be related to the kinds of intellectual structures our mind can produce."

Characteristically, Chomsky had to interrupt our conversation to attend a meeting of dissident professors at M.I.T. His colleague Morris Halle —who collaborated with Chomsky on the enormously difficult and technical book *The Sound Pattern of English*—replaced him on the dilapidated chair.

"What Chomsky has done is invent a kind of formal structure in terms of which you record your observations," said Professor Halle. "When Mendeleev invented the Periodic Table he told people to arrange chemical elements in a particular way. People said: 'Why shouldn't we do it alphabetically?' Mendeleev said the reason you should do it this way is because you will discover other things by doing this."

"One of the striking things was that they found holes in the table and errors in weights of certain elements—errors found in terms of his structure. They could then correct the errors, discover the reasons for them, and hunt for missing elements.

"This is what has happened in linguistics. There's a formal structure in terms of which facts are organized, and this structure allows you to organize additional facts.

"*Finding* facts is no problem. You can easily discover that the word 'America' is stressed on the second syllable. But that fact is interesting only if it tells you something about structure. What you're trying to understand in chemistry is the nature of matter, and what you're trying to understand in linguistics is the nature of language.

"Just as you can find out lots of facts about chemical elements, the interesting question is how they're related, what do they mean, and this comes only when you invent a theory. It tells you about things you have never seen.

"In chemistry you discover the elements you didn't know. In language the things you discover are things you know—unconsciously. If what we're describing is a realistic description of language, the man on the street must 'know' how to use the machinery even if he is not conscious of its existence.

"He uses linguistic transformations without ever learning that such things exist. He doesn't learn that there are other things called phonemes, though he uses them all the time in speech. How does he manage to speak so fluently while he understands so poorly? Chomsky's answer is that this ability depends on an innate structure."

Halle, like Chomsky, reaches across to psychology to make the meaning clearer. A cat presumably sees a chair, yet a cat doesn't learn intellectually. How does the cat discover that there are objects such as chairs or people or other cats? The only reasonable explanation, says Halle (following Chomsky), is that this knowledge of objects is built in.

Analogously, pursues Halle, part of the genetic equipment of man is the ability to perform the activity called language use. "We've studied hundreds of languages," Halle notes. "We find differences in them, of course. But the deep properties, like transformations and phonemes, are in all languages."

"Until Chomsky came along, the dominant school in linguistics was structural. The idea was that you could find out relevant facts in language by comparing almost identical cases. To show the difference between *t* and *p,* for example, you might offer 'tick' and 'pick.' The idea was that differences in sound that don't signal differences of meaning don't count, and you can ignore them. But our idea is that the important thing is for linguistics not simply to accumulate facts, which you can cherish as an antiquarian would, but to develop theoretical explanations for evidence. Grammar used to be 'natural history' and we are trying to make it 'natural science.'

"Just as chemistry tells you what structure a possible element must have, an element that we have seen as well as one yet to be discovered, linguistic theory defines a possible language, indeed every possible language. It thus tells you about thought, about behavior, about what it means to be a human being making choices through the filter of the mind."

Professor Halle waved one hand as though he wanted to seize the essence of thought within his fist and present it to me. "The use of language is certainly the most complicated intellectual process accessible to every man of normal intelligence," he said, "so it stands to reason that it may lead to an understanding of other intellectual processes, for example the ability to reason and to make computations."

"The most obvious field in which we can expect advances is psychology, and some people are already trying to apply the methods of linguistics in studying myths. Unfortunately, every field demands a different approach, not slavish transfer of a method that happens to work elsewhere. The example of the invention of particular methods to solve linguistic problems should spur scientists in other fields to devise methods applicable to their own problems."

Chomsky has no way of knowing how successful these efforts will be, and indeed, he has no desire to be a prophet. These days it is difficult enough merely to be a revolutionary.

It is probably fair to say that physical science progresses by a series of successive approximations to the true state of affairs in nature. Social science progresses in the same manner, and ideas which seemed reasonable—in view of evidence available at the time—had to be given up and replaced as new data was acquired. A clear example of this successive-approximations approach to the real state of affairs in social science is provided by the evolution of our ideas about the language of disadvantaged children. In her article, Susan Houston details some of the history of our changing conceptions about the language of children who come from "disadvantaged" environments.

A Reexamination of Some Assumptions About the Language of the Disadvantaged Child

Susan H. Houston

Although research on the language of the disadvantaged child is now receiving much impetus, few extant studies have been helpful to the teacher. Linguistic science has only recently become concerned with this topic; thus, most studies have been pursued without the requisite linguistic and sociolinguistic base. As a result, the field has developed a body of misconception and mythology centering around the notion of linguistic deprivation, and from this incorrect concept no useful correction programs can stem. The purpose of this article is to reexamine widely held misconceptions about disadvantaged-child language in light of modern linguistic and psycholinguistic advances.

A major concern of modern American education is the coexistence within our schools of several different child populations. Many factors have interacted to produce this situation, including increased geographic mobility and progress in school integration. However, advances in educational theory and practice and in the development of teaching materials have not kept pace with the rate of change in school populations. Most educators now recognize this situation as the cause of many serious problems.

Probably nowhere is the crisis so acute as in the area of language arts and communications skills programs, where rapid theoretical advancements in linguistic science over the last 12 years would have hastened the obsolescence of extant materials even without the added difficulties of adapting the materials to speakers of seemingly quite divergent variants of English. It is not surprising that teachers of such courses feel inadequate in the face of this situation (Strom 1965, p. 41). Unfortunately, these teachers can find few answers,

Source: Reprinted by permission from *Child Development,* December 1970, *41,* 947–963. Copyright © 1970 by The Society for Research in Child Development, Inc.

algorithmic or heuristic, in the current literature on the language of disadvantaged or minority children. In fact, the literature is rarely able even to define
the problems cogently enough that solutions to them might be proposed.

This lack of analytical viewpoint has resulted chiefly from the disciplinary origins of researches on disadvantaged and minority language variants. Such researches have typically been carried out by linguists on the one
hand and by educators and other social scientists on the other. Linguistic
attacks on the subject have been either dialect-atlas-type studies or, more recently, technical descriptions of certain specific features of the target language
forms. Neither type of study is likely to provide information directly helpful to
teachers attempting to deal with ongoing language-contact situations for the
following reasons. The dialect atlas is concerned with amassing data, typically
lexical and non-systematic phonological, bearing on regional dialect-boundary
determination. It tends to ignore the social, situational, and other variations
often of greatest relevance to educators. The descriptive linguistic study is
usually based on principles and techniques still unfamiliar to the majority of
teachers and provides no direct means of applying its results to the classroom,
although it may be of great value to linguistic investigations (an example of
the dialect-atlas study is Kurath and McDavid 1961; an exmple of the linguistic study is Labov 1967).

More important than the new techniques of language description,
however, are the new theories of language acquisition and production which
underlie them. It is these theories which are absent from most social-science-
oriented work on the language of disadvantaged children. Within education
and educational psychology, nearly all such work has been concerned with the
putative problems of linguistic and cognitive deprivation or disability and with
attempts to find means to alleviate or "remediate" such problems. Because
modern linguistic and psycholinguistic theory has not yet filtered through to
these fields, a traditional body of mythology and empirically derived educational philosophy pervades extant research on the so-called disadvantaged
child. It is the purpose of the present paper to reexamine some of the most
widely held assumptions and beliefs about the language and communication of
the disadvantaged child in light of psycho- and sociolinguistic knowledge
gained since the late 1950s, and perhaps to indicate some fruitful directions for
further research efforts based thereon.

Among the most fascinating and significant of recent discoveries in
child development is the realization that the neonatal or newborn infant is
equipped with many capabilities for learning and perception (for not overly
technical summaries of such work, see Kessen 1965; Pines 1966, pp. 169–182;
Vernon 1962, pp. 16–30). A neonatal infant is capable of tracking an object
with his eyes, an activity which presumes some sort of attention mechanism as
well as neuromuscular control of optic processes. A child 1 or 2 months old
can be taught to react differentially to objects. These abilities are apparently
innate, or at least have sizable innate components.

It is in fact the opinion of growing numbers of psychologists that whole areas of behavior formerly considered conditioned or learned are instead supported by large innate or biologically determined components. It should not be thought from this that current psychology or psycholinguistics is totally "hereditarian" or "naticist" in outlook. There is in reality no heredity-environment debate, nor is any important form of human behavior so simple as to be creditable solely to heredity or to environmental factors. Rather, cognitive and surely linguistic development are products of interaction between the two, due both to learning and to what Hebb has termed "psychological maturation" (1966, pp. 157–158).

On the other hand, there is now some evidence supporting the viewpoint that learning may not play quite so important a role in all facets of cognitive development as was formerly thought. One of the chief forms of evidence for this is the apparent universality of certain types of human behavior. Since no two organisms have the same learning environment (including, of course, identical twins) and since, in fact, stimulus input for any two babies selected randomly is likely to be practically incommensurable, the appearance of highly similar or identical developmental patterns across environments is a good indication of the innate nature of the patterns. It can thus be stated that a psychological or a linguistic universal generally implies an innate component, and vice versa. This is important because once it is proposed that the basic set of Gestalt perceptions, for example, is innate, then one can expect them to be present throughout the species, and similarly for other innately determined behavioral or cognitive processes. Although individual development comes about through constant bilateral interaction between innate and noninnate processes, as has been stated, it is still assumed that man as a species possesses a single type of hereditary equipment, so that changes in environmental structure will not prevent the development of behaviors which are not due principally to environmental factors (an obvious example is bipedal gait or walking; see Lenneberg 1964).

In particular, it has been accepted during the past few years that language, formerly considered to be learned behavior similar to simple acquired skills (e.g., Mowrer 1960; Osgood 1957; Skinner 1957; Staats and Staats 1964), is instead an endogenously or innately caused construct different from habit structures based on stimulus-response conditioning. One reason for this conclusion is that both the language-acquisition process and the structure of language itself have a number of significant universal features. For instance, it is a universal fact that all children learn language merely by being placed in the environment of the language and that they do not need any special training or conditioning whatever to achieve this (e.g., Chomsky 1959; Langacker 1967, pp. 13–16; Lenneberg 1967, pp. 125, 139; McNeill 1966a). Further, all children appear to learn language in about the same length of time, namely, from 4 to 6 years. There is some evidence (e.g., Slobin 1966) that relatively infrequent constructions in some languages may take longer to master, but this is of little importance when compared with the startling uniformity in language-acquisition stages throughout the world. Given the open-ended variation

in learning environments previously noted and given the lack of directed reinforcement for language or other behavior in children characteristic of many
societies, the argument for a biological basis for language acquisition is convincing. This is especially so since alternative explanations, such as attribution
of language learning to conditioning, have been rather conclusively shown to
be inadequate (e.g., Miller, Galanter, and Pribram 1960, pp. 139–148). It is
now believed by linguists that man has an innate biological capacity for language acquisition, a capacity which has been described as a species-specific
and species-uniform language-acquisition device (McNeill 1966a, 1966b)
which functions uniquely in the language-acquisition process and the operation
of which is constant for all children. Various biological and neurophysiological
correlates of the language-learning process have been discovered, so that this
position is strengthened (Lenneberg 1967, e.g., pp. 142–182).

All these new hypotheses about language have certain important
implications for the study of language acquisition and function among disadvantaged or minority children. It is a common hypothesis among educators, for
instance, that such children may be considered linguistically deprived, presumably because they have not been specifically taught how to speak by their
parents as well as because of other environmental reasons. Clearly, however,
if it is accepted that language learning is a species universal and that it occurs
merely by placing the child in the environment of the language, then this hypothesis is shown to be invalid. That disadvantaged children are not taught
language in the same way as nondisadvantaged, a proposition itself still somewhat in doubt, will not prevent them from acquiring the language of their sur-
roundings, if we assume only that they are not brain damaged or psychotic.
To be sure, lack of reinforcement for linguistic behavior must have an effect
on the young child. Most probably, its effect is to limit the use of language in
nonreinforcing contexts. But since it is now believed that linguistic competence,
or the internalized ability to use and understand language, is separate from
and may develop even without linguistic performance or the ability to speak
(e.g., Chomsky 1967, pp. 397–401; Lenneberg 1962), the limited use of language in certain situations is not evidence of the lack of capacity to handle
language. In other words, linguistic deprivation, in the traditional sense, does
not seem to exist.

A further factor leading to notions of linguistic deprivation is the
concept of the primitive language. This is relevant since some specialists have
argued that, whereas disadvantaged children may have command of a form of
language, the language which they do speak is stunted and erratic, composed,
presumably, of a random amalgam of mistakes and conceptual lacunae
(Bereiter and Englemann 1966). The conclusion from this position is that these
children's language is not adequate for their needs or environment, because of
its sparse vocabulary, simple and inflexible syntax, or other (generally unspecified) deficiency. However, there is no such thing as a primitive language, nor
is there evidence that primitive languages, whatever one wishes to imply by the
term, ever existed (Lenneberg 1964, pp. 587–588). In fact, it is not immedi-

ately clear what a primitive language would be composed of, since the basic structuring principles on which language is founded appear to be universal and are extremely complex. All written records of now-extinct languages, as well as all historical linguistic reconstructions of past linguistic forms, seem to be based on these same structuring principles.

In regard to linguistic variation, it should be noted that language is not correlated with technological sophistication, depth or age of culture, or other anthropological or sociological measures; some societies with unsophisticated technology have incredibly complex languages. Most linguists now assume that languages do not differ greatly in their underlying structures (e.g., Chomsky 1965, p. 118) or in their other formal characteristics, such as, for example, redundancy in the mathematical sense. In other words, all forms of language, taken in the aggregate, are about equally complicated, and furthermore none is produced in random fashion. Whereas child language always differs qualitatively as well as quantitatively from adult language, no childhood stage of any language is appreciably simpler or more randomized than the corresponding stage of any other language. Thus, for example, all 6-year-old children seem to have similar linguistic proficiency, a fact not surprising in light of the overwhelming preponderance of evidence for a sizable innate component in language development. It has been indicated previously that language-acquisition stages seem invariant; it should be additionally noted that all children have rules by which they produce their language at each stage of the acquisition process, irrespective of the particular language or form of language they are acquiring (Brown and Fraser 1964, p. 45; Menyuk 1969; Miller and Ervin 1964). As Chomsky (1968) has proposed, this, too, may be a fact about the structuring of the human mind.

Several conclusions may be drawn from even this brief discussion of the language-acquisition process. In particular, it will be seen that modern linguistic and psycholinguistic knowledge casts serious doubts on many standard comments about the language development of the disadvantaged child. It may be helpful to the reader for us to consider individually some of these frequently appearing notions and to comment upon them based upon what has been reviewed above and other relevant material.

1. *The language of the disadvantaged child is deficient.*—Different approaches are needed to this postulate, depending on the nature of the deficiency intended. I have already discussed the invalidity of suggesting that the language of disadvantaged children is generally primitive and simple, any more than that of other children. However, a number of more specific statements along the same lines have also gained currency of late. For example, Bernstein (1961) and others have commented upon the apparent great limitations of disadvantaged and minority children's language, the lack of willingness or perhaps ability of these children to use language as easily or as often as nondisadvantaged children, and the peculiar characteristics of the language they do use. Among relevant characteristics frequently cited are short utterance length, one-word replies to questions, limited expressed affect (e.g., Blank and Solomon

1968, p. 379), strange intonational and paralinguistics features, and similar manifestations. Such a set of characteristics is said to demonstrate either that language use somehow does not come naturally to these children, who prefer to express themselves in other ways, or that their language remains fixed at an early stage and so becomes inappropriate to their environments as they become older.

In fact, all these observations do have some basis. They are, however, apparently all due to the occurrence in disadvantaged language of a single phenomenon, that which we term "register" (Houston 1969a, 1969b). A register consists of a range of styles of language which have in common their appropriateness to a given situation or environment. Register is a broader concept than style, since there may be much stylistic variation within a single register, but it can nevertheless be viewed as one register if there are linguistic and behavioral features common to that one unified situation alone. The concept of register became relevant in a study I conducted (under the auspices of the Southeastern Education Laboratory, a regional lab of the U.S. Office of Education) of Child Black English in rural northern Florida. The children studied had at least two distinct registers, termed by us the School and the Nonschool register, because the first appeared primarily in school settings and with teachers and the second in other settings. However, the School register also was used with all persons perceived by the children as in authority over them or studying them in any way (the author excluded, for various reasons too lengthy to be detailed here) and in formal and constrained situations. A description of either register is a linguistic task of some complexity and is not relevant for our purposes. But one may note that the characteristics of the School register include most of the observations given above as indications of disadvantaged nonfluency, notably foreshortened utterances, simplified syntax, and phonological hypercorrection. It should be added that the content expressed in this register tends to be rather limited and non-revelatory of the children's attitudes, feelings, and ideas.

It is my current opinion, then, that the majority of postulations of linguistic deficiency among speakers of Uneducated English, Black or White, are due to observation of the school register only, since the possession of two or more registers is nearly universal, among such child speakers. Clearly, most investigations and research carried out among these children involve situations in which the school register is almost certain to be used, especially when the children are black and the researcher is both white and unknown to them— and this register does give an impression of nonfluency and strange language use. But it must be borne in mind that this is neither the whole of the children's linguistic performance nor in any way representative of their linguistic competence.

In regard to performance, the Nonschool register presents an entirely different picture from the School register. It is the language which the children use naturally, with friends and family, and in which they express themselves with greatest ease and fluency. To the observer able to elicit the

Nonschool register, as I did in Florida, the natural linguistic creativity and frequent giftedness of the so-called linguistically deprived child become apparent. The children worked with, perhaps because they were quite poor and had little material with which to play, engaged in constant language games, verbal contests, and narrative improvisations far removed from linguistic disability. Moreover, the Nonschool register shows a complete set of the expected syntactic patterns characteristic of children of this age, namely, about 11 years, insofar as these are known (see the works cited by Houston [1969a, 1969b] for technical details). This should come as no surprise, considering the rather minimal syntactic variation characteristic of subforms, geographic or otherwise, of any given language.

As to linguistic competence, it has been pointed out that the internalized ability to comprehend and produce an infinite variety of sentences in one's language is not mirrored isomorphically by linguistic performance. Indeed, it cannot be, since competence is open-ended and performance is finite. That the children of disadvantaged environments are able to understand outside researchers, their teachers, their parents, and each other—often four very different kinds of language—indicates that competence goes far beyond spoken performance, as is the case for all speakers.

The remarks above concerning the syntax of the disadvantaged child bring up another often cited kind of language deficiency, namely, what can be described as an unusually high rate of error or deviation from "standard English" on some or all levels of language (e.g., Blank and Solomon 1968; Dillard 1967; Hurst and Jones 1966). In fact, this notion contains two separate claims: Whereas it is not the case that the language of the disadvantaged child contains mistakes in the most literal sense, that is, departures from his own system of grammatical rules, it may be true that disadvantaged child language does differ considerably from standard text-book English. It has already been pointed out that the first claim cannot be valid, since all forms of all languages are systematic. This is in the nature of a fact rather than a theory still in doubt. The second claim is somewhat more complicated to discuss, however, largely because there is almost no data save an occasional anecdote either to substantiate or disconfirm it. But there do exist some indications which cast doubt on the theory of numerous differences between disadvantaged and nondisadvantaged child language, at least on the syntactic level. One bit of evidence considered relevant by some linguists, among them myself, is that dialects or regional variants of a language tend to differ mainly in phonology. Although deeper underlying differences between dialects do exist, they are fewer in number than the phonological and lexical differences which in fact often define dialect boundaries. Whereas in a strict sense neither disadvantaged nor minority language can be called dialects, nevertheless as variants of a single language they can be expected to differ much in the same way as do dialects. Further, studies such as the one I conducted indicate that nonstandard forms often classed as syntactic deviations might better be treated as phonological. For example, to oversimplify somewhat, one may say either that uneducated Child

Black English lacks regular past tense forms or that it lacks final /t/ and /d/. In my study I observed fewer than a half-dozen main syntactic divergences between the target language and standard English, although these divergences occur frequently in speech. Other differences between the nonstandard and standard variants of language were phonological. This implies no comment about the relative importance of phonological and syntactic differences from educated English, a problem on which almost no data have yet been collected.

2. *The disadvantaged child does not use words properly.*—Several studies, for example, the widely quoted Bereiter and Englemann work (1966, e.g., p. 34), have stated that the disadvantaged child does not use words in the same way as the nondisadvantaged, that the former does not construct sentences from words at all but rather from differently structured units, perhaps larger conceptual groupings. Along with this proposition, it is often remarked that such children tend to omit certain words in their speech, for instance articles and prepositions. The Bereiter and Englemann discussion of this point also adds that, when one has listened to such children for awhile, one may be deceived into thinking that such items are in fact present—due, presumably, to the tendency to interpret language according to customary patterns—whereas the children invariably omit them.

Now, few observers would want to suggest that disadvantaged American children speak something other than English or, in other words, that their language differs enough from the standard to be considered a separate language. This being the case, clearly utterances in the language of the disadvantaged child must be formed the same way as utterances of standard English, whatever this method may be. No language can properly be described as a simple concatenation of words, as was held by linguists prior to the 1950s, since sentences are hierarchically constructed and manifest complicated interrelationships (Chomsky 1959 and many subsequent dates). The important point here is that the fact of hierarchical organization does not vary from language to language, so that it could scarcely be expected to vary within one single language. However disadvantaged children may use words, linearly or otherwise, all children and surely all English-speaking children use them in the same way.

The range of comments illustrated by statement 2 above seems essentially to be caused by unfamiliarity with phonological theory, and in particular with the phonology of the target children. Several phenomena acting together produce the impression described by Bereiter and Englemann and others. First, the language of the disadvantaged black child at least differs considerably from standard White English in its phonological structure. This does not mean that the children keep making mistakes or are unable to pronounce the sounds of English. It does mean, however, that their phonological system is constructed somewhat differently, on one level, from that of the average adult White English speaker. Note that the level on which the differences occur is one of systematic performance, as we term it, rather than competence. This is manifested in the nearly universal ability among disadvantaged black children to comprehend utterances in Educated White English (if they are familiar with the lexicon used, of course). All forms of all languages are produced by regular rules, and this is true on all levels of language. Thus, the children do not eliminate sounds at random but, rather, have a regular and fully describable set of rules by which they pronounce their language. The effect of some of these rules is to eliminate certain sounds, notably final consonants and consonant clusters, /r/ and /l/, and some intervocalic nasals. Others of the rules function in determining the shape of vowels in the children's language; often the children produce vowels which do not occur in the same context in standard English, for instance, Southern Child Black English /flow/ for standard English /flor/ "floor."

Also, English in general shows many so-called Sandhi phenomena, or changes in the phonological shape of morphemes (minimal meaning units) when the morphemes are concatenated or strung together. The Sandhi rules of Child Black English are undoubtedly different from those of standard White English, although the latter has them also. Some of these rules are in effect what is often called elision, as when the final /d/ of the first word in "good morning" is not pronounced. They do not constitute errors, although the appearance of some of these rules seems to strike some listeners as unaesthetic. It is not known whether Child Black English, or any disadvantaged child language, has any greater preponderance of Sandhi rules than standard English. At any rate, since Child Black English does tend to eliminate many final consonants present in standard English, the former often sounds as though it has numerous elisions or omissions of phonological items. This is not equivalent to stating that speakers of this language do not use words or that they use them in an aberrant manner. Their words are simply sometimes shaped differently from the corresponding words in standard English.

Bereiter and Englemann in particular add an interesting note to their discussion when they observe that the listener may sometimes be deceived into believing that he hears some of the omitted items, whether sounds or words. The linguist would say that the reason the listener is led to believe this is that in fact he has heard something, even if it is not the same thing that he would have said in the context. Rarely are items simply left out of Child Black English or other variants of language. They are almost always replaced by something, at least if the items are phonological units. Omission of final consonants, /l/ and /r/, and nasals nearly always leaves something in place of the omitted unit. This something may be a pause, a glide, a lengthening of the preceding vowel segment or syllable, or a combination of these. It is this that the listener hears.

3. *The language of the disadvantaged child does not provide him with an adequate basis for (abstract or other) thinking.*—This assumption also seems to have appeared very frequently and has been stated in a form similar to this by Bernstein (1961), Blank and Solomon (1968, p. 381), and others. It is most commonly presented in connection with programs designed to impart various types of abstract thinking and conceptualization to so-called disad-

vantaged children. The importance of this proposition is great, since it presents the underlying rationale for the majority of programs as well as a leading cause for their frequent failure (for a report on the failure of Operation Head Start, perhaps the best known of programs to aid disadvantaged children, see Westinghouse Learning Corporation 1969).

Evidence for remarks such as statement 3 is sometimes considered to be the children's lack of abstract terminology. This is probably the most usual basis for the notion that disadvantaged children cannot think properly, since deductions about the thought processes of the children seem to be based primarily or entirely on evidence from language. Unfortunately, this tends to render the conclusions invalid for the following reasons.

Although this fact remains largely unrecognized by persons not specializing in language science or psychology, the direction of dependence between language and cognition is still undetermined. However, it is no longer considered possible to extrapolate cognitive patterns directly from specific linguistic patterns, a notion sometimes incorrectly attributed to the 1930–1940 writings of Benjamin Lee Whorf (Whorf 1956). That a language is highly inflecting, for instance, does not necessarily indicate that its speakers are more complex or more energetic than the speakers of an isolating language such as Chinese; that a language contains many consonant clusters or velar fricatives (popularly termed "gutterals") does not mean that its speakers are primitive and bestial in their thinking; and so forth. Likewise, if a language or form of language is found to lack a unitary term for a certain phenomenon, this does not indicate either that its speakers are unaware of the phenomenon or that they cannot deal with it when it occurs. It does not in fact indicate anything whatever, save that the language lacks the term. This matter has been experimentally supported on a number of occasions (e.g., Lenneberg 1961). Thus, a lack of specific lexical items on the part of disadvantaged children does not imply a lack of sophisticated cognition, nor does their putative failure to use abstract terms necessarily imply inability to conceptualize in this manner.

An additional difficulty with assertions such as statement 3 above is that it is not at all clear precisely what constitutes abstract thinking or how one is to determine whether a subject is engaging in it at a given moment. Abstract thinking is sometimes said to consist of the ability to generalize and categorize. Such abilities are usually considered innate, however, and are implied in the use of language itself; it is not certain that portions of language can be considered more abstract than other portions, or more involved with categorization and generalization. Presumably, grammatical utterances could not be constructed at all without internalized notions of grammatical category, and novel utterances could not be formed without generalization from previously experienced patterns. Furthermore, it is not the case exactly that language provides a conceptual base for thinking, abstract or otherwise; more accurately, the innate ability to abstract, generalize, conceptualize, and so forth is necessary in order for language, generically speaking, to be present. In all members of the human species, save the genetically damaged, these abilities do exist, although of course they show a developmental progression with age, since their ontogenesis is maturationally determined. But the universal existence of these abilities implies, among other things, that much of language is impregnable to environmental forces and that those environmental forces which do in some way act upon language nevertheless fail to alter the innate component of intellection.

In regard to child language and the ability, or lack of it, to generalize, it has been proposed (e.g., Blank and Solomon 1968, p. 382) that the disadvantaged child is unable to use his language efficiently enough to extract information from what is said to him. This is presumably either because such children are unable to think in this way since their language does not provide them with the necessary tools or simply because they have not been taught to do so. The following small example of this assertion comes from Blank and Solomon (1968). It purports to demonstrate the disadvantaged child's lack of a linguistic framework for extracting information from the environment and consists of a dialogue between such a child and his teacher: "For example, the teacher put on her coat at the end of a session. The child said, 'Why are you going home?' The teacher replied, 'How do you know I am going home?' to which the child said, "You're not going home?' This response meant that the child had dropped any attempt at reasoning; he had interpreted the teacher's query to mean that he must negate his earlier inference."

The problem demonstrated by the above instance is not technically one of linguistics but rather of psychology; it is, however, rather typical of the incidents cited by teachers and others to substantiate statement 3 above. However, there is actually nothing anomalous in the child's use of language in this situation. Of the large number of ways the teacher's query could have been answered, it seems to me that the child chose the most sensible. At the point where the teacher asked how the child knew she was going home, there is little else that he could have inferred except that his original answer had been wrong, since this is one of the standard ways in which a teacher indicates this. In other words, the child was making a rather subtle and complex generalization from past experience with teachers, a process quite distant from "dropping any attempt at reasoning." It is not especially the case that the disadvantaged child communicates in peculiar ways, except insofar as these are necessitated by his environment. It should be recognized that a school setting is utterly alien to any other setting in regard to the child's linguistic interaction with the teacher and to his permitted interaction with his age mates. To be sure, the child's remark would have been inappropriate, or at the very least, facetious, in most other social contexts, but for that matter the teacher's question would have been considered quite rude under ordinary social circumstances. The concept of rudeness applied to adult-child conversations is an unusual one. It is clear that this is a unique communication situation in which different rules apply for both parties. One should also bear in mind that children in a school setting are tacitly or otherwise threatened with far more sanctions for incorrect behavior than are participants in most other types of social interaction. Had the child in the above example not been fearful of being "wrong," it is doubtful that he would have needed his original deduction verified. And once again, the entire incident was described in such detail here because it strikes me as representative of teachers' comments about the behavior of the disadvantaged child, behavior cited as atypical and demonstrative of conceptualization deficiencies. It is our purpose to indicate that such incidents can often be interpreted in a number of ways, some of which often show extremely adaptive and reasoned behavior.

4. *To the disadvantaged child, language is dispensable; such children tend to communicate nonverbally in preference to verbally.*—It is, of course, scarcely necessary to point out that language is dispensable to nobody and is not used because of choice or necessity. This is because language acquisition is not a skill—neither is it acquisition of a skill—and so does not depend on environmental exigencies, except in that children must hear a language in order to learn it. But it is natural for children to learn and employ language, which they do without regard to their needs. Probably all children's use of language is similar in some respects (McNeill 1966a). On the other hand, it is also clear that verbal proficiency and skill at handling words are differently valued in many communities here and elsewhere (Kochman 1969; Labov and Cohen 1967) and that the rules of communication must differ in different social groups. Many children's games are nonverbal and are based primarily on physical contact. It is not known whether this is more typical of the disadvantaged child than of the nondisadvantaged. However, the nondisadvantaged child is almost by definition far better supplied with actual things with which to play and so is less constrained to develop any sort of game on his own. Contact between individuals is either verbal or nonverbal; the disadvantaged children I observed engaged in much ritualized fighting and roughhousing, and they also engaged in constant verbal play. There are few other alternatives open to the child without playthings, after all.

It should not be thought, on the other hand, that we wish to deny the possibility that the use of language differs among disadvantaged children. There is simply no solid evidence on this point to date. One might wish to ascertain, for instance, whether parent-child use of language is qualitatively or quantitatively different in this setting, as has been proposed by Bernstein (1961) and many others. The researcher must remember the existence of register, however; perhaps one of the reasons why these children have been said to use language strangely or in limited ways is that only the limited register had been perceived by outside researchers.

5. *The language of the disadvantaged child, since it represents his culture and environment, should be left alone and not changed in any way.*— This proposal, at the opposite end of the spectrum from the proposals con-

sidered previously, is sometimes expressed by linguists and others in the spirit that the sociolinguist Charles Ferguson has characterized as "sentimental egalitarianism." Now, it is perfectly correct to state that the language of the disadvantaged child is useful to him, systematic and regular in its rules of construction, not syntactically or semantically deficient, and as good a basis for thinking and conceptualization as any other form of language. However, statement 5 above does not follow from these facts, because there are other considerations which must be taken into account by educators.

In the first place, it is quite conceivable that the disadvantaged child, especially if rural, may lack some of the lexicon he needs in order to succeed at school, read newspapers, get professional or managerial jobs, and so forth. If this is found to be the case, then disadvantaged children must be taught those items they do not know. However, this is a weighty "if." It is possible that the target child may be able to comprehend such lexicon even though he never uses it. This means in effect that he already "knows" it in some sense and must be given contexts in which to use it along with encouragement to do so. Or, possibly, he both understands and uses it already, only not in a school setting but rather in other registers. It is very difficult to ascertain this, but it is a possibility which must not be overlooked, especially with the prevalence of television and the expanded linguistic environment which it provides.

A far more important consideration, although one more difficult to deal with, is the status of the target child's language in relation to others and standard-English speakers' perception of it. Although *Webster's Dictionary* (3rd ed.) has removed the label of "substandard" from such items as "ain't," nevertheless it is a sociolinguistic fact that some forms of language are an irrevocable block to social, academic, economic, and even geographic upward mobility. If some social prejudice is based on language, as seems to be the case, then this is all the justification necessary for altering those features which elicit such reactions. Note that one can speak of Educated and Uneducated English, a distinction obtaining throughout the English-speaking world regardless of other factors, and that no particular dialect or regional set of characteristics is in itself substandard or uneducated, although some may be considered as unaesthetic by speakers from other regions. It should also be pointed out here that there is Uneducated White English and Uneducated Black English, as well as Educated varieties of each (Houston 1969a). In order to proceed rationally with programs of language change in the schools, it is of course necessary to discover precisely which features of the language of the disadvantaged child are likely to be deleterious (not, I might note, "debilitating"). This is not known at present.

Finally, it has been suggested (e.g., Blank and Solomon 1968) that a useful task might be to lead the disadvantaged child to an awareness that he possesses language and to impart to him sensitivity to differences in the ways people talk. This is obviously a most worthwhile goal. There is no reason to confine it to the disadvantaged child, either, since an awareness of the diversity and functioning of language can be of inestimable value to any child. The way in which this should be done, I believe, is as directly as possible. If the disadvantaged or other child is to be taught about how he talks, he should be told that he is being taught this and should be encouraged to perceive and discuss language itself.

The usual proposed alternative to this suggestion seems to be to engage in a series of word games in which the child is asked to first draw something and then draw something else belonging to a different class from the first object drawn, told to select "two red blocks and one green block" (Blank and Solomon 1968, p. 383) from a pile in order to become habituated to the selective use of adjectives, directed to repeat commands aloud before obeying them, and so on. None of these activities is the least bit atypical of programs designed to augment the linguistic capacity of the disadvantaged child, and none of them is furthermore at all likely to achieve this goal, because they are merely exercises to the child and not learning activities. As Joos (1964, p. 207) has pointed out, to most children school requires a whole new way of thinking and is unrelated to any real situation encountered elsewhere. Thus, a child will accept the necessity for stacking blocks and following other commands which seem silly to him because school activities are designed for this purpose. It "never occurs to him that there is such a thing as a geography of his home town, or a rhetoric of persuasion within his circle of friends" (Joos 1964). If it is found that the language of the disadvantaged child actually needs certain types of augmentation, which I presume would be in lexicon, this can be done through conversation; if such children are to be made aware of language, this should be done through direct reference to language. Most likely, the linguistic aid they need most is encouragement to use their nonschool or natural language in the presence of adults, teachers, and otherwise, since this register of language often turns out to possess all the features said to be lacking in the language of the disadvantaged child.

References

BEREITER, C., & ENGLEMANN, S. *Teaching disadvantaged children in the preschool.* Englewood Cliffs, N.J.: Prentice-Hall, 1966.

BERNSTEIN, B. Social structure, language, and learning. *Educational Research,* 1961, *3,* 163–176.

BLANK, M., & SOLOMON, F. A tutorial language program to develop abstract thinking in socially disadvantaged preschool children. *Child Development,* 1968, *39,* 379–389.

BROWN, R., & FRASER, C. The acquisition of syntax. In U. Bellugi & R. Brown (Eds.), The acquisition of language. *Monographs of the Society for Research in Child Development,* 1964, *29* (1, Serial No. 92), 43–79.

CHOMSKY, N. *Syntactic structures.* The Hague: Mouton, 1959.

————. *Aspects of the theory of syntax.* Cambridge, Mass.: M.I.T. Press, 1965.

————. The formal nature of language. In E. Lenneberg, *Biological foundations of language.* New York: Wiley, 1967. Pp. 397–442.

———. Language and the mind. *Psychology Today,* 1968, *1*(9), 48–68.

DILLARD, J. L. Negro children's dialect in the inner city. *Florida FL Reporter,* Fall 1967, pp. 1–3.

HEBB, D. O. *A textbook of psychology.* Philadelphia: Saunders, 1966.

HOUSTON, S. H. A sociolinguistic consideration of the black English of children in northern Florida. *Language,* 1969, *45,* 599–607. (a)

———. Child Black English: the School register. Paper presented to the 44th Annual Meeting of the Linguistic Society of America, San Francisco, 1969. (b)

HURST, C. C., & JONES, W. L. Psychosocial concomitants of substandard speech. *Journal of Negro Education,* 1966, Fall, 409–421.

JOOS, M. Language and the school child. *Harvard Educational Review,* 1964, *34,* 203–210.

KESSEN, W. Research in the psychological development of infants: an overview. In I. J. Gordon (Ed.), *Human development.* Glenview, Ill.: Scott, Foresman, 1965. Pp. 83–90.

KOCHMAN, T. "Rapping" in the black ghetto. *Trans-action,* 1969, *6*(4), 26–34.

KURATH, H., & McDAVID, R. I., JR. *The pronunciation of English in the Atlantic states.* Ann Arbor: University of Michigan Press, 1961.

LABOV, W. Deletion, contraction, and inherent variability of the English copula. Paper presented to the Forty-second Annual Meeting of the Linguistic Society of America, Chicago, 1967.

LABOV, W., & COHEN, P. Systematic relations of standard and non-standard rules in the grammars of Negro speakers. *Project Literacy Reports,* July 1967, No. 8, Cornell University. Pp. 66–84.

LANGACKER, R. W. *Language and its structure.* New York: Harcourt, Brace, 1967.

LENNEBERG, E. H. Color naming, color recognition, color discrimination: a reappraisal. *Perceptual and Motor Skills,* 1961, *2,* 375–382.

———. Understanding language without the ability to speak: a case report. *Journal of Abnormal Social Psychology,* 1962, *65,* 419–425.

———. The capacity for language acquisition. In J. A. Fodor & J. J. Katz (Eds.), *The structure of language.* Englewood Cliffs, N.J.: Prentice-Hall, 1964. Pp. 579–603.

———. *Biological foundations of language.* New York: Wiley, 1967.

McNEILL, D. Developmental psycholinguistics. In F. Smith & G. A. Miller (Eds.), *The genesis of language.* Cambridge, Mass.: M.I.T. Press, 1966. Pp. 15–84. (a)

———. The creation of language by children. In J. Lyons & R. J. Wales (Eds.), *Psycholinguistics papers.* Edinburgh: Edinburgh University Press, 1966. Pp. 99–115 (b)

MENYUK, P. *Sentences children use.* Cambridge, Mass.: M.I.T. Press, 1969.

MILLER, G. A., GALANTER, E., & PRIBRAM, K. H. *Plans and the structure of behavior.* New York: Holt, Rinehart and Winston, 1960.

MILLER, W., & ERVIN, S. The development of grammar in child language. In U. Bellugi & R. Brown (Eds.), The acquisition of language. *Monographs of the Society for Research in Child Development,* 1964, *29* (1, Serial No. 92), 9–34.

MOWRER, O. H. *Learning theory and the symbolic processes.* New York: Wiley, 1960.

OSGOOD, C. E., SUCI, G. J., & TANNENBAUM, P. H. *The measurement of meaning.* Urbana: University of Illinois Press, 1957.

PINES, M. *Revolution in learning.* New York: Harper & Row, 1966.

SKINNER, B. F. *Verbal behavior.* New York: Appleton-Century-Crofts, 1957.

SLOBIN, D. I. The acquisition of Russian as a native language. In F. Smith & G. A. Miller (Eds.), *The genesis of language*. Cambridge, Mass.: M.I.T. Press, 1966. Pp. 129–148.

STAATS, A. W., & STAATS, C. K. *Complex human behavior*. New York: Holt, Rinehart and Winston, 1964.

STROM, R. D. *Teaching in the slum school*. Columbus, Ohio: Merrill, 1965.

VERNON, M. D. *The psychology of perception*. Harmondsworth, U.K.: Pelican, 1962.

WESTINGHOUSE LEARNING CORPORATION. *The impact of Headstart*. Washington, D.C.: Westinghouse, 1969.

WHORF, B. L. *Language, thought and reality*. Cambridge, Mass.: M.I.T. Press, 1956.

The curve of intelligence for blacks is displaced some 10 or 15 IQ points in relation to that of whites; that is, blacks, on the average, score 10 to 15 IQ points lower than whites. (But 50 percent of the blacks are still brighter than 33 percent of the whites). A continuing debate has raged about the explanation of this generally accepted finding. Unfortunately, the debate is clouded by emotions that have nothing to do with the question at hand. In the following article, Sandra Scarr-Salapatek presents a balanced, sane discussion of hypotheses suggested to explain the observed difference in white and black intelligence test performance. Although the following article is somewhat technical, it is included here because of its truly great importance. A few of the terms used in the article are defined below:

Genotype, *the individual's genetic makeup. The term may refer to one, some, or all of his genes and their locations on chromosomes.*
Genetic variance, *the genetic variability among individuals.*
Phenotype, *the sum total of the individual's observable characteristics.*
Phenotypic variance, *the observable differences among individuals.*
Heritability index, *the ratio of genetic variance to phenotypic variance.*

For any given trait this index tells the extent to which the observed differences can be attributed to genetic factors.

Race, Social Class, and IQ

Sandra Scarr-Salapatek

Population differences in heritability of IQ scores were found for racial and social class groups.

The heritability of intelligence in white, middle-class populations of school-aged children and adults has been repeatedly estimated to account for 60 to 80 percent of the total variance in general intelligence scores, however measured (1–4). Yet Jensen (3, pp. 64–65) has noted many limitations to the available data on heritability.

> It is sometimes forgotten that such [heritability] estimates actually represent *average* values in a population that has been sampled and that they do not necessarily apply either to differences *within* various subpopulations or to differences *between* subpopulations. . . . All the major heritability studies have been based on samples of white European and North American populations, and our knowledge of intelligence in different racial and cultural groups within these populations is nil. For example, no adequate heritability studies have been based on samples of the Negro population of the United States [italics added].

Source: Reprinted by permission from *Science*, 24 December 1971, *174* (4016), 1285–1295. Copyright © 1971 by The American Association for the Advancement of Science.

After carefully examining the intelligence data on the black and white populations, Jensen (3, 4) hypothesized that the average genetic potential of the black population may not be equal to that of the white population. Others (5, 6) have interpreted the same racial differences in mean IQ (intelligence quotient) within an environmental framework, often naively and without good evidence for their competing hypotheses. Dislike of a genetic hypothesis to account for racial differences in mean IQ scores does not equal disproof of that hypothesis. Evidence for genetic or environmental hypotheses must come from a critical examination of both explanations, with data that support one.

As every behavioral geneticist knows, the heritability of a behavioral characteristic is a function of the population in which it is measured (7, 8). There is no reason to assume that behaviors measured in one population will show the same proportion of genetic and environmental variances when measured in a second population whose distributions of genetic or environmental characteristics, or both, differ in any way from those of the first population. Racial and social class groups are, for many purposes, sufficiently different populations to make a generalization from one to another highly questionable (9–11).

The sociological literature on social class and racial differences in style of life, nutrition, child-rearing practices, and the like describes *population* differences in distributions of environments. These population differences must affect the development of phenotypic (observed) IQ (12) and the relative proportions of genetic and environmental variances in IQ scores.

Distributions of genotypes for the development of behavioral characteristics may also vary from one population to another. Except for single-gene characteristics such as Huntington's chorea, microcephaly, and the like, we know very little about genotypic variability among populations for behavioral development. Because identified single-gene characteristics are known to occur with varying frequencies among populations, it is assumed that genes for polygenic characteristics may also be distributed somewhat differently among groups.

The sources of within-group and between-group variation can be assessed, although they are seldom effectively studied. Thoday (13, pp. 4–5) reviewed the problems of cross-population studies and concluded:

> While discontinuous variables such as blood groups present us with little difficulty [in studying differences between populations], continuous variables such as IQ are a different matter, for it is not possible with these to identify specific genotypes and it is therefore not possible to determine gene frequencies. Furthermore, there are always environmental as well as genetic causes of variation. We may measure the relative importance of environmental as well as genetic causes of variation or heritability within a population, and if the heritabilities are very high, that is, variation is almost entirely a consequence of genetic variety, we may know more than if they are low. But even if they are high, as with

fingerprint ridge counts, we are already in difficulties with population comparisons, for there is no warrant for equating within-group heritabilities and between-group heritabilities.

In this article, I outline important concepts and methods in the study of individual and group variation and describe a new study of genetic and environmental variances in aptitude scores in black and white, and advantaged and disadvantaged populations.

Two Models of IQ, Social Class, and Race

There are two major, competing hypotheses for predicting the relation among social class, race, and IQ—the environmental disadvantage hypothesis and the genotype distribution hypothesis. Both hypotheses make differential predictions about the proportions of genetic and environmental variance in IQ within lower and higher social class groups.

The term "environmental disadvantage" refers to the largely unspecified complex of environmental factors associated with poverty that prevents an organism from achieving its optimum development. The biological environmental disadvantages have been reviewed by Birch and Gussow (14), and references to social environmental disadvantages have been reviewed by Deutsch, Katz, and Jensen (15).

Race and social class are terms that refer to socially defined subgroups of the human population. Reproduction is more likely to occur between people in the same subgroup than between people in different subgroups. There is no question that races are partially closed breeding groups with a great deal more endogamy than exogamy (10). It is also true that social class groups (groups whose members have attained a certain educational and occupational status) within races practice more endogamy than exogamy (11). Social mobility from generation to generation does not upset the notion of social classes as somewhat different breeding groups, in terms of IQ levels, because the distribution of IQ's within each occupational level is reestablished in each generation of adults (16). Brighter children in families at all but the top social levels tend to be upwardly mobile, whereas duller siblings at all but the bottom class level tend to be downwardly mobile (17). Social class groups may be thought of as endogamous primarily for IQ (as expressed in occupational and educational achievements).

Social class groups may represent both different distributions of parental genotypes for IQ and different rearing environments for children. Although fathers' average IQ scores may vary by 50 points or more from top professional groups to unskilled laborers, their children's average IQ's differ by 25 points or less (16, 17).

The mean differences in children's IQ's by social class reflect differences in both parental genotypes and rearing environments, which covary to a large extent in the development of IQ. Crucial evidence on the genetic and environmental components from adopted children is very limited, but Skodak and Skeels (18) revealed a 20 point rise in the IQ of adopted children over that of their biological mothers. The distribution of adopted children's IQ's was also shifted beyond the values expected by regression to a mean above the average of the population, presumably by their better social environments.

Social class groups, then, are subdivisions of races and represent different distributions of parental genotypes, as well as different rearing environments. There is no comparable statement that can be made about racial groups: whereas races represent different rearing environments, no statements can be made concerning different distributions of parental genotypes for IQ. Since there is no direct test possible for distributions of genotypic IQ (13), it is impossible to assert that such distributions for the two races are "equal" or "different." Races do constitute different rearing environments in two respects. First, proportionately more blacks than whites are socially disadvantaged, thus more black children are reared under lower-class conditions; second, being black in the United States may carry with it a social burden not inflicted on any white.

The environmental disadvantage hypothesis assumes that lower-class whites and most blacks live under suppressive (19, 20) conditions for the development of IQ. In brief, the disadvantage hypothesis states: (i) unspecified environmental factors affect the development of IQ, thereby causing the observed differences in mean IQ levels among children of different social classes and races; (ii) blacks are more often biologically and socially disadvantaged than whites; and (iii) if disadvantage were equally distributed across social class and racial groups, the social class and racial correlations with IQ would disappear. The environmental disadvantage hypothesis predicts that IQ scores within advantaged groups will show larger proportions of genetic variance and smaller proportions of environmental variance than IQ scores for disadvantaged groups. Environmental disadvantage is predicated to reduce the genotype-phenotype correlation (21) in lower-class groups and in the black group as a whole.

The genetic differences hypothesis, as it applies to social class groups within races, centers on the issues of assortative mating by IQ and selective migration, based on intelligence, within the social structure. Social class differences in mean IQ are assumed to be principally genetic in origin and to result from the high heritability of IQ throughout the population, assortative mating for IQ, and a small covariance term that includes those educational advantages that brighter parents may provide for their brighter children (3, 10). Social class differences in phenotypic IQ are assumed to reflect primarily the mean differences in genotype distribution by social class; environmental differences between social class groups (and races) are seen as insignificant in determining total phenotypic variance in IQ. Therefore, the proportion of genetic variance in IQ scores is predicted to be equally high for all social class groups (and for both races). Figures 1 and 2 present models 1 and 2, respectively, as they apply to social class.

Model 1: Environmental advantage as the determinant of group differences in IQ.

Assumptions:

1. Genotypic distribution by social class for phenotypic IQ of children (no differences).

2. Environmental effects on the development of IQ by SES (large effect).

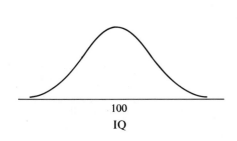

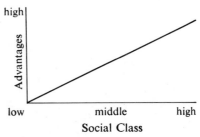

Prediction: lower h^2 in disadvantaged groups.

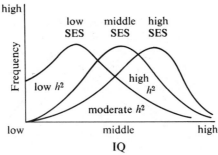

FIGURE 1.   Environmental disadvantage, model 1 (h^2 is heritability for twins; SES is socioeconomic status).

In model 1, there are assumed to be equal distributions of genotypes across social classes. In model 2, there are assumed to be unequal distributions of genotypes for IQ, the lower class having proportionally more genotypes for low IQ and the upper social groups having proportionally more genotypes for high IQ. Environmental effects of social class are posited to be strong in model 1 and very weak in model 2.

Competing Predictions

Both models account for the observed social class data on IQ, but they make competing predictions about the proportion of genetic variance. In model 1, environmental factors are predicted to reduce the mean and the heritability of IQ in the lower social class groups and raise both in the higher social groups. Model 2 predicts equally high heritabilities for all groups, regardless of rearing environments and regardless of mean scores. Estimated heritabilities by social class and race provide a new way of evaluating the adequacy with which the two hypotheses account for observed differences in mean

Model 2: Genetic differences as the primary determinant of group differences in IQ.

Assumptions:

1. Genotypic distribution by social class for   2. Environmental effects on the develop-
   phenotypic IQ of children (differences).   ment of IQ by SES (small effect).

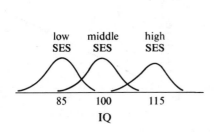

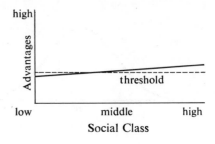

Prediction: equal h^2 in all groups.

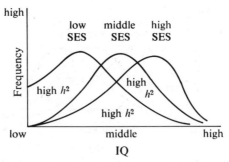

FIGURE 2.   Genetic differences, model 2 (h^2 is heritability for twins;
SES is socioeconomic status).

IQ by social class. Racial differences may also be examined if the following
rationale is always considered.

        To the extent that the *same* environmental factors are assumed to
affect the development of IQ in the same way in both black and white populations, predictions can be made about the sources of racial differences in
mean IQ scores. If certain biological deprivation (such as low weight at birth,
poor nutrition) are known to be more prevalent in lower class groups of both
populations and more prevalent among blacks than whites, then the two
models can make differential predictions about the effects of these sources
of environmental variance on the proportion of genetic variance in each population. Given a larger proportion of disadvantaged children within the black
group, the environmental disadvantage hypothesis must predict smaller proportions of genetic variance to account for differences in phenotypic IQ
among blacks than among whites, as whole populations. Since the genotype
distribution hypothesis predicts no differences in the proportion of genetic

variance for social class groups within the races, it should predict the same proportions of genetic variance in the two races.

To the extent that *different* environmental factors are assumed to affect the development of IQ in black and white populations, or the same environmental factors are assumed not to affect the development of IQ in the same way, or both, no differential predictions about the origin of racial differences can be made by the two models. If all black children are disadvantaged to an unknown degree by being reared as blacks in a white-dominated society, and no white children are so disadvantaged, it is impossible to estimate genetic and environmental variances between the races. Only if black children could be reared as though they were white, and vice versa, could the effects of different rearing environments on the genotype distribution of the two races be estimated.

Some combinations of models 1 and 2 may be found to account best for phenotypic variability within and between groups. The clear opposition of models 1 and 2 as explanations for the same IQ, racial, and social class data was presented to demonstrate the differential predictions that can be generated about proportions of genetic variance in different populations.

Twin Sample

An alphabetic roster of all students enrolled in the Philadelphia public schools in April 1968 was examined for children with the same last name, the same birth dates, and the same home address. Children who met the three criteria were identified as twins.

Of the 250,258 children in kindergarten through grade 12, 3042 were identified as twins, including 493 opposite-sex pairs and 1028 same-sex pairs.

The racial distribution of these twins was 36 percent white and 64 percent black. The corresponding figures for the entire public school population were 41 percent white and 59 percent black. The twins' racial distribution was discrepant from the total population by 5 percent, which can be accounted for by the substantially higher rate of fraternal twinning among blacks (22).

In a large sample of twins it is tactically difficult to differentiate the monozygotic and dizygotic groups directly. Direct approaches to zygocity could be discarded in favor of the indirect, statistical approach, which is advocated by Burt (2), Vandenberg (23), Sandon (24), and Husen (25). The reasoning is as follows: the percentage of opposite-sex pairs is known in any complete population survey. By applying the Weinberg formula, the proportion of monozygotic twins can be easily obtained (21). There will always be approximately the same proportion of same-sex pairs as opposite-sex pairs because of the distribution of sexes. It is then a simple matter to estimate the percentage of monozygotic pairs as follows: $100 - 2$ (percent of opposite-sex pairs) = percent of monozygotic pairs. Percentage estimates for monozygotic and dizygotic groups were done separately for each racial group.

Once the proportion of monozygotic and dizygotic twins is known, the correlations for same-sex and opposite-sex groups can be used to estimate the correlation coefficients for monozygotic and dizygotic twins within the same-sex sample. By converting correlation coefficients to z scores, the same-sex intraclass coefficient can be apportioned according to the percentages of monozygotic pairs in the same-sex group, so that:

$$r_{iss} = \frac{\% \ SS_{dz}(r_{ios}) + \% \ SS_{mz}(X)}{\% \ SS_{mz+dz}}$$

On the basis of seven independent studies including more than 1000 pairs of same-sex and 100 pairs of opposite-sex twins, Burt (2) found the average correlations for intelligence to be .76 and .57, respectively. From these coefficients, he was able to estimate the correlation for monozygotic and dizygotic groups as .89 and .56, respectively. These estimates match very closely the correlations found for intelligence in samples of monozygotic and dizygotic twins whose zygosity had been determined by blood-grouping procedures.

In the Philadelphia sample, 30 percent of the white pairs and 34 percent of the black pairs were found to be of opposite sexes. Therefore, by the Weinberg formula, 40 percent of the whites and 32 percent of the blacks were estimated to be monozygotic pairs. The higher proportion of monozygotic twins in the white population matched the figures reported (24) for a complete age-group of British children taking the 11+ examinations.

The final samples were considerably smaller than the original 1521 pairs found, for several reasons. First, since standardized tests were not administered to the kindergarten or first-grade groups, 282 pairs were lost. Second, one or both members of 124 pairs were found to be enrolled in special classes, to whom the tests used in this study were not given (26). Third, the absence of one or both twins on the days that tests were administered eliminated an additional 123 pairs. Combined losses of 529 pairs reduced the final sample to 992 pairs with aptitude or achievement scores, or both, for each twin, as shown in Table 1.

TABLE 1. Final sample pairs by race and test scores

Test Scores	Black	White
Aptitude only	315	194
Achievement only	129	75
Aptitude and achievement	191	88
Total pairs	635	357

Social Class Measures

Within both the black and white groups, social class variables were used to assign pairs to relatively advantaged and disadvantaged groups. The public school data on parental occupation, income, and education were incomplete and too unreliable for these purposes. Instead, census tract information from the 1960 U.S. Census was used.

Every pair had a census tract designation for which median income and educational data were available. Although census tracts in an urban area are designed to provide maximum homogeneity within tracts, they are still imperfect measures of individual SES (socioeconomic status) characteristics. Relatively advantaged and disadvantaged groups could be designated by neighborhood SES, however, since peer associations and school characteristics would be reflected in the census tract data. To the extent that the social disadvantage hypothesis pertains to the life-style, in addition to within-family environment, the census tract data were appropriate.

Social-class assignment was made by establishing a median level of income and educational characteristics for the total number of census tracts from which the twin sample was drawn, regardless of race. Cross-tabulations of above- and below-median levels of income and education provided three groups: one below the census tract medians for both income and education; one above the medians of both; and a third above in one and below in the other. On this basis, the three groups were designated as below median, above median, and middle status.

Aptitude and Achievement Tests

Results from several tests were available in the 1968–69 school year for children in the Philadelphia school district from second through twelfth grade (27). All children in grades three through eight who were in regular academic classrooms were given the Iowa Tests of Basic Skills, which test long-term development of intellectual skills (28). These are highly reliable group tests (29) that are used to measure scholastic achievement in many school districts across the nation. The vocabulary, reading, language total, arithmetic total, and composite scores were obtained. A total of 319 black and 163 white pairs had scores on all subtests for each twin.

Since a different aptitude test was given in every second school grade, it was impossible to obtain a sufficiently large number of pairs for reliable test-by-test results. It was decided, therefore, to combine aptitude test results across tests and age ranges, and to treat them as age-appropriate, equivalent forms of the same test. This radical decision was based primarily on the roughly equivalent structure of the aptitude tests. All have at least two principal subtests, a verbal and a nonverbal (or numerical), as well as a total score. Some tests, such as the Differential Abilities Test, have additional subtests to measure spatial, mechanical, and other abilities not included in more scholastically-oriented tests, such as the School and College Ability Tests. Thus, the total scores based on all subtests are not strictly equivalent; nor are the nonverbal tests, which may be based primarily on arithmetic reasoning or may include abstract reasoning as well. The verbal scores are the most nearly equivalent from test to test, and thus are the most reliable for comparisons across grades.

No a priori assumptions were made about the appropriateness of standardized aptitude tests for different social-class and racial groups. Although there exists a popular notion that standardized tests are less predictive of scholastic achievement in disadvantaged groups, this has generally been unsupported by research (30). This hypothesis was tested, however, by examining the correlations between aptitude and achievement scores for each racial and social-glass group.

Since the generalizations were never intended to exceed the limits of aptitude test and IQ scores, no extensive discussion of the epistemological issue, "What do IQ tests measure?" will be attempted here. Suffice it to say that variance in IQ and aptitude test scores have been shown to have strong genetic components in other studies of white populations, and that the appropriateness of these measures for other racial and social-class samples will be considered in the results section.

Statistics

Statistics in studies of twins are based on the variances in scores among individuals of different genetic and environmental relatedness. The total phenotypic variance in the populations studied can be apportioned into between-family and within-family variances for both same- and opposite-sex twins. The comparison of between- and within-family mean squares is usually expressed as an F ratio.

$$F = \frac{\sigma_b^2}{\sigma_w^2}$$

The intraclass correlation expresses the proportion of variance arising from family influences, both genetic and environmental. It compares the between-family variances minus the within-family variances to the total phenotypic variance in the population from which the related persons are drawn.

$$r_1 = \frac{\sigma_b^2 - \sigma_w^2}{\sigma_b^2 + \sigma_w^2} = \frac{F - 1}{F + 1}$$

where σ_b^2 is the mean squares between pairs, and σ_w^2 is the mean squares within pairs.

The comparison of intraclass correlation coefficients and variance ratios for two or more related sets of individuals leads to the calculation of heritability estimates. The heritability of a trait is an expression of the ratio of total genetic variance to total phenotypic variance.

In the simplest form for studies of twins, the restricted model for broad heritability (h_r^2) was defined by

$$h_r^2 = \frac{2(r_{ims} - r_{idz})}{1 - \sigma_E^2}$$

where r_{imz} is the intraclass correlation for monozygotic pairs, r_{idz} is the intraclass correlation for dizygotic pairs, and σ_E^2 is the percentage of variance due to errors in measurement. In this study, σ_E^2 was estimated to be .073, or the minimum unreliability for group aptitude tests.

Another version of the h^2 statistic for broad heritability using twins was offered by Jensen (31) to include the available data on assortative mating for IQ in the white population. The assortative-mating model for data on twins takes into account the positive correlation between IQ scores of parents, which are generally found to be around .40. Nonrandom mating patterns produce a genetic correlation between siblings that is somewhat higher than the .50 expected under mating patterns that are random with respect to IQ. The formula for computing the heritability coefficient with assortative mating (h_a^2) is

$$h_a^2 = \frac{c(r_{ims} - r_{idz})}{1 - \sigma_E^2}$$

where $c = 1 / 1 - p$, or 2.222, when $p = .55$; and σ_E^2 is the percentage of variance due to errors in measurement.

If the heritability of a trait is known, the total variance can be apportioned into four major components: within-family genetic variance (σ_{wg}^2), within-family environmental variance (σ_{we}^2), between-family genetic variance (σ_{bg}^2), and between-family environmental variance (σ_{be}^2). Regardless of the absolute size of the total variance, the proportions of variance can be estimated (32).

Distributions of Scores

An initial look at the distribution of scores within the samples of twins from Philadelphia indicated that the scores were far from normal. The low mean value, especially in the black population, and the skew of the distributions required careful normalization of the scores before any heritability analyses could be attempted. Thus, the results are reported in three sections: first, the distributions of scores and their transformations; second, the analyses of data on twins; and third, the heritability and estimated proportions of variance in the scores by race and social class.

The distributions of aptitude scores, based on national norms were divided first by race and then by race and social class. The means and standard deviations of the scores were markedly different by race; the mean aptitude scores of whites were slightly below the national mean of .50, while the mean aptitude scores of blacks were one standard deviation ($\sigma = 19$) below the national mean. There was almost one standard deviation between the means of the two races. The standard deviations of the whites were slightly higher than those of the blacks, as Jensen (3, 4) and others have noted; but the ratios of standard deviations to the means (proportional variance) were higher in the black than in the white groups (see Table 2).

TABLE 2. Means and standard deviations (σ) of national scores for individuals by race

Aptitude Test	Black (N = 1006) Mean	σ	White (N = 560) Mean	σ
Verbal	30.3	18.2	45.9	21.2
Nonverbal	32.7	19.1	47.9	21.8
Total	28.9	18.5	46.1	20.8

On measures of aptitude, the racial groups had surprisingly large differences, once social class was considered (Table 3). The mean of the below-median (in income and education) white group equalled or surpassed the mean of the above-median black children on verbal, nonverbal, and total aptitude scores. The quartile (q) boundaries showed the distributions of below-median whites and above-median blacks to have similar properties, except that the total variance among advantaged black children was somewhat higher than that among disadvantaged whites.

TABLE 3. Mean and standard deviations (σ) of national scores on combined aptitude tests for individuals by race and social class. (Q indicates quartile)

Statistics	Black Below (N = 634)	Middle (N = 236)	Above (N = 134)	White Below (N = 114)	Middle (N = 106)	Above (N = 340)
			Verbal			
Mean	29.0	30.9	35.3	36.4	43.9	49.8
σ	(17.7)	(17.2)	(20.8)	(18.6)	(22.6)	(20.4)
Q	15-28-39	19-31-43	23-32-46	22-38-50	28-42-56	38-41-63
			Nonverbal			
Mean	32.0	32.7	35.9	38.3	44.5	52.2
σ	(19.2)	(18.7)	(19.3)	(18.0)	(22.5)	(21.5)
Q	17-32-44	20-32-46	20-34-50	25-39-50	29-43-59	36-51-68
			Total			
Mean	27.7	29.7	33.0	34.8	43.4	50.9
σ	(18.1)	(18.1)	(20.3)	(16.9)	(21.4)	(20.2)
Q	15-26-39	15-30-41	19-29-47	23-37-47	29-42-56	38-52-65

The social-class divisions among whites separated the aptitude means of the subpopulations by approximately four-fifths of a standard deviation. The comparable divisions among blacks produced a difference of one-quarter of a standard deviation between children below and above the medians for the 280 census tracts in which the twins lived. Social-class groups of children were far more differentiated among whites than among blacks, despite the same criteria for assignment.

Comparisons across racial groups showed that disadvantaged white children scored in a pattern similar to that of black children, while the middle and above-median white groups had much higher means. Variances were not reliably different across races.

Compared to the national distribution, the twins in Philadelphia scored poorly. Instead of mean scores of 50, all black groups and white groups of below-median and middle status had mean performance scores in the 20 to 40 range. Only the above-median whites had mean scores close to the national average. A comparison of the means and variances of the twins' scores with those of all Philadelphia children showed that the twins were indeed representative of their respective racial and social-class groups, and were only slightly handicapped by their twinship.

Since the scores based on national norms were skewed within the Philadelphia samples, the scores for each test were normalized, separately by racial groups, to a mean of 50 and a standard deviation of 10, in order to develop comparable data for blacks and whites. Since the means and variances of the two racial groups were arbitrarily set as equal, there were no longer any differences based on race in the distributions of scores. In every test, there were significant social-class differences and significant class-by-race interaction terms, which reflected the fact that social-class differences in mean scores were much greater among whites than blacks.

Correlational analyses of all test scores by race and social class were done to examine the equivalence of measurement among groups. As Table 4 shows, the patterns of correlation among aptitude and achievement scores were quite similar in all groups, regardless of race or social class. It is difficult to argue that the dimensions of performance measured in the different racial and social-class groups were not comparable. The most parsimonious explanation of similar patterns of correlations is that there are similar underlying dimensions. It is impossible to argue that "nothing" is being measured by these tests in disadvantaged groups, because the prediction from aptitude to achievement scores is approximately as good in the below-median as in the middle black groups, and is certainly as good in the black groups as it is in the white groups.

Analyses of Twins by Race

The four major groups of same-sex and opposite-sex, black and white twins were treated separately for the first set of analyses. Analyses of

TABLE 4. Intercorrelations of test scores by race and social class [nonverbal (NV), total (T), vocabulary (Vo), reading (R), language (L), arithmetic (A), composite (C)]

| | Black | | | | | | |
| | Aptitude | | | Achievement | | | |
Test	verbal	non-verbal	total	vocab-ulary	read-ing	lan-guage	arith-metic
	Below-median group (N = 351)						
NV	.57						
T	.84	.87					
Vo	.56	.44	.54				
R	.56	.47	.59	.64			
L	.59	.54	.64	.67	.67		
A	.53	.58	.62	.57	.66	.67	
C	.64	.57	.67	.82	.84	.86	.83
	Middle group (N = 125)						
NV	.71						
T	.90	.89					
Vo	.54	.47	.56				
R	.64	.56	.66	.66			
L	.67	.54	.65	.66	.75		
A	.60	.53	.60	.64	.72	.73	
C	.70	.59	.70	.83	.89	.90	.85
	Above-median group (N = 51)						
NV	.53						
T	.82	.86					
Vo	.60	.35	.53				
R	.62	.56	.68	.71			
L	.68	.55	.71	.74	.87		
A	.55	.65	.68	.61	.81	.77	
C	.67	.57	.71	.83	.94	.93	.87

variance comparing within-pair and between-pair variances were applied to each test score in the four groups. Table 5 gives the twins' results by race for the three aptitude scores. Intraclass correlations for the monozygotic group are estimated by the method described earlier.

Same-sex twins were, in general, more similar than were opposite-sex pairs. In both the black and white groups, the presence of monozygotic pairs in the same-sex group increased their correlation above that of the opposite-sex dizygotic pairs, so that the estimated monozygotic correlation was higher than the dizygotic correlation for four of the six comparisons. The two exceptions are total aptitude score for the blacks and nonverbal aptitude for the whites. Correlations between the two children in each same-sex and opposite-sex black pair were consistently lower than for their white counterparts. Black twins were not found to be as similar to each other as white twins, when compared to randomly paired members of the same groups.

	White						
	Aptitude			Achievement			
Test	verbal	non-verbal	total	vocab-ulary	read-ing	lan-guage	arith-metic
	Below-median group (N = 60)						
NV	.44						
T	.81	.83					
Vo	.53	−.04	.31				
R	.62	.30	.51	.61			
L	.76	.28	.61	.69	.79		
A	.67	.37	.59	.58	.77	.79	
C	.75	.26	.58	.81	.87	.92	.89
	Middle group (N = 43)						
NV	.57						
T	.88	.85					
Vo	.81	.49	.71				
R	.84	.59	.79	.88			
L	.71	.51	.69	.75	.85		
A	.60	.52	.63	.64	.71	.77	
C	.78	.61	.77	.86	.93	.94	.85
	Above-median group (N = 147)						
NV	.66						
T	.81	.88					
Vo	.71	.49	.59				
R	.68	.53	.60	.78			
L	.69	.61	.66	.73	.74		
A	.70	.70	.74	.66	.71	.78	
C	.77	.64	.72	.87	.90	.88	.87

Analyses of Twins by Race and Social Class

It was hypothesized in model 1 that social-class conditions of life would affect twin similarities and resulting estimates of genetic variances. The potentially restricting effects of lower-class life on the development of genetically based individual differences could tend to reduce within-pair correlation coefficients in the lower-class groups, whereas better environmental opportunities could allow a greater range of phenotypic individual differences in the middle-class groups. Model 2 predicted that similar proportions of genetic variance would be found across social-class groups because mean differences in scores were assumed to arise from differences in genotype distributions.

Within-pair similarities were analyzed for those pairs below the median and then for those of middle and above status combined—the small number of black pairs above the median made it advantageous to combine

TABLE 5.   Analysis of variance of aptitude scores of twin pairs by race

Mean Squares	Black		White	
	Same Sex	*Opposite Sex*	*Same Sex*	*Opposite Sex*
		Verbal		
	($N = 333$)	($N = 169$)	($N = 192$)	($N = 82$)
σ_b^2	129.1	113.7	149.4	133.2
σ_w^2	38.2	44.8	29.6	33.9
F	3.38	2.54	5.05	3.93
r_1	0.543	0.435	0.669	0.594
r_{1mz}		0.653		0.719
		Nonverbal		
	($N = 332$)	($N = 169$)	($N = 192$)	($N = 82$)
σ_b^2	130.5	115.2	149.7	131.7
σ_w^2	39.6	39.4	33.8	26.8
F	3.30	2.92	4.42	4.92
r_1	0.535	0.490	0.631	0.662
r_{1mz}		0.594		0.601
		Total		
	($N = 334$)	($N = 169$)	($N = 193$)	($N = 82$)
σ_b^2	127.4	119.2	168.0	156.9
σ_w^2	35.1	31.2	23.7	28.4
F	3.62	3.82	7.10	5.53
r_1	0.567	0.585	0.753	0.694
r_{1mz}		0.544		0.791

TABLE 6.   Analysis of variance of verbal aptitude scores of twin pairs by race and social class

Mean Squares	Black		White	
	Same Sex	*Opposite Sex*	*Same Sex*	*Opposite Sex*
		Below-median group		
	($N = 211$)	($N = 107$)	($N = 41$)	($N = 16$)
σ_b^2	120.7	102.9	81.8	105.8
σ_w^2	41.7	42.1	28.7	31.0
F	2.89	2.44	2.85	3.41
r_1	0.486	0.419	0.481	0.546
r_{1mz}		0.558		0.430
		Middle and above-median group		
	($N = 123$)	($N = 62$)	($N = 153$)	($N = 70$)
σ_b^2	136.0	134.0	154.1	119.9
σ_w^2	32.2	49.4	29.8	34.5
F	4.23	2.71	5.17	3.47
r_1	0.618	0.460	0.676	0.553
r_{1mz}		0.753		0.749

the latter two groups. Tables 6, 7, and 8 give the analysis of variance results of the aptitude tests for the below-median and the combined middle and above-median groups for both races.

In the below-median SES groups of both races, the same-sex correlation exceeded the opposite-sex coefficient only once (black verbal aptitude). The failure of opposite-sex correlations to exceed same-sex coefficients left the estimated monozygotic correlations and heritability statistics indeterminant. It is unlikely that the correlations for monozygotic twins were lower than those for the same-sex dizygotic twins, but it is senseless to assign a value when r_{ios} is greater than r_{iss}. The most likely interpretation of this result is that the greater genetic correlation between monozygotic twins was not sufficient to increase the same-sex correlations above the values obtained for opposite-sex twins. Thus, genetic factors cannot be seen as strong determinants of aptitude scores in the disadvantaged groups of either race.

TABLE 7. Analysis of variance of nonverbal aptitude scores of twin pairs by race and social class

Mean Squares	Black		White	
	Same Sex	Opposite Sex	Same Sex	Opposite Sex
	Below-median group			
	(N = 211)	(N = 107)	(N = 41)	(N = 16)
σ_b^2	128.9	120.3	111.1	87.8
σ_w^2	41.4	37.8	34.8	20.7
F	3.11	3.19	3.20	4.25
r_i	0.513	0.523	0.524	0.619
r_{imz}		0.508		0.445
	Middle and above-median group			
	(N = 123)	(N = 62)	(N = 152)	(N = 68)
σ_b^2	132.5	107.8	149.9	122.3
σ_w^2	36.3	42.2	33.6	28.1
F	3.65	2.55	4.46	4.34
r_i	0.570	0.437	0.634	0.625
r_{imz}		0.698		0.642

In the middle- to above-median SES groups, the same-sex correlations exceeded the opposite-sex correlations for all three aptitude scores in both races. The most likely inference from these data is that both genetic and environmental components of variance contributed to the similarity of within-pair scores in the advantaged group. For the disadvantaged group, the failure of same-sex correlations to exceed opposite-sex coefficients makes it doubtful that the proportion of genetic variance in the lower-class group equals that of the advantaged group.

Total variance was generally larger in the advantaged than in the disadvantaged groups of both races. For whites, total variance was larger

TABLE 8. Analysis of variance of total aptitude scores of twin pairs by race and social class

Mean Squares	Black		White	
	Same Sex	Opposite Sex	Same Sex	Opposite Sex
		Below-median group		
	(N = 212)	(N = 107)	(N = 41)	(N = 16)
σ_b^2	122.7	109.7	83.1	109.1
σ_w^2	38.1	27.5	20.5	24.7
F	3.22	3.99	4.05	4.42
r_i	0.526	0.599	0.604	0.631
r_{imz}		0.434		0.585
		Middle and above-median group		
	(N = 123)	(N = 62)	(N = 155)	(N = 70)
σ_b^2	130.6	137.4	174.7	139.1
σ_w^2	30.1	37.5	24.5	29.2
F	4.34	3.66	7.13	4.76
r_i	0.625	0.571	0.754	0.653
r_{imz}		0.680		0.813

TABLE 9. Estimated heritability ratios by race and social class for aptitude scores

Aptitude Test Scores	Black					White				
	r_{ios}	r_{iss}	r_{imz}	h_r^2	h_a^2	r_{ios}	r_{iss}	r_{imz}	h_r^2	h_a^2
				Below-median group						
Verbal	0.419	0.486	0.558	0.309	0.343	0.546	0.481	*	*	*
Nonverbal	0.523	0.513	*	*	*	0.619	0.524	*	*	*
Total	0.599	0.526	*	*	*	0.631	0.604	*	*	*
				Middle and above-median group						
Verbal	0.460	0.618	0.753	0.651	0.723	0.553	0.676	0.749	0.436	0.484
Nonverbal	0.437	0.570	0.698	0.580	0.644	0.625	0.634	0.642	0.038	0.042
Total	0.571	0.625	0.680	0.242	0.269	0.653	0.754	0.813	0.356	0.395
				All						
Verbal	0.435	0.543	0.653	0.470	0.522	0.594	0.669	0.719	0.270	0.299
Nonverbal	0.490	0.535	0.594	0.224	0.249	0.662	0.631	*	*	*
Total	0.585	0.567	*	*	*	0.694	0.753	0.791	0.209	0.232

* Cannot be estimated.

in all six comparisons of advantaged and disadvantaged groups. For blacks, total variance was larger in four of six comparisons. This finding reflects the greater phenotypic variability of advantaged children, as predicted in model 1. The intraclass correlations were found to be comparable for blacks and whites within classes (see Table 9).

Assuming that the comparison of estimated monozygotic correla-

TABLE 10. Percentage of variance in verbal aptitude scores for opposite-sex twins by race and social class

Source	Disadvantaged			Advantaged		
	Between Family	Within Family	Total	Between Family	Within Family	Total
		Black				
Genetic	18.8	15.5	34.3	39.7	32.6	72.3
Environmental	23.1	42.6	65.7	6.3	21.4	27.7
Total	41.9	58.1	100.0	46.0	54.0	100.0
		White				
Genetic	*	*	*	24.0	19.6	43.6
Environmental	54.6	45.4	*	31.3	25.1	56.4
Total	54.6	45.4	*	55.3	44.7	100.0

* Cannot be estimated.

TABLE 11. Percentages of variance in nonverbal aptitude scores for opposite-sex twins by race and social class

Source	Disadvantaged			Advantaged		
	Between Family	Within Family	Total	Between Family	Within Family	Total
		Black				
Genetic	*	*	*	35.4	29.0	64.4
Environmental	52.3	47.7	*	8.3	27.3	35.6
Total	52.3	47.7	*	43.7	56.3	100.0
		White				
Genetic	*	*	*	2.3	1.9	4.2
Environmental	61.9	38.1	*	60.2	35.6	95.8
Total	61.9	38.1	*	62.5	37.5	100.0

* Cannot be estimated.

tions and opposite-sex dizygotic correlations can be used to estimate heritability ratios, the proportion of genetic to total variance was calculated by the restricted and assortative mating formulas. Table 10 gives the intraclass correlations and estimated heritabilities for aptitude scores by race and social class.

As noted earlier, the proportion of genetic variance in disadvantaged groups was low, but indeterminant—except for verbal aptitude among blacks. Aptitude scores in advantaged groups all showed heritability estimates of greater than zero, except in the nonverbal scores of whites. Verbal aptitude scores had the highest heritability for both blacks and whites.

Based on the estimated heritability ratios, genetic and environmental variances can be apportioned. The apportionment between and within families is based on the ratio of between-family to total variance, expressed in the intraclass correlation. Only opposite-sex pairs were used, because their correlations were known to be based on a common inheritance of about 55 percent.

From Tables 11, 12, and 13, one can see that the percentage of total variance attributable to genetic sources was always higher in the advantaged groups of both races. In most cases, genetic variance could not be estimated for the aptitude scores of lower-class children. For both advantaged and disadvantaged children, however, there were approximately equal vari-

TABLE 12. **Percentages of variance in total aptitude for opposite-sex twins by race and social class**

Source	Disadvantaged			Advantaged		
	Between Family	Within Family	Total	Between Family	Within Family	Total
Black						
Genetic	*	*	*	14.3	11.7	26.0
Environmental	59.9	40.1	*	42.7	31.3	74.0
Total	59.9	40.1	*	57.0	43.0	100.0
White						
Genetic	*	*	*	21.5	17.5	39.0
Environmental	63.1	36.9	*	43.5	17.5	61.0
Total	63.1	36.9	*	65.0	35.0	100.0

* Cannot be estimated.

TABLE 13. **Analysis of variance of aptitude scores for same-sex pairs by race**

Mean Squares	Black		White	
	Male (N = 139)	Female (N = 194)	Male (N = 96)	Female (N = 96)
Verbal				
σ_b^2	144.3	119.0	162.5	134.8
σ_w^2	43.1	34.7	34.7	24.4
F	3.35	3.43	4.68	5.52
r_1	0.540	0.549	0.648	0.693
Nonverbal				
σ_b^2	131.6	129.1	156.3	144.6
σ_w^2	47.6	33.7	28.7	39.0
F	2.76	3.83	5.45	3.71
r_1	0.468	0.586	0.690	0.575
Total				
σ_b^2	127.6	127.3	202.0	135.0
σ_w^2	43.0	29.5	26.1	21.2
F	2.97	4.31	7.75	6.36
r_1	0.496	0.623	0.771	0.728

ances between and within families, the between-family variance being some-what larger more often. Thus, the major finding of the analysis of variance is that advantaged and disadvantaged children differ primarily in what pro-portion of variance in aptitude scores can be attributed to environmental sources.

To check on the validity of the findings, the aptitude data were analyzed separately for male-male and female-female pairs who were found to have correlations of similar magnitude. The overall results of the study were not due to the greater similarity of male or female pairs, as seen in Table 14.

TABLE 14. Analysis of variance of white, advantaged, opposite-sex twins, by aptitude level

Mean Squares	Both < 50 (N = 22)	Both ≥ 50 (N = 31)
	Verbal	
σ_b^2	54.8	65.7
σ_w^2	30.1	20.3
F	1.82	3.24
r_1	0.291	0.528
	Nonverbal	
σ_b^2	44.7	59.4
σ_w^2	18.7	20.9
F	2.39	2.84
r_1	0.41	0.479
	Total	
σ_b^2	34.6	57.5
σ_w^2	17.8	19.8
F	1.94	2.90
r_1	0.320	0.487

Genotype-Environment Interaction

While neither model 1 nor model 2 predicted statistical interaction, a combination of the two models could predict an interaction between geno-types and environments in producing phenotypic ability. Wiseman (33) has suggested that children with lower IQ's are less affected by environmental deprivations than are children with higher IQ's. If lower IQ children are less affected by differential family environments, then the between-family variance and the correlations between siblings with lower IQ's will be smaller than among siblings with higher IQ's, on whom family environment presumably has a greater effect. Burt (34) reported a correlation of .61 between siblings both of whose IQ's were above 100, and a correlation of .43 between siblings with IQ's below 100.

The possible explanations for these findings include (i) restriction of total variance in the group with lower IQ's because of a "floor effect" in the tests used; (ii) larger within-pair variances for children with lower IQ's as a function of a poor family environment; and (iii) smaller between-pair variances for children with lower IQ's as a function of less responsiveness to different family environments.

A test for restriction in total variance was made by dividing all opposite-sex pairs into those with both twins above the mean of 50 and those with both twins below. Mixed cases were eliminated from the samples. Neither black nor white twins with aptitude scores below the mean had lower total variances than the above-mean groups. Since total variances were equal in the two groups, a test of the interaction hypothesis could be made.

To test for the effects of lower IQ alone on patterns of sibling correlation in the white group, only those children with social class ratings at the median and above were included. Intraclass correlations for the 22 white, advantaged, opposite-sex pairs with aptitude scores below 50, and the 31 above 50 were found to be consistently different. As Table 14 shows, siblings below the aptitude mean had consistently lower correlations between their scores than siblings above the mean. The lower correlations between siblings with lower IQ's were not a function of social class, but of smaller between-pair variances, primarily. This suggests that white children with lower IQ's are less susceptible to environmental differences between families than are children with higher IQ's, even in an advantaged population. There was no evidence of interaction between IQ and environment in the black population.

Mean Scores and Genetic Variance

The lower mean scores of disadvantaged children of both races can be explained in large part by the lower genetic variance in their scores. A "deprived" or unfavorable environment for the development of phenotypic IQ unfavorably affects mean scores, phenotypic variability, genetic variance in phenotypes, and the expression of individual differences (21, pp. 64–65). No study of human family correlations to date has looked at all of these effects of suppressive environments. In a landmark study of mice, however, Henderson (8) has demonstrated that suppressive environments reduce the amount of genetic variance in performance, reduce phenotypic variability, and reduce mean performance scores. The percentage of genetic variance in the scores of standard-cage-reared animals was one-fourth that of animals with enriched environments (10 percent versus 40 percent). Not only did genetic variance account for a larger portion of the variance among animals with enriched environments, but their performance on the learning task was vastly superior to that of their relatively deprived littermates.

Although generalizations from genetic studies of the behavior of mice to genetic studies of the behavior of human beings are generally unwarranted (because mechanisms of development vary greatly among species), the role that a better rearing environment played in the development of genetic individual differences among Henderson's mice finds an obvious parallel with the effects of advantaged SES homes in this study.

From studies of middle-class white populations, investigators have reached the conclusion that genetic variability accounts for about 75 percent of the total variance in IQ scores of whites. A closer look at children reared under different conditions shows that the percentage of genetic variance and the mean scores are very much a function of the rearing conditions of the population. A first look at the black population suggests that genetic variability is important in advantaged groups, but much less important in the disadvantaged. Since most blacks are socially disadvantaged, the proportion of genetic variance in the aptitude scores of black children is considerably less than that of the white children, as predicted by model 1.

"Disadvantage" has been used as a term throughout this paper to connote all of the biological and social deficits associated with poverty, regardless of race. As long as these environmental factors were considered to be the same, and to act in the same way on children of both races, then racial differences in scores could be discussed. Unquantified environmental differences between the races—either different factors or the same factors acting in different ways—preclude cross-racial comparisons. Informed speculation is not out of order at this point, however.

Those cultural differences between races that affect the *relevance* of home experience to scholastic aptitudes and achievement may be of primary importance in understanding the remaining racial differences in scores, once environmental deficits have been accounted for. In a series of studies of African children's scholastic performance, Irvine found that many sources of variation that are important for European and American scores are irrelevant for African children (35, p. 93).

> Of environmental variables studied in population samples, including socio-economic status, family size, family position, and school quality, only school quality showed significant and consistent relation to ability and attainment tests. Other sources of variation were irrelevant to the skills being learned.

For the black child in Philadelphia, the relevance of extrascholastic experience is surely greater than it is for the tribal African. But one may question the equivalence of black and white cultural environments in their support for the development of scholastic aptitudes. As many authors of an environmental persuasion have indicated (6, 36), the black child learns a different, not a deficient, set of language rules, and he may learn a different style of thought. The transfer of training from home to school performance is probably less direct for black children than for white children.

The hypothesis of cultural differences in no way detracts from the predictive validity of aptitude tests for the scholastic achievement of black children. The correlations between aptitude and achievement are equally good in both racial groups. But the cultural differences hypothesis does speak to the issue of genetic and environmental components of variance. If most black children have limited experience with environmental features that contribute to the development of scholastic skills, then genetic variation will not be as prominent a source of individual phenotypic variation; nor will other between-family differences, such as SES level, be as important as they are in a white population. School-related experiences will be proportionately more important for black children than for white children in the development of scholastic aptitudes. The Coleman report (37) suggested that scholastic environment does have more influence on the performance of black children than it does on the performance of white children. The generally lower scores of black children can be fit adequately to the model 1 hypothesis, with the additional inter-pretation of cultural differences to account for the lower scores of black children at each social-class level.

The differences in mean IQ between the races can be affected by giving young black children rearing environments that are more conducive to the development of scholastic aptitudes. Or the differences in performance can simply be accepted as differences, and not as deficits. If there are alter-nate ways of being successful within the society, then differences can be valued variations on the human theme (38), regardless of their environmental or genetic origins. Haldane (39) has suggested that, ideally, different human genotypes would be found to respond most favorably to different environ-mental conditions—that genotype-environment interactions would exist for many human characteristics. From a genetic point of view, varied adapta-tions are useful to the species and permit the greatest flowering of individual differences. Socially invidious comparisons, however, can destroy the useful-ness of such differences.

Group differences in mean scores and phenotypic variability that exist because of environmental deprivation can and should be ameliorated. To the extent that children are not given supportive environments for the full development of their individual genetic differences, changes can be made in their prenatal and postnatal environments to improve both their overall per-formance and the genetic variance in their scores. If all children had optimal environments for development, then genetic differences would account for most of the variance in behavior. To the extent that better, more supportive environments can be provided for all children, genetic variance and mean scores will increase for all groups. Contrary to the views of many naive en-vironmentalists, equality of opportunity leads to bigger and better genotype-phenotype correlations. It is toward this goal that socially concerned citizens should work.

References and Notes

1. L. ERLENMEYER-KIMLING, & L. F. JARVIK, Science, 142, 1477 (1963); S. G. VAN-DENBERG, in Genetics, D. Glass (Ed.) (Rockefeller Univ. Press, New York, 1968), pp. 3–58; Acta Genet. Med. Gemellol. 19, 280 (1970).

2. C. Burt, *Brit. J. Psychol. 57*, 137 (1966).

3. A. R. Jensen, *Harv. Educ. Rev. 39*, 1 (1969a).

4. ———, in *Disadvantaged child*, J. Hellmuth, Ed. (Brunner-Mazel, New York, 1970), vol. 3, pp. 124–157.

5. T. F. Pettigrew, *A profile of the Negro American* (Van Nostrand, Princeton, N.J., 1964).

6. S. Baratz, & J. Baratz, *Harv. Educ. Rev. 40*, 29 (1970).

7. M. Manosevitz, G. Lindzey, D. Thiessen, *Behavioral genetics: Method and research* (Appleton-Century-Crofts, New York, 1969).

8. N. Henderson, J. *Comp. Physiol. Psychol. 3*, 505 (1970).

9. I. Gottesman, in *Handbook of mental deficiency: psychological theory and research*, N. Ellis, Ed. (McGraw-Hill, New York, 1963), pp. 253–295; F. Weizmann, *Science 171*, 589 (1971).

10. I. Gottesman, in *Social class, race, and psychological development*, M. Deutsch, I. Katz, A. Jensen, Eds. (Holt, Rinehart and Winston, New York, 1968), pp. 11–51.

11. C. V. Kiser, *Eugen. Quart. 15*, 98 (1968).

12. A genotype is the genetic makeup of an individual. The term may refer to one, several, or all loci. Genetic variance refers to the differences among individuals that arise from differences in genotypes. A phenotype is the sum total of all observable characteristics of an individual. Phenotypic variance refers to the observable differences among individuals.

13. J. Thoday, *J. Biosoc. Sci. 1* (Suppl.), 3 (1969).

14. H. Birch, & J. Gussow, *Disadvantaged children: Health, nutrition and school failure* (Harcourt, Brace & World, New York, 1970).

15. M. Deutsch, I. Katz, A. Jensen, Eds., *Social class, race and psychological development* (Holt, Rinehart and Winston, New York, 1968).

16. C. Burt, *Brit. J. Statist. Psychol. 14*, 3 (1961); R. Herrnstein, *Atl. Mon. 228*, 43 (September 1971).

17. J. Waller, thesis, University of Minnesota (1970).

18. M. Skodak, & H. Skeels, *J. Genet. Psychol. 75*, 85 (1949).

19. Suppressive environments are those which do not permit or evoke the development of a genetic characteristic. "Suppose, for example, that early experience in the manipulation of objects is essential for inducing hoarding behavior. Genetic differences in this form of behavior will not be detected in animals reared without such experience" (21, p. 65).

20. J. L. Fuller, & W. R. Thompson, *Behavior genetics* (Wiley, New York, 1960).

21. The genotype-phenotype correlation is generally expressed as the square root of the heritability of a characteristic in a given population ($p_{pg} = \sqrt{h^2}$).

22. H. Strandskov, & E. Edelen, *Genetics 31*, 438 (1946).

23. S. G. Vandenberg, quoted in C. Burt (2).

24. F. Sandon, *Brit. J. Statist. Psychol. 12*, 133 (1959).

25. T. Husen, *Psychological twin research* (Almquist and Wiksele, Stockholm, 1959).

26. Of the 124 pairs in special classes, one or both members of 99 pairs were enrolled in "retarded educable" and "retarded trainable" classes. The racial distribution of the "retarded" twins was 80 percent black and 20 percent white, which represents a 15 percent discrepancy from the racial distribution of twins in the public schools. The exclusion of "retarded" twins attenuates the sample and restricts the conclusions of the study to children in normal classrooms.

27. Aptitude tests used in this study are Primary Mental Abilities (2nd grade): *verbal meaning, perceptual speed, *number facility, spatial relations, and *total; Lorge-Thorndike Intelligence Tests (4th grade): *verbal, *nonverbal, and *total; Academic Promise Tests (6th grade): abstract reasoning, numerical, *nonverbal total, language usage, verbal, *verbal total, and *total; Differential Abilities Tests (8th grade): *verbal reasoning, *numerical ability, abstract reasoning, space relations, mechanical reasoning, clerical speed and accuracy, language usage, and *total (scholastic aptitude); School and College Ability Tests (10th grade): *verbal, *quantitative, and *total; Test of Academic Progress (12th grade): *verbal, *numerical, and *total. Achievement tests used are Iowa Tests of Basic Skills (3rd through 8th grades): *vocabulary, *reading comprehension, *language total, work-study skills, *arithmetic total, and *composite (average of five scores). Asterisks indicate scores reported.

28. H. STEVENSON, A. FRIEDRICHS, W. SIMPSON, *Child Develop. 41*, 625 (1970).

29. O. BUROS, Ed. *The sixth mental measurements yearbook* (Gryphon Press, Highland Park, N.J., 1965).

30. J. STANLEY, *Science 171*, 640 (1971).

31. A. JENSEN, *Proc. Nat. Acad. Sci. U.S. 58*, 149 (1967).

32. My gratitude to Prof. V. Elving Anderson and Dr. Paul Nichols for suggesting this analysis.

33. S. WISEMAN, in *Genetic and environmental factors in human ability*, J. Meade and A. Parkes, Eds. (Oliver and Boyd, London, 1966), pp. 64–80.

34. C. BURT, *Brit. J. Educ. Psychol. 13*, 83 (1943).

35. S. IRVINE, *J. Biosoc. Sci. 1* (Suppl.), 91 (1969).

36. S. HOUSTON, *Child Develop. 41*, 947 (1970); F. WILLIAMS, in *Language and poverty*, F. Williams, Ed. (Markham, Chicago, 1970), pp. 1–10; C. Cazden, *ibid.*, pp. 81–101.

37. U.S. COMMISSION ON CIVIL RIGHTS, *Racial isolation in the public schools* (Government Printing Office, Washington, D.C., 1967).

38. D. FREEDMAN, in *Progress in human behavior genetics*, S. G. Vandenburg, Ed. (Johns Hopkins Press, Baltimore, 1968), pp. 1–5.

39. J. B. S. HALDANE, *Ann. Eugen. 13*, 197 (1946).

40. My gratitude goes to Heidelise Rivinus and Marsha Friefelder, who collected much of the data; to William Barker and Melvin Kuhbander, who ran many of the analyses; to Professors I. I. Gottesman, Arthur R. Jensen, Harold W. Stevenson, Leonard Heston, V. Elving Anderson, Steven G. Vandenberg, and Lee Willerman, and to Dr. Paul Nichols, all of whom critically read an earlier draft of this article. The research was supported by a grant from the National Institute of Child Health and Human Development (HD-04751).

The academic achievement of children is dependent upon a variety of factors both within and outside of the classroom. Within the classroom, it is not only the teacher's skill that determines his or her effectiveness. As the authors of the following article demonstrate, the teacher's orientation (concrete or abstract) determines the general tone or atmosphere of the classroom, and this in turn affects the children in significant ways. An important contribution of this study is its demonstration of how facets of the teacher's personality (the affective or emotional domain) play a significant part in academic learning (the cognitive domain). It is clear from this study that academic learning is never simply cognitive; it is always affected by "feeling" dimensions.

Teachers' Beliefs, Classroom Atmosphere and Student Behavior

O. J. Harvey, Misha Prather, B. Jack White, and James K. Hoffmeister

Harvey, White, Prather, Alter and Hoffmeister (1966) found recently that preschool teachers of concrete and abstract belief systems differed markedly in the class room environments they created for their students. Teachers representing System 4, the most abstract belief system treated by Harvey, Hunt and Schroder (1961) differed from representatives of System 1, the most concrete mode of functioning characterized by Harvey and others (1961), in what was presumed to be an educationally desirable direction on all 26 dimensions of classroom behavior on which they were rated.

The difference was statistically significant on 14 dimensions: System 4 teachers expressed greater warmth toward children, showed greater perceptiveness of the children's wishes and needs, were more flexible in meeting the interests and needs of the children, were more encouraging of individual responsibility, gave greater encouragement to free expression of feelings, were more encouraging of creativity, displayed greater ingenuity in improvising teaching and play materials, invoked unexplained rules less frequently, were less rule oriented, were less determining of classroom and playground procedure, manifested less need for structure, were less punitive, and were less anxious about being observed.

Source: Reprinted by permission from *American Educational Research Journal,* March 1968, 5 (2), 151–166. Copyright © 1968 by the American Educational Research Association.

Note: The collection of these data and part of their analyses were supported by the Office of Economic Opportunity, Contract OEO–1274 with the Extension Division of the University of Colorado. Harvey's participation in the data collection part of this study occurred while he was a Fellow at the Center for Advanced Study in the Behavioral Sciences. His subsequent participation has been supported by a Career Development Award from the National Institute of Mental Health, No. K03 MH28117.

A cluster analysis of these 14 dimensions (Tyron & Bailey, 1965, 1966) yielded three factors of resourcefulness, dictatorialness and punitiveness. System 4 teachers were more resourceful, less dictatorial and less punitive than System 1 teachers.

While consistent both with our theoretical stance and a wide range of other differences found between the more concretely and the more abstractly functioning individuals (Adams, Harvey, & Heslin, 1966; Harvey, 1963; 1966; Harvey & Ware, 1967; Ware & Harvey, 1967; White & Harvey, 1965), the finding that teachers' belief systems affect their overt behavior in the classroom does not bear directly upon the more educationally significant question of the influence of teachers' beliefs and behavior upon the learning and performance of their students. It is with this later question that the present study is concerned.

More specifically, the main aim of this study was to assess the relationship between students' performance and teachers' resourcefulness, dictatorialness and punitiveness. In addition, the study provided a test of the replicability of the early findings that concrete and abstract teachers differ in the kinds of classroom behavior they manifest.

The general expectancies were that teachers of more concrete belief systems would display less resourcefulness, more dictatorialness and more punitiveness in the classroom than the more abstract teachers, as found in the previous study (Harvey, and others, 1966); and that greater abstractness, greater resourcefulness, less dictatorialness and less punitiveness on the part of the teacher would be associated with more educationally preferable performances of the children.

Method

Concrete and abstract teachers of kindergarten and first grade were rated on the 14 dimensions found by Harvey and others (1966) to discriminate significantly between concrete and abstract teachers. Their students were rated, as a class, on a specially constructed 31-item rating scale.

TEACHER RATING SCALE. This instrument, while providing the necessary information for a test of the replicability of the earlier results (Harvey and others, 1966), was intended primarily as a measure of teachers' overt resourcefulness, dictatorialness and punitiveness. It consisted of the 14 items from which these three factors were derived: (1) warmth toward the children, (2) perceptiveness of the children's needs and wishes, (3) flexibility in meeting the needs and interests of the children, (4) maintenance of relaxed relationships with the children, (5) encouragement of individual responsibility, (6) encouragement of free expression of feeling, (7) encouragement of creativity, (8) ingenuity in improvising teaching and play materials, (9) use of unexplained rules, (10) rule orientation, (11) determination of classroom procedures, (12) need for structure, (13) punitiveness and (14) anxiety induced by the observers' presence.

STUDENT RATING SCALE.   This measure of student behavior, which provided the major dependent variables of this study, consisted of the following items: (1) overall adherence to the teacher's rules, (2) immediacy of response to the rules, (3) adherence to the spirit (vs. the letter) of the rules, (4) information seeking, (5) independence, (6) cooperativeness with the teacher (7) task attentiveness, (8) enthusiasm, (9) voice in classroom activities, (10) voluntary participation in classroom activities, (11) free expression of feelings, (12) diversity of goal relevant activities, (13) student-initiated activity, (14) amount of activity, (15) considerateness toward classmates, (16) reciprocal affection between classmates, (17) cooperation with classmates, (18) taking turns with classmates, (19) amount of interaction with classmates, (20) novelty of response to problem or teacher's question, (21) appropriateness of response, (22) accuracy of facts, (23) integration of facts, (24) orientation toward specificity of facts (vs. more general principles), (25) roteness of answers or solutions, (26) active hostility toward the teacher, (27) passive hostility toward the teacher, (28) fear attentiveness (anxiety), (29) aggression toward classmates, (30) guidance seeking, and (31) approval seeking.

Each of the dimensions in both the teacher and student rating scale was rated on a six-point scale: 3, 2, and 1 for "far," "considerably" and "slightly," above average respectively; and —1, —2, and —3 for "slightly," "considerably" and "far" below average respectively. The "average" category was omitted with the aim (by creating a forced choice condition) of avoiding the common tendency of observers (Os) to assign a wide variety of discriminably different behaviors to this category. Through a training program described later, an attempt was made to establish equivalent "averages" for all Os.

Subjects

Since the present study was part of a larger investigation concerned with the effects of prior participation in Head Start, classrooms were selected for observation if they contained at least one kindergarten or first grade student who had gone to Head Start nine months earlier (i.e., during the summer of 1965) and who was attending public school for the first time. These criteria yielded 118 classes, 92 kindergarten and 26 first grade, in 18 rural and urban Colorado school districts. The 92 kindergarten classes were taught by 64 teachers while the 26 first grade classes were taught by 26 teachers. Each of the 118 classes, with an average of 26 students, was observed and rated *as a class,* not as individual students, on the student rating scale.

Of the 90 teachers, 67 completed the "This I Believe" (TIB) Test and 66 completed the Conceptual Systems Test (CST). Both the TIB and CST are tests of concreteness-abstractness of belief systems, the former being based upon sentence completions and the latter upon response to objective items.

THE "THIS I BELIEVE" (TIB) TEST.   This test, developed specifically as a measure of concreteness-abstractness of conceptual or belief systems (e.g., Harvey, 1964, 1966; Harvey, and others, 1966; Ware & Harvey, 1967;

White & Harvey, 1965), requires S to indicate his beliefs about a number of socially and personally relevant concept referents by completing in two or three sentences the phrase "This I believe about————," the blank being replaced successively by one of the referents. The referents employed in the present study were "religion," "friendship," "the American way of life," "sin," "education," "the family," "people on welfare," "punishment," "teaching" and "sex."

From the relativism, tautologicalness, novelty and connotative implications or richness of the completions, together with criteria implied below, respondents may be classified into one of the four principal systems posited by Harvey and others (1961) or into some mixture of two or more systems.

More specifically, Ss are classified as representing predominantly System 1, the most concrete mode of dimensionalizing and construing the world, if their completions denote such characteristics as high absolutism, high tautologicalness, high frequency of platitudes and normative statements, high ethnocentrism, high religiosity, assertion of the superiority of American morality and expression of highly positive attitudes toward institutional referents.

Subjects are categorized as representing System 2, the next to the lowest level of abstractness, if, in addition to being highly evaluative and absolute, they express strong negative attitudes toward such referents as marriage, religion, the American way of life—the same referents toward which System 1 representatives manifest highly positive attitudes.

Responses to the TIB are scored as representing System 3 functioning, the next to the highest level of abstractness posited by Harvey and others (1961) if they indicate more relativism and less evaluativeness than Systems 1 and 2 and at the same time express strongly positive beliefs about friendship, people and interpersonal relations.

System 4 functioning, the highest of the four levels of abstractness, is indicated by TIB responses that imply a high degree of novelty and appropriateness, independence without negativism, high relativism and contingency of thought, and the general usage of multidimensional rather than unidimensional interpretive schemata.

Of the 67 teachers who completed the TIB, 50 were classified as System 1, none was categorized as System 2, four were scored as System 3, eight were classified as weak instances of System 4, and five were scored as admixtures of Systems 1 and 3. In the analysis involving the TIB the admixtures were omitted; Systems 3 and 4 were combined into the *more abstract group;* and System 1 teachers were treated as the *more concrete group.* Of the 50 concrete teachers, 30 taught 44 classes of kindergartners and 20 taught 20 classes of first-graders. Seven of the 12 abstract teachers taught 11 kindergarten classes while the other five abstract teachers taught five first-grade classes. Thus it should be noted that while both concrete and abstract first grade teachers each taught only one class, kindergarten teachers, both concrete and abstract, each taught an approximate average of 1½ classes.

THE CONCEPTUAL SYSTEMS TEST (*CST*). All but one of the 67 teachers who completed the TIB Test also completed the objective measure of belief systems, the CST. From a pool of several hundred items and numerous runs through Tryon's program of cluster analysis (Tryon & Bailey, 1965; 1966) seven factors have been extracted and replicated which are theoretically consistent with the major characteristics of the four principal belief systems posited by Harvey and others (1961). These factors as we have tentatively labeled them (Harvey, 1967) are (1) Divine Fate Control, (2) Need for Simplicity-Certainty, (3) Need for Structure-Order, (4) Distrust of Social Authority, (5) Friendship Absolutism, (6) Moral Absolutism, and (7) General Pessimism.

While the CST was administered in its entirety, for purposes of this study scores were derived for only the three clusters of Divine Fate Control, Need for Simplicity-Certainty and Need for Structure-Order. The combined scores from these three factors were treated as our second measure of a teacher's concreteness-abstractness. Representative items comprising each of the three of these component factors include:

1. Divine Fate Control (DFC) is assessed by such items as "There are some things which God will never permit man to know," "In the final analysis, events in the world will be in line with the master plan of God," and "I believe that to attain my goals it is only necessary for me to live as God would have me live."

2. Need for Simplicity-Certainty (NS-C) is inferred from response to such statements as "I dislike having to change my plans in the middle of a task," "It is annoying to listen to a lecturer who cannot seem to make up his mind as to what he really believes," and "A group which tolerates extreme differences of opinion among its own members cannot exist for long."

3. Need for Structure-Order (NS-O) is derived from such items as "I don't like to work on a problem unless there is a possibility of coming out with a clear-cut, definite answer," "I don't like for things to be uncertain and unpredictable," and "I like to have a place for everything and everything in its place."

TRAINING OF OBSERVERS AND ASSESSMENT OF INTER-OBSERVER RELIABILITY. Each of the nine *O*s, all females, participated in six training sessions during which six teachers and their classes were observed and independently rated. Each observation session was followed by a lengthy group discussion among the *O*s and other staff members aimed at increasing the reliability of the ratings through improving observation techniques and clarifying and standardizing meaning and usage for the rating categories.

Inter-judge reliability for the nine Os was assessed for both the teacher and student rating scales at three points: immediately following the last training session, one week after field observations began, and immediately preceding completion of the experimental observations, 2 weeks later. The mean correlation between every pair of judges for the teacher scale was .78, .76 and .70 for the three periods respectively; the corresponding reliability values for the student scale were .84, .75 and .77.

PROCEDURE.   Each teacher and her students were observed in the classroom on a single occasion by a single O for approximately two hours. All teachers had been advised earlier by their principals of the dates on which they were to be observed.

Observation occurred during normal classroom activities on a day free of special events in order to render the conditions of observation as comparable as possible across classrooms. The O arrived before class, introduced herself, explained (with the aim of allaying the teacher's apprehension and fostering her cooperation) that the purpose of the visit was to gather examples of good teaching procedure that could be utilized as bases for future teacher training programs, and requested that she be allowed to observe while remaining as inconspicuous as possible in order to minimize the effects of her presence upon the children. To further O's unobtrusiveness and simultaneously to increase the likelihood of both the teacher and her students behaving in their usual fashion, each teacher was asked not to converse with O during the observation period.

The teacher and her class were rated by the same O, the students being observed and rated first as independently as possible of the teacher's behavior. This procedure was aimed at minimizing the contamination between the dependent and independent variables likely to result from the students and teacher being rated by the same O. Extensive pretesting indicated that this procedure, of having the O first concentrate on and rate the behavior of the students as a class before focusing on the teacher, yielded a relationship between student and teacher ratings that was no higher than that between separate ratings of the teacher and her students by different judges. In fact, the evidence indicated clearly that, while the use of a single O for both the teacher and her students may have produced contamination, at the same time it produced seemingly more valid ratings than those yielded by the practice of one judge observing only the teacher while the other O noted only the responses of the children. Thus the degree of contamination inherent in the method of observation we employed appears to be preferable to the loss of validity that results from attempts of Os to rate the behavior of the teacher and her students without the use of the other as a referent.

In rating the children, care was exercised to rate the class as a whole and not to give inordinate weight to a small minority by concentrating on the behavior of a single child or a few children.

Results

Tests of Assumptions

Before analyzing the effects of teachers' overt behavior upon students' performance, it was first necessary to test two basic assumptions: (1) that the 14 items of the teacher rating scale would yield the three factors of resourcefulness, dictatorialness and punitiveness, as they had in the earlier study (Harvey, and others, 1966); and (2) that variations in the concreteness-abstractness of the teachers' beliefs would lead them to score differently on these three behavioral factors.

The validity of the first assumption was demonstrated by the results of a factor analysis of the teacher rating scale by Tryon's method of cluster analysis (Tryon & Bailey, 1965; 1966) which yielded the three anticipated clusters.

Resourcefulness was comprised of four behavioral items. They, together with their factor loadings (represented by the values in the parentheses) were: utilization of physical resources (.77), diversity of simultaneous activities (.77), encouragement of creativity (.72) and ingenuity in improvising teaching and play materials (.71).

Dictatorialness contained seven items: need for structure (.90), flexibility (−.90), rule orientation (.86), encouragement of free expression of feelings, (−.84), teacher determination of classroom procedures (.81) and the of unexplained rules (.70).

Punitiveness was based on three items: warmth toward the children (−.86), perceptiveness of the children's needs and wishes (−.85) and punitiveness (.77).

The second assumption also proved to be warranted. Teachers classified on the basis of the TIB as being concrete were significantly less resourceful ($t = 4.03$, $p < .001$), significantly more dictatorial ($t = 1.67$, $p < .05$), and were more punitive, although not significantly more, ($t = 1.05$, $p > .10$) than teachers classified as abstract. Moreover, the abstractness measure from the CST correlated significantly positively with teacher resourcefulness ($r = .37$, $p < .005$), and significantly negatively with both teacher dictatorialness ($r = −.19$, $p < .05$) and punitiveness ($r = −.19$, $p < .05$). These results, through replicating the more essential findings of our earlier study (Harvey, and others, 1966), make it clear that variation in the concreteness-abstractness of teachers' beliefs generates theoretically consistent and predictable parallels in the overt behavior of these individuals. Thus an examination of the effects of teachers' beliefs and behavior upon their students, the major concern of this study, becomes appropriate.

Concreteness-Abstractness of Teachers' Beliefs and Student Performance.

FACTOR ANALYSIS OF THE STUDENT RATING SCALE.   In order to extricate the more generic dimensions encompassed within the 31-item student rating scale and thus enhance the coherency of the presentation of results, the student rating scale was factorized by Tryon's method of cluster analysis (Tryon & Bailey, 1965; 1966) and the resulting factors related to variation in teachers' beliefs and overt behavior.

Seven factors were derived from the student rating scale. The first cluster, termed *cooperation,* was comprised of five items, which with their factor loadings were: immediacy of response to rules (.91), overall adherence to teachers' rules (.86), child-sustained activity (.68), cooperativeness with teacher (.57) and adherence to the spirit of the rules (.55). The second factor, which centered around *student involvement,* consisted of eight items: enthusiasm (.89), voluntary participation in classroom activity (.82), free expression of feelings (.78), voice of students in classroom activity (.78), independence (.76), information seeking (.72), insecurity (−.66) and task attentiveness (.63). The third factor, labeled *activity level,* was derived from two items: amount of activity (.81) and diversity of goal-relevant activity (.81). The fourth factor, *nurturance seeking,* contained two items: guidance seeking (.68) and approval seeking (.59). The fifth factor, termed *achievement level,* included three items: accuracy of facts (.81), appropriateness of solution (.80) and integration of facts (.71). The sixth factor, *helpfulness,* was comprised of four items: considerateness toward classmates (.79), cooperativeness with classmates (.71), taking turns (.56) and aggression (−.49). The seventh cluster, referred to as *concreteness of response,* contained three items: roteness of answers or solutions (.88), orientation toward specificity of facts (.71) and novelty of answer or solution (−.56.) Factor scores were obtained by computing the mean score on the items constituting the factor.

Four of the items from the student rating scale were not included in any of the seven clusters: amount of interaction, reciprocal affection, passive and active hostility. Results relating to these four items will not be reported.

TIB CLASSIFICATION AND STUDENT PERFORMANCE.   Comparisons were made between the 64 classes taught by the 50 teachers classified by the TIB as being concrete and the 16 classes taught by the 12 abstract teachers on each of the seven factors derived from the student rating scale.

As indicated in Table 1, students of more abstract teachers, in comparison to their counterparts, were significantly more involved in classroom activities, more active, higher in achievement and less concrete in their responses. They were also less nurturant seeking, more cooperative and more helpful, but not significantly so, than students of concrete teachers.

CST FACTORS AND STUDENT PERFORMANCE.   Teachers' scores on the abstractness measure from the CST and on each of the three factors going into

TABLE 1.   Performances of students of concrete and abstract teachers (as classified by the TIB)

Student Rating Scale Factors	Concrete Teachers		Abstract Teachers		t
	Mean	*SD*	*Mean*	*SD*	
Cooperation	4.05	0.82	4.34	0.75	1.26
Involvement	3.60	0.87	4.09	0.90	1.96*
Activity	3.29	1.01	4.22	1.02	3.29**
Nuturance seeking	2.91	0.99	2.56	0.95	−1.27
Achievement	3.90	0.71	4.25	0.56	1.81*
Helpfulness	4.03	0.65	4.20	0.63	0.97
Concreteness	3.78	0.88	3.27	0.80	−2.12*

Note:—*df* for all tests $= 78$
* one-tailed $p < .05$
** one-tailed $p < .01$

this measure were correlated with each of the seven factors from the student rating scale. These relationships are presented in Table 2.

The CST measure of abstractness related significantly to every one of the student performance factors. Greater abstractness of the teacher was accompanied by greater involvement, greater cooperation, more activity, less nurturance seeking, higher achievement, greater helpfulness and less concreteness on the part of the students.

While all three of the factors constituting the measure of teacher abstractness correlated in the predicted direction with performance of the children, the teachers' need for structure-order correlated the highest and most consistently. In fact, the teachers' need for structure-order had greater in-

TABLE 2.   Correlations between clusters from the conceptual systems test and the student rating scale

Student Rating Scale Factors	Teacher Variables: CST Clusters			
	1. Divine Fate Control	*2. Simplicity-Consistency*	*3. Structure-Order*	*4. Abstractness (ε 1-2-3)*
Cooperation	−.14	−.21*	−.22*	.21*
Involvement	−.10	−.18*	−.21*	.18*
Activity	−.12	−.13	−.34**	.19*
Nurturance Seeking	.14	.12	.24*	−.18*
Achievement	−.22*	−.21*	−.30**	.27**
Helpfulness	−.17	−.17	−.15**	.19*
Concreteness	.06	.23*	.29**	−.19*

Note:—*df* for all tests $= 84$
* one-tailed $p < .05$
** one-tailed $p < .01$

fluence on the performance of the children than her belief in divine fate control, need for simplicity-consistency and overall abstractness.

TEACHERS' OVERT BEHAVIOR AND STUDENT PERFORMANCE. Teachers' scores on the behavioral factors of resourcefulness, dictatorialness and punitiveness were correlated with the seven student performance clusters. These results are included in Table 3.

TABLE 3. Correlations of teacher dictatorialness, punitiveness and resourcefulness with student performance factors

Student Behavior	Teacher Behavior		
	Resourcefulness	Dictatorialness	Punitiveness
Cooperativeness	.23**	—.18*	—.34**
Involvement	.69**	—.84**	—.73**
Activity	.76**	—.33**	—.29**
Nurturance Seeking	—.12	—.05	—.01
Achievement	.28**	—.28**	—.32**
Helpfulness	.02	—.23**	—.32**
Concreteness	—.60**	.67**	.56**

Note:—df for all tests of significance = 116
* one-tailed $p < .05$
** one-tailed $p < .01$

The resourcefulness of the teacher correlated significantly positively with student cooperation, involvement, activity and achievement and significantly negatively with the concreteness of students' responses.

The teachers' dictatorialness correlated significantly negatively with the students' cooperation, involvement, activity; achievement and helpfulness and significantly positively with students' concreteness of responses.

Teachers' punitiveness correlated significantly negatively with student cooperation, involvement, activity, achievement and helpfulness and significantly positively with the concreteness of the students' responses.

Nuturance seeking was the only one of the seven student performance clusters that did not relate significantly to any one of the teacher behaviors.

Discussion

By replicating the findings of our earlier study (Harvey, and others, 1966), these results make it clear that the concreteness-abstractness of teachers' belief systems affect their overt resourcefulness, dictatorialness and punitiveness in the classroom. In addition, the results show that the classroom behavior of the teacher and the behavior of the students are significantly related. Clearly, this relationship does not tell us the nature of the causality. Theoretically, the teacher's behavior could determine the childrens' behavior, the reverse could be true, both could be determined by a third factor, such as the organizational climate, or the effects could be produced by the inter-action among all of these factors. The possibility that the relationship be-tween teachers' and students' behavior is a result of organizational climate is minimized by the fact that the concrete and abstract teachers, while se-lected from the same organizational climates, nevertheless differed markedly in their classroom behaviors, as did their students. Further, while students no doubt affect the behavior of their teachers, it appears more likely that, because of her socially prescribed power, her influence is greater and more direct than theirs.

The obtained differences between concrete and abstract teachers probably would have been accentuated had the group of more abstract teachers been comprised only of clear instances of System 4. Instead unclear instances, together with cases of System 3, were combined with clear instances of Sys-tem 4 to constitute the abstract group in this study. Yet, if our experiences from the earlier (Harvey, and others, 1966) and the present study are typical, a large sample of teachers would be necessary to yield an adequate number of clear cases of System 4. Of the 292 teachers to whom we have admin-istered the TIB, only 18, or six percent, have been classified as System 4, not all of which were ideal cases. While strongly suggesting that in terms of absolute numbers few teachers operate at the System 4 level, it should be noted that this percentage is almost identical to the seven percent of System 4 individuals we have found from among approximately 3000 undergradu-ates administered the TIB. In fact, this percentage appears to be so constant across a large sample of subjects that some special factor(s) may be necessary to account for it.

Indeed the whole question of the determinants of the different belief systems is far from being answered, having been resolved only partially at the theoretical level and even less empirically. One of the more theoretically viable determinants seems to be the freedom the individual had as a child to explore the world of values and to evolve and internalize rules on the basis of direct experience and pragmatic outcomes (Adams, and others, 1966; Harvey, 1967). Although this freedom and the differential evolution of sys-tems should be expected to relate to a host of sociological factors, the only significant demographic variable we have found, from the study of two large samples of subjects made up of college students and school teachers, centers around religion. Thus while representatives of the belief systems did not differ in such background factors as socio-economic status, educational level of themselves or their parents, or even in intelligence, they did differ in such religion related behavior as frequency of church attendance. This kind of evidence, together with background information on the present teachers, which showed the representatives of the different systems did not differ in level of education, kind of degrees, years of teaching, indicate that the results obtained in this study can more parsimoniously and directly be attributed to differences in teachers' belief systems than to possible sociological correlates.

References

ADAMS, D. K., HARVEY, O. J., & HESLIN, R. E. Variation in flexibility and creativity as a function of hypnotically induced past histories." In O. J. Harvey (Ed.), *Experience, structure and adaptability.* New York: Springer, 1967. Pp. 217–234.

HARVEY, O. J. Cognitive determinants of role playing. *Technical report No. 3,* Contract Nonr 1147(07). University of Colorado, 1963. 22 pp.

——. Some cognitive determinants of influencibility. *Sociometry,* June 1964, *27,* 208–221.

——. System structure, flexibility and creativity. In O. J. Harvey (Ed.), *Experience, structure and adaptability.* New York: Springer, 1966. Pp. 242–262.

——. Conceptual systems and attitude change. In C. W. Sherif & M. Sherif (Eds.), *Attitude, ego-involvement and attitude change.* New York: Wiley, 1967. Pp. 201–226.

HARVEY, O. J., HUNT, D. E., & SCHRODER, H. M. *Conceptual systems and personality organization.* New York: Wiley, 1961. Pp. 85–112; 158–203.

HARVEY, O. J., & WARE, R. Personality differences in dissonance resolution. *Journal of Personality and Social Psychology,* October 1967, *7,* 227–230.

HARVEY, O. J., WHITE, B. J., PRATHER, M., ALTER, R. D., & HOFFMEISTER, J. K. Teachers' belief systems and preschool atmospheres. *Journal of Educational Psychology,* December 1966, *57,* 373–381.

TRYON, R. C., & BAILEY, D. E. *Try user's manual.* Boulder: University of Colorado Computing Center, 1965. 186 pp.

——. *The B. C. try system of cluster analysis.* Boulder: University of Colorado Computing Center, 1966. Pp. 3–35.

WARE, R., & HARVEY, O. J. A cognitive determinant of impression formation. *Journal of Personality and Social Psychology,* January 1967, *5,* 38–44.

WHITE, B. J., & HARVEY, O. J. Effects of personality and own stand on judgment and production of statements about a central issue. *Journal of Experimental Social Psychology,* October 1965, *1,* 334–347.

Section Six
LEARNING
AND
MEMORY

The articles in this section have been chosen to illustrate the richness and diversity of research in the field of learning and memory. They span the range from fairly traditional interference-theory interpretations of forgetting to information-processing approaches, models of memory, and unusual effects such as the tip-of-the-tongue phenomenon. The variety in method of presentation, style, terminology, and theoretical preferences illustrates some of the many differing shades of opinion still remaining about the nature of learning and memory.

The selection by Underwood illustrates the need to be skeptical of dogma. His is an interference-theory orientation toward learning and memory, which at the human level has much in common with the views of Solomon on animal learning. These viewpoints can be traced to early theoretical development from the literature of conditioning that originally grew out of the work of Pavlov and Skinner. The domain of application, however, is clearly different as Solomon cites experiments from the animal field while Underwood cites experiments from the human field.

Miller's work is an early landmark in the development of an information-processing view of memory. Along with a book published at about the same time by Broadbent (*Perception and Communication,* 1958), this article represented a change in the basic approach to learning and memory. Rather than relying on the associationistic concepts of classical association theory and the conditioning laboratory, these authors show that the concepts developed by Shannon and others in communication theory could apply to human memory. This is the beginning of emphasis on the encoding, storage, and retrieval of information from memory.

The tip-of-the-tongue phenomenon is well known to everyone. A particular incident of fact seems to be almost accessible, but not quite. Psychologists have long known not to trust introspections and are skeptical of anecdotes unless they can be studied under controlled conditions in the laboratory. Brown and McNeill describe the results of studying this phenomenon under such laboratory conditions.

The article by Craik and Lockhart summarizes and evaluates some of the recent thinking in the field of human memory. Current models of memory processes (such as those of Broadbent, Waugh and Norman, and the buffer model of Atkinson and Shiffrin) are based on what Craik and Lockhart feel to be a questionable assumption—namely, a partitioning of memory into temporally discrete stores. This "boxes-in-the-head" approach has certain basic weaknesses, and an alternative viewpoint is suggested instead. As one can see, theoretical ideas about learning and memory change, and they may change rapidly. As we come to learn more about them, the conceptualizations change. We clearly have not reached a final understanding, but later theories build upon earlier theories, and in this way progress is being made.

Bennet B. Murdock, Jr.

After first discussing the basic concept of information, which was less well known when this article was written than it is now, George Miller develops the notion of channel capacity and shows how it is revealed by studies of absolute judgment. His article shows that our channel capacity is severely limited in the unidimensional case, but it increases (though not proportionally) as the number of different stimulus dimensions increases. When he applies the same informational principles to memory span, however, a discrepancy arises; memory span seems more accurately characterized by chunks of information than by bits of information. Recoding is seen as a way of enriching these limited chunks of information so that we can expand, but not exceed, our channel capacity.

The Magical Number Seven, Plus or Minus Two: Some Limits on Our Capacity for Processing Information

George A. Miller

My problem is that I have been persecuted by an integer. For seven years this number has followed me around, has intruded in my most private data, and has assaulted me from the pages of our most public journals. This number assumes a variety of disguises, being sometimes a little larger and sometimes a little smaller than usual, but never changing so much as to be unrecognizable. The persistence with which this number plagues me is far more than a random accident. There is, to quote a famous senator, a design behind it, some pattern governing its appearances. Either there really is something unusual about the number or else I am suffering from delusions of persecution.

I shall begin my case history by telling you about some experiments that tested how accurately people can assign numbers to the magnitudes of various aspects of a stimulus. In the traditional language of psychology these would be called experiments in absolute judgment. Historical accident, however, has decreed that they should have another name. We now call them experiments on the capacity of people to transmit information. Since these

Source: Reprinted by permission from *Psychological Review,* 1956, *63*, 81–97. Copyright © 1956 by the American Psychological Association.

Note: This paper was first read as an Invited Address before the Eastern Psychological Association in Philadelphia on April 15, 1955. Preparation of the paper was supported by the Harvard Psycho-Acoustic Laboratory under Contract N5ori–76 between Harvard University and the Office of Naval Research, U.S. Navy (Project NR142–201, Report PNR–174). Reproduction for any purpose of the U.S. Government is permitted.

experiments would not have been done without the appearance of information theory on the psychological scene, and since the results are analyzed in terms of the concepts of information theory, I shall have to preface my discussion with a few remarks about this theory.

Information Measurement

The "amount of information" is exactly the same concept that we have talked about for years under the name of "variance." The equations are different, but if we hold tight to the idea that anything that increases the variance also increases the amount of information we cannot go far astray.

The advantages of this new way of talking about variance are simple enough. Variance is always stated in terms of the unit of measurement —inches, pounds, volts, etc.—whereas the amount of information is a dimensionless quantity. Since the information in a discrete statistical distribution does not depend upon the unit of measurement, we can extend the concept to situations where we have no metric and we would not ordinarily think of using the variance. And it also enables us to compare results obtained in quite different experimental situations where it would be meaningless to compare variances based on different metrics. So there are some good reasons for adopting the newer concept.

The similarity of variance and amount of information might be explained this way: When we have a large variance, we are very ignorant about what is going to happen. If we are very ignorant, then when we make the observation it gives us a lot of information. On the other hand, if the variance is very small, we know in advance how our observation must come out, so we get little information from making the observation.

If you will now imagine a communication system, you will realize that there is a great deal of variability about what goes into the system and also a great deal of variability about what comes out. The input and the output can therefore be described in terms of their variance (of their information). If it is a good communication system, however, there must be some systematic relation between what goes in and what comes out. That is to say, the output will depend upon the input, or will be correlated with the input. If we measure this correlation, then we can say how much of the output variance is attributable to the input and how much is due to random fluctuations or "noise" introduced by the system during transmission. So we see that the measure of transmitted information is simply a measure of the input-output correlation.

There are two simple rules to follow. Whenever I refer to "amount of information," you will understand "variance." And whenever I refer to "amount of transmitted information," you will understand "covariance" or "correlation."

The situation can be described graphically by two partially overlapping circles. Then the left circle can be taken to represent the variance of the input, the right circle the variance of the output, and the overlap the covariance of input and output. I shall speak of the left circle as the amount of input information, the right circle as the amount of output information, and the overlap as the amount of transmitted information.

In the experiments on absolute judgment, the observer is considered to be a communication channel. Then the left circle would represent the amount of information in the stimuli, the right circle the amount of information in his responses, and the overlap the stimulus-response correlation as measured by the amount of transmitted information. The experimental problem is to increase the amount of input information and to measure the amount of transmitted information. If the observer's absolute judgments are quite accurate, then nearly all of the input information will be transmitted and will be recoverable from his responses. If he makes errors, then the transmitted information may be considerably less than the input. We expect that, as we increase the amount of input information, the observer will begin to make more and more errors; we can test the limits of accuracy of his absolute judgments. If the human observer is a reasonable kind of communication system, then when we increase the amount of input information the transmitted information will increase at first and will eventually level off at some asymptotic value. This asymptotic value we take to be the *channel capacity* of the observer; it represents the greatest amount of information that he can give us about the stimulus on the basis of an absolute judgment. The channel capacity is the upper limit on the extent to which the observer can match his responses to the stimuli we give him.

Now just a brief word about the *bit* and we can begin to look at some data. One bit of information is the amount of information that we need to make a decision between two equally likely alternatives. If we must decide whether a man is less than six feet tall or more than six feet tall and if we know that the chances are 50–50, then we need one bit of information. Notice that this unit of information does not refer in any way to the unit of length that we use—feet, inches, centimeters, etc. However you measure the man's height, we still need just one bit of information.

Two bits of information enable us to decide among four equally likely alternatives. Three bits of information enable us to decide among eight equally likely alternatives. Four bits of information decide among 16 alternatives, five among 32, and so on. That is to say, if there are 32 equally likely alternatives, we must make five successive binary decisions, worth one bit each, before we know which alternative is correct. So the general rule is simple: every time the number of alternatives is increased by a factor of two, one bit of information is added.

There are two ways we might increase the amount of input information. We could increase the rate at which we give information to the observer, so that the amount of information per unit time would increase. Or we could ignore the time variable completely and increase the amount of input information by increasing the number of alternative stimuli. In the absolute judgment experiment we are interested in the second alternative. We give the observer as much time as he wants to make his response; we simply increase the number of alternative stimuli among which he must discriminate and look to see where confusions begin to occur. Confusions will appear near the point that we are calling his "channel capacity."

Absolute Judgments of Unidimensional Stimuli

Now let us consider what happens when we make absolute judgments of tones. Pollack (17) asked listeners to identify tones by assigning numerals to them. The tones were different with respect to frequency, and covered the range from 100 to 8000 cps in equal logarithmic steps. A tone was sounded and the listener responded by giving a numeral. After the listener had made his response he was told the correct identification of the tone.

When only two or three tones were used the listeners never confused them. With four different tones confusions were quite rare, but with five or more tones confusions were frequent. With fourteen different tones the listeners made many mistakes.

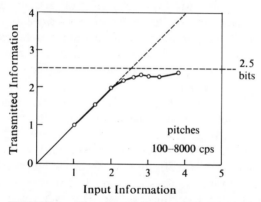

FIGURE 1.   Data from Pollack (17, 18) on the amount of information that is transmitted by listeners who make absolute judgments of auditory pitch. As the amount of input information is increased by increasing from 2 to 14 the number of different pitches to be judged, the amount of transmitted information approaches as its upper limit a channel capacity of about 2.5 bits per judgment.

These data are plotted in Figure 1. Along the bottom is the amount of input information in bits per stimulus. As the number of alternative tones was increased from 2 to 14, the input information increased from 1 to 3.8 bits. On the ordinate is plotted the amount of transmitted information. The amount of transmitted information behaves in much the way we would expect a commnucation channel to behave; the transmitted information increases linearly up to about 2 bits and then bends off toward an asymptote at about 2.5 bits. This value, 2.5 bits, therefore, is what we are calling the channel capacity of the listener for absolute judgments of pitch.

So now we have the number 2.5 bits. What does it mean? First, note that 2.5 bits corresponds to about six equally likely alternatives. The result means that we cannot pick more than six different pitches that the listener will never confuse. Or, stated slightly differently, no matter how many alternative tones we ask him to judge, the best we can expect him to do is to assign them to about six different classes without error. Or, again, if we know that there were N alternative stimuli, then his judgment enables us to narrow down the particular stimulus to one out of $N/6$.

Most people are surprised that the number is as small as six. Of course, there is evidence that a musically sophisticated person with absolute pitch can identify accurately any one of 50 or 60 different pitches. Fortunately, I do not have time to discuss these remarkable exceptions. I say it is fortunate because I do not know how to explain their superior performance. So I shall stick to the more pedestrian fact that most of us can identify about one out of only five or six pitches before we begin to get confused.

It is interesting to consider that psychologists have been using seven-point rating scales for a long time, on the intuitive basis that trying to rate into finer categories does not really add much to the usefulness of the ratings. Pollack's results indicate that, at least for pitches, this intuition is fairly sound.

Next you can ask how reproducible this result is. Does it depend on the spacing of the tones or the various conditions of judgment? Pollack varied these conditions in a number of ways. The range of frequencies can be changed by a factor of about 20 without changing the amount of information transmitted more than a small percentage. Different groupings of the pitches decreased the transmission, but the loss was small. For example, if you can discriminate five high-pitched tones in one series and five low-pitched tones in another series, it is reasonable to expect that you could combine all ten into a single series and still tell them all apart without error. When you try it, however, it does not work. The channel capacity for pitch seems to be about six and that is the best you can do.

While we are on tones, let us look next at Garner's (7) work on loudness. Garner's data for loudness are summarized in Figure 2. Garner went to some trouble to get the best possible spacing of his tones over the intensity range from 15 to 110 db. He used 4, 5, 6, 7, 10, and 20 different stimulus intensities. The results shown in Figure 2 take into account the differences among subjects and the sequential influence of the immediately preceding judgment. Again we find that there seems to be a limit. The channel capacity for absolute judgments of loudness is 2.3 bits, or about five perfectly discriminable alternatives.

Since these two studies were done in different laboratories with slightly different techniques and methods of analysis, we are not in a good position to argue whether five loudnesses is significantly different from six pitches. Probably the difference is in the right direction, and absolute judgments of pitch are slightly more accurate than absolute judgments of loudness.

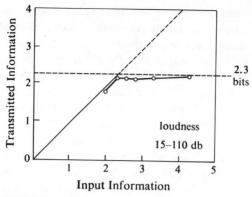

FIGURE 2.   Data from Garner (7) on the channel capacity for absolute judgments of auditory loudness

The important point, however, is that the two answers are of the same order of magnitude.

The experiment has also been done for taste intensities. In Figure 3 are the results obtained by Beebe-Center, Rogers, and O'Connell (1) for absolute judgments of the concentration of salt solutions. The concentrations ranged from 0.3 to 34.7 gm. NaCl per 100 cc. tap water in equal subjective steps. They used 3, 5, 9, and 17 different concentrations. The channel capacity is 1.9 bits, which is about four distinct concentrations. Thus taste intensities seem a little less distinctive than auditory stimuli, but again the order of magnitude is not far off.

On the other hand, the channel capacity for judgments of visual position seems to be significantly larger. Hake and Garner (8) asked observers to interpolate visually between two scale markers. Their results are shown in Figure 4. They did the experiment in two ways. In one version they let the observer use any number between zero and 100 to describe the position, al-

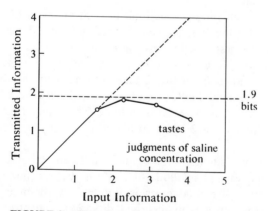

FIGURE 3.   Data from Beebe-Center, Rogers, and O'Connell (1) on the channel capacity for absolute judgments of saltiness

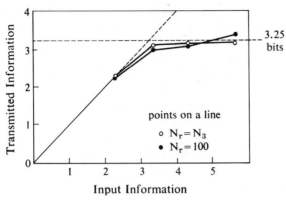

FIGURE 4.   Data from Hake and Garner (8) on the channel capacity for absolute judgments of the position of a pointer in a linear interval.

though they presented stimuli at only 5, 10, 20, or 50 different positions. The results with this unlimited response technique are shown by the filled circles on the graph. In the other version the observers were limited in their responses to reporting just those stimulus values that were possible. That is to say, in the second version the number of different responses that the observer could make was exactly the same as the number of different stimuli that the experimenter might present. The results with this limited response technique are shown by the open circles on the graph. The two functions are so similar that it seems fair to conclude that the number of responses available to the observer had nothing to do with the channel capacity of 3.25 bits.

The Hake-Garner experiment has been repeated by Coonan and Klemmer. Although they have not yet published their results, they have given me permission to say that they obtained channel capacities ranging from 3.2 bits for very short exposures of the pointer position to 3.9 bits for longer exposures. These values are slightly higher than Hake and Garner's, so we must conclude that there are between 10 and 15 distinct positions along a linear interval. This is the largest channel capacity that has been measured for any unidimensional variable.

At the present time these four experiments on absolute judgments of simple, unidimensional stimuli are all that have appeared in the psychological journals. However, a great deal of work on other stimulus variables has not yet appeared in the journals. For example, Eriksen and Hake (6) have found that the channel capacity for judging the sizes of squares is 2.2 bits, or about five categories, under a wide range of experimental conditions. In a separate experiment Eriksen (5) found 2.8 bits for size, 3.1 bits for hue, and 2.3 bits for brightness. Geldard has measured the channel capacity for the skin by placing vibrators on the chest region. A good observer can identify about four intensities, about five durations, and about seven locations.

One of the most active groups in this area has been the Air Force Operational Applications Laboratory. Pollack has been kind enough to furnish me with the results of their measurements for several aspects of visual displays. They made measurements for area and for the curvature, length, and direction of lines. In one set of experiments they used a very short exposure of the stimulus—¼₀ second—and then they repeated the measurements with a 5-second exposure. For area they got 2.6 bits with the short exposure and 2.7 bits with the long exposure. For the length of a line they got about 2.6 bits with the short exposure and about 3.0 bits with the long exposure. Direction, or angle of inclination, gave 2.8 bits for the short exposure and 3.3 bits for the long exposure. Curvature was apparently harder to judge. When the length of the arc was constant, the result at the short exposure duration was 2.2 bits, but when the length of the chord was constant, the result was only 1.6 bits. This last value is the lowest that anyone has measured to date. I should add, however, that these values are apt to be slightly too low because the data from all subjects were pooled before the transmitted information was computed.

Now let us see where we are. First, the channel capacity does seem to be a valid notion for describing human observers. Second, the channel capacities measured for these unidimensional variable range from 1.6 bits for curvature to 3.9 bits for positions in an interval. Although there is no question that the differences among the variables are real and meaningful, the more impressive fact to me is their considerable similarity. If I take the best estimates I can get of the channel capacities for all the stimulus variables I have mentioned, the mean is 2.6 bits and the standard deviation is only 0.6 bit. In terms of distinguishable alternatives, this mean corresponds to about 6.5 categories, one standard deviation includes from 4 to 10 categories, and the total range is from 3 to 15 categories. Considering the wide variety of different variables that have been studied, I find this to be a remarkably narrow range.

There seems to be some limitation built into us either by learning or by the design of our nervous systems, a limit that keeps our channel capacities in this general range. On the basis of the present evidence it seems safe to say that we possess a finite and rather small capacity for making such unidimensional judgments and that this capacity does not vary a great deal from one simple sensory attribute to another.

Absolute Judgments of Multidimensional Stimuli

You may have noticed that I have been careful to say that this magical number seven applies to one-dimensional judgments. Everyday experience teaches us that we can identify accurately any one of several hundred faces, any one of several thousand words, any one of several thousand objects, etc. The story certainly would not be complete if we stopped at this point. We must have some understanding of why the one-dimensional variables we judge in the laboratory give results so far out of line with what we do constantly in our behavior outside the laboratory. A possible explanation lies in the number of independently variable attributes of the stimuli that are being judged. Objects, faces, words, and the like differ from one another in many ways, whereas the simple stimuli we have considered thus far differ from one another in only one respect.

Fortunately, there are a few data on what happens when we make absolute judgments of stimuli that differ from one another in several ways. Let us look first at the results Klemmer and Frick (13) have reported for the absolute judgment of the position of a dot in a square. In Figure 5 we see their results. Now the channel capacity seems to have increased to 4.6 bits, which means that people can identify accurately any one of 24 positions in the square.

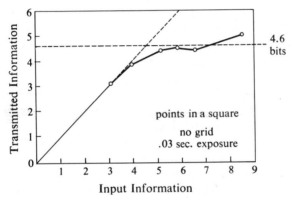

FIGURE 5.   Data from Klemmer and Frick (13) on the channel capacity for absolute judgments of the position of a dot in a square

The position of a dot in a square is clearly a two-dimensional proposition. Both its horizontal and its vertical position must be identified. Thus it seems natural to compare the 4.6-bit capacity for a square with the 3.25-bit capacity for the position of a point in an interval. The point in the square requires two judgments of the interval type. If we have a capacity of 3.25 bits for estimating intervals and we do this twice, we should get 6.5 bits as our capacity for locating points in a square. Adding the second independent dimension gives us an increase from 3.25 to 4.6, but it falls short of the perfect addition that would give 6.5 bits.

Another example is provided by Beebe-Center, Rogers, and O'Connell. When they asked people to identify both the saltiness and the sweetness of solutions containing various concentrations of salt and sucrose, they found that the channel capacity was 2.3 bits. Since the capacity for salt alone was 1.9, we might expect about 3.8 bits if the two aspects of the compound stimuli were judged independently. As with spatial locations, the second dimension adds a little to the capacity but not as much as it conceivably might.

A third example is provided by Pollack (18), who asked listeners to judge both the loudness and the pitch of pure tones. Since pitch gives 2.5 bits and loudness gives 2.3 bits, we might hope to get as much as 4.8 bits for pitch and loudness together. Pollack obtained 3.1 bits, which again indicates that the second dimension augments the channel capacity but not so much as it might.

A fourth example can be drawn from the work of Halsey and Chapanis (9) on confusions among colors of equal luminance. Although they they did not analyze their results in informational terms, they estimate that there are about 11 to 15 identifiable colors, or, in our terms, about 3.6 bits. Since these colors varied in both hue and saturation, it is probably correct to regard this as a two-dimensional judgment. If we compare this with Eriksen's 3.1 bits for hue (which is a questionable comparison to draw), we again have something less than perfect addition when a second dimension is added.

It is still a long way, however, from these two-dimensional examples to the multidimensional stimuli provided by faces, words, etc. To fill this gap we have only one experiment, an auditory study done by Pollack and Ficks (19). They managed to get six different acoustic variables that they could change: frequency, intensity, rate of interruption, on-time fraction, total duration, and spatial location. Each one of these six variables could assume any one of five different values, so altogether there were 5^6, or 15,625 different tones that they could present. The listeners made a separate rating for each one of these six dimensions. Under these conditions the transmitted information was 7.2 bits, which corresponds to about 150 different categories that could be absolutely identified without error. Now we are beginning to get up into the range that ordinary experience would lead us to expect.

Suppose that we plot these data, fragmentary as they are, and make a guess about how the channel capacity changes with the dimensionality of the stimuli. The result is given in Figure 6. In a moment of considerable daring I sketched the dotted line to indicate roughly the trend that the data seemed to be taking.

Clearly, the addition of independently variable attributes to the stimulus increases the channel capacity, but at a decreasing rate. It is interesting to note that the channel capacity is increased even when the several variables are not independent. Eriksen (5) reports that, when size, brightness, and hue all vary together in perfect correlation, the transmitted information is 4.1 bits as compared with an average of about 2.7 bits when these attributes are varied one at a time. By confounding three attributes, Eriksen increased the dimensionality of the input without increasing the amount of input information; the result was an increase in channel capacity of about the amount that the dotted function in Figure 6 would lead us to expect.

The point seems to be that, as we add more variables to the display, we increase the total capacity, but we decrease the accuracy for any particular variable. In other words, we can make relatively crude judgments of several things simultaneously.

We might argue that in the course of evolution those organisms were most successful that were responsive to the widest range of stimulus energies in their environment. In order to survive in a constantly fluctuating world,

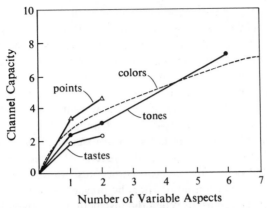

FIGURE 6.   The general form of the relation between channel capacity and the number of independently variable attributes of the stimuli

it was better to have a little information about a lot of things than to have a lot of information about a small segment of the environment. If a compromise was necessary, the one we seem to have made is clearly the more adaptive.

Pollack and Ficks's results are very strongly suggestive of an argument that linguists and phoneticians have been making for some time (11). According to the linguistic analysis of the sounds of human speech, there are about eight or ten dimensions—the linguists call them *distinctive features*—that distinguish one phoneme from another. These distinctive features are usually binary, or at most ternary, in nature. For example, a binary distinction is made between vowels and consonants, a binary decision is made between oral and nasal consonants, a ternary decision is made among front, middle, and back phonemes, etc. This approach gives us quite a different picture of speech perception than we might otherwise obtain from our studies of the speech spectrum and of the ear's ability to discriminate relative differences among pure tones. I am personally much interested in this new approach (15), and I regret that there is not time to discuss it here.

It was probably with this linguistic theory in mind that Pollack and Ficks conducted a test on a set of tonal stimuli that varied in eight dimensions, but required only a binary decision on each dimension. With these tones they measured the transmitted information at 6.9 bits, or about 120 recognizable kind of sounds. It is an intriguing question, as yet unexplored, whether one can go on adding dimensions indefinitely in this way.

In human speech there is clearly a limit to the number of dimensions that we use. In this instance, however, it is not known whether the limit is imposed by the nature of the perceptual machinery that must recognize the sounds or by the nature of the speech machinery that must produce them. Somebody will have to do the experiment to find out. There is a limit, however, at about eight or nine distinctive features in every language that has been studied, and so when we talk we must resort to still another trick for increasing our channel capacity. Language uses sequences of phonemes, so we make several judgments successively when we listen to words and sentences. That is to say, we use both simultaneous and successive discriminations in order to expand the rather rigid limits imposed by the inaccuracy of our absolute judgments of simple magnitudes.

These multidimensional judgments are strongly reminiscent of the abstraction experiment of Külpe (14). As you may remember, Külpe showed that observers report more accurately on an attribute for which they are set than on attributes for which they are not set. For example, Chapman (4) used three different attributes and compared the results obtained when the observers were instructed before the tachistoscopic presentation with the results obtained when they were not told until after the presentation which one of the three attributes was to be reported. When the instruction was given in advance, the judgments were more accurate. When the instruction was given afterwards, the subjects presumably had to judge all three attributes in order to report on any one of them and the accuracy was correspondingly lower. This is in complete accord with the results we have just been considering, where the accuracy of judgment on each attribute decreased as more dimensions were added. The point is probably obvious, but I shall make it anyhow, that the abstraction experiments did *not* demonstrate that people can judge only one attribute at a time. They merely showed what seems quite reasonable, that people are less accurate if they must judge more than one attribute simultaneously.

Subitizing

I cannot leave this general area without mentioning, however briefly, the experiments conducted at Mount Holyoke College on the discrimination of number (12). In experiments by Kaufman, Lord, Reese, and Volkmann random patterns of dots were flashed on a screen for ⅕ of a second. Anywhere from 1 to more than 200 dots could appear in the pattern. The subject's task was to report how many dots there were.

The first point to note is that on patterns containing up to five or six dots the subjects simply did not make errors. The performance on these small numbers of dots was so different from the performance with more dots that it was given a special name. Below seven the subjects were said to *subitize;* above seven they were said to *estimate.* This is, as you will recognize, what we once optimistically called "the span of attention."

This discontinuity at seven is, of course, suggestive. Is this the same basic process that limits our unidimensional judgments to about seven categories? The generalization is tempting, but not sound in my opinion. The data on number estimates have not been analyzed in informational terms; but on the basis of the published data I would guess that the subjects transmitted something more than four bits of information about the number of dots.

Using the same arguments as before, we would conclude that there are about 20 or 30 distinguishable categories of numerousness. This is considerably more information that we would expect to get from a unidimensional display. It is, as a matter of fact, very much like a two-dimensional display. Although the dimensionality of the random dot patterns is not entirely clear, these results are in the same range as Klemmer and Frick's for their two-dimensional display of dots in a square. Perhaps the two dimensions of numerousness are area and density. When the subject can subitize, area and density may not be the significant variables, but when the subject must estimate perhaps they are significant. In any event, the comparison is not so simple as it might seem at first thought.

This is one of the ways in which the magical number seven has persecuted me. Here we have two closely related kinds of experiments, both of which point to the significance of the number seven as a limit on our capacities. And yet when we examine the matter more closely, there seems to be a reasonable suspicion that it is nothing more than a coincidence.

The Span of Immediate Memory

Let me summarize the situation in this way. There is a clear and definite limit to the accuracy with which we can identify absolutely the magnitude of a unidimensional stimulus variable. I would propose to call this limit the *span of absolute judgment,* and I maintain that for unidimensional judgments this span is usually somewhere in the neighborhood of seven. We are not completely at the mercy of this limited span, however, because we have a variety of techniques for getting around it and increasing the accuracy of our judgments. The three most important of these devices are (*a*) to make relative rather than absolute judgments; or, if that is not possible, (*b*) to increase the number of dimensions along which the stimuli can differ; or (*c*) to arrange the task in such a way that we make a sequence of several absolute judgments in a row.

The study of relative judgments is one of the oldest topics in experimental psychology, and I will not pause to review it now. The second device, increasing the dimensionality, we have just considered. It seems that by adding more dimensions and requiring crude, binary, yes-no judgments on each attribute we can extend the span of absolute judgment from seven to at least 150. Judging from our everyday behavior, the limit is probably in the thousands, if indeed there is a limit. In my opinion, we cannot go on compounding dimensions indefinitely. I suspect that there is also a *span of perceptual dimensionality* and that this span is somewhere in the neighborhood of ten, but I must add at once that there is no objective evidence to support this suspicion. This is a question sadly needing experimental exploration.

Concerning the third device, the use of successive judgments, I have quite a bit to say because this device introduces memory as the handmaiden of discrimination. And, since mnemonic processes are at least as complex as are perceptual processes, we can anticipate that their interactions will not be easily disentangled.

Suppose that we start by simply extending slightly the experimental procedure that we have been using. Up to this point we have presented a single stimulus and asked the observer to name it immediately thereafter. We can extend this procedure by requiring the observer to withhold his response until we have given him several stimuli in succession. At the end of the sequence of stimuli he then makes his response. We still have the same sort of input-output situation that is required for the measurement of transmitted information. But now we have passed from an experiment on absolute judgment to what is traditionally called an experiment on immediate memory.

Before we look at any data on this topic I feel I must give you a word of warning to help you avoid some obvious associations that can be confusing. Everybody knows that there is a finite span of immediate memory and that for a lot of different kinds of test materials this span is about seven items in length. I have just shown you that there is a span of absolute judgment that can distinguish about seven categories and that there is a span of attention that will encompass about six objects at a glance. What is more natural than to think that all three of these spans are different aspects of a single underlying process? And that is a fundamental mistake, as I shall be at some pains to demonstrate. This mistake is one of the malicious persecutions that the magical number seven has subjected me to.

My mistake went something like this. We have seen that the invariant feature in the span of absolute judgment is the amount of information that the observer can transmit. There is a real operational similarity between the absolute judgment experiment and the immediate memory experiment. If immediate memory is like absolute judgment, then it should follow that the invariant feature in the span of immediate memory is also the amount of information that an observer can retain. If the amount of information in the span of immediate memory is a constant, then the span should be short when the individual items contain a lot of information and the span should be long when the items contain little information. For example, decimal digits are worth 3.3 bits apiece. We can recall about seven of them, for a total of 23 bits of information. Isolated English words are worth about 10 bits apiece. If the total amount of information is to remain constant at 23 bits, then we should be able to remember only two or three words chosen at random. In this way I generated a theory about how the span of immediate memory should vary as a function of the amount of information per item in the test materials.

The measurements of memory span in the literature are suggestive on this question, but not definitive. And so it was necessary to do the experiment to see. Hayes (10) tried it out with five different kinds of test materials: binary digits, decimal digits, letters of the alphabet, letters plus decimal digits, and with 1,000 monosyllabic words. The lists were read aloud at the rate of one item per second and the subjects had as much time as they needed to give their responses. A procedure described by Woodworth (20) was used to score the responses.

The results are shown by the filled circles in Figure 7. Here the dotted line indicates what the span should have been if the amount of information in the span were constant. The solid curves represent the data. Hayes repeated the experiment using test vocabularies of different sizes but all containing only English monosyllables (open circles in Figure 7). This more homogeneous test material did not change the picture significantly. With binary items the span is about nine and, although it drops to about five with monosyllabic English words, the difference is far less than the hypothesis of constant information would require.

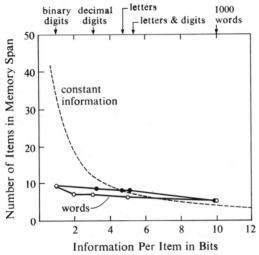

FIGURE 7. Data from Hayes (10) on the span of immediate memory plotted as a function of the amount of information per item in the test materials.

There is nothing wrong with Hayes's experiment, because Pollack (16) repeated it much more elaborately and got essentially the same result. Pollack took pains to measure the amount of information transmitted and did not rely on the traditional procedure for scoring the responses. His results are plotted in Figure 8. Here it is clear that the amount of information transmitted is not a constant, but increases almost linearly as the amount of information per item in the input is increased.

And so the outcome is perfectly clear. In spite of the coincidence that the magical number seven appears in both places, the span of absolute judgment and the span of immediate memory are quite different kinds of limitations that are imposed on our ability to process information. Absolute judgment is limited by the amount of information. Immediate memory is limited by the number of items. In order to capture this distinction in somewhat picturesque terms, I have fallen into the custom of distinguishing between *bits*

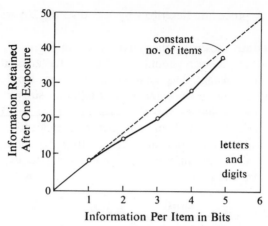

FIGURE 8.   Data from Pollack (16) on the amount of information retained after one presentation plotted as a function of the amount of information per item in the test materials.

of information and *chunks* of information. Then I can say that the number of bits of information is constant for absolute judgment and the number of chunks of information is constant for immediate memory. The span of immediate memory seems to be almost independent of the number of bits per chunk, at least over the range that has been examined to date.

The contrast of the terms *bit* and *chunk* also serves to highlight the fact that we are not very definite about what constitutes a chunk of information. For example, the memory span of five words that Hayes obtained when each word was drawn at random from a set of 1000 English monosyllables might just as appropriately have been called a memory span of 15 phonemes, since each word had about three phonemes in it. Intuitively, it is clear that the subjects were recalling five words, not 15 phonemes, but the logical distinction is not immediately apparent. We are dealing here with a process of organizing or grouping the input into familiar units or chunks, and a great deal of learning has gone into the formation of these familiar units.

Recoding

In order to speak more precisely, therefore, we must recognize the importance of grouping or organizing the input sequence into units or chunks. Since the memory span is a fixed number of chunks, we can increase the number of bits of information that it contains simply by building larger and larger chunks, each chunk containing more information than before.

A man just beginning to learn radiotelegraphic code hears each *dit* and *dah* as a separate chunk. Soon he is able to organize these sounds into letters and then he can deal with the letters as chunks. Then the letters organize themselves as words, which are still larger chunks, and he begins to hear whole phrases. I do not mean that each step is a discrete process, or that plateaus must appear in his learning curve, for surely the levels of organization are achieved at different rates and overlap each other during the learning process. I am simply pointing to the obvious fact that the dits and dahs are organized by learning into patterns and that as these larger chunks emerge the amount of message that the operator can remember increases correspondingly. In the terms I am proposing to use, the operator learns to increase the bits per chunk.

In the jargon of communication theory, this process would be called *recoding*. The input is given in a code that contains many chunks with few bits per chunk. The operator recodes the input into another code that contains fewer chunks with more bits per chunk. There are many ways to do this recoding, but probably the simplest is to group the input events, apply a new name to the group, and then remember the new name rather than the original input events.

Since I am convinced that this process is a very general and important one for psychology, I want to tell you about a demonstration experiment that should make perfectly explicit what I am talking about. This experiment was conducted by Sidney Smith and was reported by him before the Eastern Psychological Association in 1954.

Begin with the observed fact that people can repeat back eight decimal digits, but only nine binary digits. Since there is a large discrepancy in the amount of information recalled in these two cases, we suspect at once that a recoding procedure could be used to increase the span of immediate memory for binary digits. In Table 1 a method for grouping and renaming is illustrated.

TABLE 1. Ways of recoding sequences of binary digits

Binary Digits (Bits)	*1 0 1 0 0 0 1 0 0 1 1 1 0 0 1 1 1 0*								
2:1 Chunks	10	10	00	10	01	11	00	11	10
Recoding	2	2	0	2	1	3	0	3	2
3:1 Chunks	101		000		100		111	001	110
Recoding	5		0		4		7	1	6
4:1 Chunks	1010			0010		0111		0011	10
Recoding	10			2		7		3	
5:1 Chunks	10100			01001			11001		110
Recoding	20			9			25		

Along the top is a sequence of 18 binary digits, far more than any subject was able to recall after a single presentation. In the next line these same binary digits are grouped by pairs. Four possible pairs can occur: 00 is renamed 0, 01 is renamed 1, 10 is renamed 2, and 11 is renamed 3. That is to say, we recode from a base-two arithmetic to a base-four arithmetic. In the recoded sequence there are now just nine digits to remember, and this is almost within the span of immediate memory. In the next line the same sequence of binary digits is regrouped into chunks of three. There are eight possible sequences of three, so we give each sequence a new name between 0 and 7. Now we have recoded from a sequence of 18 binary digits into a sequence of 6 octal digits, and this is well within the span of immediate memory. In the last two lines the binary digits are grouped by fours and by fives and are given decimal-digit names from 0 to 15 and from 0 to 31.

It is reasonably obvious that this kind of recoding increases the bits per chunk, and packages the binary sequence into a form that can be retained within the span of immediate memory. So Smith assembled 20 subjects and measured their spans for binary and octal digits. The spans were 9 for binaries and 7 for octals. Then he gave each recoding scheme to five of the subjects. They studied the recoding until they said they understood it—for about 5 or 10 minutes. Then he tested their span for binary digits again while they tried to use the recoding schemes they had studied.

The recoding schemes increased their span for binary digits in every case. But the increase was not as large as we had expected on the basis of their span for octal digits. Since the discrepancy increased as the recoding ratio increased, we reasoned that the few minutes the subjects had spent learning the recoding schemes had not been sufficient. Apparently the translation from one code to the other must be almost automatic or the subject will lose part of the next group while he is trying to remember the translation of the last group.

Since the 4:1 and 5:1 ratios require considerable study, Smith decided to imitate Ebbinghaus and do the experiment on himself. With Germanic patience he drilled himself on each recoding successively, and obtained the results shown in Figure 9. Here the data follow along rather nicely with the results you would predict on the basis of his span for octal digits. He could remember 12 octal digits. With the 2:1 recoding, these 12 chunks were worth 24 binary digits. With the 3:1 recoding they were worth 36 binary digits. With the 4:1 and 5:1 recodings, they were worth about 40 binary digits.

It is a little dramatic to watch a person get 40 binary digits in a row and then repeat them back without error. However, if you think of this merely as a mnemonic trick for extending the memory span, you will miss the more important point that is implicit in nearly all such mnemonic devices. The point is that recoding is an extremely powerful weapon for increasing the amount of information that we can deal with. In one form or another we use recoding constantly in our daily behavior.

In my opinion the most customary kind of recoding that we do all the time is to translate into a verbal code. When there is a story or an argument or an idea that we want to remember, we usually try to rephrase it "in our own words." When we witness some event we want to remember, we make a verbal description of the event and then remember our verbalization. Upon recall we recreate by secondary elaboration the details that seem consistent with the particular verbal recoding we happen to have made. The well-known experiment by Carmichael, Hogan, and Walter (3) on the influence that names have on the recall of visual figures is one demonstration of the process.

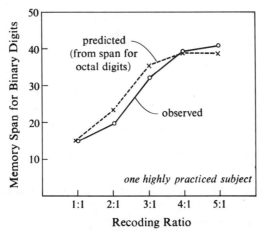

FIGURE 9.   The span of immediate memory for binary digits is plotted as a function of the recoding procedure used. The predicted function is obtained by multiplying the span for octals by 2, 3 and 3.3 for recoding into base 4, base 8, and base 10, respectively.

The inaccuracy of the testimony of eyewitnesses is well known in legal psychology, but the distortions of testimony are not random—they follow naturally from the particular recoding that the witness used, and the particular recoding he used depends upon his whole life history. Our language is tremendously useful for repackaging material into a few chunks rich in information. I suspect that imagery is a form of recoding, too, but images seem much harder to get at operationally and to study experimentally than the more symbolic kinds of recoding.

It seems probable that even memorization can be studied in these terms. The process of memorizing may be simply the formation of chunks, or groups of items that go together, until there are few enough chunks so that we can recall all the items. The work by Bousfield and Cohen (2) on the occurrence of clustering in the recall of words is especially interesting in this respect.

Summary

I have come to the end of the data that I wanted to present, so I would like now to make some summarizing remarks.

First, the span of absolute judgment and the span of immediate memory impose severe limitations on the amount of information that we are able to receive, process, and remember. By organizing the stimulus input simultaneously into several dimensions and successively into a sequence of chunks, we manage to break (or at least stretch) this informational bottleneck.

Second, the process of recoding is a very important one in human psychology and deserves much more explicit attention than it has received. In particular, the kind of linguistic recoding that people do seems to me to be the very lifeblood of the thought processes. Recoding procedures are a constant concern to clinicians, social psychologists, linguists, and anthropologists and yet, probably because recoding is less accessible to experimental manipulation than nonsense syllables or **T** mazes, the traditional experimental psychologist has contributed little or nothing to their analysis. Nevertheless, experimental techniques can be used, methods of recoding can be specified, behavioral indicants can be found. And I anticipate that we will find a very orderly set of relations describing what now seems an uncharted wilderness of individual differences.

Third, the concepts and measures provided by the theory of information provide a quantitative way of getting at some of these questions. The theory provides us with a yardstick for calibrating our stimulus materials and for measuring the performance of our subjects. In the interests of communication I have suppressed the technical details of information measurement and have tried to express the ideas in more familiar terms; I hope this paraphrase will not lead you to think they are not useful in research. Informational concepts have already proved valuable in the study of discrimination and of language; they promise a great deal in the study of learning and memory; and it has even been proposed that they can be useful in the study of concept formation. A lot of questions that seemed fruitless twenty or thirty years ago may now be worth another look. In fact, I feel that my story here must stop just as it begins to get really interesting.

And finally, what about the magical number seven? What about the seven wonders of the world, the seven seas, the seven deadly sins, the seven daughters of Atlas in the Pleiades, the seven ages of man, the seven levels of hell, the seven primary colors, the seven notes of the musical scale, and the seven days of the week? What about the seven-point rating scale, the seven categories for absolute judgment, the seven objects in the span of attention, and the seven digits in the span of immediate memory? For the present I propose to withhold judgment. Perhaps there is something deep and profound behind all these sevens, something just calling out for us to discover it. But I suspect that it is only a pernicious, Pythagorean coincidence.

References

1. BEEBE-CENTER, J. G., ROGERS, M. S., & O'CONNELL, D. N. Transmission of information about sucrose and saline solutions through the sense of taste. *J. Psychol.,* 1955, *39,* 157–160.

2. BOUSFIELD, W. A., & COHEN, B. H. The occurrence of clustering in the recall of randomly arranged words of different frequencies-of-usage. *J. Gen. Psychol.,* 1955, *52,* 83–95.

3. CARMICHAEL, L., HOGAN, H. P., & WALTER, A. A. An experimental study of the effect of language on the reproduction of visually perceived form. *J. Exp. Psychol.,* 1932, *15,* 73–86.

4. CHAPMAN, D. W. Relative effects of determinate and indeterminate *Aufgaben. Amer. J. Psychol.,* 1932, *44,* 163–174.

5. ERIKSEN, C. W. Multidimensional stimulus differences and accuracy of discrimination. *USAF, WADC Tech. Rep.*, 1954, No. 54–165.

6. ERIKSEN, C. W., & HAKE, H. W. Absolute judgments as a function of the stimulus range and the number of stimulus and response categories. *J. Exp. Psychol.*, 1955, *49*, 323–332.

7. GARNER, W. R. An informational analysis of absolute judgments of loudness. *J. Exp. Psychol.*, 1953, *46*, 373–380.

8. HAKE, H. W., & GARNER, W. R. The effect of presenting various numbers of discrete steps on scale reading accuracy. *J. Exp. Psychol.*, 1951, *42*, 358–366.

9. HALSEY, R. M., & CHAPANIS, A. Chromaticity-confusion contours in a complex viewing situation. *J. Opt. Soc. Amer.*, 1954, *44*, 442–454.

10. HAYES, J. R. M. Memory span for several vocabularies as a function of vocabulary size. In *Quarterly Progress Report*. Cambridge, Mass.: Acoustics Laboratory, Massachusetts Institute of Technology, Jan.–June, 1952.

11. JAKOBSON, R., FANT, C. G. M., & HALLE, M. *Preliminaries to speech analysis.* Cambridge, Mass.: Acoustics Laboratory, Massachusetts Institute of Technology, 1952. (Tech. Rep. No. 13.)

12. KAUFMAN, E. L., LORD, M. W., REESE, T. W., & VOLKMANN, J. The discrimination of visual number. *Amer. J. Psychol.*, 1949, *62*, 498–525.

13. KLEMMER, E. T., & FRICK, F. C. Assimilation of information from dot and matrix patterns. *J. Exp. Psychol.*, 1953, *45*, 15–19.

14. KÜLPE, O. Versuche über Abstraktion. *Ber. ü. d. I Kongr. f. exper. Psychol.*, 1904, 56–68.

15. MILLER, G. A., & NICELY, P. E. An analysis of perceptual confusions among some English consonants. *J. Acoust. Soc. Amer.*, 1955, *27*, 338–352.

16. POLLACK, I. The assimilation of sequentially encoded information. *Amer. J. Psychol.*, 1953, *66*, 421–435.

17. ———. The information of elementary auditory displays. *J. Acoust. Soc. Amer.*, 1952, *24*, 745–749.

18. ———. The information of elementary auditory displays. II. *J. Acoust. Soc. Amer.*, 1953, *25*, 765–769.

19. POLLACK, I., & FICKS, L. Information of elementary multi-dimensional auditory displays. *J. Acoust. Soc. Amer.*, 1954, *26*, 155–158.

20. WOODWORTH, R. S. *Experimental psychology.* New York: Holt, 1938.

Benton Underwood shows that forgetting, which previously had been attributed exclusively to retroactive inhibition, depends critically on the prior laboratory experience of the subject. If he is learning his first list, he will forget only about 25 per cent a day later, whereas if he has learned a number of prior lists, he will forget approximately 75 percent a day later. This finding was suggested by some pilot experiments and then substantiated by a thorough review of the literature. This examples illustrates the constant interplay between current research findings and past knowledge. One builds on the other, and the development is cumulative. This article resulted in a major shift of research activity, in that henceforth forgetting was seen as a joint function of two variables. They were retroactive and proactive inhibition, with proactive inhibition becoming steadily more important in the understanding of human memory.

Interference and Forgetting

Benton J. Underwood

I know of no one who seriously maintains that interference among tasks is of no consequence in the production of forgetting. Whether forgetting is conceptualized at a strict psychological level or at a neural level (e.g., neural memory trace), some provision is made for interference to account for at least some of the measured forgetting. The many studies on retroactive inhibition are probably responsible for this general agreement that interference among tasks must produce a sizable proportion of forgetting. By introducing an interpolated interfering task very marked decrements in recall can be produced in a few minutes in the laboratory. But there is a second generalization which has resulted from these studies, namely, that most forgetting must be a function of the learning of tasks which interfere with that which has already been learned (19). Thus, if a single task is learned in the laboratory and retention measured after a week, the loss has been attributed to the interference from activities learned outside the laboratory during the week. It is this generalization with which I am concerned in the initial portions of this paper.

Now, I cannot deny the data which show large amounts of forgetting produced by an interpolated list in a few minutes in the laboratory. Nor do I deny that this loss may be attributed to interference. But I will try to show that use of retroactive inhibition as a paradigm of forgetting (via interference) may be seriously questioned. To be more specific: if a subject learns a single task, such as a list of words, and retention of this task is measured

Source: Reprinted by permission from *Psychological Review*, 1957, *64* (1), 49–60. Copyright © 1957 by the American Psychological Association.

Note: Address of the president, Mideastern Psychological Association, St. Louis, Missouri, May, 1956. Most of the data from the author's own research referred to in this paper were obtained from work done under Contract N7 onr-45008, Project NR-154–057, between Northwestern University and The Office of Naval Research.

after a day, a week, or a month, I will try to show that very little of the forgetting can be attributed to an interfering task learned outside the laboratory during the retention interval. Before pursuing this further, I must make some general comments by way of preparation.

Whether we like it or not, the experimental study of forgetting has been largely dominated by the Ebbinghaus tradition, both in terms of methods and materials used. I do not think this is due to sheer perversity on the part of several generations of scientists interested in forgetting. It may be noted that much of our elementary knowledge can be obtained only by rote learning. To work with rote learning does not mean that we are thereby not concerning ourselves with phenomena that have no counterparts outside the laboratory. Furthermore, the investigation of these phenomena can be handled by methods which are acceptable to a science. As is well known, there are periodic verbal revolts against the Ebbinghaus tradition (e.g., 2, 15, 22). But for some reason nothing much ever happens in the laboratory as a consequence of these revolts. I mention these matters neither by way of apology nor of justification for having done some research in rote learning, but for two other reasons. First, it may very well be true, as some have suggested (e.g., 22), that studies of memory in the Ebbinghaus tradition are not getting at all of the important phenomena of memory. I think the same statement—that research has not got at all of the important processes—could be made about all areas in psychology; so that the criticism (even if just) should not be indigenous to the study of memory. Science does not deal at will with all natural events. Science deals with natural events only when ingenuity in developing methods and techniques of measurement allow these events to be brought within the scope of science. If, therefore, the studies of memory which meet scientific acceptability do not tap all-important memorial processes, all I can say is that this is the state of the science in the area at the moment. Secondly, because the bulk of the systematic data on forgetting has been obtained on rote-learned tasks, I must of necessity use such data in discussing interference and forgetting.

Returning to the experimental situation, let me again put in concrete form the problem with which I first wish to deal. A subject learns a single task, such as a list of syllables, nouns, or adjectives. After an interval of time, say, 24 hours, his retention of this list is measured. The explanatory problem is what is responsible for the forgetting which commonly occurs over the 24 hours. As indicated earlier, the studies of retroactive inhibition led to the theoretical generalization that this forgetting was due largely to interference from other tasks learned during the 24-hour retention interval. McGeoch (20) came to this conclusion, his last such statement being made in 1942. I would, therefore, like to look at the data which were available to McGeoch and others interested in this matter. I must repeat that the kind of data with which I am concerned is the retention of a list without formal interpolated learning introduced. The interval of retention with which I am going to deal in this, and several subsequent analyses, is 24 hours.

First, of course, Ebbinghaus' data were available and in a sense served as the reference point for many subsequent investigations. In terms of percentage saved in relearning, Ebbinghaus showed about 65 per cent loss over 24 hours (7). In terms of recall after 24 hours, the following studies are representative of the amount forgotten: Youtz, 88 per cent loss (37); Luh, 82 per cent (18); Krueger, 74 per cent (16); Hovland, 78 per cent (11); Cheng, 65 per cent and 84 per cent (6); Lester, 65 per cent (17). Let us assume as a rough average of these studies that 75 per cent forgetting was measured over 24 hours. In all of these studies the list was learned to one perfect trial. The percentage values were derived by dividing the total number of items in the list into the number lost and changing to a percentage. Thus, on the average in these studies, if the subject learned a 12-item list and recalled three of these items after 24 hours, nine items (75 per cent) were forgotten.

The theory of interference as advanced by McGeoch, and so far as I know never seriously challenged, was that during the 24-hour interval subjects learned something outside the laboratory which interfered with the list learned in the laboratory. Most of the materials involved in the investigations cited above were nonsense syllables, and the subjects were college students. While realizing that I am viewing these results in the light of data which McGeoch and others did not have available, it seems to me to be an incredible stretch of an interference hypothesis to hold that this 75 per cent forgetting was caused by something which the subjects learned outside the laboratory during the 24-hour interval. Even if we agree with some educators that much of what we teach our students in college is nonsense, it does not seem to be the kind of learning that would interfere with nonsense syllables.

If, however, this forgetting was not due to interference from tasks learned outside the laboratory during the retention interval, to what was it due? I shall try to show that most of this forgetting was indeed produced by interference—not from tasks learned outside the laboratory, but from tasks learned previously in the laboratory. Following this I will show that when interference from laboratory tasks is removed, the amount of forgetting which occurs is relatively quite small. It then becomes more plausible that this amount could be produced by interference from tasks learned outside the laboratory, although, as I shall also point out, the interference very likely comes from prior, not interpolated, learning.

In 1950 a study was published by Mrs. Greenberg and myself (10) on retention as a function of stage of practice. The orientation for this study was crassly empirical; we simply wanted to know if subjects learn how to recall in the same sense that they learn how to learn. In the conditions with which I am concerned, naive subjects learned a list of ten paired adjectives to a criterion of eight out of ten correct on a single trial. Forty-eight hours later this list was recalled. On the following day, these same subjects learned a new list to the same criterion and recalled it after 48 hours. This continued for two additional lists, so that the subjects had learned and recalled four lists, but the learning and recall of each list was complete before another list was learned. There was low similarity among these lists as far as conventional symptoms

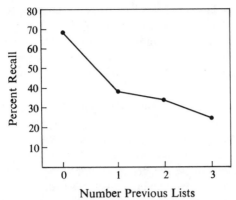

FIGURE 1.   Recall of paired adjectives as a function of number of previous lists learned (10)

of similarity are concerned. No words were repeated and no obvious similarities existed, except for the fact that they were all adjectives and a certain amount of similarity among prefixes, suffixes, and so on must inevitably occur. The recall of these four successive lists is shown in Figure 1.

As can be seen, the more lists that are learned, the poorer the recall, from 69 per cent recall of the first list to 25 per cent recall of the fourth list. In examining errors at recall, we found a sufficient number of intrusion responses from previous lists to lead us to suggest that the increasing decrements in recall were a function of proactive interference from previous lists. And, while we pointed out that these results had implications for the design of experiments on retention, the relevance to an interference theory of forgetting was not mentioned.

Dr. E. J. Archer has made available to me certain data from an experiment which still is in progress and which deals with this issue. Subjects learned lists of 12 serial adjectives to one perfect trial and recalled them after

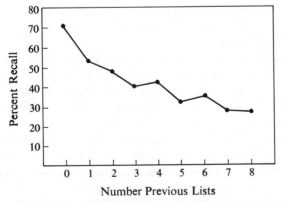

FIGURE 2.   Recall of serial adjective lists as a function of number of previous lists learned. Unpublished data, courtesy of Dr. E. J. Archer.

24 hours. The recall of a list always took place prior to learning the next list. The results for nine successive lists are shown in Figure 2. Let me say again that there is no laboratory activity during the 24-hour interval; the subject learns a list, is dismissed from the laboratory, and returns after 24 hours to recall the list. The percentage of recall falls from 71 per cent for the first list to 27 per cent for the ninth.

In summarizing the more classical data on retention above, I indicated that a rough estimate showed that after 24 hours 75 per cent forgetting took place, or recall was about 25 per cent correct. In viewing these values in the light of Greenberg's and Archer's findings, the conclusion seemed inescapable that the classical studies must have been dealing with subjects who had learned many lists. That is to say, the subjects must have served in many conditions by use of counterbalancing and repeated cycles. To check on this I have made a search of the literature on the studies of retention to see if systematic data could be compiled on this matter. Preliminary work led me to establish certain criteria for inclusion in the summary to be presented. First, because degree of learning is such an important variable, I have included only those studies in which degree of learning was one perfect recitation of the list. Second, I have included only studies in which retention was measured after 24 hours. Third, I have included only studies in which recall measures were given. (Relearning measures add complexities with which I do not wish to deal in this paper.) Fourth, the summary includes only material learned by relatively massed practice. Finally, if an investigator had two or more conditions which met these criteria, I averaged the values presentation in this paper. Except for these restrictions, I have used all studies I found (with an exception to be noted later), although I do not pretend to have made an exhaustive search. From each of these studies I got two facts: first, the percentage recalled after 24 hours, and second, the average number of previous lists the subjects had learned before learning the list on which recall after 24 hours was taken. Thus, if a subject had served in five experimental conditions via counterbalancing, and had been given two practice lists, the average number of lists learned before learning the list for which I tabulated the recall was four. This does not take into account any previous experiments in rote learning in which the subject might have served.

For each of these studies the two facts, average number of previous lists learned and percentage of recall, are related as in Figure 3. For example, consider the study by Youtz. This study was concerned with Jost's law, and had several degrees of learning, several lengths of retention interval, and the subjects served in two cycles. Actually, there were 15 experimental conditions and each subject was given each condition twice. Also, each subject learned six practice lists before starting the experimental conditions. Among the 15 conditions was one in which the learning of the syllables was carried to one perfect recitation and recall was taken after 24 hours. It is this particular condition in which I am interested. On the average, this condition would have been given

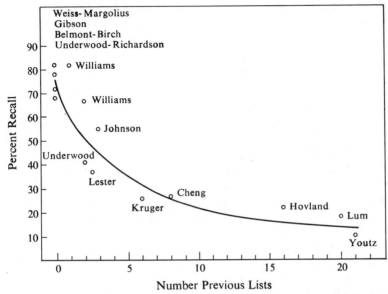

FIGURE 3.   Recall as a function of number of previous lists learned as determined from a number of studies. From life to right: Weiss and Margolius (35), Gibson (9), Belmont and Birch (3), Underwood and Richardson (33), Williams (36), Underwood (27, 28, 29 30) Lester (17), Johnson (14), Krueger (16), Cheng (6), Hovland (11), Luh (18), Youtz (37)

at the time when the subject had learned six practice lists and 15 experimental lists, for a total of 21 previous lists.

The studies included in Figure 3 have several different kinds of materials, from geometric forms to nonsense syllables to nouns; they include both paired-associate and serial presentation, with different speeds of presentation and different lengths of lists. But I think the general relationship is clear. The greater the number of previous lists learned the greater the forgetting. I interpret this to mean that the greater the number of previous lists the greater the *proactive* interference. We know this to be true (26) for a formal proactive-inhibition paradigm; it seems a reasonable interpretation for the data of Figure 3. That there are minor sources of variance still involved I do not deny. Some of the variation can be rationalized, but that is not the purpose of this report. The point I wish to make is the obvious one of the relationship between number of previous lists learned—lists which presumably had no intentionally built-in similarity—and amount of forgetting. If you like to think in correlational terms, the rank-order correlation between the two variables is − .91 for the 14 points of Figure 3.

It may be of interest to the historian that, of the studies published before 1942 which met the criteria I imposed, I did not find a single one in which subjects had not been given at least one practice task before starting experimental conditions, and in most cases the subjects had several practice lists and several experimental conditions. Gibson's study (1942) was the first I found in which subjects served in only one condition and were not given practice tasks. I think it is apparent that the design proclivities of the 1920s and 1930s have been largely responsible for the exaggerated picture we have had of the rate of forgetting of rote-learned materials. On the basis of studies performed during the 1920s and 1930s, I have given a rough estimate of forgetting as being 75 per cent over 24 hours, recall being 25 per cent. On the basis of modern studies in which the subject has learned no previous lists —where there is no proactive inhibition from previous laboratory tasks—a rough estimate would be that forgetting is 25 per cent; recall is 75 per cent. The values are reversed. (If in the above and subsequent discussion my use of percentage values as if I were dealing with a cardinal or extensive scale is disturbing. I will say only that it makes the picture easier to grasp, and in my opinion no critical distortion results.)

Before taking the next major step, I would like to point out a few other observations which serve to support my general point that proactive inhibition from laboratory tasks has been the major cause of forgetting in the more classical studies. The first illustration I shall give exemplifies the point that when subjects have served in several conditions, forgetting after relatively short periods of time is greater than after 24 hours if the subject has served in only one condition. In the Youtz study to which I have already referred, other conditions were employed in which recall was taken after short intervals. After 20 minutes recall was 74 per cent, about what it is after 24 hours if the subject has not served in a series of conditions. After two hours recall was 32 per cent. In Ward's (34) well-known reminiscence experiment, subjects who on the average had learned ten previous lists showed a recall of only 64 per cent after 20 minutes.

In the famous Jenkins-Dallenbach (13) study on retention following sleep and following waking, two subjects were used. One subject learned a total of 61 lists and the other 62 in addition to several practice lists. Roughly, then, if the order of the conditions was randomized, approximately 30 lists had been learned prior to the learning of a list for a given experimental condition. Recall after eight waking hours for one subject was 4 per cent and for the other 14 per cent. Even after sleeping for eight hours the recall was only 55 per cent and 58 per cent.

I have said that an interpolated list can produce severe forgetting. However, in one study (1), using the A-B, A-C paradigm for original and interpolated learning, but using subjects who had never served in any previous conditions, recall of the original list was 46 per cent after 48 hours, and in another comparable study (24), 42 per cent. Thus, the loss is not nearly as great as in the classical studies I have cited where there was no interpolated learning in the laboratory.

My conclusion at this point is that, in terms of the gross analysis I have made, the amount of forgetting which might be attributed to interference from tasks learned outside the laboratory has been "reduced" from 75 per cent to about 25 per cent. I shall proceed in the next section to see if we have grounds for reducing this estimate still more. In passing on to this section, however, let me say that the study of factors which influence proactive inhibition in these counterbalanced studies is a perfectly legitimate and important area of study. I mention this because in the subsequent discussion I am going to deal only with the case where a subject has learned a single list in the laboratory, and I do not want to leave the impression that we should now and forevermore drop the study of interference produced by previous laboratory tasks. Indeed, as will be seen shortly, it is my opinion that we should increase these studies for the simple reason that the proactive paradigm provides a more realistic one than does the retroactive paradigm.

When the subject learns and recalls a single list in the laboratory, I have given an estimate of 25 per cent as being the amount forgotten over 24 hours. When, as shown above, we calculate percentage forgotten of lists learned to one perfect trial, the assumption is that had the subjects been given an immediate recall trial, the list would have been perfectly recalled. This, of course, is simply not true. The major factor determining how much error is introduced by this criterion-percentage method is probably the difficulty of the task. In general, the overestimation of forgetting by the percentage method will be directly related to the difficulty of the task. Thus, the more slowly the learning approaches a given criterion, the greater the drop on the trial immediately after the criterion trial. Data from a study by Runquist (24), using eight paired adjectives (a comparatively easy task), shows that amount of forgetting is overestimated by about 10 per cent. In a study (32) using very difficult consonant syllables, the overestimation was approximately 20 per cent. To be conservative, assume that on the average the percentage method of reporting recall overestimates the amount forgotten by 10 per cent. If we subtract this from the 25 per cent assumed above, the forgetting is now re-estimated as being 15 per cent over 24 hours. That is to say, an interference theory, or any other form of theory, has to account for a very small amount of forgetting as compared with the amount traditionally cited.

What are the implications of so greatly "reducing" the amount of forgetting? There are at least three implications which I feel are worth pointing out. First, if one wishes to hold to an interference theory of forgetting (as I do), it seems plausible to assert that this amount of forgetting could be produced from learning which has taken place outside of the laboratory. Furthermore, it seems likely that such interference must result primarily from proactive interference. This seems likely on a simple probability basis. A 20-year-old college student will more likely have learned something during his 20 years prior to coming to the laboratory that will interfere with his retention than he will during the 24 hours between the learning and retention test. However, the longer the retention interval the more important will retroactive interference become relative to proactive interferences.

The second implication is that these data may suggest greater homogeneity or continuity in memorial processes than hitherto supposed. Although no one has adequately solved the measurement problem of how to make comparisons of retention among conditioned responses, prose material, motor tasks, concept learning, and rote-learned tasks, the gross comparisons have indicated that rote-learned tasks were forgotten much more rapidly than these other tasks. But the rote-learning data used for comparison have been those derived with the classical design in which the forgetting over 24 hours is approximately 75 per cent. If we take the revised estimate of 15 per cent, the discrepancies among tasks become considerably less.

The third implication of the revised estimate of rate of forgetting is that the number of variables which appreciably influence rate of forgetting must be sharply limited. While this statement does not inevitably follow from the analyses I have made, the current evidence strongly supports the statement. I want to turn to the final section of this paper which will consist of a review of the influence of some of the variables which are or have been thought to be related to rate of forgetting. In considering these variables, it is well to keep in mind that a variable which produces only a small difference in forgetting is important if one is interested in accounting for the 15 per cent assumed now as the loss over 24 hours. If appropriate for a given variable, I will indicate where it fits into an interference theory, although in no case will I endeavor to handle the details of such a theory.

TIME.   Passage of time between learning and recall is the critical defining variable for forgetting. Manipulation of this variable provides the basic data for which a theory must account. Previously, our conception of rate of forgetting as a function of time has been tied to the Ebbinghaus curve. If the analysis made earlier is correct, this curve does not give us the basic data we need. In short, we must start all over and derive a retention curve over time when the subjects have learned no previous materials in the laboratory. It is apparent that I expect the fall in this curve over time to be relatively small.

In conjunction with time as an independent variable, we must, in explanations of forgetting, consider why sleep retards the processes responsible for forgetting. My conception, which does not really explain anything, is that since forgetting is largely produced by proactive interference, the amount of time which a subject spends in sleep is simply to be subtracted from the total retention interval when predicting the amount to be forgotten. It is known that proactive interference increases with passage of time (5); sleep, I believe, brings to a standstill whatever these processes are which produce this increase.

DEGREE OF LEARNING.   We usually say that the better or stronger the learning the more or better the retention. Yet, we do not know whether or not the *rate* of forgetting differs for items of different strength. The experimental problem is a difficult one. What we need is to have a subject learn a single association and measure its decline in strength over time. But this is difficult to carry out with verbal material, since almost of necessity we must have the subject learn a series of associations, to make it a reasonable task. And, when a series of associations are learned, complications arise from interaction effects among associations of different strength. Nevertheless, we may expect, on the basis of evidence from a wide variety of studies, that given a constant degree of similarity, the effective interference varies as some function of the strength of associations.

DISTRIBUTION OF PRACTICE. It is a fact that distribution of practice during acquisition influences retention of verbal materials. The facts of the case seem to be as follows. If the subject has not learned previous lists in the laboratory, massed practice gives equal or better retention than does distributed practice. If, on the other hand, the subject has learned a number of previous lists, distributed practice will facilitate retention (32). We do not have the theoretical solution to these facts. The point I wish to make here is that whether or not distribution of learning inhibits or facilitates retention depends upon the amount of interference from previous learning. It is reasonable to expect, therefore, that the solution to the problem will come via principles handling interference in general. I might also say that a theoretical solution to this problem will also provide a solution for Jost's laws.

SIMILARITY. Amount of interference from other tasks is closely tied to similarity. This similarity must be conceived of as similarity among materials as such and also situational similarity (4). When we turn to similarity within a task, the situation is not quite so clear. Empirically and theoretically (8) one would expect that intratask similarity would be a very relevant variable in forgetting. As discussed elsewhere (31), however, variation in intratask similarity almost inevitably leads to variations in intratask similarity. We do know from a recent study (33) that with material of low meaningfulness forgetting is significantly greater with high intralist similarity than with low. While the difference in magnitude is only about 8 per cent, when we are trying to account for a total loss of 15 per cent, this amount becomes a major matter.

MEANINGFULNESS. The belief has long been held that the more meaningful the material the better the retention—the less the forgetting. Osgood (21) has pointed out that if this is true it is difficult for an interference theory to handle. So far as I know, the only direct test of the influence of this variable is a recent study in which retention of syllables of 100 per cent association value was compared with that of zero association value (33). There was no difference in the recall of these syllables. Other less precise evidence would support this finding when comparisons are made among syllables, adjectives, and nouns, as plotted in Figure 3. However, there is some evidence that materials of very low meaningfulness are forgotten more rapidly than nonsense syllables of zero association value. Consonant syllables, both serial (32) and paired associates (unpublished), show about 50 per cent loss over 24 hours. The study using serial lists was the one mentioned earlier as knowingly omitted from Figure 3. These syllables, being extremely difficult to learn, allow a correction of about 20 per cent due to criterion overestimation, but even with this much correction the forgetting (30 per cent) is still appreciably more than the estimate we have made for other materials. To invoke the interference theory to account for this discrepancy means that we must demonstrate how interference from other activities could be greater for these consonant syllables than for nonsense syllables, nouns, adjectives, and other materials. Our best guess at the present time is that the sequences of letters in consonant syllables are contrary to other well-established language habits. That is to say, letter sequences which commonly occur in our language are largely different from those in consonant syllables. As a consequence, not only are these consonant syllables very difficult to learn, but forgetting is accelerated by proactive interference from previously well-learned letter sequences. If subsequent research cannot demonstrate such a source of interference, or if some other source is not specified, an interference theory for this case will be in some trouble.

AFFECTIVITY.   Another task dimension which has received extensive attention is the affective tone of the material. I would also include here the studies attaching unpleasant experiences to some items experimentally and not to others, and measuring retention of these two sets of items. Freud is to a large extent responsible for these studies, but he cannot be held responsible for the malformed methodology which characterizes so many of them. What can one say by way of summarizing these studies? The only conclusion that I can reach is a statistical one, namely, that the occasional positive result found among the scores of studies is about as frequent as one would expect by sampling error, using the 5 per cent level of confidence. Until a reliable body of facts is established for this variable and associated variables, no theoretical evaluation is possible.

OTHER VARIABLES.   As I indicated earlier, I will not make an exhaustive survey of the variables which may influence rate of forgetting. I have limited myself to variables which have been rather extensively investigated, which have immediate relevance to the interference theory, or for which reliable relationships are available. Nevertheless, I would like to mention briefly some of these other variables. There is the matter of *warm-up* before recall: some investigators find that this reduces forgetting (12); others, under as nearly replicated conditions as is possible to obtain, do not (23). Some resolution must be found for these flat contradictions. It seems perfectly reasonable, however, that inadequate set or context differences could reduce recall. Indeed, an interference theory would predict this forgetting if the set or context stimuli are appreciably different from those prevailing at the time of learning. In our laboratory we try to reinstate the learning set by careful instructions, and we simply do not find decrements that might be attributed to inadequate set. For example, in a recent study (33) subjects were given a 24-hour recall of a serial list after learning to one perfect trial. I think we would expect that the first item in the list would suffer the greatest decrement due to inadequate set, yet this item showed only .7 per cent loss. But let it be clear that when we are attempting to account for the 15 per cent loss over 24 hours, we should not overlook any possible source for this loss.

Thus far I have not said anything about forgetting as a function of characteristics of the subject, that is, the personality or intellectual characteristics. As far as I have been able to determine, there is not a single valid study which shows that such variables have an appreciable influence on forgetting. Many studies have shown differences in learning as a function of these variables, but not differences in rate of forgetting. Surely there must be some such variables. We do know that if subjects are severely insulted, made to feel stupid, or generally led to believe that they have no justification for continued existence on the earth just before they are asked to recall, they will show losses (e.g., 25, 38), but even the influence of this kind of psychological beating is short lived. Somehow I have never felt that such findings need explanation by a theory used to explain the other facts of forgetting.

Concerning the causes of forgetting, let me sum up in a somewhat more dogmatic fashion than is probably justified. One of the assumptions of science is finite causality. Everything cannot influence everything else. To me, the most important implication of the work on forgetting during the last ten years is that this work has markedly *reduced* the number of variables related to forgetting. Correspondingly, I think the theoretical problem has become simpler. It is my belief that we can narrow down the cause of forgetting to interference from previously learned habits, from habits being currently learned, and from habits we have yet to learn. The amount of this interference is primarily a function of similarity and associative strength, the latter being important because it interacts with similarity.

Summary

This paper deals with issues in the forgetting of rote-learned materials. An analysis of the current evidence suggests that the classical Ebbinghaus curve of forgetting is primarily a function of interference from materials learned previously in the laboratory. When this source of interference is removed, forgetting decreases from about 75 per cent over 24 hours to about 25 per cent. This latter figure can be reduced by at least 10 per cent by other methodological considerations, leaving 15 per cent as an estimate of the forgetting over 24 hours. This estimate will vary somewhat as a function of intratask similarity, distributed practice, and with very low meaningful material. But the overall evidence suggests that similarity with other material and situational similarity are by far the most critical factors in forgetting. Such evidence is consonant with a general interference theory, although the details of such a theory were not presented here.

References

1. ARCHER, E. J., & UNDERWOOD, B. J. Retroactive inhibition of verbal associations as a multiple function of temporal point of interpolation and degree of interpolated learning. *J. Exp. Psychol.*, 1951, *42*, 283–290.

2. BARTLETT, F. C. *Remembering: a study in experimental and social psychology.* London: Cambridge Univer. Press, 1932.

3. BELMONT, L., & BIRCH, H. G. Re-individualizing the repression hypothesis. *J. Abnorm. Soc. Psychol.*, 1951, *46*, 226–235.

4. BILODEAU, I. McD., & SCHLOSBERG, H. Similarity in stimulating conditions as a variable in retroactive inhibition. *J. Exp. Psychol.*, 1951, *41*, 199–204.

5. BRIGGS, G. E. Acquisition, extinction, and recovery functions in retroactive inhibition. *J. Exp. Psychol.*, 1954, *47*, 285–293.

6. CHENG, N. Y. Retroactive effect and degree of similarity. *J. Exp. Psychol.*, 1929, *12*, 444–458.

7. EBBINGHAUS, H. *Memory: a contribution to experimental psychology.* (Trans. by H. A. Ruger, and C. E. Bussenius.) New York: Bureau of Publications, Teachers College, Columbia Univer., 1913.

8. GIBSON, E. J. A systematic application of the concepts of generalization and differentiation to verbal learning. *Psychol. Rev.*, 1940, *47*, 196–229.

9. ———. Intra-list generalization as a factor in verbal learning. *J. Exp. Psychol.*, 1942, *30*, 185–200.

10. GREENBERG, R., & UNDERWOOD, B. J. Retention as a function of stage of practice. *J. Exp. Psychol.*, 1950, *40*, 452–457.

11. HOVLAND, C. I. Experimental studies in rote-learning theory. VI. Comparison of retention following learning to same criterion by massed and distributed practice. *J. Exp. Psychol.*, 1940, *26*, 568–587.

12. IRION, A. L. The relation of "set" to retention. *Psychol. Rev.*, 1948, *55*, 336–341.

13. JENKINS, J. G., & DALLENBACH, K. M. Oblivescence during sleep and waking. *Amer. J. Psychol.*, 1924, *35*, 605–612.

14. JOHNSON, L. M. The relative effect of a time interval upon learning and retention. *J. Exp. Psychol.*, 1939, *24*, 169–179.

15. KATONA, G. *Organizing and memorizing: studies in the psychology of learning and teaching.* New York: Columbia Univer. Press, 1940.

16. KRUEGER, W. C. F. The effect of overlearning on retention. *J. Exp. Psychol.*, 1929, *12*, 71–78.

17. LESTER, O. P. Mental set in relation to retroactive inhibition. *J. Exp. Psychol.*, 1932, *15*, 681–699.

18. LUH, C. W. The conditions of retention. *Psychol. Monogr.*, 1922, *31*, No. 3 (Whole No. 142).

19. McGEOCH, J. A. Forgetting and the law of disuse. *Psychol. Rev.*, 1932, *39*, 352–370.

20. ———. *The psychology of human learning.* New York: Longmans, Green, 1942.

21. OSGOOD, C. E. *Method and theory in experimental psychology.* New York: Oxford Univer. Press, 1953.

22. RAPAPORT, D. Emotions and memory. *Psychol. Rev.*, 1943, *50*, 234–243.

23. ROCKWAY, M. R., & DUNCAN, C. P. Pre-recall warming-up in verbal retention. *J. Exp. Psychol.*, 1952, *43*, 305–312.

24. RUNQUIST, W. Retention of verbal associations as a function of interference and strength. Unpublished doctor's dissertation, Northwestern Univer., 1956.

25. RUSSELL, W. A. Retention of verbal material as a function of motivating instructions and experimentally-induced failure. *J. Exp. Psychol.*, 1952, *43*, 207–216.

26. UNDERWOOD, B. J. The effect of successive interpolations on retroactive and proactive inhibition. *Psychol. Monogr.*, 1945, *59*, No. 3 (Whole No. 273).

27. ————. Studies of distributed practice: VII. Learning and retention of serial nonsense lists as a function of intralist similarity. *J. Exp. Psychol.*, 1952, *44*, 80–87.

28. ————. Studies of distributed practice: VIII. Learning and retention of paired nonsense syllables as a function of intralist similarity. *J. Exp. Psychol.*, 1953, *45*, 133–142.

29. ————: Studies of distributed practice: IX. Learning and retention of paired adjectives as a function of intralist similarity. *J. Exp. Psychol.*, 1953, *45*, 143–149.

30. ————. Studies of distributed practice: X. The influence of intralist similarity on learning and retention of serial adjective lists. *J. Exp. Psychol.*, 1953, *45*, 253–259.

31. ————. Intralist similarity in verbal learning and retention. *Psychol. Rev.*, 1954, *3*, 160–166.

32. UNDERWOOD, B. J., & RICHARDSON, J. Studies of distributed practice: XIII. Interlist interference and the retention of serial nonsense lists. *J. Exp. Psychol.*, 1955, *50*, 39–46.

33. ————. The influence of meaningfulness, intralist similarity, and serial position on retention. *J. Exp. Psychol.*, 1956, *52*, 119–126.

34. WARD, L. B. Reminiscence and rote learning. *Psychol. Monogr.*, 1937, *49*, No. 4 (Whole No. 220).

35. WEISS, W., & MARGOLIUS, G. The effect of context stimuli on learning and retention. *J. Exp. Psychol.*, 1954, *48*, 318–322.

36. WILLIAMS, M. The effects of experimentally induced needs upon retention. *J. Exp. Psychol.*, 1950, *40*, 139–151.

37. YOUTZ, A. C. An experimental evaluation of Jost's laws. *Psychol. Monogr.*, 1941, *53*, No. 1 (Whole No. 238).

38. ZELLER, A. F. An experimental analogue of repression: III. The effect of induced failure and success on memory measured by recall. *J. Exp. Psychol.*, 1951, *42*, 32–38.

Brown and McNeill report a method to study the tip-of-the-tongue effect under controlled laboratory conditions; this phenomenon occurs when you can't remember a word or a name, but you feel that it is right at the tip of your tongue. In the experimental method, the target words are known to the experimenter but not the subjects. By extensive testing they can find a number of cases where this effect occurs, even though the probability of its occurrence in any particular instance is quite small. They are able to go one step beyond and classify the way in which the generated item is similiar to the target item. It is interesting to note that in some cases the similarity is on the basis of meaning and in some cases is on the basis of sound. The phonemic similarity reported here (which actually outnumbers the cases of semantic similarity) shows the similarity between short- and long-term memory (cf. the acoustic confusion effect of Conrad). At the end of this selection, the authors suggest a "neural dictionary" model for memory which includes semantic markers or attributes.

The "Tip of the Tongue" Phenomenon

Roger Brown and David McNeill

William James wrote, in 1893: "Suppose we try to recall a forgotten name. The state of our consciousness is peculiar. There is a gap therein; but no mere gap. It is a gap that is intensely active. A sort of wraith of the name is in it, beckoning us in a given direction, making us at moments tingle with the sense of our closeness and then letting us sink back without the longed-for term. If wrong names are proposed to us, this singularly definite gap acts immediately so as to negate them. They do not find into its mould. And the gap of one word does not feel like the gap of another, all empty of content as both might seem necessarily to be when described as gaps" (p. 251).

The "tip of the tongue" (TOT) state involves a failure to recall a word of which one has knowledge. The evidence of knowledge is either an eventually successful recall or else an act of recognition that occurs, without additional training, when recall has failed. The class of cases defined by the conjunction of knowledge and a failure of recall is a large one. The TOT state, which James described, seems to be a small subclass in which recall is felt to be imminent.

For several months we watched for TOT states in ourselves. Unable to recall the name of the street on which a relative lives, one of us thought of *Congress* and *Corinth* and *Concord* and then looked up the address and learned that it was *Cornish*. The words that had come to mind have certain properties in common with the word that had been sought (the "target word"):

Source: Reprinted by permission of Academic Press from *Journal of Verbal Learning and Verbal Behavior*, 1966, *5*, 325–337.

all four begin with *Co;* all are two-syllable words; all put the primary stress on the first syllable. After this experience we began putting direct questions to ourselves when we fell into the TOT state, questions as to the number of syllables in the target word, its initial letter, etc.

Woodworth (1934), before us, made a record of data for naturally occurring TOT states and Wenzl (1932, 1936) did the same for German words. Their results are similar to those we obtained and consistent with the following preliminary characterization. When complete recall of a word is not presently possible but is felt to be imminent, one can often correctly recall the general type of the word; *generic* recall may succeed when particular recall fails. There seem to be two common varieties of generic recall. (a) Sometimes a part of the target word is recalled, a letter or two, a syllable, or affix. Partial recall is necessarily also *generic* since the class of words defined by the possession of any *part* of the target word will include words other than the target. (b) Sometimes the abstract form of the target is recalled, perhaps the fact that it was a two-syllable sequence with the primary stress on the first syllable. The whole word is represented in *abstract form recall* but not on the letter-by-letter level that constitutes its identity. The recall of an abstract form is also necessarily *generic,* since any such form defines a class of words extending beyond the target.

Wenzl and Woodworth had worked with small collections of data for naturally occurring TOT states. These data were, for the most part, provided by the investigators; were collected in an unsystematic fashion; and were analyzed in an impressionistic nonquantitative way. It seemed to us that such data left the facts of generic recall in doubt. An occasional correspondence between a retrieved word and a target word with respect to number of syllables, stress pattern or initial letter is, after all, to be expected by chance. Several months of "self-observation and asking-our-friends" yielded fewer than a dozen good cases and we realized that an improved method of data collection was essential.

We thought it might pay to "prospect" for TOT states by reading to *S* definitions of uncommon English words and asking him to supply the words. The procedure was given a preliminary test with nine *S*s who were individually interviewed for 2 hrs. each.[1] In 57 instances an *S* was, in fact, "seized" by a TOT state. The signs of it were unmistakable; he would appear to be in mild torment, something like the brink of a sneeze, and if he found the word his relief was considerable. While searching for the target *S* told us all the words that came to his mind. He volunteered the information that some of them resembled the target in sound but not in meaning; others he was sure were similar in meaning but not in sound. The *E* intruded on *S*'s agony with two questions: (a) How many syllables has the target word? (b) What is its first letter? Answers to the first question were correct in 47% of all cases and answers to the second question were correct in 51% of the cases. These out-

---

[1] We wish to thank Mr. Charles Hollen for doing the pretest interviews.

comes encouraged us to believe that generic recall was real and to devise a group procedure that would further speed up the rate of data collection.

Method

Subjects

Fifty-six Harvard and Radcliffe undergraduates participated in one of three evening sessions; each session was 2 hrs. long. The *S*s were volunteers from a large General Education Course and were paid for their time.

WORD LIST. The list consisted of 49 words which according to the Thorndike-Lorge *Word Book* (1952) occur at least once per four million words but not so often as once per one million words. The level is suggested by these examples: *apse, nepotism, cloaca, ambergris,* and *sampan.* We thought the words used were likely to be in the passive or recognition vocabularies of our *S*s but not in their active recall vocabularies. There were 6 words of 1 syllable; 19 of 2 syllables; 20 of 3 syllables; 4 of 4 syllables. For each word we used a definition from *The American College Dictionary* (Barnhart, 1948) edited so as to contain no words that closely resembled the one being defined.

RESPONSE SHEET. The response sheet was laid off in vertical columns headed as follows:

> *Intended word (+ One I was thinking of).*
> > *(− Not).*
> *Number of syllables (1–5).*
> *Initial letter.*
> *Words of similar sound. (1. Closest in sound)*
> > *(2. Middle)*
> > *(3. Farthest in Sound)*
> *Words of similar meaning.*
> *Word you had in mind if not intended word.*

Procedure

We instructed *S*s to the following effect.

In this experiment we are concerned with that state of mind in which a person is unable to think of a word that he is certain he knows, the state of mind in which a word seems to be on the tip of one's tongue. Our technique for precipitating such states is, in general, to read definitions of uncommon words and ask the subject to recall the word.

(1) We will first read the definition of a low-frequency word.

(2) If you should happen to know the word at once, or think you do, or, if you should simply not know it, then there is nothing further for you to do at the moment. Just wait.

(3) If you are unable to think of the word but feel sure that you

know it and that it is on the verge of coming back to you then you are in a TOT state and should begin at once to fill in the columns of the response sheet.

(4) After reading each definition we will ask whether anyone is in the TOT state. Anyone who is in that state should raise his hand. The rest of us will then wait until those in the TOT state have written on the answer sheet all the information they are able to provide.

(5) When everyone who has been in the TOT state has signalled us to proceed, we will read the target word. At this time, everyone is to write the word in the left-most column of the response sheet. Those of you who have known the word since first its definition was read are asked not to write it until this point. Those of you who simply did not know the word or who had thought of a different word will write now the word we read. For those of you who have been in the TOT state two eventualities are possible. The word read may strike you as definitely the word you have been seeking. In that case please write '+' after the word, as the instructions at the head of the column direct. The other possibility is that you will not be sure whether the word read is the one you have been seeking or, indeed, you may be sure that it is not. In this case you are asked to write the sign '−' after the word. Sometimes when the word read out is not the one you have been seeking your actual target may come to mind. In this case, in addition to the minus sign in the leftmost column, please write the actual target word in the rightmost column.

(6) Now we come to the column entries themselves. The first two entries, the guess as to the number of syllables and the initial letter, are required. The remaining entries should be filled out if possible. When you are in a TOT state, words that are related to the target word do almost always come to mind. List them as they come, but separate words which you think resemble the target in sound from words which you think resemble the target in meaning.

(7) When you have finished all your entries, but before you signal us to read the intended target word, look again at the words you have listed as 'Words of similar sound.' If possible, rank these, as the instructions at the head of the column direct, in terms of the degree of their seeming resemblance to the target. This must be done without knowledge of what the target actually is.

(8) The research procedure of a person in the TOT state will sometimes serve to retrieve the missing word before he has finished filling in the columns and before we read out the word. When this happens please mark the place where it happens with the words "Got it" and *do not provide any more data.*

Results

Classes of Data

There were 360 instances, across all words and all *S*s, in which a TOT state was signalled. Of this total, 233 were positive TOTs. A positive

TOT is one for which the target word is known and, consequently, one for which the data obtained can be scored as accurate or inaccurate. In those cases where the target was not the word intended but some other word which *S* finally recalled and wrote in the rightmost column his data were checked against that word, his effective target. A negative TOT is one for which the *S* judged the word read out not to have been his target and, in addition, one in which *S* proved unable to recall his own functional target.

The data provided by *S* while he searched for the target word are of two kinds: explicit guesses as to the number of syllables in the target and the initial letter of the target; words that came to mind while he searched for the target. The words that came to mind were classified by *S* into 224 words similar in sound to the target (hereafter called "SS" words) and 95 words similar in meaning to the target (hereafter called "SM" words). The *S*'s information about the number of syllables in, and the initial letter of the target may be inferred from correspondences between the target and his SS words as well as directly discovered from his explicit guesses. For his knowledge of the stress pattern of the target and of letters in the target, other than the initial letter, we must rely on the SS words alone since explicit guesses were not required.

To convey a sense of the SS and SM words we offer the following examples. When the target was *sampan* the SS words (not all of them real words) included: *Saipan, Siam, Cheyenne, sarong, sanching,* and *sympoon.* The SM words were: *barge, houseboat,* and *junk.* When the target was *caduceus* the SS words included *Casadesus, Aeschelus, cephalus,* and *leucosis.* The SM words were: *fasces, Hippocrates, lictor,* and *snake.* The spelling in all cases is *S*'s own.

We will, in this report, use the SM words to provide baseline data against which to evaluate the accuracy of the explicit guesses and of the SS words. The SM words are words produced under the spell of the positive TOT state but judged by *S* to resemble the target in meaning rather than sound. We are quite sure that the SM words are somewhat more like the target than would be a collection of words produced by *S*s with no knowledge of the target. However, the SM words make a better comparative baseline than any other data we collected.

General Problems of Analysis

The data present problems of analysis that are not common in psychology. To begin with, the words of the list did not reliably precipitate TOT states. Of the original 49 words, all but *zither* succeeded at least once; the range was from one success to nine. The *S*s made actual targets of 51 words not on the original list and all but five of these were pursued by one *S* only. Clearly none of the 100 words came even close to precipitating a TOT state in all 56 *S*s. Furthermore, the *S*s varied in their susceptibility to TOT states. There were nine who experienced none at all in a 2-hr. period; the largest number experienced in such a period by one S was eight. In our data, then, the entries for one word will not usually involve the same Ss or even the same number of Ss as the entries for another word. The entries for one S need not involve the same words or even the same number of words as the entries for another S. Consequently for the tests we shall want to make there are no significance tests that we can be sure are appropriate.

In statistical theory our problem is called the "fragmentary data problem."[2] The best thing to do with fragmentary data is to report them very fully and analyze them in several different ways. Our detailed knowedge of these data suggests that the problems are not serious for, while there is some variation in the pull of words and the susceptibility of Ss there is not much variation in the quality of the data. The character of the material recalled is much the same from word to word and S to S.

Number of Syllables

As the main item of evidence that S in a TOT state can recall with significant success the number of syllables in a target word he has not yet found we offer Table 1. The entries on the diagonal are instances in which guesses were correct. The order of the means of the explicit guesses is the same as the order of the actual number of syllables in the target words. The rank order correlation between the two is 1.0 and such a correlation is significant with a $p < .001$ (one-tailed) even when only five items are correlated. The modes of the guesses correspond exactly with the actual numbers of syllables, for the values one through three; for words of four and five syllables the modes continue to be three.

TABLE 1.   Actual numbers of syllables and guessed numbers for all TOTs in the main experiment

Actual Numbers	Guessed Numbers					No Guess	Mode	Mean
	1	2	3	4	5			
1	9	7	1	0	0	0	1	1.53
2	2	55	22	2	1	5	2	2.33
3	3	19	61	10	1	5	3	2.86
4	0	2	12	6	2	3	3	3.36
5	0	0	3	0	1	1	3	3.50

When all TOTs are combined, the contributions to the total effects of individual Ss and of individual words are unequal. We have made an analysis in which each word counts but once. This was accomplished by calculating the mean of the guesses made by all Ss for whom a particular word precipi-

[2] We wish to thank Professor Frederick Mosteller for discussing the fragmentary data problem with us.

tated a TOT state and taking that mean as the score for that word. The new means calculated with all words equally weighted were, in order: 1.62; 2.30; 2.80; 3.33; and 3.50. These values are close to those of Table 1 and *rho* with the actual numbers of syllables continues to be 1.0.

We also made an analysis in which each *S* counts but once. This was done by calculating the mean of an *S*'s guesses for all words of one syllable, the mean for all words of two syllables, etc. In comparing the means of guesses for words of different length one can only use those *S*s who made at least one guess for each actual length to be compared. In the present data only words of two syllables and three syllables precipitated enough TOTs to yield a substantial number of such matched scores. There were 21 *S*s who made guesses for both two-syllable and three-syllable words. The simplest way to evaluate the significance of the differences in these guesses is with the Sign Test. In only 6 of 21 matched scores was the mean guess for words of two syllables larger than the mean for words of three syllables. The difference is significant with a $p = .039$ (one-tailed). For actual words that were only one syllable apart in length, *S*s were able to make a significant distinction in the correct direction when the words themselves could not be called to mind.

The 224 SS words and the 95 SM words provide supporting evidence. Words of similar sound (SS) had the same number of syllables as the target in 48% of all cases. This value is close to the 57% that were correct for explicit guesses in the main experiment and still closer to the 47% correct already reported for the pretest. The SM words provide a clear contrast; only 20% matched the number of syllables in the target. We conclude that *S* in a positive TOT state has a significant ability to recall correctly the number of syllables in the word he is trying to retrieve.

In Table 1 it can be seen that the modes of guesses exactly correspond with the actual number of syllables in target words for the values one through three. For still longer target words (four and five syllables) the means of guesses continue to rise but the modes stay at the value three. Words of more than three syllables are rare in English and the generic entry for such words may be the same as for words of three syllables; something like "three or more" may be used for all long words.

Initial Letter

Over all positive TOTs, the initial letter of the word *S* was seeking was correctly guessed 57% of the time. The pretest result was 51% correct. The results from the main experiment were analyzed with each word counting just once by entering a word's score as "correct" whenever the most common guess or the only guess was in fact correct; 62% of words were, by this reckoning, correctly guessed. The SS words had initial letters matching the initial letters of the target words in 49% of all cases. We do not know the chance level of success for this performance but with 26 letters and many words that began with uncommon letters the level must be low. Probably the results for the SM words are better than chance and yet the outcome for these words was only 8% matches.

We did an analysis of the SS and SM words, with each S counting just once. There were 26 Ss who had at least one such word. For each S we calculated the proportion of SS words matching the target in initial letter and the same proportion for SM words. For 21 Ss the proportions were not tied and in all but 3 cases the larger value was that of the SS words. The difference is significant by Sign Test with $p = .001$ (one-tailed).

The evidence for significantly accurate generic recall of initial letters is even stronger than for syllables. The absolute levels of success are similar but the chance baseline must be much lower for letters than for syllables because the possibilities are more numerous.

Syllabic Stress

We did not ask S to guess the stress pattern of the target word but the SS words provide relevant data. The test was limited to the syllabic location of the primary or heaviest stress for which *The American College Dictionary* was our authority. The number of SS words that could be used was limited by three considerations. (a) Words of one syllable had to be excluded because there was no possibility of variation. (b) Stress locations could only be matched if the SS word had the same number of syllables as the target, and so only such matching words could be used. (c) Invented words and foreign words could not be used because they do not appear in the dictionary. Only 49 SS words remained.

As it happened all of the target words involved (whatever their length) placed the primary stress on either the first or the second syllable. It was possible, therefore, to make a 2 × 2 table for the 49 pairs of target and SS words which would reveal the correspondences and noncorrespondences. As can be seen in Table 2 the SS words tended to stress the same syllable as the

TABLE 2. Syllables receiving primary stress in target words and SS words

	Target Words	
SS Words	*1st syllable*	*2nd Syllable*
1st syllable	25	6
2nd syllable	6	12

target words. The χ^2 for this table is 10.96 and that value is significant with $p < .001$. However, the data do not meet the independence requirement, so we cannot be sure that the matching tendency is significant. There were not enough data to permit any other analyses, and so we are left suspecting that S in a TOT state has knowledge of the stress pattern of the target, but we are not sure of it.

Letters in Various Positions

We did not require explicit guesses for letters in positions other then the first, but the SS words provide relevant data. The test was limited to the following positions: first, second, third, third-last, second-last, and last. A target word must have at least six letters in order to provide data on the six positions; it might have any number of letters larger than six and still provide data for the six (relatively defined) positions. Accordingly we included the data for all target words having six or more letters.

Figure 1 displays the percentages of letters in each of six positions of SS words which matched the letters in the same positions of the corresponding targets. For comparison purposes these data are also provided for SM words. The SS curve is at all points above the SM curve; the two are closest together at the third-last position. The values for the last three positions of the SS curve quite closely match the values for the first three positions. The values for the last three positions of the SM curve, on the other hand, are well above the values for the first three positions. Consequently the *relative* superiority of the SS curve is greater in the first three positions.

The letter-position data were also analyzed in such a way as to count each target word just once, assigning each position in the target a single score representing the proportion of matches across all Ss for that position in that word. The order of the SS and SM points is preserved in this finer analy-

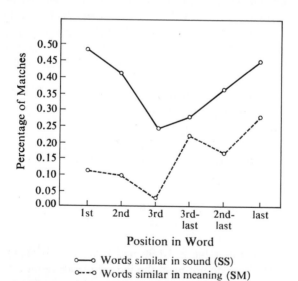

Position in Word

o——o Words similar in sound (SS)
o---o Words similar in meaning (SM)

FIGURE 1. Percentages of letter matches between target words and SS words for six serial positions

sis. We did Sign Tests comparing the SS and SM values for each of the six positions. As Figure 1 would suggest the SS values for the first three positions all exceeded the SM values with p's less than .01 (one-tailed). The SS values for the final two positions exceeded the SM values with p's less than .05 (one-tailed). The SS values for the third-last position were greater than the SM values but not significantly so.

The cause of the upswing in the final three positions of the SM curve may be some difference in the distribution of information in early and late positions of English words. Probably there is less variety in the later positions. In any case the fact that the SS curve lies above the SM curve for the last three positions indicates that S in a TOT state has knowledge of the target in addition to his knowledge of English word structure.

Chunking of Suffixes

The request to S that he guess the initial letter of the target occasionally elicited a response of more than one letter; e.g., *ex* in the case of *extort* and *con* in the case of *convene*. This result suggested that some letter (or phoneme) sequences are stored as single entries having been "chunked" by long experience. We made only one test for chunking and that involved three-letter suffixes.

It did not often happen that an S produced an SS word that matched the target with respect to all of its three last letters. The question asked of the data was whether such three-letter matches occurred more often when the letters constituted an English suffix than when they did not. In order to determine which of the target words terminated in such a suffix, we entered *The American College Dictionary* with final trigrams. If there was an entry describing a suffix appropriate to the grammatical and semantic properties of the target we considered the trigram to be a suffix. There were 20 words that terminated in a suffix, including *fawning, unctuous,* and *philatelist.*

Of 93 SS words produced in response to a target terminating in a suffix, 30 matched the target in their final three letters. Of 130 SS words supplied in response to a target that did not terminate in a suffix only 5 matched the target in their final three letters. The data were also analyzed in a way that counts each S just once and uses only Ss who produced SS words in response to both kinds of target. A Sign Test was made of the difference between matches of suffixes and matches of endings that were not suffixes; the former were more common with $p = .059$ (one-tailed). A comparable Sign Test for SM words was very far from significance. We conclude that suffix-chunking probably plays a role in generic recall.

Proximity to the Target and Quality of Information

There were three varieties of positive TOT states: (*1*) Cases in which S *recognized* the word read by E as the word he had been seeking; (*2*) Cases in which S *recalled* the intended word before it was read out; (*3*) Cases in which *S* *recalled* the word he had been seeking before *E* read the intended word and the recalled word was not the same as the word read. Since *S* in a TOT state of either type 2 or type 3 reached the target before the intended word was read and *S* in a TOT state of type 1 did not, the TOTs of the second and third types may be considered "nearer" the target than TOTs of the first type. We have no basis for ordering types 2 and 3 relative to one another. We predicted that *S*s in the two kinds of TOT state that ended in recall (types 2 and 3) would produce more accurate information about the target than *S*s in the TOT state that ended in recognition (type 1).

The prediction was tested on the explicit guesses of initial letters since these were the most complete and sensitive data. There were 138 guesses from *S*s in a type 1 state and 58 of these, or 42%, were correct. There were 36 guesses from *S*s in a type 2 state and, of these, 20, or 56%, were correct. There were 59 guesses from *S*s in a type 3 state and of these 39, or 66%, were correct. We also analyzed the results in such a way as to count each word only once. The percentages correct were: for type 1, 50%; type 2, 62%; type 3, 63%. Finally, we performed an analysis counting each *S* just once but averaging together type 2 and type 3 results in order to bring a maximum number of *S*s into the comparison. The combining action is justified since both type 2 and type 3 were states ending in recall. A Sign Test of the differences showed that guesses were more accurate in the states that ended in recall than in the states that ended in recognition; one-tailed $p < .01$. Supplementary analyses with SS and SM words confirmed these results. We conclude that when *S* is nearer his target his generic recall is more accurate than when he is farther from the target.

Special interest attaches to the results from type 2 TOTs. In the method of our experiment there is nothing to guarantee that when *S* said he recognized a word he had really done so. Perhaps when *E* read out a word, *S* could not help thinking that that was the word he had in mind. We ourselves do not believe anything of the sort happened. The single fact that most *S*s claimed fewer than five positive TOTs in a 2-hr. period argues against any such effect. Still it is reassuring to have the 36 type 2 cases in which *S* recalled the intended word *before* it was read. The fact that 56% of the guesses of initial letters made in type 2 states were correct is hard-core evidence of generic recall. It may be worth adding that 65% of the guesses of the number of syllables for type 2 cases were correct.

Judgments of the Proximity of SS Words

The several comparisons we have made of SS and SM words demonstrate that when recall is imminent *S* can distinguish among the words that come to mind those that resemble the target in form from those that do not resemble the target in form. There is a second kind of evidence which shows that *S* can tell when he is getting close (or "warm").

In 15 instances *S*s rated two or more SS words for comparative similarity to the target. Our analysis contrasts those rated "most similar" (*1*) with those rated next most similar (*2*). Since there were very few words rated (*3*) we attempted no analysis of them. Similarity points were given for all the features of a word that have now been demonstrated to play a part in generic recall—with the single exception of stress. Stress had to be disregarded because some of the words were invented and their stress patterns were unknown.

The problem was to compare pairs of SS words, rated 1 and 2, for overall similarity to the target. We determined whether each member matched the target in number of syllables. If one did and the other did not, then a single similarity point was assigned the word that matched. For each word, we counted, beginning with the initial letter, the number of consecutive letters in common with the target. The word having the longer sequence that matched the target earned one similarity point. An exactly comparable procedure was followed for sequences starting from the final letter. In sum, each word in a pair could receive from zero to three similarity points.

We made Sign Tests comparing the total scores for words rated most like the target (1) and words rated next most like the target (2). This test was only slightly inappropriate since only two target words occurred twice in the set of 15 and only one S repeated in the set. Ten of 12 differences were in the predicted direction and the one-tailed $p = .019$. It is of some interest that similarity points awarded on the basis of letters in the middle of the words did not even go in the right direction. Figure 1 has already indicated that they also do not figure in *S*s' judgments of the comparative similarity to the target of pairs of SS words. Our conclusion is that *S* at a given distance from the target can accurately judge which of two words that come to mind is more like the target and that he does so in terms of the features of words that appear in generic recall.

Conclusions

When complete recall of a word has not occurred but is felt to be imminent there is likely to be accurate generic recall. Generic recall of the *abstract form* variety is evidenced by *S*'s knowledge of the number of syllables in the target and of the location of the primary stress. Generic recall of the *partial* variety is evidenced by *S*'s knowledge of letters in the target word. This knowledge shows a bowed serial-position effect since it is better for the ends of a word than for the middle and somewhat better for beginning positions than for final positions. The accuracy of generic recall is greater when *S* is near the target (complete recall is imminent) than when *S* is far from the target. A person experiencing generic recall is able to judge the relative similarity to the target of words that occur to him and these judgments are based on the features of words that figure in partial and abstract form recall.

Discussion

The facts of generic recall are relevant to theories of speech perception, reading the understanding of sentences, and the organization of memory. We have not worked out all the implications. In this section we first attempt a model of the TOT process and then try to account for the existence of generic memory.

A Model of the Process

Let us suppose (with Katz and Fodor, 1963, and many others) that our long-term memory for words and definitions is organized into the functional equivalent of a dictionary. In real dictionaries, those that are books, entries are ordered alphabetically and bound in place. Such an arrangement is too simple and too inflexible to serve as a model for a mental dictionary. We will suppose that words are entered on keysort cards instead of pages and that the cards are punched for various features of the words entered. With real cards, paper ones, it is possible to retrieve from the total deck any subset punched for a common feature by putting a metal rod through the proper hole. We will suppose that there is in the mind some speedier equivalent of this retrieval technique.

The model will be described in terms of a single example. When the target word was *sextant*, *S*s heard the definition: "A navigational instrument used in measuring angular distances, especially the altitude of sun, moon, and stars at sea." This definition precipitated a TOT state in 9 *S*s of the total 56. The SM words included: *astrolabe, compass, dividers,* and *protractor.* The SS words included: *secant, sextet,* and *sexton.*

The problem begins with a definition rather than a word and so *S* must enter his dictionary backwards, or in a way that would be backwards and quite impossible for the dictionary that is a book. It is not impossible with keysort cards, providing we suppose that the cards are punched for some set of semantic features. Perhaps these are the semantic "markers" that Katz and Fodor (1963) postulate in their account of the comprehension of sentences. We will imagine that it is somehow possible to extract from the definition a set of markers and that these are, in the present case: "navigation, instrument, having to do with geometry." Metal rods thrust into the holes for each of these features might fish up such a collection of entries as: *astrolabe, compass, dividers,* and *protractor.* This first retrieval, which is in response to the definition, must be semantically based and it will not, therefore, account for the appearance of such SS words as *sextet* and *sexton.*

There are four major kinds of outcome of the first retrieval and these outcomes correspond with the four main things that happen to *S*s in the TOT experiment. We will assume that a definition of each word retrieved is entered on its card and that it is possible to check the input definition against those on the cards. The first possible outcome is that *sextant* is retrieved along with *compass* and *astrolabe* and the others and that the definitions are specific enough so that the one entered for *sextant* registers as matching the input and all the others as not-matching. This is the case of correct recall; S has found a word that matches the definition and it is the intended word. The second possibility is that *sextant* is not among the words retrieved and, in addition, the definitions entered for those retrieved are so imprecise that one of them (the definition for *compass,* for example) registers as matching the input. In this case S thinks he has found the target though he really has not. The third possibility is that *sextant* is not among the words retrieved, but the definitions entered for those retrieved are specific enough so that none of them will register a match with the input. In this case, S does not know the word and realizes the fact. The above three outcomes are the common ones and none of them represents a TOT state.

In the TOT case the first retrieval must include a card with the definition of *sextant* entered on it but with the word itself incompletely entered. The card might, for instance, have the following information about the word: two-syllables, initial s, final t. The entry would be a punchcard equivalent of S__ __T. Perhaps an incomplete entry of this sort is James's "singularly definite gap" and the basis for generic recall.

The S with a correct definition, matching the input, and an incomplete word entry will know that he knows the word, will feel that he almost has it, that it is on the tip of his tongue. If he is asked to guess the number of syllables and the initial letter he should, in the case we have imagined, be able to do so. He should also be able to produce SS words. The features that appear in the incomplete entry (two-syllables, initial s, and final t) can be used as the basis for a second retrieval. The subset of cards defined by the intersection of all three features would include cards for *secant* and *sextet*. If one feature were not used then *sexton* would be added to the set.

Which of the facts about the TOT state can now be accounted for? We know that Ss were able, when they had not recalled a target, to distinguish between words resembling the target in sound (SS words) and words resembling the target in meaning only (SM words). The basis for this distinction in the model would seem to be the distinction between the first and second retrievals. Membership in the first subset retrieved defines SM words and membership in the second subset defines SS words.

We know that when S had produced several SS words but had not recalled the target he could sometimes accurately rank-order the SS words for similarity to the target. The model offers an account of this ranking performance. If the incomplete entry for *sextant* includes three features of the word then SS words having only one or two of these features (e.g., *sexton*) should be judged less similar to the target than SS words having all three of them (e.g., *secant*).

When an SS word has all of the features of the incomplete entry (as do *secant* and *sextet* in our example) what prevents its being mistaken for the target? Why did not the S who produced *sextet* think that the word was "right?" Because of the definitions. The forms meet all the requirements of the incomplete entry but the definitions do not match.

The TOT state often ended in recognition; i.e., S failed to recall the word but when E read out *sextant* S recognized it as the word he had been seeking. The model accounts for this outcome as follows. Suppose that there is only the incomplete entry S___ ___T in memory, plus the definition. The E now says (in effect) that there exists a word *sextant* which has the definition in question. The word *sextant* then satisfies all the data points available to S; it has the right number of syllables, the right initial letter, the right final letter, and it is said to have the right definition. The result is recognition.

The proposed account has some testable implications. Suppose that E were to read out, when recall failed, not the correct word *sextant* but an invented word like *sekrant* or *saktint* which satisfies the incomplete entry as well as does *sextant* itself. If S had nothing but the incomplete entry and E's testimony to guide him then he should "recognize" the invented words just as he recognizes *sextant*.

The account we have given does not accord with intuition. Our intuitive notion of recognition is that the features which could not be called were actually in storage but less accessible than the features that were recalled. To stay with our example, intuition suggests that the features of *sextant* that could not be recalled, the letters between the first and the last, were entered on the card but were less "legible" than the recalled features. We might imagine them printed in small letters and faintly. When, however, the E reads out the word *sextant,* then S can make out the less legible parts of his entry and, since the total entry matches E's word, S recognizes it. This sort of recognition should be "tighter" than the one described previously. *Sekrant* and *saktint* would be rejected.

We did not try the effect of invented words and we do not know how they would have been received but among the outcomes of the actual experiment there is one that strongly favors the faint-entry theory. Subjects in a TOT state, after all, sometimes recalled the target word without any prompting. The incomplete entry theory does not admit of such a possibility. If we suppose that the entry is not S___ ___T but something more like S*èx tan*T (with the italicized lower-case letters representing the faint-entry section) we must still explain how it happens that the faintly entered, and at first inaccessible, middle letters are made accessible in the case of recall.

Perhaps it works something like this. The features that are first recalled operate as we have suggested, to retrieve a set of SS words. Whenever an SS word (such as *secant*) includes middle letters that are matched in the faintly entered section of the target then those faintly entered letters become accessible. The match brings out the missing parts the way heat brings out anything written in lemon juice. In other words, when *secant* is retrieved the target entry grows from S*èx tan*T to SE*x t*ANT. The retrieval of *sextet* brings out the remaining letters and S recalls the complete word—*sextant.*

It is now possible to explain the one as yet unexplained outcome of the TOT experiment. Subjects whose state ended in recall had, before they found the target, more correct information about it than did *S*s whose state ended in recognition. More correct information means fewer features to be brought out by duplication in SS words and so should mean a greater likelihood that all essential features will be brought out in a short period of time.

All of the above assumes that each word is entered in memory just once, on a single card. There is another possibility. Suppose that there are entries for *sextant* on several different cards. They might all be incomplete, but at different points, or, some might be incomplete and one or more of them complete. The several cards would be punched for different semantic markers and perhaps for different associations so that the entry recovered would vary with the rule of retrieval. With this conception we do not require the notion of faint entry. The difference between features commonly recalled, such as the first and last letters, and features that are recalled with difficulty or perhaps only recognized, can be rendered in another way. The more accessible features are entered on more cards or else the cards on which they appear are punched for more markers; in effect, they are wired into a more extended associative net.

The Reason for Generic Recall

In adult minds words are stored in both visual and auditory terms and between the two there are complicated rules of translation. Generic recall involves letters (or phonemes), affixes, syllables, and stress location. In this section we will discuss only letters (legible forms) and will attempt to explain a single effect—the serial position effect in the recall of letters. It is not clear how far the explanation can be extended.

In brief overview this is the argument. The design of the English language is such that one word is usually distinguished from all others in a more-than-minimal way, i.e., by more than a single letter in a single position. It is consequently *possible* to recognize words when one has not stored the complete letter sequence. The evidence is that we do not store the complete sequence if we do not have to. We begin by attending chiefly to initial and final letters and storing these. The order of attention and of storage favors the ends of words because the ends carry more information than the middles. An incomplete entry will serve for recognition, but if words are to be produced (or recalled) they must be stored in full. For most words, then, it is eventually necessary to attend to the middle letters. Since end letters have been attended to from the first they should always be more clearly entered or more elaborately connected than middle letters. When recall is required, of words that are not very familiar to *S*, as it was in our experiment, the end letters should often be accessible when the middle are not.

In building pronounceable sequences the English language, like all other languages, utilizes only a small fraction of its combinatorial possibilities (Hockett, 1958). If a language used all possible sequences of phonemes (or letters) its words could be shorter, but they would be much more vulnerable to misconstruction. A change of any single letter would result in reception of a different word. As matters are actually arranged, most changes result in no word at all; for example: *textant, sixtant, sektant.* Our words are highly redundant and fairly indestructible.

Underwood (1963) has made a distinction for the learning of nonsense syllables between the "nominal" stimulus which is the syllable presented and the "functional" stimulus which is the set of characteristics of the syllable actually used to cue the response. Underwood reviews evidence showing that college students learning paired-associates do not learn any more of a stimulus trigram than they have to. If, for instance, each of a set of stimulus trigrams has a different initial letter, then *S*s are not likely to learn letters other than the first, since they do not need them.

Feigenbaum (1963) has written a computer program (EPAM) which simulates the selective-attention aspect of verbal learning as well as many other aspects. ". . . EPAM has a *noticing order for letters of syllables,* which prescribes at any moment a letter-scanning sequence for the matching process. Because it is observed that subjects generally consider end letters before middle letters, the noticing order is initialized as follows: first letter, third letter, second letter" (p. 304). We believe that the differential recall of letters in various positions, revealed in Figure 1 of this paper, is to be explained by the operation in the perception of real words of a rule very much like Feigenbaum's.

Feigenbaum's EPAM is so written as to make it possible for the noticing rule to be changed by experience. If the middle position were consistently the position that differentiated syllables, the computer would learn to look there first. We suggest that the human tendency to look first at the beginning of a word, then at the end and finally the middle has "grown" in response to the distribution of information in words. Miller and Friedman (1957) asked English speakers to guess letters for various open positions in segments of English text that were 5, 7, or 11 characters long. The percentages of correct first guesses show a very clear serial position effect for segments of all three lengths. Success was lowest in the early positions, next lowest in the final positions, and at a maximum in the middle positions. Therefore, information was greatest at the start of a word, next greatest at the end, and least in the middle. Attention needs to be turned where information is, to the parts of the word that cannot be guessed. The Miller and Friedman segments did not necessarily break at word boundaries but their discovery that the middle positions of continuous text are more easily guessed than the ends applies to words.

Is there any evidence that speakers of English do attend first to the ends of English words? There is no evidence that the eye fixations of adult readers consistently favor particular parts of words (Woodworth and Schlosberg, 1954). However, it is not eye fixation that we have in mind. A considerable stretch of text can be taken in from a single fixation point. We are suggesting that there is selection within this stretch, selection accomplished centrally; perhaps by a mechanism like Broadbent's (1958) "biased filter."

Bruner and O'Dowd (1958) studied word perception with tachisto-scopic exposures too brief to permit more than one fixation. In each word presented there was a single reversal of two letters and the *S* knew this. His task was to identify the *actual* English word responding as quickly as possible. When the *actual* word was AVIATION, *S*s were presented with one of the following: VAIATION, AVITAION, AVIATINO. Identification of the actual word as AVIATION was best when *S* saw AVITAION, next best when he saw AVIATINO, and most difficult when he saw VAIATION. In general, a reversal of the two initial letters made identification most difficult, reversal of the last two letters made it somewhat less difficult, reversal in the middle made least difficulty. This is what should happen if words are first scanned initially, then finally, then medially. But the scanning cannot be a matter of eye movements; it must be more central.

Selective attention to the ends of words should lead to the entry of these parts into the mental dictionary, in advance of the middle parts. However, we ordinarily need to know more than the ends of words. Underwood has pointed out (1963), in connection with paired-associate learning, that while partial knowledge may be enough for a stimulus syllable which need only be recognized it will not suffice for a response item which must be produced. The case is similar for natural language. In order to speak one must know all of a word. However, the words of the present study were low-frequency words, words likely to be in the passive or recognition vocabularies of the college-student *S*s but not in their active vocabularies; stimulus items, in effect, rather than response items. If knowledge of the parts of new words begins at the ends and moves toward the middle we might expect a word like *numismatics,* which was on our list, to be still registered as NUM_____ICS. Reduced entries of this sort would in many contexts serve to retrieve the definition.

The argument is reinforced by a well-known effect in spelling. Jensen (1962) has analyzed thousands of spelling errors for words of 7, 9, or 11 letters made by children in the eighth and tenth grades and by junior college freshmen. A striking serial position effect appears in all his sets of data such that errors are most common in the middle of the word, next most common at the end, and least common at the start. These results are as they should be if the order of attention and entry of information is first, last, and then, middle. Jensen's results show us what happens when children are forced to produce words that are still on the recognition level. His results remind us of those blue-books in which students who are uncertain of the spelling of a word write the first and last letters with great clarity and fill in the middle with indecipherable squiggles. That is what should happen when a word that can be only partially recalled must be produced in its entirety. End letters and a stretch of squiggles may, however, be made quite adequate for recognition purposes. In the TOT experiment we have perhaps placed adult *S*s in a situation comparable to that created for children by Jensen's spelling tests.

There are two points to clarify and the argument is finished. The *S*s in our experiment were college students, and so in order to obtain words on the margin of knowledge we had to use words that are very infrequent in English as a whole. It is not our thought, however, that the TOT phenomenon occurs only with rare words. The absolute location of the margin of word knowledge is a function of S's age and education, and so with other Ss we would expect to obtain TOT states for words more frequent in English. Finally the need to produce (or recall) a word is not the only factor that is likely to encourage registration of its middle letters. The amount of detail needed to specify a word uniquely must increase with the total number of words known, the number from which any one is to be distinguished. Consequently the growth of vocabulary, as well as the need to recall, should have some power to force attention into the middle of a word.

References

BARNHART, C. L. (Ed.) *The American college dictionary.* New York: Harper, 1948.

BROADBENT, D. E. *Perception and communication.* New York: Macmillan, 1958.

BRUNER, J. S., & O'DOWD, D. A note on the informativeness of words. *Language and Speech,* 1958, *1,* 98–101.

FEIGENBAUM, E. A. The simulation of verbal learning behavior. In E. A. Feigenbaum & J. Feldman (Eds.), *Computers and thought.* New York: McGraw-Hill, 1963. Pp. 297–309.

HOCKETT, C. F. *A course in modern linguistics.* New York: Macmillan, 1958.

JAMES, W. *The principles of psychology.* Vol. I. New York: Holt, 1893.

JENSEN, A. R. Spelling errors and the serial-position effect. *Journal of Educational Psychology,* 1962, *53,* 105–109.

KATZ, J. J., & FODOR, J. A. The structure of a semantic theory. *Language,* 1963, *39,* 170–210.

MILLER, G. A., & FRIEDMAN, E. A. The reconstruction of mutilated English texts. *Information Control,* 1957, *1,* 38–55.

THORNDIKE, E. L., & LORGE, I. *The teacher's word book of 30,000 words.* New York: Columbia University, 1952.

UNDERWOOD, B. J. Stimulus selection in verbal learning. In C. N. Cofer & B. S. Musgrave (Eds.), *Verbal behavior and learning: Problems and processes.* New York: McGraw-Hill, 1963.

WENZL, A. Empirische und theoretische Beiträge zur Erinnerungsarbeit bei erschwerter Wortfindung. *Archiv für die Gesamte Psychologie,* 1932, *85,* 181–218.

———. Empirische und theoretische Beiträge zur Erinnerungsarbeit bei erschwerter Wortfindung. *Archiv für die Gesamte Psychologie,* 1936, *97,* 294–318.

WOODWORTH, R. S. *Psychology.* 3d ed. New York: Holt, 1934.

WOODWORTH, R. S., & SCHLOSBERG, H. *Experimental psychology.* Rev. ed. New York: Holt, 1954.

Craik and Lockhart suggest a reinterpretation of current memory data in terms of a "levels of processing" point of view. They suggest that various active processes can occur upon presentation of the stimulus coding. Type I processing, which might be illustrated by simple rehearsing does little to enhance or enrich the memory trace. Type II processing involves a deeper analysis of the stimulus and leads to a more durable trace. What is referred to as "primary memory" by Waugh and Norman is seen here as continued attention to an item. Many of the basic empirical phenomena of short-term memory are then reinterpreted in a way consistent with this levels-of-processing view.

Levels of Processing: A Framework for Memory Research

Fergus I. M. Craik and Robert S. Lockhart

This paper briefly reviews the evidence for multistore theories of memory and points out some difficulties with the approach. An alternative framework for human memory research is then outlined in terms of depth or levels of processing. Some current data and arguments are reexamined in the light of this alternative framework and implications for further research considered.

Over the past decade, models of human memory have been dominated by the concept of stores and the transfer of information among them. One major criterion for distinguishing between stores has been their different retention characteristics. The temporal properties of stored information have, thus, played a dual role: Besides constituting the basic phenomenon to be explained, they have also been used to generate the theoretical constructs in terms of which the explanation is formulated. The apparent circularity has been avoided by the specification of additional properties of the stores (such as their capacity and coding characteristics) thereby characterizing them independently of the phenomena to be explained. The constructs, thus formulated, have been used to account for data across a variety of paradigms and experimental conditions. The essential concept underlying such explanations is that of information being transferred from one store to another, and the store-to-store transfer models may be distinguished, at least in terms of emphasis, from explanations which associate different retention characteristics with qualitative changes in the memory code.

Source: Reprinted by permission of Academic Press from *Journal of Verbal Learning and Verbal Behavior*, 1972, *11*, 671–684.

Note: This research was supported by Grants A8261 and A0355 from the National Research Council of Canada to the first and second author, respectively. We thank our colleagues who read a preliminary version of the paper and made many helpful suggestions.

In the present paper we will do three things: (*a*) examine the reasons for proposing multistore models, (*b*) question their adequacy, and (*c*) propose an alternative framework in terms of levels of processing. We will argue that the memory trace can be understood as a byproduct of perceptual analysis and that trace persistence is a positive function of the depth to which the stimulus has been analyzed. Stimuli may also be retained over short intervals by continued processing at a constant depth. These views offer a new way to interpret existing data and provide a heuristic framework for further research.

Multistore Models

The Case in Favor

When man is viewed as a processor of information (Miller, 1956; Broadbent, 1958), it seems necessary to postulate holding mechanisms or memory stores at various points in the system. For example, on the basis of his dichotic listening studies, Broadbent (1958) proposed that information must be held transiently before entering the limited-capacity processing channel. Items could be held over the short term by recycling them, after perception, through the same transient storage system. From there, information could be transferred into and retained in a more permanent long-term store. Broadbent's ideas have been developed and extended by Waugh and Norman (1965), Peterson (1966), and Atkinson and Shiffrin (1968). According to the modal model (Murdock, 1967), it is now widely accepted that memory can be classified into three levels of storage: sensory stores, short term memory (STM) and long-term memory (LTM). Since there has been some ambiguity in the usage of terms in this area, we shall follow the convention of using STM and LTM to refer to experimental situations, and the terms "short-term store" (STS) and "long-term store" (LTS) to refer to the two relevant storage systems.

Stimuli can be entered into the sensory stores regardless of whether or not the subject is paying attention to that source; that is, sensory stores are "preattentive" (Neisser, 1967). The input is represented in a rather literal form and can be overwritten by further inputs in the same modality (Neisser, 1967; Crowder & Morton, 1969). Further features which distinguish the sensory registers from later stores are the modality-specific nature and moderately large capacity of sensory stores and the transience of their contents.

Attention to the material in a sensory register is equivalent to reading it out and transferring it to STS. Here, verbal items are coded in some phonemic fashion (Shulman, 1971) or in auditory–verbal–linguistic terms (Atkinson & Shiffrin, 1968). The STS is further distinguished from sensory memories by virtue of its limited capacity (Miller, 1956; Broadbent, 1958), by the finding that information is lost principally by a process of displacement (Waugh & Norman, 1965), and by the slower rate of forgetting from STS: 5–20 seconds as opposed to the ¼–2-second estimates for sensory storage.

While most research has concentrated on verbal STS, there is evidence that more literal "representational" information may also be held over the short term (Posner, 1967), although the relationship between such modality-specific stores and the verbal STS has not been made clear.

The distinctions between STS and LTS are well-documented. Whereas STS has a limited capacity, LTS has no known limit; verbal items are usually coded phonemically in STS but largely in terms of their semantic features in LTS (Baddeley, 1966); forgetting from STS is complete within 30 seconds or less while forgetting from LTS is either very slow or the material is not forgotten at all (Shiffrin & Atkinson, 1969). In the free-recall paradigm, it is generally believed that the last few items are retrieved from STS and prior items are retrieved from LTS; it is now known that several variables affect one of these retrieval components without affecting the other (Glanzer, 1972). Further persuasive evidence for the STS/LTS dichotomy comes from clinical studies (Milner, 1970; Warrington, 1971). The distinguishing features of the three storage levels are summarized in Table 1.

TABLE 1. Commonly accepted differences between the three stages of verbal memory (see text for sources)

Feature	Sensory Registers	Short-Term Store	Long-Term Store
Entry of information	Preattentive	Requires attention	Rehearsal
Maintenance of information	Not possible	Continued attention Rehearsal	Repetition Organization
Format of information	Literal copy of input	Phonemic Probably visual Possibly semantic	Largely semantic Some auditory and visual
Capacity	Large	Small	No known limit
Information loss	Decay	Displacement Possibly decay	Possibly no loss Loss of accessibility or discriminability by interference
Trace duration	¼–2 Seconds	Up to 30 seconds	Minutes to years
Retrieval	Readout	Probably automatic Items in consciousness Temporal/phonemic cues	Retrieval cues Possibly search process

The attractiveness of the "box" approach is not difficult to understand. Such multistore models are apparently specific and concrete; information flows in well-regulated paths between stores whose characteristics have intuitive appeal; their properties may be elicited by experiment and described either behaviorally or mathematically. All that remains, it seems, is to specify the properties of each component more precisely and to work out the transfer functions more accurately.

Despite all these points in their favor, when the evidence for multistore models is examined in greater detail the stores become less tangible. One warning sign is the progressively greater part played by "control processes" in more recent formulations (for example, Atkinson & Shiffrin, 1971). In the next section we consider the adequacy of multistore notions more critically.

The Case Against

The multistore approach has not been without its general critics (Melton, 1963; Murdock, 1972). Other workers have objected to certain aspects of the formulation. For example, Tulving and Patterson (1968) argued against the notion of information being transferred from one store to another. Similarly, Shallice and Warrington (1970) presented evidence against the idea that information must necessarily "pass through" STS to enter LTS.

In our view, the criteria listed in the previous section do not provide satisfactory grounds for distinguishing between separate stores. The adequacy of the evidence will be considered with reference to the concepts of capacity, coding, and finally, the retention function itself.

Capacity

Although limited capacity has been a major feature of the information flow approach, and especially a feature of STS in multistore models, the exact nature of the capacity limitation is somewhat obscure. In particular, it has been unclear whether the limitation is one of processing capacity, storage capacity, or is meant to apply to some interaction between the two. In terms of the computer analogy on which information flow models are based, the issue is whether the limitation refers to the storage capacity of a memory register or to the rate at which the processor can perform certain operations. The notion of a limited-capacity channel (Broadbent, 1958) appears to emphasize the second interpretation while later models of memory, such as that of Waugh and Norman (1965), appear to favor the storage interpretation. Both interpretations are present in Miller (1956) but the relationship between the two is not explicitly worked out.

Attempts to measure the capacity of STS have leant towards the storage interpretation, and considered number of items to be the appropriate scale of measurement. Such attempts have provided quite a range of values. For example, recent estimates of primary memory size (Baddeley, 1970; Murdock, 1972) have yielded values between two and four words. However, measures of memory span (which have been said to reflect the limited capacity of the STM box) are typically between five and nine items, depending on whether the items in question are words, letters or digits (Crannell & Parrish, 1957). Finally, if the words in a span test form a sentence, young subjects can accurately reproduce strings of up to 20 words (Craik & Masani, 1969). Thus, if capacity is a critical feature of STM operation, a box model has to account for this very wide range of capacity estimates.

The most widely accepted explanation of this variation is that capacity is limited in terms of chunks, and that few or many items can be recoded into a chunk depending on the meaningfulness of the material. Apart from the difficulty of defining a chunk independently from its memorial consequences, this view entails a rather flexible notion of STS as a storage compartment which can accept a variety of codes from simple physical features to complex semantic ones.

From the standpoint of the present paper, the concept of capacity is to be understood in terms of a limitation on processing; limitations of storage are held to be a direct consequence of this more fundamental limitation.

Coding

Working with verbal material, Conrad (1964) and Baddeley (1966) provided one plausible basis for distinguishing STS and LTS. They concluded that information in STS was coded acoustically and that coding was predominantly semantic in LTS. Further research has blurred this distinction, however. First, it has been shown that STS coding can be either acoustic or articulatory (Levy, 1971; Peterson & Johnson, 1971). Second, recent papers by Kroll and his colleagues (Kroll *et al.,* 1970) have demonstrated that even with verbal material, STS can sometimes be visual. Apparently STS can accept a variety of physical codes.

Can STS also hold semantic information? The persistence of contradictory evidence suggests either that the question has been inappropriately formulated or that the answer depends on the paradigm used. When traditional STM paradigms are considered, the answer seems to be "no" (Kintsch & Buschke, 1969; Craik & Levy, 1970), although Shulman (1970, 1972) has recently presented persuasive evidence in favor of a semantic STS. While type of coding may originally have seemed a good basis for the distinction between short-term and long-term memory, the distinction no longer appears satisfactory. A defender of the multistore notion might argue that STS coding is flexible, but this position removes an important characteristic by which one store is distinguished from another.

We will argue that the coding question is more appropriately formulated in terms of the processing demands imposed by the experimental paradigm and the material to be remembered. In some paradigms and with certain material, acoustic coding may be either adequate or all that is possible. In other circumstances processing to a semantic level may be both possible and advantageous.

Forgetting Characteristics

If memory stores are to be distinguished in terms of their forgetting characteristics, a minimal requirement would seem to be that the retention function should be invariant across different paradigms and experimental conditions. While this invariance has not been rigorously tested, there are cases where it clearly breaks down. We will give two examples. First, in the finite-state models of paired-associate learning, the state commonly identified as STS shows forgetting characteristics which are different from those established for STS in other paradigms (Kintsch, 1970, p. 206). In the former case, STS retention extends over as many as 20 intervening items while in the free-recall and probe paradigms (Waugh & Norman, 1965), STS information is lost much more rapidly. As a second example, the durability of the memory trace for visual stimuli appears to depend on the material and the paradigm. According to Neisser (1967), the icon lasts 1 second or less, Posner (1969) and his colleagues have found evidence for visual persistence of up to 1.5 seconds, while other recent studies by Murdock (1971), Phillips and Baddeley (1971) and by Kroll *et al.* (1970) have yielded estimates of 6, 10, and 25 seconds, respectively. Estimates are even longer in recognition memory for pictures (Shepard, 1967; Haber, 1970). Given that we recognize pictures, faces, tunes, and voices after long periods of time, it is clear that we have long-term memory for relatively literal nonverbal information. Thus, it is difficult to draw a line between "sensory memory" and "representational" or "pictorial" memory.

We will argue that retention depends upon such aspects of the paradigm as study time, amount of material presented and mode of test; also upon the extent to which the subject has developed systems to analyze and enrich particular types of stimuli; that is, the familiarity, compatibility, and meaningfulness of the material.

Although we believe that the multistore formulation is unsatisfactory in terms of its capacity, coding, and forgetting characteristics, obviously there are some basic findings which any model must accommodate. It seems certain that stimuli are encoded in different ways within the memory system: A word may be encoded at various times in terms of its visual, phonemic, or semantic features, its verbal associates, or an image. Differently encoded representations apparently persist for different lengths of time. The phenomenon of limited capacity at some points in the system seems real enough and, thus, should also be taken into consideration. Finally, the roles of perceptual, attentional, and rehearsal processes should also be noted.

One way of coping with the kinds of inconsistencies we have described is to postulate additional stores (see, Morton, 1970; Sperling, 1970). However, we think it is more useful to focus on the encoding operations themselves and to consider the proposal that rates of forgetting are a function of the type and depth of encoding. This view is developed in the next section.

Levels of Processing

Many theorists now agree that perception involves the rapid analysis of stimuli at a number of levels or stages (Selfridge & Neisser, 1960; Triesman, 1964; Sutherland, 1968). Preliminary stages are concerned with the analysis of such physical or sensory features as lines, angles, brightness, pitch, and loudness, while later stages are more concerned with matching the input against stored abstractions from past learning; that is, later stages are concerned with pattern recognition and the extraction of meaning. This conception of a series or hierarchy of processing stages is often referred to as "depth of processing" where greater "depth" implies a greater degree of semantic or cognitive analysis. After the stimulus has been recognized, it may undergo further processing by enrichment or elaboration. For example, after a word is recognized, it may trigger associations, images or stories on the basis of the subject's past experience with the word. Such "elaboration coding" (Tulving & Madigan, 1970) is not restricted to verbal material. We would argue that similar levels of processing exist in the perceptual analysis of sounds, sights, smells and so on. Analysis proceeds through a series of sensory stages to levels associated with matching or pattern recognition and finally to semantic–associative stages of stimulus enrichment.

One of the results of this perceptual analysis is the memory trace. Such features of the trace as its coding characteristics and its persistence thus arise essentially as byproducts of perceptual processing (Morton, 1970). Specifically, we suggest that trace persistence is a function of depth of analysis, with deeper levels of analysis associated with more elaborate, longer lasting, and stronger traces. Since the organism is normally concerned only with the extraction of meaning from the stimuli, it is advantageous to store the products of such deep analyses, but there is usually no need to store the products of preliminary analyses. It is perfectly possible to draw a box around early analyses and call it sensory memory and a box around intermediate analyses called short-term memory, but that procedure both oversimplifies matters and evades the more significant issues.

Although certain analytic operations must precede others, much recent evidence suggests that we perceive at meaningful, deeper levels before we perceive the results of logically prior analyses (Macnamara, 1972; Savin & Bever, 1970). Further elaborative coding does not exist in a hierarchy of necessary steps and this seems especially true of later processing stages. In this sense, "spread" of encoding might be a more accurate description, but the term "depth" will be retained as it conveys the flavor of our argument.

Highly familiar, meaningful stimuli are compatible, by definition, with existing cognitive structures. Such stimuli (for example, pictures and sentences) will be processed to a deep level more rapidly than less meaningful stimuli and will be well-retained. Thus, speed of analysis does not necessarily predict retention. Retention is a function of depth, and various factors, such as the amount of attention devoted to a stimulus, its compatibility with the analyzing structures, and the processing time available, will determine the depth to which it is processed.

Thus, we prefer to think of memory tied to levels of perceptual processing. Although these levels may be grouped into stages (sensory analyses, pattern recognition, and stimulus elaboration, for example) processing levels may be more usefully envisaged as a continuum of analysis. Thus, memory, too, is viewed as a continuum from the transient products of sensory analyses to the highly durable products of semantic–associative operations. However, superimposed on this basic memory system there is a second way in which stimuli can be retained—by recirculating information at one level of processing. In our view, such descriptions as "continued attention to certain aspects of the stimulus," "keeping the items in consciousness," "holding the items in the rehearsal buffer," and "retention of the items in primary memory" all refer to the same concept of maintaining information at one level of processing. To preserve some measure of continuity with existing terminology, we will use the term primary memory (PM) to refer to this operation, although it should be noted that our usage is more restricted than the usual one.

We endorse Moray's (1967) notion of a limited-capacity central processor which may be deployed in a number of different ways. If this processing capacity is used to maintain information at one level, the phenomena of short-term memory will appear. The processor itself is neutral with regard to coding characteristics: The observed PM code will depend on the processing modality within which the processor is operating. Further, while limited capacity is a function of the processor itself, the number of items held will depend upon the level at which the processor is operating. At deeper levels the subject can make greater use of learned rules and past knowledge; thus, material can be more efficiently handled and more can be retained. There is apparently great variability in the ease with which information at different levels can be maintained in PM. Some types of information (for example, phonemic features of words) are particularly easy to maintain while the maintenance of others (such as early visual analyses—the "icon") is apparently impossible.

The essential feature of PM retention is that aspects of the material are still being processed or attended to. Our notion of PM is, thus, synonymous with that of James (1890) in that PM items are still in consciousness. When attention is diverted from the item, information will be lost at the rate appropriate to its level of processing—slower rates for deeper levels. While PM retention is, thus, equivalent to continued processing, this type of processing merely prolongs an item's high accessibility without leading to formation of a more permanent memory trace. This Type I processing, that is, repetition of analyses which have already been carried out, may be contrasted with Type II processing which involves deeper analysis of the stimulus. Only this second type of rehearsal should lead to improved memory performance. To the extent that the subject utilizes Type II processing, memory will improve with total study time, but when he engages in Type I processing, the "total time hypothesis" (see Cooper & Pantle, 1967) will break down. Stoff and Eagle (1971) have reported findings in line with this suggestion.

To summarize, it is suggested that the memory trace is better described in terms of depth of processing or degree of stimulus elaboration. Deeper analysis leads to a more persistent trace. While information may be held in PM, such maintenance will not in itself improve subsequent retention; when attention is diverted, information is lost at a rate which depends essentially on the level of analysis.

Existing Data Reexamined

Incidental Learning

When memory traces are viewed as the product of a particular form of processing, much of the incidental learning literature acquires a new significance. There are several reviews of this literature (Postman, 1964; McLaughlin, 1965), and we will make no attempt to be comprehensive. An important characteristic of the incidental learning paradigm is that the subject processes the material in a way compatible with or determined by the orienting task. The comparison of retention across different orienting tasks, therefore, provides a relatively pure measure of the memorial consequences of different processing activities. According to the view of the present paper, and in agreement with Postman (1964), the instruction to learn facilitates performance only insofar as it leads the subject to process the material in a manner which is more effective than the processing induced by the orienting task in the incidental condition. Thus, it is possible, that with an appropriate orienting task and an inappropriate intentional strategy, learning under incidental conditions could be superior to that under intentional conditions.

From the point of view of this paper, then, the interesting thing to do is to systematically study retention following different orienting tasks within the incidental condition, rather than to compare incidental with intentional learning. Under incidental conditions, the experimenter has a control over the processing the subject applies to the material that he does not have when the subject is merely instructed to learn and uses an unknown coding strategy.

We will consider several examples which illustrate this point. Tresselt and Mayzner (1960) tested free recall after incidental learning under three different orienting tasks: crossing out vowels, copying the words, and judging the degree to which the word was an instance of the concept "economic". Under the last condition, the number of words recalled was four times higher than that of the first and twice that of the second condition. Similar results using the free-recall paradigm have been obtained by Hyde and Jenkins (1969), and Johnston and Jenkins (1971). The experiments by Jenkins and his colleagues showed that with lists of highly associated word pairs, free recall and organization resulting from an orienting task which required the use of the word as a semantic unit, was equivalent to that of an intentional control group with no incidental task, but both were substantially superior to an incidental group whose task involved treating the word structurally (checking for certain letters or estimating the number of letters in the word). These results are consistent with those of Mandler (1967) who showed that incidental learning during categorization of words yielded a similar recall level to that of a group who performed the same activity but who knew that their recall would be tested.

Experiments involving the incidental learning of sentences (Bobrow & Bower, 1969; Rosenberg & Schiller, 1971) have shown that recall after an orienting task that required processing the sentence to a semantic level was substantially superior to recall of words from equivalently exposed sentences which were processed nonsemantically.

Schulman (1971) had subjects scan a list of words for targets defined either structurally (such as words containing the letter A) or semantically (such as words denoting living things). After the scanning task, subjects were given an unexpected test of recognition memory. Performance in the semantically defined target conditions was significantly better than that in the structurally defined conditions although scanning time per word was approximately the same in most cases.

These results support the general conclusion that memory performance is a positive function of the level of processing required by the orienting task. However, beyond a certain stage, the form of processing which will prove optimal depends on the retrieval or trace utilization requirements of the subsequent memory test. There is clear evidence in the incidental learning literature that the relative value of different orienting tasks is not the same for all tests of memory.

This conclusion is supported by comparisons of the differential effects of orienting tasks on recognition and recall. Eagle and Leiter (1964) found that whereas free recall in an unhindered intentional condition was superior to that of an incidental group and to a second intentional group who had also to perform the orienting task, these latter two conditions showed superior recognition performance. Such a result poses no difficulty provided it is assumed that optimal processing does not take the same form for both memory tests. In the Eagle and Leiter (1964) experiment, the orienting task, while almost certainly involving some degree of semantic analysis, might have served to prevent the kind of elaborative processing necessary for later access to the stored information. On the other hand, such elaborative coding might hinder subsequent discrimination between target words and the associatively related distractors used in this experiment. Results consistent with this kind of analysis have also been reported by Dornbush and Winnick (1967) and Estes and DaPolito (1967).

While the orienting tasks used by Wicker and Bernstein (1969) in their study of incidental paired-associate learning all required analysis to a semantic level, they did not facilitate subsequent performance to the same degree. When the orienting task involved the production of mediating responses, performance was equal to that of unhindered intentional learning and superior to when the orienting task was rating words for pleasantness. In single-trial free recall, this latter orienting task produces performance equal to that of intentional learning (Hyde & Jenkins, 1969). Identical orienting tasks do not seem to have equivalent effects across different paradigms. The interaction between initial encoding and subsequent retrieval operations is worth emphasizing. Although the distinction between availability and accessibility (Tulving & Pearlstone, 1966) is a useful one, the effectiveness of a retrieval cue depends on its compatibility with the item's initial encoding or, more generally, the extent to which the retrieval situation reinstates the learning context.

Selective Attention and Sensory Storage

Moray (1959) showed that words presented to the nonattended channel in a dichotic listening test were not recognized in a later memory test. Similarly, Neisser (1964) has shown that nontarget items in a visual search task left no recognizable trace. Thus, if stimuli are only partially analyzed, or processed only to peripheral levels, their record in memory is extremely fleeting. This point was neatly demonstrated by Treisman (1964). When the same prose passage was played to both ears dichotically, but staggered in time with the unattended ear leading, the lag between messages had to be reduced to 1.5 seconds before the subject realized that the messages were identical. When the attended (shadowed) ear was leading, however, subjects noticed the similarity at a mean lag of 4.5 seconds. Thus, although the subjects were not trying to remember the material in either case, the further processing necessitated by shadowing was sufficient to treble the durability of the memory trace. Treisman also found that meaningfulness of the material (reversed speech versus normal speech, and random words versus prose) affected the lag necessary for recognition, but only when the attended channel was leading. If the message was rejected after early analyses, meaningfulness played no part; but when the message was attended, more meaningful material could be processed further and was, thus, retained longer. The three estimates of memory persistence in these experiments (1.5 seconds for all nonattended material, 3 seconds for attended reversed speech and attended strings of random words, and 5 seconds for attended prose) can be attributed to the functioning of different stores, but it is more reasonable, in our view, to postulate that persistence is a function of processing level.

While further studies will not be reviewed in such detail, it may be noted that the findings and conclusions of many other workers in the area of sensory memory can also be accommodated in the present framework. Neisser (1967, p. 33) concluded that "longer exposures lead to longer-lasting icons." Studies by Norman (1969), Glucksberg and Cowen (1970), and Peterson and Kroener (1964) may all be interpreted as showing that nonattended verbal material is lost within a few seconds.

Massaro (1970) suggested that memory for an item is directly related to the amount of perceptual processing of the item, a statement which is obviously in line with the present proposals, although his later arguments (Massaro, 1972), that echoic memory inevitably lasts only 250 milliseconds, are probably overgeneralizations. Shaffer and Shiffrin concluded from an experiment on picture recognition that "it might prove more fruitful to consider the more parsimonious view that there is just a single short-term visual memory. This short-term visual memory would decay quickly when the information content of the visual field was high and more slowly when the information content was greatly reduced" (Shaffer & Shiffrin, 1972, p. 295). Plainly this view is similar to our own, although we would argue that the continuum extends to long-term retention as well. We would also suggest that it is processing level, rather than information content, which determines the rate of decay.

The STS/LTS Distinction

The phenomenon of a limited-capacity holding mechanism in memory (Miller, 1956; Broadbent, 1958) is handled in the present framework by assuming that a flexible central processor can be deployed to one of several levels in one of several encoding dimensions, and that this central processor can only deal with a limited number of items at a given time. That is, items are kept in consciousness or in primary memory by continuing to rehearse them at a fixed level of processing. The nature of the items will depend upon the encoding dimension and the level within that dimension. At deeper levels the subject can make more use of learned cognitive structures so that the item will become more complex and semantic. The depth at which primary memory operates will depend both upon the usefulness to the subject of continuing to process at that level and also upon the amenability of the material to deeper processing. Thus, if the subject's task is merely to reproduce a few words seconds after hearing them, he need not hold them at a level deeper than phonemic analysis. If the words form a meaningful sentence, however, they are compatible with deeper learned structures and larger units may be dealt with. It seems that primary memory deals at any level with units or "chunks" rather than with information (see Kintsch, 1970, pp. 175–181). That is, we rehearse a sound, a letter, a word, an idea, or an image in the same way that we perceive objects and not constellations of attributes.

As pointed out earlier, a common distinction between memory stores is their different coding characteristics; STS is said to be predominantly acoustic (or articulatory) while LTS is largely semantic. According to the present argument, acoustic errors will predominate only insofar as analysis has not proceeded to a semantic level. There are at least three sources of the failure of processing to reach this level; the nature of the material, limited available processing capacity, and task demands. Much of the data on acoustic confusions in short-term memory is based on material such as letters and digits which have relatively little semantic content. The nature of this material itself tends to constrain processing to a structural level of analysis and it should be no surprise, therefore, that errors of a structural nature result. Such errors can also occur with meaningful material if processing capacity is diverted to an irrelevant task (Eagle & Ortoff, 1967).

A further set of results relevant to the STS/LTS distinction are those that show that in free recall, variables such as presentation rate and word frequency, affect long-term but not short-term retention (Glanzer, 1972). Our interpretation of these findings is that increasing presentation rate, or using unfamiliar words, inhibits or prevents processing to those levels necessary to support long-term retention, but does not affect coding operations of the kind that are adequate for short-term retention. It follows from this interpretation that diverting processing capacity as in the Eagle and Ortoff (1967) experiments should result in a greater decrement in long-term than in short-term retention and, indeed, there is good evidence that such is the case (Murdock, 1965; Silverstein & Glanzer, 1971).

Conversely, manipulations that influence processing at a structural level should have transitory, but no long-term, effects. Modality differences (Murdock, 1966) provide a clear example. Finally, long-term recall should be facilitated by manipulations which induce deeper or more elaborative processing. We suggest that the encoding variability hypothesis as it has been used to account for the spacing effect in free recall (Madigan, 1969; Melton, 1970) is to be understood in these terms.

The Serial Position Curve

Serial-position effects have been a major source of evidence for the STS/LTS distinction (see Broadbent, 1971, pp. 354–361; Kintsch, 1970, pp. 153–162). In free recall, the recency effect is held to reflect output from STS while previous items are retrieved from LTS (Glanzer & Cunitz, 1966). Several theoretical accounts of the primacy effect have been given, but perhaps the most plausible is that initial items receive more rehearsals and are, thus, better registered in LTS (Atkinson & Shiffrin, 1968; Bruce & Papay, 1970). We agree with these conclusions. Since the subject knows he must stop attending to initial items in order to perceive and rehearse subsequent items, he subjects these first items to Type II processing; that is, deeper semantic processing. Final list items can survive on phonemic encoding, however, which gives rise to excellent immediate recall (since they are still being processed in primary memory) but is wiped out by the necessity to process interpolated material. In fact, if terminal items have been less deeply processed than initial items, the levels of processing formulation would predict that in a subsequent recall attempt, final items should be recalled least well of all list items. The finding of negative recency (Craik, 1970) supports this prediction. An alternative explanation of negative recency could be that recency items were rehearsed fewer times than earlier items (Rundus, 1971). However, recent studies by Jacoby and Bartz (1972), Watkins (1972), and Craik (1972) have shown that it is the type rather than the amount of processing which determines the subsequent recall of the last few items in a list.

In serial recall, subjects must retain the first few items so that they can at least commence their recall correctly. The greatly enhanced primacy effect is thus probably attributable, in part at least, to primary-memory retention. The degree to which subjects also encode initial items at a deeper level is likely to depend on the material and the task. Using a relatively slow (2.5 seconds) presentation rate and words as visually presented stimuli, Palmer and Ornstein (1971) found that an interpolated task only partially eliminated the primacy effect. However, Baddeley (1968) presented digits auditorily at a 1-second rate and found that primacy was entirely eliminated by the necessity to perform a further task.

Repetition and Rehearsal Effects

One suggestion in the present formulation is that Type I processing does nothing to enhance memory for the stimulus; once attention is diverted, the trace is lost at the rate appropriate to its deepest analyzed level. Thus, the concept of processing has been split into Type I or same-level processing and Type II processing which involves further, deeper analysis of the stimulus and leads to a more durable trace. Similarly, the effects of repeated presentation depend on whether the repeated stimulus is merely processed to the same level or encoded differently on its further presentations. There is evidence, both in audition (Moray, 1959; Norman, 1969), and in vision (Turvey, 1967), that repetition of an item encoded only at a sensory level does not lead to an improvement in memory performance.

Tulving (1966) has also shown that repetition without intention to learn does not facilitate learning. Tulving's explanation of the absence of learning in terms of interitem organization cannot easily be distinguished from an explanation in terms of levels of processing. Similarly, Glanzer and Meinzer (1967) have shown that overt repetition of items in free recall is a less effective strategy than that normally used by subjects. Although both Waugh and Norman (1965), and Atkinson and Shiffrin (1968) have suggested that rehearsal has the dual function of maintaining information in primary memory and transferring it to secondary memory, the experiments by Tulving (1966) and by Glanzer and Meinzer (1967) show that this is not necessarily so. Thus, whether rehearsal strengthens the trace or merely postpones forgetting depends on what the subject is doing with his rehearsal. Only deeper processing will lead to an improvement in memory.

Concluding Comments

Our account of memory in terms of levels of processing has much in common with a number of other recent formulations. Cermak (1972), for example, has outlined a theoretical framework very similar to our own. Perceptually oriented attribute-encoding theories such as those of Bower (1967) and Norman and Rumelhart (1970) have a close affinity with the present approach as does that of Posner (1969) who advocates stages of processing with different characteristics associated with each stage.

If the memory trace is viewed as the byproduct of perceptual analysis, an important goal of future research will be to specify the memorial consequences of various types of perceptual operations. We have suggested the comparison of orienting tasks within the incidental learning paradigm as one method by which the experimenter can have more direct control over the encoding operations that subjects perform. Since deeper analysis will usually involve longer processing time, it will be extremely important to disentangle such variables as study time and amount of effort from depth as such. For example, time may be a correlate of memory to the extent that time is necessary for processing to some level, but it is possible that further time spent in merely recycling the information after this optimal level will not predict trace durability.

Our approach does not constitute a theory of memory. Rather, it provides a conceptual framework—a set of orienting attitudes—within which memory research might proceed. While multistore models have played a useful role, we suggest that they are often taken too literally and that more fruitful questions are generated by the present formulation. Our position is obviously speculative and far from complete. We have looked at memory purely from the input or encoding end; no attempt has been made to specify either how items are differentiated from one another, are grouped together and organized, or how they are retrieved from the system. While our position does not imply any specific view of these processes, it does provide an appropriate framework within which they can be understood.

References

ATKINSON, R. C., & SHIFFRIN, R. M. Human memory: A proposed system and its control processes. In K. W. Spence & J. T. Spence (Eds.), *The psychology of learning and motivation: Advances in research and theory,* Vol. II. New York: Academic Press, 1968. Pp. 89–195.

———. The control of short-term memory. *Scientific American,* 1971, *224,* 82–89.

BADDELEY, A. D. Short-term memory for word sequences as a function of acoustic, semantic, and formal similarity. *Quarterly Journal of Experimental Psychology,* 1966, *18,* 362–365.

———. How does acoustic similarity influence short-term memory? *Quarterly Journal of Experimental Psychology,* 1968, *20,* 249–264.

———. Estimating the short-term component in free recall. *British Journal of Psychology,* 1970, *61,* 13–15.

BOBROW, S. A., & BOWER, G. H. Comprehension and recall of sentences. *Journal of Experimental Psychology,* 1969, *80,* 455–461.

BOWER, G. H. A multicomponent theory of the memory trace. In K. W. Spence & J. T. Spence (Eds.), *The psychology of learning and motivation: Advances in research and theory,* Vol. 1. New York: Academic Press, 1967. Pp. 230–325.

BROADBENT, D. E. *Perception and communication.* New York: Pergamon Press, 1958.

————. *Decision and stress.* New York: Academic Press, 1971.

BRUCE, D., & PAPAY, J. P. Primacy effect in single-trial free recall. *Journal of Verbal Learning and Verbal Behavior,* 1970, *9,* 473–486.

CERMAK, L. S. *Human memory. Research and theory.* New York: Ronald, 1972.

CONRAD, R. Acoustic confusions in immediate memory. *British Journal of Psychology,* 1964, *55,* 75–84.

COOPER, E. H., & PANTLE, A. J. The total-time hypothesis in verbal learning. *Psychological Bulletin,* 1967, *68,* 221–234.

CRAIK, F. I. M. The fate of primary memory items in free recall. *Journal of Verbal Learning and Verbal Behavior,* 1970, *9,* 143–148.

————. A 'levels of analysis' view of memory. Paper presented at the 2nd Erindale Symposium on Communication and Affect, March, 1972.

CRAIK, F. I. M., & LEVY, B. A. Semantic and acoustic information in primary memory. *Journal of Experimental Psychology,* 1970, *86,* 77–82.

CRAIK, F. I. M., & MASANI, P. A. Age and intelligence differences in coding and retrieval of word lists. *British Journal of Psychology,* 1969, *60,* 315–319.

CRANNELL, C. W., & PARRISH, J. M. A comparison of immediate memory span for digits, letters, and words. *Journal of Psychology,* 1957, *44,* 319–327.

CROWDER, R. G., & MORTON, J. Precategorical acoustic storage. *Perception and Psychophysics,* 1969, *5,* 365–373.

DORNBUSH, R. L., & WINNICK, W. A. Short-term intentional and incidental learning. *Journal of Experimental Psychology,* 1967, *73,* 608–611.

EAGLE, M., & LEITER, E. Recall and recognition in intentional and incidental learning. *Journal of Experimental Psychology,* 1964, *68,* 58–63.

EAGLE, M., & ORTOFF, E. The effect of level of attention upon "phonetic" recognition errors. *Journal of Verbal Learning and Verbal Behavior,* 1967, *6,* 226–231.

ESTES, W. K., & DAPOLITO, F. Independent variation of information storage and retrieval processes in paired-associate learning. *Journal of Experimental Psychology,* 1967, *75,* 18–26.

GLANZER, M. Storage mechanisms in recall. In G. H. Bower (Ed.), *The psychology of learning and motivation: Advances in research and theory,* Vol. 5. New York: Academic Press, 1972. Pp. 129–193.

GLANZER, M., & CUNITZ, A. R. Two storage mechanisms in free recall. *Journal of Verbal Learning and Verbal Behavior,* 1966, *5,* 351–360.

GLANZER, M., & MEINZER, A. The effects of intralist activity on free recall. *Journal of Verbal Learning and Verbal Behavior,* 1967, *6,* 928–935.

GLUCKSBERG, S., & COWEN, G. N. Memory for nonattended auditory material. *Cognitive Psychology,* 1970, *1,* 149–156.

HABER, R. N. How we remember what we see. *Scientific American,* 1970, *222,* 104–112.

HYDE, T. S., & JENKINS, J. J. The differential effects of incidental tasks on the organization of recall of a list of highly associated words. *Journal of Experimental Psychology,* 1969, *82,* 472–481.

JACOBY, L. L., & BARTZ, W. H. Encoding processes and the negative recency effect. *Journal of Verbal Learning and Verbal Behavior,* 1972, *11,* 561–565.

JAMES, W. *Principles of psychology.* New York: Holt, 1890.

JOHNSTON, C. D., & JENKINS, J. J. Two more incidental tasks that differentially affect associative clustering in recall. *Journal of Experimental Psychology,* 1971, *89,* 92–95.

KINTSCH, W. *Learning, memory, and conceptual processes.* New York: Wiley, 1970.

KINTSCH, W., & BUSCHKE, H. Homophones and synonyms in short-term memory. *Journal of Experimental Psychology,* 1969, *80,* 403–407.

KROLL, N. E. A., PARKS, T., PARKINSON, S. R., BIEBER, S. L., & JOHNSON, A. L. Short-term memory while shadowing. Recall of visually and aurally presented letters. *Journal of Experimental Psychology,* 1970, *85,* 220–224.

LEVY, B. A. Role of articulation in auditory and visual short-term memory. *Journal of Verbal Learning and Verbal Behavior,* 1971, *10,* 123–132.

MACNAMARA, J. Cognitive basis of language learning in infants. *Psychological Review,* 1972, *79,* 1–13.

MADIGAN, S. A. Intraserial repetition and coding processes in free recall. *Journal of Verbal Learning and Verbal Behavior,* 1969, *8,* 828–835.

MANDLER, G. Organization and Memory. In K. W. Spence & J. T. Spence (Eds.), *The psychology of learning and motivation: Advances in research and theory,* Vol. 1. New York: Academic Press, 1967. Pp. 328–372.

MASSARO, D. W. Perceptual processes and forgetting in memory tasks. *Psychological Review,* 1970, *77,* 557–567.

————. Preperceptual images, processing time, and perceptual units in auditory perception. *Psychological Review,* 1972, *79,* 124–145.

McLAUGHLIN, B. "Intentional" and "incidental" learning in human subjects: The role of instructions to learn and motivation. *Psychological Bulletin,* 1965, *63,* 359–376.

MELTON, A. W. Implications of short-term memory for a general theory of memory. *Journal of Verbal Learning and Verbal Behavior,* 1963, *2,* 1–21.

————. The situation with respect to the spacing of repetitions and memory. *Journal of Verbal Learning and Verbal Behavior,* 1970, *9,* 596–606.

MILLER, G. A. The magical number seven, plus or minus two: Some limits on our capacity for processing information. *Psychological Review,* 1956, *63,* 81–97.

MILNER, B. Memory and the medial temporal regions of the brain. In K. H. Pribram & D. E. Broadbent (Eds.), *Biology of memory.* New York: Academic Press, 1970. Pp. 29–50.

MORAY, N. Attention in dichotic listening: affective cues and the influence of instructions. *Quarterly Journal of Experimental Psychology,* 1959, *9,* 56–60.

————. Where is capacity limited? A survey and a model. In A. Sanders (Ed.), *Attention and performance.* Amsterdam: North-Holland, 1967.

MORTON, J. A functional model of memory. In D. A. Norman (Ed.), *Models of human memory.* New York: Academic Press, 1970. Pp. 203–254.

MURDOCK, B. B. JR. Effects of a subsidiary task on short-term memory. *British Journal of Psychology,* 1965, *56,* 413–419.

————. Visual and auditory stores in short-term memory. *Quarterly Journal of Experimental Psychology,* 1966, *18,* 206–211.

————. Recent developments in short-term memory. *British Journal of Psychology,* 1967, *58,* 421–433.

————. Four channel effects in short-term memory. *Psychonomic Science,* 1971, *24,* 197–198.

————. Short-term memory. In G. H. Bower (Ed.), *Psychology of learning and motivation,* Vol. 5. New York: Academic Press, 1972. Pp. 67–127.

NEISSER, U. Visual search. *Scientific American,* 1964, *210,* 94–102.

————. *Cognitive psychology.* New York: Appleton-Century-Crofts, 1967.

NORMAN, D. A. Memory while shadowing. *Quarterly Journal of Experimental Psychology*, 1969, *21*, 85–93.

NORMAN, D. A., & RUMELHART, D. E. A system for perception and memory. In D. A. Norman (Ed.), *Models of human memory*. New York: Academic Press, 1970. Pp. 21–64.

PALMER, S. E., & ORNSTEIN, P. A. Role of rehearsal strategy in serial probed recall. *Journal of Experimental Psychology*, 1971, *88*, 60–66.

PETERSON, L. R. Short-term verbal memory and learning. *Psychological Review*, 1966, *73*, 193–207.

PETERSON, L. R., & JOHNSON, S. T. Some effects of minimizing articulation on short-term retention. *Journal of Verbal Learning and Verbal Behavior*, 1971, *10*, 346–354.

PETERSON, L. R., & KROENER, S. Dichotic stimulation and retention. *Journal of Experimental Psychology*, 1964, *68*, 125–130.

PHILLIPS, W. A., & BADDELEY, A. D. Reaction time and short-term visual memory. *Psychonomic Science*, 1971, *22*, 73–74.

POSNER, M. I. Short-term memory systems in human information processing. *Acta Psychologica*, 1967, *27*, 267–284.

————. Abstraction and the process of recognition. In G. H. Bower & J. T. Spence (Eds.), *The psychology of learning and motivation: Advances in research and theory*, Vol. III. New York: McGraw-Hill, 1969. Pp. 152–179.

POSTMAN, L. Short-term memory and incidental learning. In A. W. Melton (Ed.), *Categories of human learning*. New York: Academic Press, 1964. Pp. 145–201.

ROSENBERG, S., & SCHILLER, W. J. Semantic coding and incidental sentence recall. *Journal of Experimental Psychology*, 1971, *90*, 345–346.

RUNDUS, D. Analysis of rehearsal processes in free recall. *Journal of Experimental Psychology*, 1971, *89*, 63–77.

SAVIN, H. B., & BEVER, T. G. The nonperceptual reality of the phoneme. *Journal of Verbal Learning and Verbal Behavior*, 1970, *9*, 295–302.

SCHULMAN, A. I. Recognition memory for targets from a scanned word list. *British Journal of Psychology*, 1971, *62*, 335–346.

SELFRIDGE, O. G., & NEISSER, U. Pattern recognition by machine. *Scientific American*, 1960, *203*, 60–68.

SHAFFER, W. O., & SHIFFRIN, R. M. Rehearsal and storage of visual information. *Journal of Experimental Psychology*, 1972, *92*, 292–296.

SHALLICE, T., & WARRINGTON, E. K. Independent functioning of verbal memory stores: A neuropsychological study. *Quarterly Journal of Experimental Psychology*, 1970, *22*, 261–273.

SHEPARD, R. N. Recognition memory for words, sentences, and pictures. *Journal of Verbal Learning and Verbal Behavior*, 1967, *6*, 156–163.

SHIFFRIN, R. M., & ATKINSON, R. C. Storage and retrieval processes in long-term memory. *Psychological Review*, 1967, *76*, 179–193.

SHULMAN, H. G. Encoding and retention of semantic and phonemic information in short-term memory. *Journal of Verbal Learning and Verbal Behavior*, 1970, *9*, 499–508.

————. Similarity effects in short-term memory. *Psychological Bulletin*, 1971, *75*, 399–415.

————. Semantic confusion errors in short-term memory. *Journal of Verbal Learning and Verbal Behavior*, 1972, *11*, 221–227.

SILVERSTEIN, C., & GLANZER, M. Concurrent task in free recall: Differential effects of LTS and STS. *Psychonomic Science*, 1971, *22*, 367–368.

SPERLING, G. Short-term memory, long-term memory, and scanning in the processing of visual information. In A. Young & D. B. Lindsley (Eds.), *Early experience and visual information processing in perceptual and reading disorders*. Washington: National Academy of Sciences, 1970. Pp. 198–215.

STOFF, M., & EAGLE, M. N. The relationship among reported strategies, presentation rate, and verbal ability and their effects on free recall learning. *Journal of Experimental Psychology*, 1971, *87*, 423–428.

SUTHERLAND, N. S. Outlines of a theory of visual pattern recognition in animals and man. *Proceedings of the Royal Society. Series B*, 1968, *171*, 297–317.

TREISMAN, A. Monitoring and storage of irrelevant messages in selective attention. *Journal of Verbal Learning and Verbal Behavior*, 1964, *3*, 449–459.

TRESSELT, M. E., & MAYZNER, M. S. A study of incidental learning. *Journal of Psychology*, 1960, *50*, 339–347.

TULVING, E. Subjective organization and effects of repetition in multi-trial free-recall learning. *Journal of Verbal Learning and Verbal Behavior*, 1966, *5*, 193–197.

TULVING, E., & MADIGAN, S. A. Memory and verbal learning. *Annual Review of Psychology*, 1970, *21*, 437–484.

TULVING, E., & PATTERSON, R. D. Functional units and retrieval processes in free recall. *Journal of Experimental Psychology*, 1968, *77*, 239–248.

TULVING, E., & PEARLSTONE, Z. Availability versus accessibility of information in memory for words. *Journal of Verbal Learning and Verbal Behavior*, 1966, *5*, 381–391.

TURVEY, M. T. Repetition and the preperceptual information store. *Journal of Experimental Psychology*, 1967, *74*, 289–293.

WARRINGTON, E. K. Neurological disorders of memory. *British Medical Bulletin*, 1971, *27*, 243–247.

WATKINS, M. J. The characteristics and functions of primary memory. Unpublished Ph.D. thesis, University of London, 1972.

WAUGH, N. C., & NORMAN, D. A. Primary memory. *Psychological Review*, 1965, *72*, 89–104.

WICKER, F. W., & BERNSTEIN, A. L. Association value and orienting task in incidental and intentional paired-associate learning. *Journal of Experimental Psychology*, 1969, *81*, 308–311.

Section Seven
THE PSYCHOLOGY OF PERCEPTION

If we ask how we obtain information about the environment, the answer at first seems obvious. Through our sense organs, of course. So it seems reasonable to begin by looking at the *sensory bases of perception:* how our sense organs work, and how subjective impressions of a stimulus (its intensity, for example) correspond to its physical characteristics. Research soon shows that there is no simple one-to-one correspondence between the physical characteristics of a particular stimulus and the psychological attributes of the resulting sensation; we don't just passively record the absolute physical values of the world "out there." Instead, we tend to perceive the characteristics of the world in relation to each other; perceptual qualities and intensities are fundamentally relative. The next step is to leave a simplistic one-to-one correspondence model of perception and to examine instead an interactive form of analysis, concentrating on the *relativity of perception.* But even this orientation does not do justice to the full, rich complexity of perception since it, too, implicitly assumes that perception is a passive rather than an active process. During the last decade researchers and theorists in sensation and perception have recognized increasingly that perception is a matter of active construction rather than of passive registration; hence it is appropriate to emphasize the *creativity of perception.*

The following readings exhibit this sequence. We begin with a study that exemplifies a sensory orientation. It describes an ingenious technique for communicating with pigeons in such a way as to measure the course of their dark adaptation—a course, incidentally, that closely resembles the human dark-adaptation function.

The next two selections illustrate relational phenomena in perception: the first experiment demonstrates that rhesus monkeys can categorize visual stimuli relative to a standard, or adaptation level, in a manner that is analogous to the categorical features of human speech perception; and the second describes an interesting visual motion aftereffect that is relational in a number of respects (relative textures and relative directions of motion).

The remaining excerpts concern the active information-processing feature of perception, or the creativity of perception. First is a brief passage from a book that was pivotal in the recent development that reemphasized the active nature of the perceptual process, a passage that states the problem vividly and succinctly. The last two excerpts are typical of recent research on speech perception, a process that many studies have shown to be highly constructive and creative. The first shows how errors in the apparent location of a click depend upon the structure of the sentence in which the click is heard, and the second shows how the visual detection of misspellings depends upon complex cognitive processes, such as word meanings and the subject's expectations.

It is impossible to do justice to a field as broad and diverse as sensation and perception with just a handful of readings. Nevertheless, the selections here do provide the flavor of recent original work in the area and are broadly representative of it. It is technically a rather sophisticated field, with a long history, careful experimental design, well-developed methodology, and complex apparatus. It is also multidisciplinary, with close ties to mathematics, physiology, and physics. Most of all, it is a rapidly changing field, as new, increasingly precise methods are employed and as the physiological mechanisms involved in perceptual processes become better understood.

Michael Wertheimer

How do you measure sensory experiences in animals? The selection by Donald S. Blough, based on his doctoral dissertation at Harvard, describes a truly ingenious method that could be used to measure a wide variety of psychophysical functions in many different animals. It has, in fact, been used to determine animal audiograms and has been adapted for other purposes. In a paper published a year after this one, Blough used it to show how lysergic acid diethylamide-25 (LSD) raises the visual threshold of pigeons. The key to the method, based on an idea of Georg von Békésy, is that when the organism senses the stimulus, it makes one response, A; when it cannot sense the stimulus, it makes another response, B—and the organism's responses are linked to the intensity of the stimulus, such that making response A diminishes the stimulus while making response B increases its intensity. A continuous record is thus generated over time, with the stimulus intensity hovering around the subject's threshold.

Dark Adaptation in the Pigeon

Donald S. Blough

Information on sensory thresholds is relevant to research topics that range from discrimination learning to the chemistry of receptive processes. Unfortunately, experiments on many of these topics involve the use of subhuman species from which few precise psychophysical data have as yet been obtained. In improving this situation with respect to visual psychophysics, the choice of the pigeon as a subject is particularly advantageous. The pigeon's vision is good, perhaps comparable to that of man (3, 9, 15); physiological and anatomical studies have been made of its visual apparatus (4, 7, 8, 11); Ferster and Skinner have outlined (6, 14) attributes that make it an excellent subject for closely controlled behavioral investigation.

This paper reports experiments in which the absolute visual thresholds of pigeons were traced during dark adaptation. The method involves behavior control techniques based on the work of Skinner and his associates (6, 14) and a stimulus control technique similar to Békésy's (1) method of human audiometry. The method, together with the reasons for various training and testing procedures, has been described in some detail elsewhere (2, 10). It has two fundamental features: (*a*) the stimulus controls the bird's responses as a result of differential reinforcement; (*b*) the bird's responses control the stimulus through an automatic switching circuit. This reciprocal control pro-

Source: Reprinted from *Journal of Comparative and Physiological Psychology*, 1956, *49*, 425–430. Copyright © 1956 by the American Psychological Association.

Note: This research was supported, in part, by Contract N5ori–07663 (Proj. NR140–072) between Harvard University and the Office of Naval Research, directed by Dr. Floyd Ratliff. It represents part of a thesis submitted to the Department of Psychology, Harvard University, in partial fulfillment of the requirements for the Ph.D. degree. The writer is indebted to Dr. Ratliff for his constant interest and helpful advice.

cess is arranged as follows. The pigeon confronts two response keys and a small lighted stimulus patch. On a random schedule, pecking key A blacks out the stimulus patch; pecking key B raises a food magazine within reach if the patch is dark. Although only a small proportion of pecks on the two keys is reinforced in this way, the bird gradually learns to peck key A when the patch is visible and key B when the patch is dark. The bird's responses control the stimulus through a separate, automatic switching circuit; pecks on key A reduce the luminance of the stimulus patch, while pecks on key B increase the luminance of the patch. As a result, the stimulus is kept oscillating about the bird's absolute threshold. When the luminance rises above threshold, the bird pecks key A, driving the stimulus dimmer again. When the stimulus disappears below threshold, the bird pecks key B and the stimulus gets brighter. A record of the stimulus luminance traces the absolute threshold of the pigeon through time.

Method

Subjects

Three male domestic pigeons ("white Carneaux") were used. The birds were secured from a commercial pigeon farm. They had differing histories of visual discrimination training prior to these experiments.

Apparatus

DARK-ADAPTATION BOX.   The pigeon worked in a light-tight aluminium picnic ice box. A plywood partition divided the box into two chambers. The bird stood in one chamber and placed its head through a round hole in the partition; the head and neck of the bird were then in a small "response compartment" 6 cm. deep and 5 cm. wide (Figure 1). The bird faced a window,

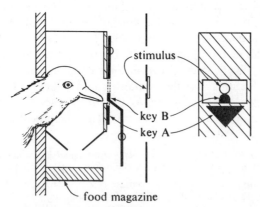

FIGURE 1.   Response chamber of the adaptation box. *Left,* side view, showing relative positions of pigeon, food magazine, response keys, and stimulus patch. *Right,* keys and patch seen from the pigeon's position.

through which it viewed a milk-plastic stimulus patch 1 cm. in diameter 4 cm. beyond the frame of the window. Two response keys were in the plane of the window. One (*key A*) was just below the window. The other (*key B*) protruded 1 cm. up within the frame. During reinforcement, a solenoid raised a magazine containing grain to a hole in the floor of the compartment. To eat, the bird lowered its head from the response position and pecked through the hole. The metal sides of the compartment reduced head-turning and lateral head movement. The top of the response compartment was open for ventilation. A fan ventilated the entire adaptation box, drawing air in and out through a light-tight series of baffles.

PRE-EXPOSURE BOX.   Before each experimental run, the pigeon was kept in a box 30 cm. wide, 25 cm. deep, and 25 cm. high. The walls and floor of this box were lined with white cardboard. The ceiling was a glass plate covered by a white paper diffusing screen. This screen could be illuminated from above by an incandescent bulb. When this bulb was off, the box was completely dark inside. A fan and baffle system ventilated the box. A removable side gave quick access to the box.

STIMULUS SOURCE AND CONTROL.   A strip filament lamp (G.E. 18 A, 1–6 V, T–10) run at 14 amp, d.c. supplied light for the stimulus. A beam of light from the lamp passed to the stimulus patch through a simple optical system. Neutral density filters and a neutral optical wedge were placed near a real image of the lamp filament. These controlled the brightness of the patch. A silent, reversible motor drove the wedge on a rack and pinion and also moved a pen that recorded the position of the wedge continuously on a moving strip of paper. A telechron motor powered a silent blanking shutter that blocked the light beam entirely when closed.

SWITCHING CIRCUIT.   Each peck on one of the keys momentarily opened a switch. The switches acted through a series of relays and timers to control the movement of the optical wedge, the shutter, and the solenoid that delivered reinforcement.

Training Procedure

The pigeon's basic task was to peck key A when the stimulus patch was visible and key B when the patch was dark. Training proceeded in several stages. When the bird became proficient at one stage, the next was introduced; about fifty training hours were needed before experimental data could be collected. The only light in the adaptation box came from the stimulus patch, except in the earliest stages of training, when a supplementary overhead light was used.

First, the hungry bird (70 per cent to 80 per cent of free-feeding cage weight) was trained to peck the two keys at random by the "response differentiation" technique described by Ferster (6). Next, the stimulus patch was illuminated and the control circuit adjusted so that a peck on key A closed the shutter, blacking out the patch. After a peck on key A blacked out the patch a peck on key B caused the food magazine to be raised within reach for about 5 sec. After most reinforcements, the shutter opened, and the lighted patch reappeared. Continued darkness followed one reinforcement in five; in this case, a peck on key B brought food a second time.

In the next stage of training, several pecks in a row, rather than a single peck, were required on key A to close the shutter and on key B to obtain food. The number of pecks required varied randomly between one and eight. An interval during which no amount of pecking could close the shutter was introduced after each reinforcement. The duration of this interval varied randomly between 0 and 15 sec., with a mean of 7.5 sec. The longest interval was later increased to 30 sec., and the mean to 15 sec.

When training was nearly complete, the luminance of the stimulus patch was put under the control of the bird's responses during the intervals between reinforcements. Each peck on key A reduced the luminance of the patch by .03 log unit, while each peck on key B increased the luminance of the patch by this amount. The pen coupled to the wedge drive recorded these luminance changes continuously. When the patch reappeared following a reinforcement, it always had the same luminance that it had had just before it was blacked out.

Testing Procedure

In the last stage of the training just described the procedure was such that absolute thresholds were obtained. When these thresholds became stable from day to day, the collection of experimental data began. At about the same time each day, the bird was carried from its home cage and placed in total darkness in the pre-exposure box. After the pigeon had been in the dark at least 1 hr., the pre-exposure light was turned on for a predetermined interval, following which the bird was transferred to the adaptation box. The transfer, done in dim light, took less than 5 sec. The bird usually began to respond within 1 min. after the box was sealed. If it did not peck within 3 min., the bird was returned to its home cage until the next day.

Supplementary grain given the birds after their experimental sessions maintained them at approximately constant body weight. Birds No. 191 and 192 were kept between 70 per cent and 80 per cent of ad lib. cage weight. Number 121, a very active bird, was kept between 75 per cent and 85 per cent of ad lib. weight.

EXPERIMENT I: VARIABLE PRE-EXPOSURE DURATION.   In this experiment, a 25-w. frosted bulb illuminated the pre-exposure box. When this bulb was on, the ceiling of the box had a nearly uniform luminance of 55 mL., the walls of 22 mL., and the floor of 23 mL. This pre-exposure condition was designated "22 mL." because observation indicated that birds almost never looked toward the floor or ceiling while in the pre-exposure box. The pigeon was pre-exposed at this luminance for 1, 3, 5, 10, or 20 min. before being placed in the adaptation box. These five pre-exposure conditions were presented in a random order from day to day. Following pre-exposure the birds' thresholds were traced for 60 min. Each bird was run three times under each of the pre-exposure conditions.

EXPERIMENT II: BRIGHT PRE-EXPOSURE.   After Experiment I was completed, a 300-w. frosted bulb was placed above the pre-exposure box. When this bulb was on, the walls of the box had a luminance of 411 mL., the ceiling of 31,210 mL., and the floor of 46 mL. This was designated the "411 mL." condition; the sole pre-exposure interval was 5 min. Following this pre-exposure the birds' thresholds were traced for 70 min. Bird 121 was run three times following the bright pre-exposure; 191 and 192 were each run once.

EXPERIMENT III: RED STIMULUS PATCH.   For this experiment, one thickness of Polaroid XDA-12 red dark-adaptation plastic was placed in the stimulus beam path. Polaroid XDA-12 has a sharp wavelength cutoff with 50 per cent transmission at about 610 mμ. The brightness of the resulting red stimulus patch was calibrated by heterochromatic matching with the Macbeth Illumino-meter. The thresholds of the birds were tested with this red stimulus patch following a 10-min. pre-exposure at 22 mL. as in Experiment I. The birds were run after completing Experiment II; bird 121 was run three times; 191 and 192 were each run once.

Results

A sample dark-adaptation curve appears in Figure 2. This curve was produced by bird 192 in a single hour, following a 10-min. pre-exposure at 22 mL. The luminance of the stimulus patch is represented on the ordinate; time in dark is on the abscissa. The curve can readily be separated into two continuous segments, joined at a rather sharp "break." These divisions will be

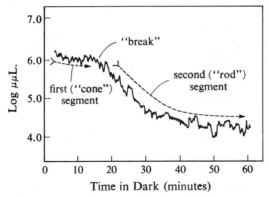

FIGURE 2.   Sample dark adaptation curve secured from a bird in a single hour. Pre-exposure was 10 min. at 22 mL. The luminance of the stimulus patch, in log micromicrolamberts, is on the ordinate.

referred to as the "first (or 'cone') segment" and the "second (or 'rod') segment." No threshold is shown for 3 min. at the beginning of the adaptation period. This due to the fact that each run began with the stimulus at a super-threshold luminance (7.2 log $\mu\mu$ L); the first responses were all to key A and served only to reduce the luminance to threshold. Consequently, a record of the luminance in this period was a rapidly falling curve that bore no relation to the threshold.

Figures 3a, 3b, and 3c each show all the curves collected from one of the three birds in Experiment I. The three curves collected from one bird after the same pre-exposure have been superimposed. The ordinate scale reads

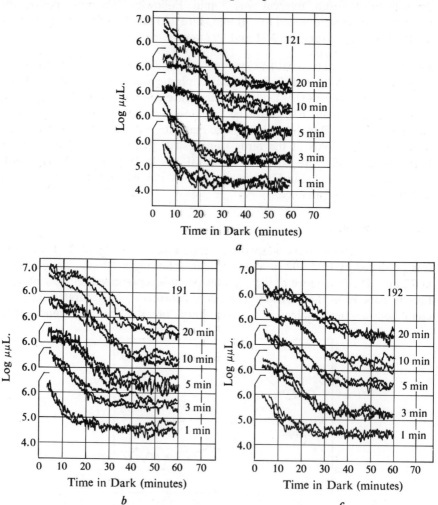

FIGURE 3. Dark adaptation curves from birds 121, 191, and 192. Pre-exposure luminance was 22 mL. The parameter is pre-exposure duration. Curves with a common pre-exposure duration are superimposed. Successive pre-exposure groups are shifted up the ordinate in 1 log unit steps.

correctly only for the 1-min. pre-exposure group of curves; each successive pre-exposure group has been shifted up one log unit from the preceding group. The curves differ in a regular fashion with increasing pre-exposure. The first segment is absent after the 1-min. pre-exposure; it appears following the 3- or the 5-min. pre-exposure, and its duration increases with increasing pre-exposure. The level of the first segment rises only slightly, if at all, with increasing pre-exposure. The total time for adaptation increases from between 20 and 30 min. following the 1-min. pre-exposure to between 40 and 60 min. after the 20-min. pre-exposure. These effects are especially clear in the very consistent data from bird 192. Maximum sensitivity under all conditions is approximately 4.4 log $\mu\mu$L.; the second segment contributes about 1.7 log unit to sensitivity. A large variability between days may be noted in some groups of curves, especially those following the 20-min. pre-exposure. The rather poor control of pre-exposure may account for some of this variability.

Figure 4 shows the results of Experiment II. One graph again

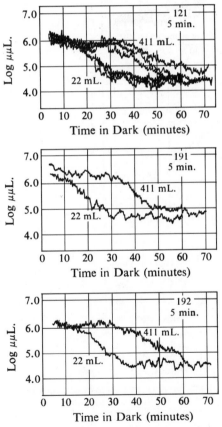

FIGURE 4.   Dark-adaptation curves of three birds following 5-min. pre-exposures to 411 mL. and to 22 mL. Three hours' data following each pre-exposure are superimposed for bird 121.

represents each bird. Curves for the less bright 5-min. pre-exposure of Experiment I are included on the same coordinates for purposes of comparison. The higher luminance pre-exposure of Experiment II yielded a very late "break" and a subsequent slow attainment of maximum sensitivity. In only one instance (bird 191) did the level of the first segment appear to rise with increased pre-exposure luminance.

In Figure 5, adaptation curves obtained with the red stimulus are plotted together with corresponding curves from Experiment I. The "red" and "white" curves approximately coincide during the first 20 min. of adaptation. Thereafter, they pull apart. Slight breaks in the "red" curves from bird 121 are partially obscured by the superimposition of the curves.

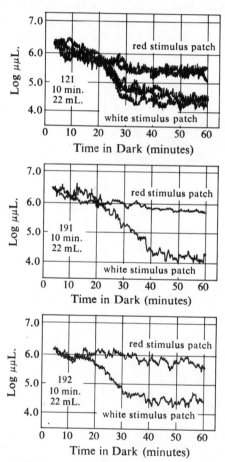

FIGURE 5. Dark-adaptation curves of three birds following 10-min. pre-exposure to 22 mL. Results with a red and with a white stimulus patch are superimposed for each bird. Three hours' data for each condition are superimposed for bird 121.

Discussion

A variety of findings (12) relates the first segment of the human adaptation curve to cone function and photopic sensitivity and relates the second segment to rods and scotopic sensitivity. In man, rods far outnumber cones except in or near the fovea, and unless the test stimulus is restricted to the fovea, the second segment characteristically dominates the dark-adaptation picture.

The pigeon possesses a duplex retina with elements grossly similar to their counterparts in the human retina, except for the fact that the pigeon cones contain red, orange, or yellowish oil droplets. Schultze's diagrams (11) of the pigeon retina show up to 20 of these cones for each rod in the temporal retina, while in the nasal region the proportion falls to about two cones to a rod; the fovea is rod-free. This cone dominance in the pigeon retina appears to be expressed in the bird's dark adaptation; a short, low-luminance pre-exposure suffices to produce an identifiable first segment; a long initial plateau results from a moderately bright or long pre-exposure; the threshold falls slowly from this plateau to its final level, and this fall accomplishes a relatively small gain in sensitivity.

The comparison of adaptation with red and white stimuli shown in Figure 5 suggests the presence of the Purkinje shift in the pigeon's relative sensitivity to different wavelengths as it becomes dark-adapted. The presence of such a shift has been clearly indicated by studies of electrical responses in the pigeon retina (7, 8). It is of interest that the pigeon's photopic thresholds for the red and white stimuli lie at about the same luminance on the ordinate of Figure 5. Since this luminance scale was calibrated by a human match of the red and white stimuli, the coincidence of these thresholds suggests that the relative photopic sensitivities to these red and white stimuli are comparable in the pigeon and man.

Despite the appearance of familiar features in the pigeon data, it would not do to draw the conclusion that differences between pigeon and human dark adaptation are solely a function of the different distributions of elements on the two retinas. Even at the retinal level other important factors may operate. It has been reported (5) that when the retina of the pigeon is exposed to strong light, considerable pigment migration occurs, and the receptor cells change shape and position. These changes seem to proceed in such a way as to reduce the amount of light reaching the receptors in bright light and to increase it in the dark. The pigmentation of the pigeon's retinal cones may also affect the absolute threshold in ways as yet unclear.

Summary

A new method was used to study dark adaptation in the pigeon. The bird was trained to peck one key when a stimulus patch was lighted and a second key when the patch was dark. These responses controlled the luminance of the stimulus patch in such a way that it fluctuated about the bird's absolute threshold. A record of the stimulus luminance through time traced the course of dark adaptation following a controlled pre-exposure to white light.

The principal independent variable was the duration of a 22-mL. pre-exposure to white light. The effects of a 411-mL. pre-exposure and of a red stimulus patch were also studied briefly.

The following results were obtained:

1. The new method appeared to be a reliable and efficient means for studying dark adaptation in the pigeon.

2. The pigeons produced two-segment adaptation curves grossly similar to human adaptation data. However, as compared with human curves, the pigeon curves had very prominent first ("cone") segments, and the second ("rod") segments appeared to contribute less to sensitivity (about 1.7 log unit).

3. As the 22-mL. pre-exposure increased from a minimum duration of 1 min., the pigeons' adaptation became progressively less rapid, with a "cone-rod break" appearing first with 3 or 5 min. of pre-exposure, and coming later with the longer pre-exposures.

4. A 5-min., 411-mL. pre-exposure yielded a "cone" segment lasting more than 30 min., followed by a "rod" segment with sensitivity increasing for at least an additional 30 min.

5. With a red stimulus patch (50 per cent cutoff at about 610 mμ), the first portion of the adaptation curve appeared as it had with the white stimulus, but the threshold fell little or not at all below this initial plateau.

References

1. Békésy, G. V. A new audiometer. *Acta Oto-laryngol.*, 1947, *35*, 411–422.

2. Blough, D. S. Method for tracing dark adaptation in the pigeon. *Science,* 1955, *121*, 703–704.

3. Chard, R. D. Visual acuity in the pigeon. *J. Exp. Psychol.*, 1939, *24*, 588–608.

4. Chard, R. D., & Gundlach, R. H. The structure of the eye of the homing pigeon. *J. Comp. Psychol.*, 1938, *25*, 249–272.

5. Detweiler, S. R. *Vertebrate photoreceptors.* New York: Macmillan, 1943.

6. Ferster, C. B. The use of the free operant in the analysis of behavior. *Psychol. Bull.*, 1953, *50*, 263–274.

7. Graham, C. H., Kemp, E. H., & Riggs, L. A. An analysis of the electrical retinal responses of a color-discriminating eye to light of different wavelengths.. *J. Gen. Psychol.*, 1935, *13*, 275–296.

8. Granit, R. The photopic spectrum of the pigeon. *Acta Physiol. Scand.*, 1942, *4*, 118–124.

9. Hamilton, W. F., & Coleman, T. B. Trichromatic vision in the pigeon as illustrated by the spectral hue discrimination curve. *J. Comp. Psychol.*, 1933, *15*, 183–191.

10. Ratliff, F., & Blough, D. S. Behavioral studies of visual processes in the pigeon. USN, ONR, Tech. Rep., 1954 (Contract N5 ori-07663, Proj. NR140-072).

11. Schultze, M. Zur Anatomie und Physiologie der Retina. *Arch. F. Mikr. Anat.*, 1866, *2*, 175.

12. Sheard, C. Dark adaptation: some physical, physiological, clinical, and aeromedical considerations. *J. Opt. Soc. Amer.*, 1944, *34*, 464–508.

13. Skinner, B. F. *The behavior of organisms.* New York: Appleton-Century-Crofts, 1938.

14. ————. Some contributions of an experimental analysis of behavior to psychology as a whole. *Amer. Psychologist*, 1953, *8*, 69–78.

15. Walls, G. L. *The vertebrate eye and its adaptive radiation.* Bloomfield Hills, Mich.: Cranbrook Institute of Science, 1942.

Martha Wilson, daughter of Harry Helson, the originator of adaptation-level (AL) theory, is a distinguished comparative psychologist in her own right. In this article she shows that monkeys exhibit assimilative and contrast effects in visual perception much as humans do. Using lines of different lengths, angles from the vertical, and density of surface structure, she demonstrates that the response to a given line depends upon its relation to the neutral point, or AL, of the series in which it occurs. This experiment is particularly interesting, since the stimuli she uses vary along dimensions that have recently been the focus of attention of neuro-physiologically oriented sensory psychologists who, following Hubel and Wiesel, have begun to determine the physiological mechanisms behind the discrimination of such features as the slant of a line. It is also particularly noteworthy because, as the author points out, it may be the first clear demonstration in nonhuman primates of a kind of categorical behavior that has been assumed to be basic to the encoding and decoding of speech stimuli.

Assimilation and Contrast Effects in Visual Discrimination by Rhesus Monkeys

Martha Wilson

Sets of visual stimuli which differed on one of three dimensions, length, orientation, or density, were judged by 12 rhesus monkeys in a paired-comparison procedure. It was found that the discriminability of any pair of stimuli was a function of two factors: the physical distance between the stimuli and the relationship of the stimuli to the adaptation level of the series. The results point to categorical perception in a non-speech mode, independent of identification training.

A great deal of evidence suggests that a special perceptual decoder is required for the analysis of speech as opposed to nonspeech stimuli. The existence of categorical perception has been taken as one indicator that a unique mechanism is involved in the encoding and decoding of speech stimuli (cf. Liberman, Cooper, Shankweiler, & Studdert-Kennedy, 1967, for a comprehensive review). Several recent experiments have examined the question of whether categorical perception of nonspeech stimuli can be demonstrated, and this problem has been taken as critical for disconfirming the theory referred to above. Although the experimental conditions were almost identical, two

Source: Reprinted by permission from *Journal of Experimental Psychology*, 1972, *93*, 279–282. Copyright © 1972 by the American Psychological Association.

Note: This research was supported by Grant MH-18217 from the National Institute of Mental Health, United States Public Health Service. The author is grateful to Peter Van Gelder for his helpful comments.

studies have provided contradictory results. It appeared in the Cross, Lane, and Sheppard study (1965, Exp. II) that discrimination of stimuli in two different categories was better than that within either category. A later study, which attempted to reproduce this result, failed to find superior intercategory as opposed to intracategory discrimination (Parks, Wall, & Bastian, 1969). Both studies used verbal labels to define the two categories.

The results presented here arose from entirely different considerations. Sets of visual stimuli on three dimensions were judged by rhesus monkeys so that perceptually equivalent, unidimensional stimulus sets could be constructed. However, the results also provided evidence for categorical perception in a nonhuman primate in a nonspeech mode.

Method

SUBJECTS.   Twelve sophisticated rhesus monkeys, previously trained on visual object and pattern discrimination, were used as *S*s. Of the original sample of 14, 2 failed to learn the initial phases and were discarded.

APPARATUS.   Testing was done in a Wisconsin General Test Apparatus (WGTA) with a stimulus board having foodwells spaced 32 cm. apart. Stimulus sets for each dimension consisted of 10 white cardboard squares, 6.5 cm. on a side, with an appropriate figure centered on each card. These were covered with transparent plastic. Two identical sets were constructed and were interchanged frequently during testing. All stimulus figures were bars, 4 mm. wide and were outlined in black Chartpak tape, 1/32 in. wide. Stimuli were constructed from Letratone printed papers. The two dimensions not varied in a given set were made constant at the middle values of these dimensions. Stimulus values are given in Table 1, and representative stimuli are shown in Figure 1.

TABLE 1.   Physical values of stimuli in three dimensions

Dimension	Stimulus Value									
	1	*2*	*3*	*4*	*5*	*6*	*7*	*8*	*9*	*10*
Length (cm.)	1.0	1.5	2.0	2.5	3.0	3.5	4.0	4.5	5.0	5.5
Orientation (degrees)	0	10	20	30	40	50	60	70	80	90
Density (lines/cm)	3.0	4.0	4.8	6.2	9.5	12.5	15.8	19	22	23

PROCEDURE.   Monkeys were given 30 trials/day with a raisin reward for choosing the correct stimulus. First, *S*s were trained to choose between Stimulus 1 (+) and Stimulus 10 (−) on a given dimension to a criterion of 28 correct in 30 trials.[1] Then all 10 stimuli were presented in a paired comparison

---

[1] The reward contingencies were inadvertently reversed on the density dimension, so that Stimulus 1 was avoided rather than approached.

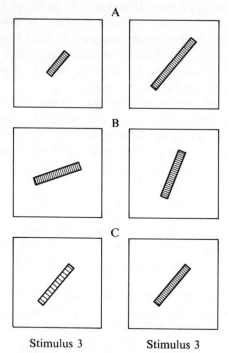

Stimulus 3   Stimulus 3

FIGURE 1.   Representative stimuli on (A) length, (B) orientation, and
(C) density dimensions. (The two dimensions not varied in a given stimulus
set were kept constant at the middle value of those dimensions.)

design. The stimulus in a pair that was closer to the positive stimulus in training was rewarded. Each pair was presented two times, making a total of 90
judgments by each monkey on each dimension. Every stimulus appeared
equally often, once in each position for a given pairing. A quasirandom order
of presentation insured that no particular stimulus value was presented on 2
successive trials, and neither position was rewarded on more than 3 successive
trials. All monkeys judged the three dimensions in the same order: length,
orientation, density.

Results

The proportion of choices of the rewarded stimulus in each pair
was calculated for all monkeys and the scale value of each stimulus in the set,
based on Thurstone's Case V, was derived as shown in Guilford (1954). The
scale values obtained are shown in Figure 2. The algebraic signs of the scale
values are retained since the scale value of 0 represents a true psychological
zero (cf. Guilford, 1954, p. 171). The stimulus which is given a scale value of
0 thus represents the adaptation level (AL) or neutral point of the series
(Helson, 1964).

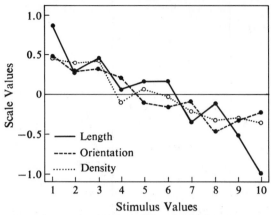

FIGURE 2.   Scale values of 10 stimuli in each dimension derived from paired comparisons

It was noted during testing that responses to pairs in which the stimuli were closely spaced seemed to be correct more often when the stimuli were somewhere in the middle of the range than when they were at the extremes. Since a first approximation to the AL for a stimulus series without an anchor is also somewhere in the middle of the stimulus range, it seemed worthwhile to explore the possibility that this phenomenon depended upon the relationship of the stimuli to the AL. This led to an analysis of performance in terms of two factors: the number of steps between the stimuli in a pair, and the relationship of the stimuli to each other in terms of the AL for the series.

The neutral point for each dimension is, as noted above, that stimulus value which yields a scale value of 0 on the stimulus versus scale value curves. Stimulus pairs were classified into those in which both stimuli were on the same side of the AL (same algebraic sign) and those in which the stimuli were on different sides of the AL (opposite algebraic signs). The frequency of correct choices was then computed for each number of steps of separation between the stimuli. For example, two-step separations of stimuli lying on the same side of the AL for length (Stimulus 1 vs. 3; 2 vs. 4; 3 vs. 5; 7 vs. 9; etc.) were compared with two-step separations of stimuli lying on either side of the AL (5 vs. 7; 6 vs. 8). This was done for all step separations from one to five: these constituted all of the possible stimulus pairs in which a given step difference could lie either on one side or both sides of the AL.

The results of the analyses are shown in Figure 3. In all three dimensions, with the exception of one unexplained value for length, and one for density, there is a striking improvement in discriminability of stimulus differences when the stimuli lie on opposite sides of the AL. For example, a stimulus difference of 20° in orientation on one side of AL was not discriminable ($p = .53$), while the same difference was clearly discriminated ($p = .65$) when the stimuli lay on opposite sides. There is a tendency for the differences in discriminability to become smaller as the steps get larger. However, if only

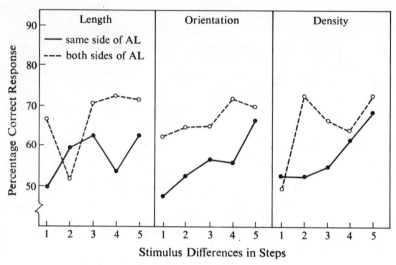

FIGURE 3.   Percentage of correct choices as a function of the physical differences between the stimuli, and the relationship of the stimuli to the adaptation level

the smaller stimulus steps are considered, the results appear to approach categorical perception. The overall difference between the two kinds of stimulus pairs is significant for length ($\chi^2 = 13.26$, $p < .001$), orientation ($\chi^2 = 20.83$, $p < .001$), and density ($\chi^2 = 10.40$, $p < .01$). The better discrimination noted in the middle of the range is thus seen to depend upon the way in which the AL structures the dimensional perceptually. Furthermore, equal sense distances derived from average discriminability may mask the differential sensitivity to stimulus differences that exists in different parts of the stimulus range.

Discussion

These results show that the perceptual characteristics of stimuli depend upon their relationship to the prevailing AL for stimuli in that universe. It has previously been shown that the *identifiability* of a visual stimulus depends upon its psychophysical distance from AL (Wilson, 1971): these data show that the *discriminability* of stimuli also depends upon the way in which the AL structures the stimulus set.

The relevance of the data for the question of categorical perception in a nonspeech mode is obvious. The neutral point divides the stimulus set into two categories, longer/shorter, denser/less dense, etc., and discrimination within categories is more difficult than between categories. These effects have been studied as contrast and assimilation effects, and their dependence upon a single underlying mechanism has been clearly spelled out (Helson, 1964).

While the AL can be changed by variations in stimulus input, the absence of an explicit anchor in the Cross et al. (1965) experiment makes it likely that their stimulus continuum was divided in the middle of the stimulus range. This could explain the differences in discriminability obtained without the necessity of invoking the identification training. On the other hand, since there were only four stimuli in the set, the two extreme stimuli should be highly identifiable, while the two middle stimuli should be highly discriminable. This would lead to the result obtained by Parks et al. (1969). Only with a larger number of stimuli, as in the present experiment, should differences in intra- and intercategory judgment be obvious.

These data provide evidence for tendencies toward categorical responding in a nonhuman primate which are totally independent of identification training. The effects can be explained in terms of AL theory, which postulates a labile, stimulus-sensitive, interval level to which stimuli are referred. This kind of mechanism appears superficially to be of a different order than that responsible for the invariances characteristic of speech decoding. However, one could speculate that speech perception is categorical because the discontinuous articulatory mechanisms underlying speech production provide extreme and stable anchors to which speech stimuli are assimilated. On this view, speech production and perception are intimately associated, as the motor theory suggests, but via a perceptual mechanism that is shared with nonspeech perception.

References

CROSS, D. V., LANE, H. L., & SHEPPARD, W. C. Identification and discrimination functions for a visual continuum and their relation to the motor theory of speech perception. *Journal of Experimental Psychology*, 1965, *70*, 63–74.

GUILFORD, J. P. *Psychometric methods.* (2d ed.) New York: McGraw-Hill, 1954.

HELSON, H. *Adaptation level theory.* New York: Harper & Row, 1964.

LIBERMAN, A. M., COOPER, F. S., SHANKWEILER, D. P., & STUDDERT-KENNEDY, M. Perception of the speech code. *Psychological Review*, 1967, *74*, 431–461.

PARKS, T., WALL, C., & BASTIAN, J. Intercategory and intracategory discrimination for one visual continuum: Contributions of identification training and of individual differences. *Journal of Experimental Psychology*, 1969, *81*, 241–245.

WILSON, M. Shifts in categorization and identifiability of visual stimuli by rhesus monkeys. *Perception & Psychophysics*, 1971, *10*, 271–272.

The article by James T. Walker, prepared for oral presentation at a convention of the American Psychological Association, represents a now well-established tradition, but one that is currently undergoing rapid change. Various perceptual aftereffects have been known for centuries. They are, of course, relational by definition, since the perception of a stimulus pattern now is affected by its relation to a preceding stimulus pattern. The kinds of aftereffects investigated in recent years by such distinguished scientists as Richard Held, Ivo Kohler, Charles Harris, and Celeste McCollough have become increasingly more complex and harder to account for by the relatively simple physiological mechanisms of yesteryear. Particular simultaneous aftereffects in opposite directions but in the same sense organ have been demonstrated, with the direction of the aftereffect contingent upon the color of the adapting stimulus, its orientation, and, in the present study, its texture. Sensory neurophysiology is making major strides toward uncovering the neural mechanisms that may be responsible for such phenomena.

A Texture-Contingent Visual Motion Aftereffect

James T. Walker

The following procedure produces a new visual motion aftereffect. Two visually textured discs, one fine and the other coarse, rotating in opposite directions at 8 RPM are presented alternately for 4 seconds each (see Figure 1). The observer fixates the center of each rotating disc, and after 4 minutes of repeated presentations the discs stop. Each stationary disc, when fixated, then appears to rotate in the direction opposite to its prior objective rotation. Thus, opposite negative motion aftereffects occur when the same visual receptors are alternately stimulated by oppositely rotating fine and coarse visual textures. This phenomenon, a texture-contingent negative motion aftereffect, is analogous in some respects to the orientation-contingent color aftereffect discovered by McCollough (1965).

In the first demonstrations of the present phenomenon, the two discs were placed side by side a few feet in front of the observer. After the inspection period, the fine and coarse stationary discs remained in the same left-right positions they had occupied during the inspection period. Since the directions of eye movements (left and right) required to fixate the rotating discs were correlated with directions of rotation, it could be argued that the direction of negative motion aftereffect might have been mediated by a conditioned relationship between left-right eye movements and possible cyclotor-

Source: Reprinted by permission of Psychonomic Journals, Inc., from *Psychonomic Science*, 1972, 28, 333–335.

Note: This research was supported in part by National Institute of Mental Health Grant Number USPH 1 R03 MH 18809–01.

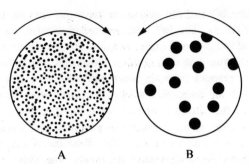

FIGURE 1.   Fine visual texture (A) and coarse visual texture (B) rotate in opposite directions

sional movements induced by the rotations of the discs. In order to rule out the above explanation, in the experiment described below, the left-right positions of the fine and coarse discs were interchanged after the inspection period.

Subjects

Eight men and 8 women, introductory psychology students, participated as a course requirement.

Apparatus

The visual textures were selected from a specially prepared set of quasi-random textures comprising a logarithmic scale. Regular dot arrays, such as printing screens, are readily available commercially, but irregular textures produce greater conventional motion aftereffects (Dixon & Meisels, 1966). There was a difference of .8 log unit between the coarseness of the two textures chosen for this experiment; thus, the coarse texture is 6.31 times as coarse as the fine. Both textures were .20 black and .80 white.

The discs were 6 inches in diameter and were presented at a viewing distance of 8 feet against a flat black background. Each disc was enclosed in a box with a large circular hole in the front. The boxes were placed side by side and were of such a size that the centers of the discs were separated by a distance of 29 inches. Each disc was illuminated from the front by a 100-W slide projector with a circular aperture in the slide plane. The discs were rotated at 8 RPM.

Procedure

The experiment was run with the room lights off. The discs were alternately lighted for 4 seconds each, and S was instructed to fixate the center of each disc as steadily as possible as long as the disc was lighted. During the inspection period, S was asked which direction the discs were rotating in order to make sure S was capable of indicating directions of rotation. For half the

*S*s, the fine disc was on the left and the coarse on the right, and these *positions* were reversed for the other *S*s. The left disc rotated clockwise and the right counterclockwise for half the *S*s, and these *rotation directions* were balanced across the positions of the fine and coarse discs. Positions and rotation directions were balanced with respect to each other and also with respect to the sex variable. After a 4-minute inspection period, the discs were stopped. The projectors were turned off for about 1 minute while the fine and coarse discs were interchanged. Both stationary discs were then lighted and *S* was asked to fixate the center of each disc and to indicate the direction of apparent rotation. If either disc, or both discs, appeared stationary, the experimenter (E) said, "If I told you the disc on the left (right) really was rotating, which direction would you *guess* it to be rotating?" A similar forced-choice procedure has been used in connection with studies of the McCollough effect (Harris & Gibson, 1968). The projectors were turned off while the discs were again interchanged so that the fine and coarse discs occupied the same left-right positions they had occupied during the inspection period. The stationary discs were again lighted, and *S* indicated directions of apparent rotation, as above.

Results

Texture-contingent negative motion aftereffects occurred. After the inspection period, each visual texture appeared to move in a direction opposite to its prior objective rotation.

Aftereffect scores were found by the following procedure: A free choice of direction opposite to the prior objective rotation of a texture was given a value of +2, and a forced choice in this direction was given a value of +1. Free and forced choices in the same direction as the prior objective rotation were given values of −2 and −1 respectively, since these choices represent responses contrary to those expected if texture-contingent negative motion aftereffects were to occur. An *S*'s aftereffect score is the sum of the above values, and since the stationary fine and coarse textures were presented twice to each *S,* aftereffect scores could range between −8 and +8 inclusive. The mean aftereffect score was 4.75, and this score is significantly different from zero ($t = 6.29$, $df = 15$, $p < .001$). However, the aftereffect scores for 2 *S*s were zero. Table 1 shows the distribution of aftereffect scores.

TABLE 1.   Distribution of aftereffect scores

Score	0	1	2	3	4	5	6	7	8
Frequency	2	0	3	2	1	0	0	4	4

The mean aftereffect score, above, takes into account forced as well as free choices. In order to rule out any contamination from any possible forced-choice biases, aftereffect scores were found utilizing only the data from the first presentation of the stationary textures. Free choices at this stage of the experiment were made before any forced choices had been made. Assigning values of $+1$ and -1 respectively to those free choices which support and do not support the occurrence of a texture-contingent aftereffect yields a mean aftereffect score of .94 out of 2 possible, and this mean is significantly different from zero ($t = 4.39$, $df = 15$, $p < .001$).

The aftereffect scores found by combining free and forced choices were subjected to a 3-way analysis of variance. The factors were Sex, Position of Test Textures (switched vs. not switched with respect to left-right positions of inspection textures) and Texture Magnitude (fine vs. coarse). There were repeated measures on the last two factors. There was no significant Sex effect ($F < 1.00$). Since the within-subjects error terms were not heterogeneous, these error terms were pooled as recommended by Winer (1962). The only significant effect was that of Texture Magnitude ($F = 6.98$, $df = 1/42$, $p < .02$). The mean aftereffect scores for the fine and coarse textures were respectively 1.75 and 3.00 out of 4 possible. Since these means differ from each other, and since the smaller mean differs significantly from zero ($t = 4.39$, $df = 15$, $p < .001$), it follows that a texture-contingent negative motion aftereffect occurred in both textures.

Discussion

The apparatus used in the present experiment required that Ss move their eyes left and right in order to fixate the fine and coarse discs. The experimental procedure probably rules out any simple conditioning between left-right eye movements and cyclotorsional movements as an explanation of the texture-contingent motion aftereffect, but it would nevertheless be desirable to present the discs in such a way that no eye movements would be required. An improved apparatus utilizing a two-way mirror allows the discs to be presented alternately in the same portion of the visual field. Preliminary observations carried out using this new apparatus confirm the occurrence of the texture-contingent motion aftereffect.

The present phenomenon appears related in some respects to the McCollough effect (McCollough, 1965). In this latter effect, a display consisting, for example, of a grid of red and black vertical bars alternates with a display of green and black horizontal bars. After fixating these alternating displays for a few minutes, black and white vertical bars appear greenish, and black and white horizontal bars appear reddish. Thus, the McCollough effect can be described as an orientation-contingent color aftereffect. Motion-contingent color aftereffects have also been described, where red-and-black and green-and-black moving stimuli produce color aftereffects when black-and-white moving stimuli are subsequently presented (Hepler, 1968; Stromeyer, 1970).

McCollough (1965) argued that her aftereffect could be explained by color adaptation of edge detectors, although no such color-sensitive edge detectors were known to exist at that time. While McCollough's explanation has been questioned (Harris & Gibson, 1968), orientation detectors have been found in the visual cortex of the monkey which respond to colors in an opponent-process manner (Hubel & Wiesel, 1968). Adapting a set of such color-sensitive orientation detectors simultaneously to color and orientation should produce not only orientation-contingent color aftereffects but color-contingent orientation aftereffects as well, depending primarily on the arrangement of the test stimuli. Indeed, Held and Shattuck (1971) have recently produced a color-contingent orientation aftereffect which reverses the contingency relationship observed in the McCollough effect.[1]

There is indirect evidence that texture-sensitive detectors may exist in the visual system, since inspecting a coarse visual texture makes a subsequently viewed intermediate texture look finer (Walker, 1966; Blakemore & Sutton, 1969). There is also evidence that visual texture is a factor in the apparent velocity of objective motion and motion aftereffects (Cann, 1962; Walker, in preparation). If there are texture detectors in the visual system which are also responsive to motion, then such motion-sensitive texture detectors might account for the present texture-contingent negative motion aftereffect.

References

BLAKEMORE, C. P., & SUTTON, P. Size adaptation: A new aftereffect. *Science,* 1969, *166,* 245–247.

CANN, M. A. The negative aftereffect of motion as a function of test stimulus texture. Doctoral dissertation, Boston University, 1961.

DIXON, N. F., & MEISELS, L. The effects of information content upon the perception and after-effects of a rotating field. *Quarterly Journal of Experimental Psychology,* 1966, *18,* 310–318.

FAVREAU, O. E., EMERSON, V. F., & CORBALLIS, M. C. Motion perception: A color-contingent aftereffect. *Science,* 1972, *176,* 78–79.

HARRIS, C. S., & GIBSON, A. R. Is orientation-specific color adaptation in human vision due to edge detectors, afterimages, or "dipoles"? *Science,* 1968, *162,* 1506–1507.

HELD, R., & SHATTUCK, S. R. Color- and edge-sensitive channels in the human visual system: Tuning for orientation. *Science,* 1971, *174,* 314–316.

HEPLER, N. Color: A motion-contingent aftereffect. *Science,* 1968, *162,* 376–377.

MAYHEW, J. E. W., & ANSTIS, S. M. Movement after-effects contingent on color, intensity and pattern. *Perception & Psychophysics,* in press.

McCOLLOUGH, C. Color adaptation of edge-detectors in the human visual system. *Science,* 1965, *149,* 1115–1116.

---

[1] After this paper was accepted for presentation, Favreau, Emerson, and Corballis (1972) reported a *color*-contingent motion aftereffect which appears analogous to the present texture-contingent effect. The above paper refers to unpublished observations of color-contingent motion aftereffects by Stromeyer (1968) and also refers to observations of motion aftereffects contingent on color, intensity, spatial frequency of gratings, and size of dots in visual textures by Mayhew and Anstis (in press).

STROMEYER, C. F., III. Informal observations of color-contingent motion aftereffects. Unpublished, 1968. Noted in O. E. Favreau, V. F. Emerson, & M. C. Corballis. Motion perception: A color-contingent aftereffect. *Science*, 1972, *176*, 78–79.

STROMEYER, C. F., III, & MANSFIELD, R. J. W. Colored aftereffects produced with moving edges. *Perception & Psychophysics*, 1970, *7*, 108–114.

WALKER, J. T. Textural aftereffects: Tactual and visual. Doctoral dissertation, University of Colorado, 1966.

―――. Some effects of visual texture on real and apparent visual motion. In preparation.

WINER, B. J. *Statistical principles in experimental design*. New York: McGraw-Hill, 1962.

Ulric Neisser, professor of psychology at Cornell University, won the Century Psychology Series Award in 1966 for his seminal book, Cognitive Psychology. *The theme of his volume is "the continuously creative processes by which the world of experience is constructed" (p. 11). He writes, "The central assertion is that seeing, hearing and remembering are all acts of* construction, *which may make more or less use of stimulus information depending on circumstances" (p. 10). Most succinctly, to take a phrase from the brief excerpt from the book, "The world of experience is produced by the man who experiences it." Neisser's thought has had a profound effect upon research of information processing in general and upon work in perceptual psychology in particular. His* Cognitive Psychology *is recognized as the most complete, integrated, and convincing statement of the new orientation toward perception as a constructive activity, a statement which ingeniously synthesizes a wealth of diverse data from a wealth of diverse empirical studies. The selection here presents the first few paragraphs of the first chapter.*

The Cognitive Approach

Ulric Neisser

It has been said that beauty is in the eye of the beholder. As a hypothesis about localization of function, the statement is not quite right—the brain and not the eye is surely the most important organ involved. Nevertheless it points clearly enough toward the central problem of cognition. Whether beautiful or ugly or just conveniently at hand, the world of experience is produced by the man who experiences it.

This is not the attitude of a skeptic, only of a psychologist. There certainly is a real world of trees and people and cars and even books, and it has a great deal to do with our experiences of these objects. However, we have no direct, *im*mediate access to the world, nor to any of its properties. The ancient theory of *eidola,* which supposed that faint copies of objects can enter the mind directly, must be rejected. Whatever we know about reality has been *mediated,* not only by the organs of sense but by complex systems which interpret and reinterpret sensory information. The activity of the cognitive systems results in—and is integrated with—the activity of muscles and glands that we call "behavior." It is also partially—very partially—reflected in those private experiences of seeing, hearing, imagining, and thinking to which verbal descriptions never do full justice.

Physically, this page is an array of small mounds of ink, lying in certain positions on the more highly reflective surface of the paper. It is this physical page which Koffka (1935) and others would have called the "distal

Source: Reprinted by permission of Appleton-Century-Crofts from *Cognitive Psychology,* by Ulric Neisser.

stimulus," and from which the reader is hopefully acquiring some information. But the sensory input is not the page itself; it is a pattern of light rays, originating in the sun or in some artificial source, that are reflected from the page and happen to reach the eye. Suitably focused by the lens and other ocular apparatus, the rays fall on the sensitive retina, where they can initiate the neural processes that eventually lead to seeing and reading and remembering. These patterns of light at the retina are the so-called "proximal stimuli." They are not the least bit like *eidola*. One-sided in their perspective, shifting radically several times each second, unique and novel at every moment, the proximal stimuli bear little resemblance to either the real object that gave rise to them or to the object of experience that the perceiver will construct as a result.

Visual cognition, then, deals with the processes by which a perceived, remembered, and thought-about world is brought into being from as unpromising a beginning as the retinal patterns. Similarly, auditory cognition is concerned with transformation of the fluctuating pressure-pattern at the ear into the sounds and the speech and music that we hear. The problem of understanding these transformations may usefully be compared to a very different question that arises in another psychological context. One of Freud's papers on human motivation is entitled "Instincts and their Vicissitudes" (1915). The title reflects a basic axiom of psychoanalysis: that man's fundamental motives suffer an intricate series of transformations, reformulations, and changes before they appear in either consciousness or action. Borrowing Freud's phrase—without intending any commitment to his theory of motivation—a book like this one might be called "Stimulus Information and its Vicissitudes." As used here, the term "cognition" refers to all the processes by which the sensory input is transformed, reduced, elaborated, stored, recovered, and used. It is concerned with these processes even when they operate in the absence of relevant stimulation, as in images and hallucinations. Such terms as *sensation, perception, imagery, retention, recall, problem-solving,* and *thinking,* among many others, refer to hypothetical stages or aspects of cognition. . . .

When clicks are sounded at the same time a sentence is spoken, people tend to hear the clicks as if they occur during "natural breaks" in a sentence. This promising finding has opened up a whole new line of research, of which the experiments on click location and syntactic structure done in Australia by V. M. Holmes and K. I. Forster are a fine example. Their work is influenced by the revolution in psycholinguistics occasioned by Noam Chomsky's theory of generative transformational grammar; they use such concepts as the "matrix S" (sometimes referred to as the "deep structure" of an utterance, as the "kernel sentence," or as the basic meaning behind a sentence) and "NP" (noun phrase, typically consisting of such components as an article like the *or* an, *an adjective, and a noun). Their experiments show that the errors made in judging where in a sentence a click was sounded, and the shifting of the apparent location of the click, depend upon the syntactic structure of the sentence. They suggest that click location accuracy can be used as an index of perceptual-processing load during the decoding of sentences. When we are listening to someone speak, we construct meanings that fit the auditory input.*

Click Location and Syntactic Structure

V. M. Holmes and K. I. Forster

Four experiments are reported in which Ss had to judge the location of clicks superimposed on recorded sentences. The first experiment showed that the accuracy of locating the clicks was a function of the position of the click in the constituent structure, the greatest accuracy being for clicks at major clause boundaries. The second experiment showed that this effect was independent of migration, i.e., the tendency for judgments to be displaced towards the major clause break. In the third experiment, it was shown that the requirement that S reproduce the sentence did not influence the response distribution. Finally, in the fourth experiment, a small but significant trend for location accuracy to decrease with decreasing separation of the click from the major break was found. However, this trend was much smaller than the differences in accuracy for various positions in the constituent structure. It was concluded that click location accuracy can be used as an index of perceptual processing load during recognition of individual sentences.

In experiments by Fodor and Bever (1965), Garrett, Bever, and Fodor (1966), Bever, Kirk, and Lackner (1969), Bever, Lackner, and Kirk (1969), and Bever, Lackner, and Stolz (1969), Ss were required to judge the location of an extraneous signal (usually a click) which occurred during a recorded sentence. The results showed that Ss systematically mislocated the clicks towards the nearest major clause boundary within the sentence. This "migration" or "attraction" of the judgments of click location has been interpreted as demonstrating that the clause is a major perceptual unit in sentence recognition. According to Bever, Lackner, and Kirk (1969) and Bever (1970), the click migration effect shows that the listener initially segments the input into those sequences which correspond to a sentence in the underlying structure of the sentence. As well as obtaining the migration effect, Fodor and Bever (1965) found that clicks at major constituent boundaries were more accurately located than were the clicks adjacent to such boundaries. They took the results to be merely a consequence of their main conclusion about click migration, i.e., Ss were less likely to mislocate clicks at major breaks because the clicks would not be attracted away from such positions.

It can be argued that variations in the accuracy of click location are not just a byproduct of the click migration effect but are a result of differential interference from processing the sentence structure in the immediate context of the click. Using a click detection task, Holmes and Forster (1970) showed that reaction time to clicks varies at different locations in the sentence structure: the fastest reactions to clicks occurred at major clause breaks. This effect is presumably a result of differences in attention required by concurrent sentence processing, suggesting that there is a temporary lull in processing activity at the major syntactic break. Such variations in processing load may also underlie Fodor and Bever's (1965) accuracy effect of click location. At points where S is able to react relatively rapidly to a click, he may also be able to remember its location more accurately.

While these remarks about click location accuracy are not incompatible with the interpretation of the click migration effect proposed by Fodor and Bever (1965), they provide a different perspective for viewing the processes operating in the click location task. Furthermore, click location accuracy seems much more straightforward as a measure of performance than does click migration. Criteria for determining whether click migration has occurred are somewhat arbitrary, a fact which is evidenced by the variety of procedures used to assess the magnitude of the effect. The measure of click location accuracy is simply whether the judgment is correct.

The following experiments aimed to explore the use of click location accuracy as an index of processing load during sentence recognition. Specifically, it was intended to see whether Fodor and Bever's (1965) result, that accuracy of click location is greater at major constituent breaks than within major constituents, is a general one or is specific to conditions where migration occurs. That is, the accuracy of locating clicks occurring near the major break may have been reduced simply by the migration effect and not by increased sentence processing load. In that case, the lower error rate for locating clicks at the major break might only reflect lowered accuracy at the adjacent positions. To eliminate this possibility, it is necessary to demonstrate that differences in accuracy can occur independently of migration effects. It seems reasonable to expect that migration effects would be less likely to occur for clicks placed far from the break instead of the one-to-four-syllable distances used in all the studies of click migration. Hence, in comparing the accuracy of locating clicks at the major break with that of clicks at other positions in the structure of the sentence, we used click positions which were at a considerable distance from the break. If accuracy of click location indicates the processing load imposed by those parts of the sentence surrounding the click, then accuracy should still be dependent on the position of the click in the syntactic structure of the sentence, even in the absence of a click migration effect.

General Design and Procedure of Experiments

In each experiment, a randomly ordered list of sentences was recorded on one track of a stereophonic tape recorder. A short burst of noise, a "click," was recorded on the other tape track. In Experiments 1 and 2 the duration of the click was about 80 msec, while in Experiments 3 and 4 the duration of the click was 1 msec. Owing to the smoothing effect of the headphones, the 1-msec click was effectively about 20 msec, and, in fact, there appeared to be little difference subjectively between the two click lengths. The intensity of the clicks was adjusted so that it was approximately equal perceptually to the loudest speech sound. None of the clicks was located within a word; instead, each click was placed just at the end of a word so that it did not occur during the acoustic pause possible between words. The energy level of the two tape tracks was analyzed, using a two-channel pen recorder, and the results verified the assumption that the clicks did not occur during acoustic pauses.

The experiments were designed so that repeated measurements were obtained from each S. Each S heard every one of the sentences, which were presented in one of four orders arranged from a Latin square design. The sentences in each experiment varied in syntactic structure, except for one important constraint: each sentence had a major surface structure boundary where no constituents except the matrix S itself were interrupted. This boundary divided the sentence into two clauses.[1] The sentences were either coordinate clause constructions or adverbial clause constructions with the adverbial clause either first or second. In order to avoid stereotyped responding owning to monotony of the sentences, the semantic content was made as varied and interesting as possible. Some examples are: *Until the Foreign Office states the facts, we will not believe the wild rumors; The young doctor cannot join the team, if the test's results are not satisfactory; The crowd cheered, as the cast of the play returned on stage for an encore; Tongues of flame licked up from the burning building, and sparks shot into the sky.*[2]

[1] A clause is defined for present purposes as a surface constituent, except an adjective, dominated by an S in the underlying structure.
[2] A complete list of the sentences used in each experiment, together with the mean click location accuracy and mean migration scores for each sentence, can be obtained from ASIS National Auxiliary Publications Service (c/o CCM Information Sciences, Inc., 22 West 34th Street, New York, New York 10001).

The stimuli were presented through headphones, and presentation of sentences in one ear and clicks in the other was alternated across the orders. *S*s were instructed to write the sentence out as accurately as possible and to place a slash mark to indicate as accurately as possible the location of the click. *S*s were given several practice examples. All the *S*s used in each experiment were native speakers of English.

Experiment 1

Clicks were placed at three positions in the constituent structure of sentences. First, clicks were located at the major clause break which separated coordinate clauses or the adverbial clause from the main clause. In most analyses of surface constituent structure, no constituents except the matrix *S* itself are interrupted at this point. Secondly, clicks were placed at divisions within one of the major clauses, either at the boundaries of embedded clauses or between phrases. These locations were considered to be at "minor" breaks in the constituent structure. Thirdly, clicks were placed at points either within simple noun phrases or within the auxiliary expansion of verb phrases. Since these click locations interrupt a large number of constituents, they were classified as being not at a break in the structure. No attempt was made to specify the number of constituents interrupted by the clicks in the latter two conditions because a particular sentence may be given different surface structure analyses according to different theoretical orientations. The three kinds of click positions are shown in the following example: *When they arrived/, they found/ the woman was/ screaming and in a state of hysteria.* In our classification, the first slash represents a click at a major clause break, the second click is at a minor break, and the third click is not at a break.

Two hypotheses were tested: (1) Click location judgments should be more accurate at a major clause break than either at a minor break or not at a break. This prediction is based on Holmes and Forster's (1970) conclusion that attention to sentence processing is reduced at major clause breaks compared with other parts of the sentence; (2) location accuracy should be greater for clicks at a minor break than for clicks not at a break if a decrease in sentence processing load also occurs at minor breaks in the constituent structure. In addition, it was predicted that migration would *not* occur because the relevant click positions were so far away from the major clause break.

Design

The 24 stimulus sentences were the same as those listed in Holmes and Forster (1970). The position of the click in the constituent structure was the main treatment condition (constituent break type): the click was either at a major clause break, at a minor break, or not at a break. For the latter two conditions, the average separations of the click from the major clause boundary were 6.3 and 16.9 syllables, respectively. Clicks were also located at different serial positions in the sentence: either in the first half of the sentence (early) or in the second half of the sentence (late). As a form of internal replication, two sets of stimuli were prepared. The same 24 sentences were recorded twice, with clicks placed in different positions, and each set of sentences was presented to a separate group of 20 Ss.[3]

Subjects

The Ss were 40 volunteers from a undergraduate psychology course at the University of Melbourne.

Results

The sum of each S's accurate click locations for the four sentences in each condition was obtained. The location accuracy means over all Ss are shown as percentages in Figure 1. A four-way analysis of variance was per-

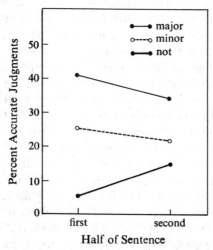

FIGURE 1.   Percentage of accurate click location judgments in Experiment 1 as a function of position of the click serially in the sentence and of position of the click in the constituent structure (at a major clause break, at a minor break, and not at a break)

formed on the data (Ss by Groups by Constituent Break Type by Serial Position). The sum of squares (SS) for the constituent break type factor was divided into two components corresponding to the two orthogonal predicted contrasts (Hays, 1963). Setting the Type I error rate at $\alpha = .05$, both con-

---

[3] It could be argued that two of the sentences do not fit the classification exactly. In one sentence (Sentence 14 in Holmes & Forster, 1970), where the click is said to be at a minor break, the click is between two NPs, but may interrupt more constituents than some of those in the not-at-break condition. In another (Sentence 19 in Holmes & Forster, 1970), where the click is said to be not at a break, the click may not interrupt as many constituents as others in this condition.

trasts were significant.[4] More accurate judgments were made for clicks at a major break than for clicks either at a minor break or not at a break, with $F(1,76) = 35.75$; more accurate judgments were made for clicks at a minor break than for clicks not at a break, with $F(1,76) = 11.56$. The only other significant term from the analysis was the interaction between constituent break type and serial positions, where $F(2,76) = 3.87$. From Figure 1, it appears that the effects of different constituent break positions decreased when clicks occurred late in the sentence.

The test for migration towards the major clause break was concerned only with the conditions in which the click was either at a minor break or not at a break. In order to maximize the probability of obtaining an effect, the data were scored in the same way as that reported by Bever, Lackner, and Kirk (1969). Not only were the accurate responses excluded from the analysis, but also excluded were responses which were beyond the major break ("overshoots"). Responses which were *not* in the direction of the break but were displaced by an amount greater than the distance between the break and the objective click location were also excluded. For each S, the number of responses going towards or into the major clause break was expressed as a proportion of the number of remaining errors. The overall mean proportion of migration errors was .576. On the assumption that a majority of the errors specified should go towards or into the major clause break, the appropriate test was to compare this value with .5, using the error mean square (MSE) calculated from an analysis of variance. This test showed that .576 was significantly higher than .5, with $F(1,38) = 6.63$, indicating that a small, but significant, migration effect had occurred.

That responses migrated towards the break from click positions so far away from it seemed surprising. However, a post hoc analysis showed that the only mean from the four relevant conditions which differed significantly from .5 was that for clicks which were not at a break and were late in the sentence, with $F(3,38) = 9.73$. An explanation for this result is implied by Ladefoged and Broadbent (1960) and more recently by Bertelson and Tisseyre (1970), who reported that clicks heard during sentences were judged as occurring *prior* to their actual location.[5] Seventy-five percent of all location errors in the present experiment placed the click prior to its objective location. This preposition tendency creates a problem for interpreting the migration effect, since all early clicks which were not at a break occurred before the major break, while all late clicks which were not at a break followed the major break. Thus, preposition and migration were confounded in the very

---

[4] All subsequent decisions were based on a Type I error rate of $\alpha = .05$.

[5] A general preposing tendency was not discussed by Garrett et al. (1966), Bever, Lackner, and Kirk (1969), and Bever, Lackner, and Stolz (1969). Bever, Kirk and Lackner (1969) found that shocks presented during sentences were judged to occur a fraction of a syllable prior to their objective location. However, Fodor and Bever (1965) found almost no overall preposition effect: 52% of the error responses were placed prior to the objective location and 48% were placed after the objective location.

condition which post hoc analysis showed to be the source of the migration effect.

Experiment 2

This experiment aimed to balance the preposition tendency with the migration tendency by placing clicks both before and after the major clause break, thereby demonstrating an effect of syntactic structure on click location accuracy apart from a migration effect. It was hypothesized that migration towards major clause breaks would not occur and that location accuracy would remain higher for clicks at a major clause break than for clicks not at a break. Again, large separations of the click and the break were employed.

Design

Clicks were located either in the first half (early) or in the second half (late) of 16 sentences which were 15 words long. Clicks were also placed either at the major clause break or not at a break. For clicks not at a break, half the clicks were before the clause break and half were after it. The average separation of such clicks from the major clause break was 7.1 syllables.

Subjects

Twenty graduate students and members of staff in the Department of Psychology at the University of Melbourne acted as Ss.

Results

Of all the erroneous click location judgments, 84% were recorded prior to the objective click location. Migration was calculated in the same way as above: the obtained proportion of .571 errors migrating towards the major clause break was not significantly different from .5, with $F(1,19) = 2.94$. Assuming that migration should disappear when the click and the break are widely separated, the failure to find a migration effect was anticipated. However, it is possible for an effect to be obscured by a large amount of variance. Setting $\alpha = \beta = .05$, an experiment having two observations on each of 20 Ss can detect a difference from .5 of .151, with $MSE = .0685$. This value is well within the magnitude of the difference (.27) reported by Bever, Lackner, and Kirk (1969), who found .77 errors in favor of migration using the same scoring procedure with clicks very close to the break. Thus, the present experiment was sensitive enough to detect a migration effect equal in magnitude to that previously reported, although a smaller migration tendency may have gone undetected. The point was to demonstrate not that migration effects do not occur at all, but that differences in the accuracy of click location may occur independently of significant migration.

The mean proportions of accurate judgments over Ss were as follows: .438 for early clicks at a break, .388 for late clicks at a break, .125 for early clicks not at a break, and .100 for late clicks not at a break. Analysis of variance of the scores showed that the only significant effect was constituent break type, with $F(1,19) = 22.61$. Thus, it has been shown that location accuracy was significantly better for clicks at major clause breaks than for clicks not at such breaks, in the absence of migration.

Experiment 3

This experiment was designed to assess the effect of the requirement that Ss reproduce the sentence in the click location task. The obvious reason for instructing S to write out the sentence is to force him to process and retain the sentence while trying to judge the location of the click. However, it may be the case that writing out the sentence alters, or even creates, errors in click location. Therefore, a situation was devised where Ss were forced to process the sentence but did not always have to write it out. Two response conditions were used: either Ss had to reproduce the sentence, or they were supplied with a correct version after the sentence had been presented. These two conditions were interspersed randomly for a given S. The second variable of interest was the separation of the click from the major clause break. It has been assumed that the tendency for migration towards the break would be greater the nearer the click was to the break. Two click-break separations were included in the experiment to give a preliminary indication of any effects on either migration or accuracy.

Design

Twenty sentences were presented in the immediate response condition, in which the sentence was supplied for the S; and 20 sentences were presented in the delayed response condition, in which S had to reproduce the sentence. All 40 sentences were 14 words long and were constructed so that a major surface structure break occurred after the seventh word and separated the sentence into two clauses. The position of the click was the same for each response condition. In 4 sentences, the click occurred at the major clause break; in 16, the click was not at a break. In the latter sentences, the click occurred six syllables prior to the break, two syllables prior to the break, six syllables after the break, or two syllables after the break. The five locations are shown by slashes in the following example: *Just after John ordered/ his new/ car/, he/ saw a/ better bargain somewhere else.* Response booklets were prepared in such a way that S knew as soon as he turned the page at the end of each recorded sentence whether to write out the sentence before marking the location of the click.

Subjects

Thirty-eight undergraduate students from the University of Melbourne, who were paid for their participation, acted as Ss. The data for one S

were rejected after it was found that he had recorded judgments only in one response condition.

Results

The mean percent of accurate judgments for the various conditions is shown in Figure 2, where little difference between the two response conditions can be observed. Analysis of variance of the scores showed that the response condition factor was not significant, with $F(1,36) = 0.59$. The SS for click-break separation and response condition were divided into six orthogonal contrasts, leaving a residual with two degrees of freedom. The first two contrasts compared location accuracy at the break with the four not-at-break conditions. The contrasts were significant in both response conditions: for delayed responding, $F(1,144) = 33.75$, and for immediate responding, $F(1,144) = 26.49$. Significantly more errors were made for clicks located after the break than before the break, with $F(1,144) = 6.49$ for delayed responding, and with $F(1,144) = 8.63$ for immediate responding. The final two contrasts compared performance for clicks two syllables from the break with that for clicks six syllables from the break. For neither delayed responding, where $F(1,144) = 0.16$, nor immediate responding, where $F(1,144) = 1.39$, was there a significant effect. The results support those found in Experiments 1 and 2 and show that reproduction of the sentence does not increase the probability of forgetting the available click location information.

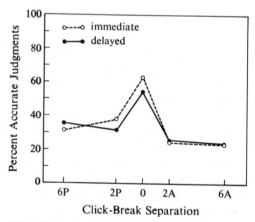

FIGURE 2.   Percentage of accurate click location judgments in Experiment 3 as a function of the separation (in syllables) between the click and the major clause break and of immediate compared with delayed responding

The mean proportions of errors migrating towards or into the major clause break are shown in Table 1. Analysis of variance of the data showed that there was no significant effect due to delayed or immediate responding, with $F(1,36) = 0.14$. The SS for click-break separation plus Click-Break

TABLE 1.   Mean proportion of click location errors migrating toward or into the major clause break in Experiment 3

Response Condition	Click-Break Separation			
	6 Prior	2 Prior	2 After	6 After
Delayed	.385	.464	.806	.854
Immediate	.495	.419	.798	.743

Separation by Response Condition were again divided into six components, four of which were orthogonal contrasts and two of which were noncontrast hypotheses. There was no significant difference between migration for clicks six or two syllables from the break: for delayed responding, $F(1,108) = 0.08$, and for immediate responding, $F(1,108) = 0.04$. However, migration was significantly greater for clicks after the break than before the break: for delayed responding, $F(1,108) = 55.56$; and for immediate responding, $F(1,108) = 33.21$. The two noncontrast hypotheses tested whether the proportion of migration errors both before and after the break were different from .5. After the break, the proportion was significantly *greater* than .5, with $F(1,108) = 120.73$, while before the break it was significantly *less* than .5, with $F(1,108) = 4.71$.

The results of this experiment demonstrate that Ss' having to reproduce the sentence affects neither the accuracy of judgments of click location nor the tendency for location judgments to migrate towards the syntactic break. Accuracy was highest for clicks at the major clause boundary in both response conditions, independent of the migration effects. While before-break clicks migrated less than after-break clicks, they were still located much less accurately than clicks at the break. Finally, the failure to show that click-break separation affected migration argues against the assumption that migration should increase as clicks occur closer to the break.

Experiment 4

The aim of this experiment was to evaluate more precisely the effect of the separation of the click from the major clause break. The reason that no effect of click-break separation on either migration or accuracy was found in Experiment 3 might be that the relation is a nonlinear one. Since more than two conditions are required to detect such a trend, a larger number of click-break separations were used in this experiment.

Design

Twenty-seven 14-word sentences were constructed with one-syllable words in the 5th to 10th positions (i.e., the middle 6 words) and with two-syllable words in the 4th and 11th positions. The first and last 3 words varied in syllable length. There were three sentences in each of nine conditions of click-break separation: the click was either at the major clause break (which was always after the seventh word) or at nine, six, four, or two syllables prior to or after the break. Thus, the clicks were located after the 3rd, 4th, 5th, 6th, 7th, 8th, 9th, 10th, or 11th words. The following sentence illustrates the possible click positions: *Because it was/ snowing/ at/ the/ lodge/, we/ left/ our/ luggage/ in the hotel.*

Subjects

Forty students from an undergraduate psychology course at the University of Melbourne volunteered to be *S*s.

Results

Figure 3 shows the mean percent accurate responses as a function of click-break separation. In the analysis of variance, the eight degrees of freedom were taken up by the following tests. First, the location of clicks occurring at the major clause break was judged significantly more accurately than the location of clicks at all other positions, with $F(1,312) = 70.44$. Secondly, the comparison of the conditions with the click prior to the break and after the break was also significant, with $F(1,312) = 21.02$. The third to eighth contrasts tested three components of trend for clicks prior to and after the break.

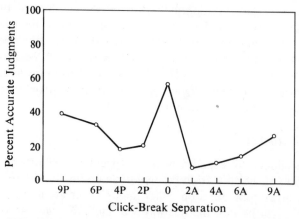

FIGURE 3.   Percentage of accurate click location judgments in Experiment 4 as a function of the separation (in syllables) between the click and the major clause break

There was a significant linear trend for responses both prior to the break, with $F(1,312) = 15.57$, and after the break, with $F(1,312) = 11.07$. The quadratic and cubic components did not approach significance. Thus, the accuracy of the judgments was dependent on click-break separation; fewer accurate judgments were made when the click was close to the break.

The mean proportions of migration errors are shown in Table 2. Three components of trend were tested for responses to clicks prior to and after the break. The only significant component was a linear trend for clicks prior to the break, with $F(1,273) = 6.57$. The linear trend for clicks after the break was not significant, with $F(1,273) = 1.29$; $F < 1$ for all other tests. The proportion of migration errors prior to the break was significantly lower than .5, with $F(1,273) = 36.47$; the proportion of migration errors after the break was significantly greater than .5, with $F(1,273) = 191.47$.

TABLE 2.   Mean proportion of click location errors migrating toward or into the major clause break in Experiment 4

Position of Click	Click-Break Separation			
	9	6	4	2
Prior to Break	.233	.304	.400	.408
After Break	.917	.908	.867	.808

The results show that as click-break separation decreased, Ss' judgments to before-break clicks became less accurate, apparently due to an increasing tendency to locate the clicks towards the major clause break. The fact that the proportion of migrating before-break clicks was a minority, however, demonstrates that the tendency to prepose the clicks is even stronger as a determinant of the location judgments. For after-break clicks, the picture is not so clear. While Ss did become less accurate in locating the clicks as the distance between the click and the break decreased, there was no corresponding increase in the proportion of errors migrating towards the break. The only plausible explanation of these results for after-break clicks seems to be that the preposing tendency is stronger than the migration tendency. That is, any increase in the tendency for the break to attract errors as click-break separation decreases might be counteracted by a decrease in the tendency to locate the clicks prior to their objective positions, as clicks become closer to the beginning of the sentence. Thus, the preposing tendency might have prevented the detection of an increasing trend in the migration effect for after-break clicks.

Discussion

The results of Experiment 1 have shown that accuracy of click location varies as a function of the position of the click in the constituent structure of sentences. Clicks were found to be located most accurately at the boundaries between major clauses, with intermediate accuracy between major phrases within clauses, and least accurately within simple phrases. Experiments 2–4 were designed to provide support for the claim that these results can be explained by variations in processing difficulty during sentence recognition. In Experiment 2, it was shown that such location results obtain under conditions where there is no detectable click migration towards the major clause break.

Thus, differences in accuracy of click location are not necessarily dependent on migration effects. The results of Experiment 3 demonstrated that the pattern of click location judgments obtained is the same when S is required to reproduce the sentence as when he is not required to do so. This is an important confirmation of the view that accuracy of click location reflects perceptual processing load.

The fact that the separation of the click from the major clause break influences accuracy of click location, as found in Experiment 4, suggests that location accuracy and migration are not always independent. Therefore, in tests of hypotheses about finer aspects of structure than those features examined in the present experiments, the distance of the click from the break may have to be controlled. However, the trends in accuracy of click location as a function of click-break separation were small compared with the differences obtained between different positions in the constituent structure. Thus, this result does not seriously challenge the basic finding of Experiment 1.

It should be stressed that the failure to find a significant tendency for judgments of click location to migrate towards major clause breaks in Experiment 2, and the partial confirmations of migration in Experiments 3 and 4, is not necessarily inconsistent with prior research. The aim of the present experiments was to set up conditions where migration would be minimal. Previous investigations, in which a migration effect has been clearly demonstrated, have all used click positions near the relevant constituent break, where the migration effect is strongest. Because it was not the purpose of Experiments 3 and 4 to detect a migration effect, the tendency to prepose judgments was left confounded with the tendency for judgments to migrate. While the evidence from these experiments suggests that the preposing tendency is a stronger determinant of the direction of the responses than migration, this conclusion may not apply in other experimental situations.

Given that accuracy of click location is a valid index of sentence processing load, the question to be asked is: At what stage in processing of the sentence do the location errors arise? The main result of Experiment 1 is in strong agreement with that of Holmes and Forster (1970), who found that reaction times (RTs) were faster to clicks at a major clause break than to clicks at a minor break or not at a break. This result indicates that the high location accuracy at the major clause break is at least partly due to the reduction in attention necessary for processing the sentence at the time such clicks occur.

The results of Holmes and Forster (1970) and those of the present experiments are not parallel in every respect. First, the difference between RTs to clicks at a minor break and clicks not at a break was weak and inconsistent in Holmes and Forster (1970), whereas location accuracy for these click positions was substantially different in the present experiments. This implies that, although attention to sentence processing may not differ reliably within major clauses according to minor constituent structure, subsequent processing into these minor constituents must occur. Secondly, RTs in Holmes and Forster (1970) were markedly faster to clicks late in the sentence than to early clicks. In Experiments 1 and 2, location accuracy was no higher for late than for early clicks. (In fact, in Experiments 3 and 4, early clicks were more accurately located than late clicks. This probably reflects the confounding of the preposition and the migration tendencies.) Hence, the absence of an analogous serial position effect for location accuracy implies that judgments of click location are influenced by processing input subsequent to the click.

The differences between the results of Holmes and Forster (1970) and those of the present experiments indicate that additional processing must affect judgments of click location, but they do not lead to the conclusion that "the psychological mechanism for reacting to clicks is distinct from the mechanism for locating clicks [Abrams & Bever, 1969, p. 286]." Abrams and Bever placed clicks in the syllable prior to the major clause break, at the break, or in the first syllable after the break. They reported that "Although before-break clicks receive slower RT than after-break clicks, in-break clicks do not receive the fastest RT [1969, p. 283]" and inferred that "attention to non-speech activity is reduced at the ends of clauses rather than enhanced [1969, p. 287]." However, in their two experiments, the mean of the RTs to clicks before and after the break was almost the same as that for RTs to clicks in the break. That after-break RTs were faster than before-break RTs might as plausibly be explained by a decreasing serial position effect as by an effect of syntactic structure. Moreover, placing the clicks for the three conditions so close to one another would not only make it difficult to detect reliable differences in RTs, but also would make the conditions different from those in Holmes and Forster (1970), in which large click-break separations were used. Thus, Abrams and Bever's conclusion about the relation of RTs and location accuracy is based on quite different evidence from that considered in our experiments.

In conjunction with the results of Holmes and Forster (1970), the present findings suggest the following view of the processes operating during the click location task. A marked reduction in attention to sentence processing at major clause boundaries, which produces comparatively fast RTs, allows clicks to be more accurately located there than at other parts of the sentence. While it is not clear whether attention varies within major clauses, judgments of click location are subject to less interference from subsequent sentence processing at minor breaks within these clauses than within phrases. This implies that the words of sentences may not be coded into phrases immediately as they are heard but may be recoded into major phrases for storage in short-term memory (at least where verbatim recall is required). The general proposing tendency found in the experiments may result from S's delaying his coding of the sentential input slightly by making use of his echoic storage system (Neisser, 1967). The click, on the other hand, has to be dealt with rapidly before it is forgotten and so tends to be judged in relation to the objectively earlier input which the S is now processing.

The processes described attempt to explain the determinants of accuracy of click location, but they do not preclude the possibility of a migration effect occurring. In Bever, Lackner, and Kirk (1969) and Bever (1970), it has been argued that the tendency for migration arises from a very early stage in processing, as a result of an initial perceptual segmentation strategy.[6] However, it seems to us that migration errors are more likely to arise from later stages in processing. If interference from the requirements of sentence processing has made the S unclear as to the location of the click, then the more processing he is required to do, the more likely is the S to integrate his location response with concurrent processing. Hence, S may erroneously locate the click towards the boundary of a unit he is recoding in short-term memory. This might lead one to expect a tendency for clicks to be located towards minor constituent boundaries as well as towards major clause boundaries. However, this is a difficult hypothesis to test, owing to the problems in constructing criteria for assessing the strength of the effects at minor breaks. The available evidence does not support the prediction that clicks migrate towards minor breaks (Bever, Lackner, & Kirk, 1969).

A final issue needing further investigation is whether it is essential for the major constituent break to be a boundary between S-dominated constituents (clauses) in order for there to be the greatest possible reduction in processing load. Correspondingly, it would be interesting to know whether minor breaks in the sentence structure produce decreased processing load more effectively if they are clause rather than phrase boundaries.

References

ABRAMS, K., & BEVER, T. G. Syntactic structure modifies attention during speech perception and recognition. *Quarterly Journal of Experimental Psychology,* 1969, *21,* 280–290.

BERTELSON, P., & TISSEYRE, F. Perceiving the sequence of speech and nonspeech stimuli. *Quarterly Journal of Experimental Psychology,* 1970, *22,* 653–662.

BEVER, T. G. The cognitive basis for linguistic structures. In J. R. Hayes (Ed.), *Cognition and the development of language.* New York: Wiley, 1970.

BEVER, T., KIRK, R., & LACKNER, J. An autonomic reflection of syntactic structure. *Neuropsychologia,* 1969, *7,* 23–28.

BEVER, T. G., LACKNER, J. R., & KIRK, R. The underlying structures of sentences are the primary units of immediate speech processing. *Perception & Psychophysics,* 1969, *5,* 225–234.

BEVER, T. G., LACKNER, J. R., & STOLZ, W. Transitional probability is not a general mechanism for the segmentation of speech. *Journal of Experimental Psychology,* 1969, *79,* 387–394.

FODOR, J. A., & BEVER, T. G. The psychological reality of linguistic segments. *Journal of Verbal Learning & Verbal Behavior,* 1965, *4,* 414–420.

[6] Abrams and Bever have also claimed that "the systematic nature of errors in click location are due to perceptual processing which follows the initial segmentation of the speech stimulus [1969, p. 288]." This view is more compatible with the explanations expressed in the present paper.

GARRETT, M., BEVER, T. G., & FODOR, J. A. The active use of grammar in speech perception. *Perception & Psychophysics,* 1966, *1,* 30–32.

HAYS, W. L. *Statistics for psychologists.* New York: Holt, Rinehart & Winston, 1963.

HOLMES, V. M., & FORSTER, K. I. Detection of extraneous signals during sentence recognition. *Perception & Psychophysics,* 1970, *7,* 297–301.

LADEFOGED, P., & BROADBENT, D. E. Perception of sequence in auditory events. *Quarterly Journal of Experimental Psychology,* 1960, *12,* 162–170.

NEISSER, U. *Cognitive psychology.* New York: Appleton-Century-Crofts, 1967.

The final article in this section is by Donald G. MacKay, of the University of California at Los Angeles. He has made many contributions to the new field of psycholinguistics as well as to perception proper. Here he applies his input-testing theory of perception—one of the active models of a construction approach to perception—to the detection of misspellings, and his findings clearly present difficulties for a passive model of perception. This experiment, like the preceding ones by Holmes and Forster, is typical of the massive current research effort in the perception of language.

Input Testing in the Detection of Misspellings

Donald G. MacKay

Two types of misspellings (phonetically compatible, WERK for WORK; or phonetically incompatible, WARK for WORK) were tachistoscopically presented to 24 subjects. Telling them what word would be misspelled increased the probability of detecting phonetically incompatible misspellings, but not phonetically compatible ones. The findings present difficulties for passive models of perception; an active, input-testing model is more promising.

It may seem surprising that spelling errors should provide a testing ground for general issues in perception. But current data on detection of misspellings contradict the general assumption that perception results from direct or passive activation of analyzers for orthographic input. Rather, an active or mismatch process seems to be involved, whereby perception results from a comparison of the input (at various stages of coding) with a self-generated model of that input.

Consider these two types of misspellings: *phonetically compatible* and *phonetically incompatible*. Compatible misspellings can be pronounced the same as the original word (say, VURSE for VERSE) whereas the incompatible ones cannot (VORSE for VERSE). MacKay (1968) showed that incompatible misspellings were easier to detect in a sentence than compatible ones, a finding in accord with a mismatch model of perception (after Teuber, 1960). According to this model, the context of the sentence leads the subject to expect a particular word at the phonetic level, and detecting the misspellings depends in part on a mismatch between this expectation and the internal pro-

Source: Reprinted by permission of the University of Illinois Press from *American Journal of Psychology*, 1972, *85*, 121–127.

Note: This investigation was supported by UCLA Grant 2428 and USPHS Grant 166668–01. The author thanks K. Achevski for running the experiment and analyzing the data, and M. Friedman for lending the experimental equipment.

nunciation of the actual input. Since the internal pronunciation of phonetically compatible misspellings matches that of the expected word, these misspellings pass undetected at the phonetic level. But the expectation fails to match the internal pronunciation of phonetically incompatible misspellings, which are therefore easily detected at the phonetic level according to the mismatch model.

The present study was a replication and extension of the 1968 MacKay study. To control for exposure duration, the phonetically compatible and incompatible misspellings were presented tachistoscopically. The subject's expectations were controlled by instructing or not instructing him to expect a particular word. According to the mismatch model, phonetically incompatible misspellings should be easier to detect in the instructed condition than in the uninstructed condition. And phonetically compatible misspellings should be harder to detect than incompatible ones in the instructed condition but not in the uninstructed condition.

We also presented misspellings that form new words; for example, the misspelling of GREET as GREAT. Our question was whether subjects would identify GREAT more readily if they expected GREET than if they had no expectation at all. The mismatch model predicts that these 'new word' misspellings should behave like phonetically incompatible ones, being easy to detect in the instructed condition because of an internal mismatch at the pronunciation level and perhaps at the semantic level as well. We will see that the failure of this prediction leads to a theoretical reformulation of the mechanisms underlying the detection of misspellings.

Method

Subjects and Procedure

Twenty-four UCLA undergraduates received course credit for their participation in the 40-minute experiment. Each subject was warned that the words to be presented would sometimes be correctly spelled and sometimes not. He was to write down exactly what he saw, guessing at the spelling if necessary.

The materials consisted of 14 correctly spelled words (say, INCITE), 14 phonetically compatible misspellings (INSITE), and 14 phonetically incompatible misspellings (INBITE). The stimuli were typed in capital letters on 46 5-by-4-in. cards, which were shuffled thoroughly for each subject. The two types of misspelling were formed by changing exactly the same letter in one of the correctly spelled words. The misspellings altered neither word length nor letter height. The first letter was always correct but the position of the substituted letter varied from word to word. In addition, 5 new-word misspellings were formed by changing exactly the same letter in the original, correctly spelled words (say, INVITE for INCITE). The new-word misspellings slightly exceeded the original words in average Thorndike-Lorge frequency, but this is irrelevant here, since we were interested in comparing each word with itself in the 'set' and 'no-set' conditions described below.

In the *no-set* condition, a warning tone sounded 4 sec before the stimulus appeared. The *set* condition was identical except that the subjects were verbally told what word to expect in the 4 sec between the tone and stimulus onset. The order of the set and no-set conditions was counterbalanced across subjects. Half the stimuli were presented in the set condition and the remainder in the no-set condition (counterbalanced across subjects so that each stimulus appeared equally often in both conditions). In both conditions all the materials were first exposed for 120 msec and then for 160 msec.

Apparatus

A two-channel tachistoscope (Scientific Prototype 800F) presented the materials. One channel displayed a fixation point, and the other exposed the stimuli for either 120 or 160 msec. The words were 14 min (visual angle) in height and 30.5 min to 61 min in length. The luminance level of the stimuli was about 78 ftL as measured with a Spectra brightness spot meter. The tachistoscope was connected in series to three general purpose timers: one triggered the stimulus onset 4 sec after a warning tone, another fixed the duration of the warning tone (1 sec), and the third began the next trial by triggering the warning tone 12 sec after offset of the stimulus. An HP audio oscillator (201C) generated the 2,000-Hz warning tone.

Results

Detection of Misspellings

Compatible misspellings were no harder to detect than incompatible ones in the no-set condition. Here the probability of detecting compatible misspellings (averaged across subjects, words, and exposure durations) was .27; incompatible misspellings, .26. Nor did the set condition have a significant effect on the recognition of compatible misspellings (p at the .50 level, Friedman two-way analysis of variance on ranks). But the set condition did facilitate detection of incompatible misspellings. Significantly more incompatible misspellings were detected in the set than no-set condition ($p < .05$, same test). Similarly, incompatible misspellings were significantly easier to detect than compatible ones in the set condition ($p < .05$, same test).

We categorized incorrect responses as incorrect-word responses and as incorrect-set responses. An incorrect-set response was scored whenever the subject erroneously responded with the 'set' word, and an incorrect-word response whenever he erroneously responded with a correctly spelled English word. Table 1 shows the frequency of incorrect-set and -word responses for compatible and incompatible misspellings. As can be seen there, incorrect-word responses were no more frequent for compatible than incompatible misspellings in the no-set condition, but much more frequent in the set con-

TABLE 1. The probability of incorrect-word responses and incorrect-set responses given an incorrect identification of phonetically compatible and incompatible misspellings

	Incorrect-word Responses		Incorrect-set Responses	
	Compatible Misspellings	Incompatible Misspellings	Compatible Misspellings	Incompatible Misspellings
Set condition	.71	.56	.40	.33
No-set condition	.54	.53	.10	.09

dition ($p < .05$, Friedman two-way analysis of variance on ranks). This difference was only partly due to the slightly higher frequency of incorrect-set responses for phonetically compatible misspellings. In the set condition (also shown in Table 1), incorrect-word responses remained about 8% higher for compatible than incompatible misspellings when the incorrect-set responses were subtracted out. Thus compatible misspellings were mistaken for correctly spelled words more often than incompatible misspellings, but only in the set condition.

Detection of Correctly Spelled Words

'Set' words (say, HERD) and new-word misspellings (say, HARD for HERD) made up the correctly spelled words. The set words were correctly identified more frequently in the set than the no-set condition ($p < .01$, Friedman two-way analysis of variance on ranks). But the opposite was true of new-word misspellings, which were correctly recognized significantly more often in the no-set than in the set condition ($p < .05$, same test).

Incorrect-set responses and incorrect-word responses were scored as before, with the results shown in Table 2. Incorrect-word responses were no more frequent for new-word misspellings than set words in the no-set condition, but were significantly more frequent for new-word misspellings in the set condition (84% versus 0%). This difference is only partly due to the high frequency of incorrect-set responses for new-word misspellings (also shown in Table 2). With these incorrect-set responses subtracted out, 50%

TABLE 2. The probability of incorrect-word responses given an incorrect response to two types of normally spelled words, along with the probability of incorrect-set responses for new-word misspellings

	Incorrect-word Responses		Incorrect-set Responses
	Set Words	New-word Misspellings	New-word Misspellings
Set condition	.0	.84	.34
No-set condition	.40	.41	.08

of the erroneous responses to new-word misspellings were incorrect-word responses (as compared to 0% for the set words). Apparently the subjects realized the new-word misspellings were words, but were unsure *which* words.[1]

Discussion

Our findings present difficulties for passive models of perception. But the mismatch model developed in the introduction also fails to explain certain aspects of our data. According to this model, new-word misspellings should be easier to detect in the set than the no-set condition. Since the reverse was true, we were forced to develop a new model to explain our results. Our model can be considered an input-testing theory (after MacKay, 1967; Miller, Galanter, and Pribram, 1960), since perception is considered to follow a series of tests on the input.

Four possible input tests in the set condition of our experiment are shown in Table 3. Exposure duration was undoubtedly too brief to allow com-

TABLE 3.   The outcomes of four possible input tests in the set condition for the four types of stimuli

Input Tests	Phonetically Compatible Misspellings	Phonetically Incompatible Misspellings	Set Words	New-word Misspellings
1. Is the input identical to the set word at the orthographic level?	No	No	Yes	No
2. Is the input a familiar configuration (is it a word) at the orthographic level?	No	No	Yes	Yes
3. Is the input identical to the set word at the phonetic level?	Yes	No	Yes	No
4. Is the input familiar (is it a word) at the phonetic level?	Yes	No	Yes	Yes

plete application of the first test (Is the input identical to the set word at the orthographic level?). And assuming that only one or two of the remaining tests can be applied on a probabilistic basis, this model seems capable of handling virtually all of our results.

Consider the possibility that a new-word misspelling has only passed test 3 (Is the input identical to the set word at the phonetic level?),

[1] A curious response bias was noted for set words in the set condition. Here the subjects frequently created phonetically compatible misspellings of the set word. For example, they misspelled WORK as WURK, ADJOURN as ADJURN, and SURVEY as SERVEY. Moreover, these responses were inventions rather than carry-overs from the experimental misspellings WERK, ADJERN, and SURVAY that could have appeared earlier in the session. This response bias suggests that the subjects realized that the stimuli matched the expected word at the phonetic level but were unsure of its orthographic representation.

without time for further tests. Given no further information, the subject's best response is that the set word was presented, which accounts for both the high frequency of incorrect-set responses and the low probability of detecting new-word misspellings in the set condition. Note too that phonetically compatible misspellings pass tests 3 and 4, making the set word the best possible response if time permits no further tests. The input-testing model therefore explains the high frequency of incorrect-set responses for phonetically compatible misspellings.

The model also explains the ease of detecting phonetically incompatible misspellings, which fail all four input tests. The high frequency of incorrect-word responses for phonetically compatible misspellings and new-word misspellings can be handled in similar fashion. Both classes of stimuli pass test 4 (Is the input a word at the phonetic level?), forcing the subject to respond with a word if no further tests can be run. Finally, the model explains why erroneous responses for set words in the set condition were usually phonetically compatible. If the exposure duration permits all but test 1 (Is the input identical to the expected word at the orthographic level?), only two responses are feasible in this condition: one a possible incorrect-set response, and the other a phonetically compatible response. By chance alone, some of the responses will fall into this latter class, explaining the tendency to make errors that are phonetically compatible with the set word.

An input-testing model also captures the difficulty in detecting the absence of silent E's, as in HORDE, or silent K's, as in KNIGHT (Corcoran, 1966, 1967, 1968), since the missing element is absent both in the phonetic test and in the internal pronunciation of the misspelling. The model likewise predicts difficulty in detecting the addition of silent letters as in CORDE.

The findings of Rommetveit (1968) also fit an input-testing model. Rommetveit found that when SHAR is exposed to one eye along with SHAP to the other eye, the subjects reported SHARP, as if the input passed all the tests for perceiving SHARP. Similarly, Day (1967) found that when RODUCT is presented to one ear, along with PODUCT to the other, the subjects heard PRODUCT, as if the input passed all the tests for hearing PRODUCT.

In conclusion, further research on input-testing models is recommended to discover the order (if any) in which the tests are usually run; to determine whether different individuals apply different tests to the same input, leading to subject-specific misperceptions (such as Freud's misreading of *Hasdrubal* as *Hamilcar;* 1914), and to determine the nature of input testing in other modalities.

References

CORCORAN, D. W. J. An acoustic factor in letter cancellation. *Nature,* 1966, *210,* 658.

———. Acoustic factors in proof reading. *Nature,* 1967, *214,* 851.

CORCORAN, D. W. J., & WEENING, D. L. Acoustic factors in visual search. *Quarterly Journal of Experimental Psychology,* 1968, *20,* 83–85.

DAY, R. Fusion in dichotic listening. Paper read to the Psychonomic Society, Chicago, 1967.

FREUD, S. *Psychopathology of everyday life,* trans. A. Brill. New York: Penguin, 1914.

MACKAY, D. G. Phonetic favors in the perception and recall of spelling errors. *Neuropsychologia,* 1968, *6,* 321–325.

MACKAY, D. M. Ways of looking at perception. In *Models for the perception of speech and visual form,* ed. W. Wathen-Dunn. Cambridge, Mass.: The M.I.T. Press, 1967.

MILLER, G. A., GALANTER, E., & PRIBRAM, K. D. Plans and the structure of behavior. New York: Holt, 1960.

ROMMETVEIT, R. *Words, meanings, and messages.* New York: Academic Press, 1968.

TEUBER, H. L. Perception. In J. Field (Ed.), *Handbook of physiology,* Vol. 3. Washington, D.C.: American Physiological Society, 1960. Pp. 1595–1668.

Section Eight

BIOLOGICAL PSYCHOLOGY

Unexpected and significant findings about human behavior can often be discovered by studying physiological processes that take place under the skin. Quite often knowledge of animal physiology and behavior leads to new observations and new understanding of human behavior. The goal of biological psychology is to promote understanding of behavior by studying its biological mechanisms.

The articles in this section take up several questions that are representative of this area of psychology: How do fat people differ from normal-weight people in interpreting stimuli from inside and from outside the body? What unexpected facts about obese people have been discovered by studying the behavior of rats whose obesity was caused by experimentally induced brain lesions? If you distort visual input in a kitten, what changes occur in the connections within its brain? Can emotional responses—psychosomatic symptoms—be learned? When two rats receive exactly the same amount of shock, what psychological factors determine which one will develop more stomach ulcers?

The experimental techniques employed by these authors are also representative of the field—recording electrical activity of the brain from the surface of the head and recording the activity of single brain cells with microelectrodes; altering behavior by administering alcohol, barbiturates, and other drugs; analyzing the relationship between levels of biochemical substances in the brain and behavioral conditions. Investigators draw on techniques of all the biological sciences in their attempts to understand behavior more fully. Often two or more techniques are used in a study to cross-check results.

Each of these studies is based on earlier work which provided important information while leaving certain questions unanswered. Each study advances our knowledge of the problem; some take one clear step forward, while others take several steps. And in each case, while we obtain new knowledge, we are also left with further questions. Each of these selections was prepared as a lecture presenting an overview of the integrated research programs carried on by the authors in their laboratories.

Mark R. Rosenzweig

In this article, David Hubel summarizes a series of studies which show that distorting visual input in kittens alters connections in their brains. Hubel uses a microelectrode as he studies the response of one brain cell (or neuron) at a time. Each visual cell typically responds only to certain specific visual stimuli. If one eye is closed for several months in a kitten, few cortical cells will later respond to stimulation of that eye. But closing the eye of an adult cat for several months has no effect on the ability of that eye to command central cells. The result in kittens cannot be explained as establishment of neural connections by learning or as loss of connections by disuse, Hubel says. Hubel's challenging work with the visual system leads him to speculate: "Could it be that . . . abnormal emotion situations early in life may lead to a deterioration or distortion of connections in the same yet unexplored part of the brain?"

The results of Hubel and others, showing changes induced in animal brains by distorted sensory input, have led recently to a search for similar effects in man. Freeman and Thibos (1973) have found that a common visual defect—astigmatism—can have permanent effects on the brain. Unless an astigmatic child is given corrective glasses at a very early age, he will always see better in some orientations than in others.

Effects of Distortion of Sensory Input on the Visual System of Kittens

David H. Hubel

A prime objective of neurophysiology is to learn how cells in the nervous system function during the everyday and moment-to-moment activities of an organism. This amounts to learning how the brain is constructed and how the parts function when the organism perceives, thinks or acts. An equally important though perhaps less obvious objective is to understand how the structure and function of the nervous system are affected by the previous history of the organism. The ability to undergo long term alteration as a result of experience is an essential property of nervous systems of all animals, and in higher forms the very act of learning presumably involves such changes. To understand the nervous system one must sooner or later address both phases of the problem—the day-to-day functioning and the modification of function by experience.

In designing experiments one soon realizes that the two problems

Source: Reprinted by permission from *The Physiologist*, 1967, *10*, 17–45. Copyright © 1967 by The American Physiological Society.

Note: The material from this lecture represents the condensation of work published in six papers (see references 8, 10, 20, 21, 22, 23).

must be undertaken in sequence—that at least a sketchy outline of the everyday workings of the normal nervous system is necessary before there can be much hope of detecting effects of varied experience. One difficulty in understanding the function of neural structures arises largely from the extreme specialization of the nerve cells themselves. Of course it is well known that a structure like the cerebral cortex is divided into a number of areas, some concerned with audition, others with motor function, and so on. However, within any one of these, a given piece of tissue such as the cortical grey matter contains many classes of cells that are more or less intermixed. Different types of cells, and even cells in the same class which may morphologically appear the same, tend to respond to very special and quite distinct stimuli. This characteristic of the nervous system makes it profoundly different from any other tissue in the body, and arises from the intricate and highly organized interconnections between cells. The system is thus virtually inaccessible except at a single-cell level. Because techniques for recording from single cells have only been available in the last few decades, knowledge of how most parts of the brain work is still very scanty. The most rapid progress has been made in the spinal cord where relatively simple reflexes can be isolated, and in sensory systems such as the somatic, auditory, and visual, where one can study the responses of neurones close to the input end of the nervous system. The visual system, which concerns us here, has the advantage of a relatively simple and direct anatomical pathway from the retina through geniculate to striate cortex (Figure 1): here it is possible to examine and compare cells from one structure to the next with the hope of reaching some conclusions about how information is handled as the pathway is traversed.

During the past 10–15 years a number of studies have been made at various levels in the vertebrate visual system (1, 2, 3, 6, 9, 11, 12, 13, 14, 15, 24, 25). Our own work in normal visual physiology has been done mainly in the cat and monkey, and provides a background for a series of experiments in animals deprived of normal visual experience. To make these deprivation experiments understandable it is necessary to start by summarizing some of this work on the normal cat.

Normal Visual Physiology

In trying to understand the normal visual system we begin by examining how a single cell in the pathway is linked to the environment. How, by its connections to retinal receptors, does a cell "see" the outside world, and what combination of retinal stimuli will best activate the cell? In a typical experiment we record from single cells or fibers at various points in the visual pathway and stimulate the eyes with light. The cat or monkey is anesthetized, its head is fastened securely in a stereotaxic apparatus, and the eyes are held open and face a large white screen at a distance of 1½ meters. The stimulus consists of lights or shadows varying in size, shape, or wavelength projected

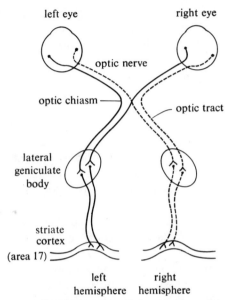

FIGURE 1.   Diagram of visual pathway from retina to cortex in a higher mammal. Note that the left hemisphere receives its input from the two left half-retinas and hence from the right visual field, and that each hemisphere receives input from both eyes.

on the screen and hence onto the two retinas, which can be stimulated together or separately. An electrode consisting of a fine wire insulated to within 10–20 μ of the tip is inserted into the retina, optic nerve, or brain, until it comes close enough to a single cell or fiber to sample the small extracellular currents associated with the all-or-none impulses. In any particular recording situation the relative constancy in size and shape from one impulse deflection of the oscilloscope to the next provides the evidence that the electrode is recording from one cell body or axon.

We then observe the effects of stimulating the retina upon single elements in the visual system, and try to determine the optimum stimulus for each cell. Having observed one cell for a few minutes or hours, we advance the electrode and study others, going from cell to cell along a straight line path. Electrolytic lesions can be made at 2 or 3 points along a track, so that later when the brain is sectioned in the plane of the track the positions of all the cells studied in a penetration can be determined. A cell's behavior can thus be correlated with its anatomical position.

Responses of Single Cells in Visual Cortex

In the visual cortex, as in other areas of the central nervous system, cells are extremely specialized. The great majority give practically no response to an abrupt increase or decrease in the total illumination of the retina. This comes at first as a surprise—it seems natural to expect that a stimulus capable of activating all of the retinal receptors should have a powerful influence on any visual cell. The reasoning of course fails because the visual pathway presumably contains inhibitory as well as excitatory synapses, and the effects of simultaneously stimulating different sets of receptors can cancel one another with unexpected precision.

Nevertheless, if the stimuli are properly chosen, all cells in the striate cortex can probably be influenced, and most can be made to fire vigorously. Each cell responds only to stimulation of a limited retinal region called the receptive field of the cell, and ignores stimuli applied outside this region. The receptive field of a cortical cell in the cat may be as small as about $\frac{1}{2}°$, or about 125 μ on the retina, or as large as 10°. Presumably the rods and cones outside the receptive field have too few connections, or connections that are too indirect, for them to have any easily detectable effect on the cell.

Uniform illumination of the cell's receptive field then, is without any appreciable effect on the cell's firing, since this amounts to the same thing as diffusely illuminating the retina. More specific stimuli must be used to make the cell respond. It turns out that for most cells the receptive field must be crossed by some kind of straight-line stimulus. The line may be made up of a bright slit on a dark background, a dark bar on a bright background, or a boundary between darkness and light; a given cell prefers one of these types of line and responds less well or even ignores the others. If the line crosses the receptive field in just the appropriate orientation the cell will fire vigorously. The orientation that elicits the optimal response varies from cell to cell, some cells preferring vertical, others horizontal, and others oblique, with all possible orientations represented. A typical cell will respond vigorously over a range of orientations of about 10–30°, the response declining outside this range, and failing completely for stimuli 90° from the optimum. Sweeping an optimally oriented line across the receptive field is usually a powerful stimulus, as in the cell whose responses are shown in Figure 2. Here a stationary line had little influence on the cell, but a line moving up and to the right evoked a brisk response consisting of several impulses, whereas movement in the opposite direction was without effect. Almost all cells are sensitive to this sort of movement, but many show less selectivity, responding almost equally to movement in the two diametrically opposite directions.

This kind of highly specific response has been seen in chronically prepared animals in the absence of anesthesia and with the animal fully alert. They have also been seen in the monkey cortex. It seems clear that the connections underlying the specificity of response to line stimuli must be in the cortex, since neither retinal nor geniculate cells show any tendency to prefer one orientation over another. Furthermore, while reacting best to restricted stimuli, many retinal and geniculate cells respond well to diffuse light. Various models have been proposed to explain the behavior of the cells in terms of neural connections (6, 9).

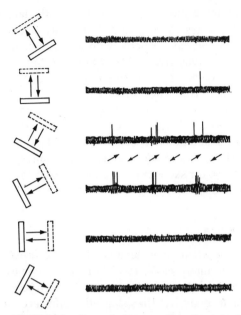

FIGURE 2.   Records from a cell in the right striate cortex of a normal adult cat. A retinal region about 1½ mm x 1½ mm (about 4° x 4° in the projected visual field) is illuminated by a small rectangle of light subtending 0.5° x 8°, which is moved back and forth over the region in different orientations as shown. Microelectrode recordings photographed from an oscilloscope are shown to the right; time, 1 sec. From (5).

Functional Architecture

From anatomical studies and work with evoked potentials recorded with gross electrodes it has long been clear that the retina is mapped upon the cortex in an orderly fashion (16, 18). Our single-cell work confirms this, but also tells something about the detailed arrangement of cells. All the cells in any small region of cortex have their receptive fields in roughly the same part of the retina, and usually the fields overlap extensively. As one goes from cell to cell in a penetration through the cortex there is a small more or less random variation or staggering in the positions of the fields. Cells situated a centimeter apart will have their fields in separate regions of the retina, the exact position depending on the detailed topographic map. More interesting and unexpected is the finding that almost invariably the receptive field orientations of two neighboring cells are, as far as one can tell, identical. As an electrode advances through the cortex there are usually long sequences of cells all having the same receptive field orientation, with sudden shifts in orientation between the sequences. The cells turn out to be aggregated into more or less cylindrical regions of common receptive field orientation which extend from surface to white matter. These columns probably vary considerably in size, with cross-sectional diameters ranging from about 50–100 μ in up to around 0.5 mm.

The number of cells in a column is hard to estimate, but for the largest column it might be a few tens of thousands. A column is apparently a functional unit of cortex, its cells having rich interconnections, with few interconnections between cells in different columns. Any given small region of retina is thus represented in the cortex by many columns subserving different orientations, vertical, oblique or horizontal. There is no suggestion that cells with any particular receptive-field orientation, such as vertical or horizontal, are more common than cells with any other. To look after the entire retina, with all possible orientations represented, and additional specialization within the individual columns for light lines, dark lines, and edges, obviously requires a vast number of cells, but this is no cause for skepticism or concern, since a vast number of cells is just what the cortex has.

Binocular Interaction

It is obviously important to understand how the inputs from the two eyes combine, if we are to interpret the results of closing one eye. As seen in Figure 1, the first structure in the retino-cortical path to receive binocular input is the lateral geniculate body. At that stage the influences of the two eyes are for all practical purposes kept strictly separate, the geniculate being divided into discrete layers, with the arriving optic fibers segregated so that all cells in a given layer get input from one eye only. In the 3-layered geniculate of the cat the uppermost and the inferior layers receive input from the contralateral eye, the middle from the ipsilateral.

In the cortex the situation is more complex. In the cat we find that about 80% of cells receive input from both eyes, the remaining 20% having input from a single eye, either the ipsilateral or the contralateral. It is therefore important to learn how, in a cell with binocular input, the influences of the two eyes compare. Putting the question in concrete terms, one can record from a single cell, and map out the receptive field first in one eye and then in the other, comparing the two with respect to position, orientation, optimum stimulus, and so on.

The results are clear and consistent. First, the receptive fields are situated, as far as one can tell with present methods, on exactly corresponding points in the two retinas. This means that if a cell's receptive field as measured in the left eye is 2° above and 3° to the left of the fovea, in the right eye it will also be 2° up and 3° to the left of the fovea (Figure 3A). Second, for each cell the properties of the optimal stimulus for the left eye are exactly the same as those for the right. If an edge works best in the left eye, it will work best for the right; if orientation is 2.30 o'clock for the left it will also be 2.30 o'clock for the right; if downward movement is favored in the left eye, it will be favored in the right; whatever rate of movements is optimal for one eye will be optimal for the other. Finally, in one important respect the two eyes do not necessarily have identical effects: when the retinas are stimulated separately with the optimum stimulus the two resulting responses are not necessarily

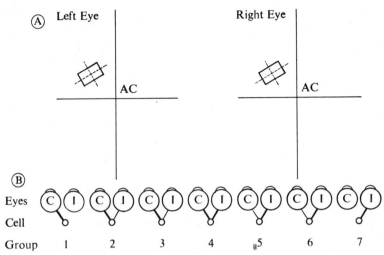

FIGURE 3.   A. Receptive fields of a typical cell in cat striate cortex, as
mapped for the left and right eyes. Each diagram represents the visual field
as seen by one eye; AC represents the *area centralis* (equivalent of the fovea
of primates), or center of gaze. Receptive fields are in corresponding regions
of the visual fields of the two eyes, and the orientation and preferred direction of movement are the same.

B. Diagram illustrating the seven ocular dominance groupings. A cell
(small circle) in the right hemisphere may be influenced equally from the 2
eyes (Group 4); it may receive input only from the contralateral (C) eye
(Group 1) or only from the ipsilateral (I) eye (Group 7). For the intermediate groups one eye may influence the cell much more than the other
(Groups 2 and 6) or the difference may be slight (Groups 3 and 5).

equal in strength. The response evoked by the ipsilateral eye may exceed that
from the contralateral eye (measuring the response by the number of impulses in a unit of time), or it may be less or the two may be equal. All shades
of relative ocular dominance are found, from complete dominance by the
contralateral eye, through equality, to complete dominance by the ipsilateral.
Cells thus apparently vary in the relative richness of connections from the two
eyes, though in other respects the two sets of connections seem to be exact
duplicates.

Proceeding from cell to cell in a penetration through the cortex,
one can observe the relative influence of the two eyes on each cell. From one
cell to the next this generally differs, and it becomes convenient to have a
rough way of measuring the relative dominance. We therefore divide cells into
seven categories depending on their ocular dominance. As illustrated in Figure
3B, a group 1 cell receives its input exclusively from the contralateral eye, a
group 7 cell exclusively from the ipsilateral. Groups 2–6 represent the binocularly driven cells: Group 4 represents cells driven equally from the two, while
for groups 2 and 3 the contralateral eye predominates markedly or slightly:
and for 6 and 5 the ipsilateral eye predominates markedly or slightly. Thus for
a given cell one has only to decide whether the two eyes have equal influence

or not, and if not whether the dominance is slight (groups 3 and 5) marked (groups 2 and 6) or complete (groups 1 and 7). The classification is rough and the decision is occasionally arbitrary, since two observers may disagree on whether, for example, one eye predominates slightly or markedly. Nevertheless it is unlikely that a cell would ever be misassigned by more than one group.

When a cell with connections to both eyes is stimulated by both eyes in corresponding parts of the two retinas, as happens when an animal fixes on an object, the response evoked is much greater than that from either eye alone. This is illustrated in Figure 4 for a cell that responded optimally to a

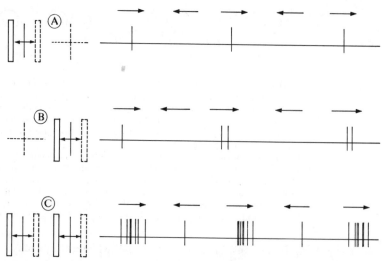

FIGURE 4.   Movement of a ¼ x 2° slit back and forth horizontally across the receptive field of a binocularly influenced cell. A, left eye; B, right eye; C, both eyes. The cell clearly preferred left-to-right movement, but when both eyes were stimulated together it responded also to the reverse direction. Field diameter, 2°, situated 5° from the area centralis. Time, 1 sec. From (6).

vertical slit moved across its field from left to right. With either eye alone this stimulation evoked only one or two spikes, but with both together a burst of 8–12 spikes was evoked. Even leftward movement, which produced no response to a single eye, now gave a weak but clear response.

To examine animals brought up under conditions of asymmetric eye input, one needs to know as accurately as possible what to expect from an electrode penetration in a normal cortex. A typical experiment done for this purpose in a normal adult cat is shown in Figure 5. The center of the slide shows tracings of two coronal sections through striate cortex, the upper from the right hemisphere, the lower from the left. In each hemisphere the electrode track, traced from histological sections, is shown entering the cortex and extending through about one-half of the thickness of grey matter. A small elec-

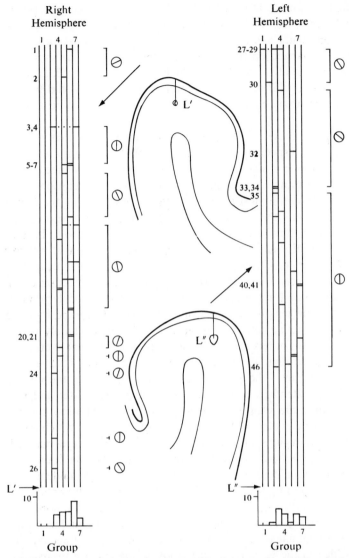

FIGURE 5. Reconstruction of two penetrations, one in each hemisphere, through striate cortex of a normal adult cat. In the middle of figure are shown tracings of coronal sections through the postlateral gyri. The electrode tracks are shown terminated by electrolytic lesions L′ and L″. To either side the tracks are reconstructed, each cell indicated by a short horizontal line placed in its appropriate ocular-dominance group. Two horizontal lines close together, or dots between pairs of lines, indicate two-unit recordings. For each group, the total number of cells are shown in the histogram below. Lines to the right within the circles indicate by their tilt the receptive-field orientation of the cells within the brackets. From (10).

trolytic lesion made at the end of each track for marking purposes is shown as a small circle. For each cell studied the electrode depth was noted, and the ocular dominance and receptive field orientation were recorded. This information is summarized on the sides of the figure, where the short horizontal bars indicate the relative depths at which cells were recorded, and the vertical columns the ocular-dominance group of each cell. At the bottom the results are summed up by histograms indicating the number of cells recorded in each group.

In these two penetrations it can be seen that most ocular-dominance groups, especially the middle ones (3–5) are fairly well represented. In addition there is a suggestion of segregation of dominance groups within the cortex. For example, in the penetration in the right hemisphere (shown to the left in the figure), almost all of the cells recorded during the first two-thirds of the penetration either favored the ipsilateral eye or were neutral, whereas in the final one-third most cells favored the contralateral. In the penetration through the left hemisphere there was no such emphasis, but instead a mixture of group 4 cells and cells favoring one or other eye; there were also simultaneous recordings of cells many groups apart. Studies of this type indicate a tendency for the cortex to be subdivided by ocular-dominance grouping, with some regions of cortex predominantly influenced by the contralateral eye and containing few cells in groups 5–7, others mainly ipsilateral in emphasis, and still others mixed. It should be stressed that even in a contralaterally dominated region the great majority of the cells receive input also from the ipsilateral eye; the point is that most cells favor the contralateral. The regions can extend from cortical surface to white matter and may be columnar, but they are clearly independent of the orientation columns. Figure 6 shows a surface map of a small area of cortex in which both orientation columns and regions of ipsilateral eye dominance were mapped by making many very superficial microelectrode penetrations. The boundaries in the two systems, far from being superimposed, seem quite independent.

The importance of a segregation of cells by ocular dominance for our present discussion is a practical one. In assessing the normality of the cortex in a deprived animal by making a small sampling of cells in a few penetrations, the regional variation on ocular dominance may become important. To get an idea of the variation in the adult normal cat we prepared ocular-dominance histograms from 12 successive penetrations (Figure 7). In most penetrations all but one or two groups were represented, but as expected, some, such as numbers 4, 5, and 6, were predominantly contralateral in emphasis, and others, such as number 9, were predominantly ipsilateral. Clearly a penetration must give results far more asymmetric than numbers 2, 4, or 5 in Figure 7 before one can consider the cortex abnormal. The problem of sampling becomes less important of course as more cells are studied in a penetration or when several long penetrations are made in one animal.

An idea of the relative ocular dominance in the cortex as a whole can be obtained from the pooled results of many penetrations. A histogram

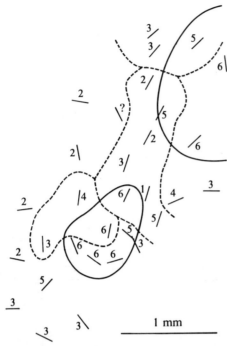

FIGURE 6.   Map in normal adult cat showing receptive-field orientations and ocular-dominance of first cells, encountered near the surface, in 31 penetrations. The region of the right striate cortex covered by the entire map measures about 1½ x 4 mm. Interrupted lines separate regions of relatively constant receptive-field orientation, partly outlining 3 columns. The numbers refer to ocular-dominance groups. Continuous lines separate areas of strong ipsilateral dominance from areas of mixed or contralateral dominance. From (7, 10).

based on 223 cells from 45 penetrations is shown in Figure 8. Groups 1–3 contain about twice as many cells as groups 5–7, suggesting a minor overall skew distribution in favor of the contralateral eye. The extreme groups 1 and 7 together make up about 14% of the total.

   To sum up: in judging an individual penetration, one can consider Figure 8 to represent the normal, and regard as probably abnormal only departures much greater than those of penetration 2 and 4 of Figure 7.

Physiology in Visually Deprived Animals

Opaque Occlusion

   A few years ago it seemed to us that with the knowledge of the normal visual system of cats and monkeys, visual physiology had reached the stage where the effects on the central nervous system of gross changes in past experience might be detectable. We therefore did the preliminary experiment

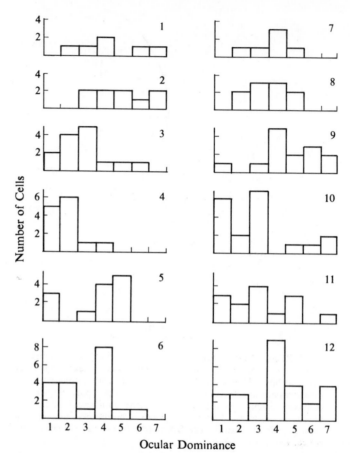

FIGURE 7. Ocular-dominance histograms from 12 separate consecutive penetrations in striate cortex of normal adult cats. Each histogram is compiled as illustrated in Figure 5. From (21).

of sewing shut the lids of the right eye of a newborn kitten, and letting the animal live a relatively normal life for three months. A recording was then made from the visual cortex, with the object of looking for any possible abnormalities, particularly any changes in relative dominance of the two eyes. The kitten was anesthetized and the right eye opened. The cornea and media were clear, the fundus seemed normal, and the direct and consensual pupillary reflexes were normal, indicating that at least some of the retina and optic nerve fibers must have survived.

The results of a recording from the left hemisphere, shown in Figure 9, could hardly have been more extreme. None of the cells examined could be influenced by the eye that had been closed. Most cells responded to the left eye only—the eye that had been open all along. A small number were driven by neither eye, something that one does not see in normal cortex.

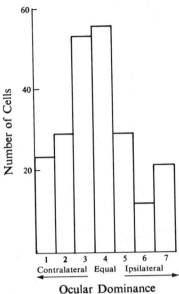

FIGURE 8.   Ocular-dominance distribution of 223 cells recorded from striate cortex of adult cats, in a series of 45 penetrations. From (6).

Encouraged by this unexpected result we quickly repeated the experiment in two other kittens with much the same outcome. Of the first 84 cells recorded, only one was affected by the closed eye, and this was abnormal in its responses.

Finding even one cell that responded to the eye that had been closed suggested that there probably were others, and for reasons that will become apparent later it seemed important to find out just how scarce or plentiful these cells were. Given a tendency to spatial aggregation of cells favoring one or other eye, it seemed possible that in the deprived animals there might persist groups or pockets of cells still capable of responding to the occluded eye. We therefore made an intensive search for such cells, doing 5 more penetrations in two right-eye deprived kittens, recording from 115 more cells. The results are shown in Figure 10. In the first kitten (Figure 10 left) no cells were influenced from the right eye, compared with 50 normally driven from the left. In the second kitten, however, there were a few cells that could be driven from the right eye, and these indeed showed a tendency to be aggregated. The largest cluster of cells was seen near the end of penetration 4 in the left hemisphere.

Figure 11 shows a final histogram containing information on all cells recorded from kittens raised from birth with monocular eye closure. Of 199 cells only 13 responded to the deprived eye, and it is interesting that of these, 12 responded to the previously closed eye in an abnormal way, either inconsistently or without the orientation specificity seen in normal cells.

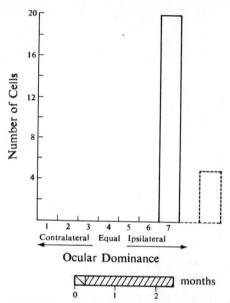

FIGURE 9.   Ocular-dominance distribution of 25 cells recorded in the
visual cortex of a 2½-month-old kitten. Experimental procedures are indicated beneath; during the first week the eyes were not yet open; on the
eighth day the lids of the right eye were sutured, and they remained closed
until the time of the experiment (shaded region). The left eye opened
normally on the ninth day. Recordings were made from the left visual cortex, contralateral to the eye that had been closed. Five of the cells, represented by the interrupted column on the right, could not be driven from
either eye. The remaining 20 were driven only from the normally exposed
(left, or ipsilateral) eye, and were therefore classed as group 7. From (21).

The conclusion from this first set of experiments is that monocular
occlusion for three months is capable of producing a profound abnormality in
the visual pathway. The results raised a number of obvious questions, which
we now set about trying to answer.

Site of Abnormality

One cannot conclude, from the above experiments alone, that anything was wrong with the cortex itself. Cortical cells, it is true, failed to respond to stimulation of one eye, but there was no guarantee that the abnormality was not in the retina or geniculate. This was easily tested in the
same experiments by putting electrodes also into the geniculate. Here there
were plenty of cells that responded apparently normally to stimulation of the
previously occluded eye. One had the impression that the activity was not
quite as rich in the layers receiving afferents from the deprived eye, but there
certainly was no abnormality comparable to that seen in the cortex. This
made it very likely that the site of the abnormality was the cortex, a conclusion
strongly reinforced by subsequent findings.

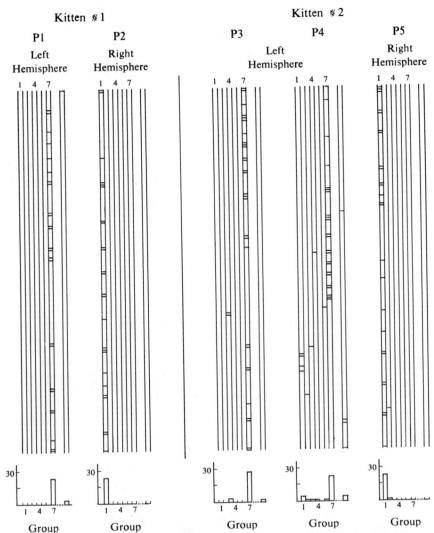

FIGURE 10. Schematic reconstructions of five microelectrode penetrations in two kittens. Kitten 1 was 8 weeks old and kitten 2, 10 weeks; both had the right eye closed by lid suture at 8 days. Each penetration extended into cortical gray matter for about 1.5 mm. The penetrations are drawn so as to indicate relative positions of individual cells; each cell is represented by a short horizontal line placed in the appropriate vertical row according to ocular-dominance group. The separate row to the right of group 7 is for unresponsive cells. The total number of cells in each group is indicated in the histogram at the bottom. From (22).

In view of this relative normality of geniculate-cell responses it came as a great surprise to find that histologically the cells were quite abnormal. Cells in the layers that received input from the eye that had been closed were smaller, paler, and more closely packed than those in the other layers.

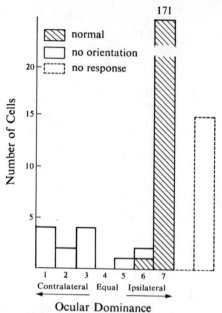

FIGURE 11.   Ocular-dominance distribution of 199 cells recorded in the visual cortex of 5 monocularly deprived kittens. The animals were 8–14 weeks old and all had the right eye closed by lid suture from the time of normal eye opening. Shading indicates cells that had the usual specific response properties to visual stimulation; absence of shading indicates cells that lacked the normal orientation specificity. Interrupted lines indicate cells that did not respond to either eye. From (22).

Careful measurements showed these cells to be decreased in cross sectional area by 40%. We have learned subsequently that the small size of the geniculate cells represents chiefly a failure of cells to grow at the normal rate, rather than a genuine atrophy. At birth the cross sectional area of geniculate cells in the dorsal layer is about ⅓ of the normal adult size. With one eye closed the cells in the layers getting input from that eye increase in size, but at a reduced rate, attaining ⅔ of normal size in three months. By contrast, a normal kitten's geniculate cells seem to be fully grown by that time. If instead of occluding an eye it is removed one week after birth, the cells at 3 months seem not to have grown at all.

Thus while physiologically most geniculate cells seemed normal, anatomically there were rather marked changes. Conceivably the size of a cell may be related to its overall activity or use, and not necessarily to its ability to respond normally. Our present impression is that there are probably abnormalities at all levels of the visual system, from retina on.

Translucent Occluders

It seemed appropriate at this point to ask what it was about the eye closures that led to such profound effects. Suturing the eyes certainly prevents any stimulation of the retina by forms or contours. It can also be shown to reduce the entering light by about 4–5 log units (a factor of 10,000 to 100,000): but the light that does reach the eyes is probably not insignificant, given a dynamic range of some 10 log units, and the great sensitivity of the dark adapted cat eye. Any diffuse light reaching the retina would undoubtedly activate the geniculate cells to some extent, but should have practically no influence on cortical cells.

To learn whether our results were related to deprivation of form or of light, we brought up a few kittens by covering one eye with a translucent contact occluder—a plastic with the consistency of opal glass or a ping-pong ball. This undoubtedly abolished all form vision, but reduced the incident light by only about 1–2 log units. On recording from the cortex after 2–3 months the results were practically identical to those obtained with lid suture, with cells virtually unresponsive to the occluded eye, and a small number that failed to respond to either eye. Our conclusion is that form deprivation rather than light deprivation was the important thing in eye-suture experiments, so far as the cortical abnormality is concerned. In the geniculate of the kittens deprived with translucent occluders the cells receiving input from the deprived eyes were again shrunken, but this time the decrease in cross sectional area amounted to only about 10%, a change that was difficult to be sure of by simple inspection under a microscope. Form deprivation, then, is not nearly as damaging to geniculate cells as is deprivation by eye suture—a finding that is reasonable in view of the responsiveness of geniculate cells to diffuse light.

Behavioral Testing

The vision of these animals, deprived by lid suture or a translucent occluder, when tested at 2–3 months, was of course normal in the eye that had been open, but seemed very defective if not entirely absent in the deprived eye. With the good eye covered, the animal when placed on the floor bumped into obstacles such as table legs; when put up on a table it groped towards the edge and on jumping failed to land on its feet. Objects moved in front of the kitten were not followed, and visual placing reactions were absent. These behavioral results agree with these obtained by rearing kittens in darkness (17).

Studies on Newborn Kittens

In thinking about the results of dark rearing it has been customary to attribute the resulting blindness to a sort of failure to learn, as though the animal had been born without the necessary connections, and had not gone on to develop them because of the absence of a normal visual learning experience. However attractive this idea may be, it is not the only possibility. Connections already present and fully developed at birth might be lost through disuse. To test this second possibility we did some recordings on kittens a few days after birth, before the time at which the eyes normally open. (In the cat this occurs at about the 8th to 10th day.) To our surprise we found that all of the specific types of response seen in the adult cat's striate cortex are present in the newborn visually naive animal. Figure 12 for example, shows the responses of a cortical cell in an 8-day-old kitten; here active firing occurred when a 1:00 oriented slit was moved across the receptive field, but there was no response to a 4:00 slit. The newborn animal also possesses a columnar arrangement of cells by receptive field orientation, and the binocular apparatus described above.

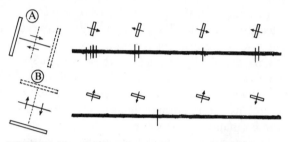

FIGURE 12.   Single-cell responses from cortex of an 8-day-old kitten with no previous visual experience. A rectangle of light 1° x 5° is moved back and forth across the receptive field in the contralateral eye. Unit binocularly activated, ocular-dominance group 3. Receptive-field sizes about 5° x 5°; fields situated in the central part of the contralateral visual field. A; stimulus oriented 12:30–6:30 (parallel to receptive-field axis). B; stimulus oriented 9:30–3:30 (at right angles to the optimal orientation). Rate of movement, 5°/sec. Time, 1 sec. From (8).

This is not to say that the system is necessarily fully developed at birth. Histologically the cortex of the newborn kitten is in many ways different from that of the adult. Physiologically, the sensitivity to orientation of lines tends to be somewhat less impressive in the newborn animal than in the adult. This seems to have nothing to do with experience but to be a matter simply of development, since if one or both eyes are kept closed by suturing the lids for 3–4 weeks after birth (too short a time for deprivation effects to take place) the responses are then just as precise and specific as in the adult. Up to the level of the striate cortex the connections are thus innately determined and do not require visual experience for their development. Needless to say this puts a certain burden on the underlying genetic mechanisms.

Delay of Eye Closure

From the evidence so far given, one would conclude that the connections up to the striate cortex are for all practical purposes formed at birth or develop soon after, even without visual stimulation; if the connections are not used, they tend to become non-functional. Preliminary studies in which deprivation is begun on the 8–10th day and continued for varying lengths of time indicate that the critical period is somewhere around the 4th and 6th week; monocular deprivation ending before the 4th week of life produces little or no physiological defect, while lid closure for more than 6 weeks gives the full-blown picture seen at 3 months. In some ways this is not surprising, since for the first 4 weeks a kitten seems to make little use of its vision but stays with its mother and litter mates under the sofa.

If it is true that our eye-closure results are related to deterioration of connections already formed, rather than to a failure of a pathway to develop, is it really necessary to raise the animals with an eye closed from birth, or might one just as well work with older cats? To test this we delayed the time of operation for several weeks and then closed an eye for a few months. Figure 13 shows histograms from an animal whose right eye was closed from

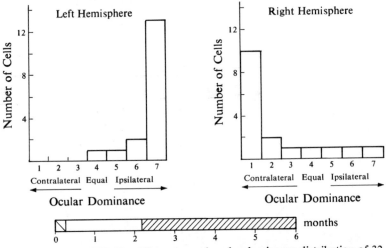

FIGURE 13.   Histograms of ocular-dominance distribution of 32 cells recorded in two penetrations, one in the left visual cortex and one in the right. Kitten whose right eye was closed by lid suture at 9 weeks, for a period of 4 months. Seventeen cells recorded from each hemisphere. All cells were influenced by patterned-light stimulation. From (21).

the second to the sixth month. The cortex was unquestionably abnormal in that only a very few cells favored the deprived eye, while a pathologically high proportion failed to respond to it at all. On the other hand the abnormality was nothing like as severe as in animals deprived from birth. Apparently each month of normal vision makes the animal less susceptible, and an adult deprived from three months failed to show any abnormality at all. This animal was by definition an adult, being the mother of one of our litters. It seems, then, that at birth this part of the nervous system possesses a certain flexibility, expressed as a sensitivity to the effects of distorted sensory input, and that somewhere between infancy and adulthood this flexibility is lost.

The importance of age on the effects of sensory deprivation will come as no surprise to the clinical ophthalmologist. A man of sixty who has a cataract removed after five years of blindness sees well as soon as the loss of his lens is compensated for by glasses. In contrast, when congenital cataracts are removed in a child or adult the subject cannot see immediately, and vision returns at a painfully slow rate, possibly never reaching normal (19). In the cat recovery likewise seems to be very slow. Figure 14 shows the result of closing the right eye for the first three months of life and then having it open for the next year and two months. During the time the right eye was open we closed the left eye in an attempt to promote recovery as much as possible, just as a clinician patches the normal eye in treating *amblyopia ex anopsia*. The result was that all of the cells we observed strongly favored the eye that had been open for the first three months, even though that eye had subsequently been closed for more than a year! There was thus very little recovery from the early eye closure, though there was clearly some. In this and other

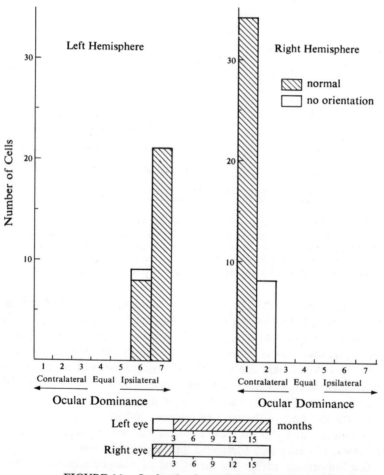

FIGURE 14.   Ocular dominance of 72 cells recorded from a cat in which the right eye was closed for the first 3 months of life, following which the right eye was opened and left eye closed for the next 14 months. From (23).

experiments many of the cells that could be driven from the originally deprived eye were abnormal, responding inconsistently and without the usual sharply defined optimum stimulus orientation. It was as if some connections had become re-established, but more or less at random.

Behaviorally also the recovery of these animals seems limited and incomplete. After months with an eye open an animal will still react inappropriately or be slow to react to visual stimuli. Ultimately it becomes able to follow large objects, and after a year or more it may develop some ability to discriminate form. Whether vision ever becomes entirely normal is not yet clear.

Binocular Closures

Up to this point the results seem to be accounted for in a straightforward way by assuming that at an early age deterioration of cortical connections is the result of disuse. Two further experiments have made us realize that the situation is more complicated and far more interesting.

The first experiment was to take four kittens and suture both eyes closed for the first 3 months. We had hoped to avoid this radical procedure, but became convinced that we must do it if our results were to be compared with those obtained in dark reared animals. We assumed that, unless the two pathways from eye to brain interacted in an unexpected way, the results should be predictable from the one-eye closures. Just as closing one eye gave a cortex with large areas devoid of cells responsive to that eye, so on closing both eyes we expected to find large areas of cortex containing no responsive cells, with only occasional islands of cells responding aberrantly to one or other eye. This was not at all the result. Most cells that were recorded (73%) responded to visual stimuli, and of those that responded more than half were, as far as one could tell, quite normal. The number of unresponsive cells may well have been greater than 27%, since such cells are only detected by their spontaneous activity or their firing when injured by the electrode. Nevertheless there were not large regions of unresponsive cortex. The results from 126 cells recorded in 4 kittens are given in Figure 15. While the unexpected thing in these animals was the large number of normal cells, it should be emphasized that the cortex was still far from normal, both with respect to the unresponsive cells and to those that fired inconsistently and lacked the normal response specificity.

This result means that the effects of a right-eye closure upon a single cortical cell cannot be predicted unless one is told whether the left eye was also closed: it seems that the chances of the connections surviving are much less if the left eye is kept open. We have no idea of the detailed mechanisms involved, and though it is tempting to imagine the left eye taking over control of a cell when the connections from the right are at a disadvantage, there is no direct evidence that anything like this occurs. But in any case it is not entirely easy to account for the results of monocular closure in terms of simple disuse.

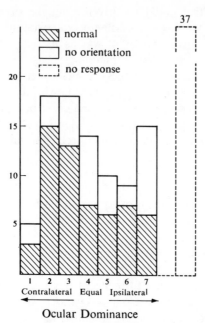

FIGURE 15.   Ocular-dominance distribution of 126 cells recorded from the 4 binocularly deprived kittens in 10 penetrations. From (22).

When tested behaviorally these animals seemed to be quite blind. This may seem strange in view of the normally responding cells in the cortex, but it must be remembered that the striate cortex represents only one stage, and surely an early one, in the visual pathway, and nothing is known about the integrity of connections at later stages. In the monocularly closed animals many cells in the striate cortex and beyond receive normal input from the good eye, whereas in binocular closure they are obviously cut off from all visual input.

Strabismus

The second surprising experiment was motivated by clinical considerations. An adult who develops a squint (strabismus, or non-parallel eyes) usually continues to see double indefinitely if vision in both eyes is normal. In an infant or child with squint, vision in one eye is apparently soon suppressed, so that double vision is ordinarily only transient. If the squint persists one of two things happen—the vision in one eye may deteriorate, so that ultimately the eye becomes useless (*amblyopia ex anopsia*), or the eyes may alternate, each fixing in turn. In alternating squint, vision in both eyes may remain normal.

We decided to produce a squint in newborn kittens to see whether we could obtain an amblyopia and study the mechanisms involved. We therefore cut the medial rectus muscles in each of four kittens, producing florid divergent squints in all of them. The result was disappointing, for three months later the cats all had perfectly normal vision in both eyes. Even before testing the animals we had expected this, since they all appeared to be fixating first with one eye and then with the other.

With little idea of what might be found, we decided to record from the cortex of one of the animals. The result is shown in Figure 16. At the outset the penetration seemed unremarkable, with many cells responding perfectly normally. As the penetration progressed, however, we were surprised to find a decided lack of binocularly driven cells. Cell after cell would fall into group 7, then there might be a mixture of sevens and ones with occasional cells from other groups interspersed, and finally there would occur another long sequence, either all group 7 again or all group 1. The resulting histogram, shown at the bottom of the track reconstruction, was quite unlike anything we had ever seen in normal animals. The squint had evidently produced a sharp decline in binocularly activated cells.

Very similar results were found in the other three animals. The most extreme result was obtained in an animal brought up with squint for a year; here only four cells out of 64 could be driven from both eyes, these belonging to groups 2 and 6. Out of a total of 384 cells recorded in all 4 animals with squint, 79% were monocularly driven compared with 20% in the normal cat (Figure 17).

In these experiments it seems clear that the decline in cells of groups 2–6 does not represent a simple dropping out of these cells. Not only were the penetrations (such as that of Figure 16) especially rich in cells, hardly supporting the idea that 80% of the cells were missing, but there were long sequences of group 1 cells or of group 7 cells, instead of an almost random mixture of groups 1 and 7, as would have occurred had the other cells simply become unresponsive. On the other hand, a shift in ocular dominance, with cells of groups 2 and 3 moving into group 1, and 5 and 6 moving to group 7, explains the findings perfectly, given the normal tendency for segregation of cells by eye preference (see Figures 5 and 6). With squint, then, it seems that for each cell the dominant eye tends to take over, at least relative to the nondominant eye: whether the influence of the dominant eye increases absolutely is not known. The scarcity of group 4 cells suggests that for a given cell even a slight imbalance in the influence from the two eyes tends to increase, leading finally to a complete loss of the control from one eye.

The squint experiments seem to us particularly interesting in that the overall input from the two eyes is presumably normal. What is not normal is the time relationships between the impulses from the two eyes. This becomes easier to visualize if one considers a particular binocularly driven cell in the cortex, say a group 3. As described above, the two receptive fields of this cell occupy corresponding positions on the two retinas, and are similar in organization. Furthermore, when the eyes fix normally on an object the image falls on corresponding parts of the retina. From this (and neglecting parallax) it follows that when the cell receives input tending to activate it from the

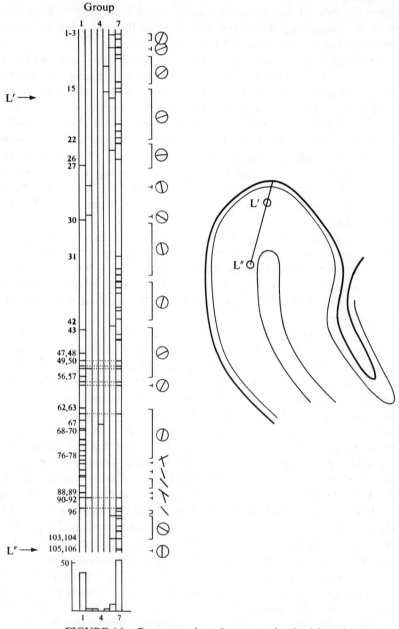

FIGURE 16.   Reconstruction of a penetration in right striate cortex of kitten age 3 months, with divergent strabismus from 8 days. For conventions see Figure 5. From (10).

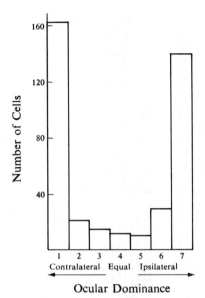

FIGURE 17.   Ocular-dominance histogram for 384 cells recorded from 4 kittens with strabismus. From (10).

dominant eye, it will also receive an activating input from the nondominant eye. This is true whether the cell under consideration itself represents the site of convergence of inputs from the 2 eyes, or is further downstream. In an animal with strabismus the relationship is entirely changed: if the cell is excited from one eye, it may be excited or inhibited or it may receive no input from the other, depending on what contours happen to cross the receptive field in that eye. Somehow, if the situation persists in the young animal, the non-dominant input apparently declines and ultimately is lost. Just as in the monocular versus the binocular closures, the detailed mechanisms are at present a mystery, but from both lines of evidence one can at least say that the two pathways are interdependent.

A final experiment was done with the idea of testing whether the squint results were produced by the lack of synergism between the 2 eyes, or whether they were related more to some kind of active antagonism or competition. To prevent the eyes from working together we brought up two animals for three months with an opaque occluder placed over one eye on one day and the other eye the next, alternating eyes each day. After three months the animals seemed to have normal vision. The experimental results are seen in Figure 18. The effect was similar, and if anything was even more extreme than that produced by squint. It seems, then, the squint result comes from the eyes not working together, rather than from some form of active competition. Binocular occlusion (Figure 15) did not give any radical decline in binocularly activated cells, so that one must stipulate that, for the squint result, one must have stimulation of the eyes, but no cooperation.

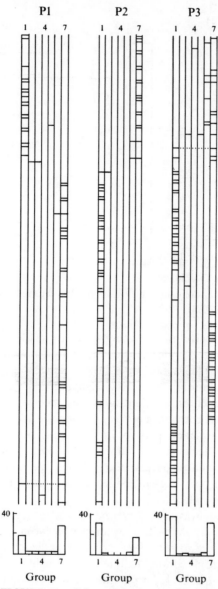

FIGURE 18.   Schematic reconstruction of three penetrations in the
striate cortex of two 10-week-old kittens raised from the time of normal eye
opening with an opaque contact occluder covering one eye one day, and the
other eye the next. Each penetration extended into cortical gray matter for
about 1.5 mm. From (10).

Final Comments

In summing up this work, one may say that in the cat's visual system the cortical connections may be seriously damaged by distortion of sensory input in the early months of life, in the absence of any direct tampering with any part of the pathway. The effects may depend on disuse, but this can only be part of the story: a full account must take into consideration the interrelationships between the different inputs to the systems.

There is a remarkable correspondence between the form of the sensory distortion and the damage produced. Deprivation of form with continued exposure to light tends to spare the geniculate, most of whose cells respond to diffuse light, but it affects the cortex, whose cells are influenced by form but not by light as such. In light deprivation (which includes form deprivation) the geniculate is also affected, at least morphologically. Finally, interference with the ability of the two eyes to work together produces adverse effects strictly confined to the connections that presumably are important for binocular vision. The extent to which this list may be expanded by future work can only be guessed at now, especially since the main obstacle to extending such studies is our ignorance of the brain mechanisms involved in much of perception, to say nothing of emotions or motor activity. Some of the next steps are rather obvious: as one comes to understand more about things like color physiology, binocular stereopsis, or form recognition, appropriate deprivation experiments will become possible. It will be important to compare visual deprivation results in the cat and monkey, once enough is known about the physiology of vision in the normal monkey, especially because the time course of the susceptible period may be quite different in different species, with the monkey intermediate between cat and man, and probably considerably closer to man. Perhaps the most exciting possibility for the future is the extension of this type of work to other systems besides sensory. Experimental psychologists and psychiatrists both emphasize the importance of early experience on subsequent behavior patterns—could it be that deprivation of social contacts or the existence of other abnormal emotional situations early in life may lead to a deterioration or distortion of connections in some yet unexplored parts of the brain? If so, one may hope that someday even the concepts of Freud may be explained in neurophysiological terms.

References

1. Barlow, H. B., Hill, R. M., & Levick, W. R. Retinal ganglion cells responding selectivity to direction and speed of image motion in the rabbit. *J. Physiol.,* 1964, *173,* 377–407.

2. Dejours, S. F. Receptive fields of optic tract fibers in lizards. (Sceloporus SPP). (Doctoral dissertation). Harvard Univ., Cambridge, Mass., 1965.

3. DeValois, R. L., & Jones, A. E. Single-cell analysis of the organization of the primate color-vision system. In R. Jung & H. Kornhuber (Eds.), *The visual system: Neurophysiology and psychophysics.* Berlin: Springer, 1961. Pp. 178–191.

4. GREGORY, R. L., & WALLACE, J. G. Recovery from early blindness: A case study. *Exp. Psychol. Monographs.* London: W. Heffer & Sons, 1963.

5. HUBEL, D. H., & WIESEL, T. N. Receptive fields of single neurons in the cat's striate cortex. *J. Physiol.,* 1959, *148,* 574–591.

6. ———. Receptive fields, binocular interaction and functional architecture in the cat's visual cortex. *J. Physiol.,* 1962, *160,* 106–154.

7. ———. Shape and arrangement of columns in cat's striate cortex. *J. Physiol.,* 1963, *165,* 559–568.

8. ———. Receptive fields of cells in striate cortex of very young, visually inexperienced kittens. *J. Neurophysiol.,* 1963, *26,* 994–1002.

9. ———. Receptive fields and functional architecture in two non-striate visual areas (18 and 19) of the cat. *J. Neurophysiol.,* 1965, *28,* 229–289.

10. ———. Binocular interaction in striate cortex of kittens reared with artificial squint. *J. Neurophysiol.,* 1965, *28,* 1041–1059.

11. JUNG, R., & BAUMGARTNER, G. Hemmungs-mechanismen und bremsende Stabilisierung an einzelnen Neuronen des optischen cortex. *Pflügers Arch. Bd. Physiol.,* 1955, *261,* 434–456.

12. KUFFLER, S. W. Discharge patterns and functional organization of mammalian retina. *J. Neurophysiol.,* 1953, *16,* 37–68.

13. LETTVIN, J. Y., MATURANA, H. R., McCULLOCH, W. S., & PITTS, W. H. What the frog's eye tells the frog's brain. *Proc. Inst. Radio Engrs.,* 1959, *47,* 1940–1951.

14. MATURANA, H. R. Functional organization of the pigeon retina. In R. W. Gerard & J. W. Duyff (Eds.), *Information processing in the nervous system. Vol. III Proc. XXII. Intern. Congr. Physiol. Sci.* Leiden, 1962. Exerpta Medica Fndn., Amsterdam. Pp. 170–178.

15. MICHAEL, C. R. Receptive fields of directionally selective units in the optic nerve of the ground squirrel. *Science,* 1966, *152,* 1092–1094.

16. MINKOWSKI, M. Experimentelle Untersuchungen uber die Beziehungen der Grosshirnrinde und der Netzhaut zu den Primären *Arb. hirnanat. Inst. Zürich,* 1913, *7,* 259–362.

17. RIESEN, A. H. Stimulation as requirement for growth and function in behavioral development. In D. W. Fiske & S. R. Maddi, (Eds.), *Functions of varied experience.* Homewood, Ill.: Dorsey Press, 1961. Pp. 57–105.

18. TALBOT, S. A., & MARSHALL, W. H. Physiological studies on neural mechanisms of visual localization and discrimination. *Am. J. Ophthal.,* 1941, *24,* 1255–1263.

19. VONSENDEN, M. *Raum- und Gestaltauffassung bei operierten Blindgeborenen vor und nach der Operation,* J. Barth (Ed.). Leipzig, 1932. English trans. under title: *Space and Sight.* Glencoe, Ill.: Free Press, 1960.

20. WIESEL, T. N., and HUBEL, D. H. Effects of visual deprivation on morphology and physiology of cells in the cat's lateral geniculate body. *J. Neurophysiol.,* 1963, *26,* 978–993.

21. ———. Single cell responses in striate cortex of kittens deprived of vision in one eye. *J. Neurophysiol.,* 1963, *26,* 1003–1017.

22. ———. Comparison of the effects of unilateral and bilateral eye closures on cortical unit responses in kittens. *J. Neurophysiol.,* 1965, *28,* 1029–1040.

23. ———. Extent of recovery from the effects of visual deprivation in kittens. *J. Neurophysiol.,* 1965, *28,* 1060–1072.

24. ———. Spatial and chromatic interactions in the lateral geniculate body of the rhesus monkey. *J. Neurophysiol.,* 1966, *29,* 1115–1156.

25. WOLBARSHT, M. L., WAGNER, H. G., & MACNICHOL, E. F., JR. Receptive fields of retinal ganglion cells: extent and spectral sensitivity. In R. Jung & H. Kornhuber (Eds.), *The visual system: Neurophysiology and biophysics.* Berlin: Springer, 1961. Pp. 170–175.

In the early 1940's it was discovered that small lesions made in a precise area of the hypothalamus lead to overeating; the condition is called "hypothalamic hyperphagia." Many subsequent experiments have been done to study the behavioral characteristics of animals with such lesions and to trace the brain circuits that are involved. The hyperphagia rats gain weight much more rapidly on a soft, palatable high-fat diet than on the usual hard laboratory chow pellets. That is, the lesioned rats are sensitive to the external food stimuli, but they are not sensitive to internal bodily cues related to their food consumption. Obese human beings also appear to be sensitive to external food stimulation but insensitive to internal bodily stimuli, as Schachter shows in his entertaining article.

After noticing some striking similarities between the behavior of obese humans and of hypothalamic hyperphagic rats, Schachter makes a detailed comparison of the two kinds of subjects. The behavior of obese rats and humans corresponded in many ways, most of which would not have been predicted on a commonsense basis. In some cases there were interesting observations on the rats for which no human counterparts were known—we often know more about other species than about ourselves. Schachter, a behavioral psychologist rather than a physiological psychologist, designed experiments to fill in gaps in our knowledge of human behavior. A great deal of novel and nonobvious information about people was obtained from experiments modeled on research with rats. Then Schachter set about to generalize his interpretation. Rather than restricting it to food sensitivity, Schachter proposed that obese people are generally more sensitive to external stimuli than are normal-weight people. His research includes several ingenious experiments to test this hypothesis. Using this information, Schachter turns back to the animal studies and attempts to give a more complete interpretation of the behavior of rats with hypothalamic lesions—an interpretation which accounts for not only eating, but also activity and emotional behavior.

Some Extraordinary Facts About Obese Humans and Rats

Stanley Schachter

Several years ago, when I was working on the problem of the labeling of bodily states, I first became aware of Stunkard's (Stunkard & Koch, 1964) work on obesity and gastric motility. At that time, my students and I had been working on a series of studies concerned with the interaction of cognitive and physiological determinants of emotional state (Schachter, 1964). Our experiments had all involved manipulating bodily state by injections of adrenaline or placebo and simultaneously manipulating cognitive and situa-

Source: Reprinted by permission from *American Psychologist*, 1971, 26, 129–144. Copyright © 1971 by the American Psychological Association.

Note: The research reported has been supported by National Science Foundation Grant GS 732.

tional variables that were presumed to affect a subject's interpretation of his bodily state. In essence, these experiments had demonstrated that cognitive factors play a major role in determining how a subject interprets his bodily feelings. Precisely the same set of physiological symptoms—an adrenaline-induced state of sympathetic arousal—could be interpreted as euphoria, or anger, or anxiety, or indeed as no emotional state at all, depending very largely on our cognitive and situational manipulations. In short, there is not an invariant, one-to-one relationship between a set of physiological symptoms and a psychological state.

This conclusion was based entirely on studies that manipulated bodily state by the exogenous administration of adrenaline or some other agent. My interest in Stunkard's research was generated by the fact that his work suggested that the same conclusion might be valid for endogenous physiological states. In his study, Stunkard had his subjects do without breakfast and come to his laboratory at 9:00 A.M. They swallowed a gastric balloon, and for the next four hours, Stunkard continuously recorded stomach contractions. Every 15 minutes, he asked his subjects, "Do you feel hungry?" They answered "Yes" or "No," and that is all there was to the study. He has then a record of the extent to which stomach contractions coincide with self-reports of hunger. For normally sized subjects, the two coincide closely. When the stomach contracts, the normal subject is likely to report hunger; when the stomach is quiescent, the normal subject is likely to say that he does not feel hungry. For the obese, on the other hand, there is little correspondence between gastric motility and self-reports of hunger. Whether or not the obese subject describes himself as hungry seems to have almost nothing to do with the state of his gut. There are, then, major individual differences in the extent to which this particular bodily activity—gastric motility—is associated with the feeling state labeled "hunger."

To pursue this lead, we (Schachter, Goldman, & Gordon, 1968) designed an experiment in which we attempted to manipulate gastric motility and the other physiological correlates of food deprivation by the obvious technique of manipulating food deprivation so that some subjects had empty stomachs and others full stomachs before entering an experimental eating situation. The experiment was disguised as a study of taste, and subjects had been asked to do without the meal (lunch or dinner) that preceded the experiment.

When a subject arrived, he was, depending on condition, either fed roast beef sandwiches or fed nothing. He was then seated in front of five bowls of crackers, presented with a long set of rating scales and told, "We want you to judge each cracker on the dimensions (salty, cheesy, garlicky, etc.) listed on these sheets. Taste as many or as few of the crackers of each type as you want in making your judgments; the important thing is that your ratings be as accurate as possible."

The subject then tasted and rated crackers for 15 minutes, under the impression that this was a taste test, and we simply counted the number of crackers that he ate. There were, of course, two types of subjects: obese subjects (from 14% to 75% overweight) and normal subjects (from 8% underweight to 9% overweight).

To review expectations: If it is correct that the obese do not label as hunger the bodily states associated with food deprivation, then this manipulation should have no effect on the amount eaten by obese subjects; on the other hand, the eating behavior of normal subjects should directly parallel the effects of the manipulation on bodily state.

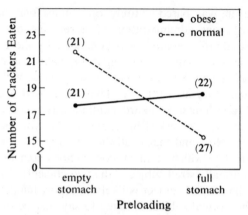

FIGURE 1.   The effects of preloading on eating

It will be a surprise to no one to learn, from Figure 1, that normal subjects ate considerably fewer crackers when their stomachs were full of roast beef sandwiches than when their stomachs were empty. The results for obese subjects stand in fascinating contrast. They ate as much—in fact slightly more—when their stomachs were full as when they were empty. Obviously, the actual state of the stomach has nothing to do with the eating behavior of the obese.[1]

In similar studies (Schachter, 1967; Schachter et al., 1968), we have attempted to manipulate bodily state by manipulating fear and by injecting subjects with epinephrine. Both manipulations are based on Cannon's (1915) and Carlson's (1916) demonstrations that both the state of fear and the injection of epinephrine will inhibit gastric motility and increase blood sugar—both peripheral physiological changes associated with low hunger. These manipulations have no effect at all on obese subjects, but do affect the amounts eaten by normal subjects.

It seems clear that the set of bodily symptoms the subject labels "hunger" differs for obese and normal subjects. Whether one measures gastric motility as Stunkard did, or manipulates motility and the other physiological

[1] The obese subject's failure to regulate when preloaded with sandwiches or some other solid food has now been replicated three times. Pliner's (1970) recent work, however, indicates that the obese will regulate, though not as well as normals, when preloaded with liquid food.

correlates of food deprivation, as I assume my students and I have done, one finds, for normal subjects, a high degree of correspondence between the state of the gut and eating behavior and, for obese subjects, virtually no correspondence.

Whether or not they are responsive to these particular visceral cues, the obese *do* eat, and the search for the cues that trigger obese eating occupied my students' and my attention for a number of years. Since the experimental details of this search have been published (Schachter, 1967, 1968, 1971), and I believe are fairly well known, I will take time now only to summarize our conclusions—eating by the obese seems unrelated to any internal, visceral state, but is determined by external, food-relevant cues such as the sight, smell, and taste of food. Now, obviously, such external cues to some extent affect anyone's eating behavior. However, for normals these external factors clearly interact with internal state. They may affect what, where, and how much the normal eats, but chiefly when he is in a state of physiological hunger. For the obese, I suggest, internal state is irrelevant, and eating is determined largely by external cues.

As you may know, there have been a number of experiments testing this hypothesis about the external sensitivity of the obese. To convey some feeling for the nature of the supporting data, I will describe two typical experiments. In one of these, Nisbett (1968a) examined the effects of the sight of food. He reasoned that if the sight of food is a potent cue, the externally sensitive, obese person should eat just as long as food is in sight, and when, in effect, he has consumed all of the available cues, he should stop and make no further attempt to eat. In contrast, the amounts eaten by a normal subject should depend on his physiological needs, not on the quantity of food in sight. Thus, if only a small amount of food is in sight but the subject is given the opportunity to forage for more, the normal subject should eat more than the obese subject. In contrast, if a large amount of food is in sight, the obese should eat more than the normal subject.

To test these expectations, Nisbett provided subjects, who had not eaten lunch, with either one or three roast beef sandwiches. He told them to help themselves and, as he was leaving, pointed to a refrigerator across the room and said, "There are dozens more sandwiches in the refrigerator. Have as many as you want." His results are presented in Table 1. As you can see,.

TABLE 1.   Effect of quantity of visible food on amounts eaten

	No. Sandwiches	
Subjects	*One*	*Three*
Normal	1.96	1.88
Obese	1.48	2.32

Note: From Nisbett (1968a).

obese subjects ate significantly more than normals when presented with three sandwiches, but ate significantly less than normals when presented with only one sandwich.

In another study, Decke (1971) examined the effects of taste on eating. She reasoned that taste, like the sight or smell of food, is essentially an external cue. Good taste, then, should stimulate the obese to eat more than normals, and bad taste, of course, should have the reverse effect.

TABLE 2.   Effect of taste on eating

Subjects	Ounces Consumed In	
	Good Taste	Bad Taste
Normal	10.6	6.4
Obese	13.9	2.6

Note: From Decke (1971).

In a taste test context, Decke provided her subjects with either a decent vanilla milk shake or with a vanilla milk shake plus quinine. The effects of this taste manipulation are conveyed in Table 2 where, as you can see, obese subjects drank more than normals when the milk shake was good and drank considerably less when the milk shake had been laced with quinine.

Now, anyone who sees Decke's milk shake data and who is familiar with physiological psychology will note that this is precisely what Miller, Bailey, and Stevenson (1950) found and what Teitelbaum (1955) found in the lesioned hyperphagic rat. For those of you who are unfamiliar with this preparation, let me review the facts about this animal. If you make bilateral lesions in the ventromedial nuclei of the hypothalamus, you are likely to get an animal that will eat prodigious amounts of food and will eventually achieve monumental weight—a creature of nightmares. This has been demonstrated for rats, cats, mice, monkeys, rabbits, goats, dogs, and sparrows. Classic descriptions of these preparations portray an animal that immediately after the operation staggers over to its food hopper and shovels in food. For several weeks, this voracious eating continues, and there is, of course, very rapid weight gain. This is called the dynamic phase of hyperphagia. Finally, a plateau is reached, at which point the animal's weight levels off, and its food intake drops to a level only slightly above that of the normal animal. This is called the static phase. During both the static and the dynamic stages, the lesioned animal is also characterized as markedly inactive, and as irascible, emotional, and generally bitchy.

Now it turns out that though the lesioned animal is normally a heavy eater, if you add quinine to its food it drastically decreases its intake to levels far below that of a normal animal's whose food has been similarly tainted. On the other hand, if to its normal food you add dextrose, or lard, or something that is apparently tasty to a rat, the lesioned animal increases its intake to levels considerably above its regular intake and above the intake of a control rat whose food has also been enriched.

The similarity of these facts about the finickiness of the lesioned rat to Decke's findings in her milk shake experiment is, of course, striking, and many people (notably Nisbett, 1968a, 1970) have pointed to this and other similarities between our data on obese humans and the physiologist's data on the obese rat. In order to determine if there was anything more to this than an engaging, occasional resemblance between two otherwise remotely connected sets of data, Judith Rodin and I decided to treat the matter dead seriously and, where possible, to make a point-for-point comparison of every fact we could learn about the hypothalamic, obese rat with every fact we could learn about the obese human. Before describing the results of our work, I would like, however, to be sure that you are aware of the areas of my expertise. I am not a physiological psychologist. Though I am pretty sure that I've eaten a hypothalamus, I doubt that I've ever seen one. When I say something like "bilateral lesions of the ventromedial nuclei of the hypothalamus," you can be sure that I've memorized it. I make this personal confession because of the dilemma that Rodin, also a physiological innocent, and I faced in our work. Though we couldn't have succeeded, we attempted to read *everything* about the ventromedial lesioned rat. If you've ever made this sort of attempt, you may have been seized by the same despair as were we when it sometimes seemed as if there were no such thing as a fact that *someone* had not failed to confirm. (I include in this sweeping generalization, by the way, the apparent fact that a ventromedial lesion produces a hyperphagic, obese animal—see Reynolds, 1963, and Rabin and Smith, 1968). And it sometimes seemed as if there were no such thing as an experiment which *someone* had not failed to replicate. Since I happen to have spent my college physics lab course personally disproving most of the laws of physics, I cannot say that I find this particularly surprising, but if one is trying to decide what is the fact, it is a depressing state of affairs. In our own areas of expertise, this probably isn't too serious a problem. Each of us in our specialities knows how to evaluate a piece of work. In a field in which you are not expert, you simply cannot, except in the crudest of cases, evaluate. If several experimenters have different results, you just don't know which to believe. In order to cope with this dilemma, Rodin and I decided to treat each of our facts in batting average terms. For each fact, I will inform you of the number of studies that have been concerned with the fact and the proportion of these studies that work out in a given direction. To be included in the batting average, we required only that a study present all or a substantial portion of its data, rather than report the author's impressions or present only the data of one or two presumably representative cases. I should also note that in all cases we have relied on the data and not on what the experimenter said about the data. It may seem silly to make this point explicit, but it is the case that in a few studies, for some perverse reason, the experimenter's conclusions simply have nothing to do with this data. Finally, I should note that in all comparisons of animal and human data, I will consider the data only for animals in the static phase of obesity, animals who, like our human subjects, are already fat. In general, however, the results for dynamic and static animals are quite similar.

As a shorthand method of making comparisons between studies and species, I shall throughout the rest of this article employ what we can call a Fat to Normal (F/N) ratio in which we simply get an index by dividing the magnitude of the effect for fat subjects by the magnitude of the effect for normal control subjects. Thus, if in a particular study the fat rats ate an average of 15 grams of food and normal rats ate 10 grams, the F/N ratio would be 1.50, indicating that the fat rats ate 50% more food than normal rats.

To begin our comparisons, let us return to the effects of taste on eating behavior. We know that fat human beings eat more of a good-tasting food than do normal human beings and that they eat less of bad-tasting food than do normals. The physiologists have done almost identical experiments to ours, and in Line 1 of Table 3 we can compare the effects of good-tasting

TABLE 3.   Effects of taste on eating

Condition	Animals		Humans	
	Batting Average	Mean F/N	Mean F/N	Batting Average
Good food	5/6	1.45	1.42	2/2
Bad food	3/4	.76	.84	1/2

Note: F/N = Fat to normal ratio.

food on lesioned animals and on men. You will notice on the left that Rodin and I found six studies on lesioned animals, in this case largely rats. Batting average: five of the six studies indicate that lesioned, static, obese animals eat more of a good-tasting food than do their normal controls. The average F/N ratio for these six studies is 1.45, indicating that fat rats on the average eat 45% more of good-tasting food than do normal rats. On the right side of the table, you can see that there have been two human studies, and that both of these studies indicate that fat humans eat more of good-tasting food than do normal humans. The average F/N ratio for humans is 1.42, indicating that fat humans eat 42% more of good-tasting food than do normally sized humans.[2]

Incidentally, please keep in mind throughout this exercise that the left side of each table will always contain the data for lesioned animals, very largely rats, that have been abused by a variety of people named Epstein, and

[2] The technically informed reader undoubtedly will wish to know precisely which studies and what data are included in Tables 3 and 4. There are so many studies involved that, within the context of this paper, it is impossible to supply this information. Dr. Rodin and I are preparing a monograph on this work which will, of course, provide full details on such matters.

Teitlebaum, and Stellar, and Miller, and so on. The right side of each table will always contain the data for humans, mostly Columbia College students, nice boys who go home every Friday night, where, I suppose, they too are abused by a variety of people named Epstein, and Teitelbaum, and Stellar, and Miller.

In Line 2 of Table 3, we have the effects of bad taste on consumption. For both animals and men, in all of these studies bad taste was manipulated by the addition of quinine to the food. There are four animal studies; three of the four indicate that fat animals eat less than normal animals, and the average F/N ratio is .76. There are two human studies: one of the two indicates that fats eat considerably less bad food than normals; the other indicates no significant difference between the two groups, and the mean F/N ratio for these two studies is .84. For this particular fact, the data are more fragile than one would like, but the trends for the two species are certainly parallel.

To continue this examination of parallel facts: the eating habits of the lesioned rats have been thoroughly studied, particularly by Teitelbaum and Campbell (1958). It turns out that static obese rats eat on the average slightly, not considerably, more than normal rats. They also eat fewer meals per day, eat more per meal, and eat more rapidly than do normal animals. For each of these facts, we have parallel data for humans. Before presenting these data, I should note that for humans, I have, wherever possible, restricted myself to behavioral studies, studies in which the investigators have actually measured how much their subjects eat. I hope no one will be offended, I assume no one will be surprised, if I say that I am skeptical of the self-reports of fat people about how much they eat or exercise.[3] For those of you who feel that this is high-handed selection of studies, may I remind you of Stunkard's famous chronic fat patients who were fed everything that, in interviews, they admitted to eating daily, and who all steadily lost weight on this diet.

Considering first the average amount eaten per day when on ad-lib feeding of ordinary lab chow or pellets, you will note in Line 1 of Table 4 that consistently static obese rats eat somewhat (19%) more than do their normal

TABLE 4.   Eating habits

	Animals		Humans	
Variable	Batting Average	Mean F/N	Mean F/N	Batting Average
Amount of food eaten ad lib	9/9	1.19	1.16	2/3
No. meals per day	4/4	.85	.92	3/3
Amount eaten per meal	2/2	1.34	1.29	5/5
Speed of eating	1/1	1.28	1.26	1/1

Note: F/N = Fat to normal ratio.

[3] In three of four such self-report studies, fat people report eating considerably less food than do normals.

counterparts. The data for humans are derived from all of the studies I know of in which eating is placed in a noshing, or ad-lib, context; that is, a bowl of ordinary food, usually nuts or crackers, is placed in the room, the experiment presumably has nothing to do with eating, and the subject is free to eat or not, as he chooses, just as is a rat in its cage. In two of the three experiments conducted in this context, obese subjects eat slightly more than do normals; in the third experiment, the two groups eat precisely the same number of crackers. For both humans and rats, then, the fat subject eats only slightly more than the normal subject.

Turning next to the number of meals per day, we note on Line 2 of Table 4 that for both rats and humans, fatter subjects consistently eat fewer meals per day. (A rat meal is defined by Teitelbaum and Campbell, 1958, as "any burst of food intake of at least five pellets separated by at least 5 min. from any other burst [p. 138].") For humans, these particular data are based on self-report or interview studies, for I know of no relevant behavioral data. In any case, again the data for the lesioned rat and the obese human correspond very closely indeed.

From the previous two facts, it should, of course, follow that obese subjects will eat more per meal than normal subjects, and, as can be seen in Line 3 of Table 4, this is the case for both lesioned rats and obese humans. The data for rats are based on two experiments that simply recorded the amount of food eaten per eating burst. The data for humans are based on all experiments in which a plate of food, usually sandwiches, is placed before a subject, and he is told to help himself to lunch or dinner.

Our final datum on eating habits is the speed of eating. Teitelbaum and Campbell (1958) simply recorded the number of pellets their animals ate per minute. Since there is nothing else to do when you are sitting behind a one-way screen watching a subject eat, Nisbett (1968b—data not reported in paper) recorded the number of spoonfuls of ice cream his subjects ate per minute. The comparison of the two studies is drawn in Line 4 of Table 4, where you will note an unsettling similarity in the rate at which lesioned rats and obese humans outspeed their normal counterparts.[4]

All told, then, in the existing literature, Rodin and I found a total of six items of behavior on which it is possible to make rather precise comparisons between lesioned rats and obese humans. These are mostly nonobvious facts, and the comparisons drawn between the two sets of experiments do not attempt to push the analogies beyond the point of common sense. I do not think there can be much debate about pellets versus spoonfuls of ice cream consumed per minute as equivalent measures of eating rate. For all six facts in the existing literature, the parallels between the species are striking. What the lesioned, fat rat does, the obese human does.

In addition to these facts, we identified two other areas of behavior in which it is possible to draw somewhat more fanciful, though still not ridicu-

[4] Fat rats do not drink more rapidly than do normals. There are no comparable data for humans.

lous, comparisons between the species. These are the areas of emotionality and of activity. Though there has been little systematic study of emotionality, virtually everyone who has worked with these animals agrees that the lesioned animals are hyperexcitable, easily startled, overemotional, and generally bitchy to handle. In addition, work by Singh (1969) and research on active avoidance learning do generally support this characterization of the lesioned animal as an emotional beast.

For humans, we have two experiments from which it is possible to draw conclusions about emotionality. In one of these (Schachter et al., 1968), we manipulated fear by threat of painful electric shock. On a variety of rating scales, fat subjects acknowledged that they were somewhat more frightened and anxious than did normal subjects. In a second experiment, Rodin (1970) had her subjects listen to an audio tape while they were working at either a monitoring or a proofreading task. The tapes were either neutral (requiring the subject to think about either rain or seashells) or emotionally charged (requiring the subject to think about his own death or about the bombing of Hiroshima). The emotionally charged tapes produced dramatic differences between subjects. On a variety of rating scales, the obese described themselves as considerably more upset and disturbed than did normal subjects; they reported more palpitations and changes in breathing rate than did normals; and performance, at either the proofreading or monitoring tasks, deteriorated dramatically more for obese than for normal subjects. Again, then, the data are consistent, for both the lesioned animal and the obese human seem to react more emotionally than their normal counterparts.

Finally, on activity, numerous studies using stabilimeter cages or activity wheels have demonstrated that the lesioned animal is markedly less active than the normal animal. This is not, I should add, a totally trivial fact indicating only that the lesioned animal has trouble shlepping his immense bulk around the cage, for the dynamic hyperphagic rat—who though not yet fat, will be—is quite as lethargic as his obese counterpart. On the human side, Bullen, Reed, and Mayer (1964) have taken movies of girls at camp during their scheduled periods of swimming, tennis, and volleyball. They categorize each camper for her degree of activity or exertion during these periods, and do find that the normal campers are more active than are the obese girls.

All told, then, Rodin and I found a total of eight facts, indicating a perfect parallel between the behavior of the lesioned rat and the obese human. We have, so far, found no fact on which the two species differ. Now all of this has proved such an engaging exercise that my students and I decided to play "real" scientist, and we constructed a matrix. We simply listed every fact we could find about the lesioned animals and every fact we could find about obese humans. I have told you about those facts for which parallel data exist. There are, however, numerous holes in the matrix—facts for rats for which no parallel human data have yet been collected, and vice versa. For the past year, we have been engaged in filling in these holes—designing for humans, experiments that have no particular rhyme or reason except that someone once did such an experiment on lesioned rats. For example, it is a fact that though lesioned rats will outeat normal rats when food is easily available, they will not lift a paw if they have to work to get food. In a Skinner box setup, Teitelbaum (1957) finds that at FR1, when one press yields one pellet, fat lesioned rats outpress normal. As the payoff decreases, however, fat rats press less and less until at FR256, they do not manage to get a single pellet during a 12-hour experimental session, whereas normal rats are still industriously pressing away. Similarly, Miller et al. (1950) found that though lesioned rats ate more than normal controls when an unweighted lid covered the food dish, they ate less than did the controls when a 75-gram weight was fastened to the lid. They also found that the lesioned rats ran more slowly down an alley to food than controls did and pulled less hard when temporarily restrained by a harness. In short, fat rats will not work to get food.

Since there was no human parallel to these studies, Lucy Friedman and I designed a study in which, when a subject arrived, he was asked simply to sit at the experimenter's desk and fill out a variety of personality tests and questionnaires. Besides the usual student litter, there was a bag of almonds on the desk. The experimenter helped herself to a nut, invited the subject to do the same, and then left him alone with his questionnaires and nuts for 15 minutes. There were two sets of conditions. In one, the nuts had shells on them; in the other, the nuts had no shells. I assume we agree that eating nuts with shells is considerably more work than eating nuts with no shells.

TABLE 5. Effects of work on the eating behavior of normal and fat subjects

Nuts Have	Number Who	
	Eat	Don't Eat
Normal subjects		
Shells	10	10
No shells	11	9
Fat subjects		
Shells	1	19
No shells	19	1

The top half of Table 5 presents for normal subjects the numbers who do and do not eat nuts in the two conditions. As you see, shells or no shells has virtually no impact on normal subjects. Fifty-five percent of normals eat nuts without shells, and 50% eat nuts with shells. I am a little self-conscious about the data for obese subjects, for it looks as if I were too stupid to know how to fake data. I know how to fake data, and were I to do so, the bottom half of Table 5 certainly would not look the way it does. When the nuts have no shells, 19 of 20 fat subjects eat nuts. When the nuts have shells on them, 1 out of 20 fat subjects eats. Obviously, the parallel to Miller's and to Teitelbaum's rats is perfect. When the food is easy to get at, fat subjects, rat or human, eat more than normals; when the food is hard to get at, fat subjects eat less than normals.

Incidentally, as a casual corollary of these and other findings, one could expect that, given acceptable food, fat eaters would be more likely than normals to choose the easiest way of eating. In order to check on this, Lucy Friedman, Joel Handler, and I went to a large number of Chinese and Japanese restaurants, categorized each patron as he entered the restaurant as obese or normal, and then simply noted whether he ate with chopsticks or with silverware. Among Occidentals, for whom chopsticks can be an ordeal, we found that almost five times the proportion of normal eaters ate with chopsticks as did obese eaters—22.4% of normals and 4.7% of the obese ate with chopsticks.

In another matrix-hole-filling experiment, Patricia Pliner (1970) has demonstrated that obese humans, like lesioned rats, do not regulate food consumption when they are preloaded with solids but, again like the rats, do regulate when they are preloaded with liquids.

In addition to these experiments, we are currently conducting studies on pain sensitivity and on passive versus active avoidance learning— all designed to fill in more holes in our human–lesioned rat matrix. To date, we have a total of 12 nonobvious facts in which the behaviors of lesioned rats parallel perfectly the behaviors of obese humans. Though I cannot believe that as our matrix-hole-filling experiments continue, this perfect parallelism will continue, I submit that even now these are mind-boggling data. I would also submit, however, that we have played this enchanting game just about long enough. This is, after all, science through analogy—a sport I recommend with the same qualifications and enthusiasms with which I recommend skiing—and it is time that we asked what on earth does it all mean? To which at this point I can only answer ruefully that I wish to God I knew.

On its most primitive level, I suppose that I would love to play doctor and issue pronouncements such as, "Madam, you have a very sick hypothalamus." And, indeed, I do know of one case of human obesity (Reeves & Plum, 1969) accompanied by a precisely localized neoplasm that destroyed the ventromedial hypothalamus. This is an astonishing case study, for the lady reads like a lesioned rat—she ate immense amounts of food, as much as 10,000 calories a day, grew impressively fat and was apparently a wildly emotional creature given to frequent outbursts of laughing, crying, and rage. Now I am not, of course, going to suggest that this lady is anything but a pathological extreme. The only vaguely relevant study I know of is a morphological study (Maren, 1955) of the hypothalami of genetically obese mice, an animal whose behavior also resembles the lesioned rat's, which found no structural differences between obese and normal mice.

Mrosovsky (1971) has been developing a more sober hypothesis. Comparing the hibernator and the ventromedial lesioned rat, Mrosovsky has been playing much the same analogical game as have I, and he, too, has noted the marked behavioral similarities of his two species to the obese human. He hypothesizes that the unlesioned, obese animal, rodent or human, has a ventromedial hypothalamus that is functionally quiescent. Though I would be willing to bet that when the appropriate biochemical and electrophysiological studies are done, Mrosovsky will be proven correct, I do not believe that this is a fact which is of fundamental interest to psychologists. Most of us, I suspect, have long been convinced, psychodynamics notwithstanding, that there is *something* biologically responsible for human obesity, and to be able suddenly to point a finger at an offending structure would not really put us much ahead. After all, we've known about the adrenal medulla and emotion for more than 50 years, and I doubt that this particular bit of knowledge has been of much help in our understanding of aggression, or fear, or virtually any other emotional state.

If it is true that the ventromedial hypothalamus is functionally quiescent, for us the question must be, for what function, psychologically speaking, is it quiescent? What processes, or inputs, or outputs are mediated by this particular structure? Speculation and theorizing about the functions of this area have tended to be cautious and modest. Essentially, two suggestions have been made—one that the area is a satiety center, and the other that the area is an emotionality center. Both Miller (1964) and Stellar (1954) have tentatively suggested that the ventromedial area is a satiety center—that in some fashion it monitors the signals indicating a sufficiency of food and inhibits the excitatory (Eat! Eat!) impulses initiated in the lateral hypothalamus. This inhibitory-satiety mechanism can account for the hyperphagia of the lesioned animals and, consequently, for their obesity. It can also account for most of the facts that I outlined earlier about the daily eating habits of these animals. It cannot by itself, however, account for the finickiness of these animals, nor can it, as I believe I can show, account for the apparent unwillingness of these animals to work for food. Finally, this hypothesis is simply irrelevant to the demonstrated inactivity and hyperemotionality of these animals. This irrelevance, however, is not critical if one assumes, as does Stellar, that discrete neural centers, also located in the ventromedial area, control activity and emotionality. The satiety theory, then, can account for some, but by no means all, of the critical facts about eating, and it has nothing to say about activity or emotionality.

As a theoretically more ambitious alternative, Grossman (1966, 1967) has proposed that the ventromedial area be considered the emotionality center and that the facts about eating be derived from this assumption. By definition, Grossman's hypothesis accounts for the emotionality of these animals, and his own work on active avoidance learning certainly supports the emotionality hypothesis. I must confess, however, that I have difficulty in understanding just why these emotional animals become fat. In essence, Grossman (1966) assumes that "lesions in or near the VMH sharply increase an animal's affective responsiveness to apparently all sensory stimuli [p. 1]." On the basis of this general statement, he suggests that "the 'finickiness' of the ventromedial animal might then reflect a change in its affective response to taste." This could, of course, account for the fact that lesioned animals eat more very good- and less very bad-tasting food than do normals. However, I simply find it hard to believe that this affective hypothesis can account for the basic fact about these animals—that for weeks on end, the lesioned animals eat grossly more of ordinary, freely available lab chow.

Grossman (1967) attributes the fact that lesioned animals will not work for food to their "exaggerated response to handling, the test situation, the deprivation regimen, and the requirement of having to work for their daily bread [p. 358]." I suppose all of this is possible, I simply find it farfetched. At the very least, the response to handling and to the deprivation regime should be just as exaggerated whether the reinforcement schedule is FR1 or FR256 and the lesioned animals do press more than the normals at FR1.

My skepticism, however, is irrelevant, and Grossman may be correct. There are, however, at least two facts with which, it seems to me, Grossman's hypothesis cannot cope. First, it would seem to me that an animal with an affective response to food would be likely to eat more rather than less often per day, as is the fact. Second, it is simply common sense to expect that an animal with strong "affective responsiveness to all sensory stimuli" will be a very active animal indeed, but the lesioned animal is presumably hypoactive.

None of the existing theories, then, can cope with all of the currently available facts. For the remainder of this article, I am going to try my hand at developing a hypothesis that I believe can cope with more of the facts than can the available alternatives. It is a hypothesis that derives entirely from our work on human obesity. I believe, however, that it can explain as many of the facts about ventromedial-lesioned rats as it can about the human obese. If future experimental work on animals proves this correct, it would certainly suggest that science by analogy has merits other than its entertainment value.

The gist of our findings on humans is this—the eating behavior of the obese is under external, rather than internal, control. In effect, the obese seem stimulus-bound. When a food-relevant cue is present, the obese are more likely to eat and to eat a great deal than are normals. When such a cue is absent, the obese are less likely to try to eat or to complain about hunger. Though I have not, in this article, developed this latter point, there is evidence that, in the absence of food-relevant cues, the obese have a far easier time fasting than do normals, while in the presence of such cues, they have a harder time fasting (Goldman, Jaffa, & Schachter, 1968).

Since it is a little hard to believe that such stimulus-binding is limited to food-relevant cues, for some time now my students and I have been concerned with the generalizability of these facts. Given our starting point, this concern has led to some rather odd little experiments. For example, Judith Rodin, Peter Herman, and I have asked subjects to look at slides on which are portrayed 13 objects or words. Each slide is exposed for five seconds, and the subject is then asked to recall what he saw. Fat subjects recall more objects than do normal subjects. The experiment has been replicated, and this appears to be a reliable phenomenon.

In another study, Rodin, Herman, and I compared fat and normal subjects on simple and on complex or disjunctive reaction time. For simple reaction time, they are instructed to lift their finger from a telegraph key as soon as the stimulus light comes on. On this task, there are no differences between obese and normal subjects. For complex reaction time, there are two stimulus lights and two telegraph keys, and subjects are instructed to lift their left finger when the right light comes on and lift their right finger when the left light comes on. Obese subjects respond more rapidly and make fewer errors. Since this was a little hard to believe, this study was repeated three times—each time with the same results—the obese are simply better at complex reaction time than are normals. I do not pretend to understand these results, but they do seem to indicate that, for some reason, the obese are more efficient stimulus or information processors.

At this stage, obviously, this is shotgun research which, in coordination with the results of our eating experiments, seems to indicate that it may be useful to more generally characterize the obese as stimulus-bound and to hypothesize that any stimulus, above a given intensity level, is more likely to evoke an appropriate response from an obese than from a normal subject.

Our first test of implications of this hypothesis in a noneating setting is Rodin's (1970) experiment on the effects of distraction on performance. She reasoned that if the stimulus-binding hypothesis is correct, distracting, irrelevant stimuli should be more disruptive for obese than for normal subjects when they are performing a task requiring concentration. Presumably, the impinging stimulus is more likely to grip the attention of the stimulus-bound obese subject. To test this guess, she had her subjects work at a simple proofreading task. In one condition, the subjects corrected proof with no distractions at all. In the three other conditions, they corrected proof while listening to recorded tapes that varied in the degree to which they were likely to grip a subject's attention, and therefore distract him. The results are presented in Figure 2, where, as you can see, the obese are better at proofreading when undistracted but their performance seriously deteriorates as they are distracted until, at extreme distraction, they are considerably worse than normals. Rodin finds precisely the same pattern of results, by the way, in a similar study in which she uses the complex reaction time task I have already described rather than the proofreading task. For humans, then, there is evidence, outside of the eating context, to support the hypothesis.

Let us return to consideration of the ventromedial lesioned animal and examine the implications of the hypothesis that any stimulus, above a given intensity level, is more likely to evoke an appropriate response from a lesioned than from an intact animal. This is a hypothesis which is, in many ways, similar to Grossman's hypothesis and, on the face of it, would appear to be vulnerable to exactly the same criticisms as I have leveled at his theory.

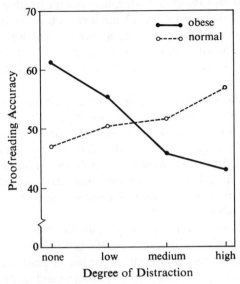

FIGURE 2.   The effects of distraction on performance (from Rodin, 1970)

There are, however, crucial differences that will become evident as I elaborate this notion. I assume it is self-evident that my hypothesis can explain the emotionality of the lesioned animals and, with the exception of meal frequency—a fact to which I will return—can account for virtually all of our facts about the daily eating habits of these animals. I will, therefore, begin consideration of the hypothesis by examining its implications for those facts that have been most troubling for alternative formulations and by examining those facts that seem to most clearly contradict my own hypothesis.

Let us turn first to the perverse and fascinating fact that though lesioned animals will outeat normals when food is easily available they simply will not work for food. In my terms, this is an incomplete fact which may prove only that a remote food stimulus will not evoke a food-acquiring response. It is the case that in the experiments concerned with this fact, virtually every manipulation of work has covaried the remoteness or prominence of the food cue. Food at the end of a long alleyway is obviously a more remote cue than food in the animal's food dish. Pellets available only after 256 presses of a lever are certainly more remote food stimuli than pellets available after each press of a lever. If the stimulus-binding hypothesis is correct, it should be anticipated that, in contrast to the results when the food cue is remote, the lesioned animal will work harder than the normal animal when the food stimulus is prominent and compelling. Though the appropriate experiment has not yet been done on rats, to my delight I have learned recently that such an experiment has been done on humans by William Johnson (1970), who independently has been pursuing a line of thought similar to mine.

Johnson seated his subject at a table, fastened his hand in a harness, and, to get food, required the subject for 12 minutes to pull, with his index finger, on a ring that was attached by wire to a seven-pound weight. He received food on a VR50 schedule—that is, on the average, a subject received a quarter of a sandwich for every 50 pulls of the ring. Obviously, this was moderately hard work.

To vary stimulus prominence, Johnson manipulated food visibility and prior taste of food. In "food visible" conditions, he placed beside the subject one desirable sandwich covered in a transparent wrap. In addition, as the subject satisfied the VR requirements, he placed beside him quarter sandwiches similarly wrapped. In "food invisible" conditions, Johnson followed exactly the same procedures, but wrapped the sandwiches in white, non-transparent shelf paper. Subjects, of course, did not eat until they had completed their 12 minutes of labor.

As a second means of varying cue prominence, half of the subjects ate a quarter of a very good sandwich immediately before they began work. The remaining subjects ate a roughly equivalent portion of plain white bread.

In Figure 3, you can see the effects of these manipulations on effort. I have arranged the conditions along the dimension of food cue prominence—ranging from no prominent food cues to two prominent food cues—that is, the subjects ate a quarter sandwich and the food was visible. As you

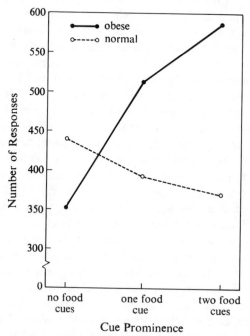

FIGURE 3.   The effect of food cue prominence on effort (from Johnson, 1970)

can see, the stimulus prominence manipulations have a marked effect on the obese, for they work far harder when the food cues are prominent and compelling than when they are inconspicuous. In contrast, cue prominence has relatively little effect on normal subjects.

Please note also that these results parallel Miller's and Teitelbaum's results with lesioned rats. When the food cues are remote, the obese human works less hard for food than the normally sized human. The fact that this relationship flips when the cues are prominent is, of course, a delight to me, and wouldn't it be absorbing to replicate this experiment on lesioned rats?

Let us turn next to the fact that lesioned rats are hypoactive. If ever a fact were incompatible with a hypothesis, this one is it. Surely an animal that is more responsive to any stimulus should be hyper-, not hypoactive. Yet this is a most peculiar fact—for it remains a fact only because one rather crucial finding in the literature has been generally overlooked and because the definition of activity seems restricted to measures obtained in running wheels or in stabilimeter-type living cages.

Studies of activity have with fair consistency reported dramatically less activity for lesioned than for normal rats. Within one exception, these studies report data in terms of total activity per unit time, making no distinction between periods when the animal room was quiet and undisturbed and periods involving the mild ferment of animal-tending activities. Gladfelter and Brobeck (1962), however, report activity data separately for the "43-hour period when the constant-temperature room was dark and quiet and the rats were undisturbed" and for the "five-hour period when the room was lighted and the rats were cared for [p. 811]." During the quiet time, these investigators find precisely what almost everyone else does—lesioned rats are markedly less active. During the animal-tending period, however, lesioned animals are just about as active as normal animals. In short, when the stimulus field is relatively barren and there is little to react to, the ventromedial animal is inactive; when the field is made up of the routine noises, stirrings, and disturbances involved in tending an animal laboratory, the lesioned animal is just about as active as the normal animal.

Though this is an instructive fact, it hardly proves my hypothesis, which specifies that above a given stimulus intensity the lesioned animal should be *more* reactive than the normal animal. Let us, then, ask—is there any evidence that lesioned animals are more active than normal animals? There is, if you are willing to grant that specific activities such as lever pressing or avoidance behavior are as much "activity" as the gross, overall measures obtained in stabilimeter-mounted living cages.

In his study of activity, Teitelbaum (1957) has distinguished between random and food-directed activity. As do most other investigators, he finds that in their cages, lesioned rats are much less active than are normals. During a 12-hour stint in a Skinner box, however, when on an FR1 schedule, the lesioned animals are more active; that is, they press more than do normals. Thus, when the food cue is salient and prominent, as it is on an FR1 schedule, the lesioned animal is very active indeed. And, as you know, when the food cue is remote, as it is on an FR64 or FR256 schedule, the lesioned animal is inactive.

Since lever pressing is activity in pursuit of food, I suppose one should be cautious in accepting these data as support for my argument. Let us turn, then, to avoidance learning where most of the experiments are unrelated to food.

In overall batting average terms,[5] no area could be messier than this one, for in three of six studies, lesioned animals are better and in three worse at avoidance than normals. However, if one distinguishes between passive and active avoidance, things become considerably more coherent.

In active avoidance studies, a conditioned stimulus, such as a light or buzzer, precedes a noxious event such as electrifying the floor grid. To avoid the shock, the animal must perform some action such as jumping into the nonelectrified compartment of a shuttle box. In three of four such studies, the lesioned animals learn considerably more rapidly than do normal animals. By this criterion, at least, lesioned animals are more reactive than normal animals.[6] Parenthetically, it is amusing to note that the response latencies of the lesioned animal are smaller (Grossman, 1966) than those of the normal animal, just as in our studies of complex reaction time, obese humans are faster than normal humans.

In contrast to these results, lesioned animals do considerably worse than normal animals in passive avoidance studies. In these studies, the animal's water dish or the lever of a Skinner box are electrified so that if, during the experimental period, the animal touches these objects he receives a shock. In both of the studies we have so far found on passive learning, the lesioned animals do considerably worse than normal animals. They either press the lever or touch the water dish more than do normals and accordingly are shocked far more often. Thus, when the situation requires a response if the animal is to avoid shock, the lesioned animal does better than the normal

[5] Of all the behavioral areas so far considered, avoidance learning is probably the one for which it makes least sense either to adopt a batting average approach or to attempt to treat the research as a conceptually equivalent set of studies. Except in this area, the great majority of experiments have used, as subjects, rats with electrolytically produced lesions. In the avoidance learning area, the subjects have been mice, rats, and cats; the lesions are variously electrolytically produced, produced by gold thioglucose injections, or are "functional" lesions produced by topical application of atropine or some other agent.

[6] Reactive, yes, but what about activity in the more primitive sense of simply moving or scrambling about the experimental box? Even in this respect, the lesioned animals appear to outmove the normals, for Turner, Sechzer, and Liebelt (1967) report that,

> The experimental groups, both mice and rats, emitted strong escape tendencies prior to the onset of shock and in response to shock. Repeated attempts were made to climb out of the test apparatus. This group showed much more vocalization than the control group. . . . In contrast to the behavior of the experimental animals, the control animals appeared to become immobilized or to "freeze" both before and during the shock period. Thus, there was little attempt to escape and little vocalization [p. 242].

animal. Conversely, if the situation requires response quiescence if the animal is to avoid shock, the lesioned animal does far worse than the normal animal. This pair of facts, I suggest, provides strong support for the hypothesis that beyond a given stimulus intensity, the lesioned animal is more reactive than the normal animal. I would also suggest that without some variant of this hypothesis, the overall pattern of results on avoidance learning is incoherent.

All in all, then, one can make a case of sorts for the suggestion that there are specifiable circumstances in which lesioned animals will be more active. It is hardly an ideal case, and only an experiment that measures the effects of systematically varied stimulus field richness on gross activity can test the point.

These ruminations on activity do suggest a refinement of the general hypothesis and also, I trust, make clear why I have insisted on inserting that awkward phrase "above a given intensity level" in all statements of the hypothesis. For activity, it appears to be the case that the lesioned animal is less active when the stimulus is remote and more active when the stimulus is prominent. This interaction between reactivity and stimulus prominence is presented graphically in Figure 4. This is a formulation which I believe fits almost all of the available data, on both animals and men, remarkably well. It is also a formulation which for good ad-hoc reasons bears a striking resemblance to almost every relevant set of data I have discussed.

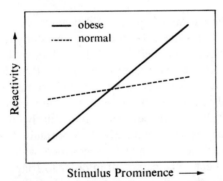

FIGURE 4.   Theoretical curves of relationship of reactivity to stimulus prominence

For human eating behavior, virtually every fact we have supports the assertion that the obese eat more than normals when the food cue is prominent and less when the cue is remote. In Johnson's study of work and cue prominence, the obese do not work as hard as normals when there are no prominent food cues, but work much harder when the food cues are highly salient. In Nisbett's one- and three-sandwich experiment, the obese subjects eat just as long as food cues are prominent—that is, the sandwiches are directly in front of the subject—but when these immediate cues have been consumed, they stop eating. Thus, they eat more than normals in the three-sandwich condition and less in the one-sandwich condition. We also know that the obese have an easy time fasting in the absence of food cues and a hard time in the presence of such cues, and so on.

About eating habits we know that the obese eat larger meals (what could be a more prominent cue than food on the plate?), but eat fewer meals (as they should if it requires a particularly potent food cue to trigger an eating response). Even the fact that the obese eat more rapidly can be easily derived from this formulation.

For rats, this formulation in general fits what we know about eating habits, but can be considered a good explanation of the various experimental facts only if you are willing to accept my reinterpretation, in terms of cue prominence, of such experiments as Miller et al.'s (1950) study of the effects of work on eating. If, as would I, you would rather suspend judgment until the appropriate experiments have been done on lesioned rats, mark it down as an engaging possibility.

Given the rough state of what we know about emotionality, this formulation seems to fit the data for humans and rats about equally well. The lesioned rats are vicious when handled and lethargic when left alone. In the Rodin (1970) experiment which required subjects to listen to either neutral or emotionally disturbing tapes, obese subjects described themselves (and behaved accordingly) as less emotional than normals when the tapes were neutral and much more emotional than normals when the tapes were disturbing.

All in all, given the variety of species and behaviors involved, it is not a bad ad-hoc hypothesis. So far there has been only one study deliberately designed to test some of the ideas implicit in this formulation. This is Lee Ross's (1969) study of the effects of cue salience on eating. Ross formulated this experiment in the days when we were struggling with some of the data inconsistent with our external-internal theory of eating behavior (see Schachter, 1967). Since the world is full of food cues, it was particularly embarrassing to discover that obese subjects ate less frequently than normals. Short of invoking denial mechanisms, such a fact could be reconciled with the theory only if we assumed that a food cue must be potent in order to trigger an eating response in an obese subject—the difference between a hot dog stand two blocks away and a hot dog under your nose, savory with mustard and steaming with sauerkraut.

To test the effects of cue prominence, Ross simply had his subjects sit at a table covered with a variety of objects among which was a large tin of shelled cashew nuts. Presumably, the subjects were there to take part in a study of thinking. There were two sets of experimental conditions. In high-cue-saliency conditions, the table and the nuts were illuminated by an unshaded table lamp containing a 40-watt bulb. In low-saliency conditions, the lamp was shaded and contained a 7½-watt red bulb. The measure of eating was simply the difference in the weight of the tin of nuts before and after the subject thought his experimentally required thoughts. The results are presented

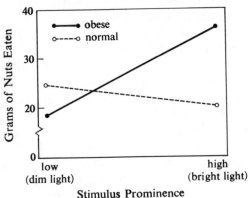

FIGURE 5.   The effects of stimulus intensity on amount eaten (from Ross, 1969)

in Figure 5, which, needless to say, though I will say it, bears a marked resemblance to our theoretical curves.

So much for small triumphs. Let us turn now to some of the problems of this formulation. Though I do not intend to detail a catalog of failings, I would like to make explicit some of my discomforts.

1. Though there has been no direct experimental study of the problem, it seems to be generally thought that the lesioned rat is hyposexual, which, if true, is one hell of a note for a theory which postulates superreactivity. It is the case, however, that gonadal atrophy is frequently a consequence of this operation (Brooks & Lambert, 1946; Hetherington & Ransom, 1940). Possibly, then, we should consider sexual activity as artifactually quite distinct from either gross activity or stimulus-bound activity such as avoidance behavior.

2. I am made uncomfortable by the fact that the obese, both human and rat, eat less bad food than do normals. I simply find it difficult to conceive of nonresponsiveness as a response. I suppose I could conceptually pussyfoot around this difficulty, but I cannot imagine the definition of response that would allow me to cope with both this fact and with the facts about passive avoidance. I take some comfort from the observation that of all of the facts about animals and humans, the fact about bad taste has the weakest batting average. It may yet turn out not to be a fact.

3. Though the fact that obese humans eat less often is no problem, the fact that obese rats also eat less often is awkward, for it is a bit difficult to see how food stimulus intensity can vary for a caged rat on an ad-lib schedule. This may seem farfetched, but there is some experimental evidence that this may be due to the staleness of the food. Brooks, Lockwood, and Wiggins (1946), using mash for food, demonstrated that lesioned rats do not outeat normals when the food is even slightly stale. Only when the food was absolutely fresh and newly placed in the cage did lesioned rats eat conspicu-

ously more than normal rats. It seems doubtful, however, that this could be the explanation for results obtained with pellets.

4. As with food, one should expect from this formulation that the animal's water intake would increase following the lesion. There does not appear to have been much systematic study of the problem, but what data exist are inconsistent from one study to the next. Several studies indicate decreased water intake; at least one study (Krasne, 1964) indicates no change following the operation: and there are even rare occasional case reports of polydipsia. Possibly my interactional hypothesis can cope with this chaos, and systematically varying the salience of the water cue will systematically affect the water intake of the ventromedial animal. It is also possible that under any circumstance, water, smell-less and tasteless, is a remote cue.

There are, then, difficulties with this formulation. These may be the kinds of difficulties that will ultimately damn the theory, or at least establish its limits. Alternatively, these may mostly be apparent difficulties, and this view of matters may help us clarify inconsistent sets of data, for I suspect that by systematically varying cue prominence we can systematically vary the lesioned animal's reactivity on many dimensions. We shall see. Granting the difficulties, for the moment this view of matters does manage to subsume a surprisingly diverse set of facts about animals and men under one quite simple theoretical scheme.

Since I have presented this article as a more or less personal history of the development of a set of ideas, I would like to conclude by taking a more formal look at this body of data, theory, and speculation, by examining what I believe we now know, what seems to be good guesswork, and what is still out-and-out speculation.

1. With some confidence, we can say that obese humans are externally controlled or stimulus-bound. There is little question that this is true of their eating behavior, and evidence is rapidly accumulating that eating is a special case of the more general state.

I have suggested that stimulus prominence and reactivity are key variables in understanding the realms of behavior with which I have been concerned, and Figure 4 represents a first guess as to the nature of the differential functions involved for obese and normal humans. The specific shapes of the curves are, of course, pure guesswork, and the only absolute requirement that I believe the data impose on the theory is that there be an interaction such that at low levels of stimulus prominence, the obese are less reactive, and at high levels of prominence more reactive, than normals.

2. With considerably less confidence, I believe we can say that this same set of hypotheses may explain many of the differences between the ventromedial lesioned rat and his intact counterpart. This conclusion is based on the fact that so much of the existing data either fit or can be plausibly reinterpreted to fit these ideas. Obviously, the crucial experiments have yet to be done.

3. Finally, and most tentatively, one may guess that the obesity of rats and men has a common physiological locus in the ventromedial hypothalamus. I must emphasize that this guess is based *entirely* on the persistent and tantalizing analogies between lesioned rats and obese humans. There is absolutely no relevant independent evidence. However, should future work support this speculation, I suspect, in light of the evidence already supporting the stimulus-binding hypotheses, that we are in for a radical revision of our notions about the hypothalamus.

References

BROOKS, C. McC., & LAMBERT, E. F. A study of the effect of limitation of food intake and the method of feeding on the rate of weight gain during hypothalamic obesity in the albino rat. *American Journal of Physiology*, 1946, *147*, 695–707.

BROOKS, C. McC., LOCKWOOD, R. A., & WIGGINS, M. L. A study of the effect of hypothalamic lesions on the eating habits of the albino rat. *American Journal of Physiology*, 1946, *147*, 735–741.

BULLEN, B. A., REED, R. B., & MAYER, J. Physical activity of obese and nonobese adolescent girls appraised by motion picture sampling. *American Journal of Clinical Nutrition*, 1964, *14*, 211–223.

CANNON, W. B. *Bodily changes in pain, hunger, fear and rage.* (2d ed.) New York: Appleton, 1915.

CARLSON, A. J. *The control of hunger in health and disease.* Chicago: University of Chicago Press, 1916.

DECKE, E. Effects of taste on the eating behavior of obese and normal persons. Cited in S. Schachter, *Emotion, obesity, and crime.* New York: Academic Press, 1971.

GLADFELTER, W. E., & BROBECK, J. R. Decreased spontaneous locomotor activity in the rat induced by hypothalamic lesions. *American Journal of Physiology*, 1962, *203*, 811–817.

GOLDMAN, R., JAFFA, M., & SCHACHTER, S. Yom Kippur, Air France, dormitory food, and the eating behavior of obese and normal persons. *Journal of Personality and Social Psychology*, 1968, *10*, 117–123.

GROSSMAN, S. P. The VMH: A center for affective reactions, satiety, or both? *International Journal of Physiology and Behavior*, 1966, *1*, 1–10.

――――. *A textbook of physiological psychology.* New York: Wiley, 1967.

HETHERINGTON, A. W., & RANSON, S. W. Hypothalamic lesions and adiposity in the rat. *Anatomical Record*, 1940, *78*, 149–172.

JOHNSON, W. G. The effect of prior-taste and food visibility on the food-directed instrumental performance of obese individuals. Unpublished doctoral dissertation, Catholic University of America, 1970.

KRASNE, F. B. Unpublished study cited in N. E. Miller, Some psycho-physiological studies of motivation and of the behavioural effects of illness. *Bulletin of the British Psychological Society*, 1964, *17*, 1–20.

MAREN, T. H. Cited in J. L. Fuller & G. A. Jacoby, Central and sensory control of food intake in genetically obese mice. *American Journal of Physiology*, 1955, *183*, 279–283.

MILLER, N. E. Some psycho-physiological studies of motivation and of the behavioural effects of illness. *Bulletin of the British Psychological Society*, 1964, *17*, 1–20.

MILLER, N. E., BAILEY, C. J., & STEVENSON, J. A. F. Decreased "hunger" but increased food intake resulting from hypothalamic lesions. *Science*, 1950, *112*, 256–259.

MROSOVSKY, N. *Hibernation and the hypothalamus.* New York: Appleton-Century-Crofts, 1971.

NISBETT, R. E. Determinants of food intake in human obesity. *Science,* 1968, *159,* 1254–1255. (a)

———. Taste, deprivation, and weight determinants of eating behavior. *Journal of Personality and Social Psychology,* 1968, *10,* 107–116. (b)

———. Eating and obesity in men and animals. In press, 1971.

PLINER, P. Effects of liquid and solid preloads on the eating behavior of obese and normal persons. Unpublished doctoral dissertation, Columbia University, 1970.

RABIN, B. M., & SMITH, C. J. Behavioral comparison of the effectiveness of irritative and non-irritative lesions in producing hypothalamic hyperphagia. *Physiology and Behavior,* 1968, *3,* 417–420.

REEVES, A. G., & PLUM, F. Hyperphagia, rage, and dementia accompanying a ventromedial hypothalamic neoplasm. *Archives of Neurology,* 1969, *20,* 616–624.

REYNOLDS, R. W. Ventromedial hypothalamic lesions with hyperphagia. *American Journal of Physiology,* 1963, *204,* 60–62.

RODIN, J. Effects of distraction on performance of obese and normal subjects. Unpublished doctoral dissertation, Columbia University, 1970.

ROSS, L. D. Cue- and cognition-controlled eating among obese and normal subjects. Unpublished doctoral dissertation, Columbia University, 1969.

SCHACHTER, S. The interaction of cognitive and physiological determinants of emotional state. In L. Berkowitz (Ed.), *Advances in experimental social psychology.* Vol. 1. New York: Academic Press, 1964.

———. Cognitive effects on bodily functioning: Studies of obesity and eating. In D. C. Glass (Ed.), *Neurophysiology and emotion.* New York: Rockefeller University Press and Russell Sage Foundation, 1967.

———. Obesity and eating. *Science,* 1968, *161,* 751–756.

———. *Emotion, obesity, and crime.* New York: Academic Press, 1971.

SCHACHTER, S., GOLDMAN, R., & GORDON, A. Effects of fear, food deprivation, and obesity on eating. *Journal of Personality and Social Psychology,* 1968, *10,* 91–97.

SINGH, D. Comparison of hyperemotionality caused by lesions in the septal and ventromedial hypothalamic areas in the rat. *Psychonomic Science,* 1969, *16,* 3–4.

STELLAR, E. The physiology of motivation. *Psychological Review,* 1954, *61,* 5–22.

STUNKARD, A., & KOCH, C. The interpretation of gastric motility: I. Apparent bias in the reports of hunger by obese persons. *Archives of General Psychiatry,* 1964, *11,* 74–82.

TEITELBAUM, P. Sensory control of hypothalamic hyperphagia. *Journal of Comparative and Physiological Psychology,* 1955, *48,* 156–163.

———. Random and food-directed activity in hyperphagic and normal rats. *Journal of Comparative and Physiological Psychology,* 1957, *50,* 486–490.

TEITELBAUM, P., & CAMPBELL, B. A. Ingestion patterns in hyperphagic and normal rats. *Journal of Comparative and Physiological Psychology,* 1958, *51,* 135–141.

TURNER, S. G., SECHZER, J. A., & LIEBELT, R. A. Sensitivity to electric shock after ventromedial hypothalamic lesions. *Experimental Neurology,* 1967, *19,* 236–244.

The last article in this section is based on a thirty-year research program on interactions between learning and physiological factors in mental illness. It is written by Neal E. Miller, a well-known psychologist who began by interpreting abnormal behavior in terms of learning and who has made increasing use of biological techniques and concepts since the 1950's.

Beginning in 1966, Miller and his colleagues demonstrated that internal autonomic responses, such as changes in heart rate and in intestinal contractions, could be conditioned. This research has attracted much attention, especially since it suggests that many clinical symptoms (abnormal heart rates and digestive disorders, for example) may be learned. But Miller urges caution in attempting to apply these findings before further basic research is done. In fact, as he shows in his article, the strength of heart-rate conditioning has been dwindling since the effect was first reported, and it is clear that not all of the important factors are yet under control.

Other research in Miller's laboratory has focused on coping responses and their physiological concomitants. Rats have been given problems where their successful response may enable them to avoid electric shocks or it may not. Even among animals receiving the same amount of shock, aspects of the psychological situation—control or lack of control, coping or induced helplessness—determine the incidence of both stomach ulcers and chemical measures in the brain. The results of these animal experiments combined with his human experience lead Miller to speculate, "Perhaps we have evolved so that our mental health depends on an environment that forces us to perform coping responses."

Interactions Between Learned and Physical Factors in Mental Illness

Neal E. Miller

Since this paper briefly covers some 30 years of work, my discussion will be limited to a few unrelated high points with an effort to relate them to our interdisciplinary goals.

The basic hypothesis that John Dollard and I (4) formulated many years ago was that, to the extent that functional neuroses are acquired during one's lifetime, they must be learned either by known laws of learning or by new laws yet to be discovered. In this review, primary emphasis will be placed on the neuroses rather than on the psychoses. Since it is obvious that there is no completely clear-cut distinction between the two, in that learning does enter into both, it remains to be seen whether its role is primary or secondary. The

Source: Reprinted by permission of Grune and Stratton, Inc., from *Seminars in Psychiatry*, August 1972, *4* (3), 239–254.

Note: Supported by USPHS Grants MH 13189, MH 19183, and MH 19991.

effect of learning on psychoses is demonstrated quite clearly by the contents of delusions. People no longer are likely to be deluded into thinking that they are Napoleon Bonaparte or Franklin Delano Roosevelt, but their delusions have other, more modern contents.

Fear as a Learned Drive Motivating Further Learning

Figure 1 shows the apparatus used in an experiment illustrating some of the properties of fear. The left side is white and has a grid; the right side is black and has a smooth floor. If animals are placed within this apparatus, with the door separating the two compartments open, they will wander casually about. But their behavior will be radically changed if for a number

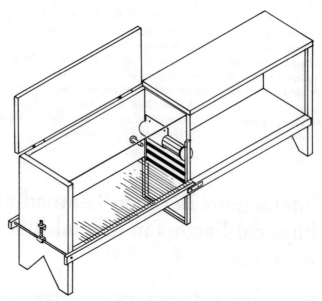

FIGURE 1.   Apparatus for demonstrating that fear functions as a learned drive and a reduction in fear as a reward. (By permission [12].)

of trials, they are put into the left side, where a strong shock is sent through the grid and where they are allowed to escape through the open door to the other compartment. On subsequent trials where the shock is absent they will run rapidly from the left to the right. But is this running the automatic persistence of a habit or is a learned drive involved? From the urination and defecation of the animals and their generally agitated behavior, one might think that they had learned to be afraid. The way to test this is to prevent the door from dropping open. With his escape blocked, the animal will indeed get very excited. He will scramble around and eventually turn the wheel which is connected so that it causes the door to drop open. Figure 2 shows that during a

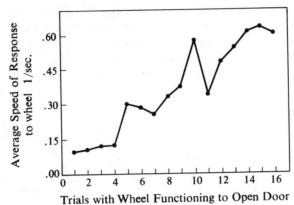

FIGURE 2.   Learning of a new response, that of rotating a wheel, which allows the rat to escape from a situation that elicits fear. (By permission [12].)

series of such trials the rats will learn the new habit of promptly rotating the wheel.[1]

Learning of Symptoms

If you observe the animal, you will see that his behavior is very peculiar—he has a compulsion to rotate the wheel and run through into the other compartment. But, if you know the history, this bizarre behavior is perfectly understandable. It is compatible with the idea that the rat is motivated by a learned drive to fear the white compartment, which acts just the same as any other drive such as hunger, and that the escape from this fear functions as a reward for rotating the wheel just as food does for a hungry animal. As the animal becomes skillful at rotating the wheel, his behavior becomes more and more casual, so that you would not notice any overt symptoms of fear at all and might indeed be puzzled by the way the animal calmly and persistently performs this act. One might note an analogy with the "belle indifference" of some hysterical patients about their symptoms. But, if you block the habit so that animal can no longer get to the wheel or if the wheel no longer works to drop the door open, the fear immediately returns, as is shown by urination, defecation, and agitated behavior. Again one can note an analogy to the fact that the blocking of at least certain neurotic symptoms produces an increase in anxiety which is concealed, so to speak, behind the symptom.

Figure 3 shows that if you make the wheel nonfunctional, the habit of turning the wheel extinguishes, demonstrating that the reduction in fear by

[1] Although the original experiment described here is subject to the criticism that the electric shocks might potentiate an innate preference for a specific compartment or that the motivation might come from the blocking of a learned habit of running, instead of from fear, similar results have been secured in a subsequent experiment on cats that was designed to eliminate both of these alternative explanations (17).

escaping to the other compartment was essential for maintaining this habit. But, as Figure 3 also shows, if you make the bar functional so that it will cause the door to drop, the animal will learn a new habit of pressing the bar. This seems like the symptom substitution which sometimes occurs if a symptom is merely blocked without solving the patient's emotional problem.

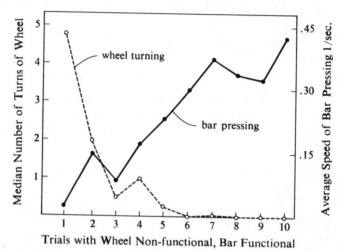

FIGURE 3.   Extinction of the response of rotating the wheel when it is no longer rewarded by escape from fear; learning of a second response, pressing a bar, after it begins to be rewarded by escape from fear. (By permission [12].)

If you merely continue to give the animal additional trials without electric shocks, it takes an enormous length of time for this habit to extinguish. With the rat, the habit may last for as many as 500 trials. In a similar habit with a higher organism, such as a dog, the habit may persist for thousands of trials without extinguishing (26). But if eventually you do extinguish or counter-condition the fear, not only the performance of the original habit disappears but also the tendency to learn any new substitute disappears. I think that this removal of the underlying drive of fear may be analogous to the goal of various types of psychotherapy, be they Freudian or behavioral. It is interesting that as the behavior therapists are becoming more experienced, they are finding that it is necessary to locate and deal with the patient's real phobia rather than some subsidiary symptom (20).

The animal model just described is quite applicable to phobias and also to certain compulsions whose interruption induces fear (4). It also seems to be readily applicable to combat neuroses, where the source of the fear often is quite clear and the fear-reducing value of the symptom that allows the soldier to escape from combat provides a clear explanation for the reinforcement of that symptom. The hysterical paralysis of the trigger finger or of the legs of an infantryman or an interference with the depth perception of a pilot are examples. Certain types of combat amnesia that are not readily explainable by head injury are another example. Our analysis is that the intense fear aroused by the terrifying memories motivates one to stop thinking about them and the consequent relief reinforces the inhibition of thought. If those of you who have a mild fear of heights had to jump across a 5-foot gap from the roof of a skyscraper to a ledge, you might well run up to the edge and suddenly find yourself unable to jump. Our hypothesis is that a train of thought is a series of responses just like running and that stopping a specific train of thought is a response just like the stopping of running.

Now, if you were given a drug that reduced your fear enough, it is conceivable that you would be able to jump. But, if you landed on a precarious ledge, you might find yourself still more frightened. Grinker and Spiegel (6) found that intravenous injections of a barbiturate often could relax a patient with combat amnesia so that he could recover his memories which were indeed terrifying. To quote their vivid description:

> The terror exhibited in the moments of supreme danger, such as at the imminent explosion of shells, the death of a friend before the patient's eyes, the absence of cover under a heavy dive-bombing attack, is electrifying to watch. The body becomes increasingly tense and rigid; the eyes widen and the pupils dilate, while the skin becomes covered with fine perspiration. The hands move about convulsively, seeking a weapon, or a friend to share the danger. The breathing becomes incredibly rapid and shallow. The intensity of the emotion sometimes becomes unbearable; and frequently, at the height of the reaction, there is a collapse and the patient falls back in bed and remains quiet a few minutes, usually to resume the story at a more neutral point.[2]

According to the theory that Dollard and I have put forward, other forms of repression are motivated in very much the same way as is combat amnesia. When the subject loses the ability to remember and to think about certain topics, he reduces his ability to make fine discriminations and to solve problems adaptively. In our analysis, we have emphasized fear (or, anxiety as it is called when its source is vague) as the motivation and a reduction in fear as the reinforcement, or, as psychiatrists frequently call it, the secondary gain. But other drives and rewards may be involved, such as anger, the need for love, the need for social approval, which may even be based on an innate human gregariousness, guilt, and the needs for achievement and self-assertiveness. Most of these motivations still are not well understood; studying them rigorously in the laboratory presents a highly significant challenge. (See Miller, 13, pp. 262–272.)

As Grey Walter contends, one way of reducing an overwhelming and incapacitating chronic fear is by minute lesions at appropriate points in

---

[2] For a detailed discussion of the mechanism for such an increase in fear, commonly called the negative therapeutic effect, and for the rationale resistances first, see Miller (13, 15).

the brain. We would expect such a reduction to eliminate a considerable variety of symptoms. But it is interesting that he found that the points that were most effective for eliminating extreme obsessive-compulsive behavior were somewhat different from those that were most effective for anxiety. This finding seems to rule out mere placebo effects. It suggests either that there may be different places in the brain for fears of different origins or, more probably, that some other kind of motivation besides pure fear is involved in obsessive-compulsive behavior. Additional investigation should be fruitful.

Drug Effects and Addiction

The foregoing analysis has assumed that barbiturates reduce fear, and, indeed, the clinical observations by Grinker and Spiegel were the basis of a series of experiments in my laboratory, which showed that sodium amytal can reduce the fear in rats (14). But, if this barbiturate specifically reduces fear, then we might expect a quick painless dose of it, via a chronic catheter into a vein, to act as a reward for a frightened animal. Thus, such an animal should learn to press a bar to administer the drug to itself. And, as Figure 4 shows, this is the case (3). While rats without shocks did not learn to press the bar for either of the two barbiturates, in two separate experiments rats, frightened by occasional inescapable shocks, did learn to press the bar for amobarbital. But, after several days, the rewarding effect weakened and disappeared. Unfortunately, in clinical practice the initial excellent fear-reducing properties of a drug often weaken with repeated administration.

Since immediate rewards are more effective than delayed ones, we would expect a quicker-acting barbiturate to be more effective than a slower-acting one. And the quicker-acting of the two drugs, hexobarbital, was more effective as a persistent reward.

I believe that the foregoing experiment illustrates one of the mechanisms that may be involved in addiction. Escape from the aversive withdrawal symptoms is another well-known mechanism. It may be that some drugs have also a direct rewarding effect (22). The foregoing mechanisms do not need to be mutually exclusive; in some cases they may potentiate each other.

The social and behavioral effects of alcohol have been a puzzle. It is supposed to be a central nervous system depressant, but the increase in the decibel level at a cocktail party does not seem to be an obvious symptom of such depression. It is supposed to depress higher functions first, but it is not clear that standing mutely and shyly in a corner involves higher cortical functions than becoming the life of the party. Conger (1) solved some of these paradoxes by showing that in an approach-avoidance conflict, alcohol reduces the fear-motivating avoidance more than the appetitive drive of the hunger-motivating approach. Thus, hungry animals that have been prevented from approaching food by receiving an electric shock at the goal resume running completely up to the goal if they are given a mild dose of alcohol. Figure 5 shows the results of an experiment in which separate groups of animals were

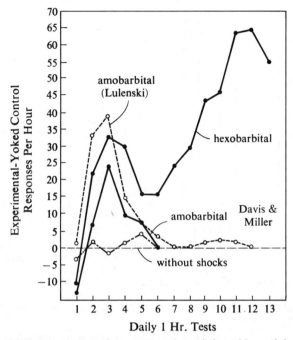

FIGURE 4. Learning to press a bar reinforced by an injection of a fear-reducing drug. When an experimental rat pressed a bar both he and a yoked control (whose bar functioned only to record his presses) received an immediate injection via a chronic catheter into a vein. The experimental rats learned when periodic inescapable brief electric shock created a chronic fear situation but did not learn if they received no shocks. The control rats did not learn. In two experiments on sodium amytal the rewarding effect of the drug wears off after several days while the effect of the faster-acting hexobarbital appears to be more permanent (3).

trained either to approach or to avoid, and the strength of each tendency was measured by the force which the animal exerted when temporarily restrained. It is clear that the alcohol reduced the avoidance motivated by fear more than the approach motivated by hunger. Many other experiments on conflict behavior are relevant to mental illness, but it would require a separate paper to do them justice (13).

Visceral Learning and Choice of Psychosomatic Symptom

I would like you to recall the first experiment in which rats learned to rotate the wheel to escape from the white compartment into the black one. This experiment involved two stages of learning: (1) By a classical conditioning procedure, the fear originally elicited by an electric shock was transferred to the white compartment; and (2) by an instrumental training procedure, the response of rotating the wheel was learned in order to escape from the fear-inducing white compartment. This second step is what Thorndike (27) called

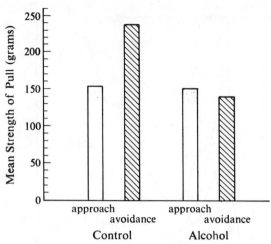

FIGURE 5.   The effect of 1.5 ml of 10% alcohol per 100 g of body weight given intraperitoneally on approach and avoidance responses measured separately by strength of pull exerted during temporary restraint halfway down a runway. (By permission [1].)

trial-and-error learning, and what Skinner (24) has renamed and popularized as operant conditioning.

It is widely believed that classical conditioning is a simpler type of learning and that the autonomic nervous system that mediates glandular and visceral responses is less intelligent so that it can be modified only by classical conditioning. Conversely, it is believed that only the skeletal responses mediated by the presumably brighter somatic nervous system are subject to the more sophisticated type of instrumental learning. Similarly, many, but not all, psychiatrists believe that the psychosomatic symptoms mediated by the autonomic nervous system are a more primitive type of symptom that cannot be influenced by symbolic factors or the secondary gains that I would call rewards. The problem is important because a classically conditioned response must be reinforced by an unconditioned stimulus that elicits exactly the same response that is to be learned. But in instrumental learning, the reward does not elicit the response to be learned; it reinforces any immediately preceding response. Thus the same reward may be used to reinforce any one of a number of different responses, as when one uses food to train a dog to sit up or lie down. Similarly, a given response may be reinforced by a number of different rewards—food for a hungry dog or water for a thirsty one. If the instrumental learning of glandular and visceral responses is possible, there are many more chances for psychosomatic symptoms to be reinforced and learned.

Determining whether or not visceral responses are subject to instrumental learning runs into the problem of separating out the effects of the skeletal muscles since the two systems are intimately and adaptively interrelated in maintaining homeostasis during normal behavior. If I offered you $100 to speed up your heart rate, you would probably think for a moment and then run up a flight of stairs and come back to collect your money. But from my point of view that would be cheating because you would be using the control of your skeletal muscles to produce an indirect effect on your heart rather than directly controlling your heart rate. A subtler method of affecting your heart rate is to change the depth or rate of your respiration. In order to rule out such indirect effects, we paralyzed the skeletal muscles of our rats with curare, which left the autonomic responses relatively unaffected, and maintained them on artificial respiration. It was shown later that curarization also improved visceral learning, presumably by removing a lot of "noise" from the situation and reducing the possibility that rewarding skeletal responses produced indirect effects that masked the direct ones.

Our procedure was to record accurately the visceral response, and immediately reward those small spontaneous fluctuations that were in the desired direction. After the animal had learned small changes, we shaped him by gradually requiring larger and larger ones to reach the criterion level that automatically and immediately delivered the reward.

But how does one reward an animal that is paralyzed by curare? We have used two different types of reward: the direct electrical stimulation of rewarding areas in the brain, and the escape from mild electric shocks to the tail.

Figure 6 shows an experiment in which half of the rats were rewarded for changes in heart rate and the other half were rewarded for changes

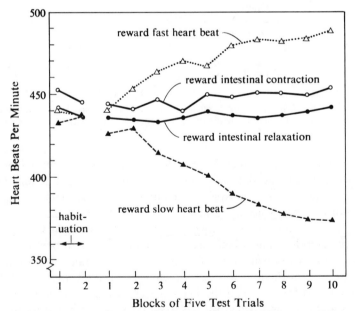

FIGURE 6. Curarized rats rewarded for increase in heart rate will increase it but those rewarded for decrease will decrease it. (By permission [18].)

in intestinal contraction. Half of each group were rewarded for increases and the other half for decreases. The animals that were rewarded for a fast heart rate learned to increase their heart rate while those that were rewarded for a slow heart rate learned to decrease it. This technique of training groups in opposite directions controls for classical conditioning and for other effects of the procedure. You will notice that those rats rewarded for increased or decreased intestinal contraction did not change their heart rates at all.

Figure 7 shows that if the animals were rewarded for increasing their intestinal contractions, they learned to increase them; if they were re-

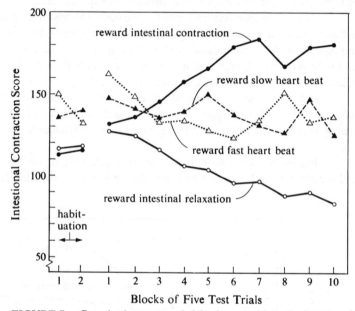

FIGURE 7.   Curarized rats rewarded for increased intestinal contraction learn to increase while those rewarded for decreases learn to decrease. (By permission [18].)

warded for decreases, they learned to decrease. But the rats rewarded for changes in heart rate did not change their intestinal contractions. This specificity of the learning controls for a number of other factors, e.g., that we were not just increasing the general arousal of the rats.

To summarize a large amount of other work in this area (16), we have successfully trained both increases and decreases in blood pressure without any changes in heart rate. Similarly, we have trained rats to increase and decrease urine formation without any changes in heart rate or blood pressure. But the blood flow through the kidneys was increased when we rewarded increases and decreased when we rewarded decreases in urine formation. Other responses have been trained, such as contraction of the uterus and vasomotor responses. Perhaps the most interesting study was an experiment where we specifically rewarded and trained differential vasomotor responses in two ears. I think you will agree that it is hard to imagine any skeletal response or even any thoughts which would cause the rat to blush in one ear but not in the other. With the specificity that it is possible to achieve in visceral training, I hope that such training will be useful in investigating the mechanisms of the control of these responses and in investigating the effects of drugs on them.

So far, the results of visceral learning are good. But now we come to an extraordinarily perplexing and vexing phenomenon, which is shown in Figure 8. In this summary of the results of a number of studies on heart rate,

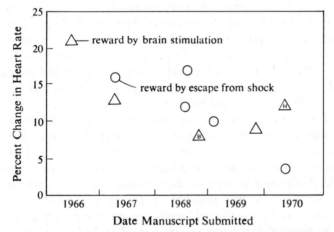

FIGURE 8. Progressive decline in amount of learned change in heart rate during a 5-yr period. Experiments are performed under approximately similar conditions in the author's laboratory, except for point B, which is from data by Hothersall and Brener (7) and point H, which is from data by Slaughter et al. (25). For each experiment, the increases and decreases are converted to percentage changes and then averaged.

most of them involving relatively similar procedures in our own laboratory, it can be seen that as time has marched on the learned differences have become progressively smaller! In fact, right now the differences that we are obtaining are still smaller, as might be expected from an extrapolation of the curve.

In addition to the decline in learned changes of heart rate, the baseline heart rates before training are from 50–100 beats per min higher than those in the earliest experiments, and at this higher rate they are much less variable, which may be a part of the difficulty. The high initial rate can be reduced by respirating the rats on a mixture of 95% air, and 5% carbon dioxide. This procedure seems to restore the general reactivity of the system and at first also seemed definitely to improve the learning, although that now seems to be another false lead.

Gorski (5) has found that the amount of testosterone necessary to sterilize a neonatal female rat has changed over the past 10 yr from an initial level of approximately $9\mu g$ to a present one of approximately $90\mu g$. I would be very interested to learn of any similar changes that others have observed in the behavioral, pharmacologic, or physiologic reactions of rats during the last 10 yr. Are there strain differences caused by the procedure of mass breeding for rats that do not bite experimenters? Can the widespread use of antibiotics in animal husbandry be a culprit? Is there some subtle form of contamination in the environment that is polluting our results?

One aspect of Figure 8 is reassuring. The two points distinguished by letters represent results from other laboratories of replications that are statistically highly reliable.

Now let us turn to the really interesting problem, namely, evidence on human visceral learning. A number of ingenious and courageous investigators have shown that people can learn to change their heart rate, blood pressure, or vasomotor responses. In general, the changes have been smaller than those achieved in our earlier experiments on curarized animals. It has been harder to rule out mediation via changes in breathing and other skeletal responses, so the interpretation has been more controversial (2, 8, 9). On the other hand, recent experiments have shown that certain selected subjects can produce small changes in blood pressure without changes in heart rate, or changes in heart rate without changes in blood pressure (23). This specificity suggests that the changes are not indirect ones unless there is some way of using skeletal responses to produce independently these two changes.

Some of the best evidence for human visceral learning, available for some time, has been neglected because of our disciplinary compartmentalization. The urethral sphincters are innervated exclusively by the autonomic nervous system but man has learned to control his urination. The conditions are favorable for such learning; there is strong motivation and immediate knowledge of results. But there has been some controversy about whether skeletal musculature may be involved indirectly in such control. This point has been resolved by a heroic experiment in which Lapides et al. (10), completely paralyzed 16 human subjects—some by curare and some by succinylcholine—so that they had to be maintained on artificial respiration. As has been known by clinicians who have used curare for treating tetanus, these subjects did not become incontinent. The new finding was that these subjects could initiate urination on command about as fast as ever, and could terminate it in about twice the time required when they were not paralyzed, stopping in spite of the fact that a large amount of fluid still remained in the bladder. Thus, it is quite clear that these people could control urination when all effects of contractions of the skeletal musculature were ruled out.

Other evidence, which has not been verified in such elegant detail, comes from the observation that many small boys learn to control their tears in the presence of their peers but may release them in the presence of a more sympathetic audience, such as their mothers. Furthermore, some actors and actresses can cry at will. Some of these claim they do it by recreating the details of an extremely sad situation, but others claim that they do not need to feel sad in order to cry, any more than they need to feel mad to clench their fists convincingly. It would be interesting to study the pattern of autonomic responses of these two schools of thought to see if the responses of the latter would be more specific than those of the former.

I believe that further study of animal and human visceral learning, and its possible therapeutic application, is a highly significant area of research. But I deplore the exaggerated publicity in the newspapers about this and other kinds of work commonly called biofeedback. Such exaggerated articles are raising impossible hopes which will result in a premature disillusionment, thus preventing the hard work necessary to prove what therapeutic usefulness or etiologic understanding can be derived from this type of research.

It is quite natural that the first investigations have concentrated on producing an effect. The experienced investigator has learned that it is a waste of time to devise elaborate, time-consuming controls before he has evidence that there may be a phenomenon to control. But once we reach the stage of being able to get clinically significant effects, it will be extremely important to put in careful controls for placebo effects, i.e., the effects of the hope and the suggestion produced by the impressive apparatus and of the personal attention that the therapeutic coach gives to the patient.

Effects of Learning on Stress; Psychosomatic Consequences

In conclusion, I would like to talk about another way in which learning can affect psychosomatic symptoms. The right side of Figure 9 illustrates the kinds of learned effect that we have just been discussing; e.g., a rat may learn to escape fear by either increasing or decreasing his heart rate, depending on which type of change is rewarded by a reduction in the fear. The left side of Figure 9 shows that it is possible also for learning to affect the amount and duration of the fear elicited in a given danger situation. Fear can innately produce psychosomatic effects, such as changes in heart rate or

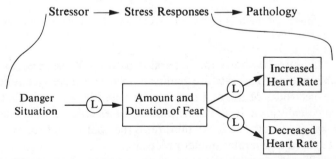

FIGURE 9.   Two different ways in which learning may affect a psychomatic symptom: (1) it may affect the amount and duration of an emotional response such as fear, which in turn may have a direct innate tendency to produce psychosomatic change; and (2) it may affect the type and amount of change that is elicited in response to a given emotional stimulus.

even lesions in the stomach. It is the type of learning illustrated in the left part of the diagram that will concern us here.

Observations of combat indicate that fear in situations of intermittent danger can be reduced by learning exactly what to expect and what to do (Miller, 13, p. 268). The first part of this proposition has been verified experimentally by Myers (19). He used a conditional emotional response type of test, in which the animal's fear inhibited drinking. Animals that had a signal that enabled them to learn when to expect an electric shock (and hence when they were safe) showed less chronic fear than those for which the shocks were completely unpredictable.

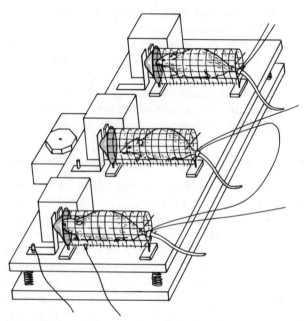

FIGURE 10.   Apparatus for studying psychologic factors affecting psychosomatic effects of shocks that are equally strong because the electrodes on the tails of the two yoked animals are wired in series. (By permission [32].)

Figure 10 shows the apparatus used by Weiss (28) to verify and extend this finding. The rats are semirestrained and have electrodes on their tails. The electrodes of the first two rats are wired in series, so that they must receive physically exactly the same amount of electric current. Such rats are called yoked partners. The lucky third rat is the control and receives no shock. Myers (19) used a generally similar procedure.

The rats are placed in separate, soundproof compartments. In one type of experiment (29), the shock for one rat is predictable because a signal precedes it, but for the other rat the shock is not predictable since the signal is given at random. Figure 11, from the experiment by Weiss (28), shows the

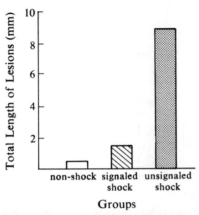

FIGURE 11. The amount of stomach lesions that are produced by signaled (predictable) as compared with unsignaled (unpredictable) electric shocks of equal physical intensity (29).

effects of this procedure as measured by total length of lesions in the stomach. You can see that the rats with the predictable, signaled shock scarcely have more lesions than the control rats, which are confined for an equal time without food or shock. The large lesions are in the stomach of the rats with the unsignaled and hence unpredictable shock. When both rats receive physically the same electric shock, the psychologic variable of knowing when the shock is coming produces a large difference.

Returning again to Figure 10, in a different use of the apparatus, the first rat can actuate an electronic relay by poking his nose through a hole in the tip of the cone to touch the L-shaped metal plate in front of the hole. If he performs this coping response soon enough after the danger signal comes on, he turns off that signal and avoids the shock. If he waits too long, he gets the shock but can turn it off by touching the plate. The second, or yoked, animal can perform the same response but, since the plate is not connected to any relay, the response does not have any effect. He is at the mercy of his partner. Figure 12 shows that this helpless, yoked rat gets by far the most stomach lesions. Although both rats receive exactly the same shocks, being able to perform the avoidance-coping response produces a great reduction in the stomach lesions (28).

If the avoidance-coping rats are given a feedback signal which clearly informs them when they have performed a correct response, the number of stomach lesions is reduced still more. The opposite is true if a conflict is introduced by giving a brief electric shock to rats who correctly perform the response that avoids the long train of shocks. This procedure reduces the safety-signal value of performing the correct response. Under this condition, the avoidance-coping rats have many more stomach lesions than their yoked controls. This result is shown in Figure 13, where the left-hand bars are a replication of the preceding experiment and the right-hand bars show the ef-

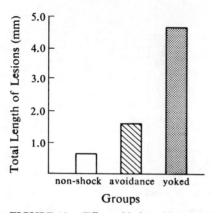

FIGURE 12. Effect of being able to perform an avoidance-coping response on the amount of stomach lesions. Each yoked rat received exactly
the same electric shocks as his avoidance partner, because the electrodes
on their tails were wired in series (29).

fects of conflict (30). In short, having to perform the response that controls
the situation is greatly beneficial if the task is simple and straightforward but
can be greatly detrimental if the task is difficult and produces conflict. Again
we see the extreme importance of psychologic factors even though for the two
groups the physical strength of the shocks, including those inducing the conflict, are held equal.

Effects of Learned Coping vs. Helplessness on Norepinephrine

In these experiments the psychosomatic effects of stress were
measured by stomach lesions, but the effects are similar for temperature
changes and also for levels of plasma corticosterone. One of the most interesting of the additional measures is the level of norepinephrine in the brain.
Figure 14 shows that, compared with the normal control animals, the rats that
can perform a successful escape response in a simple, nonconflictual situation have a higher level of norepinephrine in the brain. Conversely, those who
are helpless because none of their responses can affect the shock have norepinephrine levels in the brain that are lower than that of the nonshocked control
rats (32). With the help of a pharmacologist, Dr. Larissa Pohorecky, Dr.
Weiss is beginning to replicate these results and to extend them by determining the effects on synthesis and utilization. We also plan to see if there are
any effects on the other biogenic amines.

In conclusion, I would like to point out the relationship of these
last results to those presented by Dr. Axelrod in this volume and to clinical
observations of the type summarized by Schildkraut (21). As you know from
such work, the drugs that are useful in treating some, but unfortunately not all,
cases of depression are those that increase the effectiveness of norepinephrine
(and possibly other biogenic amines) at the synapse. The drugs that have the

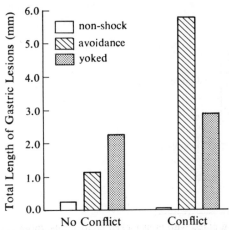

FIGURE 13.   Being the "executive" rat that learns the avoidance task reduces the amount of stomach lesions when the task is simple and clear-cut but increases it when the task involves conflict (30).

opposite effect of reducing the effectiveness of norepinephrine (and possibly other amines) at the synapse also have the opposite effect of causing or intensifying depressions if they are given to the wrong patient. Schildkraut (21) has hypothesized that situationally produced depressions may involve the same reduction in the effectiveness of norepinephrine at the synapse. (For a study on the more complex effects of chlorpromazine, see Leibowitz and Miller [11]).

In Figure 14 we have experimental evidence that a hopeless situation does indeed produce a reduction in the norepinephrine level in the brain, which presumably will decrease its effectiveness at the synapse. Perhaps this is a normal mechanism for producing a mildly depressed mood, which often is adaptive in preventing the animal from wasting too much energy by struggling with a hopeless situation. But perhaps when this mechanism is intensified by either a biochemical error or an extraordinarily hopeless environmental situation, it may lead to a maladaptive level of depression which in turn may create further failure, thus producing a vicious circle of reduced norepinephrine levels and continued depression. We hope to verify experimentally the other links in this hypothetical chain.

Finally, the increased level in norepinephrine in the animals that can perform a coping response may be a normal mechanism for producing an elevation of mood that helps to keep successful responses going at a high level. To continue with a possibly ridiculous speculation, many of our college students today seem to have vague symptoms of depression. They ask "Is there anything worthwhile?" But, when I grew up during the Great Depression after the stock market crash of 1929, I don't remember any of my young friends having that feeling. It seemed to me that we were so busy scrambling that we didn't get depressed. Perhaps, in an affluent section of society, a lack of need for and successful performance of coping responses results in a failure to raise

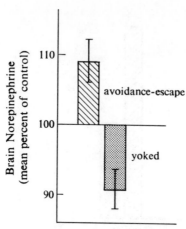

FIGURE 14.   Compared with nonshocked control rats, those that are able
to perform an avoidance-escape response have an increased level of norepinephrine in their brain while their helpless yoked partners, who have no
coping response available, have a decreased level of norepinephrine (32).

the level of norepinephrine to adequate levels, and hence leads to feelings of
vague depression. Perhaps we have evolved so that our mental health depends
on an environment that forces us to perform coping responses.

Whether or not this last speculation is true, I trust that it is clear
that learned and innate factors can interact to produce effects that are important for both mental and physical health and that the problem of understanding the details of such interactions requires interdisciplinary research of
the type exemplified by the contributors to this volume.

References

1. CONGER, J. J. The effects of alcohol on conflict behavior in the albino rat. *Quart. J. Stud. Alcohol,* 1951, *12,* 1.

2. CRIDER, A., SCHWARTZ, G. E., & SHNIDMAN, S. On the criteria for instrumental auto- nomic conditioning: A reply to Katkin and Murray. *Psychol. Bull.,* 1969, *71,* 455.

3. DAVIS, J. D., LULENSKI, G. C., & MILLER, N. E. Comparative studies of barbiturate self-administration. *Int. J. Addictions,* 1968, *3,* 207.

4. DOLLARD, J., & MILLER, N. E. *Personality and psychotherapy.* New York: McGraw-Hill, 1950.

5. GORSKI, R. A. Personal communication.

6. GRINKER, R. R., & SPIEGEL, J. P. *War neurosis.* New York: Blakiston, 1945. P. 80.

7. HOTHERSALL, D., & BRENER, J. Operant conditioning of changes in heart rate in curarized rats. *J. Comp. Physiol. Psychol.,* 1969, *68,* 338.

8. KATKIN, E. S., & MURRAY, E. N. Instrumental conditioning of autonomically medi- ated behavior: Theoretical and methodological issues. *Psychol. Bull.,* 1968, *70,* 52.

9. KATKIN, E. S., MURRAY, E. N., & LACHMAN, R. Concerning instrumental autonomic conditioning: A rejoinder. *Psychol. Bull.,* 1969, *71,* 462.

10. LAPIDES, J., SWEET, R. B., & LEWIS, L. W. Role of striated muscle in urination. *J. Urol.*, 1957, *77*, 247.

11. LEIBOWITZ, S. F., & MILLER, N. E. Unexpected adrenergic effect of chlorpromazine: Eating elicited by injection into rat hypothalamus. *Science*, 1969, *165*, 609.

12. MILLER, N. E. Studies of fear as an acquirable drive: I. Fear as motivation and fear reduction as reinforcement in the learning of new responses. *J. Exp. Psychol.*, 1948, *38*, 89.

13. ———. Liberalization of basic S-R concepts: Extensions to conflict behavior, motivation and social learning. In S. Koch (Ed.), *Psychology: A study of a science.* Study 1, Vol. 2. New York: McGraw-Hill, 1959. P. 196.

14. ———. The analysis of motivational effects illustrated by experiments on amylobarbitone sodium. In H. Steinberg, A. C. S. de Rueck, & J. Knight (Eds.), *Animal behaviour and drug action.* London: Churchill, 1964. P. 1.

15. ———. Some implications of modern behavior therapy for personality change and psychotherapy. In D. Byrne & P. Worchel (Eds.), *Personality change.* New York: Wiley, 1964. P. 149.

16. ———. Learning of visceral and glandular responses. *Science,* 1969, *163*, 434.

17. ———. *Neal E. Miller: Selected papers.* Chicago: Aldine-Atherton, 1971. P. 576.

18. MILLER, N. E., & BANUAZIZI, A. Instrumental learning by curarized rats of a specific visceral response, intestinal or cardiac. *J. Comp. Physiol. Psychol.*, 1968, *65*, 1.

19. MYERS, A. K. The effects of predictable vs. unpredictable punishment in the albino rat. Ph.D. thesis, Yale University, 1956.

20. PORTER, R. (Ed.). *The role of learning in psychotherapy.* London: Churchill, 1968.

21. SCHILDKRAUT, J. J. *Neuropsychopharmacology and the affective disorders.* Boston: Little, Brown, 1969.

22. SCHUSTER, C. R., JR., & THOMPSON, T. Self administration of and behavioral dependence on drugs. *Ann. Rev. Pharmacol.*, 1969, *10*, 483.

23. SHAPIRO, D., TURSKY, B., & SCHWARTZ, G. E. Differentiation of heart rate and systolic blood pressure in man by operant conditioning. *Psychosom. Med.*, 1970, *32*, 417.

24. SKINNER, B. F. *The behavior of organisms.* New York: Appleton-Century, 1938.

25. SLAUGHTER, J., HAHN, W., & RINALDI, P. Instrumental conditioning of heart rate in the curarized rat with varied amounts of pretraining. *J. Comp. Physiol. Psychol.*, 1970, *72*, 356.

26. SOLOMON, R. L., KAMIN, L. J., & WYNNE, L. C. Traumatic avoidance learning: The outcomes of several extinction procedures with dogs. *J. Abnorm. Psychol.*, 1953, *48*, 291.

27. THORNDIKE, E. L. Animal intelligence: An experimental study of the associative processes in animals. *Psychol. Rev. Monogr.* No. 2, 1898.

28. WEISS, J. M. Effects of coping responses on stress. *J. Comp. Physiol. Psychol.*, 1968, *65*, 251.

29. ———. Somatic effects of predictable and unpredictable shock. *Psychosom. Med.*, 1970, *32*, 397.

30. ———. Effects of punishing the coping response (conflict) on stress pathology in rats. *J. Comp. Physiol. Psychol.*, 1971, *77*, 14.

31. ———. Effects of coping behavior with and without a feedback signal on stress pathology in rats. *J. Comp. Physiol. Psychol.*, 1971, *77*, 22.

32. WEISS, M. J., STONE, E. A., & HARRELL, N. Coping behavior and brain norepinephrine level in rats. *J. Comp. Physiol. Psychol.*, 1970, *72*, 153.

Section Nine

COMPARATIVE PSYCHOLOGY

The modern study of animal behavior is an interdisciplinary effort involving the contributions of anthropologists, psychologists, and zoologists that finds common roots in the work of Charles Darwin. In the latter half of the nineteenth century, Darwin's account of evolution through natural selection provided a broad theoretical framework which encouraged: (a) a search for the survival-promoting features of behavior in each species under study, and (b) an attempt to trace the actual evolution of various behavior patterns or traits. This latter endeavor is necessarily complicated by the fact that the actual ancestors of existent species are nearly always long extinct and any behavioral reconstruction must involve numerous assumptions about the relations between existent types and ancestral types.

Although contemporary research and theorizing in animal behavior represents a synthesis of approaches, for many years there was a division between the comparative psychologists and the behaviorally oriented zoologists known as ethologists. The former were nearly always laboratory experimenters, used mammals as subjects, emphasized the study of learning, and tended to search for environmental influences on the development of animal behavior. In contrast, the "classical" ethologists focused upon the study of insects, birds, and fish in their natural habitats and emphasized species-characteristic "instinctive" units of behavior. Vigorous controversies ensued between the adherents of these two approaches over such issues as the usefulness of the "instinct" concept or the relative virtues of laboratory rigor and field relevance. The readings in this section have been selected to provide a brief glimpse of what ethologists and comparative psychologists think about such issues and how they perform their work. The work involves the study of many species under both laboratory and natural habitat conditions. However, the mere

483

gathering of data is not sufficient. There are conceptual issues to be dealt with and theoretical frameworks to be constructed and evaluated. Some theoretical issues, and some traces of old theoretical controversies, still remain and can be seen in the article by Tinbergen, which is the second article of this section. However, the remaining articles point out the nature of research that emerges from a combined approach, as when Kummer and Kurt directly compare field and laboratory behavior of baboons; when a psychologist and anthropologist carry out a field study of elephant seal behavior (Le Bouef & Peterson), or when laboratory-oriented psychologists carry out studies of learning that emphasize the survival benefits of learning certain kinds of associations with special efficiency (Garcia *et al.* and Wilcoxen *et al.*).

Stephen E. Glickman

The study of aggression is one of the most topical, yet one of the most controversial subjects under discussion by comparative psychologists. Some workers have emphasized the role of experience and particularly the idea that aggressive behavior is no different from any other operant; that it will be strengthened by reinforcement and that it can be extinguished by punishment or nonreinforcement. On the other hand, ethologists, exemplified by Konrad Lorenz and Desmond Morris, have argued that aggression is a fundamental aspect of the biology of animals and that certain species have evolved with social systems that emphasized continuous genetic selection for successful aggression. The study by Le Boeuf and Peterson certainly depicts a natural habitat situation in which reproductive succcess is closely linked to aggression. However, it must be remembered that the Le Boeuf and Peterson data do not carry any weighing of genetic and environmental factors in the ultimate production of adult aggressive behavior. In the second article, by Niko Tinbergen, a distinguished ethologist analyzes the controversy provoked by the publication of Lorenz's and Morris's popular books. He attempts to present a biologist's reasoned perspective on the implications of studying animal aggression for the understanding of human aggression.

Social Status and Mating Activity in Elephant Seals

Burney J. Le Boeuf and Richard S. Peterson

Individually marked male elephant seals, *Mirounga angustirostris,* observed on an island off central California participate in a social hierarchy resembling the peck order of domestic chickens. Individuals achieve status by fighting and maintain it by stereotyped threat displays. The higher the status of a male, the more readily he approaches and copulates with females. Four percent of the males inseminated 85 percent of the females.

Patterns of social organization in vertebrates have been generally categorized as territories or social hierarchies (1). Many pinnipeds are territorial; a few males defend specific sites where breeding females gather in "harems" (2). *Mirounga angustirostris* and *M. leonina,* the northern and southern elephant seals, are exceptions. Males of these species establish social hierarchies in which the males of highest rank remain near the breeding females but do not defend specific sites (3). Previous studies of the hierarchies were severely limited since few animals were recognizable as individuals, and since an observer must know the members of a group individually to obtain accurate data on social order. During the 1967–1968 breeding season of *M. angustirostris* at Año Nuevo Island, San Mateo County, California, we marked virtually

Source: Reprinted by permission from *Science,* 3 January 1969, *163,* 91–93. Copyright © 1969 by the American Association for the Advancement of Science.

all of the males that landed; thus we are able to provide the first quantitative description of the hierarchy and to relate individual status to breeding success.

In December of each year male elephant seals land at Año Nuevo Island, and many of them remain there continuously until March (4). In January, after many males have been on land for several weeks, the adult females come ashore, give birth, suckle their young for an average of 28 days, breed, and depart. We observed this population, on an average, for 6.0 hours per day, from 10 December 1967 to 15 March 1968, from blinds overlooking two beaches. We put individual markings on 93 of approximately 115 males as they landed on the island, and on 46 of 225 females (5). The males that we did not mark were immature transients rarely seen near the females.

As they came ashore, the adult males exhibited mutual rivalry which kept them apart from each other. Rivalry was evidenced most often by stereotyped threat patterns; a male elevated his forequarters, reared back his head allowing his proboscis to hang into his opened mouth, and emitted a series of loud, low-pitched, gutteral sounds (6). Normally, the threatened male halted his approach or retreated. If, instead, he held his ground or answered the display with one of his own, a confrontation often followed in which the males came together and attempted to butt, bite, and slash each other on the neck. We saw only 90 clashes, but more than 6000 threat displays. Fights lasted from a few seconds to 15 minutes and ended when one participant turned and fled.

We determined the direction of dominance between pairs of marked animals by noting which individual retreated after every threat or fight. Some pairs of individuals interacted as often as 65 times in 10 days. The social rank of an individual was determined by the number and identity of animals from which he retreated when threatened.

The relations between the seven top-ranking males on area 17, one of the two study areas, when displayed at 10-day intervals, demonstrates the dynamic nature of the social system (Table 1). The hierarchies were either linear (28 February to 8 March, Table 1), or complicated by triangular relations. An example of the latter occurred from 19 to 28 January when subject NIC moved subject GL, GL moved CLS, and CLS moved NIC. The direction of dominance between a pair of males did not change unless a fight occurred between them. The relation reversed when the previously dominant male retreated. The animals recognized each other individually.

The most important animal in the system was the alpha bull, the male that dominated all others on the beach. Activity centered around him since he usually remained in or near the aggregation of females toward which the other males were also oriented. Much of the alpha bull's activity involved keeping other males away from the females.

Copulation frequencies (in parentheses, Table 1) show that social rank was highly correlated with breeding success (7). We estimate that four of the highest ranking males (GL, CLS, GLS, and YLN), representing 6 percent of 71 individuals observed in area 17, inseminated 88 percent of the 120 fe-

TABLE 1. Social rank and copulation frequency of highest ranking males on area 17. Each male dominates those listed below it; deviations from a linear hierarchy are indicated by arrows. Dotted arrows denote a change in relation which occurred toward the end of the 10-day period. Copulation frequencies are in parentheses.

21 Dec. to 30 Dec.	30 Dec. to 8 Jan.	9 Jan. to 18 Jan.	19 Jan. to 28 Jan.	29 Jan to 7 Feb.	8 Feb. to 17 Feb.	18 Feb. to 27 Feb.	28 Feb. to 8 Mar.	Total copulations (No.)
NIC	NIC	CLS*	NIC(1)	GL(6)	GL(15)	GL(19)	GL(5)	46
UG	UG†	NIC	GL(1)	CLS(13)	CLS(7)	CLS(9)	CLS(1)	31
GL	GL	GL*	CLS(2)	NIC‡	GLS(4)	GLS(8)	GLS(1)	15
WN	WN	GLS	GLS(1)	GLS(5)	TWO(2)	PIN	PIN	8
HSN	TWO	TWO	TWO(2)	TWO(1)	PIN(3)	YLN(3)	YLN	9
TWO	YDB	PIN	PIN	PIN	YLN(3)	TWO‡	BLB	3
BRS	PIN	YLN	YLN	YLN(1)	BO	BLB(2)	BO	3
Copulations (No.)								
0	0	0	7	26	34	41§	7	
Females present (range)								
0–2	2–21	24–58	66–102	70–89	54–79	19–51	6–15	
Males present (range)								
15–27	19–26	19–28	22–29	24–34	24–34	23–35	24–31	

*Indeterminate relation during period despite two bloody fights.
† Moved to area 3 after losing fight to YLN at end of period.
‡ Left island during period and did not return.
§ Three other copulations were observed during this period; two by BO, one by WN.

males on that beach. The alpha bull from 29 January to 8 March (GL) copulated more frequently than any other male.

Among the four males that copulated most frequently, high rank was positively correlated with (i) demonstrating dominance over other males, (ii) preventing others from mounting and copulating, and (iii) mounting and copulating without interruption (Table 2).

On the other beach under study, area 3, one individual maintained the alpha position during the entire breeding season. This bull was involved in 73 percent of the copulations observed on area 3.

The extent to which social structure restricted mating to only a few males is illustrated by the combined statistics of the entire island. The four highest ranking males on area 17, plus the alpha bull on area 3 accounted for 123 of 144 copulations observed during the season. Thus 4 percent of the males apparently inseminated 85 percent of the females.

Social hierarchies exist in several mammalian species (8), but the type we observed in male elephant seals is especially comparable to that of domestic fowl (9). In both systems, the hierarchy may be linear, or may show

TABLE 2. Correlates of social rank in four males on area 17 during the period when GL was the alpha male

Males (in order of rank)	Times Other Males Moved by Threats (No.)	Mounts Prevented by Male (No.)	Copulations Interrupted by Male (No.)*	Mounts Prevented by Others (%)	Copulations Interrupted by Others (%)
GL	726	213	15	0	0
CLS	332	52	5	24	15
GLS	332	23	1	71	47
YLN	215	9	0	83	57

* Taken from all copulations observed, a total of 152.

triangular relations. The relations between individuals are stable unless fighting leads to reversals. However, among male fowl, high status confers access to food and roosting and nesting sites as well as to females, whereas in elephant seals the competition during the breeding season relates primarily to females. A male elephant seal shows no preference for a particular site, except one close to the females. As the females shift location, the males follow them. High-ranking males do not eat during the 3-month haul-out, and therefore do not compete for food. In addition, all the male elephant seals in our population exhibited a dominance relation with each other, whereas "no-contest" relations occur between some individuals in chicken peck orders.

A social system in which only a few males mate might have important genetic consequences for the evolution of the species, particularly if the same males continue to mate for more than one season. We do not know how many seasons one male successfully competes for females, or whether he fertilizes all those with whom he mates (10).

References

1. GUHL, A. M. In F. S. E. Hafez (Ed.), *The behavior of domestic animals*. London: Bailliere, Tindall, & Cox, 1962. P. 96.
2. BARTHOLOMEW, G. A., & HOEL, P. G. *J. Mammal.*, 1953, *34*, 417; HEWER, H. R., & BACKHOUSE, K. M. *J. Zool. Proc. Zool. Soc. London*, 1960, *134*, 157; CAMERON, A. W. *Can. J. Zool.*, 1967, *45*, 161; RAND, R. W. *Invest. Rep. Div. Sea Fish. Un. S. Afr.*, 1967, *60*, 1; PETERSON, R. S., & BARTHOLOMEW, G. A. *The natural history and behavior of the California sea lion*, American Society of Mammalogists, Spec. Publ. No. 1, 1967; SCHUSTERMAN, R. J., & DAWSON, R. G. *Science*, 1968, *160*, 434.
3. BARTHOLOMEW, G. A. *Univ. Calif. Publ. Zool*, 1952, *47*, 369; ANGOT, M. *Mammalia*, 1954, *15*, 1; LAWS, R. M. *Falkland Is. Dependencies Sur. Sci. Rep.*, 1956, No. 13; CARRICK, R. L., CSORDAS, S. E., & INGHAM, S. E. *Commonw. Sci. Ind. Res. Organ. Wildlife Res.*, 1962, *7*, 161.
4. RADFORD, K. W., ORR, R. T., & HUBBS, C. L. *Proc. Calif. Acad. Sci. 4th Ser.*, 1965, *31*, 601; ORR, R. T., & POULTER, T. C. *Ibid.*, 1965, *32*, 377.

5. Our best marks were obtained by slowly dripping 30 percent hydrogen peroxide, mixed with a cosmetic emulsifier, on the pelage of sleeping animals. The marks were easily recognizable from the blinds and lasted throughout the breeding season. We thank Clairol, Inc., for providing the emulsified "Lady Clairol Ultra Blue."

6. BARTHOLOMEW, G. A., & COLLIAS, N. E. *Anim. Behav.*, 1962, *10*, 7.

7. Copulation frequencies include only the first of a female's copulations that we observed. Additional copulations by the same female are excluded because we assumed that insemination occurred most likely as a result of the initial mating.

8. For example: KAUFMANN, J. A. In S. A. Altman (Ed.), *Social communication among primates*. Chicago: Univ. of Chicago Press, 1967. P. 73; GUHL, A. M., & ATKESON, F. W. *Trans. Kans. Acad. Sci.*, 1959, *62*, 80.

9. GUHL, A. M. In F. S. E. Hafez (Ed.), *The behavior of domestic animals*. London: Baillere, Tindall, and Cox, 1962. P. 491.

10. We attached permanent monel metal tags to many of the seals to identify them in future seasons and study the reproductive rates of males and females.

11. Our studies in Año Nuevo State Reserve were authorized by the California Department of Parks and Recreation, W. P. Mott, Jr., director; and permission to tag seals was granted by the California Department of Fish and Game, W. T. Shannon, director. We acknowledge the field assistance of M. Skeel, D. Ramsey, G. Eaton, and R. Gentry.

On War and Peace in Animals and Man: An Ethnologist's Approach to the Biology of Aggression

Niko Tinbergen

In 1935 Alexis Carrel published a best seller, *Man—The Unknown* (1). Today, more than 30 years later, we biologists have once more the duty to remind our fellowmen that in many respects we are still, to ourselves, unknown. It is true that we now understand a great deal of the way our bodies function. With this understanding came control: medicine.

The ignorance of ourselves which needs to be stressed today is ignorance about our behavior—lack of understanding of the causes and effects of the function of our brains. A scientific understanding of our behavior, leading to its control, may well be the most urgent task that faces mankind today. It is the effects of our behavior that begin to endanger the very survival of our species and, worse, of all life on earth. By our technological achievements we have attained a mastery of our environment that is without precedent in the history of life. But these achievements are rapidly getting out of hand. The consequences of our "rape of the earth" are now assuming critical proportions. With shortsighted recklessness we deplete the limited natural resources, including even the oxygen and nitrogen of our atmosphere (2). And Rachel Carson's warning (3) is now being followed by those of scientists, who give us an even gloomier picture of the general pollution of air, soil, and water. This pollution is seriously threatening our health and our food supply. Refusal to curb our reproductive behavior has led to the population explosion. And, as if all this were not enough, we are waging war on each other—men are fighting and killing men on a massive scale. It is because the effects of these behavior patterns, and of attitudes that determine our behavior, have now acquired such truly lethal potentialities that I have chosen man's ignorance about his own behavior as the subject of this paper.

I am an ethologist, a zoologist studying animal behavior. What gives a student of animal behavior the temerity to speak about problems of human behavior? Of course the history of medicine provides the answer. We all know that medical research uses animals on a large scale. This makes sense because animals, particularly vertebrates, are, in spite of all differences, so similar to us; they are our blood relations, however distant.

But this use of zoological research for a better understanding of ourselves is, to most people, acceptable only when we have to do with those bodily functions that we look upon as parts of our physiological machinery—

Source: Reprinted by permission from *Science*, 1968, *160*, 1411–1418. Copyright © 1968 by the American Association for the Advancement of Science.

the functions, for instance, of our kidneys, our liver, our hormone-producing glands. The majority of people bridle as soon as it is even suggested that studies of animal behavior could be useful for an understanding, let alone for the control, of our own behavior. They do not want to have their own behavior subjected to scientific scrutiny; they certainly resent being compared with animals, and these rejecting attitudes are both deep-rooted and of complex origin.

But now we are witnessing a turn in this tide of human thought. On the one hand the resistances are weakening, and on the other, a positive awareness is growing of the potentialities of a biology of behavior. This has become quite clear from the great interest aroused by several recent books that are trying, by comparative studies of animals and man, to trace what we could call "the animal roots of human behavior." As examples I select Konrad Lorenz's book *On Aggression* (4) and *The Naked Ape* by Desmond Morris (5). Both books were best sellers from the start. We ethologists are naturally delighted by this sign of rapid growth of interest in our science (even though the growing pains are at times a little hard to endure). But at the same time we are apprehensive, or at least I am.

We are delighted because, from the enormous sales of these and other such books, it is evident that the mental block against self-scrutiny is weakening—that there are masses of people who, so to speak, want to be shaken up.

But I am apprehensive because these books, each admirable in its own way, are being misread. Very few readers give the authors the benefit of the doubt. Far too many either accept uncritically all that the authors say, or (equally uncritically) reject it all. I believe that this is because both Lorenz and Morris emphasize our knowledge rather than our ignorance (and, in addition, present as knowledge a set of statements which are after all no more than likely guesses). In themselves brilliant, these books could stiffen, at a new level, the attitude of certainty, while what we need is a sense of doubt and wonder, and an urge to investigate, to inquire.

Potential Usefulness of Ethological Studies

Now, in a way, I am going to be just as assertive as Lorenz and Morris, but what I am going to stress is how much we do not know. I shall argue that we shall have to make a major research effort. I am of course fully aware of the fact that much research is already being devoted to problems of human, and even of animal, behavior. I know, for instance, that anthropologists, psychologists, psychiatrists, and others are approaching these problems from many angles. But I shall try to show that the research effort has so far made insufficient use of the potential of ethology. Anthropologists, for instance, are beginning to look at animals, but they restrict their work almost entirely to our nearest relatives, the apes and monkeys. Psychologists do study a larger variety of animals, but even they select mainly higher species. They also ignore certain major problems that we biologists think have to be studied. Psychiatrists, at least many of them, show a disturbing tendency to apply the *results* rather than the *methods* of ethology to man.

None of these sciences, not even their combined efforts, are as yet parts of one coherent science of behavior. Since behavior is a life process, its study ought to be part of the mainstream of biological research. That is why we zoologists ought to "join the fray." As an ethologist, I am going to try to sketch how my science could assist its sister sciences in their attempts, already well on their way, to make a united, broad-fronted, truly biological attack on the problems of behavior.

I feel that I can cooperate best by discussing what it is in ethology that could be of use to the other behavioral sciences. What we ethologists do not want, what we consider definitely wrong, is uncritical application of our results to man. Instead, I myself at least feel that it is our method of approach, our rationale, that we can offer (6), and also a little simple common sense, and discipline.

The potential usefulness of ethology lies in the fact that, unlike other sciences of behavior, it applies the method or "approach" of biology to the phenomenon behavior. It has developed a set of concepts and terms that allow us to ask:

1. In what ways does this phenomenon (behavior) influence the survival, the success of the animal?
2. What makes behavior happen at any given moment? How does its "machinery" work?
3. How does the behavior machinery develop as the individual grows up?
4. How have the behavior systems of each species evolved until they became what they are now?

The first question, that of survival value, has to do with the effects of behavior; the other three are, each on a different time scale, concerned with its causes.

These four questions are, as many of my fellow biologists will recognize, the major questions that biology has been pursuing for a long time. What ethology is doing could be simply described by saying that, just as biology investigates the functioning of the organs responsible for digestion, respiration, circulation, and so forth, so ethology begins now to do the same with respect to behavior; it investigates the functioning of organs responsible for movement.

I have to make clear that in my opinion it is the comprehensive, integrated attack on all four problems that characterizes ethology. I shall try to show that to ignore the questions of survival value and evolution—as, for instance, most psychologists do—is not only shortsighted but makes it impossible to arrive at an understanding of behavioral problems. Here ethology can make, in fact is already making, positive contributions.

Having stated my case for animal ethology as an essential part of the science of behavior, I will now have to sketch how this could be done. For this I shall have to consider one concrete example, and I select aggression, the most directly lethal of our behaviors. And, for reasons that will become clear, I shall also make a short excursion into problems of education.

Let me first try to define what I mean by aggression. We all understand the term in a vague, general way, but it is, after all, no more than a catchword. In terms of actual behavior, aggression involves approaching an opponent, and, when within reach, pushing him away, inflicting damage of some kind, or at least forcing stimuli upon him that subdue him. In this description the effect is already implicit: such behavior tends to remove the opponent, or at least to make him change his behavior in such a way that he no longer interferes with the attacker. The methods of attack differ from one species to another, and so do the weapons that are used, the structures that contribute to the effect.

Since I am concentrating on men fighting men, I shall confine myself to intraspecific fighting, and ignore, for instance, fighting between predators and prey. Intraspecific fighting is very common among animals. Many of them fight in two different contexts, which we can call "offensive" and "defensive." Defensive fighting is often shown as a last resort by an animal that, instead of attacking, has been fleeing from an attacker. If it is cornered, it may suddenly turn round upon its enemy and "fight with the courage of despair."

Of the four questions I mentioned before, I shall consider that of the survival value first. Here comparison faces us right at the start with a striking paradox. On the one hand, man is akin to many species of animals in that he fights his own species. But on the other hand he is, among the thousands of species that fight, the only one in which fighting is disruptive.

In animals, intraspecific fighting is usually of distinctive advantage. In addition, all species manage as a rule to settle their disputes without killing one another; in fact, even bloodshed is rare. Man is the only species that is a mass murderer, the only misfit in his own society.

Why should this be so? For an answer, we shall have to turn to the question of causation: What makes animals and man fight their own species? And why is our species "the odd man out"?

Causation of Aggression

For a fruitful discussion of this question of causation I shall first have to discuss what exactly we mean when we ask it.

I have already indicated that when thinking of causation we have to distinguish between three subquestions, and that these three differ from one another in the stretch of time that is considered. We ask, first: Given an adult animal that fights now and then, what makes each outburst of fighting happen? The time scale in which we consider these recurrent events is usually one of seconds, or minutes. To use an analogy, this subquestion compares with asking what makes a car start or stop each time we use it.

But in asking this same general question of causation ("What makes an animal fight?") we may also be referring to a longer period of time; we may mean "How has the animal, as it grew up, developed this behavior?" This compares roughly with asking how a car has been constructed in the factory. The distinction between these two subquestions remains useful even though we know that many animals continue their development (much slowed down) even after they have attained adulthood. For instance, they may still continue to learn.

Finally, in biology, as in technology, we can extend this time scale even more, and ask: How have the animal species which we observe today—and which we know have evolved from ancestors that were different —how have they acquired their particular behavior systems during this evolution? Unfortunately, while we know the evolution of cars because they evolved so quickly and have been so fully recorded, the behavior of extinct animals cannot be observed, and has to be reconstructed by indirect methods.

I shall try to justify the claim I made earlier, and show how all these four questions—that of behavior's survival value and the three subquestions of causation—have to enter into the argument if we are to understand the biology of aggression.

Let us first consider the short-term causation; the mechanism of fighting. What makes us fight at any one moment? Lorenz argues in his book that, in animals and in man, there is an internal urge to attack. An individual does not simply wait to be provoked, but, if actual attack has not been possible for some time, this urge to fight builds up until the individual actively seeks opportunity to indulge in fighting. Aggression, Lorenz claims, can be spontaneous.

But this view has not gone unchallenged. For instance, R. A. Hinde has written a thorough criticism (7), based on recent work on aggression in animals, in which he writes that Lorenz's "arguments for the spontaneity of aggression do not bear examination" and that "the contrary view, expressed in nearly every textbook of comparative psychology . . ." is that fighting "derives principally from the situation"; and even more explicitly: "There is no need to postulate causes that are purely internal to the aggressor" (7, p. 303). At first glance it would seem as if Lorenz and Hinde disagree profoundly. I have read and reread both authors, and it is to me perfectly clear that loose statements and misunderstandings on both sides have made it appear that there is disagreement where in fact there is something very near to a common opinion. It seems to me that the differences between the two authors lie mainly in the different ways they look at internal and external variables. This in turn seems due to differences of a semantic nature. Lorenz uses the unfortunate term "the spontaneity of aggression." Hinde takes this to mean that external stimuli are in Lorenz's view not necessary at all to make an animal fight. But here he misrepresents Lorenz, for nowhere does Lorenz claim that the internal urge ever makes an animal fight "in vacuo"; somebody or something is attacked. This misunderstanding makes Hinde feel that he has refuted Lorenz's views by saying that "fighting derives principally from the situation." But both authors are fully aware of the fact that fighting is started by a number of variables, of which some are internal and some external. What both authors know, and what cannot be doubted, is that fighting behavior is not like the simple slot machine that produces one platform ticket every time one threepenny bit is inserted. To mention one animal example: a male stickleback does not always show the full fighting behavior in response to an approaching standard opponent; its response varies from none at all to the optimal stimulus on some occasions, to full attack on even a crude dummy at other times. This means that its internal state varies, and in this particular case we know from the work of Hoar (8) that the level of the male sex hormone is an important variable.

Another source of misunderstanding seems to have to do with the stretch of time that the two authors are taking into account. Lorenz undoubtedly thinks of the causes of an outburst of fighting in terms of seconds, or hours—perhaps days. Hinde seems to think of events which may have happened further back in time; an event which is at any particular moment "internal" may well in its turn have been influenced previously by external agents. In our stickleback example, the level of male sex hormone is influenced by external agents such as the length of the daily exposure to light over a period of a month or so (9). Or, less far back in time, its readiness to attack may have been influenced by some experience gained, say, half an hour before the fight.

I admit that I have now been spending a great deal of time on what would seem to be a perfectly simple issue: the very first step in the analysis of the short-term causation, which is to distinguish at any given moment between variables within the animal and variables in the environment. It is of course important for our further understanding to unravel the complex interactions between these two worlds, and in particular the physiology of aggressive behavior. A great deal is being discovered about this, but for my present issue there is no use discussing it as long as even the first step in the analysis has not led to a clearly expressed and generally accepted conclusion. We must remember that we are at the moment concerned with the human problem: "What makes men attack each other?" And for this problem the answer to the first stage of our question is of prime importance: Is our readiness to start an attack constant or not? If it were—if our aggressive behavior were the outcome of an apparatus with the properties of the slot machine—all we would have to do would be to control the external situation: to stop providing threepenny bits. But since our readiness to start an attack is variable, further studies of both the external and the internal variables are vital to such issues as: Can we reduce fighting by lowering the population density, or by withholding provocative stimuli? Can we do so by changing the hormone balance or other physiological variables? Can we perhaps in addition control our development in such a way as to change the dependence on internal and external factors in adult man? However, before discussing development, I must first return to the fact that I have mentioned before, namely, that man is, among the thousands of other species that fight, the only mass murderer. How do animals in their intraspecific disputes avoid bloodshed?

The Importance of "Fear"

The clue to this problem is to recognize the simple fact that aggression in animals rarely occurs in pure form; it is only one of two components of an adaptive system. This is most clearly seen in territorial behavior, although it is also true of most other types of hostile behavior. Members of territorial species divide, among themselves, the available living space and opportunities by each individual defending its home range against competitors. Now in this system of parceling our living space, avoidance plays as important a part as attack. Put very briefly, animals of territorial species, once they have settled on a territory, attack intruders, but an animal that is still searching for a suitable territory or finds itself outside its home range withdraws when it meets with an already established owner. In terms of function, once you have taken possession of a territory, it pays to drive off competitors; but when you are still looking for a territory (or meet your neighbor at your common boundary), your chances of success are improved by avoiding such established owners. The ruthless fighter who "knows no fear" does not get very far. For an understanding of what follows, this fact, that hostile clashes are controlled by what we could call the "attack-avoidance system," is essential.

When neighboring territory owners meet near their common boundary, both attack behavior and withdrawal behavior are elicited in both animals; each of the two is in a state of motivational conflict. We know a great deal about the variety of movements that appear when these two conflicting, incompatible behaviors are elicited. Many of these expressions of a motivational conflict have, in the course of evolution, acquired signal function; in colloquial language, they signal "Keep out!" We deduce this from the fact that opponents respond to them in an appropriate way: instead of proceeding to intrude, which would require the use of force, trespassers withdraw, and neighbors are contained by each other. This is how such animals have managed to have all the advantages of their hostile behavior without the disadvantages: they divide their living space in a bloodless way by using as distance-keeping devices these conflict movements ("threat") rather than actual fighting.

Group Territories

In order to see our wars in their correct biological perspective one more comparison with animals is useful. So far I have discussed animal species that defend individual or at best pair territories. But there are also animals which possess and defend territories belonging to a group, or a clan (10).

Now it is an essential aspect of group territorialism that the members of a group unite when in hostile confrontation with another group that approaches, or crosses into their feeding territory. The uniting and the aggression are equally important. It is essential to realize that group territorialism does not exclude hostile relations on lower levels when the group is on its own. For instance, within a group there is often a peck order. And within the group there may be individual or pair territories. But frictions due to these relationships fade away during a clash between groups. This temporary elimination is done by means of so-called appeasement and reassurance signals. They indicate "I am a friend," and so diminish the risk that, in the general flare-up of anger, any animal "takes it out" on a fellow member of the same group (11). Clans meet clans as units, and each individual in an intergroup clash, while united with its fellow-members, is (as in interindividual clashes) torn between attack and withdrawal, and postures and shouts rather than attacks.

We must now examine the hypothesis (which I consider the most likely one) that man still carries with him the animal heritage of group territoriality. This is a question concerning man's evolutionary origin, and here we are, by the very nature of the subject, forced to speculate. Because I am going to say something about the behavior of our ancestors of, say, 100,000 years ago, I have to discuss briefly a matter of methodology. It is known to all biologists (but unfortunately unknown to most psychologists) that comparison of present-day species can give us a deep insight, with a probability closely approaching certainty, into the evolutionary history of animal species. Even where fossil evidence is lacking, this comparative method alone can do this. It has to be stressed that this comparison is a highly sophisticated method, and not merely a matter of saying that species A is different from species B (12). The basic procedure is this. We interpret differences between really allied species as the result of adaptive divergent evolution from common stock, and we interpret similarities between nonallied species as adaptive convergencies to similar ways of life. By studying the adaptive functions of species characteristics we understand how natural selection can have produced both these divergencies and convergencies. To mention one striking example: even if we had no fossil evidence, we could, by this method alone, recognize whales for what they are—mammals that have returned to the water, and, in doing so, have developed some similarities to fish. This special type of comparison, which has been applied so successfully by students of the structure of animals, has now also been used, and with equal success, in several studies of animal behavior. Two approaches have been applied. One is to see in what respects species of very different origin have convergently adapted to a similar way of life. Von Haartman (13) has applied this to a study of birds of many types that nest in holes—an anti-predator safety device. All such hole-nesters center their territorial fighting on a suitable nest hole. Their courtship consists of luring a female to this hole (often with the use of bright color patterns). Their young gape when a general darkening signals the arrival of the parent. All but the most recently adapted species lay uniformly colored, white or light blue eggs that can easily be seen by the parent.

An example of adaptive divergence has been studied by Cullen (14). Among all the gulls, the kittiwake is unique in that it nests on very narrow ledges on sheer cliffs. Over 20 peculiarities of this species have been recognized by Mrs. Cullen as vital adaptations to this particular habitat.

These and several similar studies (15) demonstrate how comparison reveals, in each species, systems of interrelated, and very intricate adaptive features. In this work, speculation is now being followed by careful experimental checking. It would be tempting to elaborate on this, but I must return to our own unfortunate species.

Now, when we include the "Naked Ape" in our comparative studies, it becomes likely (as has been recently worked out in great detail by Morris) that man is a "social Ape who has turned carnivore" (16). On the one hand he is a social primate; on the other, he has developed similarities to wolves, lions and hyenas. In our present context one thing seems to stand out clearly, a conclusion that seems to me of paramount importance to all of us, and yet has not yet been fully accepted as such. As a social, hunting primate, man must originally have been organized on the principle of group territories.

Ethologists tend to believe that we still carry with us a number of behavioral characteristics of our animal ancestors, which cannot be eliminated by different ways of upbringing, and that our group territorialism is one of those ancestral characters. I shall discuss the problem of the modifiability of our behavior later, but it is useful to point out here that even if our behavior were much more modifiable than Lorenz maintains, our cultural evolution, which resulted in the parceling-out of our living space on lines of tribal, national, and now even "bloc" areas, would, if anything, have tended to enhance group territorialism.

Group Territorialism in Man?

I put so much emphasis on this issue of group territorialism because most writers who have tried to apply ethology to man have done this in the wrong way. They have made the mistake, to which I objected before, of uncritically extrapolating the results of animal studies to man. They try to explain man's behavior by using facts that are valid only of some of the animals we studied. And, as ethologists keep stressing, no two species behave alike. Therefore, instead of taking this easy way out, we ought to study man in his own right. And I repeat that the message of the ethologists is that the methods, rather than the results, of ethology should be used for such a study.

Now, the notion of territory was developed by zoologists (to be precise, by ornithologists, 17), and because individual and pair territories are found in so many more species than group territories (which are particularly rare among birds), most animal studies were concerned with such individual and pair territories. Now such low-level territories do occur in man, as does another form of hostile behavior, the peck order. But the problems created by such low-level frictions are not serious; they can, within a community, be kept in check by the apparatus of law and order; peace within national boundaries can be enforced. In order to understand what makes us go to war, we have to recognize that man behaves very much like a group-territorial species. We too unite in the face of an outside danger to the group; we "forget our differences." We too have threat gestures, for instance, angry facial expressions. And all of us use reassurance and appeasement signals, such as a friendly smile. And (unlike speech) these are universally understood; they are cross-cultural; they are species-specific. And, incidentally, even within a group sharing a common language, they are often more reliable guides to man's intentions than speech, for speech (as we know now) rarely reflects our true motives, but our facial expressions often "give us away."

If I may digress for a moment: it is humiliating to us ethologists that many nonscientists, particularly novelists and actors, intuitively understand our sign language much better than we scientists ourselves do. Worse, there is a category of human beings who understand intuitively more about the causation of our aggressive behavior: the great demagogues. They have applied this knowledge in order to control our behavior in the most clever ways, and often for the most evil purposes. For instance, Hitler (who had modern mass communication at his disposal, which allowed him to inflame a whole nation) played on both fighting tendencies. The "defensive" fighting was whipped up by his passionate statements about "living space," "encirclement," Jewry, and Freemasonry as threatening powers which made the Germans feel "cornered." The "attack fighting" was similarly set ablaze by playing the myth of the Herrenvolk. We must make sure that mankind has learned its lesson and will never forget how disastrous the joint effects have been—if only one of the major nations were led now by a man like Hitler, life on earth would be wiped out.

I have argued my case for concentrating on studies of group territoriality rather than on other types of aggression. I must now return, in this context, to the problem of man the mass murderer. Why don't we settle even our international disputes by the relatively harmless, animal method of threat? Why have we become unhinged so that so often our attack erupts without being kept in check by fear? It is not that we have no fear, nor that we have no other inhibitions against killing. This problem has to be considered first of all in the general context of the consequences of man having embarked on a new type of evolution.

Cultural Evolution

Man has the ability, unparalleled in scale in the animal kingdom, of passing on his experiences from one generation to the next. By this accumulative and exponentially growing process, which we call cultural evolution, he has been able to change his environment progressively out of all recognition. And this includes the social environment. This new type of evolution proceeds at an incomparably faster pace than genetic evolution. Genetically we have not evolved very strikingly since Cro-Magnon man, but culturally we have changed beyond recognition, and are changing at an ever-increasing rate. It is of course true that we are highly adjustable individually, and so could hope to keep pace with these changes. But I am not alone in believing that this behavioral adjustability, like all types of modifiability, has its limits. These limits are imposed upon us by our hereditary constitution, a constitution which can only change with the far slower speed of genetic evolution. There are good grounds for the conclusion that man's limited behavioral adjustability has been outpaced by the culturally determined changes in his social environment, and that this is why man is now a misfit in his own society.

We can now, at last, return to the problem of war, of uninhibited mass killing. It seems quite clear that our cultural evolution is at the root of the trouble. It is our cultural evolution that has caused the population explosion. In a nutshell, medical science, aiming at the reduction of suffering, has, in doing so, prolonged life for many individuals as well—prolonged it to well beyond the point at which they produce offspring. Unlike the situation in any wild species, recruitment to the human population consistently surpasses losses through mortality. Agricultural and technical know-how have enabled us to grow food and to exploit other natural resources to such an extent that we can still feed (though only just) the enormous numbers of human beings on our crowded planet. The result is that we now live at a far higher density than that in which genetic evolution has molded our species. This, together with long-distance communication, leads to far more frequent, in fact to continuous, intergroup contacts, and so to continuous external provocation of aggression. Yet this alone would not explain our increased tendency to kill each other; it would merely lead to continuous threat behavior.

The upsetting of the balance between aggression and fear (and this is what causes war) is due to at least three other consequences of cultural evolution. It is an old cultural phenomenon that warriors are both brainwashed and bullied into all-out fighting. They are brainwashed into believing that fleeing—originally, as we have seen, an adaptive type of behavior—is despicable, "cowardly." This seems to me due to the fact that man, accepting that in moral issues death might be preferable to fleeing, has falsely applied the moral concept of "cowardice" to matters of mere practical importance—to the dividing of living space. The fact that our soldiers are also bullied into all-out fighting (by penalizing fleeing in battle) is too well known to deserve elaboration.

Another cultural excess is our ability to make and use killing tools, especially long-range weapons. These make killing easy, not only because a spear or a club inflicts, with the same effort, so much more damage than a fist, but also, and mainly, because the use of long-range weapons prevents the victim from reaching his attacker with his appeasement, reassurance, and distress signals. Very few aircrews who are willing, indeed eager, to drop their bombs "on target" would be willing to strangle, stab, or burn children (or, for that matter, adults) with their own hands; they would stop short of killing, in response to the appeasement and distress signals of their opponents.

These three factors alone would be sufficient to explain how we have become such unhinged killers. But I have to stress once more that all this, however convincing it may seem, must still be studied more thoroughly.

There is a frightening, and ironical paradox in this conclusion: that the human brain, the finest life-preserving device created by evolution, has made our species so successful in mastering the outside world that it suddenly finds itself taken off guard. One could say that our cortex and our brainstem (our "reason" and our "instincts") are at loggerheads. Together they have created a new social environment in which, rather than ensuring our survival, they are about to do the opposite. The brain finds itself seriously threatened by an enemy of its own making. It is its own enemy. We simply have to understand this enemy.

The Development of Behavior

I must now leave the question of the moment-to-moment control of fighting, and, looking further back in time, turn to the development of aggressive behavior in the growing individual. Again we will start from the human problem. This, in the present context, is whether it is within our power to control development in such a way that we reduce or eliminate fighting among adults. Can or cannot education in the widest sense produce non-aggressive men?

The first step in the consideration of this problem is again to distinguish between external and internal influences, but now we must apply this to the growth, the changing, of the behavioral machinery during the individual's development. Here again the way in which we phrase our questions and our conclusions is of the utmost importance.

In order to discuss this issue fruitfully, I have to start once more by considering it in a wider context, which is now that of the "nature-nurture" problem with respect to behavior in general. This has been discussed more fully by Lorenz in his book *Evolution and Modification of Behaviour* (18); for a discussion of the environmentalist point of view I refer to the various works of Schneirla (see 19).

Lorenz tends to classify behavior types into innate and acquired or learned behavior. Schneirla rejects this dichotomy into two classes of behavior. He stresses that the developmental process, of behavior as well as of other functions, should be considered, and also that this development forms a highly complicated series of interactions between the growing organism and its environment. I have gradually become convinced that the clue to this difference in approach is to be found in a difference in aims between the two authors.

Lorenz claims that "we are justified in leaving, at least for the time being, to the care of the experimental embryologists all those questions which are concerned with the chains of physiological causation leading from the genome to the development of . . . neurosensory structures" (18, p. 43). In other words, he deliberately refrains from starting his analysis of development prior to the stage at which a fully coordinated behavior is performed for the first time. If one in this way restricts one's studies to the later stages of development, then a classification in "innate" and "learned" behavior, or behavior components, can be considered quite justified. And there was a time, some 30 years ago, when the almost grotesquely environmentalist bias of psychology made it imperative for ethologists to stress the extent to which behavior patterns could appear in perfect or near-perfect form without the aid of anything that could be properly called learning. But I now agree (however belatedly) with Schneirla that we must extend our interest to earlier stages of development and embark on a full program of experimental embryology of behavior. When we do this, we discover that interactions with the environment can indeed occur at early stages. These interactions may concern small components of the total machinery of a fully functional behavior pattern, and many of them cannot possibly be called learning. But they are interactions with the environment, and must be taken into account if we follow in the footsteps of the experimental embryologists, and extend our field of interest to the entire sequence of events which lead from the blueprints contained in the zygote to the fully functioning, behaving animal. We simply have to do this if we want an answer to the question to what extent the development of behavior can be influenced from the outside.

When we follow this procedure the rigid distinction between "innate" or unmodifiable and "acquired" or modifiable behavior patterns becomes far less sharp. This is owing to the discovery, on the one hand, that "innate" patterns may contain elements that at an early stage developed in interaction with the environment, and, on the other hand, that learning is, from step to step, limited by internally imposed restrictions.

To illustrate the first point, I take the development of the sensory cells in the retina of the eye. Knoll has shown (20) that the rods in the eyes of tadpoles cannot function properly unless they have first been exposed to light. This means that, although any visually guided response of a tadpole may well, in its integrated form, be "innate" in Lorenz's sense, it is so only in the sense of "nonlearned," not in that of "having grown without interaction with the environment." Now it has been shown by Cullen (21) that male sticklebacks reared from the egg in complete isolation from other animals will, when adult, show full fighting behavior to other males and courtship behavior to females when faced with them for the first time in their lives. This is admittedly an important fact, demonstrating that the various recognized forms of learning do not enter into the programing of these integrated patterns. This is a demonstration of what Lorenz calls an "innate response." But it does not exclude the possibility that parts of the machinery so employed may, at an earlier stage, have been influenced by the environment, as in the case of the tadpoles.

Second, there are also behavior patterns which do appear in the inexperienced animal, but in an incomplete form, and which require additional development through learning. Thorpe has analyzed a clear example of this: when young male chaffinches reared alone begin to produce their song for the first time, they utter a very imperfect warble; this develops into the full song only if, at a certain sensitive stage, the young birds have heard the full song of an adult male (22).

By far the most interesting aspect of such intermediates between innate and acquired behavior is the fact that learning is not indiscriminate, but is guided by a certain selectiveness on the part of the animal. This fact has been dimly recognized long ago; the early ethologists have often pointed out that different, even closely related, species learn different things even when developing the same behavior patterns. This has been emphasized by Lorenz's use of the term "innate teaching mechanism." Other authors use the word "template" in the same context. The best example I know is once more taken from the development of song in certain birds. As I have mentioned, the males of some birds acquire their full song by changing their basic repertoire to resemble the song of adults, which they have to hear during a special sensitive period some months before they sing themselves. It is in this sensitive period that they acquire, without as yet producing the song, the knowledge of "what the song ought to be like." In technical terms, the bird formed a *Sollwert* (23) (literally, "should-value," an ideal) for the feedback they receive when they hear their own first attempts. Experiments have shown (24) that such birds, when they start to sing, do three things: they listen to what they produce; they notice the difference between this feedback and the ideal song; and they correct their next performance.

This example, while demonstrating an internal teaching mechanism, shows, at the same time, that Lorenz made his concept too narrow when he coined the term "innate teaching mechanism." The birds have developed a teaching mechanism, but while it is true that it is internal, it is not innate; the birds have acquired it by listening to their father's song.

These examples show that if behavior studies are to catch up with experimental embryology our aims, our concepts, and our terms must be continually revised.

Before returning to aggression, I should like to elaborate a little further on general aspects of behavior development, because this will enable me to show the value of animal studies in another context, that of education.

Comparative studies, of different animal species, of different behavior patterns, and of different stages of development, begin to suggest that wherever learning takes a hand in development, it is guided by such *Sollwerte* or templates for the proper feedback, the feedback that reinforces. And it becomes clear that these various *Sollwerte* are of a bewildering variety. In human education one aspect of this has been emphasized in particular, and even applied in the use of teaching machines: the requirement that the reward, in order to have maximum effect, must be immediate. Skinner has stressed this so much because in our own teaching we have imposed an unnatural delay between, say, taking in homework, and giving the pupil his reward in the form of a mark. But we can learn more from animal studies than the need for immediacy of reward. The type of reward is also of great importance, and this may vary from task to task, from stage to stage, from occasion to occasion; the awards may be of almost infinite variety.

Here I have to discuss briefly a behavior of which I have so far been unable to find the equivalent in the development of structure. This is exploratory behavior. By this we mean a kind of behavior in which the animal sets out to acquire as much information about an object or a situation as it can possibly get. The behavior is intricately adapted to this end, and it terminates when the information has been stored, when the animal has incorporated it in its learned knowledge. This exploration (subjectively we speak of "curiosity") is not confined to the acquisition of information about the external world alone; at least mammals explore their own movements a great deal, and in this way "master new skills." Again, in this exploratory behavior, *Sollwerte* of expected, "hoped-for" feedbacks play their part.

Without going into more detail, we can characterize the picture we begin to get of the development of behavior as a series, or rather a web, of events, starting with innate programing instructions contained in the zygote, which straightaway begin to interact with the environment; this interaction may be discontinuous, in that periods of predominantly internal development alternate with periods of interaction, or sensitive periods. The interaction is enhanced by active exploration; it is steered by selective *Sollwerte* of great variety; and stage by stage this process ramifies; level upon level of ever-increasing complexity is being incorporated into the programing.

Apply what we have heard for a moment to playing children (I do not, of course, distinguish sharply between "play" and "learning"). At a certain age a child begins to use, say, building blocks. It will at first manipulate them in various ways, one at a time. Each way of manipulating acts as exploratory behavior: the child learns what a block looks, feels, tastes like, and so forth, and also how to put it down so that it stands stably.

Each of these stages "peters out" when the child knows what it wanted to find out. But as the development proceeds, a new level of exploration is added: the child discovers that it can put one block on top of the other; it constructs. The new discovery leads to repetition and variation, for each child develops, at some stage, a desire and a set of *Sollwerte* for such effects of construction, and acts out to the full this new level of exploratory behavior. In addition, already at this stage the *Sollwert* or ideal does not merely contain what the blocks do, but also what, for instance, the mother does; her approval, her shared enjoyment, is also of great importance. Just as an exploring animal, the child builds a kind of inverted pyramid of experience, built of layers, each set off by a new wave of exploration and each directed by new sets of *Sollwerte,* and so its development "snowballs." All these phases may well have more or less limited sensitive periods, which determine when the fullest effect can be obtained, and when the child is ready for the next step. More important still, if the opportunity for the next stage is offered either too early or too late, development may be damaged, including the development of motivational and emotional attitudes.

Of course gifted teachers of many generations have known all these things (25) or some of them, but the glimpses of insight have not been fully and scientifically systematized. In human education, this would of course involve experimentation. This need not worry us too much, because in our search for better educational procedures we are in effect experimenting on our children all the time. Also, children are fortunately incredibly resilient, and most grow up into pretty viable adults in spite of our fumbling educational efforts. Yet there is, of course, a limit to what we will allow ourselves, and this, I should like to emphasize, is where animal studies may well become even more important than they are already.

Can Education End Aggression?

Returning now to the development of animal and human aggression, I hope to have made at least several things clear: that behavior development is a very complex phenomenon indeed; that we have only begun to analyze it in animals; that with respect to man we are, if anything, behind in comparison with animal studies; and that I cannot do otherwise than repeat what I said in the beginning: we must make a major research effort. In this effort animal studies can help, but we are still very far from drawing very definite conclusions with regard to our question: To what extent shall we be able to render man less aggressive through manipulation of the environment, that is, by educational measures?

In such a situation personal opinions naturally vary a great deal. I do not hesitate to give as my personal opinion that Lorenz's book *On Agression,* in spite of its assertativeness, in spite of factual mistakes, and in spite of the many possibilities of misunderstandings that are due to the lack of a common language among students of behavior—that this work must be taken more seriously as a positive contribution to our problem than many critics have done. Lorenz is, in my opinion, right in claiming that elimination, through education, of the internal urge to fight will turn out to be very difficult, if not impossible.

Everything I have said so far seems to me to allow for only one conclusion. Apart from doing our utmost to return to a reasonable population density, apart from stopping the progressive depletion and pollution of our habitat, we must pursue the biological study of animal behavior for clarifying problems of human behavior of such magnitude as that of our aggression, and of education.

But research takes a long time, and we must remember that there are experts who forecast worldwide famine 10 to 20 years from now; and that we have enough weapons to wipe out all human life on earth. Whatever the causation of our aggression, the simple fact is that for the time being we are saddled with it. This means that there is a crying need for a crash program, for finding ways and means for keeping our intergroup aggression in check. This is of course in practice infinitely more difficult than controlling our intranational frictions; we have as yet not got a truly international police force. But there is hope for avoiding all-out war because, for the first time in history, we are afraid of killing ourselves by the lethal radiation effects even of bombs that we could drop in the enemy's territory. Our politicians know this. And as long as there is this hope, there is every reason to try and learn what we can from animal studies. Here again they can be of help. We have already seen that animal opponents meeting in a hostile clash avoid bloodshed by using the expressions of their motivational conflicts as intimidating signals. Ethologists have studied such conflict movements in some detail (26), and have found that they are of a variety of types. The most instructive of these is the redirected attack; instead of attacking the provoking, yet dreaded, opponent, animals often attack something else, often even an inanimate object. We ourselves bang the table with our fists. Redirection includes something like sublimation, a term attaching a value judgment to the redirection. As a species with group territories, humans, like hyenas, unite when meeting a common enemy. We do already sublimate our group aggression. The Dutch feel united in their fight against the sea. Scientists do attack their problems together. The space program—surely a mainly military effort—is an up-to-date example. I would not like to claim, as Lorenz does, that redirected attack exhausts the aggressive urge. We know from soccer matches and from animal work how aggressive behavior has two simultaneous, but opposite effects: a waning effect, and one of self-inflammation, of mass hysteria, such as recently seen in Cairo. Of these two the inflammatory effect often wins. But if aggression were used successfully as the motive force behind nonkilling and even useful activities, self-stimulation need not be a danger; in our short-term cure we are not aiming at the elimination of aggressiveness, but at "taking the sting out of it."

Of all sublimated activities, scientific research would seem to offer the best opportunities for deflecting and sublimating our aggression. And, once we recognize that it is the disrupted relation between our own behavior and our environment that forms our most deadly enemy, what could be better than uniting, at the front or behind the lines, in the scientific attack on our own behavioral problems?

I stress "behind the lines." The whole population should be made to feel that it participates in the struggle. This is why scientists will always have the duty to inform their fellowmen of what they are doing, of the relevance and the importance of their work. And this is not only a duty, it can give intense satisfaction.

I have come full circle. For both the long-term and the short-term remedies at least we scientists will have to sublimate our aggression into an all-out attack on the enemy within. For this the enemy must be recognized for what it is: our unknown selves, or, deeper down, our refusal to admit that man is, to himself, unknown.

I should like to conclude by saying a few words to my colleagues of the younger generation. Of course we all hope that, by muddling along until we have acquired better understanding, self-annihilation either by the "whimper of famine" or by the "bang of war" can be avoided. For this, we must on the one hand trust, on the other help (and urge) our politicians. But it is no use denying that the chances of designing the necessary preventive measures are small, let alone the chances of carrying them out. Even birth control still offers a major problem.

It is difficult for my generation to know how seriously you take the danger of mankind destroying his own species. But those who share the apprehension of my generation might perhaps, with us, derive strength from keeping alive the thought that has helped so many of us in the past when faced with the possibility of imminent death. Scientific research is one of the finest occupations of our mind. It is, with art and religion, one of the uniquely human ways of meeting nature, in fact, the most active way. If we are to succumb, and even if this were to be ultimately due to our own stupidity, we could still, so to speak, redeem our species. We could at least go down with some dignity, by using our brain for one of its supreme tasks, by exploring to the end.

References

1. CARREL, A. L'homme, cet inconnu. Paris: Librairie Plon, 1935.
2. AAAS Annual Meeting, 1967. See New Scientist, 1968, 37, 5.
3. CARSON, R. Silent spring. Boston: Houghton Mifflin, 1962.
4. LORENZ, K. On aggression. London: Methuen, 1966.
5. MORRIS, D. The naked ape. London: Jonathan Cape, 1967.
6. TINBERGEN, N. Z. Tierpsychol., 1964, 20, 410.
7. HINDE, R. A. New Society, 1967, 9, 302.
8. HOAR, W. S. Animal behaviour, 1962, 10, 247.
9. BAGGERMAN, B. In Symp. Soc. Exp. Biol., 1965, 20, 427.
10. KRUUK, H. New scientist, 1966, 30, 849.
11. TINBERGEN, N. Z. Tierpsychol., 1959, 16, 651; Zool. Mededelingen, 1964, 39, 209.
12. ———. Behaviour, 1959, 15, 1–70.
13. VON HAARTMAN, L. Evolution, 1957, 11, 339.
14. CULLEN, E. Ibis, 1957, 99, 275.
15. CROOK, J. H. Symp. Zool. Soc. London, 1965, 14, 181.
16. FREEMAN, D. Inst. Biol. Symp., 1964, 13, 109; MORRIS, D. (Ed.), Primate ethology. London: Weidenfeld and Nicolson, 1967.
17. HOWARD, H. E. Territory in bird life. London: Murray, 1920; HINDE, R. A., et al. Ibis, 1956, 98, 340–530.
18. LORENZ, K. Evolution and modification of behaviour. London: Methuen, 1966.
19. SCHNEIRLA, T. C. Quart. Rev. Biol., 1966, 41, 283.

20. KNOLL, M. D. *Z. Vergleich. Physiol.*, 1956, *38*, 219.

21. CULLEN, E. *Final Rept. Contr. AF 61 (052)-29*, USAFRDC, 1961, 1–23.

22. THORPE, W. H. *Bird-song.* New York: Cambridge Univ. Press, 1961.

23. HOLST, E. VON, & MITTELSTAEDT, H. *Naturwissenschaften*, 1950, *37*, 464.

24. KONISHI, M. *Z. Tierpsychol.*, 1965, *22*, 770; NOTTEBOHM, F. *Proc. 14th Intern. Ornithol. Congr.*, 1967, 265–280.

25. STANDING, E. M. *Maria Montessori.* New York: New American Library, 1962.

26. TINBERGEN, N. In I. Rosen (Ed.), *The pathology and treatment of sexual deviation.* London: Oxford Univ. Press, 1964. Pp. 3–23; JONES, N. B. *Wildfowl Trust 11th Ann. Rept.*, 1960, 46–52; SEVENSTER, P. *Behaviour Suppl.*, 1961, *9*, 1–170; ROWELL, F. *Animal behaviour*, 1961, *9*, 38.

Many studies of learning carried out in the behavioristic tradition have emphasized the existence of general principles which cut across species barriers. Stated in its strongest form (as, for example, by B. F. Skinner, A case history in scientific method, Amer. Psychologist, 1956, 11, 221–223), such an approach leads to the assumption that if one has a reinforcing stimulus which is effective for a given species, that stimulus is capable of modifying the probable occurrence of any operant response in the motor repertoire of that species. On the other hand, more naturalistically oriented psychologists have emphasized that different species evolve to solve certain kinds of problems for efficiently than others. The next two selections by Garcia et al. and Wilcoxon et al. exemplify the constraints that the biological propensities of the species place on what is learned. Both rats and quail have evolved to sample novel foods to determine, on the basis of ingestive experience, whether such foods should be subsequently eaten. This learning is unusual in several respects. First, it proceeds despite extraordinary delays between tasting the food and subsequent illness. In addition, the ease with which particular classes of sensory stimuli can be attached to the aversive postingestive effects is limited. Thus, rats can associate taste but not visual stimuli with post ingestive upset, while birds, who are normally visual feeders, can use both visual and gustatory cues.

Illness-Induced Aversions in Rat and Quail: Relative Salience of Visual and Gustatory Cues

*Hardy C. Wilcoxon, William B. Dragoin,
and Paul A. Kral*

Bobwhite quail, like the rat, learn in one trial to avoid flavored water when illness is induced by a drug ½ hour after drinking. In contrast to the rat, quail also learn to avoid water that is merely darkened by vegetable dye. The visual cue is even more salient than the taste cue in quail.

Earlier work on illness-induced aversions to eating and drinking shows rather clearly that the rat, at least, must have either a gustatory or an olfactory cue in order to learn to avoid ingesting a substance if the illness that follows ingestion is delayed by ½ hour or more. Visual, auditory, and tactual cues, even though conspicuously present at the time of ingestion, do not become danger signals for the rat in such circumstances (1, 2). On the other

Source: Reprinted by permission from *Science*, 1971, *171*, 826–828. Copyright © 1971 by the American Association for the Advancement of Science.

Note: This research is part of the program of the John F. Kennedy Center for Research on Education and Human Development, George Peabody College for Teachers, Nashville, Tennessee, under a Biomedical Sciences Support grant from the National Institutes of Health.

hand, blue jays (*Cyanocitta cristata bromia* Oberholser, Corvidae) easily learn to reject toxic monarch butterflies (*Danaus plexippus* L., subfamily Danainae) on sight, although the model suggested for this learning gives emetic reinstatement of taste during illness a prominent, mediating role (3).

Impetus for our experiments came from the general view that the behavior of an organism, including what it can and cannot readily learn, is largely a product of its evolutionary history. In view of the rat's highly developed chemical senses, nocturnal feeding habits, and relatively poor vision, its ability to learn to avoid toxic substances on the basis of their taste or smell, rather than their appearance, is not surprising. But how general is this phenomenon across species? Might we not expect a diurnal bird, with its superior visual equipment and greater reliance upon vision in foraging for food and drink, to show a different pattern? Perhaps such birds, even in situations involving long delay between the time of ingestion of some food and the onset of illness, can learn to avoid ingesting substances that are distinctive in appearance only.

We report here two experiments which show that bobwhite quail (*Colinus virginianus*) can associate a purely visual cue with a long-delayed, illness consequence. In the first experiment we investigated the relative salience of a visual cue and a gustatory cue in both rats and quail. In the second experiment, in which we used quail only, we controlled for two variables which, unless accounted for, would not have allowed clear-cut interpretation of the first experiment.

Forty 90-day-old male Sprague-Dawley rats and 40 adult male bobwhite quail were subjects (4) in the first experiment. All were caged individually and had free access to food throughout the experiment. At the start, both species were trained over a period of several days to drink all of their daily water from 30-ml glass Richter tubes. Water was presented at the same time each day, and the time allowed for drinking was gradually reduced to a 10-minute period. Baseline drinking was then measured for 1 week, after which experimental treatments were imposed.

On treatment day, subgroups of each species received an initial 10-minute exposure to water that was either dark blue ($N = 8$), sour ($N = 8$), or both blue and sour ($N = 24$). Water was made blue by the addition of three drops of vegetable food coloring to 100 ml of water. Sour water consisted of a weak hydrochloric acid solution (0.5 ml per liter). One-half hour after removal of the distinctive fluid all subjects were injected intraperitoneally with the illness-inducing drug, cyclophosphamide. The dosage for the rats was 66 mg/kg, a dosage known to be effective for establishing one-trial aversions to distinctive tastes in the rat. We used a larger dose (132 mg/kg) for the quail, however, because exploratory use of the drug with the birds showed that the larger dose was necessary in order to produce the primary symptom of illness that rats exhibit, namely, extensive diarrhea.

For 2 days after treatment all subjects drank plain water at the regular 10-minute daily drinking period. This allowed them time to recover from the illness, as evidenced by remission of diarrhea and a return to baseline amounts of water consumption. Extinction tests were then begun to determine whether aversive conditioning had been established to the cues present in the water on treatment day. Five 10-minute tests were conducted, one every third day, with 2 days intervening between tests during which subjects were allowed to drink plain water to restablish the baseline.

Animals that drank sour water on treatment day were tested with sour water (S : S); those that drank blue water on treatment day received blue water in the extinction tests (B : B). However, the 24 animals of each species that had drunk blue-sour water on treatment day were divided into three subgroups for testing. One group of each species was tested on blue-sour water (BS : BS), another on sour water (BS : S), and the third on blue water (BS : B).

Figure 1 shows a comparison of the amount of water drunk by rats and quail over five extinction trials for each of the five treatment : test conditions. Differences between mean drinking scores on treatment day and the first extinction trial (E_1) were assessed for statistical significance by the t-test. Results in the S : S condition show that the sour taste by itself was an effective cue for avoidance in both rat ($P < .02$) and quail ($P < .05$). Only the quail, however, showed reduced drinking ($P < .01$) of water that was colored blue on treatment and test days (B : B). In the BS : BS condition, both species again showed significantly reduced drinking in the tests ($P < .001$).

Perhaps the most striking results were shown by the last two subgroups for which the compound cue (BS) of the treatment day conditioning trial was split for separate testing of each component. In the latter two conditions (BS : S and BS : B) rats and quail showed a remarkable difference with respect to the salience of gustatory and visual cues. When the sour element of the compound conditioning stimulus was the test cue (BS : S), rats avoided it ($P < .001$) but quail did not. On the other hand, when the blue color was the element tested (BS : B), quail avoided it ($P < .01$) but rats did not. The behavior of the quail in these split-cue tests is especially informative. Although the quail learned the aversion to taste alone (S : S condition), removal of the visual element from the compound conditioning stimulus (BS : S condition) apparently constituted such a radical change in stimulus for them that it rendered the remaining taste element ineffective. The results demonstrate, therefore, not only that quail can associate a visual cue with long-delayed illness, but also that a visual cue can be so salient as to overshadow taste when the two cues are compounded.

The most important results of this experiment is that quail were somehow able to associate blue water with a subsequent illness which we induced arbitrarily ½ hour after removal of the drinking tube. Failure of the rats used in our experiments to do so does not, of course, constitute a powerful argument that this species cannot associate a visual cue over a long delay. It is conceivable, although we think it unlikely, that rats see no difference between plain and dark blue water. In any event, Garcia and his co-workers

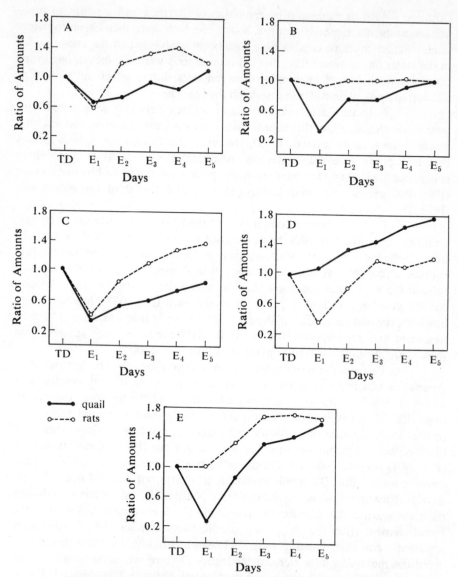

FIGURE 1.   Comparison of the amount of water consumed by quail
(solid lines) and rats (dashed lines) expressed as a ratio of the amount consumed on a given day to the amount consumed on treatment day (TD); E_1
through E_5 are the five extinction trials given at 3-day intervals after the
single conditioning trial on TD. (A) Group S : S; (B) group B : B; (C)
group BS : BS; (D) group BS : S; (E) group BS : B

(1) have reported much more convincing evidence than ours that rats do not
utilize a visual cue in delayed-illness avoidance learning. Thus, our main concern after the first experiment was whether the results for quail were unequivocal, rather than whether rats could actually see our visual cue.

In the second experiment we attempted to answer two questions: (i) Could the quail have been relying on some subtle taste of the dyed water rather than solely upon its appearance?; and (ii) Was the effective consequence that produced aversion to blue water really the drug-induced illness, or was it the considerable trauma of being caught, handled, and injected?

Birds from each of the five earlier subgroups were assigned to one of two groups, assignment being random except for the restriction that the groups be balanced with respect to prior treatment and test conditions. Procedural details were the same as in the first experiment. On treatment day, however, both groups drank from tinted blue tubes filled with the same plain water to which they were accustomed. One group ($N = 20$) was then injected with cyclophosphamide ½ hour after drinking, whereas the other group ($N = 20$) was injected with normal saline.

Figure 2 shows the result. Birds that received the illness-inducing drug drank less from the tinted tube when they next encountered it ($P < .001$), whereas those injected with saline did not.

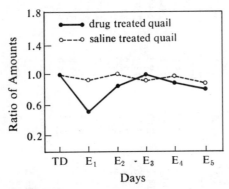

FIGURE 2.   A comparison of the amount of plain water drunk from tinted tubes by drug-treated quail (solid line) and saline-treated quail (dashed line). The amount drunk is expressed as a ratio of the amount ingested on a given day to the amount consumed on treatment day (TD).

Although Figures 1 and 2 give a clear picture of the relative changes in drinking occasioned by treatment-day and test conditions, they give no information on the absolute amounts ingested or the degree of variability. Accordingly, means and standard deviations are shown in Table 1 for all groups each day from the last baseline day through the first extinction test. Comparison of baseline scores with those of treatment day shows that sour water, whether blue or not, was somewhat aversive to both species at first encounter, that is, before induction of illness; blue water alone was not. The amount of plain water drunk on the two recovery days after treatment shows a return to baseline levels. Effects of the delayed-illness conditioning trial are seen best by comparing scores of treatment day with those of the first extinction test.

Despite the controls introduced in the second experiment, it could

TABLE 1. Means and standard deviations (S.D.) of drinking scores in all groups of both experiments from the last baseline day through the first extinction test (E_1). Probabilities (P) of differences between means of the treatment day (TD) and E_1 were calculated by the t-test for repeated measures

(t-test) Group	N	Last Baseline Day		TD		First Recovery Day		Second Recovery Day		E_1		P
		Mean (ml)	S.D.	Mean (ml)	S.D.	Mean (ml)	S.D.	Mean (ml)	S.D.	Mean (ml)	S.D.	
Experiment 1												
S : S quail	8	12.9	3.16	9.1	3.24	9.8	4.49	12.6	3.75	6.0	3.77	< .05
S : S rat	8	17.8	4.60	10.6	2.31	17.6	2.04	19.0	3.16	6.2	3.99	< .02
B : B quail	8	12.4	2.52	14.1	2.83	9.5	4.50	11.4	1.90	5.1	3.66	< .01
B : B rat	8	17.4	2.71	19.6	3.70	13.1	2.60	17.6	2.27	18.1	3.71	
BS : BS quail	8	13.0	1.80	6.8	2.49	12.2	3.03	13.0	2.35	2.2	2.68	< .001
BS : BS rat	8	20.4	2.30	13.1	2.29	15.9	3.38	19.4	3.09	5.0	2.92	< .001
BS : S quail	8	13.2	3.07	6.6	3.03	13.2	4.81	12.2	2.59	7.1	3.61	
BS : S rat	8	17.9	2.90	12.0	2.24	17.6	2.53	17.8	2.17	4.5	2.96	< .001
BS : B quail	8	11.5	2.55	8.8	3.19	11.8	3.70	11.9	2.06	2.2	3.19	< .001
BS : B rat	8	18.5	3.08	12.2	3.73	15.9	1.93	17.5	2.96	12.2	4.35	
Experiment 2, quail only (tinted tube)												
Drug-treated	20	14.1	2.61	13.2	3.58	9.5	3.24	11.4	3.44	7.0	3.63	< .001
Saline-treated	20	13.3	2.86	13.5	3.98	13.0	3.87	13.5	3.30	12.5	3.10	

be argued that the results represent not true associative learning but only the birds' increased wariness of strange-looking fluids as a result of recent illness. However, studies now completed in our laboratory (5) show that, although such sensitization or heightened neophobia contributes to the effect, there is a significant associative learning component as well. We are confident, therefore, that at least one avian species can associate a purely visual cue with a delayed illness without mediation by means of peripheral mechanisms such as reinstated taste.

It seems reasonable to expect that this capacity will be widespread among animals whose visual systems are highly developed and whose niches demand great reliance upon vision in foraging. If so, the implications for ecology, behavior theory, and evolutionary theory are of considerable importance.

References

1. GARCIA, J., & KOELLING, R. A., *Psychonom. Sci. 4*, 123 (1966); GARCIA, J., MCGOWAN, B. K., ERVIN, F. R., & KOELLING, R. A., *Science, 160*, 794 (1968).

2. ROZIN, P. *J. Comp. Physiol. Psychol.*, 1969, *67*, 421.

3. BROWER, L. P., RYERSON, W. N., COPPINGER, L. L., & GLAZIER, S. C. *Science*, 1968, *161*, 1349; BROWER, L. P. *Sci. Amer.*, Feb. 1969, *220*, 22.

4. We thank Dr. G. McDaniel of Auburn University for supplying the quail and Dr. P. Tavormina of Mead Johnson Research Center for experimental samples of cyclophosphamide.

5. WILCOXON, H.C., DRAGOIN, W. B., & KRAL, P. A., in preparation.

Cues: Their Relative Effectiveness as a Function of the Reinforcer

*J. Garcia, B. K. McGowan, F. R. Ervin,
and R. A. Koelling*

Two cues, either size or flavor of food pellet, were conditionally paired with either malaise induced by x-ray or pain induced by shock in four groups of rats. The combination of flavor and illness produced a conditioned decrement in consumption, but that of size and illness did not. Conversely, the combination of size and pain produced an inhibition of eating, but flavor and pain did not. Apparently, effective associative learning depends on central neural convergence of the paired afferent input.

Pavlov (1) proposed that "any natural phenomena chosen at will may be converted into conditioned stimuli." For example, any discriminable cue, such as an audible tone or a visible light, which precedes a food reinforcer on several occasions can elicit responses associated with feeding in the absence of the reinforcer as confirmed by much experimental evidence.

However, consideration of the adaptive responses of rodents to poisoned foods may require qualification of Pavlov's notion. Animals that survive a poisoning attempt subsequently avoid the poisonous food but not the place where the food was consumed (2). In this situation, the visual, tactual, and other stimuli defining the place of the poison do not become conditional stimuli, perhaps because they are not as intimately associated with eating as the gustatory and olfactory stimuli are.

In our experiments, we attempted to discover whether nongustatory attributes of food (for example, size of pellet) could serve as conditional stimuli (CS) with illness as the unconditioned stimulus (US). We compared the relative effectiveness of both gustatory and nongustatory stimuli as cues when the consequence of eating was either a general internal malaise or a specific peripheral pain.

Four groups of eight young adult male rats (300 g. Sprague-Dawley) were trained with one form of food that was conditionally paired with the noxious stimulus and another form of the food that was not so paired (Table 1). Two size groups received food pellets of similar flavors but different sizes. The large size was a whole Purina Chow pellet (approximately 2.5 by 1.5 cm); this was cut into four equal parts for the small size. Two groups

Source: Reprinted by permission from *Science*, 17 May 1968. *160*, 794–795. Copyright © 1968 by the American Association for the Advancement of Science.

Note: This research is supported in part by NIH research grants No. RH0067, 10329, and AEC research grant No. AT(30-1)-3698. F.R.E. was NIH career awardee No. K3-MH-19,434.

TABLE 1. Stimulus combination in conditioning four groups of animals

Groups	Cue (CS)	Reinforcer (US)
1	Size of pellet	X-ray (illness)
2	Flavor of pellet	X-ray (illness)
3	Size of pellet	Shock (pain)
4	Flavor of pellet	Shock (pain)

received pellets of the same size, but differing in flavor of the coating. Quartered pellets were rolled in flour or in powdered sugar so that their flavor differed but their appearance was similar. Some animals had small pellets associated with the noxious stimuli; others had the large pellets so associated. Flour and sugar were balanced in the same way.

The animals were habituated to eating the nonconditional form of the food for 1 hour each day. After a week, conditioning began. During each conditioning day the conditional form of the food was provided during the 1-hour feeding period, and the noxious stimulation was applied. Five conditioning days were carried out every 2 to 4 days. On the intervening days, the animals ate the nonconditional form of the food without the noxious stimulation. Two days after the final conditioning session the animals were tested with the conditional form of the food without noxious stimulation. The latency to begin eating and the total amount consumed in 1 hour were observed. Similar observations were recorded for consumption of the nonconditional food the day before and the day after the test.

One flavor group and one size group were conditioned with electric shock delivered to the paws by an electric shock generator with constant current through a grid floor of the eating compartment. Shocks (0.2-second pulses) were delivered immediately after the rat put the conditional form of the food pellet into its mouth. The intensity caused the rat to drop the pellet (approximately 2.0 ma). The animal received a shock when it placed a pellet in its mouth during the 60-minute conditioning session.

The other flavor group and the other size group were conditioned with x-ray. [Previous studies demonstrated that ionizing rays produce behavioral effects similar to those of toxins but without the peripheral pain of an injection (3).] An exposure to 50 r of 280 filtered x-ray (half-value layer, 1.4 mm of Cu) was delivered in 4.5 minutes immediately after each 60-minute conditioning session.

The flavor of the pellet was an adequate CS when combined with x-rays. Every animal in the flavor-x-ray group ate more of the nonconditional flavored food than of the conditional flavored food. The animals showed little hesitation in picking up either form of food and sampling it; thus the amount eaten was a more effective measure than latency to begin eating. However, the size of the pellet did not acquire this same conditional power although it was associated with identical x-ray treatment. By comparison, the size of the pellet was an excellent conditional stimulus when paired with shock to the paws. Latency to begin eating was a more effective measure than amount eaten since every rat in the size-shock group hesitated much longer before eating the conditional size food; but once they commenced eating they continued to do so. However, the flavor of the pellet did not acquire significant CS properties when combined with the pain of shock. By contrast to the flavor-x-ray group, no animals in the flavor-shock group showed a decrease in preference for the shocked flavor even though the rats were shocked immediately after they began eating the flavored pellet (Figure 1).

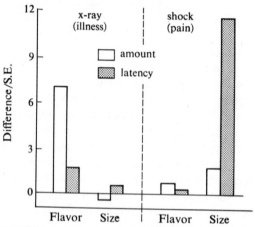

FIGURE 1.   Relative effectiveness of two attributes of food pellets (size or flavor) to act as cues after conditional pairing with two forms of noxious reinforcement (shock or x-ray) in four groups of rats. The mean difference between measures obtained with conditional and nonconditional forms of the food is scaled in terms of the standard error of that difference. (One S.E. is approximately 0.7 g or 8.2 seconds.) Amount reflects depressed consumption, and latency reflects hesitation before eating caused by the given cue on tests in absence of the reinforcer.

These data indicate: (i) that both the size cues and the taste cues were discriminable, (ii) that both x-ray and shock disrupted eating behavior, but (iii) that learning occurred only for certain stimulus combinations. Apparently, pairing a perceptible cue with an effective reinforcer does not insure effective associative learning; the cue must be "appropriate" for the consequences that ensue.

Since flavor is closely related to the chemical composition of food, natural selection would favor associative mechanisms relating flavor to the aftereffects of ingestion. The rat has such specialization in its anatomical structure, in gustatory receptors which sample food before it is incorporated by the internal viscera. Both the gustatory and visceral receptors send fibers that converge in the nucleus of the fasciculus solitarius (4). Other sensory systems do not send fibers directly to this nucleus; thus the neural organization reflects the propensity of the animal to associate flavor cues (but not size cues) with a subsequent malaise that is internally referred. When the consequences are beneficial (corrected vitamin deficit), the animal exhibits an increased preference for the flavor, and these shifts in preferences occur even though the subsequent reinforcement is delayed for hours (5).

Our evidence points toward a similar relation between the telereceptors (vision, audition) and cutaneous receptors. Externally referred sights and sounds are readily conditioned to the peripheral pain of shock. Although the mechanisms are considerably more complex, these systems also appear closely related both behaviorally and neurologically. When the consequence of eating is immediate peripheral pain, the animal exhibits fear responses (hesitation, jumping, squealing) to the nongustatory attributes of the food. But it does not display a reduced preference for either the gustatory or nongustatory attributes of the food. At higher intensities, both telereceptive and cutaneous cues produce similar orienting and startle reactions. These afferents may converge subcortically also probably at the level of the posterior thalamus (6). The probability of establishing associative learning depends in part on central integration of the particular afferent channels through which the conditionally paired stimuli are presented.

References

1. PAVLOV, I. P. *Lectures on conditioned reflexes.* New York: International Publishers, 1928.
2. BARNETT, S. A. *The rat: A study in behavior.* Chicago: Aldine Press, 1963.
3. GARCIA, J., & KOELLING, R. A. *Radiation Res.,* 1967, *7*, 439.
4. HERRICK, C. J. *J. Comp. Neurol.,* 1944, *81*, 307; HALPERN, B. P. In M. R. Kare & O. Mauer (Eds.), *The chemical senses and nutrition.* Baltimore: Johns Hopkins Univ. Press. In press.
5. GARCIA, J., ERVIN, F. R., YORKE, C. H., & KOELLING, R. A. *Science,* 1967, *155*, 716.
6. HERRICK, C. J. *The brain of the tiger salamander: Ambystoma tigrinum.* Chicago: Univ. of Chicago Press, 1948; POGGIO, G. F., & MOUNTCASTLE, V. B. *Johns Hopkins Hosp. Bull.,* 1960, *106*, 266; ERICKSON, R. P., JANE, J. A., WAITE, R., & DIAMOND, L. T. *J. Neurophysiol.,* 1964, *27*, 1026.

There has recently been considerable interest in the social behavior of
primates. This is sparked in part by a natural fascination with the behavior of these
highly social animals and also by the realization that man, monkey, and ape share a
common membership within the primate order. Certainly many workers in this field
have hoped to learn more about human evolution by expanding our knowledge of
the social behavior and habits of our primate relatives. The baboons are among the
best-studied primate groups. Because of their large size and frequent occurrence in
areas permitting naturalistic observation, studies of baboon behavior have been
carried out on a number of different species, and these studies have revealed widely
different forms of social organization from one group to the next.

The article by Kummer and Kurt is concerned with the social behavior
of the hamadryas baboon. This species was first observed in the zoo to have a
unique social organization in which single adult males maintained exclusive mating
access to groups of adult females. The existence of similar one-male groups in wild
hamadryas baboons was subsequently confirmed by Kummer and Kurt (1968), and
the selection here was designed to evaluate quantitatively the similarities and differ-
ences in social behavior between wild and captive hamadryas baboons. Two cau-
tions are necessary. First, the reader should be aware that one-male group structures
do not typify all baboon societies. Second, in other primate groups where one-male
groups exist, the males may not occupy the dominant position that they do in
hamadryas societies (K. R. L. Hall, Behaviour and ecology of the wild Patas mon-
key, Erythrocebus patas, *in* Uganda. J. Zool., *1965,* 148, *15–87).*

A Comparison of Social Behavior in Captive and Wild Hamadryas Baboons

H. Kummer and F. Kurt

In recent research on the social behavior of primates, field studies
have become increasingly important. One reason for this is the interest in eco-
logical aspects of social organization; another, the possible changes of group
structure and social behavior caused by conditions of captivity. Nonetheless,
even descriptive investigations will continue to be made in zoological gardens
and laboratories, especially with species whose observation in the field is extremely difficult. In order to properly evaluate the results of captivity studies a
number of species should be observed under both conditions, if possible, by

Source: Reprinted by permission of the University of Texas Press from *The Baboon in*
Medical Research, edited by Harold Vagtborg (1965), pp. 65–80

Note: The field study has been supported by a grant from the Schweizerischer Nation-
alfonds für wissenschaftliche Forschung to the senior author and by contributions from
the G. et A. Claraz-Schenkung as well as from the Schweizerische Naturforschende
Gesellschaft.

the same observer and according to the same quantitative methods. In this article we shall attempt such a comparative study for *Papio hamadryas*.

The captive colony of hamadryas baboons was studied in the Zürich Zoo, where it lived in an open enclosure of fourteen by twenty-five meters. The study was carried out by one of us (Kummer) in three different observation periods, namely, 1955, 1958, and 1959. In all three periods the colony was comprised of fiteen baboons; however, in 1959 only twelve animals out of the original colony were still alive, eight of them in substantially different social positions (Table 1).

TABLE 1.   Composition of the zoo colony during the three observation periods

1955	1958	1959
1 adult ♂, old, only group leader	1 unchanged, guides the ♀ ♀ 2–5 and 9–11	1 clearly senile, only the ♀ ♀ 3 and 9 still follow him
2 ⎫ 3 ⎪ adult ♀ ♀, all 4 ⎰ follow the ♂ 1 5 ⎭	2 ⎫ 3 ⎪ 4 ⎰ unchanged 5 ⎭	2 ⎫ 3 ⎪ distributed over the 4 ⎰ ♂ ♂ 1, 6, and 7 (see 5 ⎭ there)
6* juvenile ♂, 5 years	6* adult ♂, 8 years, ♀ 16 follows him	6* adult ♂, 9 years, he is followed by ♀ ♀ 2, 4, 11, and 16
7* juvenile ♂, 4.5 years	7* adult ♂, 7.5 years	7* adult ♂, 8.5 years, he is followed by ♀ ♀ 5 and 10
8* juvenile ♂, 3.5 years	(8* sold)	
9* ⎫ juvenile ♀ ♀, 3 10* ⎰ years, begin to 11* ⎭ follow the ♂ 1	9* ⎫ juvenile ♀ ♀, 6 10* ⎰ years, follow 11* ⎭ the ♂ 1	9* ⎫ adult ♀ ♀, 7 years, 10* ⎰ distributed over the 11* ⎭ ♂ ♂ 1, 6, and 7
12* ⎱ juvenile ♂ ♂, 2 13* ⎰ years	12* ⎱ subadult ♂ ♂, 5 13* ⎰ years	12* ⎱ subadult ♂ ♂, 6 13* ⎰ years
14* ⎱ juvenile ♀ ♀, 1 15* ⎰ year	(14* sold) (15* sold)	
	16* juvenile ♀, 2 years follows the ♂ 6	16* juvenile ♀, 3 years, follows the ♂ 6
	17* juvenile ♂, 2 years	17* juvenile ♂, 3 years
	18* juvenile ♀, 1–5 years	(18* sold)
		19* juvenile ♀, 1 year

*Individuals born in the zoo are indicated by an asterisk.

In 1960 and 1961 we studied wild hamadryas baboons living in the region of Erer-Gota and Dire Dawa in Ethiopia, using the same methods. The extensive investigation of group structures and individual spacing comprised four troops, totaling about 1,000 baboons; the studies of social behavior have been mostly limited to a typical troop averaging 137 individuals. For details of methods and results of both investigations see Kummer (1) where the zoo colony is described and also the report on the field study (2).

Ideally, such a comparison should consider how much social behavior varies among different captive colonies as well as among different regions of the natural habitat. Zuckerman's (3) observations in several zoos and our own superficial knowledge of hamadryas behavior in twenty-three different places of Eastern Ethiopia are not sufficient as far as this is concerned. The differences actually observed could, therefore, be the results of different geographical origin and/or different composition of samples. The relative effect of these factors can only be estimated. As to genetic similarity of captive and wild baboons, we only have one argument: following the ninth parallel from West to East, the skin and hair of the Ethiopian hamadryas baboons become gradually and considerably lighter. The Zürich colony closely corresponds to baboons of Erer-Gota as far as pigmentation is concerned. No clear evidence for genetic differences of the two samples could be found. The sex-age distribution in the zoo colony never exactly agreed with that of the wild troops (Table 2). Although it even changed from one observation period to the other, no significant effect of composition on behavior frequencies in the classes could be detected. In some single behavior patterns, however, the influence of group composition will become evident.

TABLE 2. Composition of compared samples according to sex-age-classes in per cents

	Adult	Subadult	Juvenile	Adult and Subadult	Juvenile	Total	
	♂ ♂	♂ ♂	♂ ♂	♀ ♀	♀ ♀	Individuals	%
Free-living population	22.9	6.0	17.6	32.6	21.0	1351	100.1
Zoo colony	13.3	15.6	11.1	40.0	19.9	15	99.9

When animals in a narrow enclosure are forced to reduce the distance between themselves and their neighbors their social behavior may be profoundly changed (4). The zoo colony, however, covered about five times as much surface as a similar number of wild hamadryas baboons would occupy during the periods of social behavior on the sleeping-rock. In the wild the average distance from females to their males was .65 meters when resting and about 3 meters when the troop was moving and feeding. In the zoo colony the average distance at any hour of the day was 3.1 meters. The observed differences of social behavior, therefore, cannot be traced to abnormally small distances between individuals. In the zoo the baboons were observed from a distance of four to fifteen meters. In the field we were mostly twenty to thirty meters away from the baboons, but we used 6×24 field glasses.

A. Group Structure

The most constant unit among wild hamadryas baboons is not—as with other Cercopithecoidea—a troop, but a "one-male-group" (5). It consists of one adult male and, usually, one to four females who follow the male as the leader of the group and as their sex partner. Adult members of such groups, under extreme conditions, leave the troop, but not each other. Males threaten their females as soon as they separate themselves by more than four to ten meters. The most extreme form of threat is neck biting which at once increases the following-reaction of the females. This group pattern is closely reconstructed in captivity. Zuckerman (3) describes the formation of hamadryas colonies in three different zoos. From his figures for the twenty-five one-male-groups one can deduce an average of 1.92 females per group. In the Erer-Gota population one-male-groups contained an average of 1.86 adult and 0.44 juvenile females. The largest zoo group contained 8, while the largest group observed in Ethiopia contained 10 females. This concordance is especially impressive since in the zoo colonies—because of the smaller number of females—the majority of males were bachelors with no females at all.

The zoo colony in Zürich had only a single one-male-group with four adult and three three-year-old females during the first observation period. The only adult Male No. 1 led it from one place to another quite as he would in the wild. Four years later Males Nos. 6 and 7 became adults and Male No. 1 became apparently senile. Some of the seven females then joined the young males, resulting subsequently in a colony of three one-male-groups (Table 1). The following sections are given to show to what extent characteristics of wild one-male-groups have been retained in captivity.

According to Zuckerman's observations in the London Zoo a "family group may sometimes include one or more bachelors or unmated males" (3). In the Erer-Gota population 36 per cent of seventy-eight groups were accompanied by one or two subadult males. These "followers" sleep near the group and stay with it in the daytime. However, they rarely engage in open social contacts with it except for occasional grooming with the adult females, which is likely to provoke a threat response from the group leader. Copulations between followers and the females are even more rare and, if caught in the act, the female will be severely attacked by its male. All this refers equally to wild and captive hamadryas baboons.

When Female No. 16 at the Zürich Zoo had its first swellings it started to follow the young adult Male No. 6 as his only consort. The two sometimes behaved as a group leader and his female, at other times they showed behavior which is typical for a mother and her infant. This type of one-male-group is not—as we surmised at first—a result of captivity, but fits into the normal composition of a wild troop. In a sample of sixty-eight one-male-groups thirteen were found to consist of one young adult male and one or two mostly immature females, the youngest of them being about one year old. Clearly, here too, the leader-consort and the mother-child relationships were interchangeable. Many males seem to start their career as group leaders with an immature female, and accordingly we called these units initial groups. In the wild, as in the zoo, the small females followed their males and groomed them frequently, but copulations were never attempted. Where climbing was difficult or during fights in the troop the males carried their females on their backs.

Males Nos. 6 and 7 of the zoo colony were eight and one-half and nine years old, respectively, and fully grown in the third period (Table 1). One led four, the other, two females, of which two were old and experienced members of the former group of Male No. 1. Both young males led their groups in a typical way through the enclosure, and the grooming and sexual behavior were normal. Their threat behavior, however, was imperfect. When a female left, the young group leaders hardly ever threatened her, and when two of their consorts threatened each other they did not interfere. Their rarely used bites on the neck were atypical and badly aimed, although they performed them correctly on juveniles. In the group of Male No. 6, old Female No. 4 had assumed the part of the group leader. This amazing animal threatened the other females of the group in situations similar to those in which an experienced male would have engaged in this behavior. The other females of Male No. 6 several times performed the protected threat in front of the male, but Female No. 4 would sit behind him, run forward at the appropriate moment, give one of the quarrelers a neck-bite, and then retreat again behind the male. The other females often presented to her and followed her with their eyes, when they exceeded the normal threshold of a group leader's tolerance. Males Nos. 6 and 7 were sold a little later, and we do not know whether group leader behavior was ever fully developed afterward, or whether captivity caused a definite behavioral shortcoming.

B. Frequency of Social Behavior

We shall consider behavior as "social" if, according to the observer's experience, it is motivated by the presence or the behavior of a partner of the same species. The passive part of being groomed has been included, since it is accompanied by adaptive movements and apparently reduces the readiness to react to other stimuli. The "social time" was measured as the percentage of minutes of observation which included at least one social behavior. For each sex-age-class the mean value of this percentage was calculated. In the field a baboon was observed continuously over a period of 5 to 15 minutes, while in the zoo Kummer observed each individual every 15 minutes for 1 minute. The mean observation time per class in the zoo was 96 minutes, in the wild, 282 minutes.

At the zoo, as in the field, these observations were limited to that part of the day devoted mainly to social activities. In the wild this period starts when the baboons leave their sleeping ledges and ends when the troop departs for the day's route. In the zoo it mostly ends at about 10 A.M. During these hours play, grooming, and sexual behavior dominate all activities; walking and eating are completely missing. A meaningful comparison has to be limited to this morning period, if it is not to be destroyed by the differences in feeding habits which allow the captive baboons to carry on sporadic social behavior all day.

The mean length of a social contact is approximately one minute. Therefore the minute of observation was adopted as the unit for statistical purposes, and the probability that one minute would contain social behavior was compared under both conditions. Since we are concerned only with definite changes in captivity we shall—unless otherwise indicated—consider significant only those differences which have a p value of less than 0.001.

Figure 1 demonstrates that all sex-age-classes of the zoo colony dedicated more morning time to social behavior than did those in the field.

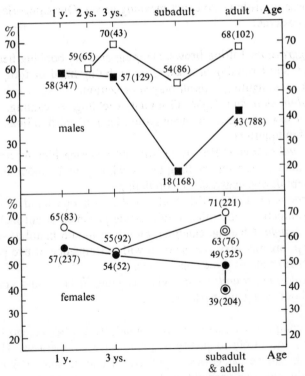

FIGURE 1. Percentages of observation minutes that contain social behavior. Black dots indicate values for wild baboons, empty circles indicate those for captive baboons, double rings represent females in estrus. The number of observation minutes is given in parentheses.

The difference concerns mostly adult animals and is significant for each adult and subadult class. The social frequency of the juveniles, however, is not clearly higher in the zoo. It can further be seen that the ontogenetical development of social time in captive baboons parallels the field values. Thus, the subadult males go through a relatively "solitary" phase in both conditions, having already outgrown the play groups, but not yet leading females. This temporary reduction is, however, only significant in the wild; in captivity it is partly overlapped by a longer period of playing. In both situations another reduction of social time is noticeable among females in estrus: this difference is significant only in wild females and only at the 0.05 level. The low value of three-year-old females results from the composition of the zoo colony: during the first observation period three of them lived with four adult females in the same one-male-group and seldom had contacts with the male. In the wild, also, males prefer adult females to subadult and juvenile females. On the whole, social time tends to diminish with increasing age in the wild while tending to increase in the zoo.

When social behavior is subdivided into categories such as aggression and play it is necessary to list the behavior patterns placed in each category, since these terms have no exact meaning as yet. Our categories consist of the following patterns:

Aggression: Lifting brows, slapping ground, bobbing head, beating with one hand, short running attacks, chasing, biting hand or foot, biting tail, biting nape of neck, fighting without play vocalization.

Submission and flight: Grinning, cackling, screaming, crouching, fleeing from or toward aggressor, fleeing onto back of third animal, presenting with lowered hindquarters.

Sexual behavior: Presenting without lowering hindquarters and excluding male-male presenting, sniffing or touching genitals, mounting or being mounted (except during aggression), copulating.

Grooming: Either with both hands, with one hand or forefinger, or just gazing intently at the other's hair. Being groomed is not included.

Play fight: Chasing, catching, mouth to mouth fighting—all accompanied by deep, breathy play vocalization with a frequency of five per second, uttered in a series of about three coughs each.

Exploring ground: (Not social) Digging in holes and cracks, turning stones without eating any particles.

A complete catalogue would include still other categories, which, however, occur too rarely to justify a quantitative comparison. The relative frequency of the above categories is given in Table 3. Since the zoo colony did not contain any one-year-old males, two-year-olds are compared with one-year-old free-living males.

Aggressive behavior was executed much more frequently by adults in the zoo than in the wild. Females in captivity threatened each other in front

TABLE 3. Frequencies of main behavioral categories in the sex-age-classes of free-living (F) and captive (C) baboons, expressed as a percentage of the observation minutes in which the behavior occurred

| | | Males | | | | Females | | | |
		1–2 yrs.	3 yrs.	Sub-adult	Adult	1 yr.	3 yrs.	Subadult and Adult Anestrous	Estrous
Aggression	F	0.3	3.1	0.0	0.4	0.0	0.0	0.3	0.0
	C	1.5	2.3	2.2	7.0	1.1	1.1	2.7	0.0
Submission and Flight	F	1.4	3.8	0.0	0.0	0.0	0.0	0.3	1.5
	C	3.0	14.0	2.2	0.0	8.4	8.8	1.8	6.6
Sexual Behavior	F	0.0	3.1	0.0	1.1	0.0	1.9	0.3	6.9
	C	3.0	11.6	2.2	9.0	2.4	4.3	2.3	4.0
Grooming	F	14.5	11.5	11.0	12.0	13.3	23.0	28.1	19.7
	C	1.5	7.2	8.0	8.1	1.2	16.3	34.8	26.3
Being Groomed	F	5.8	15.8	8.2	19.4	22.5	29.2	20.7	8.3
	C	3.1	16.2	15.0	50.5	4.8	1.1	19.5	7.9
Play Fighting	F	13.6	1.5	0.0	0.0	7.2	2.1	0.0	0.0
	C	38.2	21.0	18.8	1.0	32.5	18.5	0.3	0.0
Exploring Ground	F	0.6	0.0	0.0	0.0	3.5	0.0	0.0	0.0
	C	24.3	15.9	20.4	2.0	14.1	24.7	4.1	7.8

of the male, a behavior which was very rare in Ethiopia. Using the wild population as standard, old Male No. 1 had too many females in the first period, when such scenes occurred frequently. Schaller (6) found that in captive mountain gorillas dominance behavior is increased, probably because of the limited and concentrated food supply. In the hamadryas colony in Zürich food was a minor cause of threatening.

Submission and flight occurred more often in the zoo than in the field. Although mainly among juveniles, the increase is significant for all classes. In the first period the very appearance of the adult male with his silver coat provoked cackling or screaming from the infants. Later, when the colony had three fully grown adult males, fewer reactions of this kind were observed. They were completely missing in the field where each infant continually found several adult males around it. After a phase of low frequency in submission and flight behavior, there is an increase again in the three-year-old zoo baboons. Females of this age, when copulating with Male No. 1, usually showed a high degree of flight motivation. The three-year-old males, who in the field kept away from adult males, were attracted in the zoo by Male No. 1, but thereby often uttered flight vocalizations. The increase of flight behavior in adult females during estrus was observed under both conditions. Estrous females often do not follow the male at the first threat, probably because their submissive behavior, thanks to the effective stimulus of the swelling, protects them more efficiently from being bitten. Females in estrus submit more often, but with little intensity. Sexual presenting, of course, was not considered as submissive behavior.

The significant increase in *sexual* behavior can hardly be explained by the composition of the colony. Copulation was not more frequent in the captive baboons, but presenting, mounting, inspecting of genital regions, and similar activities were. Females often mounted other females in captivity; they very rarely did this in the wild. This corresponds to Schaller's (6) statement that "various forms of erotic behavior, commonly exhibited by captive gorillas, were never observed in the wild." In the wild, as in captive baboons, the high frequency of sexual activity of three-year-old males is remarkable. Part of this activity is responsible for their frequent flight reaction. At the beginning of subadulthood hamadryas males cease to copulate until they have their own females.

The influence of group composition on *grooming* is easily discerned. There is much evidence that the more a baboon's relation to his partner is in danger of loosening, the more he will groom her. To be clearer, grooming is an "expression of high interest" in the partner. During the first period Male No. 1 never groomed any of his seven females, but when he became senile he started to groom his two remaining consorts. Grooming frequency of adult, anestrous females diminished from 43 per cent in the first period to 32 per cent in the third, when they together had three males instead of one. The field report will provide further evidence of this hypothesis. It also seems that grooming can be replaced by other stimuli: during estrus females in both environments groomed about one-third less; this difference is significant. The most important influence of captivity on grooming is observed in the development of grooming behavior in the juveniles. In the wild, one-year-old infants already spend 15 per cent of their minutes in social grooming, whereas the juveniles in the zoo made this a regular habit only at three years. The difference is significant at the 0.01 level for the one- and three-year-old baboons of each sample combined.

While grooming starts about two years late in captive juveniles, *play fighting* continues much longer than in the wild. In the Ethiopian troops three-year-olds play only occasionally; in the Zürich Zoo, however, even subadult males continued to spend about 20 per cent of their time in play fighting. These results indicate a retarding influence of captivity on the development of some behavior patterns.

The last figures in Table 3 refer to a nonsocial behavior which, aside from eating, deviates more from the corresponding field values than any other nonsocial behavior. Infants and juveniles in the zoo frequently explored the stone ground of the enclosure with their hands. Small pebbles were loosened out of cracks, but unearthed particles were never eaten. One-year-old infants in the wild sometimes turned small stones on their sleeping-rock without paying any further attention to what was uncovered. This behavior should be regarded as nonfunctional search for food. As captivity does not afford any opportunity for real foraging, juveniles in the zoo probably extended the turning over of stones which is only a part of the foraging in the wild. Here an infantile behavior, prolonged by captivity, seems to unite with the partial redirection of food searching behavior.

C. Differences in the Catalogue of Social Behavior

We shall deal here with only those parts of the catalogue in which the zoo colony differed from wild hamadryas baboons. Taking both samples together we found a total of seventy patterns of social behavior, defined only according to their form and disregarding their functions. This figure comprises just simple patterns, but not stereotyped sequences or combinations of them. Further, only the basic form of each pattern, not its variants, was counted. For instance, sexual presenting of estrous females and presenting among males, which communicates an imminent change of their spatial relations, is considered as one pattern. While Altmann (7) recognizes only mutually exclusive patterns as elements of his catalogue, we include all different patterns, even when executed simultaneously by the same individual. Before we traveled to Ethiopia sixty-eight of these patterns were known to us from the zoo, and we expected to find several new ones in the natural habitat. In reality we found only two new patterns but missed nine others which had occurred regularly in the zoo colony. The two gestures occurring only in the wild were:

1. The swing step—a straight march with long steps, lifted tail, and sidewards swing of the pelvis in rhythm with the step. With this pattern dominant males sometimes effect a sudden departure of the resting troop.

2. Free-living males sometimes lifted their females into copulatory position by gripping the hair on their head with one hand.

More interesting are the patterns which the captive baboons added to the catalogue of the wild ones:

1. Mock attack. In the wild, adult makes rarely threaten juveniles, and then only in mild form—lifting the brows or slapping the ground. In the zoo the males often rushed at the juveniles, stopped abruptly, and quietly returned to their places. In the wild an attack is sustained until the pursued animal has been reached or has escaped.

2. Hand biting. Adults in the zoo colony gave their infants a soft bite on one hand, more rarely on a foot, when the playing infants bothered them. On such occasions wild baboons used the bite on the nape of the neck.

3. Tail biting. Adult females in the zoo sometimes attacked each other seriously, directing their bites regularly onto the base of the tail. The scars on the tail of the adult females gave a reliable picture of the dominance order among them. In the wild, adult females never bit each other.

4. Carrying dance. This is a way of playing in which a subadult male lifts an infant across his arms and rotates him upright on his feet.

5. Enticing. A juvenile baboon holds a piece of paper or a branch with his mouth and thereby entices a playmate into pursuing him.

6. Tailing. Two baboons engaged in intensive mutual grooming walk side by side to another spot, while one of them lays his tail across the back of the other.

7, 8, 9. These three patterns are closely connected with the use and result of severe threatening, primarily neck biting. In Ethiopian troops the neck bite was mainly applied by group leaders to their females when these went too far away. At the moment of the bite the screaming females pressed themselves to the ground and then closely followed the male to his spot. In the zoo colony females behaved in the same way, but would continue to scream until the male sat down and the female was allowed to run her hands through his coat. Three- to four-year-old females showed similar behavior, but restricted their grooming of the aggressor to a light touch of the hair tips with one index finger (Pattern 7) or executed this movement close to the male on the ground. In the first observation period subadult males were occasionally bitten on the neck. They would then also approach the aggressor, Male No. 1, and inspect his coat—however, only by intense observation of it (Pattern 8). Between the inspections they would get up and frantically brush the ground with one hand (Pattern 9). None of these three patterns was observed in the wild, though brushing movements and index grooming occurred a few times in vestigial forms. In the zoo report an interpretation of these movements was given. Suffice it to say here that they occur when flight and following motivations toward the aggressor are simultaneously high. In the wild the tendency to follow was predominant with females; the flight tendency with other classes. In the zoo both tendencies spread through all classes and tended to cause conflicts, in which the above forms of grooming appeared as displacement activities and redirections. All nine additional patterns were used regularly by several individuals.

Neck biting gives us an example of a behavior pattern which in captivity was used on different partner classes while in the wild it was used almost exclusively on one class. A second example of this extension is the carrying on the back. In Ethiopia only infants up to one and one-half years are carried on the back. In the zoo older juveniles carried each other frequently during play and when fleeing from or to Male No. 1. Thus, a four-year-old male jumped on the back of a four and one-half-year-old male when the group leader showed up unexpectedly near them. While they were fleeing, thus united, a three-year-old female jumped on top of both of them.

At the level of complex behavior sequences the most significant difference concerns the "protected threat." A baboon *A* thereby threatens an often more dominant baboon *R*, presenting at the same time to a male *H*, dominant over both of them. In this way *A* protects himself against an attack from *H* and keeps *R* from presenting to *H*. In addition *A*'s threat often causes

H to attack *R*. Altmann (7) found the same behavior in the semiwild rhesus monkeys of Cayo Santiago and DeVore (8) saw it in wild anubis baboons in Kenya. According to Hall (personal communication) a similar behavior exists among chacma baboons and according to Reynolds (9) a rhesus colony at the Whipsnade Zoo also used the protected threat. We therefore were amazed to find that wild hamadryas baboons do not use it. This can probably be explained by the special organization of the hamadryas. Although one-male-groups sit daily for hours at a mutual distance of about two meters, their segregation is kept very strictly. A mixing of neighboring groups leads to neck biting if not to fights between the group leaders. With the protected threat one group member would necessarily be forced into a neighboring group. Continuous mixing of groups in the field can be produced by feeding the baboons on a small spot; this leads to severe fighting for possession of females throughout the troop. At such times the flight distance of the baboons toward the observers was much reduced. Frequent use of protected threat, therefore, would be an indirect menace to the whole troop. In the evolution of the hamadryas, then, the suppression of this behavior was a condition which necessarily sprang from their organization into one-male-groups. When the zoo colony had to live with a surplus of competing females as a single one-male group in a large enclosure, the latent behavior common to related species was again brought out. Perhaps the hamadryas females just cannot possibly threaten in the direction of an adult male.

Conclusions

From a practical point of view we hope this study will aid in estimating the value of captivity research and will show the directions in which deviations of social behavior in captivity may be expected. The main tendency of the zoo colony was the enrichment of social behavior in three ways:

1. More time was spent in social behavior. It speaks for the value of captivity studies that relative frequencies of behavior categories in the sex-age-classes were mostly the same in the zoo and in the wild (subadult males, estrous females.)

2. The number of social behavior patterns was slightly increased. Patterns that could hardly be identified in the wild came to full manifestation in the zoo, as for instance, grooming with the index finger. Other types of behavior, such as the carrying dance and tailing, may be new creations since all traces of them are absent in the wild troops. Of particular interest is the reappearance of the protected threat, which was lost in the wild. It is clear, once more, that the behavior in the "natural" habitat is not *the* behavior of a species (10); captivity studies have a value of their own in this respect. Finally, only two patterns of social behavior of wild baboons did not occur in the zoo. The catalogue obtained from captive animals, therefore, was a valid basis for the field work.

3. Patterns that are limited to particular partners and situations in the wild found wider application in the zoo, for example, neck biting and carrying on the back. This despecialization can entirely obscure the function of a behavioral pattern.

A second tendency of the zoo colony was the delayed change-over from typical infantile to typical adult behavior: evident in play fighting, social grooming, and possibly in the defective group leading of the males born in the zoo.

The composition of one-male-groups described by Zuckerman (3) and observed in the Zürich Zoo was a replica of wild groups, down to the smallest detail. The unnatural composition of the Zürich colony, though not affecting the social structure, did influence certain aspects of social behavior. The presence of one adult male only led to atypical behavior in females and young animals.

One of the possible causes of behavioral change in captive animals is discussed by Hediger (10). According to him the increase of sexual behavior is due to the "Hypertrophie der Valenzen," an exaggerated influence of the stimuli remaining in the limited environment over the behavior of the captive animal. Ethological research has demonstrated that a strongly activated instinct can inhibit the activation of other instincts (11). Thus, captive animals often behave socially just because their social behavior is not suppressed by such activities as seeking food or avoiding predators. Another possibility would be that the atrophy of one class of behavior directly causes the hypertrophy of another by some displacement mechanism on a high level.

Our results parallel some of the behavioral changes known in domesticated animals. We especially refer to Lorenz's (12) paper on chickens, pigeons, and geese and Immelmann's (13) recent work on thirteen species of Australian finches (Estrildinae) and their domesticated forms; Leyhausen (14) gave a comparison of wild and domestic cats. All of these authors report that many patterns of behavior are released by a wider range of stimuli in the domesticated animals. Hediger (15) states that domestic animals are less specific in their requirements of form and behavior in their sex partner than their wild relatives. According to Immelmann domesticated Zebra finches feed nestlings not having the throat designs of their own species and court rough female dummies, whereas the wild species does not respond in such tests. The wider application of some behavior patterns by captive hamadryas baboons fits into this tendency. A delayed start of adult behavior is also found in many domesticated species. All authors agree that the relative and absolute frequencies of different parts of the species' behavior are easily changed by domestication, while the form of the single pattern is highly conservative. In none of the species were new patterns developed by domesticated forms; this last finding probably does not apply for primates. Leyhausen states that captive and domesticated animals often show similar behavioral changes. Whether and why the genetic effects of breeding really follow the same directions as the immediate effects of poor environment remains to be shown. Immelmann gives a more detailed discussion of these questions.

Summary

The social behavior of a zoo colony of fifteen *Papio hamadryas* is compared with that of a population in the wild:

1. The one-male-groups of captive baboons are similar, even down to structural details, to the comparable units in Ethiopian troops.

2. The captive baboons spend more time in social activities.

3. It was investigated as to how much time various sex-age-classes spent on the different categories of behavior. The patterns of distribution observed in the wild are also found in captivity.

4. Juveniles born in the zoo retain play fighting until subadulthood, while wild juveniles stop playing at an early stage. On the other hand, social grooming starts much earlier in the wild.

5. Of sixty-one patterns of behavior found in wild baboons only two are missing in the zoo colony. Nine patterns were performed by the zoo baboons which were not found in the free-living troops.

6. The behavior sequence of "protected threat" observed in several related species is missing among free-living hamadryas baboons but appears fully developed in captivity.

7. Patterns of behavior limited in function in the wild are carried over to other situations in the zoo.

References

1. KUMMER, H. *Soziales Verhalten einer Mantelpaviangruppe.* Bern: Hans Huber, 1957.

2. ———. *Social organization of free-living hamadryas baboons.* In preparation.

3. ZUCKERMAN, S. *The social life of monkeys and apes.* London: Kegan Paul, 1932.

4. CALHOUN, J. B. Population density and social pathology. *Sci. Am.,* 1962, *206*(2), 139–148.

5. KUMMER, H., & KURT, F. Social units of free-living Hamadryas baboons. *Folia primat,* 1963, *1*, 4–19.

6. SCHALLER, G. B. *The mountain gorilla: Ecology and behavior.* Univ. Chicago Press, 1963.

7. ALTMANN, S. A field study of the sociobiology of Rhesus monkeys, *Macaca mulatta. Ann. N.Y. Acad. Sci.,* 1962, *102*(2), 338–435.

8. DeVORE, I. The social behavior and organization of baboon troops. Unpublished doctoral dissertation. Dept. of Anthropology, U. of Chicago. 1962.

9. REYNOLDS, V. The social life of a colony of Rhesus monkeys (*Macaca mulatta*). Unpublished doctoral dissertation. Dept. of Anthropology, U. of London. 1961.

10. HEDIGER, H. *Wildtiere in Gefangenschaft.* Basel: Benno Schwabe, 1942.

11. BAERENDS, G. P. Aufbau des tierischen Verhaltens. *Kükenthals Handbuch der Zoologie.* VIII, 10. Teil, Heft 3. 1956.

12. LORENZ, K. Durch Domestikation verursachte Störungen arteigenen Verhaltens. *Z. Angew. Psychol.,* 1940, *59*, 2–81.

13. IMMELMANN, K. Vergleichende Beobachtungen uber das Verhalten domestizierter Zebrafinken in Europa und ihrer wilden Stammform in Australien. *Zeitschr. f. Tierzüchtung*, 1962, *77*, 198.

14. LEYHAUSEN, P. Domestikationsbedingte Verhaltenseigentümlichkeiten der Hauskatze. *Zeitschr. f. Tierzüchtung*, 1962, *77*, 191–197.

15. HEDIGER, H. *Tierpsychologie im Zoo und im Zirkus*. Basel: F. Reinhardt, 1961.

INDEX

Italic numbers following a name indicate material written by that individual.